AA

Discovering Britain

AA

Discovering Britain

AN ILLUSTRATED GUIDE TO
MORE THAN 500 SELECTED LOCATIONS IN BRITAIN'S
UNSPOILED COUNTRYSIDE

Published by Drive Publications Limited
for the Automobile Association,
Fanum House, Basingstoke, Hants RG21 2EA

DISCOVERING BRITAIN
was edited and designed by
The Reader's Digest Association Limited
for Drive Publications Limited
Berkeley Square House, London W1X 5PD

First Edition Copyright © 1982
Drive Publications Limited

Printed in Great Britain

Cover picture: Borrowdale, Lake District; p.1 Walna
Scar, Lake District; pp.2/3 The Cotswolds near Haresfield Beacon;
pp.4/5 Quiraing, Skye, in the Scottish Islands;
pp.6/7 Covehithe, Suffolk; p.9 Dedham Vale, Suffolk.

CONTRIBUTORS

The publishers would like to thank the
following people for major contributions to this book

PRINCIPAL AUTHORS
Ross Finlay Ted Forrest
William Foster Bryn Frank Bill Grundy
Harry Hopkins Philip Llewellin David Lloyd
Robin Mead Roy Millward Tim Ware
Diana Winsor

PHOTOGRAPHERS
Martyn J. Adelman Malcom Aird Nigel Cassidy
Robert Eames Michael Freeman
Colin Molyneux John Simms Patrick Thurston
Paul Wakefield Trevor Wood Jon Wyand
John Robert Young

ARTISTS
Graham Allen Richard Bonson
Wendy Brammal Colin Emberson Ivan Lapper
D. W. Ovenden John Rignall Gill Tomblin

CONTENTS

SPECIAL FEATURES

REGIONAL GUIDE TO BRITAIN'S COUNTRYSIDE

WHERE TO FIND THE MAPS

The index map (right) shows the limits of the maps covering the carefully chosen areas of Britain's countryside described in this book. The colours indicate the regions into which the areas have been grouped. Each area features at least one detailed map and an A–Z guide that takes you to its most interesting locations. Use the index map in conjunction with the reference list beside it to find the area map you want – for example, if you are planning a trip to Exmoor, the map you need is on p.40.

HOW TO USE THE AREA MAPS

All entries in the A–Z guides are shown on the area maps in bold capital letters. Each entry includes route instructions and a simple map reference. If there are two maps covering an area, the reference is preceded by the numeral 1 or 2, indicating the relevant map. All roads mentioned in the route instructions are included on the maps, and the symbols used to identify features and places of special interest are explained in the key below.

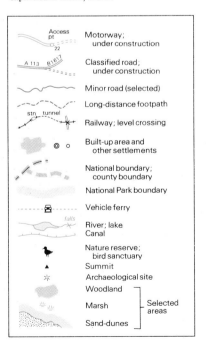

Access pt	Motorway; under construction
A 113 — B 1617	Classified road; under construction
	Minor road (selected)
	Long-distance footpath
stn. tunnel	Railway; level crossing
	Built-up area and other settlements
	National boundary; county boundary
	National Park boundary
	Vehicle ferry
falls	River; lake Canal
	Nature reserve; bird sanctuary
▲	Summit
✳	Archaeological site
	Woodland ⎫
	Marsh ⎬ Selected areas
	Sand-dunes ⎭

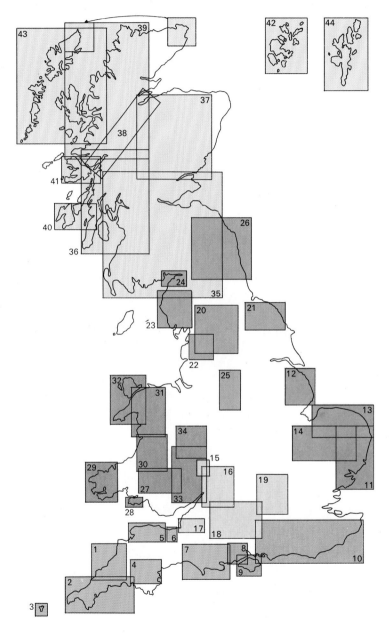

SOUTH-WEST ENGLAND
1 North Cornwall and Bodmin Moor   p.12
2 Southern Cornwall   p.20
3 Isles of Scilly   p.26
4 Dartmoor   p.30
5 Exmoor and North Devon   p.40
6 The Quantock Hills   p.54
7 The Dorset Hills   p.62

SOUTH-EAST ENGLAND
8 The New Forest   p.76
9 Isle of Wight   p.84
10 Downland and Weald   p.88

EAST ANGLIA AND THE WOLDS
11 The Suffolk Coast and Heathlands   p.102
12 The Lincolnshire Wolds and Marshes   p.110
13 Norfolk Coast and Broads   p.118
14 Fens and Breckland   p.122

ENGLAND'S SOUTHERN HILLS
15 The Malvern Hills   p.130
16 The Cotswold Hills   p.138
17 The Mendip Hills   p.150
18 The North Wessex Downs   p.158
19 The Chiltern Hills   p.170

NORTHERN ENGLAND
20 The Yorkshire Dales   p.180
21 The North York Moors   p.192
22 The Forest of Bowland   p.204
23 The Lake District   p.212
24 The Solway Coast   p.221
25 The Peak District   p.228
26 Northumberland's Coast and Hills   p.240

WALES AND THE WELSH MARCHES
27 The Brecon Beacons   p.254
28 Gower   p.266
29 The Pembrokeshire Coast   p.274
30 The Cambrian Mountains   p.286
31 Snowdonia's Peaks and Valleys   p.294
32 The Lleyn Peninsula and Anglesey   p.306
33 The Wye Valley and Welsh Borders   p.314
34 The Shropshire Hills   p.322

SCOTLAND AND ITS ISLANDS
35 The Scottish Lowlands   p.334
36 Loch Lomond and Arran   p.346
37 The Grampian Mountains   p.359
38 The Great Glen   p.372
39 The North-west Highlands   p.382
40 Islay   p.396
41 Mull   p.396
42 Orkney   p.400
43 Outer Hebrides and Skye   p.402
44 Shetland   p.408

Exploring Britain's Countryside

Even in these overcrowded islands there still remain vast tracts of countryside, of extraordinary variety and great beauty, open to us all. Much of this magnificent scenery lies within the boundaries of National Parks, Forest Parks, Areas of Outstanding Natural Beauty and Heritage Coasts; it is from these places that the 35 areas in this book have been selected. Within each area the reader will find a selection of locations, all accessible to the motorist and walker, which have been chosen to show the diversity and unspoiled nature of our countryside.

The location may be a viewpoint surrounded by magnificent scenery; a battlefield or a rounded hill scarred with fortifications of long ago; a spot associated with local legend or a famous person; or an area where animals and plants are of special interest. In the Lake District, for example, the reader, according to his mood and energy, can plan a walk through gentle woodland beside one of the lakes – or make a bracing 2,000 ft climb to a magnificent mountain viewpoint. He can tread an ancient trackway across the fells used by pedlars and shepherds centuries ago – or drive along a winding, switchback, scenic route poised high above a beautiful valley.

Many landscapes that seem to us eternal and unchanging were in fact created by our forbears, sometimes quite recently, sometimes in the distant past. The smooth green turf of the South Downs, for example, and the windy, heather-clad expanses of the Yorkshire moors are both the result of ancient clearances and grazing. The Brecklands in Norfolk are a dustbowl created by over-grazing in the Middle Ages, and the Broads in the same county were born out of the removal of millions of tons of peat during the Middle Ages. Much of the bare, wild Highlands was once a great forest, while the English chequerboard of fields and hedgerows grew out of the enclosures that took place from the Tudor age to the 19th century.

Other places change so slowly as to have hardly altered at all since man has been on the planet. These are the old, old mountains of the west and north, the peaks that legends declare to be the homes of giants and heroes, just as they fill the deep, still waters in their shadows with monsters.

Some areas, such as the Peak District, Loch Lomond, Gower and the North Downs, can be reached comparatively easily. Others require a certain spirit of adventure and exploration – the Highland hills, for instance, or the distant Shetland Islands and Hebrides, or the wilder parts of Snowdonia or the Lake District. The book is truly 'Discovering Britain'; a practical guide that will lead the reader to these beautiful places and provide him with a deeper insight into the land around him.

CORNWALL'S COAST AND MOORLAND

Virtually isolated on a sea-girt extremity, the land became the last bastion of Celtic culture in England

Dominated by its rocky, wave-lashed coastline, Cornwall is most renowned for its rugged cliffs and sandy coves, for its friendly harbours and beautiful creeks. Yet its attractions go deeper than its scenic splendours, for this Celtic country beyond the River Tamar is a land of legend and mystery, from the jagged heights of Tintagel to the brooding barrenness of Bodmin Moor. This is the land of King Arthur, among the greatest of Britain's legendary heroes. This is also the land of giants and piskies, of saints and smugglers, and of the lost land of Lyonnesse engulfed by the sea beyond Land's End.

All but 60 miles of Cornwall's 300 mile boundary is ocean, and most of its inland border with Devon is formed by the Tamar. The dramatic northern coastline, battered by the Atlantic, is the wildest and most rugged. The southern coast is gentler, still with steep headlands and stormy seas, but also with the creek-cut estuaries of the Helford, Fal and Fowey rivers. Inland Cornwall is mainly bleak moorland or stone-walled pastures, but even on Bodmin Moor in the north, the sea is never more than 20 miles away.

In prehistoric times Cornwall was quite heavily populated, as the many standing stones, stone circles and chambered tombs attest. As long as 4,000 years ago, men were extracting tin using a simple method called streaming – washing away the surface soil by diverting a stream

and so exposing the heavier tin ore. Much of the trade was with Mediterranean merchants. When the Romans arrived 2,000 years later, they hardly penetrated beyond the Tamar, and Cornish Celts were more in touch with their Irish, Welsh and Breton cousins than with the rest of Britain. Cornwall remained Celtic through most of the Dark Ages, and much Celtic legend – a mixture of folklore and shadowy romanticised history – dates from this time. So do many of the little-known Cornish saints such as St Morwenna and St Piran, the patron saint of tin miners; the remains of his 6th-century oratory were uncovered on Penhale Sands at Perranporth in 1835. They have been covered again as a protection against vandalism.

Tin and fish were the livelihood of Cornishmen for centuries. Tin mining (as opposed to streaming) began in the Middle Ages, and still continues in a small way today, although its heyday, along with copper mining, was in the 18th and 19th centuries. One of the most famous mines was Dolcoath near Camborne, 3,000 ft deep, which produced both copper and tin until early in this century. China clay is the chief extraction industry in Cornwall now, concentrated around St Austell where the huge white spoil-heaps glistening in the sunlight have earned them the nickname 'the Cornish Alps'. Many are now being sown with grass.

The many ruined and deserted engine-houses that bring a grim romance to the lonely cliffs are a legacy of Cornwall's mining past. Other relics are the huers' huts where lookouts once watched for the seasonal pilchard shoals, ready to signal the local fishermen to put to sea for a catch. The shoals ceased at the turn of the century, and fishing, like mining, is now only a shadow of the industry it once was.

ATLANTIC FURY Rollers thunder into Stanbury Mouth near Morwenstow, seething and tossing against the jagged rocks. This is Cornwall's rugged northern coast, the wave-pounded shore that faces 3,000 miles of restless ocean.

Places to visit

Map ref. 1Aa   Bedruthan Steps

Huge, irregular rock stacks shaped by the Atlantic, Bedruthan Steps are a magnificent sight at any time of the year – whether surrounded by vast stretches of sand at low tide in summer, or pounded by mountainous winter waves. Said to be stepping-stones to the 200 ft cliff used by the legendary Celtic giant Bedruthan, they are formed of slate, like the cliff itself. A number of rocky arches at the cliff base will in time probably collapse under the relentless onslaught of the sea to form more steps.

One of the rock stacks is known as the Queen Bess Rock because it is said to look like Elizabeth I in profile. Another is called the Samaritan Rock – a name that recalls the wreck of the *Good Samaritan*, an East Indiaman from Liverpool, that was smashed on to the shore by a savage Atlantic storm in 1846. Although a tragedy for the crew, the wreck was a windfall for the impoverished locals, many of whom added to their meagre living by salvaging the goods from wrecks.

About 1½ miles from the cliffs is the isolated Church of St Uvelos at St Eval, its tall tower a landmark by day to guide ships away from the wrath of the rocks. It was so valued by seamen that

in 1727 Bristol merchants paid for the tower's repair.

The Cornwall Coast Path follows the top of the cliff, in summer bright with the yellow of gorse and kidney vetch and heavy with the scent of burnet rose. There are 120 steps leading down to the beach, a restored stairway that was originally cut by smugglers and wreck robbers who probably stored their loot in caves at the cliff bottom. The caves include one known as the Great Cavern.

Bedruthan Steps lie west of the Newquay–Padstow road (B3276) about 1 mile north of Trenance. There is a large car park at the top of the cliff.

Map ref. 1Bb   Beeny Cliff

One thing sets Beeny Cliff apart from the other rugged and beautiful headlands of Cornwall's north coast – it is the only headland carved from chert, a tough, black flint-like rock. Originally a sand, the grains have been cemented together by a rock solution. Because of this the cliff-face is easy to recognise against the slate-grey of the headlands around.

From the cliff-top there are magnificent views out to sea beyond the wave-lashed reef known as the Beeny Sisters, and grey seals can sometimes be seen basking on the rocks below. South-westwards you can see the land-locked harbour of Boscastle, and north-east the towering High Cliff. Below the southern tip of Beeny Cliff is Pentargon waterfall, where a local stream plunges more than 100 ft into the ocean down a deep chasm cut into the cliff by the Atlantic.

Beeny Cliff is ½ mile west of the hamlet of Beeny, which is west off the B3263 about 1½ miles north-east of Boscastle.

Map ref. 2Ab   Cape Cornwall

The lonely stack of a deserted mine marks Cape Cornwall, where the turbulent Atlantic beats against the granite moors of the Penwith peninsula just north of Land's End. Such is the force and persistence of the breakers that parts of the cliff have worn away to leave the windswept cape almost an island.

Heather and gorse dapple the headland, and primroses and spring squill splash the cliffs with colour in the spring. In summer, clusters of thrift, or sea pink, are scattered among the rocks and clefts. Some of the clefts are relics of the headland's mining days; such clefts – in Cornish 'zawns' – were man-made when miners removed the rocks to get at the seams of copper and tin.

For hundreds of years, Cornish miners descended the zawns or the shafts to underground workings on ladders, their only light underground coming from the candles fixed with clay to

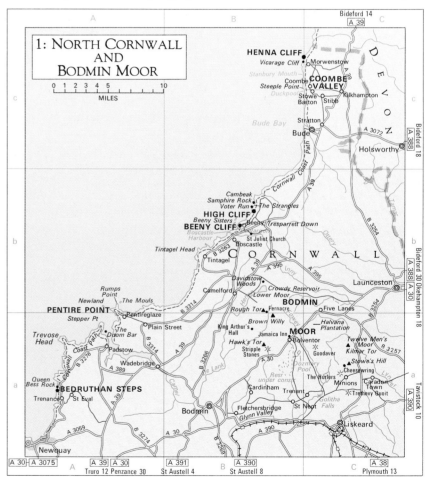

their hard felt hats. Tin streaming was known in Cornwall in prehistoric times, but tin mining first began in the 1500s, with copper mining 200 years later.

Until just over 100 years ago, Cape Cornwall and the surrounding area was a thriving mining centre, one of Britain's busiest industrial sites. Much of the world's tin and copper was produced in Cornwall until the late 1800s, when discoveries in places such as Africa and Australia caused the collapse of the Cornish industry.

The Cape Cornwall mine was abandoned in the late 1870s, and the mines at nearby Botallack in 1895 (except for a brief re-opening in the early 1900s). Now only the ruins of the engine-houses remain, chimneyed buildings which once housed the steam-engines that pumped away water – the miners' constant peril – from the workings.

No pounding pistons or thudding hammers compete with the roar of the sea and wind at Cape Cornwall now; the silent stack looks out across the grey Atlantic to where a seething line of surf marks the dangerous Brisons rocks. There is still a working tin mine at Geevor near Trewellard about 2 miles north-east. It has a visitor centre and a tin-mining museum.

Cape Cornwall lies 1¼ miles west of St Just in Penwith, along a signposted minor road.

2Bb Chysauster

It is probably 1,800 years since the Iron Age villagers of Chysauster abandoned their courtyard homes high on the Gulval Downs north of Penzance, yet the drystone walls still stand about 3 ft high in places, and you can still distinguish the outlines of their walled and

CLIFF WATERFALL Pentargon waterfall plunges 100 ft down the face of Beeny Cliff to meet the Atlantic in the creek below.

terraced gardens. The village was inhabited from about 100 BC until the 2nd century AD, and here the Celtic occupants tilled their fields on the terraced green hillsides and streamed for tin in the valley below.

Castle-an-Dinas, an Iron Age hillfort, and Roger's Tower, an early 19th-century folly, overlook the village from the 760 ft summit about a mile to the east. The village itself is about 600 ft above sea-level, with magnificent views south to Mount's Bay.

The remains of nine houses are visible in Chysauster, eight of them in two rows of four on each side of a narrow lane. All the main entrances faced north-east, away from the prevailing south-west winds. Roughly oval in shape and nearly 100 ft across, the houses had thick walls enclosing circular rooms that opened on to a central courtyard. In each house, a long, narrow passage with stone-faced earthen walls led to the courtyard; recesses in the courtyard walls may have been cattle byres. The main room of each house, opposite the passage entrance, contains a central stone with a socket for a roof-post, which probably supported a thatched or turved roof.

Most of the floors are paved and have drainage channels, and some of the side chambers have a sump. Granite mortars and hand grindstones have been found in the village, and to the south of the houses there is a fougou – an underground chamber that was probably used as a food store by the whole community.

To reach Chysauster, turn north-west at Badger's Cross on the Penzance–St Ives road, the B3311. The village lies about 1½ miles along a signposted minor road. There is a small car park near the site.

—BODMIN MOOR—

*Cornwall's granite upland – a remote and silent world
of mist and mystery*

WHEN THE RAINCLOUDS hang threateningly over its craggy tors and barren peat-bogs, Bodmin Moor appears sinister and forbidding – a land of legend and mystery haunted by the shadows of ancient men and ancient myths, where the brooding silence is broken only by the sudden cry of a startled bird whirring from the gorse. Here, the relics of prehistory reveal, men lived, worked and died for thousands of years before the coming of the Roman legions. The remains of their sacred sites and burial grounds, their huts and corn plots, are evident on all sides.

Rivers and tors

Although the 80 sq. miles of Bodmin Moor contain rough and rolling moorland in plenty, there is also a gentler face to the moor, particularly on the borders where the rivers tumble from the granite plateau through wooded valleys on their course to the sea. The four main rivers, joined by many moorland streams, are the Lynher bordering the moor in the east, the Camel in the west, the Inny in the north flowing eastwards to the Tamar, and the Fowey that winds through the heart of the moor and then along its southern border.

Crowned by castle-like columns of balanced granite boulders, the tors stand stark and spectacular above the moorland tracts, and there are wonderful views from their summits.

High peaks and ancient stones

Two of the highest peaks in Cornwall rise above the northern moor – Brown Willy (1,377 ft) and Rough Tor (1,311 ft). Looming large on the south-east moor are Kilmar Tor, overlooking Twelve Men's Moor, and Stowe's Hill, with the strange rockpile known as the Cheesewring on its western slopes.

Hauntingly poignant among the moorland wastes, the countless relics of forgotten times include the Stripple Stones on the southern slopes of Hawk's Tor Downs, a circular earthen mound enclosing a few remaining standing stones. Once it was an ancient temple, built perhaps 4,000 years ago. The Hurlers near Minions, Goodaver near Dozmary Pool and King Arthur's Hall 2 miles south-west of Rough Tor are three of the many stone groups scattered over the moor. Compared with Salisbury Plain's Stonehenge the stones are small and less impressive, but in the ghostly atmosphere

GOLITHA FALLS HERE THE RIVER FOWEY TUMBLES FROM THE GRANITE UPLANDS.

MYSTIC WATER DOZMARY POOL, WHERE SIR BEDIVERE IS SAID TO HAVE FLUNG KING ARTHUR'S SWORD, TO BE CAUGHT BY AN ARM RISING FROM THE DEPTHS.

of Bodmin Moor they cast a strange enchantment over the grey-green grassland.

Trethevy Quoit on the south-east fringe of the moor is all that remains of an eight-stone prehistoric burial chamber that includes an 11 ft long capstone; the earthen mound that once covered it has gone.

The moor was the most heavily populated part of Cornwall in prehistoric times, but during Celtic and Roman times, and the Dark Ages that followed, the population dwindled away; for centuries the area remained a seldom-visited wilderness. But by the 13th century, Cornwall's swelling population had begun to look for new pastures, and people turned once again to the upland moor. Peasant cattle farmers built their granite homes near running water in hollows sheltered from the moorland winds, such as Fernacre beside the upper reach of the De Lank river, where the remains of medieval holdings can still be seen.

TIME-WORN ROCKS GRANITE BOULDERS LITTER ROUGH TOR (LEFT), SHATTERED AND SCATTERED BY ICE AGE FROSTS. GRANITE SLABS LINE KING ARTHUR'S HALL (ABOVE), A MYSTERIOUS ANCIENT ENCLOSURE IN THE HEART OF THE MOOR.

18th-century industry

Tin and copper had been mined in Cornwall even before the Romans came, but on Bodmin Moor the mining boom began in the 18th century at Caradon. It lasted 100 years, and in their heyday the Caradon copper mines were among the richest in the world. Today, the gaunt stacks of the engine-houses stand as silent monuments to those prosperous times.

Another industry enjoyed by many Cornishmen was smuggling, a nefarious occupation romanticised by the novelist Daphne du Maurier in her story *Jamaica Inn*. The inspiration for the book stands beside the road at Bolventor – a slate-hung Georgian coaching inn 'alone in glory, four square to the winds'.

Modern man has also exploited the moor's riches, gouging out the china clay and defacing parts of the moor with spoil-heaps. But on the credit side he has created large tracts of woodland – acres of conifers such as at Halvana and Davidstow that give welcome relief against the huge expanses of grass and furze. And reservoirs like Crowdy have attracted water-fowl and other birds – herons, for example, that were rarely seen on the moor.

Bogs and marshes

The rainfall on Bodmin Moor is heavy – up to 80 in. a year. Bogs and marshes have formed in those areas where the water has been unable to find an easy path away from the impervious underlying granite. This has happened at Dozmary Pool, where the water has gathered to form a lake – a rarity in Cornwall. Local legends claimed it was bottomless but, in fact, it is quite shallow and has been known to dry up.

Pale yellow bog moss abounds in wet places, and purple moor grass thrives on the acid soil. Other moorland grasses include bent and fescue. Bog moss is capable of holding large quantities of water, even during high summer. Eventually, the lower parts of the moss decay and gradually form a layer of peat.

CORNISH GLORY Coombe Valley, once the home of Sir Richard Grenville,
is where the Rev. Stephen Hawker wrote *The Song of the Western Men* in 1825,
a ballad about the days when Cornishmen rebelled against James II.

1Cc Coombe Valley

A steep, wooded valley with a gentle stream comes as a surprise within a mile of the rugged, windswept coast of north Cornwall. Yet Coombe Valley is only half a mile from Steeple Point and the surfing beach of Duckpool. It stretches about 2 miles eastwards from the picturesque hamlet of Coombe – a cluster of cottages that once housed the miller and his men who worked the nearby water-mill, now disused. The cottages belong to the Landmark Trust.

Some of the stones used to build the mill in 1842 were probably taken from the old manor house that once stood in the valley – the family home of Sir Richard Grenville, immortalised in Lord Tennyson's poem *The Revenge*.

Sir Richard, who was the County Sheriff of Cornwall in 1577, commanded the *Revenge* in 1591 when it engaged single-handed a fleet of 53 Spanish warships near Flores in the Azores, having become separated from the main British fleet under Lord Howard of Effingham. The *Revenge* held off the Spaniards for 15 hours, until only

20 men survived and Sir Richard was mortally wounded. He died aboard the Spanish flagship.

Today, Coombe Valley is as green and peaceful as it must have been when Sir Richard rode there 400 years ago. A 1½ mile nature trail maintained by the Cornwall Naturalists' Trust leads along each side of the stream, among oakwoods hung with honeysuckle and through Forestry Commission plantations of conifers.

Buzzards circle above the valley, woodpeckers and treecreepers may be seen feeding on the oaks, and tiny goldcrests live among the conifers. By the stream there are dippers, wagtails and occasionally a kingfisher. Butterflies abound in the woodland clearings in summer, including the pale yellow brimstone that lays its eggs on the damp-loving alder buckthorn.

Coombe Valley is 4 miles north of Bude, and can be reached along minor roads north-west off the A 39 via Stibb and Stowe Barton. The nature trail starts at Coombe Cottages, and there is parking space near by.

2Ca Croft Pascoe

Still, silent pinewoods within sight of the sea are unusual along the Cornish coast. The Croft Pascoe pine plantation on Goonhilly Downs, only about 2 miles from the southern cliffs of the Lizard peninsula, was first planted by the Forestry Commission in 1955 as an experiment in tree-growing on the thin clay soil overlying the serpentine rock. Monterey and coastal lodgepole pines proved to be the most successful species.

Trees and surrounding heathland have provided a happy nesting and hunting ground for the buzzards to be

seen circling overhead, and the drumming of great spotted woodpeckers among the pines mixes with the trilling of soaring skylarks on the downland. Close by the plantation, Croft Pascoe Pool is a refuge for moorhens and many kinds of wildfowl.

In spring the flat, open heathlands of Goonhilly Downs are heady with the scent of gorse, its golden glow broken in places by the white flowers of blackthorn, which appear before the leaves. In late summer, by the time the blackthorn sloes are beginning to swell, the gorse flowers have given way to the purple of heather, particularly the pale lilac of Cornish heath found on the Lizard.

The highest point on Goonhilly Downs, 370 ft, is at Dry Tree about a mile north from Croft Pascoe near the GPO Satellite Earth Station with its huge dish aerials. The name Goonhilly is a corruption of the old Cornish *Gun helghy* – meaning 'hunting downs'. They were extensively populated in prehistoric times, for there are many burial mounds and some hut circles and standing stones, including the 3,000-year-old 15 ft standing stone near Dry Tree, once fallen but now re-erected. Until about 200 years ago there are said to have been wild ponies derived from Celtic stock, known as 'goonhillies', roaming the downs.

Croft Pascoe is off the B3293 Helston–St Keverne road, along a minor road about ¼ mile south from Traboe Cross.

SURFING BEACH Tiny Duckpool beach at the steep-sided mouth of the Coombe Valley shelters below 300 ft Steeple Point. The beach provides good surfing once the tide has cleared the jagged reefs.

2Eb Dodman Point

From the prominent heather-covered headland of Dodman Point, 373 ft above the English Channel, the eye can sweep, in clear weather, across a 95 mile curve of coastline from Black Head on the Lizard peninsula some 20 miles to the south-west, to Bolt Head in Devon some 45 miles to the east.

Dodman Point is marked by a tall granite cross, erected as a landmark for ships in 1896 by a local clergyman. Sailors called the point the Dodman, an old English word for a snail, but its name is probably a corruption of Deadman Point, for there are treacherous currents around the grey slate cliffs of the headland, where there have been many shipwrecks.

A pleasant pathway leads up to the point from Penare, between hedgerows banked with bluebells and primroses in spring, and with skylarks singing overhead. From Dodman Point, the Cornwall Coast Path leads northwards to Maenease Point and down to the fishing village of Gorran Haven.

Dodman Point is a ¾ mile walk south from Penare, where there is a large car park. Penare is about 3 miles south of Mevagissey along minor roads.

2Db Froe Creek

A finger of water lined in parts by centuries-old woods, Froe Creek flows between rocks into the Percuil River just north of its confluence with the famous anchorage of the Carrick Roads that opens into Falmouth Bay. Pines, beeches and scrub oaks, rising from both banks, make a wonderful canopy of varying shades of green in summer. The half-mile long creek is a haven for moorhens, mallards, mute swans and a colony of herons, and only the rustle of the reeds and the occasional splash of a diving kingfisher disturb the peace.

There is a dam at the head of the creek, once the mill-pond of a tide-mill now pulled down. The head of the creek is the starting point for a 6½ mile circular walk round the beautiful peninsula of St Anthony-in-Roseland; a field path leads first to Towan Beach, from where the route follows the coast path south-west to Porthmellin Head, and on to Zone Point and St Anthony Head. It then turns north past Carricknath Point and St Anthony and back through National Trust pinewoods to Froe Creek.

A shorter walk of 3½ miles takes you direct from Porthmellin Head westwards to St Anthony, cutting out the headland. Zone Point and St Anthony Head (also owned by the National Trust) can, however, be reached by road. They lie about 2 miles south-west of Froe Creek, and give sweeping views of Falmouth Bay.

To reach Froe Creek, turn south off the Tregony–St Mawes road, A3078, at Trewithian. Froe is 2½ miles south via Gerrans and Trewince.

1Bc Henna Cliff

From the heights of Henna Cliff the Atlantic breakers below seem hushed almost to a murmur, for it plunges a sheer 450 ft to the sea. Except for Beachy Head, this is the highest sheer drop of any sea-cliff in England.

Northwards you can see beyond Hartland Point and Lundy island to the blue haze of the Pembroke coast some 50 miles away. South-west there are views along 40 miles of the Cornish coast, gnarled with headlands such as Tintagel, to Trevose Head. Gorse and heather cover the cliff-top, despite the battering of savage Atlantic gales. In summer the pink-flowering thrift grows here in profusion.

About a quarter of a mile south of Henna Cliff is Vicarage Cliff, owned by the National Trust, where a driftwood lookout hut built by the Rev. Robert Stephen Hawker is perched on the cliff-edge. From 1834 until 1875 Hawker was the vicar of nearby Morwenstow, which takes its name from the holy well of St Morwenna set in the steep face of the cliff.

Parson Hawker was noted for his help and compassion for the many victims of shipwrecks under the cliffs, but today he is best remembered as the writer of *The Song of the Western Men*, the famous Cornish ballad.

Henna Cliff is about ¼ mile north-west of Morwenstow, where there is parking space by the church. Morwenstow is 4 miles north-west of Kilkhampton on the A39 along minor roads.

1Bb High Cliff

As you look down from High Cliff, the highest point on the Cornish coast, the silver-grey expanse of sea 700 ft or more below seems remote and unreal, although the strong onshore winds dispel any sensation of dreaminess. The cliff is not sheer; two hummocks interrupt its slope to the sea.

Just to the north, towards the headland of Cambeak, is the jagged cliff known as the Voter Run, which produces a strange roaring when wind and tide are at a certain strength. Beyond Voter Run lies the treacherous reef of The Strangles, a reminder that, despite the shimmering beauty of the sea from this vantage point, this is a dangerous coast where many sailing ships have

BIRDS OF CORNWALL

Cornwall's coast and moors are the home of a wide range of birds. On pebbly shores the turnstone is a common sight in winter, flicking over stones and shells with its pointed bill in search of food. In stormy weather, razorbills may be seen diving for fish close inshore; they nest in colonies on cliffs and rocky islets. The Montagu's harrier is a bird of the heathlands, flying low over the ground in search of frogs, snakes and small mammals. Woodlarks frequent heaths where there are scattered trees, and are present throughout the year.

Woodlark
(*Lullula arborea*)

Razorbill
(*Alca torda*)

Turnstone
(*Arenaria interpres*)

Montagu's harrier
(*Circus pygargus*)

come to grief in times past. There is little or no shelter along these cliffs for miles, save for the narrow Boscastle harbour to the south.

Samphire Rock just beyond The Strangles recalls another hazardous undertaking of past times – the collection of samphire. Cornishmen once regularly climbed down the cliffs to collect this plant from the rock clefts; its fleshy leaves were pickled and eaten and considered a delicacy. Samphire pickers were not only in danger of falling to their deaths should they miss their footing on the steep and slippery slopes, but the soft shale cliffs of this area are very susceptible to landslips.

To reach High Cliff, leave the A39 Camelford–Stratton road at Tresparrett Down, and follow the minor road northwest for about 1¼ miles.

2Ca Kynance Cove

Some of Cornwall's loveliest scenery lies along the 6 mile stretch of coast between Mullion Cove and Lizard Point, particularly at Kynance Cove where the cliffs sweep down to weathered serpentine rocks lapped by a surf-fringed azure sea, with pale golden sands revealed at low tide.

Apart from their idyllic setting, the Kynance rocks are spectacular because of their colours and shapes. The mottled grey-green or red-brown serpentine rock – named for its resemblance to snake skin – glows with streaks of red, white, yellow and black, especially in the caves at the foot of the cliff, which have names like the Parlour and the Ladies' Bathing Pool.

The cove is scattered with rocks that the sea has worn into wild shapes, such as the tall Steeple Rock, and the Bishop's Rock that looks something like a mitred head. In the weird Devil's Letterbox and Bellows in the side of Asparagus Island, the incoming tide is sucked through a narrow hole with a massive roar, then spewed out in a shower of spray. Asparagus Island is named for the wild asparagus that once grew on its slopes.

Wild flowers grow in profusion all along these cliffs, including blue-flowering spring squill from April to June, and in summer the exotic Hottentot-fig, the Cornish heath found on the Lizard peninsula, pink thrift, buttercups, foxgloves, tormentil, milkwort and blackthorn. A Victorian naturalist the Rev. Charles Johns, author of *A Week at the Lizard* (1848), claimed to have found 12 wild plants within the area covered by his hat.

Mullion Cove is a walk of about 4 miles along the cliff-tops from Kynance. Hemmed in by lichen-covered cliffs, it has a stone-jettied harbour where fish was once landed. Lizard Point is about 2 miles south from Kynance, its lighthouse the most southerly point on the English mainland. The Lizard's strange name is derived from the Cornish *lis*, a court or palace, and *arth*, meaning high or holy.

Kynance Cove is signposted off the A3083 Helston–Lizard road, from where a toll-road leads to the car park.

2Cb Loe Pool

Cornwall's largest natural lake, Loe Pool, lies at the mouth of the River Cober, dammed from the sea by a 600 ft wide ridge of shingle known as Loe Bar. Local legend says the bar was formed when Jan Tregeagle, a notorious folk-figure, was forced to clear Berepper beach of sand by the Devil. During his labours he dropped a sack of sand across the Cober estuary when a spiteful demon tripped him up. The lake is also said to be the place where King Arthur's sword Excalibur was thrown after the king was mortally wounded at the battle of Camlamm.

SEASIDE LAKE Loe Pool was formed by a shingle bar, Loe Bar, damming the Cober river mouth.

Peaceful woods of sycamore, oak and pine stretch down to both shores of the narrow, mile-long lake. Rhododendrons make a vivid splash of colour in early summer, and there are white water-lilies floating on the water. Herons hunt among the reeds, and mallards and swans frequent Carminowe Creek, which runs into the lake at its seaward end.

At one time, the Helston residents regularly had to cut a channel for the water through the shingle bar to prevent flooding in the lower part of the town, but today there is a permanent water outlet. The sandy beach on the seaward side of Loe Bar is popular with holidaymakers, but it has not always been the scene solely of leisure.

A naval frigate, HMS *Anson*, was wrecked on the bar in December 1807, and 100 lives were lost. One man who witnessed the tragedy was Henry Trengrouse, a cabinet-maker from Helston, who was appalled to see so many drowned so close to land. It led him to spend a great deal of his time and money on devising a means of rescue, and he was the originator of the line-carrying rocket that enabled a breeches-buoy to be rigged to transfer people ashore. This device has since saved many lives.

The lake is part of the Penrose estate, now owned by the National Trust. A number of small car parks have been established, set well back from the water. These are linked by a network of footpaths which provides some of the most beautiful walks in the county (no dogs are allowed).

Loe Pool can be reached from Porthleven, 2¼ miles south-west of Helston on the B3304. Park on the south-east side of the town above Porthleven Sands, from where there is a path south-eastwards to Loe Bar and Pool. Alternatively, minor roads and tracks lead south from the B3304 to Loe Pool.

2Db   Nare Head

All the flavours that are typical of the Cornish coast can be enjoyed at Nare Head, a marvellously quiet spot that overlooks Veryan Bay to the east and Gerrans Bay to the west. The flat cliff-top, 330 ft high, is bright with the chatter of birds above the dull pounding of the surf on the rocks below, and

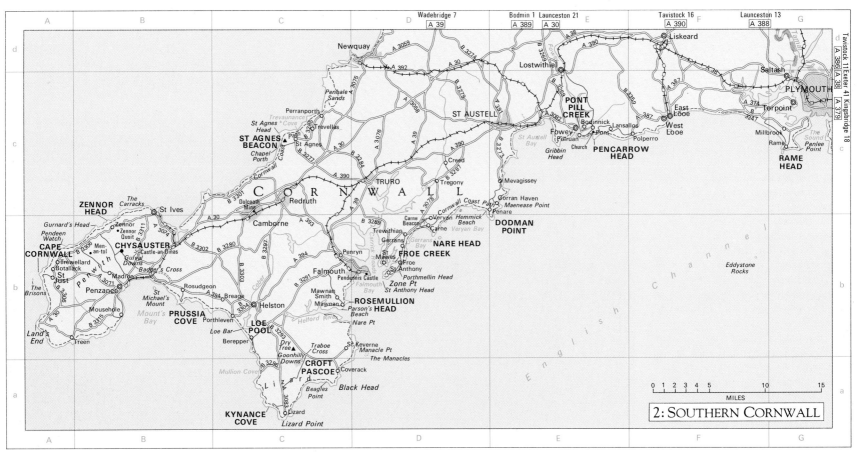

2: SOUTHERN CORNWALL

sweet with the scent of bell heather stirred by the stiff sea breezes. On Gull Rock, offshore to the south-east, cormorants can be seen sitting with wings outstretched to dry. The rock was the scene of the wreck of the sailing ship *Hera* in February 1914, with the loss of 19 lives.

The constant pounding of the waves has eaten away the slate cliffs, leaving the headland as a narrow point at its seaward tip. It broadens out inland, where there are hedgerows bright with foxgloves and red campion in summer. Cornfields cover the slopes on the headland, and a pathway leads down past a derelict fisherman's hut to the sandy coves below. On the west side of the headland a small stream runs through a bracken-covered valley to the sandy but busy Pendower Beach.

Carne Beacon, a hill with magnificent views a mile north of Nare Head, can be reached by a public footpath from the hamlet of Carne. The easiest approach is from its north-west side, and once on top there are breathtaking views of the surrounding countryside. The gorse-covered mound on the summit with its gnarled old lilac tree is a round barrow – a Bronze Age burial mound more than 3,000 years old. But legend assigns it as the grave of Gerennius, a king or saint who died some 1,400 years ago.

This semi-legendary king – who may have been the Geraint of King Arthur's Round Table – gave his name to Gerrans Bay and the village of Gerrans round the bay to the west. Believed to have been a Celtic prince who took refuge in this part of Cornwall after being driven from Wales by the Saxons, he is said to have lived at Dingerein Castle, now only an earthen mound north of Gerrans. On his

death, according to legend, Gerennius was rowed across Gerrans Bay in a golden boat with silver oars, and his boat buried with him in the Carne mound. But no boat was found when the mound was excavated in 1855.

Nare Head and Carne Beacon are both owned by the National Trust. Take the Veryan turning east off the A3078 St Mawes–Truro road and follow signposts to Carne, where cars can be parked.

THE FLAVOUR OF CORNWALL From the cliff-top at Nare Head, east of Gerrans Bay, the view is typically Cornish. Cultivated fields drop to the edge of precipitous cliffs. South-westwards the Lizard coast lines a textured-glass sea, with Zone Point guarding the entrance to Falmouth Bay and with Manacle Point on the distant horizon.

NARE HEAD ACROSS GERRANS BAY

GRANITE CLIFFS BELOW NARE HEAD

PORTHMELLIN HEAD AND MANACLE POINT FROM NARE HEAD

2Ec Pencarrow Head

One of the most attractive headlands in Cornwall, Pencarrow Head combines the intimacy of its greenery, its flowers and its birdsong with the exhilaration of its wide-ranging views – sunswept fields and sandy bays, and silent promontories reaching down to the sea.

Buzzards soar overhead while yellowhammers chirp busily in the thickets below, and in summer the bright pink of centaury and the occasional vermilion gleam of scarlet pimpernel contrast with the green of grass and bracken. Rabbits abound, prey to the circling buzzards as well as the many foxes and weasels that make their home here.

From the 447 ft summit of the headland on a clear day you can see eastwards as far as Rame Head, 20 miles away, or sometimes beyond to Bolt Head in Devon. About 15 miles southwest, the Dodman juts out into the Channel and beyond it in a blue haze is the Lizard coast around St Keverne. Inland and a mile north-west from Pencarrow Head, the 14th-century tower of St Willow, the parish church of Lanteglos by Fowey, rises above its bower of trees.

Some 200 ft below Pencarrow's sloping summit, the Cornwall Coast Path curves right round the headland, and stretches away on either side along the cliffs above the bays of Lantic to the west and Lantivet to the east. Fields slope gently down to the jagged rocks that overhang the semicircular bays, which can both be reached from the coastal path. Even in high summer you may find their sandy beaches uncrowded, and delight in the rock pools and the small coves that may have been the haunt of 18th-century smugglers. In high summer, too, the blue and mauve flowers of sea holly and the pink, white-striped flowers of sea bindweed glow among the shingle.

Pencarrow Head can be reached along the unclassified Lansallos–Polruan road west from the A387 at Polperro. After about 4 miles there is a large car park beside the road, from where a path leads to the headland, owned by the National Trust.

1Ab Pentire Point

At the western tip of a square headland that juts into the Atlantic, Pentire Point is a 260 ft high block of solidified lava known as pillow lava, for it was poured out in pillow-like masses from a submarine volcano millions of years ago. On all sides, the views are impressive. A wide sweep of the grey Atlantic stretches to the west, north and north-west. To the north-east you can see beyond Boscastle and Cambeak to the long line of cliffs near Bude, and again beyond, some 35 miles distant, to the great mass of Hartland Point on the North Devon coast.

South-westwards, Stepper Point guards the opposite, western shore of the River Camel estuary, and beyond is Trevose Head and its lighthouse. Southwards from Pentire Point, you can look down the river to the great sandbank known as The Doom Bar. This bar has blocked the mouth of the Camel for 150 years or more, reducing the river to a narrow channel and ending Padstow's prosperity as a busy port and harbour. According to legend, the bank built up because of a mermaid's curse, made after she had been fatally wounded by a Padstow fisherman who shot her with a bow and arrow in mistake for a seal. Nearly 300 ships have been driven on to the treacherous bar to be wrecked or stranded, with considerable loss of life.

The rocky islets of Newland (128 ft) and The Mouls (164 ft) that lie northwest and north-east off the Pentire headland are a haven for grey seals and puffins. The Mouls lies off Rumps

CELTIC DEFENCES Banks and ditches across the neck of Y-shaped Rumps Point once guarded an Iron Age fort.

Point at the eastern tip of the headland, a Y-shaped promontory crowned by an Iron Age fort known as The Rumps. Some 2,000 years ago a small Celtic community lived here in round thatched huts, guarded from invaders by three banks and ditches whose outlines can still be seen across the neck of the promontory. Scraps of pottery found on the site show that they may have come from Brittany in north-west France, and that they drank wine from the Mediterranean.

You can walk right round the headland, which is owned and farmed by the National Trust. Many of the cliffs are covered with bracken that glows warm brown in autumn, and in summer foxgloves and red campion are among the flowers that line the way. At Pentireglaze on the south of the headland there are remains of a mine that was worked for silver and lead ore in the 18th and 19th centuries.

Pentire Point is 6 miles north-west of Wadebridge. Leave by the B3314 and after 4 miles, at Plain Street, turn north-west along a minor road towards Pentire Farm, where there is a car park.

2Ec   Pont Pill Creek

Although it opens into Fowey harbour right opposite the town itself, Pont Pill Creek is a quiet, beautiful backwater that gives the impression it is miles from anywhere. Time seems to stand still here, but not the tide, which ebbs and flows along the narrow, mile-long creek twice daily. Woods of oak, chestnut, sycamore and hazel line the north bank, sweeping down to the water's edge, near the creek head at the hamlet of Pont, where a tiny stream filters in.

A tranquil spot where herons haunt the reeds below the leafy bank, the creek was not always so peaceful. Once it was part of the port of Fowey (pronounced 'foy'), and less than a century ago boats came regularly to the quays at Pont to collect cargoes of grain, timber, coal and sand. The quays and footbridge have been restored by the National Trust, which owns land on both shores of the creek.

At the mouth of the creek, at Pentleath Point on the north shore, there is a granite memorial to Sir Arthur Quiller-Couch, the writer known as 'Q', who died at Fowey in 1944. This is a good place for views of Fowey – until Stuart times one of the foremost ports in England. Sir Arthur's home, The Haven, overlooks the harbour. Fowey was the setting for his novel *Troy Town*. It was also 'the little grey sea town' with 'flights of stone steps overhung by great pink tufts of valerian' described by Sea Rat in Kenneth Grahame's *The Wind in the Willows* written in 1908. Grahame, a friend of Sir Arthur, was married at Fowey in 1899 and often visited the town.

From Fowey you can make a round trip along both shores of Pont Pill Creek, walking for some 3 miles along the National Trust's Hall Walk, which starts at Bodinnick ferry across the river from Fowey. It leads eastwards along the north bank of the creek and westwards along the south bank to Polruan, where there is another ferry back to Fowey.

The start of the walk leads down to the 'Q' memorial, along what was once a promenade of the old mansion of Hall, the home of the Mohun family; all that remains is the old chapel, now part of the farm buildings of Hall Farm. It was on this promenade in 1644 that Charles I was almost killed by a shot fired from a cannon at Fowey, where

A DRY LAND SKIPPER

Though often seen along coastal cliffs, the large skipper butterfly has no connection with the sea; it is named for its fast and darting flight. The butterfly lays its eggs on false brome grass, found in woods, hedges and scrubland.

False brome grass (*Brachypodium sylvaticum*)

Large skipper butterfly (*Ochlodes venata*)

Parliamentarians led by the Earl of Essex were under siege.

Fowey is on the A3082, 7 miles east of St Austell. Pont Pill Creek can also be reached along minor roads west from Polperro (signposted Bodinnick) to Pont, where there is a car park.

2Bb   Prussia Cove

A narrow inlet in the slate rocks of Bessy's Cove in Mount's Bay, Prussia Cove takes its name from a notorious smuggler, John Carter, whose nickname was the King of Prussia. No one knows for sure whether this was because he looked like Frederick the Great, or because that king was his hero. Bessy's Cove is named after the keeper of an alehouse that once stood on the cliffs above.

In the late 1700s, John Carter, from Breage, made the cove his headquarters for landing and storing contraband such as brandy, tobacco and bales of silk. The only landward approach was by a steep path down the cliff. Once when one of his cargoes was discovered and seized by Customs men, Carter raided Penzance Customs House the following night to retrieve it. The captive goods were promised to customers and Carter never broke his word. He became so bold that he ringed the cliffs above the cove with cannon to keep away the Customs cutters.

The rugged, picturesque coves are more peaceful today, along with the adjoining Piskies Cove. The caves that the smugglers found so useful were worn from the rocks by the pounding sea, and Piskies Cove in particular has been much eroded. When the seas run high, the immense clouds of spray that rise among the rocks are a spectacular sight. The climate here is generally mild, allowing a profusion of flowers such as thrift, and evergreen tamarisk shrubs line the cliff-top. Fishermen use the slender tamarisk branches for making lobster pots.

In 1947, Prussia Cove witnessed the death throes of HMS *Warspite*, a battleship of both World Wars that was at the Battle of Jutland in 1916. On her way to a breaker's yard, the 600 ft ship broke loose from her tugs in Mount's Bay in a south-westerly gale, and was eventually blown on to the rocks of the cove. Later she was refloated and moved westwards along the coast to St Michael's Mount and eventually broken up.

Prussia Cove is 5 miles east of Penzance, and is signposted south off the A394 Penzance–Helston road at Rosudgeon. Cars can be parked in a field on the cliffs above the cove.

2Cb Rosemullion Head

Sheltered by the Lizard peninsula from the full fury of the Atlantic gales, the corner of Cornwall north of the Helford river is a comparatively gentle, richly wooded area with leafy lanes and lovely creeks, and sandy beaches where it is safe to bathe. Perched on the cliff overlooking the rivermouth and Parson's Beach is 15th-century Mawnan Church. From it, a flower-lined footpath leads to Rosemullion Head about a mile to the north-east, a low promontory overlooking the western side of Falmouth Bay.

A tranquil spot where the sea laps lazily against the rocks, the headland is sea-girt on three sides, with a pathway to the south leading down to a sand and shingle beach with numerous rock pools in the wave-cut platform. Thickly covered with gorse and bracken, Rosemullion Head climbs gently inland to a height of 220 ft. More than half-a-dozen headlands come into view, including Pendennis Point with its Tudor fortress guarding the western side of Falmouth harbour, and Zone Point and the pine-clad St Anthony Head on the other side of Falmouth Bay.

St Anthony Head is distinguished by the white lighthouse at the foot of the cliff, which throws a beam of light across the harbour entrance, and also sends a red light flashing south-west to the dangerous Manacles reef. Looking south from Rosemullion Head you can

---

SMUGGLERS' HIDE-OUT Prussia Cove still echoes in the imagination to the creak of oars and the grounding of keels as contraband is smuggled ashore: 'Brandy for the Parson, 'Baccy for the Clerk . . .'

---

see Nare Point on the south shore of Helford rivermouth and beyond it Manacle Point which is north-west of The Manacles.

Nare Point was the scene of a savage shipwreck in the terrible West Country blizzards of March 1891, when the *Bay of Panama*, a clipper carrying jute from Calcutta, was hurled against its cliffs. The survivors clung to the rigging all night, some freezing to death; those still left alive were taken off by breeches-buoy next morning. Even then, the horse-bus taking them to refuge in St Keverne was caught in a snow-drift and had to be abandoned. Seventeen of the crew of 40 survived.

Rosemullion Head, owned by the National Trust, is 3 miles south of Falmouth along minor roads via Mawnan Smith and Mawnan. There is a car park by Mawnan Church, from where a path leads ½ mile to the headland.

2Gc Rame Head

The heavy seas of the English Channel beat against the grey slate rocks of Rame Head on three sides, for only a narrow neck of land links it to the mainland. It is majestic and remote, its bracken-covered slopes stretching steeply to the sea from its 300 ft summit. Rame Head is at the western tip of the headland that guards the Cornish side of Plymouth Sound, with Penlee Point 1½ miles to the east overlooking the Sound.

Gulls mewing above the roar of the sea on the rocks are the most constant sounds reaching this high vantage point, which is rich with wild flowers in summer. There are magnificent views of the Channel and its shipping, and of ships heading in and out of Plymouth Sound. On clear days it is

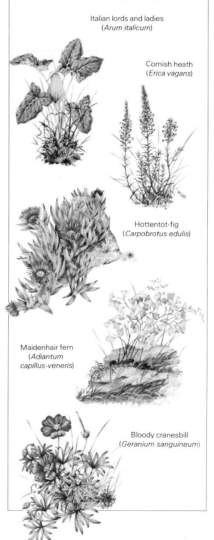

RARE AND HANDSOME BEAUTIES

The pale lilac Cornish heath grows only on the Lizard. Rare, too, is maidenhair fern, a plant of sea walls like the Hottentot-fig which is sometimes called 'Sally-my-handsome'. The yellow flower spike identifies Italian lords and ladies; bloody cranesbill is found in grassy places.

Italian lords and ladies
(*Arum italicum*)

Cornish heath
(*Erica vagans*)

Hottentot-fig
(*Carpobrotus edulis*)

Maidenhair fern
(*Adiantum capillus-veneris*)

Bloody cranesbill
(*Geranium sanguineum*)

---

sometimes possible to pick out the Lizard on the horizon some 50 miles to the south-west, and nearer at hand 9 miles out to sea is the 133 ft Eddystone Lighthouse. It was near this point, on July 20, 1588, that the English fleet first engaged the Spanish Armada.

The first lighthouse was begun on the Eddystone reef in 1696, taking nearly four years to complete. In June 1697 its designer, Henry Winstanley, was carried off by a French privateer while at work on the reef, but the Admiralty negotiated his release a month later. Only four years after its completion, the timber structure was swept away in a severe gale on November 26, 1703, and along with it its keepers and Henry Winstanley, who had gone there to supervise repairs. The second lighthouse, built by John Smeaton in 1759, was dismantled in 1877 and now stands on Plymouth Hoe.

On the summit of Rame Head there are remains of a slate-built chapel dedicated in 1397 to St Michael, the patron saint of Cornwall, and rebuilt in the 1880s. In the Middle Ages, men were paid by the Plymouth authorities to keep watch from this point and give warning of the approach of pirates or privateers. They also lit and tended beacons as a guide to ships. When gales whip up the waters of the Channel, this is a dangerous coast, particularly for sailing ships. Those sunk directly beneath Rame Head include the *Friends Endeavour*, a sloop from Fowey in January 1811, and the *Deptford*, a brig from Sunderland in January 1818.

Rame Head is about 3 miles south of Millbrook. Turn off the B3247 at Coombe Farm along a minor road leading south beyond Rame village to the Coastguard Station, where there is a car park. Rame Head is a ¼ mile walk from there.

—ISLES OF SCILLY—

Remote granite archipelago that legend claims was part of the mythical kingdom of Lyonesse

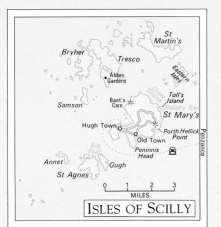

ISLES OF SCILLY

Lost land of legend

In folklore, the Isles of Scilly are said to be part of the lost Cornish kingdom of Lyonesse that was engulfed by the sea as a punishment for the dissolute life led by its inhabitants. There are similarities between the islands and the mainland that suggest that they were once linked – perhaps some 300,000 years ago. For example, there is a striking resemblance between the dramatic granite formations at Peninnis Head on St Mary's and those at Treen Cliff, 4 miles south-east of Land's End.

The early settlers

The islands were probably first colonised by Bronze Age people from the southern Iberian peninsula. They arrived around 2000 BC and settled extensively throughout the archipelago – there are three times as many prehistoric tombs there as in the rest of Cornwall. Two fine examples exist on St Mary's, one at Porth Hellick Point and the other – Bant's Carn – in the island's north-west.

Later visitors included the Phoenicians, who are believed to have discovered the Isles of Scilly while seeking tin in Cornwall. The Romans never settled there but used the islands as a place of banishment for wrongdoers. Danish raiders found them a convenient base for raids on the Bristol Channel. Later, the islands became a centre for smuggling, but by the early 19th century even this source of livelihood had slumped. It was not until the 1880s that the economy revived with the introduction of the early flower trade.

St Mary's, the largest of the islands, can be reached by boat or helicopter from Penzance.

SET like stepping-stones into the Atlantic, the southernmost fragment of Britain has the most gentle climate in the kingdom – warm summers followed by winters that are so mild that daffodils bloom in December. Yet there are extremes – one day the land cowers beneath fierce Atlantic gales, and the next day it is bathed in sunlight of startling clarity.

Lying some 28 miles west of Land's End, the low-lying, flat-topped granite islands rarely rise above 100 ft. The 200 or so islands, islets and named rocks – of which only five are inhabited – are the remnants of a granite mass formed at the same time as the great masses of Dartmoor, Bodmin Moor and Land's End. Straddling one of the busiest approaches to Britain's southwestern ports, the archipelago has been the graveyard of hundreds of ships – on one night alone in 1707, four ships and 2,000 men of Sir Cloudesley Shovell's Mediterranean Squadron were lost.

PELISTRY BAY CRYSTAL-CLEAR WATERS LAP THE SHORES OF THE BAY, ON THE EASTERN SIDE OF ST MARY'S AND ONE OF THE ISLAND'S MOST SECLUDED SPOTS, THOUGH ONLY 2 MILES FROM HUGH TOWN, CAPITAL OF THE SCILLIES.

TOLL'S ISLAND LINKED TO THE SHORES OF PELISTRY BAY BY A SLENDER STRAND, THE ISLAND LOOKS ACROSS CROW SOUND TO THE EASTERN ISLES.

2Cc   St Agnes Beacon

One of the north Cornish coast's finest scenic grandstands, St Agnes Beacon, 630 ft, gives not only superb coastal views stretching from Trevose Head and Newquay south to St Ives, but also views inland to the heights of Bodmin Moor and across the peninsula to Falmouth and St Michael's Mount.

Around the beacon itself, the hill-sides are dotted with the remains of the local mining industry that flourished in the 19th century, when St Agnes was a great centre of tin and copper mining. Gaunt, ruined engine-houses with their tall chimneys – Cornish castles – are scattered along the cliffs.

A 3 mile walk from Chapel Porth round St Agnes Head to Trevaunance Cove takes in not only the fine cliff scenery but also Wheal Coates – *wheal* is a Cornish word for 'mine'. The ruins are perched partway down the cliffs below the west slopes of the beacon, and are now owned by the National Trust. If you go in late spring or early summer, you will find the cliffs bright with wild flowers such as the pale blue, star-like spring squill, the yellow kidney vetch and the golden prostrate broom. In late summer and autumn they are aglow with the purple of heather and the gold of western gorse.

Trevaunance Cove shelters below the eastern side of St Agnes Head, and was once the harbour where tin and copper were exported. No signs of the quays remain today. They were very difficult to construct in this rock-girt cove, and four attempts between 1632 and 1736 were swept away by the sea. The narrow, rocky Trevellas Porth adjoins Trevaunance, and from here you can walk beside the stream up the lovely combe known as Trevellas Coombe

to Trevellas and Harmony Cot, about a mile north-east of the valley and the birthplace of John Opie, the 'Cornish Wonder'.

Born on May 12, 1761, John Opie was the son of a local carpenter, and on his mother's side a descendant of the local lords of the manor, the Tonkin family. Although he had no tuition in painting, he became a well-known and successful artist and portrait painter, and at the age of 26 was made a Fellow of the Royal Academy. On his death in 1807 he was buried in St Paul's Cathedral.

St Agnes is 6 miles north of Redruth via the A30 and B3277. The beacon is 1 mile south-west of the village.

CORNWALL'S CASTLES OF INDUSTRY

THE CASTLE-LIKE RUINS of engine-houses and chimney-stacks are monuments to an age when men burrowed beneath the granite cliffs and moors in search of tin, copper, lead and zinc. In the mid-19th century there were 600 mines active in Cornwall. Today the mines appear suddenly on the landscape, as the road turns a bend or climbs a hill; grey, granite buildings like tall keeps with a tapering tower, standing stark against the skyline or merging into the background of a boulder-strewn moor.

The coastal mines around St Agnes and St Just often had their engine-houses perched high on a cliff-top, where many still stand today – roofless and ivy-clad among the spoil-heaps.

WHEAL COATES MINE, CHAPEL PORTH

2Bb   Zennor Head

Backed by the bleak heather moors of Penwith, Zennor Head is a grand, lonely spot overlooking the Atlantic, with a narrow gorge known as the Horse's Mouth cutting into the headland. It is a good place for viewing a 'green flash' – a phenomenon that sometimes occurs over the sea while the sun is sinking or rising, when a green light momentarily floods the sky.

On a calm summer day the view from the 300 ft headland can be deceptively gentle, but when an Atlantic gale is blowing, mountainous seas can be heard hurling huge boulders over the rocks below. From The Carracks – rocky, seal-haunted islands 2 miles north-east – down to Pendeen Watch, 5 miles south-west beyond Gurnard's Head, this coast has been the scene of many shipwrecks.

Zennor village shelters in a hollow about half a mile inland from Zennor Head, and about half a mile south-east of the village is Zennor Quoit, a chambered tomb dating back some 5,000 years to the Stone Age. Its huge stones, including a 15 ft wide slab capstone, form a rectangular enclosure once covered by an earthen mound. Some of the support stones were taken by a 19th-century farmer for building, and another damaged the tomb by blasting in an unsuccessful treasure hunt.

Zennor is 4 miles west of St Ives on the B3306, and the headland is ¼ mile north-west from the village.

DARTMOOR

Once populated by Bronze and Iron Age farmers, the moor is now southern England's last great wilderness

Great grey granite tors rise above bleak and barren bogs and wide expanses of rolling moorland in the wild and forbidding heart of Dartmoor, where swiftly racing clouds send sinister shadows skimming across the heather, and where only the harsh croaking of a raven may break the brooding silence. Menace seems to lurk in the circling buzzards, the buffeting wind and the suddenly descending mists, yet there is also tremendous exhilaration in the invigorating upland air and in the space, solitude and might of the moor.

Dartmoor was designated a National Park in 1951 and covers 365 sq. miles, of which about half is blanket bog ringed by grass and heather moors fringed by stone-walled farmland. The high moorland covers much of a great, south-sloping 1,200 ft granite plateau, separated into two parts roughly north and south of the Yelverton–Moretonhampstead road (B3212). High Willhays (2,038 ft) and Yes Tor (2,030 ft) in the more extensive northern plateau are the highest points. The core of the National Park is the 110 sq. miles of high moorland known as Dartmoor Forest, once a royal hunting ground, that has belonged to the Duchy of Cornwall since 1307.

Wild ponies, sheep and hardy cattle such as Galloways graze among the grass and heather moors and the scattered 'clitters' of tumbled boulders. The hardy Dartmoor ponies are probably descendants of

early medieval domestic ponies, and although they run wild on the moor, all have owners and are rounded up at the annual 'pony drift' each autumn. Dartmoor's red deer died out in the 18th century, but there are sometimes a few stragglers from Exmoor to the north.

Woodland – mainly oakwoods and conifer plantations – covers just under one-tenth of the moor, much of it in the river valleys. Fourteen rivers rise in Dartmoor's upland bogs; their upland valleys are shallow, but where they leave the granite plateau there are steep wooded gorges and rocky outcrops, with beauty spots such as Dartmeet on the River Dart, Becky Falls on Becka Brook (a tributary of the Bovey) and Fingle Bridge on the River Teign.

Innumerable prehistoric remains – burial chambers, stone circles, standing stones and hut circles – bear witness to Dartmoor's heavily populated past. Lightly forested and with plenty of water and building stones, it was an attractive area in a climate warmer than today's, and from 5,000 to 3,000 years ago more people lived on the moor than have lived there since. A well-preserved settlement of that period is Grimspound, which lies 2½ miles north-east of Postbridge, near Hameldown Tor. It was within this prehistoric village that Sherlock Holmes was supposed to have concealed himself while investigating the phantom hound of the Baskervilles.

The enduring granite also provides relics of later ages, such as the stone crosses that were medieval waymarks and the stone-built homes of medieval tin miners. Tin-mining began on the moor in the 12th century, and during the Middle Ages, Dartmoor was one of Europe's main tin-producing areas. The remains of stone-built smelting-houses, or blowing-houses, can still be found near streams.

MANY FACES OF BEAUTY Dartmoor's diverse scenery is strikingly apparent at Burrator Reservoir. The boulder-strewn slopes of Yellowmead Down merge with the soft landscape of trees at the water's edge, and beyond are the wild hills and lofty crags of Leather Tor and Sharpitor.

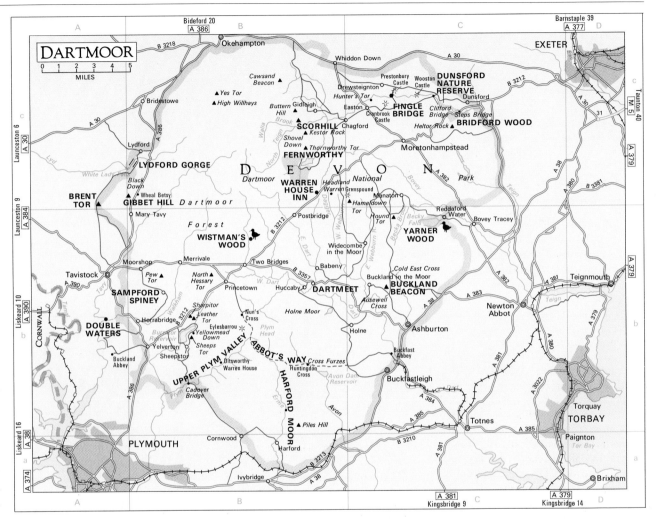

Places to visit

Map ref. Bb Abbot's Way

This romantically named track across the southern part of the moor is said to have been used by abbots travelling between Buckland Abbey and Buckfast Abbey. Since the track traceable today goes nowhere near Buckland it seems an unlikely story – more probably it was a wool-trader's packhorse route from the Plym valley to the Dart, dating from early medieval times.

Whatever its origin, Abbot's Way provides a challenging and rewarding walk from Cross Furzes to Princetown through wild, open countryside, past copses and over clapper bridges, across moorland bogs and by rivers and streams. On either side of the track are the signs of man's activities, from the cairns and hut circles of the Bronze and Iron Ages to the modern Avon Dam reservoir below Dean Moor. Medieval granite crosses such as Huntingdon Cross and Nun's Cross were waymarks, often placed where tracks crossed.

Near the source of the River Erme, which flows southwards across the moor, another track heads north for about half a mile to the remains of a smelting-house, or blowing-house. More than 70 of these buildings are scattered across Dartmoor, dating from between the 15th and 17th centuries.

Water-wheels were used to power the furnace bellows, and some had water-powered millstones for crushing the tin ore – knocking mills for coarse crushing and crazing mills for finer grinding of the stone.

Abbot's Way starts at Cross Furzes, 2½ miles west of Buckfastleigh on the A38. It fords the upper reaches of the River Plym, then heads northwards through Nun's Cross Farm to Princetown.

Ac Brent Tor

The conical peak of Brent Tor, 1,130 ft high, dominates the western side of Dartmoor, irresistibly drawing the eye towards it from miles around. The wonder of the tor lies not simply in the power of its appearance. Unlike the granite peaks around it, Brent Tor owes its character to volcanic action and also to the sturdy, medieval

Church of St Michael on its summit. Legend claims that the church was built by a merchant saved from shipwreck on the stormy Devon coast – the merchant had sworn that if he ever regained the shore, he would have a church built on the highest peak he could see. In fact, the present church was built under contract from nearby Tavistock Abbey and dedicated in 1319. It was built on the site of an earlier church, called St Michael on the Rock, dating from the middle of the 12th century.

The easiest approach to the summit is by the path that climbs gently through the gorse on the south-west side of the hill.

A signposted minor road leads from Tavistock to Brent Tor, 4 miles to the north. There is a small car park at the bottom of the hill.

Cc **Bridford Wood**

On a hillside above the River Teign lies the glorious confusion of Bridford Wood, a wilderness of ash, alder, oak, silver birch and many other species of tree. A great variety of woodland birds can be found here, including blue tits and long-tailed tits, finches, thrushes, wrens, woodpeckers and even the occasional buzzard, sparrowhawk and raven. In summer the cuckoo's call and the cooing of wood pigeons can be heard. A pleasant walk leads steeply up through the wood to the top of the hill, and then to Heltor Rock, about 1½ miles away. The route leads through Burnicombe Farm and then on to the road. Turn right to reach the stile leading up to the rock. The approach to the tor is not easy; the overgrown path leads through foxgloves, brambles and gorse. It is well worth persevering to the top, however.

The massive granite outcrop of Heltor Rock stands austerely defiant of wind and rain in the north-east corner of Dartmoor, and everything about it seems raw and revealed, as if the rock was the bones of the earth laid bare. The surrounding countryside heightens this impression, for the view is unlike that from most other Dartmoor tors, where granite-strewn peaks and

DR WATSON AND THE HOUND OF HELL

THE SHERLOCK HOLMES SOCIETY of London will no doubt continue to debate the finer points of the strange affair of *The Hound of the Baskervilles* (as recounted by Dr John Watson) for many years to come. However, its researches, it is hoped, will at last lay to rest the notion that Dr Watson was inclined to be slapdash in matters of geographical accuracy. It can now be revealed that this was a gallant attempt to protect the name of an ancient and respected family.

The confusion lies in the action of the chronicle being set within a few miles of Dartmoor prison, whereas in fact it took place over a much wider area and the names were not infrequently changed. Grimpen Mire, for example, where the hound was kennelled and Stapleton met his dreadful end, is the fearsome Foxtore Mire.

But there can be no doubt about the original of the wicked Sir Hugo Baskerville, who is said to have been killed by a phantom hound from Hell that haunted Hound Tor. It was Sir Richard Cabell of Brooke Manor, a man of evil reputation, upon whose death in 1677 black hell-hounds were seen racing across the moor to hurl themselves upon his tomb in Buckfastleigh Church.

The name Baskerville was supplied by Dr Watson's collaborator, Dr Conan Doyle. It was that of the coachman who accompanied him upon his researches.

HOUND TOR – SOURCE OF THE BASKERVILLE LEGEND

wild, open moorland stretch as far as the eye can see. The countryside around Heltor Rock is as gentle on the eye as the tor itself is bleak and unyielding, a panorama of green pastureland and, in summer, fields rippling with golden corn.

Bridford Wood is on the B3212 opposite the entrance to Dunsford Nature Reserve at Steps Bridge (see p. 32), 4 miles north-east of Moretonhampstead. There is a large car park near the entrance.

Cb **Buckland Beacon**

The view from the top of Buckland Beacon is one of the finest on the moor. To the east the River Teign winds through delightful countryside to the South Devon coast; to the south the view extends over the wide, green canopy of the Dart valley; and 10 miles to the west North Hessary Tor, marked by an unsightly television mast, stands above Princetown. The beacon itself is bare and exposed; but in summer and autumn there is no shortage of colour, when the vivid yellow of gorse and the rich purple of ling bring relief to the predominantly grey and green background. In 1928 the words of the Ten Commandments were carved on the rocks crowning Buckland Beacon, on the instructions of a former lord of the manor; and the carving aptly emphasises the Old Testament atmosphere of the scene.

A 5 mile drive north from Buckland Common to Manaton leads through the countryside that was the setting for Conan Doyle's story of *The Hound of the Baskervilles*. Some 2 miles southwest of Manaton, where the road forks three ways, a path leads south-east to the fang-like rocks crowning Hound Tor, the haunt of the phantom hound.

Buckland Beacon is 2¼ miles north-west of Ashburton on the A38. Minor roads lead from Ashburton to Buckland-in-the-Moor – the beacon is 1 mile east of the village. A path to the top starts just north of the cattle-grid on the road between Ausewell Cross and Cold East Cross.

Bb Dartmeet

A simple stone beside the road about half a mile east of Dartmeet symbolises perfectly the harsh side of life as it used to be lived on Dartmoor. The stone was a resting place in the days when men had to carry their dead across the moor for burial at Widecombe. Here they rested the coffin, while mourners gathered to sing praises and murmur prayers, before the long climb ahead. On the stone they sometimes carved the initials of the deceased. Among the lichen which surrounds the stone today, five crosses and sets of initials can still be seen.

At Dartmeet itself the East and West Dart rivers join, and here is the best of both worlds of Dartmoor. Above lies the dramatic moorland; spread out below lie the densely wooded valleys. There are many delightful walks in the area – north up the East Dart valley to Babeny, south-east to the reservoir on Holne Moor and west to Huccaby.

The path to Huccaby – just under a mile away – climbs up through pleasant pastureland to the wind-blown heights of the open moor, before dropping down again to the village. The top of the moor is a particularly marvellous sight in summer, when it is cloaked with the vivid yellow of gorse and tormentil; and in autumn, when it glows with a thick, golden cover of bracken.

Dartmeet is on the B3357, 6 miles north-west of Ashburton.

Ab Double Waters

There are many beautiful trees at Double Waters, where the rivers Tavy and Walkham meet, and they give no impression that only about 100 years ago this was an industrial area, for a copper seam lies in the ground below. Once the copper made Double Waters one of the most important mining centres in Devon, with some 200 people working at the mine. But today the only reminder of the area's industrial past is the ruined stack of the mine's engine-house.

Double Waters lies at the end of a gentle 2 mile walk from Horrabridge, a village on the River Walkham. The walk follows the course of the river downstream and crosses a bridge to the opposite bank. Sycamore, alder and ash are among the trees which grow in profusion along the river; and beneath the green canopy of trees there are wood sorrels and wood anemones, whortleberries, blackberries and many other plants and flowers. In springtime the grassy banks are thickly carpeted with bluebells. At any time of the year it is a pleasant and picturesque spot, and down by the water where the rivers join it seems a world away from the more typical, bleak, open landscape of Dartmoor.

Horrabridge is 4 miles south-east of Tavistock, on the A386. Double Waters lies to the west of the village.

Cc Dunsford Nature Reserve

This delightful stretch of woodland runs for 2 miles along the north bank of the River Teign, from Clifford Bridge downstream to Steps Bridge, with ash, alder, oak, birch and hazel, as well as open areas of scrub with saplings, low bushes and bracken. For the geologist, the reserve is chiefly interesting because the underlying rocks are shale, slates and sandstones, not the typical Dartmoor granite.

For the naturalist, its delights include many woodland birds, as well as wagtails and dippers along the river banks, and the occasional kingfisher flashing over the surface. The area also has several different kinds of grasshoppers and crickets, and more than 20 species of butterflies, including the easily recognised red admiral, painted lady, common blue and orange tip, and the rarer pearl-bordered, high-brown and silver-washed fritillaries.

One entrance to the reserve, managed by the Devon Trust for Nature Conservation, is at Steps Bridge on the B3212 between Moretonhampstead and Exeter. There is a large car park near the entrance. The other, at Clifford Bridge, is on the minor road between Dunsford and Drewsteignton.

Bc Fernworthy

The forest and reservoir of Fernworthy are set against the majestic backdrop of some of Dartmoor's highest peaks; and the fact that both are man-made in no way detracts from the natural beauty of the scene. The reservoir is fed by numerous streams tumbling down from the granite heights, and it stretches for about a mile to the forest at its south-west end. There are some 1,400 acres of woodland – mainly plantations of Norway and Sitka spruce – and a delightful, 4 mile long nature trail running through the forest.

Along the trail the yellow flowers of tormentil and the blue of milkwort, along with vetches and herb robert light up the undergrowth in summer.

BIRDS OF MOOR AND WOODLAND

The stonechat's distinctive call, like two pebbles clinking together, may be heard on rough moorland. Oakwoods provide a stage for the wood warbler's liquid song.

Wood warbler
(*Phylloscopus sibilatrix*)

Stonechat
(*Saxicola torquata*)

The banks are cloaked with bilberry patches, and lichens thrive among the boulders and on the tree stumps and felled branches. There is also a group of prehistoric hut circles, which were inhabited some 4,000 years ago by the Beaker People, so called because of their characteristic pottery.

At intervals along the trail there are views across the moor, to the ragged northern skyline of Cawsand Beacon, Shovel Down, Thornworthy Tor and Kestor Rock.

Follow the A382 north-west out of Moretonhampstead, and after 3 miles turn left at Easton to Chagford. Fernworthy Reservoir and Forest are signposted from here. There are car parks at the reservoir, and the start of the nature trail.

Cc   Fingle Bridge

Snaking west to east across the north moor the River Teign enters a deep gorge at Hunter's Tor, and for the next 5 miles flows through some of the loveliest scenery on Dartmoor. Thickly wooded slopes tower 400 ft above the sparkling river, here swirling around massive water-smoothed boulders as it races towards Fingle Bridge.

The bridge dates from the 16th or 17th centuries and was part of a pack-horse track. Its three, buttressed, granite arches span the river where brown trout leap to take an unwary fly. Occasionally salmon may be seen. High above the bridge, on the north bank, stands Prestonbury Castle, an Iron Age hill-fort with three widely spaced ramparts. Across the gorge lies Cranbrook Castle, another Iron Age hill-fort. Between them, the two forts commanded the valley below.

There are walks along the river bank from Fingle Bridge, and following the river eastwards the path leads to Clifford Bridge and Steps Bridge and passes oak woodlands and conifer plantations. In the woods above the river near Clifford Bridge is Wooston Castle, another Iron Age fort but built on a slope just below the hilltop.

Fingle Bridge is about 6 miles north of Moretonhampstead by road. Leave the A382 at Sandypark for Drewsteignton 2 miles north-east. The only access to the bridge is along a minor road east of Drewsteignton.

Bc   Gibbet Hill

The criminal's body hanging in chains on Gibbet Hill can have done little to enhance the magnificent views east over Dartmoor and west to the Church

SHADY SANCTUARY Cool, green pools formed by a River Teign weir at Fingle Bridge shelter trout and an occasional salmon.

of St Michael on Brent Tor. And still today, when the mists descend on the hill and draw a veil over the views, they seem to bring with them brooding memories of those long-forgotten, dead men, and of Lady Howard from Tavistock, who was allegedly burned here as a witch in the 17th century after murdering all four of her husbands. The flames were not hot enough to rid the moor of Lady Howard, whose ghost is still said to ride from Okehampton to Tavistock on wild Dartmoor nights, in a coach made of bones, drawn by a team of headless horses and preceded by a black hound.

Gibbet Hill is a true moorland summit, the highest point of Black Down, the focal point of a bleak, open, bracken-covered landscape where no trees grow. The shrill calls of stonechats and wheatears carry far across the moor, and high overhead buzzards wheel lazily on the wind, searching the

WATER-CARVED GORGE The White Lady Falls cascade 100 ft in a foaming skein into Lydford Gorge, a deep, 1½ mile ravine gouged out from soft rocks by the River Lyd 450,000 years ago. Its walls soar to 60 ft in places.

ground for prey. At the bottom of the hill, on the east side of the road, stands the ruined stack of the Wheal Betsy silver and lead mine – abandoned around the beginning of the century when the workings became exhausted. The mine was acquired by the National Trust in 1967 as a memorial to the mining industry of Dartmoor.

Gibbet Hill is about 1 mile north of Mary Tavy on the A386. A track leads westwards from the main road to the summit. Cars can be parked on the roadside.

Bb   Harford Moor

The earliest inhabitants of Dartmoor found much that was attractive to them on Harford Moor in the upper Erme valley, as the many cairns, stone rows, enclosures, hut circles and other Bronze Age antiquities indicate. The area is noted for its stone rows – mostly single lines of stones, one more than 2 miles long, leading to burial cairns. A fine example can be seen high on Stall Moor across the Erme.

In the Middle Ages and afterwards, the tin-miners were drawn to the place by the riches below its surface. Today it is the wildness of the moor that is attractive, the rolling countryside stretching as far as the eye can see, interspersed with moorland bog and divided by numerous streams.

Harford Church, from which a track climbs up to Piles Hill and then on to the moor, is famous for its medieval cross, one of many similar pale granite stones which once served as signposts for travellers crossing the moor.

Harford Moor can be reached by turning north off the A38 Plymouth–Exeter road at Ivybridge. There is a small car park above Harford Church, from where a footpath leads north-east on to the moor.

Bc   Lydford Gorge

Four centuries ago, so the story goes, no name was more feared on Dartmoor than that of Gubbins. This was the name of a wild gang of outlaws, as renowned for their red beards as for their ruthless pillaging of local farms and cottages. They lived like animals in the dark caves of Lydford Gorge.

But today the National Trust owns the gorge, and the dramatic scenery and abundant wildlife inspire delight, not terror. The River Lyd roars down the well-wooded valley, and crashes over 100 ft high White Lady Falls. By the river, herons wait patiently for fish, while dippers plunge into the water in search of water beetles and other aquatic insects. Great spotted woodpeckers can sometimes be heard drumming on dead boughs in the woods, and in the shadow of the trees there are many ferns and plants such as herb robert and meadowsweet.

Lydford is situated just off the A386 between Okehampton and Tavistock. Follow the road through the village to the car park beyond the church, where the walk along the gorge starts.

Bb   Sampford Spiney

The few houses and the church that make up the tiny moorland hamlet of Sampford Spiney seem remote and isolated in time as well as location, as if the centuries pass more slowly here than elsewhere, and the 20th century is

TIME-WORN GRANITE Pew Tor above Sampford Spiney is typical of the Dartmoor tors, jointed and cracked when the rock cooled 350 million years ago, then weathered by frost, wind and rain.

COLOUR ON THE WING

The green colour of its silver-spotted underwings gives the dark green fritillary its name. It lays its eggs on the common dog violet, a food plant of the butterfly's caterpillar.

Dark green fritillary
(*Argynnis aglaia*)

Common dog violet
(*Viola riviniana*)

still far off in the future. Pigs and sheep graze the common as they have always done since man first came here, wheatears breed among the boulders strewn across the harsh, unchanging landscape, buzzards wheel and call over the valley by the church.

Overlooking the hamlet and the nearby oakwoods above the Walkham valley – some of the loveliest in Devon – stands the impressive peak of Pew Tor. It is impressive not so much for its height, since it is only 1,050 ft above sea-level, as for its commanding position. From the summit there are sweeping views west across Tavistock to Bodmin Moor and east Cornwall, and south to Plymouth.

Sampford Spiney can be reached by turning south off the B3357, 2 miles east of Tavistock at Moorshop. Follow the signs to the hamlet. Cars can be parked on the roadside. Pew Tor is ¾ mile north of the village.

Bc Scorhill

A prehistoric stone circle on wild, heather-covered moorland; a primitive clapper bridge over a swiftly flowing stream; the ruins of a Norman castle in a remote village which time seems to have passed by; all the most powerful and mysterious qualities of Dartmoor can be found within easy reach of Scorhill. And the wild moorland landscape is made wilder still by the impressive views north to the agricultural lowlands of Devon, and west to the granite massif of Dartmoor proper.

Scorhill stands above Gidleigh, a remote village on the northern edge of the moor, notable for its early-16th-century church and the ruins of Gidleigh Castle, a late-Norman fortified house. The Scorhill stone circle, some 3,000 years old, stands just west of the path leading over the moor from Berrydown Farm. Beyond the circle the path drops down to the Walla Brook, just below the point where it joins the North Teign river, crossed by a clapper bridge of great but uncertain age.

The bank of the river is well wooded with conifers, and in the more sheltered parts foxgloves and tormentil grow. In late summer and autumn the moor blazes with the pink and purple flowers of ling, bell heather and cross-leaved heath. Milkwort, whortleberry and the white, sweet-smelling heath bedstraw can also be found.

To the north of Scorhill is Buttern Hill, with the foundations of Bronze Age hut circles.

Take the A382 north-west out of Moretonhampstead, and after 3 miles turn left to Chagford. Gidleigh is about 2 miles west of Chagford, and Scorhill is 1 mile south-west of the village. Parking space is limited.

Bb Upper Plym Valley

It is a 5 mile walk from Cadover Bridge to the bogs east of Eylesbarrou where the River Plym rises at Plym Head; but it is easy walking country, and there is much of interest along the way. There are stone circles, hut circles and many other relics of the prehistoric inhabit-

COLOUR IN BLOOM

The brilliant gold of the western gorse, the delicate pink of the heath spotted orchid and the sharp yellow of the tormentil are seen on the acid soils of Dartmoor during the summer.

Heath spotted orchid
(*Dactylorhiza maculata*)

Tormentil
(*Potentilla erecta*)

Western gorse
(*Ulex gallii*)

ants of the moor; spoil-heaps from tin mines abandoned less than a century ago; spectacular views, and wild, invigorating moorland scenery. The river flows in a south-westerly direction off the moor, and is fed along the way by numerous tributaries with strange and evocative names, including Calves Lake, Evil Combe Water, Shavercombe Brook, Drizzlecombe, Meavy Pool and Leggis Lake. From the moorland above Ditsworthy Warren House, 2½ miles north-east of Cadover Bridge, it is possible to see as far as Plymouth in the south-west, while Cornwall lies far away to the west, beyond the Tamar.

From Ditsworthy Warren House, a path leads north-west to the village of Sheepstor and Burrator Reservoir. The lake, in the shadow of Sheeps Tor and fringed by woodland, teems with wildfowl and is a popular beauty spot.

Cadover Bridge is 4 miles south-east of Yelverton on a minor road off the A386, signposted to Cornwood. Parking is possible beside the road near the bridge.

Bc Warren House Inn

There can be few more bleak spots on Dartmoor than Warren House Inn, a solitary public house on the high moorland road between Moretonhampstead and Two Bridges. The inn was built for the miners who, daily during the 19th century, trudged down the path 200 yds north of the inn to work in the Dagger valley below. The inn takes its name from one of the extensive warrens, or game preserves, on medieval Dartmoor – in this instance, Headland Warren on the hill slopes to the east.

At the foot of the hill, on the valley floor, the stacks of the ruined mine buildings can still be seen. A stream threads its way through the valley, and the place has all the atmosphere of a ghost town. Sheep graze the moorland turf, and along the stream gnarled oaks and hawthorns stand in ancient and splendid isolation. To the south the bracken and heather-covered moorland stretches away to a stately stand of conifers. The yellow-breasted grey wagtail can often be seen flitting over the stream in search of insects, and occasionally a buzzard soars above.

A century ago Warren House Inn was the home of Jonas Coaker, who liked to describe himself as 'the poet of the moor'. It was Jonas who moved the pub from its original site on the opposite side of the road – a move strangely lacking in business sense. The original pub stood on common land and was therefore free. When he crossed the road Jonas moved on to land owned by the Duchy of Cornwall and ended up paying rent.

Take the B3357 from Tavistock to Ashburton, and turn north at Two Bridges on to the B3212. Warren House Inn is about 2 miles beyond Postbridge. There is a car park at the inn and a smaller one by the footpath to the Dagger valley.

Bb Wistman's Wood

Mystery and legend are wrapped in the gnarled and twisted branches of this ancient forest – now a nature reserve. How ancient nobody knows, that is the mystery, but the stunted, grotesque oaks are several centuries old and the woodland itself is probably a remnant of the original native woods.

Age and mystery, as always, lead to legend, and it is said that Wistman's Wood was a sacred grove of the Druids. There is no evidence to support the belief, but it is not hard to imagine the mystic rituals taking place in such a bizarre and almost nightmarish setting. Lichen-covered boulders are strewn among the dense undergrowth of ferns, and mosses cling to the trees, cladding the misshapen trunks and branches in a velvet mantle. The air of remoteness and solitude is heightened by the silence, broken only by birdsong and the sound of a stream in the valley.

Wistman's Wood covers only 8 acres and lies on a hillside 2 miles north of Two Bridges. It can be reached by following the footpath which leads up the valley from a parking area opposite the Two Bridges Hotel on the B3357.

Two Bridges is 8 miles east of Tavistock on the B3357.

Cb Yarner Wood

On a still summer's day only the singing of the birds and the tinkling of the stream threading its way among the trees disturb the quiet of Yarner Wood National Nature Reserve. This marvellous 372 acre oak woodland spreads across two small valleys and the spur of land between them, on the eastern fringe of Dartmoor. Sessile oak, the type in which the acorn sits directly on the twig, without a stalk, is the most common tree. But there are also birch, rowan and holly. The birdlife includes all three British species of woodpeckers – the great spotted, the lesser spotted and the green – as well as wood warblers, nuthatches and yellowhammers.

Yarner Wood was not always so quiet. In the mid-19th century it rang with the sounds of a copper mine in full production. Between 1858 and 1867, 2,300 tons of copper ore were extracted at Devon Wheal Frances, as the mine was known; and the old mine building still stands today, now as still and silent as the woods around it.

Yarner Wood is about 3 miles west of Bovey Tracey, off the minor road to Manaton. There is a car park at the entrance at Reddaford Water. To avoid disturbing wildlife, visitors are asked to keep to the waymarked Woodland Walk.

MAGICAL WOOD Enchantment enfolds the dwarfed oaks and lichened boulders of age-old Wistman's Wood, high on the moor.

EXMOOR AND NORTH DEVON

Behind a spectacular coastline of hump-backed
headlands lie heather-clad heights and wooded combes

Curlews calling among the heather and buzzards wheeling in the wind proclaim the wild spirit of Exmoor, where sturdy, black-maned ponies roam in herds, where wild red deer shelter in the thickly wooded valleys, and where dippers dive in the boulder-strewn streams. In stormy weather ferocious Atlantic gales lash western Exmoor and the North Devon coast, and damp, clinging mists descend with frightening suddenness. Yet when the sun shines the air is marvellously clear and fresh, and the rapidly racing clouds give an exhilarating feeling of freedom.

Exmoor National Park covers 265 sq. miles, stretching from Dulverton northwards to the Bristol Channel and from Combe Martin eastwards to Minehead. Most of the moor is a vast green plateau rising steeply on all sides to about 1,400 ft. In the north-east Dunkery Hill, at 1,704 ft, is the highest point.

It is easy to know a little of Exmoor, but hard to know it well, for not only does it combine many different types of scenery, but some of the loveliest landscapes lie hidden from the road. Purple moor grass holds sway in the treeless central area around Simonsbath, once the old royal forest of Exmoor. The River Exe and its tributary the Barle both rise in the boglands of The Chains and flow south-eastwards through heather moors, woods and fields before converging near Dulverton.

In the northern heather moors, fast-flowing streams cut deep

combes down to the spectacular Exmoor coast, with its sloping hog's-back cliffs between Porlock and Lynton, and the magnificent towering promontories between Woody Bay and Heddon's Mouth. The Somerset and North Devon Coast Path follows the Park coastline for some 30 miles, and runs west through the area round to Braunton Burrows. On the eastern fringe of the Park lie the wooded Brendon Hills, with their deep valleys and lush pastures.

The Normans established Exmoor Forest as a royal hunting ground administered by a hereditary warden, who in later centuries became a leaseholder. During the 1649–60 Commonwealth, the freehold was sold to a wealthy merchant and adventurer named James Boevey, who built Simonsbath Lodge in Simonsbath village. After the restoration of the monarchy he stayed on as leaseholder until the 1690s, and the forest remained a royal demesne until 1818 when it was sold to John Knight, a Worcestershire farmer and foundry owner, for £50,000.

It was John Knight and his son, Sir Frederic, who, by hard work and experiment, initiated the successful farming of the moor, introducing new breeds of sheep and cattle and establishing a system of root and grass growing for winter pasture.

The Knights made Exmoor a place to farm, but the 19th-century writer Richard Doddridge Blackmore, through his novel *Lorna Doone*, made Exmoor a place to visit. Based on local legend, the story tells of the Doones of Badgworthy, an outlaw family who terrorised Exmoor in the 17th century. Blackmore admitted that he had 'romanced' the scenery, and although the Doone valley of his novel was based on Hoccombe Combe, much of his description was inspired by the beautiful Badgworthy valley that lies to the east.

HIGH AND WILD A heathery, windswept and boulder-strewn moorland height, Dunkery Hill provides sweeping views across Exmoor. To the north, east and south the hill falls away to cultivated fields and wooded valleys that lap around its foot.

Places to visit

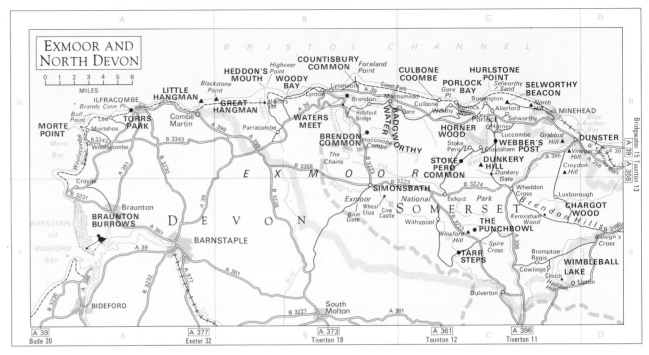

Map ref. Bb **Badgworthy Water**

The lovely valley of Badgworthy (pronounced 'Badgerry') Water lies at the east end of two large combes – Lank and Hoccombe. In its upper reaches it passes between steep hillsides covered with heather, bracken and gorse; lower down it has a gentler aspect, with a profusion of oak, ash and fir rising from the valley floor. It is the contrast between upland and lowland scenery that gives it its special charm, and adds weight to the claim that it is the most beautiful of all Exmoor's valleys.

But it is not only for its beauty that Badgworthy Water is renowned; it is also the heart of Doone country, the area of Exmoor which R. D. Blackmore immortalised in his novel *Lorna Doone* as the stronghold of the murderous outlaws, the Doones. It was in the old village of Badgworthy, which lies in Hoccombe Combe, that the outlaws are supposed to have lived, in fact as well as fiction. For Blackmore based his story on long-established Exmoor legends, which had grown out of the true exploits of a gang of desperadoes who settled in Badgworthy in the 17th century. Little remains of the old village, which may have originated as early as Saxon times. The stonework is crumbled to the ground and lies over-

grown by grass and brambles; the ruins further up the valley, known as Lorna's Cot, are the remains of a 19th-century shepherd's cottage, and have nothing to do with the original settlement.

The easiest approach to Badgworthy Water is from Malmsmead, on the road between Brendon and Oare. There is a car park, and the walk to Badgworthy, easy going on level ground, is about 3½ miles.

Aa **Braunton Burrows**

The gently undulating landscape of Braunton Burrows has an almost Sahara-like quality about it; acre upon acre of sand-dunes stretching for 4 miles along the north side of the Taw and Torridge estuaries. This is one of the finest stretches of sand-dunes in the south-west and is rich in unusual plants, as well as sea and marsh birds.

Braunton Burrows consists of two parallel groups of dunes, rising in places to 100 ft above the sea. In spring and autumn, large flocks of waders use the dunes as a resting place during migration. In winter, merlins, harriers and short-eared owls are among the birds of prey which hunt for voles, shrews and other small mammals. Resident here all the year round are herons, which stand like sentinels along the water's edge at low tide, and rabbits which breed in great numbers among the dunes. In summer, shelducks and wheatears often nest in disused rabbit burrows.

Several interesting species of moss grow here – *Tortula ruraliformis*, for example, which takes on an attractive golden-green colour after rain. Other mosses, such as the densely tufted *Tortella flavovirens* and the more common

Bryum pendulum, can also be found, as well as the rare round-headed club-rush and French toadflax.

Part of Braunton Burrows, which is situated off the B3231 Braunton–Croyde road, is a National Nature Reserve. The area is used from time to time by the military, but the footpaths can be followed except when the red flag is flying. Car parking is available.

Bb **Brendon Common**

The rolling heights of Brendon Common are as fine an example of open moorland as can be found in England today. Look out across the moor to its southern ridge, standing silhouetted against the sky; or stand in autumn sunshine on Withycombe Ridge and survey the purple heather all around, set off against the sombre browns of dying bracken. It is hard to say which response is the stronger, the sense of desolation or of the freedom that such plain, austere landscapes always inspire. The only signs of life are the sheep that graze the common – local farmers still retain common grazing rights here – the tough, little Exmoor ponies that gallop off when a stranger approaches, or perhaps a buzzard slowly turning on the wind, searching for voles, mice or rabbits hidden in the heather. But here the elements, too, seem alive: the mist that suddenly descends, cutting off the common from the outside world; the sweeping wind that carries with it all the unmistakable moorland scents; and the rain that varies from the soft drizzle that seems to hover in the air to the drenching torrents slashing and cutting across the waste with stinging ferocity.

Brendon Common is about 5 miles south-east of Lynton on the eastern side of the B3223.

Ca Chargot Wood

The narrow ridge of the Brendon Hills stretches across the easternmost part of Exmoor, linking the high moorland with the Quantocks to the east. Here there are woods and farmland, open heath on Haddon Hill to the south, and many relics of the iron mines which brought prosperity to the area in the mid-19th century. A road runs along the ridge of hills, and halfway between Wheddon Cross and Raleigh's Cross lies Chargot Wood, as tranquil a place as can be found on Exmoor. The higher parts of the Forestry Commission plantation are more than 1,000 ft above sea-level, with striking views to the north, where plantations of Douglas fir and spruce lead down to the

DOONE COUNTRY High moors enfold lovely Badgworthy Water, where the Doone family was supposed to have lived.

41

beautiful Luxborough valley, and the heavily wooded slopes of Croydon Hill dominate the skyline. Among the trees, hardly a sound can be heard louder than the rustling of leaves, the singing of birds and the occasional croak of a raven circling over the surrounding farmland. A path leads round the north of the wood and back into Kennisham Wood, just west of Chargot Wood. Here are the remains of an engine-house from a disused iron mine. On the opposite side of the Ridgeway road lies the long-forgotten railway line by which the iron ore was transported from the mine workings.

To reach Chargot Wood, take the A396 to Wheddon Cross and then follow the minor road signposted to Raleigh's Cross. There is a car park close to the entrance to the wood, on the north side of the road.

Bb Countisbury Common

The common, known locally as Barna Barrow, lies wedged between the hog-backed cliff of Foreland Point – topped by a lighthouse overlooking the Bristol Channel – and the road dropping down into Lynmouth. There are spectacular views near Countisbury Church, with its low tower and grey walls scoured by wind and rain. The panorama stretches north across the Bristol Channel to the coast of Wales, and west to where Lynton smudges the headland on the far side of Lynmouth Bay. A footpath threads its way along the cliff-top through acres of bracken, gorse and scrub; nothing disturbs the silence save the wind, the distant pounding of the waves and the sea-birds calling.

In 1899, during a savage, north-westerly gale, the wild moorland of Countisbury Common was the scene of extraordinary endeavour. A dozen horses and 100 men dragged the life-boat from Lynmouth 13 miles across the common and over the 991 ft high Countisbury Hill to Porlock. A ship was sending up distress signals off Porlock Weir, but the heavy seas at Lynmouth made it impossible to launch the lifeboat there. Mile after gruelling mile the boat was hauled on a cart, up a 1-in-4 lane and on to the common. When the cart lost a wheel they dragged the boat bodily over skids. Ten hours later, after the long, back-breaking journey, the lifeboat was launched from Porlock Weir, and the ship's crew was rescued.

Countisbury Common is north of the A39, about 2 miles east of Lynmouth. There is a small car park off the main road, ¼ mile east of the Blue Bell Inn.

WOODED HOLLOW A deep combe cuts the northern slopes of Dunkery Hill, dividing the brooding moorland from the gentler pastures. A planted line of oak and beech trees marks the moorland boundary.

Cb Culbone Coombe

There is only one way to reach the secluded cluster of buildings beneath Culbone Hill, and that is on foot. A footpath leads from the toll-gate at Worthy, about 1½ miles away, following the steep face of the coast through a splendid confusion of oak, beech and alder. The sound of the sea can be heard below, and sometimes a sparkle of waves can be glimpsed through the trees that cling to the slopes. On sunny days shafts of light strike down through the trees, illuminating the tiny brook that flows down to the coombe, and the dense banks of rhododendrons that overhang it. When the path emerges at Culbone Coombe, one of the great treasures of Exmoor lies ahead – Culbone Church, only 35 ft long and said to be the smallest parish church in England. The church dates from the 12th century and is dedicated to St Beuno, renowned for his skill as a healer in the 6th century.

Worthy is on the toll road west of Porlock Weir, which lies on the B3225, north-west of Porlock.

Cb   Dunkery Hill

Exmoor's giant hill, Dunkery, is no place for the faint-hearted: in October the treeless hillsides resound with the hoarse roaring, called belling, of red deer, as stag challenges stag for possession of the hinds; in winter the 1,705 ft high summit is frequently lost behind a dense screen of drenching rain, or made unapproachable by winds too fierce to walk through. But on a clear summer's day the view of Dunkery Hill from a distance is impressive, its wide shoulders completely dominating the surrounding countryside. A sense of space and freedom can be experienced on a soft summer morning, walking up the white ribbon of pathway from Dunkery Gate, less than a mile from the summit. Acre upon acre of heathland spreads out around the summit; far below lie the wooded Exmoor valleys, with the shimmering sea in Blue Anchor Bay peeping into view on the eastern horizon.

Dunkery Gate is 2 miles north-west of Wheddon Cross on the A396. Follow the B3224 for about ½ mile, and then take the minor road north-west to Dunkery Gate and Dunkery Hill.

Cb   Dunster

Less than a mile from the crowded streets of Dunster village lie the steep, peaceful woodlands and the heather-covered uplands of Grabbist Hill. A path leads up the hill from near where the A396 crosses the River Avill, just outside Dunster. At first, the path climbs steeply among oak, beech and holly; higher up, as gorse and heather replace the trees, the path levels out slightly. The yellow of tormentil and the blue of milkwort light up the undergrowth; and impressive views spread out around the hill.

Immediately below lies Dunster, with its castle and watch-tower – the Conygar Tower, an 18th-century folly. The waters of Blue Anchor Bay shimmer far away in the east; to the north, beyond the Bristol Channel, are the distant coast and hills of South Wales.

On the other side of the valley, across the A396, lies Vinegar Hill. A path leads from Gallox Bridge – the packhorse bridge – in Dunster, up the hill through mixed woodland, ablaze with rhododendrons in May. The route runs below Bat's Castle, an Iron Age hill-fort, a mile south of Dunster.

Stiff walking for another 2 miles leads to Croydon Hill, a Forestry Commission plantation. Legend has it that the hill is haunted by a demon – like many of the hills in this part of Somerset.

Dunster is on the A396, 2 miles south-east of Minehead. The walk up Grabbist Hill starts near the bridge over the A396, where there is a small car park. There is also a small car park near Gallox Bridge in Dunster.

Bb   Heddon's Mouth

The ravine which the River Heddon has carved on its way to the sea is cut so deep – the sides are some 700 ft high – that it is always one of the warmest and most sheltered spots on Exmoor. Yet seen from the headland of Highveer Point, at the eastern end of Heddon's Mouth, it can look uncompromisingly bleak and desolate. A giant expanse of grey scree covers the western cliff, and little grows on it except the odd clump of gorse or heather. There is more colour on the eastern side, especially in autumn when the blazing yellow of gorse blends with the green, red and brown pastel tints of waning foliage.

Walk down the valley floor to Heddon's Mouth, along the tiny footpath leading from Hunter's Inn, and a more gentle view unfolds. The path follows the east side of the river, as it dashes over rapids and slides through crystal-clear pools to the Bristol Channel; lovely woods of oak, sycamore, poplar and fir overhang the banks and cling to the steep sides of the valley. Wagtails

FORTRESS HOME ABOVE A WOODED VALLEY

DUNSTER CASTLE stands on a mound at the mouth of the Avill valley, where the Brendon Hills and Quantock Hills meet at the north-eastern corner of Exmoor. There has been a fortress on the site since Saxon times, but the present castle dates from the 13th century and was the home of the Luttrell family for 600 years.

The original castle survived the Civil War, though it changed hands twice; but after Charles I's execution in 1649 it was demolished for fear that it might become a rallying point for a Royalist uprising. Only the 13th-century gateway and Jacobean house were left standing; the splendid towers and turrets seen above the tree-tops today were the work of Anthony Salvin, a 19th-century specialist in medieval architecture. The castle is now owned by the National Trust.

DUNSTER CASTLE

and dippers dart among the boulders in search of food, and herons wade through the water, or stand silently watching for the silver glint of fish.

Heddon's Mouth is 4 miles west of Lynton. It can be reached by turning west off the A39 just north of Parracombe on to a minor road, then walking from Hunter's Inn about 2¼ miles further down the road.

Cb
Horner Wood

The woods are warm, damp and still, and yet they are always full of sound: the rushing of Horner Water as it flows down from the uplands to the Bristol Channel at Porlock Bay; the screech of jays, the shrill, piercing song of wrens, the musical trilling of warblers and other woodland songbirds. Sometimes the loud, laughing call of the green woodpecker can be heard echoing among the oaks – the call that earned the bird its country name of yaffle – or else it may be seen moving in clumsy hops across a clearing, feeding on ants in the grass. Horner Wood is one of Exmoor's most extensive deer coverts, and there is always a chance of seeing them slipping among the trees in the early morning or evening.

The stream flows gently through the woods in summer; but in winter, after heavy rain or snow, it can become a wild, roaring torrent, as dangerous as it is impressive. It is said that a horse once threw its rider into the river near Horner, when the water was high. Such was the force of the current that

JOURNEY'S END Huge cliffs tower over Heddon's Mouth, where the River Heddon meets the sea. The tumbling surf and glistening shore are a grand climax to its spirited passage through a steep-sided combe.

the drowned man's body could not be recovered before Bossington, 2 miles downstream. But in summer there is no such danger, just a lovely stream passing through one of Exmoor's most memorable stretches of woodland, with quiet paths leading along its banks and wild flowers all around.

Above the Horner valley the woods give way to the bold summit of Ley Hill, where the view extends across the roof-tops of Porlock to the sea beyond.

SWEET SONG AND SWIFT CLAW

The blackcap's rich song can be heard in woodland undergrowth in spring. But birds fall silent when the sparrowhawk pounces. Skimming the hedge-tops, it hunts small birds such as sparrows, finches and tits.

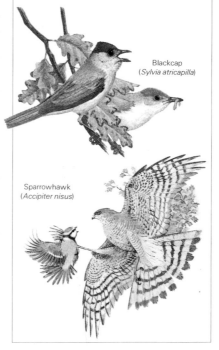

Blackcap
(*Sylvia atricapilla*)

Sparrowhawk
(*Accipiter nisus*)

To reach Horner Wood, take the Luccombe turning off the A39, ¾ mile east of Porlock. There is parking in the village of Horner, from where paths following the Horner Water lead into the wood.

Cb
Hurlstone Point

Porlock Bay was once a favourite haunt of smugglers, and nowhere offered a better lookout over the wide, surrounding sea than Hurlstone Point, at the eastern end of the bay. Many stories are still told of the smuggling days. In one of them, a keg of brandy was hidden in a nearby cottage, and when the Excise men came to search for it, the old woman who lived in the cottage sat on the keg, hiding it beneath her skirts. 'There baint nothin' here,' she said. 'Search wherever you do please.' The keg was never found.

Today a coastguard's lookout stands on Hurlstone Point, surveying the coastal waters from Minehead to the west of Porlock. The cliff also offers spectacular views over the cultivated fields at the back of Porlock Bay, to where the probing fingers of Gore Point and Foreland Point thrust into the Bristol Channel. To the south, Dunkery Hill hunches its mighty shoulders against the backdrop of the open moor, and on clear days the South Wales coast and the Brecon Beacons are visible to the north.

A fine walk leads up to the headland from the village of Bossington, about a mile away. At first the path climbs gently, later it becomes much steeper, rising to the headland through gorse, bracken, brambles and heather.

Hurlstone Point can be reached by following the signs to Bossington, off the A39 north-east of Porlock. The path to the point is signposted from the village.

FAIR-WEATHER FACE The serenity of Morte Bay and Woolacombe beach can be deceptive; this is a treacherous coast in bad weather.

Ab Little Hangman and Great Hangman

A steep climb north-east up the cliff path from Combe Martin leads to a craggy headland with two massive bluffs known as Little Hangman and Great Hangman.

The Little Hangman, which rises 716 ft above the sea, offers spectacular views in all directions: north to Wales and west to Lundy island, east and west along the towering hog-back cliff-tops, and south to the green, rolling hills of lowland Devon. The hill is at its most colourful in early autumn, when the cliff-top vegetation takes on every shade of green, red and brown. Far below, the sea surges incessantly against the rocks, and in the up-draughts off the cliff many different species of sea-bird can be seen wheeling and swooping.

The Great Hangman towers 1,043 ft above Blackstone Point, with the delightful Sherrycombe Water tumbling through a wild valley below. According to legend, the hills were named after a sheep-stealer who carried a heavy carcase on a rope over his shoulder and took a rest against a stone. Setting the carcase on the stone, he fell asleep with his back to the rock. As he slept, the carcase slipped off the rock and pulled the cord tight around his neck, strangling him to death.

The whole area is rich in scenic beauty and wildlife, and also in minerals. At Wild Pear Beach, below the Little Hangman, iron ore was discovered in the late 18th century, and soon it was being mined and shipped across the Bristol Channel to South Wales. From the 13th century to the late 19th century, silver and lead were mined in Combe Martin, and the silent stack of a deserted engine-house still stands close to the church.

Combe Martin is on the A399, 4 miles east of Ilfracombe.

Ab Morte Point

The glistening, razor-sharp slates of Morte Point are as dangerous as they are beautiful. For centuries this jutting headland west of Ilfracombe, and the deadly reef extending beyond it, have made the surrounding waters among the most treacherous off the North Devon coast.

Many a ship has come to grief at Morte Point. In the winter of 1852, no fewer than five ships ran aground there, and in the 18th century the point was a favourite place for wreckers. It is said that they tied lanterns to the horns of cows so that sailors would mistake them for the lights of Ilfracombe.

In calm weather, however, there is a beauty and serenity about the Morte Point and its surrounding coastline which belies its reputation as a graveyard for shipping. The view south takes in the long, golden sweep of surf-washed Woolacombe Sand; and the Somerset and North Devon Coast Path leads north-east across the cliff-top to Bull Point, where a lighthouse flashes out its warning to shipping in the Bristol Channel. The lighthouse standing on the headland today replaced an older one built in 1879, which gradually slipped into the sea because of coastal erosion.

Morte Point is about 1 mile west of Mortehoe, which is 1 mile north of Woolacombe on the B3343.

Cb Porlock Bay

The graceful sweep of Porlock Bay, stretching for some 3 miles from Gore Point in the west to Hurlstone Point in the east, enjoys the mildest climate on Exmoor. On three sides it is enclosed by the moorland heights – the name Porlock means a land-locked port, but the village of Porlock is a port no longer, for the sea receded in the 11th century. Porlock Weir, at the western end of the bay, was a busy little port in the 17th century, with coastal vessels loading timber and barley and unloading limestone from Wales at the stone jetty.

In summer, the breezes off the Bristol Channel keep the bay cool; in winter they check frosts, making this a perfect haven for tender plants. Among the wild flowers that can be found here are the rare silver ragwort along the shingle beach, and New Zealand willowherb.

The bay is as peaceful as it is mild: most of the time the only sounds that can be heard are the gentle lapping of sea on shore, and the plaintive cries of sea-birds. This is a perfect place for bird-watching. In winter, herring gulls, black-headed gulls and oyster catchers gather on the shingle looking for food, while immediately inland the reed-beds of Porlock Marshes teem with wintering wildfowl such as mallard, teal, wigeon and shoveler. The reed-beds also attract huge flocks of migrating waders in spring and autumn.

Take the Bossington turning off the A39 east of Porlock. At Bossington a rough track leads down to the beach.

Ca   ## The Punchbowl

Suddenly, on the northern side of the high, heather moorland called Winsford Hill, the ground drops away for more than 200 ft, forming the striking amphitheatre known as The Punchbowl. A tiny stream rises in its basin, flowing north to the Winn Brook. On the steep sides of The Punchbowl, rowan and thorn bushes grow, rising drunkenly out of the bracken. Sometimes red deer can be seen breaking through the undergrowth, then bounding to the crest of the hill.

Close to The Punchbowl, at the summit of the hill, stand the Wambarrows, one of several relics of the Bronze Age inhabitants of this area. The mysterious Caratacus Stone, a mile to the south-east at Spire Cross, is said to have supernatural visitors, in the form of a ghostly wagon and horses that rumble towards it at midnight. The stone bears an inscription – *Caraataci Nepos*, probably meaning 'Kinsman of Caratacus' – which may have been carved for a local chieftain in the Dark Ages after the Roman withdrawal.

Winsford Hill is crossed by the B3223 Exford–Dulverton road. Cars can be parked off the road near the summit. The Punchbowl is $\frac{1}{4}$ mile east of the summit.

RESCUED LAND High moorland encloses Porlock Bay, where the green fields were reclaimed from coastal marshes.

Cb   Selworthy Beacon

The long valley running eastwards from Porlock to Minehead cuts off the heights of Selworthy Beacon from the main part of Exmoor; but the Beacon belongs as surely to the moor as does the mighty, treeless bulk of Dunkery Hill, visible just a few miles away to the south. Here, too, as at Dunkery, the challenge is to reach the top. There are two ways of getting there, either by making the long, steep drive over the top of North Hill from Minehead, or by climbing up the tree-clad slopes from one of the lovely villages just south and west of the Beacon – Allerford, Bossington or Selworthy. The Somerset and North Devon Path, which starts at Minehead Quay, also passes just below the summit.

A magnificent reward awaits those who reach the top. Moorland and sea meet 1,013 ft below, where the heathery slopes plunge down to the golden edge of Selworthy Sand, with its treacherous quicksands, and Minehead Bluff. There are superb views south over the wooded valley and the bleak moors beyond, north across the Bristol Channel to South Wales and west along the North Devon coast. Between the trees the sweep of Porlock Bay can be seen, with the water looking tantalisingly inviting in almost all weathers. Because of the bay's sheltered position, the waves rarely reach more than a gentle ebb except when whipped up by a wild north-westerly gale.

Follow signs out of Minehead to North Hill and drive west along the hill road. The road ends at a car park and viewpoint. Alternatively, follow signposted footpaths from Allerford, Bossington or Selworthy – all of which are just off the A39, 4–5 miles west of Minehead.

Ba   Simonsbath

Lying at the centre of the ancient forest of Exmoor, Simonsbath provides a good starting point for exploring the valley of the River Barle as it flows south-east between steep, grassy hills towards Dulverton, swelled by numerous tributary streams where trout and dippers haunt.

South-east from the village, a path opposite the hotel leads through the beechwood planted by John Knight, who lived at Simonsbath Lodge and who developed much of the surrounding land in the mid-19th century. The path follows the River Barle downstream, and about half a mile south-east of Simonsbath a ruined cottage stands beside the river. This is all that remains of the Wheal Eliza copper and iron mine, which John Knight's son Sir Frederic and other businessmen tried to develop between 1846 and 1860. But the veins of iron ore proved too thin to be profitable.

About a mile beyond the mine stands Cow Castle, an Iron Age hillfort on a spur overlooking the river. The river can be forded a few hundred yards below the fort and the walk returns to Simonsbath along a farm lane to Blue Gate and then by a minor road running north-east.

Simonsbath is 5 miles west of Exford on the B3224.

THE DREADFUL FATE OF A MINER'S DAUGHTER

IN THE BARLE VALLEY, a miner's ruined cottage is all that remains of the Wheal Eliza mine, scene of a crime that the Victorian newspapers of the time probably described as 'murder most foul'. There had been workings on the site for centuries – Wheal is a corruption of the Cornish *hwel*, or mine, and Eliza refers to Elizabeth I – but in 1846 a group of businessmen reopened the mine with six miners who lived in cottages near by. One miner, a man named Burgess, was a widower with one daughter whom he ruled possessively, and when she became engaged to be married he objected strongly. But the daughter refused to break off the engagement, and in a fit of rage Burgess killed her and buried the body on the moor. Shortly after, sheep-stealers arrived at Wheal Eliza intent on burying a stolen carcase until a buyer could be found. Seeing the still-fresh grave, they assumed that others of their kind had been at work. This they told to Burgess, who removed the corpse in panic and threw it down the mineshaft. When the sheep-stealers later examined the grave more closely, they found human hair and part of a frock. Burgess was arrested, and was hanged at Taunton.

WHEAL ELIZA COTTAGE, NOW RUINED

Cb   Stoke Pero Common

The church at Stoke Pero, surrounded by a scattering of farms, claims to be the highest and loneliest on Exmoor. Driving up the steep, twisting road to the 1,000 ft high common it would be difficult to dispute the claim. Though the present church was built in the late 19th century, it stands on what is claimed to be the oldest Christian site on the moor, where there has been a church for almost a thousand years.

The feeling of remoteness pervading the high moorland is heightened when the wind whistles across the wide expanse of moor grass and heather, pressing the occasional gorse bushes towards the ground; or when a ghostly grey mist creeps over the land like a cold blanket. This is the hard, uncompromising Exmoor; yet the softer side of the moor is also close at hand. On the north side of the common the land falls away sharply to the woods and valleys of the Holnicote Estate, and Horner Water tumbles through the trees towards the sea.

Stoke Pero Common is a marvellous place for bird-watching. Curlews and ring ouzels can often be seen, and rarer visitors include merlins, Montagu's harriers and the elegant golden plover.

Stoke Pero Common is 3 miles south of Porlock and can be reached by following the minor road out of Luccombe towards Exford. There is a small car park near the turning for Stoke Pero.

Ca   Tarr Steps

Some experts believe that the ancient bridge across the River Barle, called Tarr Steps, is prehistoric; others claim that it is medieval, perhaps dating from the 13th century. Whatever its age, it

PREHISTORIC CROSSING? No one is sure whether Tarr Steps, a clapper bridge on the River Barle, dates back to prehistoric or medieval times. Whoever built it brought the stones to the spot – they are not of local rock.

is one of the best-preserved clapper bridges in England, a series of immense stone slabs supported on piers. The bridge is about 180 ft long from end to end and only 3 ft above the rippling water. The bridge links the ancient trackways on either side of the Barle, where numerous remains show that the area was well populated in prehistoric times. It is to this day, and is best visited on weekdays or out of season, since it is a favourite spot for visitors.

However, to find solitude there is a footpath that leads upstream on the east side of the river to Withypool, about 4 miles away. This is one of the loveliest walks on Exmoor. At any time of year the mixture of woodland and water is delightful; and the birds which may be seen include herons, king-fishers and dippers along the river bank, and stonechats, flycatchers and

finches in the woods. But the most stirring sight of all in this wild, roman-tic setting is when red deer emerge suddenly from among the shadows of the trees, and break away in full flight through the undergrowth.

To reach Tarr Steps turn south-west off the B3223 at Spire Cross, about 6 miles north-west of Dulverton. Follow this road for 1¼ miles to the large car park about ¼ mile from the Steps.

Ab Torrs Park

For 2 miles the cliffs rise and fall be-tween Torrs Park, on the outskirts of Ilfracombe, to the woods around Lee Bay. The Somerset and North Devon Coast Path leading across them offers splendid walking, with many marvell-ous views and frequent opportunities for bird-watching.

The path is steep as it leaves Ilfra-combe, and very slippery after rain; but soon it levels out, and the going is then much easier all the way to Lee. One of the finest views is from Brandy Cove Point – out across the Bristol Channel to Lundy island and South Wales, back to Ilfracombe slumbering in the lee of the point, and along the line of hog-backed cliffs stretching eastwards to Combe Martin Bay. Gorse and bram-bles cling to the steep slopes of the cliffs; further back, sheep graze on pastureland as green as any found in Exmoor's famous combes. Shags and fulmars are among the many sea-birds to be seen beneath the cliff-tops.

At Lee, the path descends to a tiny cove of rocks and sand, and a cleft in the rocks leads to another sandy bay to the west. A path leading inland follows a valley abundant with fuchsias.

A steep road on the western side of Ilfracombe leads to Torrs Park. There is a small National Trust car park near the entrance to the park.

Bb Waters Meet

In the spectacular gorge at Waters Meet, the combined Farley Water and Hoaroak Water meet the East Lyn river, and the hurrying waters tumble loudly over the boulders lining the river-bed, flowing on towards the sea at Lynmouth. The best approach is from Hillsford Bridge (where the Farley Water and Hoaroak Water combine), from where a path follows the Farley Brook to Waters Meet, three-quarters of a mile away.

The sides of the gorge are steep and well wooded, a tousled array including oak, beech and sycamore clinging pre-cariously to the slopes and spilling down to the water's edge. Wild flowers are abundant, especially in spring when the bright colours of bluebells and primroses are set against the lux-uriant green of young ferns. In spring, too, birdsong fills the woods, the sound mingling with the incessant roar of the stream. In the wild, rushing water the

RUGGED DEVON Torrs Park near Ilfracombe has some of North Devon's finest coastal scenery. Gorse-dotted cliffs sweep out to rocky headlands like Brandy Cove Point, a splendid coastal viewpoint.

aquatic dipper may be seen plunging from a rock to walk along the bottom in search of food. But in winter, when snow is melting on the uplands where the rivers rise, or heavy rain is falling, the roar of the river rises to a crescendo, drowning all other sounds, dominating all other signs of life.

During the summer, Waters Meet is a popular spot for holidaymakers.

A pleasant ¾ mile walk leads to Waters Meet from Hillsford Bridge on the A39, 1¼ miles south-east of Lynmouth, where there is a small car park.

Cb Webber's Post

South of Webber's Post the immense bulk of Dunkery Hill half blocks out the sky; the magnificent, green oakwoods of the Horner and East Water valleys spread out to the north and west. Here, at the meeting place of moorland and woodland, pathways radiate in all directions like the spokes of a wheel; and the road from Allerford forks, to pass east and west of the Dunkery Beacon.

A 2½ mile nature trail starts from Webber's Post car park and threads its way to Cloutsham through the lovely, wooded combe of East Water. It follows the stream for part of the way along the valley floor, strewn with moss-covered boulders brought down by the stream in times of flood. A quiet bridle-path leads north-east from Webber's Post through plantations of conifers, where crossbills and goldcrests can

WOODLAND WATERFALL Swift-flowing waters cascade over mossy boulders near Waters Meet, splashing the lush green gorge with effervescent white. A bank-side path follows the East Lyn River to Lynmouth.

sometimes be seen, and then past oak, beech and ash to the village of Luccombe. The path comes out of the woods just before the village, and joins the road; and a few hundred yards down the road another path leads off across the fields to the Church of St Mary, whose slender tower dominates the village.

To reach Webber's Post, follow the A39 east out of Porlock, and after about 1½ miles take the turning south to Wheddon Cross. Webber's Post is 2 miles along this road.

Ca Wimbleball Lake

Exmoor National Park's major reservoir, Wimbleball Lake, lies on the south-east side of the moor, in the shadow of Haddon Hill. The shores of the 374 acre lake are well wooded near the dam; elsewhere gentle, grassy slopes drop down to the water's edge. Footpaths lead from the southern shores of the lake up to Haddon Hill, 1,164 ft high, from which there are splendid views over rich pastureland stretching as far as the eye can see.

The lake is an ideal spot for bird-watching, with herons and kingfishers among the resident birds. Buzzards and kestrels can often be seen over the shores of the lake.

At the southern end of the lake a long creek, the Upton Arm, runs between wooded banks to Upton village. Halfway along the north shore, a footpath leads to Upton's ruined church of St James, its ivy-clad 14th-century tower and crumbling chancel walls standing desolate on a hillside. Opposite the mouth of the creek is the dam, 161 ft high and holding back 4,500 million gallons of the River Haddeo, a tributary of the Exe. West of the dam

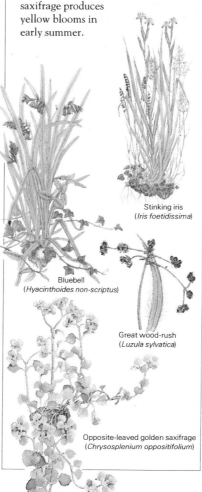

FLOWERS OF WOOD AND MOOR

Queen of the English wild flowers, the stately bluebell is common in North Devon woodlands. The great wood-rush, with its lance-shaped leaves, grows in woods and on the moors. Beautiful but deadly, the stinking iris lives up to its name when its leaves are crushed – both leaves and roots are poisonous. In the combes, by streams and among rocks, the opposite-leaved golden saxifrage produces yellow blooms in early summer.

Stinking iris
(*Iris foetidissima*)

Bluebell
(*Hyacinthoides non-scriptus*)

Great wood-rush
(*Luzula sylvatica*)

Opposite-leaved golden saxifrage
(*Chrysosplenium oppositifolium*)

the Haddeo cuts through the wooded valley of Hartford Bottom.

Wimbleball Lake lies about 10 miles south of Dunster, 3 miles east of the A396. Take the minor road to Brompton Regis, and then follow the signs to the lake. There is a large car park at Cowlings.

Bb Woody Bay

At the end of the 19th century a London solicitor planned to develop Woody Bay as a rival to Lynmouth, hoping to attract holidaymakers to travel by paddle-steamer from Weston-super-Mare, Ilfracombe and South Wales, to take tea in the shade of some of North Devon's most spectacular cliffs. But the plan misfired because of lack of financial support, and so the seclusion of Woody Bay remained delightfully undisturbed, as it still does to this day.

From the car park above this aptly named bay, a path runs westwards along the cliff-top, over the headlands of Wringapeak and The Cow and Calf to Highveer Point. The cliffs are topped with bracken, gorse and heather, and offer magnificent views over the wooded valleys, down the coast and out across the Bristol Channel to Lundy island and Wales. Another path drops down steeply through dense woodland of oaks, sycamores, beeches and conifers, to the tiny shingle beach at the bottom set in a wooded amphitheatre of oak trees. The ruined lime-kiln on the beach is a relic of the days when local farmers burned limestone here, and then hauled it up the cliff to spread on their fields.

Woody Bay, 3 miles west of Lynton, is reached by the coast road from Lynton, passing through The Valley of the Rocks and then continuing along the toll road.

THE QUANTOCK HILLS

Red deer and wild ponies roam amid the solitude
of Somerset's gentle, dreamy hills

Solitude and seclusion are the lure of the rolling, rounded Quantock Hills that lie west of the Somerset plain. Although similar in character to nearby Exmoor, with wild ponies grazing on the upland heather moors and red deer sheltering in the deep, wooded valleys, they are somehow gentler, with a softer, dreamier enchantment. Sheep-tracks finger the slopes, leading down to scattered farms and pleasant hamlets where narrow lanes seek out clusters of red-sandstone cottages and stately manor houses.

Small in extent, the Quantock Hills cover only 36 sq. miles. Their northern tip meets the Bristol Channel near Watchet, and they stretch for 12 miles south-eastwards to overlook the rich farmlands of the Vale of Taunton Deane at their southern tip. The western slopes are steep and wooded, the eastern slopes broken by deep, narrow valleys, or combes, with fast-flowing streams.

Wills Neck (1,260 ft) and Robin Upright's Hill (1,170 ft), two of the highest points (the third is Lydeard Hill at 1,197 ft), stand south and north respectively of the 1,800 acre Quantock Forest on the eastern slopes. Forestry Commission conifers have here supplanted the native oaks, but there are oakwoods among the hills, such as Shervage Wood, National Trust property near Holford, where there are some coppiced oaks. Until the beginning of this century, the Quantock oaks were used

in the tanning and charcoal industries at Holford and Nether Stowey, and the oaks were coppiced – cut at the base to produce a crop of poles – every 10–15 years.

An ancient ridgeway follows the crest of the hills for much of their length, giving fine views of the Black Down Hills to the south, the Brendon Hills and Exmoor to the west, the Mendips to the north-east, and the Bristol Channel to the north. Prehistoric man tramped this route, as evidenced by the Bronze Age round barrows, or burial mounds, and the Iron Age hill-forts such as Dowsborough and the Trendle Ring on Bicknoller Hill.

Near Stogumber below the western slopes lies Combe Sydenham, where in the 1580s the widower Sir Francis Drake courted Elizabeth Sydenham. Her parents objected to the match, and while Drake was at sea found her another suitor. According to local legend, on the day of her wedding a giant cannonball landed near the church – fired across the world by Drake. Elizabeth rejected her bridegroom and waited for Drake, and they were married in 1585. The 'cannonball' could have been a meteorite that fell in the area.

It was the solitude of the Quantocks that attracted the poet Samuel Taylor Coleridge in 1796. His cottage at Nether Stowey, now owned by the National Trust, still stands today. Although he only stayed three years, Coleridge wrote some of his best poems here, including *Kubla Khan*. In 1797 his friends William and Dorothy Wordsworth moved to Alfoxton House near Holford. Coleridge's famous poem *The Rime of the Ancient Mariner* was planned by the two poets as they walked together on the Quantocks in November 1797. There is yet another poet who sought solitude in these hills – Sir Henry Newbolt, who wrote *Drake's Drum* in 1897, lived at Aisholt in the 1930s.

QUANTOCK PROSPECT From the fine viewpoint of Aisholt Church in the southern Quantocks, sweeping landscapes extend in all directions. To the south-west the scene takes in the rich fields and woods of the Vale of Taunton Deane, with the Black Down Hills beyond.

Places to visit

Map ref. Bb Aisholt Common

This is the heart of the Quantocks, a high moorland plateau fringed by the dark green edge of Quantock Forest and dropping away to a deep valley which the poet Samuel Taylor Coleridge called 'a deep romantic chasm . . . down a green hill'. Below lies the village of Aisholt, so remote that even the solitude-seeking Coleridge rejected it as a place to settle, for fear that it would be too lonely a place for his wife. The village takes its name from the ash trees of the Quantock Forest where the Saxons settled.

The common is best seen by walking around it, using the 5¼ mile trail laid out by the Somerset Trust for Nature Conservation. The walk starts from Birches Corner. Cuckoos, buzzards and stonechats can be seen flying low above the gorse, bracken and heather, with an occasional glimpse of red deer. And along the trail there are everchanging views as the path, starting at 1,000 ft, drops to 400 ft as it passes through the village of Aisholt, and then follows the edge of the Quantock Forest, finally climbing to 1,260 ft at Wills Neck, the highest hill in the Quantocks. At one point it is possible to see three National Parks – Brecon Beacons, Exmoor and Dartmoor.

Aisholt is an attractive village of thatched cottages, oak barns and a 14th-century church. The poet Henry Newbolt lived here in the 1930s – his best-known poem is *Drake's Drum*. A short detour north from the village leads along the side of Aisholt Wood and follows a small stream. You may be lucky enough to see red deer sheltering under the beech and ash trees.

To reach Aisholt Common, take the road which climbs steeply east from West Bagborough to Birches Corner, where there is a car park. West Bagborough is 9 miles north-west of Taunton, east off the A358.

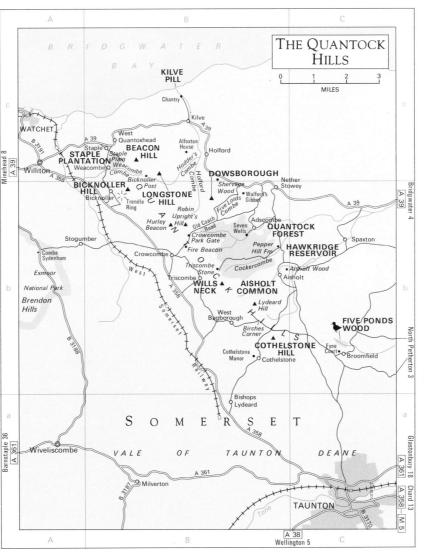

Bc Beacon Hill

Just about every range of hills in England has its Beacon Hill – sometimes more than one – where fires were lit to warn of the approaching Spanish Armada in 1588. They all have one thing in common – they can be seen for miles and are within view of other beacons. For the men who stood watch on the Quantocks Beacon Hill, the red glow on Crowcombe Fire Beacon and Hurley Beacon to the south-east would have been the signal to set ablaze their fiery warning. That warning would have been seen as far away as Dunkery Beacon on Exmoor and the Brecon Beacons across the Bristol Channel.

It was in the summer that the Spaniards came, and on any clear summer's day those far-off beacon hills can still be seen from the 1,018 ft summit in the Quantocks – and in between lie sweeping panoramas of patchwork fields, wooded combes, gorse and heather-covered slopes and silver-grey sea.

To reach Beacon Hill, take the road from West Quantoxhead to Bicknoller. The first turn on the left at Staple Farm (opposite the road to Williton and Minehead) leads to a parking place on the hills. From here there is a fine walk to the summit of the hill.

Beacon Hill is the last point in the Quantocks higher than 1,000 ft before the hills drop away to the shores of Bridgwater Bay. The summit is crossed by the prehistoric track coming up from the south-east, and marks the end of the Ridgeway, or Pack Way, for walkers setting out from Lydeard Hill 6 miles south-east.

West Quantoxhead, just over 1 mile north-west of Beacon Hill, lies on the A39 between Kilve and Williton.

Bb Bicknoller Hill

A pathway climbing up through a beech-lined combe leads to Bicknoller Hill, one of the most impressive points in the Quantocks. The route, particularly on a crisp autumn morning, provides a fusion of pastel colours, with the beeches, oaks and limes in the combe giving way to brambles and bracken as the hill is climbed. Red deer may be seen here, or may be heard in November when the throaty bellow of the stag's rutting call echoes through the woods.

Iron Age man settled on Bicknoller Hill, not on the top but on the south-western slope, and the remains of the encampment – Trendle Ring – are still visible. Its builders obviously chose the site for its wide views, and we can appreciate it today as one of the best vantage spots in the Quantocks. About 4 miles to the west are the Brendon Hills and, beyond them, the dark shape of Exmoor; 8 miles to the south lies the wide Vale of Taunton Deane and the town of Wellington, with the Black Down Hills rising behind the town. On a clear day Wellington's Monument can be seen 14 miles away on the northern edge of the hills, its narrow finger prodding the fluffy clouds above Wellington Hill. The obelisk commemorates the victor of Waterloo.

Bicknoller Hill can be reached by turning off the A358 just south of Bicknoller village, at Chilcombe Lane. There are several parking places at the lane end.

Bb Cothelstone Hill

The road climbs steeply from Cothelstone village to the crossroads on the hill. To the right a clump of wind-ravaged beeches shares the summit,

PURPLE HILLS AND BLUE SEA Beacon Hill, in the northern Quantocks, gives fine views of Exmoor and Blue Anchor Bay.

known locally as Cothelstone Beacon, with the ruins of a folly tower. Perhaps Lady Hillsborough, who built the tower about 1770, used it as a point from which to enjoy the view. It is said that several counties can be seen from here on a clear day, but at any time the view is captivating with ash and beech woods cladding the slopes, and the fields and meadows of the Vale of Taunton Deane spread out below.

The left turn at the crossroads leads to Lydeard Hill, where there is a car park, and passes through mixed oak and beech woodlands with picturesque

names, such as Paradise, Badger's Copse and Much Care Wood.

At the foot of Cothelstone Hill, near Cothelstone Church, are the grounds and buildings of Cothelstone Manor, a skilfully restored Elizabethan house of pink sandstone with its original gatehouse. There are memories here of the infamous Judge Jeffreys, who hanged two of the Duke of Monmouth's followers in the gateway after the duke's defeat at Sedgemoor in 1685. The village itself is charming, with red-sandstone cottages and a holy well. The well, called St Agnes's Well,

lies hidden in greenery in a field a little way up the hill.

Cothelstone village is signposted along minor roads from Bishops Lydeard just off the A358. There is roadside parking on Cothelstone Hill, which is reached by following the road through the village.

Bb Dowsborough

Between Nether Stowey and Crowcombe lies a magnificent winding scenic drive, with plenty of stopping places of interest along its route. It is called the Coach Road, and runs past Walford's Gibbet, Five Lords Combe, Dowsborough hill-fort, Dead Woman's Ditch, and then to a viewpoint at Crowcombe Park Gate where the road plunges down a wooded valley into Crowcombe village.

The Old Coach Road is signposted south about a mile west of Nether Stowey on the A39. Thick woods crowd in on the right-hand side of the road for about half a mile, where a sharp right turn takes the road up past Five Lords Combe. From this corner, a path leads across a field to a small quarry – a place with the sinister-sounding name of Walford's Gibbet.

On a clear day, there are fine views across the Bristol Channel to Wales. Birds sing in the hedges, and on fine summer evenings the shy deer come down from the neighbouring woods to drink at the stream.

The Old Coach Road continues past Five Lords Combe on the left – a splendid Quantocks woodland of mixed oak and beech. At the top of the combe the road turns sharp left to run across open moorland. At this turn, on the right-hand side, a path leads up through the woods to the hill called Dowsborough. Some local people call it Danesborough, though the fort on top is Iron Age and has no connection with Scandinavian invaders.

The oval, 7 acre fort occupies the higher end of the narrow ridge. Its defensive banks and ditch follow the natural contours of the land. The ditch is now full of scrub oak and the ramparts are crowned with heather. Like all Iron Age sites, little is known about the people who lived here some 2,000 years ago. This air of mystery adds to the character of Dowsborough, with its superb views across the Bristol Channel.

From below Dowsborough, the road continues to a junction at which stands a signpost with the name Dead Woman's Ditch. However, there is nothing morbid about this place; many pleasant walks lead off in all directions into the hills and combes round about, and there is adequate roadside parking.

About a mile beyond the road junction is Crowcombe Park Gate, which lies at the top of the combe above Crowcombe village. From this point, there are superb views of Fire Beacon hill, half a mile to the south, and Wills Neck – the highest point in the Quantocks – 2 miles to the south-east. The drive down the combe to the village is beautiful, with wooded banks on either side which are bright with bluebells in late spring and clothed in ferns and wild flowers in summer.

Nether Stowey, the starting point for the drive, lies on the A39, 7 miles west of Bridgwater.

Cb Five Ponds Wood

The five ponds from which this wood takes its name were dug in the 19th century, probably to enhance the grounds of nearby Fyne Court. The ponds have long since disappeared, and the wooded valley where they once lay is now a nature reserve with a trail laid out by the Somerset Trust for Nature Conservation.

The woodland is only 600 yds long and 70 yds wide. The trail follows the course of a stream that runs through the valley, where native trees mingle with introduced species, planted about the same time as the ponds were dug. Most prominent of the planted trees are beeches, in a line topping a bank along the wood's southern edge, which were originally part of a hedge. Some have now grown to an enormous size; one particularly fine tree stands where the trail enters the wood – a perfect sentinel for the leafy walk among elder, ash, hawthorn, hazel and holly. Sycamores and poplars have been added to the wood in more recent years, to join the laurels, snowberries and rhododendrons so favoured by the Victorians.

SHELTER FOR THE SKIPPER

A smaller version of the garden strawberry, the wild strawberry grows in woodland fringes and hedgebanks, flowering from April to July. During May, the grizzled skipper butterfly lays its eggs on the upper sides of the leaves, which its caterpillars roll into 'tents'. They spend nine months in cocoons at the base of the plant.

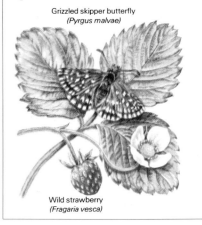

Grizzled skipper butterfly
(*Pyrgus malvae*)

Wild strawberry
(*Fragaria vesca*)

THE TRAGEDY OF JOHN WALFORD

WALFORD'S GIBBET today is a pleasant spot on a hillside, but its name recalls a tragedy of 200 years ago. John Walford was a well-liked local charcoal-burner whose true love was Ann Rice, but he married half-witted Jane who visited him in the woods, and whose two children he fathered.

One night in 1789 as the couple were going from their cottage above Bin Coombe to buy cider at the Castle of Comfort Inn, they quarrelled. He struck and killed her with a fence stake, then, panic-stricken, left her body in a ditch. He was arrested, tried and found guilty. On his way to be hanged, Walford was allowed to make a final farewell to Ann. As was the custom, his body was gibbeted at the scene of the crime.

THE SITE OF WALFORD'S GIBBET

In spring and summer the woods come alive with the colours of bluebells, red campions, snowdrops and primroses, and beside the stream the banks are speckled with the gold of kingcups and saxifrages.

Fyne Court, from where the trail starts, is close to the village of Broomfield. The most direct route is signposted west from North Petherton, which lies 5 miles to the east on the A38.

Cb Hawkridge Reservoir

One of the reservoirs that serves Taunton and Bridgwater, Hawkridge Reservoir is little more than half a mile long and about 150 yds wide. Its small size, however, adds to its charm and there is little to suggest that this is a man-made lake. At the western end the neat, rounded hills of the eastern Quantocks reach down to the water.

Hawkridge Reservoir was completed in 1961, and has become 'naturalised' with remarkable speed. Meadowsweet and cuckoo flowers grow in the damp ground, and at the water's edge the golden marsh-marigold can be seen in spring.

Water birds lost little time in taking advantage of the reservoir, particularly coots and moorhens; they are new to the Quantocks since there is no other stretch of inland water in the area apart from a reservoir on the outskirts of Bridgwater. In the dense vegetation away from the water's edge, the songs of reed warblers and sedge warblers can be heard in summer.

There are plenty of parking spaces around the reservoir, which can be reached by several roads leaving the A39 west of Bridgwater. The road from the village of Spaxton, 1 mile to the north-east of the reservoir, follows the southern shore.

Bc Kilve Pill

At the northern end of the Quantocks the hills tumble down to Bridgwater Bay, and low cliffs shelter the creek called Kilve Pill. A lane and footpath lead down to the creek, following the course of a stream between breeze-rippled fields of tall grass and corn. The path opens out to a rocky beach below the blue-grey cliffs of shale and limestone. Coiled fossils shaped like flat snails – called ammonites – are embedded in the rock-face, which was once quarried for building stone. There is a path along the cliff-top, but the edge is jagged and crumbling and care should be taken when walking there.

Early this century, the shore near Kilve was the frequent scene of 'glatting'. At the time of very low tides, the locals would go out with sticks and terriers to find and collect conger-eels hiding in the rock pools.

SHORT-LIVED INDUSTRY Between 1924 and 1926, oil was extracted from the blue-grey oil-shales around Kilve Pill.

57

Smugglers used the creek in the 18th century, and hid their brandy kegs in the lime-kilns which can still be seen in fields along the shore. They also used the abandoned 14th-century chantry which stands close to the footpath and about 500 yds from the beach. The building was founded in 1329 by Simon de Furneaux, and housed five priests who sang masses for his soul. Abandoned before the Reformation, it was used for storing farm implements. Now, its ivy-covered walls, built from the local limestone, are gaunt ruins as the result of a fire. It is said to have been caused by smugglers when they set light to their brandy kegs to thwart the Excise officers. A hollow in the field near by is the site of the priory fishpond.

Kilve Pill is reached from the village of Kilve on the A39. A lane leads from the Hood Arms to the chantry, where there is room for car parking, and the path to the beach continues from there.

Bc Longstone Hill

There are two good reasons for visiting Longstone Hill – the view from the top and the views on the way up. The climb is easy, a gentle stroll from the village of Holford along a bridle-path that leads through a magnificent tunnel of windswept beeches and oaks arching across the broad path. Between the trees the dignified, whitewashed Alfoxton House is visible. Today a hotel, it was for a year the home of William Wordsworth and his sister Dorothy, who moved there in 1797 to be near the poet Samuel Taylor Coleridge living at Nether Stowey.

Higher up the hill the beeches and oaks give way to more open ground, with bracken and clumps of gorse. Now other and more distant views attract the eye. To the south-east is Hodder's Combe, lying invitingly among the trees with a stream rushing through. Beyond it lies Holford Combe, where Wordsworth composed his poem *Lines Written in Early Spring* . . . 'through primrose tufts in that green bower, the periwinkle trailed its wreaths . . .'

The summit of Longstone Hill is 1,000 ft above sea-level, one of the highest points at the northern end of the Quantocks. To the south-east the hills and combes roll away into the distance; to the north the Bristol Channel is a glistening seascape, with the South Wales mountains making

POISED TO POUNCE

Commonest of Britain's birds of prey, the kestrel is a familiar sight as it hovers over moors and open country, and often alongside motorways. It is easily recognised by its long, pointed wings and its fanned tail. As it hovers, the bird searches the ground for voles or mice, frogs or small birds, and drops swiftly down to catch its prey, which it carries to a perch to eat. Kestrels sometimes sit on overhead cables to watch the ground below.

Kestrel
(*Falco tinnunculus*)

TOPMOST POINT Wills Neck is the highest hill in the Quantocks. Its airy moorland slopes are clothed in heather, bracken, gorse and bilberries.

occasional hazy appearances when the sea mists clear.

Holford is on the A39, 11 miles north-west of Bridgwater. The bridle-path to Longstone Hill starts from the north-west side of the village, where cars can be parked.

Bb Quantock Forest

Though large areas of Quantock Forest are now conifer plantations belonging to the Forestry Commission, it dates back to Saxon times and was a royal hunting ground. Ash trees formed much of the old forest – the nearby village of Aisholt takes its name from them – and there are parts of the forest where they still grow, along with oaks, beeches and cedars.

A forest walk of about 5 miles starts from Triscombe Stone, the highest point at 1,047 ft above sea-level. The lowest point on the walk is at Pepper Hill Farm, some 600 ft below. Although the route takes in some beautiful broad-leaved woodland in the parkland round Pepper Hill Farm, much of it is through conifers, which are not to everyone's taste. There is no denying, however, the magnificence of stately Douglas fir, Sitka spruce, Japanese larch and Scots pine – especially on a warm, summer's day when sunlight shafts through the trees and the scent of pine is heavy on the air.

There is another walk through Quantock Forest, starting at Seven Wells, where streams threading their way off the heights attract herons, dippers, kingfishers and wagtails. At Adscombe Farm, on the fringe of the forest, are the remains of a chapel built in the 10th century by the monks of Athelney Abbey.

Triscombe Stone and Seven Wells can both be reached by driving up minor roads from Nether Stowey, on the A39. There are car parks at both places.

Bc Staple Plantation

This pocket-sized patch of Forestry Commission woodland lying at the foot of Beacon Hill is barely half a mile square. It lies in an easily accessible corner of the Quantocks on their north-western fringe, where the ancient Devonian sandstone rocks give way to the lush farmland of West Somerset. From the car park at Staple Plain, above West Quantoxhead, a pathway drops down between silent stands of conifers, with westward views over the Brendon Hills, and Exmoor's lofty Dunkery Hill a purple mound in the distance.

Staple Plantation is at its best in autumn, when the beech and sweet chestnut turn to copper and gold against the never-changing green of the conifers. Beyond the woodland, Weacombe Combe runs east to Bicknoller Post, its flanks of bracken providing perfect camouflage for red deer which occasionally venture from the heights to raid the orchards and gardens in the hamlet of Weacombe. The hamlet lies at the bottom of the path from Staple Plain, at the south-west end of the plantation.

To reach Staple Plantation, turn south off the A39, ¼ mile west of West Quantoxhead, and follow the road which leads to the car park at Staple Plain.

Bb Wills Neck

From the 1,260 ft summit of Wills Neck, the patchwork quilt of the west Somerset countryside unfolds in all its splendour. To the west, the Brendon Hills and the distant purple dome of Exmoor loom on the horizon; to the north, beyond the sheen of the Bristol Channel, the South Wales mountains are visible on a clear day.

Wills Neck lies on a ridge – the name is derived from Old English and means 'Ridge of the Welshmen', referring to the Celtic tribe who probably fought a battle with the Saxons here; *walh* or *wealh* was an Anglo-Saxon word for foreigners or Welshmen. All around there is open moorland, dotted with clumps of gorse and bilberries rising from a carpet of bracken and heather. Sheep and ponies roam the paths, buzzards wheel overhead and, on sunny days in April and May, the emperor moth can be seen flitting over the heather, or in July and August the oak eggar moth.

On the south side of the hill the land falls away sharply to the tiny village of West Bagborough. In 1841, William Wordsworth and his wife, Mary, stayed as the guests of the Popham family at Bagborough House, a white, five-bayed Georgian house whose lawns are frosted with snowdrops in spring.

The easiest approach to the top of Wills Neck is from Triscombe Stone, which can be reached by taking the road from Nether Stowey (on the A39) south-west through Cockercombe in Quantock Forest. There is a car park at Triscombe Stone, from where a footpath leads to Wills Neck.

PATCHWORK FIELDS Below the steep and wooded western slope of Wills Neck, the pattern of hedgerows and fields on the low-lying land extends to the Brendon Hills on the eastern fringe of Exmoor.

THE DORSET HILLS

Thomas Hardy's country, where ancient hill-forts and
trackways straddle chalk hills, cliffs and heaths

It is the broad green sweep of the downs that makes Dorset seem such a friendly place, and the dark wilderness of the heath that makes it seem so secluded. There is an age-old stillness in its enduring rocks, and a pleasing magic in its changing moods – the sun glinting on the blue mirror of Poole Harbour, the grey fog swirling inland over the Isle of Purbeck, or the roaring sound of pebbles tumbled by the tide at Chesil Beach.

The chalk downs that enfold this world sweep south-westwards from Wiltshire and Cranborne Chase to meet the coast south of Dorchester, then branch eastwards to meet the long ridge of the Purbeck Hills. In only a few places do the Dorset hills exceed 800 ft, but to climb them gives the heady sensation of being on the roof of the world. From the steep northern slopes there are exhilarating views over Blackmoor Vale, its green surface threaded by silvery streams and rivers. To the west the chalk belt ends in the flourish of Eggardon Hill (827 ft) with its mighty Iron Age hill-fort. From the southern hills the Isle of Portland is never long out of view, and to the east they overlook the Dorset heathland and lovely Swanage Bay.

The writer Thomas Hardy described Dorset's heathland as untame-able, and even today its wilderness of gorse and heather seems to hold Dorset inviolate from the east. But there are changes – columns of

Forestry Commission conifers now march across it, an Atomic Energy Research Establishment hides behind a screen of trees on Winfrith Heath, and to the east there is an army firing range. Yet the heath survives, and when the roads are open the views from Povington and Whiteway hills still reveal its sombre charm.

The Isle of Purbeck – an island in feel but a peninsula in fact – is Dorset in miniature, its chalk hills reaching the sea at Studland cliffs, with their shining stacks and pinnacles. Running parallel with the chalk is a band of tough lime-stone that includes beds of red and green Purbeck marble. Their skill with this marble made generations of Corfe stonecutters famous all over Europe; its gleaming beauty can be seen in Westminster Abbey and a thousand other places.

The Isle of Portland stretches south from Weymouth, 4 miles of solid limestone from Castletown to the Bill of Portland, where eastwards the dangerous current of Portland Race churns the sea seething white. From Portland's quarries were hewn the stones used to build St Paul's Cathedral, and also the United Nations Headquarters in New York.

From prehistoric times, Dorset's chalk ridgeways have provided dry routes for travellers, and the hilltops were always good defensive sites. The southern ridgeway is studded with Bronze Age round barrows – burial mounds over 3,000 years old. The chain of Iron Age hill-forts, dating back more than 2,000 years, includes the most famous of them all – Maiden Castle – the largest fortified earthwork in Europe.

In the rocks of Dorset are written the last records of an even older world. The blue limestone around Lyme Regis has been famous for its fossils since 1811, when a 12-year-old girl found the first-known fossil of the 21 ft fish-lizard *Ichthyosaurus*, a relic of 180 million years ago.

SHATTERED CLIFFS Kimmeridge Ledges, cliffs of dark grey-blue clay interspersed with bands of limestone and oil-shale, lie between Kimmeridge Bay and St Aldhelm's Head. Sea erosion has caused many landslips on the cliff-face and the shore is littered with limestone blocks.

Places to visit

Map ref. Bb Abbotsbury

Nearly 450 years after the dissolution of Abbotsbury's ancient Benedictine abbey, the monks' great swannery still flourishes on the Fleet, a brackish lagoon behind Chesil Beach. The waters are rich in eel-grass and other vegetation on which the swans feed, and in April the meadow at the Fleet's end provides them with perfect nesting sites. In May, when the birds are incubating their eggs, the swannery opens to visitors. It is then, in their aggressive defence of their territories, that the birds show themselves to be every bit as wild as they are graceful.

Many of the cottages in Abbotsbury were built with stones taken from the demolished abbey, and the enormous stone-built tithe barn – 91 yds long, massively buttressed and with a cart-high porch – hints at the abbey's former riches. South-west of the village on Chapel Hill, overlooking the sea, the 14th-century St Catherine's Chapel still captures the eye. It was probably spared from destruction by Giles Strangways, Henry VIII's Dissolution Commissioner, because it was a landmark for mariners. From the chapel there are magnificent views out to sea and along the coast.

Abbotsbury is 8 miles north-west of

Weymouth on the B3157. The swannery is 1 mile south of the village, reached from New Barn Road where there is a car park.

Dc Ashmore

Its pond is the pride of Ashmore, for the village is the highest in Dorset, 711 ft above sea-level, and on the hilltops open water is a rare curiosity. The pond lies at the centre of the village, a huge circular mirror 40 yds across and 16 ft deep in the middle. Mallard and muscovy ducks dabble on its surface, and reflected in its placid waters are an old stone barn, thatched cottages of stone and flint, the Georgian Old Rectory with its spreading cedar, and the wide downland sky.

No one knows how long the pond has been there, but it probably existed in pre-Saxon times, despite the Saxon name of the village recorded in the Domesday Book – *Aisemare*, meaning 'the pond by the ash tree'. In the last half century the pond has never dried out once; sometimes, in fact, the water rises even when there has been no rain – a phenomenon characteristic of chalk country, where rain drains away through the upper layers of rock and collects in underground reservoirs. Each year around Midsummer Day the villagers honour the pond in a ceremony, called Filly Loo, of uncertain origin. A band plays from a platform in

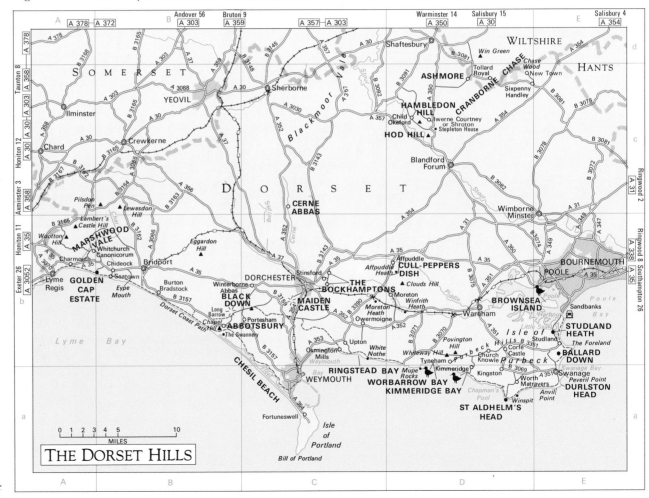

THE DORSET HILLS

ROYALIST RUIN Corfe Castle was built in 1080 to guard a gap in the Purbeck Hills. Cromwell destroyed it in 1646.

the middle of the pond and Morris Men dance on the shore.

There are fine views across the downs and combes from the ridgeway road which leads to the village from Shaftesbury.

To reach Ashmore take the B3081 south-east out of Shaftesbury towards Tollard Royal, but after 4½ miles, turn right along a minor road; Ashmore is 1 mile further.

Ballard Down
Eb

The Dorset chalklands begin dramatically at Ballard Down, where the hills of the Isle of Purbeck meet the sea. Below Studland's small Norman church, a fingerpost indicates two paths. One climbs straight ahead, first by a lane, then through blazing gorse and stone-strewn cornfields southwards to the crest of Ballard Down. About a mile west is Nine Barrow

Down with views of Corfe Castle 4 miles westwards. The other path – a more leisurely walk – descends eastwards towards the beach, turns to climb through Studland Wood, heavily scented with wild garlic and stinking iris, and finally emerges on the springy turf of the cliff-top. Do not go near the edge, for these cliffs are dangerous.

Far below, curiously sculpted chalk stacks rise dazzlingly from the sea. The great cliffs of The Foreland, a mile east of Studland, are penetrated by wave-pierced arches, and beyond lies Old Harry rock and, much eroded, Old Harry's Wife. Old Harry is a synonym for the Devil, and the area on the cliff-top is known as Old Nick's Ground. But on a sunny afternoon the place is nothing if not heavenly. Gulls circle lazily around the soaring white pinnacles, and the yellow spikes of wild cabbage brighten the cliff-edge.

The path continues along the cliff-top, with the green down and quietly grazing sheep to the right. At Ballard Point, 383 ft and a mile south-west of The Foreland, two seas come into view – to the north the great sweep of Studland Bay to Poole Harbour, and to the south the graceful crescent extending to Swanage and Peveril Point. The path then winds down into Swanage.

Ballard Down, owned by the National Trust, is 1½ miles north of Swanage. It can be reached from Swanage by taking the Studland road to New Swanage, where the southern end of the downland path starts from Ballard Way.

Black Down
Cb

Gorse and heather cover the summit of Black Down, 777 ft above the sea and surmounted by a monument to Vice-Admiral Sir Thomas Masterman

Hardy, Nelson's flag-captain at Trafalgar. The monument was erected by public subscription in 1846, and quickly became a familiar part of the Dorset landscape. The 70 ft high, octagonal stone stack captures the eye from far and wide, and from its base there are magnificent sea views across to the Isle of Wight, to Golden Cap and to Start Point almost 60 miles south-west in Devon. A bridle-path winds down from the summit of Black Down to Portesham where the admiral lived as a boy, in a modest Georgian stone house which still stands.

The downs in this area are rich in prehistoric burial mounds and standing stones. About a quarter of a mile west of the path, on the hill above Por-

tesham, there is a partly reconstructed New Stone Age chambered tomb called the Hell Stone. At the end of the Valley of Stones, in a field 1½ miles north-west of Portesham, remains of another New Stone Age tomb known as The Grey Mare and her Colts can be seen over the hedge; a Bronze Age stone circle stands a mile to its south-east near the footpath to Portesham Hill. To the north of Black Down, the outline of ancient fields can be traced in the grass.

Black Down is 5 miles west of Dorchester. Turn south off the A35 to Portesham at Winterborne Abbas. Black Down is to the east of the minor road; there is a car park near the monument.

The Bockhamptons
Cb

The heart of the writer Thomas Hardy lies buried in Stinsford churchyard, not far from the swift-flowing River Frome. His ashes are interred in Westminster Abbey. From the foot-bridge across a stream, a path leads westwards through old water-meadows to Grey's Bridge and Dorchester. Eastwards it runs alongside the stream, starred with the white flowers of river crowfoot and alive with serpentine strands of waving weed, to the stone-and-thatch village of Lower Bockhampton, where Hardy went to school.

About a mile's walk or drive northwards across the downs is Higher Bockhampton, and the wildlife sanctuary of Thorncombe Wood. From there a nature trail about 1½ miles long leads through a magnificent collection of sweet chestnuts, beeches and oaks, and on the eastern side of the wood through 20 acres of black heath, a tangle of furze, birch saplings, holly, heather and rhododendrons.

RARE RESIDENT

Its cocked tail and red eye-ring help to identify the secretive, sparrow-sized Dartford warbler. One of Britain's rarest breeding birds, it was once more widespread but the loss of heathland and some severe winters have taken their toll. These warblers stay mostly among the gorse and heather, but from March to June males sometimes sing from a bushy perch.

Dartford warbler
(*Sylvia undata*)

A side track from the trail leads up the hillside to Hardy's cottage birthplace. Where the Great Heath once swept down to the little barred back window there are now the dark conifers of the Forestry Commission's Puddletown Forest. Along the 2¼ mile Forest Walk you may glimpse Sika deer and see badger tracks.

Stinsford is just off the A35, 1½ miles east of Dorchester. Higher Bockhampton and Thorncombe Wood car park are about 1 mile north-east along minor roads.

Eb Brownsea Island

A castle overlooking the landing-stage, fields ablaze with daffodils in spring, rhododendrons forming a quarter-mile-long tunnel, and a woodland path descending to a gently shelving beach, all give Brownsea the air of a paradise island. Herring gulls nest in scores along the cliff paths, rising in shrieking protest as visitors approach. Canada geese marshal their young to grassy feeding spots, red squirrels can be seen in the pinewoods, and the island echoes with the sharp cries of peacocks in the trees or vibrating their dazzling tails in the pathways.

From the southern cliffs there are wide views across the shimmering waters of Poole Harbour to Old Harry rock and Corfe Castle tucked into its cleft in the Purbeck Hills. Near by, a chunk of Portland stone commemorates the first, experimental Boy Scouts' camp, arranged here by Baden-Powell in 1907 – only scouts and guides can camp on the island.

From a lookout hut at the start of the island nature trail you can see cormorants resting on the shingle strip, and common terns nesting on the islands built for them. A 200 acre nature reserve occupies the north side of the island, and includes one of the largest heronries in England. The Dorset Naturalists' Trust conducts a 1½ mile tour round the reserve every afternoon.

Brownsea Island, owned by the National Trust, is reached by boat from Sandbanks or Poole Quay. No dogs are allowed on the island.

Cc Cerne Abbas

The wild, aggressively masculine figure of a giant, 180 ft tall and brandishing an immense club in his right hand, is outlined in the chalk hillside above the quiet village of Cerne Abbas. Who carved the image and why is a mystery.

Some suggest that the giant is about 2,000 years old, representing a pagan fertility god, and that he was an idol at the centre of Celtic religious ritual. But another theory is that the figure portrays the Roman god Hercules, and was carved perhaps 1,700 years ago.

The pagan figure overlooks the few but impressive ruins of a Christian abbey half-hidden among beech trees just to the north of Cerne Abbas village. A path from the village leads to the sheep-grazed slopes of Giant Hill, but the stiff climb up the hill yields only glimpses of the 2 ft deep by 2 ft wide trench that forms the giant's outline, maintained by the National Trust. From the hillside there are fine views of Cerne Abbas in its bowl of green hills.

Above the giant's head lies the Trendle, or Frying Pan, a square Iron Age earthwork on the hilltop thought to have been used for Celtic ritual. Until recent times, the villagers used to set up a maypole here on May Day – a strange echo of the fertility cult that the giant may represent. According to folklore, couples who visit the giant at night can expect a fruitful marriage.

Cerne Abbas is 7 miles north of Dorchester on the A352 Sherborne road. The best view of the giant is from the lay-by on the A352 just north of the village.

Ca Chesil Beach

Seen from high above Fortuneswell, on the Isle of Portland, Chesil Beach curves away into the distance like a gigantic hawser mooring the island to the mainland. On one side lies the sea, white with surf; on the other the placid waters of the Fleet, a lagoon bordering the great bank of pebbles for half of the 16 miles to its anchorage in the tawny cliffs near Burton Bradstock. And all along the beach there is a deep and

---

A WRITER'S DORSET

THOMAS HARDY was born in a small, thatched cottage at Higher Bockhampton, Dorset, in 1840; he died in Dorchester – which he renamed 'Casterbridge' in his novels – in 1928. The centrepiece of his writing was the partly imagined 'South Wessex' – Dorset – whose rich farmlands, woods, hills, heaths, coasts, villages and towns he incorporated in his books and poems. For example, in *Under the Greenwood Tree*, Hardy

uses a description of his own cottage birthplace. *Tess of the D'Urbervilles* draws on many Dorset locations, including Bere Regis and the valleys of the Frome and Piddle. The village of 'Weatherbury' in *Far from the Madding Crowd* is Puddletown, and Woodbury Hill near by becomes 'Greenhill'.

Hardy's wild 'Egdon Heath' in *The Return of the Native* is a mixture of the scattered heathland around Puddletown Heath.

HARDY'S BIRTHPLACE, HIGHER BOCKHAMPTON

WINTER FALLOWS December snow lies upon the silent winter slopes around Black Down. The coppiced woods and shadowed fields await the return of spring to bring back life and colour to the rich Dorset landscape.

continuous hiss and roar as the waves suck back then hurl forward the millions of pebbles.

About 200 yds wide and 40 ft high at the Portland end, the beach changes shape with the sea's moods. Fishermen judge their position along the beach by the size of the pebbles, which the tide has graded in size from west to east; at Portland they are the size of a man's fist, at Burton Bradstock they are no bigger than raisins.

Chesil Beach was the scourge of sailing ships when strong south-westerly winds swept across Lyme Bay. Many a good ship has been battered to pieces on the seething pebbles. Casualties include seven ships of the line in November 1795, with the loss of more than 200 men and women. They were part of a fleet commanded by Rear-Admiral Sir Hugh Christian, on his way to the West Indies to be Commander-in-Chief. In 1824 two West-Indiamen, *Carvalho* and *Colville*, met their fate here with all hands drowned, and the sloop *Ebenezer* was flung almost into the Fleet, in which it was later re-floated.

The gales of 1824 claimed not only ships but also the village of Fleet near the eastern end of the lagoon, swept away when a freak tide roared over the bank. Only the chancel of the old village church survives.

To reach Fortuneswell, take the A354 Portland road south out of Weymouth, and cross the causeway. There is a car park in Fortuneswell.

Dc Cranborne Chase

It is easy to pass by Cranborne Chase without realising it is there, for the forest laws that protected it for a thousand years as a hunting ground for the privileged – including King John when he was Earl of Gloucester – have set it apart from the surrounding countryside. The roads that lead into it are few and narrow, and its villages are hidden haphazardly in clearings.

The chalk uplands of Cranborne Chase straddle the A354 between Salisbury and Blandford Forum. Its boundaries have varied, but at their fullest they enclosed nearly 800,000 acres within a 100 mile perimeter. The oldest part, with hunting rights dating back to Saxon times, is the Inner Chase – an area 10 miles by 3 miles to the north-west of the A354, centred around the hamlet of Tollard Royal. Win Green hill in Wiltshire, at 910 ft the highest point, is now owned by the National Trust. Its tree-crowned summit is a perfect place from which to survey the wide sweep of the Chase.

Deer-poaching is as old as the Chase itself. At Sixpenny Handley, carcases were hidden in an old tomb; the tomb cover – now inscribed – is still in the churchyard. For centuries the Chase was a battleground between an army of keepers and local farmers and poachers. Farmers put up fences to save their crops from deer; keepers tore them down. Murderous affrays became so commonplace that keepers and some poachers, 18th-century 'bloods', even wore protective clothing – straw-lined, beehive helmets and padded jackets. But the sporting ardour of the 'bloods' cooled after 1736 when the penalty for a second poaching conviction was transportation.

Hunting rights ended in 1828, and much of the ancient forest – described by Thomas Hardy as the oldest wood in England – was eventually cut down. One of the loveliest parts that still remains is Chase Wood, which can be reached by road (to New Town) or track across Handley Common.

To reach Win Green hill turn north off the B3081, 4 miles south-east of Shaftesbury. Handley Common is also off the B3081 just north-west of Sixpenny Handley, and New Town is along a minor road north off the B3081 at Sixpenny Handley.

Db Cull-peppers Dish

On Affpuddle Heath a tall tree grows from the 50 ft depths of a smooth-sided crater measuring 150 yds across. The tree and crater resemble a huge mortar and pestle, and may have been named after the 17th-century herbalist Nicholas Culpeper. Once thought to

HEATHLAND HIGHLIGHT

Rarely found outside the county, Dorset heath is one of the loveliest of Britain's seven species of heather. It bears spikes of large, brilliant rose-pink flowers from July until November, and its leaves are in whorls of three. An evergreen plant of damp heaths, it grows mainly on the Isle of Purbeck. It is sometimes found in Devon and Cornwall.

Dorset heath
(*Erica ciliaris*)

be a prehistoric temple, the crater is now recognised as a swallow-hole – one of 200 or so on the heath – a subsidence caused by underground streams eroding sand and chalk.

In the northern part of the heath, the many little bridges and decaying sluice gates tell of the once-intricate system of water-meadows around the River Piddle. The controlled flooding of these meadows early in the year resulted in early grazing for stock, because the incoming water, warmer than the soil, advanced grass growth.

To the south, tracks lead down from the heath through Forestry Commission conifers and past Rimsmoor Pond to the bridle-path to Clouds Hill. Here the National Trust maintains the cottage that was the home of Lawrence of Arabia from 1923. He bought it while, as Private Shaw of the Royal Tank Corps, he was stationed at nearby Bovington Camp. Later he transferred to the RAF, and on his discharge in 1935 returned to live at Clouds Hill until his death a few months later. Lawrence described the cottage, which lies concealed in a riot of rhododendrons, as 'earthly paradise'.

Cull-peppers Dish is 8 miles east of Dorchester. Take the A35 eastwards and turn on to the B3390 towards Affpuddle; the signpost and car park are east of the road about 1 mile south of the village.

Ea Durlston Head

The rock formations of the Isle of Purbeck are nowhere more dramatic than in the great grey cliffs of Portland stone that rise from the waves at Durlston Head. And in the park above the cliffs is a man-made rock formation – the Great Globe, a chart of the world cut from 40 tons of Portland stone and surrounded by stone slabs carved with cosmic information and quotations from the poets. It was carved in the 1880s by George Burt, a local quarryman who made his fortune supplying paving stones for Victorian London.

The Dorset County Council's Country Park here has a 'stone trail', a nature trail and geological models that tell the story of the local rocks. A path leads down through holm oaks and tamarisk to a cliff-edge sea-bird sanctuary, and then strides on towards the Anvil Point Lighthouse, descending into the gully where the Tilly Whim Caves emerge. Rock falls have forced the closure of these old quarry workings, but the great wall of Portland stone, divided into gargantuan blocks by natural joints, remains awe-inspiring. There are other impressive quarry caves at Winspit, a few miles to the west. This is an idyllic spot on a sunny day, with its great stone stacks and the sea dancing over the ledges from which generations of quarrymen winched their stone into the barges waiting below.

Durlston Head is 1 mile south of Swanage, reached by the road climbing southwards just east of Swanage pier; there is a car park just before the castle. Winspit is 4 miles west of Durlston Head, along a 1¼ mile track south from Worth Matravers, which has a car park on the Corfe road.

Bb Golden Cap Estate

When Golden Cap hill glistens in the sun, it is one of those landmarks so unforgettable that whole regions revolve around them. A flat-topped band of orange sandstone, the hill crowns the highest cliff on England's south coast, overlooking Lyme Bay. The National Trust has made Golden Cap the focal point of a miniature national park, which spans 5 miles of colourful coastline from Eype Mouth westwards to The Spittles rocks near Lyme Regis, with beaches, woods, two rivermouths, two cliff peaks and miles of downland slopes and combes. The Dorset Coast Path runs right along the estate coastline.

A narrow lane winds down to Eype Mouth, south-west of Bridport. At Seatown the River Winniford twists down a long combe to end in a small pool on the inland side of the pebble shore; here, the cliffs to the east are a subtle blend of green and grey, merging above into a tawny yellow.

The coast path crosses Seatown beach after descending westwards over Doghouse Hill from the green, 507 ft high Thorncombe Beacon; then it climbs steeply westwards to the 626 ft high summit of Golden Cap. Another, easier route to the cliff-top starts from the Langdon Hill car park west of Chideock (the only car park on the east side of the estate), and leads south through woods to the downs before finally climbing to the summit, topped with gorse and heather.

Out to sea the views from Golden Cap stretch from Start Point in Devon to the white cliffs of Bill of Portland, and inland to the west the long ridge of Stonebarrow Hill drops to the sea at the sombre cliffs called Cain's Folly. Beyond Charmouth are the tumbled landslips of Black Ven, a favourite haunt for fossil hunters.

Golden Cap is 4 miles east of Lyme Regis. A number of narrow lanes lead south from the A35 Lyme Regis–Bridport road to Golden Cap Estate. Stonebarrow Lane, at the eastern end of Charmouth, leads to Stonebarrow Hill where there is a National Trust information centre and car park.

SEA PANORAMA From the rocky shore below Golden Cap, a long, lonely beach stretches towards Wear Cliffs, which offers magnificent views eastwards taking in the great sweep of Chesil Beach and the Isle of Portland.

Dc Hod and Hambledon Hills

Two Iron Age hill-forts confront each other across the narrow valley where the road winds from Child Okeford to Stepleton House. On one side looms Hambledon Hill, grim and bare and over 600 ft high; on the other, slightly lower, stands Hod Hill. Both hills have been the scenes of local stands against invaders – both unsuccessful.

On Hod Hill in AD 43, a band of Dorset people – Durotriges Celts – tried to halt the Roman advance through southern Britain. The 2nd Augustan Legion under the Roman general Vespasian poured a deadly rain of ballista bolts on the defenders and quickly took the fort. The Romans used a corner of the 50 acre hill-fort – the largest in Dorset – to construct their own smaller fort. Behind the ramparts they built barracks for 850 legionaries and horsemen, and a house for the commander; and they cut water tanks in the chalk large enough to hold 2,000 gallons, lining them with clay.

On Hambledon Hill in 1645, during the Civil War, some 2,000 villagers made a stand against Cromwell. They belonged to a group known as the Clubmen, because of their primitive weapons; these men were sick of war and damage to their property and crops, and resisted both Royalists and Roundheads. But they were routed by 50 Roundhead dragoons, who locked some of them in Shroton Church.

South-east from Hambledon's Iron Age hill-fort are remains of a much older causewayed camp enclosing about 20 acres. Excavations in the late 1970s show that this was just part of a large Stone Age settlement on the hill where, some 4,500 years ago, men lived and kept herds of milk cattle within a defensive timber-faced earthen rampart and ditch. That they were subject to attack is evident from the discovery of a skeleton with an arrowhead embedded in the chest, and signs of fire damage to the defences.

Both Hod and Hambledon hills are privately owned and farmed, but there are public bridle-paths, one on the west side of Hod Hill, one across the Hambledon summit and by the Stone Age camp, and one on the north side of Hambledon Hill up to the hill-fort.

To reach Hod and Hambledon hills, take the A350 Shaftesbury road from Blandford Forum, and 3 miles north turn left towards Child Okeford. After ½ mile, an iron swing-gate (hidden by rising ground) in a clump of beeches on the left marks the bridle-path to Hod Hill. One mile further, a stile on the right leads to the summit of Hambledon Hill. For the hill-fort, continue on the A350 and take the turning to Iwerne Courtney or Shroton, then the path from the village.

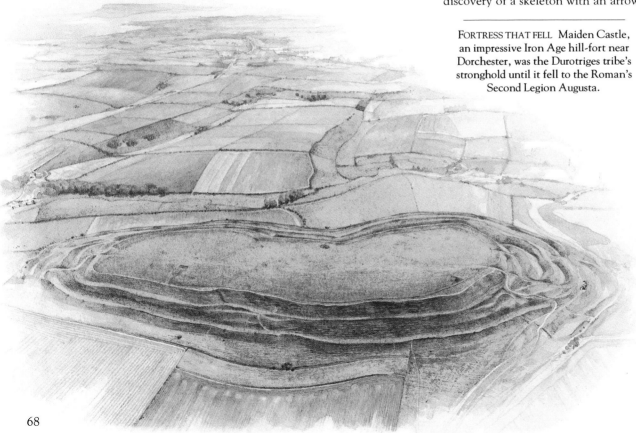

FORTRESS THAT FELL Maiden Castle, an impressive Iron Age hill-fort near Dorchester, was the Durotriges tribe's stronghold until it fell to the Roman's Second Legion Augusta.

Cb Maiden Castle

The Celtic tribe who gave their name to Dorset – the Durotriges – made Maiden Castle their hilltop capital. But the fort, whose mighty multiple ramparts wind sinuously around a saddle-backed hill outside Dorchester, was many centuries in the making.

Hardly discernible now is the New Stone Age camp that crowned the eastern summit long before 2000 BC; but a crudely shaped chalk idol, dating from this period and possibly the image of a mother-goddess, was found on the hilltop and can now be seen in the County Museum in Dorchester. Largely lost, too, is the enormous New Stone Age long-barrow burial mound that ran one-third of a mile along the top.

The first Celtic inhabitants, who arrived about 300 BC, fortified their single rampart with timber. It enclosed about 16 acres, and within its protec-

SNAKES AND LIZARDS

Dorset's heathland is a home for all six species of reptile found in Britain – three snakes and three lizards. The rarest are the sand lizard and the smooth snake. The slow (or blind) worm looks like a snake but is really a legless lizard. Of these reptiles, only the adder is venomous, but it will rarely bite unless it is frightened.

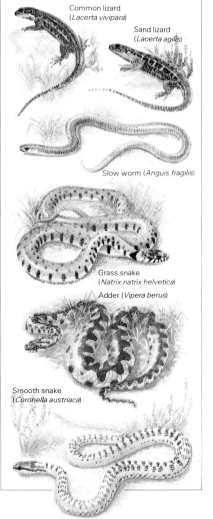

Common lizard
(*Lacerta vivipara*)

Sand lizard
(*Lacerta agilis*)

Slow worm (*Anguis fragilis*)

Grass snake
(*Natrix natrix helvetica*)

Adder (*Vipera berus*)

Smooth snake
(*Coronella austriaca*)

tion they lived in timber huts, laid out in streets, and stored their corn and water in large circular pits. The enclosure was enlarged to its present size of 47 acres – making it a small town – after 250 BC.

Maiden Castle as it is today dates from later Celtic times, largely from the 1st century BC, and was a response to the threat of a new weapon, the sling-shot, that could kill at 100 yds against the 30 yds of primitive arrows. Extra lines of ramparts were added – and were raised as high as possible. You can still walk round an inner rampart that rises 50 ft above its ditch.

But none of these fortifications offered adequate defence against the ballistae – or giant crossbows – of the Roman 2nd Legion, which attacked in AD 43. The Durotriges were routed and suffered heavy losses. By AD 70 the fort was deserted, and the survivors driven down into the new Roman town of Durnovaria, now called Dorchester. Around AD 380, the hilltop was reoccupied by the people who built the mysterious Romano-British temple whose foundations can be seen there today. Some 300 years later, about AD 635, a sacrificial victim with a hole cut in his skull was buried in the bank-barrow. By whom and for what reason is unknown.

Maiden Castle is 2 miles south-west of Dorchester. At the southern end of the town, a signposted minor road leads south-west off the A354 Weymouth road; there is a car park at the end of this road.

Ab   Marshwood Vale

A network of meandering, high-banked lanes wanders through Marshwood Vale, the valley of the River Char which winds down to Lyme Bay at Charmouth. Hidden among the lanes, villages of tawny sandstone patterned with grey-green lichen shelter below heavily wooded hills such as Wootton and Lewesdon, some of them crowned with ancient hill-forts such as Lambert's Castle. The capital of the Vale is the small hillside village of Whitchurch Canonicorum, so called because its parish tithes were split between the canons of Wells and Salisbury cathedrals. In the mainly Early English church there is a rare healing shrine, a 13th-century stone tomb containing the relics of St Wite, a Saxon saint; the three oval holes in its side were where pilgrims in hope of miracles placed their crippled limbs.

Three miles to the north-west lies Wootton Hill, where the road climbs through tunnels of beeches to a Forestry Commission car park in the shelter of tall Monterey pines. A gentle walk leads through Charmouth Forest, on the crown of the hill, where roe deer emerge from cover at dawn and dusk.

The forest road joins the B3165 which, a mile to the north-east, skirts the towering sides of Lambert's Castle, an Iron Age earthwork on the frontier between the territories of the Durotriges of Dorset and the Dumnovici, who gave their name to neighbouring Devon. From the south-west side the ascent is easy. The top is so spacious that horse races used to be run there in the 18th and 19th centuries. Now it is National Trust property, with superb views over the Vale and north-east to the distinctive Pilsdon Pen (909 ft), the highest hill in Dorset, crowned by another hill-fort.

Whitchurch Canonicorum is 4 miles north-east of Lyme Regis. A turning to the left from the A35 just east of Charmouth leads to the Vale.

Cb   Ringstead Bay

The massive chalk headland of White Nothe, called Nose locally, protects Ringstead Bay to the east. On the south-west side, the formidable stone rampart of the Isle of Portland shelters both Ringstead and Weymouth bays.

The deserted medieval village of Ringstead lies about a mile east of Osmington Mills, where John Constable painted his picture of Weymouth Bay. The village is now no more than a collection of grassy mounds and the ruined fragment of a church. Why it was deserted local records do not say.

The villagers may have succumbed to the Black Death. A more likely story

PORTLAND STONE

QUARRYING is, or was, what the Isle of Portland was all about, since it consists of a huge block of limestone some 4 miles long by 1½ miles wide. The yawning quarries are now largely abandoned, their ledges softened with turf and wild flowers. Most of the island's buildings are of Portland stone, including one of the oldest – Rufus Castle. The ruins date from the mid-15th century.

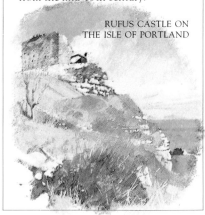

RUFUS CASTLE ON
THE ISLE OF PORTLAND

is that they were the victims of French raiders in 1420, during the Hundred Years' War.

A coastal path climbs eastwards about 2 miles to White Nothe, across sloping downland overlooking a long sweep of pebbled beach, sheltered in places by ledges of rock running into the sea. Even the chaotic, tumbled layers of the Burning Cliff in no way disrupt the bay's idyllic and tranquil atmosphere. The Burning Cliff is so called because the dark, sulphurous oil-shale – or Kimmeridge coal – of which it is composed, ignited spontaneously in 1826 and smouldered for four years.

The approach to towering White Nothe is through wooded gullies bright with red campion in summer. The final climb is very steep, but for those who make it there are superb views.

Ringstead Bay is 5 miles east of Weymouth. For Ringstead car park take the Upton turning (toll-road) south from the A353 Weymouth–Wareham road.

Da   St Aldhelm's Head

The grey wall of rock that sweeps westwards from Swanage reaches its climax at St Aldhelm's Head, a towering 350 ft cliff thrusting boldly out into the Channel. A few yards back from the cliff-edge a small Norman chapel dedicated to the evangelist St Aldhelm (c. 640–709), a Saxon Bishop of Sherborne, stands solitary on the windswept grassy plateau, heavily buttressed against the gales. Where a stone cross now stands on its roof, there was originally a fire basket whose bright glow warned sailors of the tide-race off the headland.

Westwards from the cliff the rock collapses in spectacular disarray, and strangely fretted towers and pinnacles

ADVANCE OF THE DUNES To the east of Studland Heath lies an area of sand-dunes that is slowly advancing the Dorset coast into Studland Bay. The heath and dunes were established as a National Nature Reserve in 1962, and one of the best viewing points is from the observation post at Spur Heath to the west of Little Sea, the freshwater lake that is an outstanding feature of the reserve. The dunes are developing continuously as sand blown inland piles up against seaweed or shore-line plants. Marram grass helps to hold the sand firm and the ridge is gradually colonised by other plants. Tree lupins favour the sandy soil, and gorse and Scots pine grow in the damp hollows, or 'slacks'.

TREE LUPIN

SCOTS PINE

COMMON GORSE AND MARRAM GRASS

rise from the green undercliff, wreathed in wild flowers. The Dorset Coast Path follows near the cliff-edge to Emmetts Hill overlooking Chapman's Pool, a quiet cove in a deep cleft bordered on the west by Houns-tout Cliff. The path down to the pool is so steep that 200 steps were cut into the cliffs, but now landslips in the area have made both the path and the cove unsafe, and warning notices have been posted. Keep away from the cliff-edge.

St Aldhelm's Head is 5 miles southwest of Swanage. From Worth Matravers (off B3069 west of Swanage), a pot-holed road runs westwards to Renscombe Farm, then turns south from the farmyard to St Aldhelm's Head, 1½ miles further on.

Eb   Studland Heath

The ancient wilderness of Dorset's heathland, glowing with gorse and heather, butts up against the sparkling creeks and inlets of Poole's vast, landlocked harbour. At Studland, 1,570 acres of the heath are under the protection of the Nature Conservancy, and east of the toll-road to the South Haven Point–Sandbanks chain-ferry there are two nature trails starting from the Knoll car park. One leads over the beach and sand-dunes, the other through woodland and swamp.

The sand-dunes trail first follows the superb crescent of Studland's beach, well sheltered and with wide white sands, one of the finest bathing beaches in Britain. Shells to be found along the waterline include Pandora shells, about 1¼ in. long and with a mother-of-pearl sheen; they are found only here, at Weymouth and in the Channel Isles. From the beach the trail turns inland over three lines of dunes which grow greener the further they

70

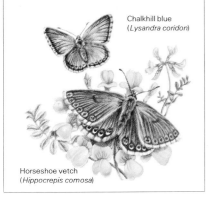
are from the sea. These sand-dunes demonstrate how the peninsula has been built up over 250 years from a small spit of land – the wind sweeping sand inshore and plants gradually colonising and anchoring the newly created dunes.

The most seaward dune is known as the Zero Ridge. The centre one is called the First Ridge, because it was the nearest dune to the sea when the area was surveyed in the 1930s. The third, innermost, ridge dates from the 18th century.

The woodland trail passes close to the south end of Studland's Little Sea, a mile-long freshwater lake edged with sallow, reedmace, yellow flag and bog bean. Until 350 years ago it was a coastal bay, but developing sand-dunes

have now completely cut it off from the sea, and drainage from inland streams has gradually replaced the salt water.

A wooden hide, reached along a short path from the ferry road, overlooks the lake, where in winter thousands of wildfowl, such as wigeon, pochard, goldeneye and shoveler, may be seen. Summer visitors include sedge and reed warblers, which can be heard singing in the reed beds. Britain's three lizard and three snake species are all found on the reserve.

Studland Heath is 4 miles north of Swanage. There are frequent ferries to the heath from Sandbanks to the north, although long queues of cars may form in summer. An alternative approach is through Wareham and Corfe via the A351 and B3351 roads. The Knoll car park is about ½ mile north of Studland along a toll-road.

Da Worbarrow and Kimmeridge Bays

A rich underwater life, flourishing on the low ledges of clay and shale that shelve into the sea, is one of the few qualities the neighbouring Worbarrow and Kimmeridge bays have in common, together with the fact that they are both part of the Purbeck Marine Nature Reserve. Otherwise they contrast dramatically.

Worbarrow Bay is flanked on the east side by the towering limestone pyramid of Worbarrow Tout; to the west – across almost 2 miles of glistening water – is Mupe Bay and the tumbling Mupe Rocks. In between, the waves have cut back the softer disarray of rock to form cliffs that are green, grey, pink or ochre, and are broken in the middle by the shining white cove of

Arish Mell, where the Purbeck-chalk range drops to the sea. A wooded gully leads to Worbarrow Bay, running down to the sea from the deserted village of Tyneham.

Kimmeridge Bay is less dramatic, backed by low green downland and with modest cliffs whose crumbly, tawny rocks alternate with dark grey shale and clay. On the bay's eastern arm stands a tower commemorating Sir William Clavell of nearby Smedmore House; in the 17th century he came close to ruin trying to develop the commercial potential of the local sulphurous oil-shale, using it as fuel first for producing alum, then for a glass works. The Celts were more successful with their use of the shale well into Romano-British times, and their bangles and ornaments made from hardened

Kimmeridge oil-shale have been found as far away as Hadrian's Wall.

Worbarrow Bay is within an army firing range, but it is open to the public most weekends and public holidays. Dates are given in the local press and on the army road boards. Marked paths lead to the bay from Tyneham car park, and it is essential to keep to the paths in case of unexploded shells.

Kimmeridge and Worbarrow bays are 8 and 10 miles west of Swanage. To reach both bays, turn off the A351 Swanage–Wareham road at Corfe Castle for Church Knowle. Just beyond Church Knowle, a turning south leads about 2 miles to Kimmeridge, from where a toll-road leads to the bay car park. For Worbarrow Bay, pass the Kimmeridge turning and continue about 4 miles via Steeple to Tyneham, where there is a car park.

SAPPHIRE SEA Pyramidal Worbarrow Tout may be the remains of a wall of limestone that kept Worbarrow Bay an inlet until the sea cut through.

THE FACE OF ANCIENT BRITAIN

MAN'S FIRST PROFOUND EFFECT UPON THE BRITISH LANDSCAPE DATES BACK TO A MERE 5,000 YEARS

MAN – *Homo sapiens sapiens* or his ancestors – has lived in Britain, off and on, for the best part of half a million years. Of the very first people, nothing is known save for a few crudely worked flints found in association with the fossilised bones of bear, lion and sabre-toothed cat. The earliest human remains – some skull bones found in Thames gravel at Swanscombe, near Tilbury – date from a staggering 250,000 years later. Swanscombe Man, and his descendants for many thousands of generations after, were big-game hunters who followed the herds over the south-east land mass that then joined Britain to the Continent. The hunters' comings and goings and the quarry they followed – reindeer and woolly mammoth, or fallow deer, giant ox and elephant – depended very much on the ebb and flow of the later Ice Ages.

Shaped by ice

The successive advances and retreats of the ice also had a tremendous effect upon the landscape. Slow-moving glaciers gouged out the valleys of the Lake District, for instance, and carved the strange, waved scarps of the Brecon Beacons; then, as they melted, they deposited great masses of accumulated scrapings, among them the glacial clays of the Lincolnshire Wolds and the sarsen ('saracen', or foreign) stones from which Stonehenge was eventually built. As the ice melted, too, a great weight was lifted from the land, permitting it to rise up, while the sea-levels also rose, gradually inundating the areas that are now the North Sea and the English Channel. By 6000 BC, Britain was an island.

However, the country was ice-free some 4,000 years before that, and in the temperate period that followed, great forests grew and game abounded, tempting hunters in ever-growing numbers over the land bridge from the Continent. Probably for most of the time they lived in skin tents, as they followed the herds of deer, wild ox and horse around, or fished in the forest streams. But they also occupied caves, from the Mendips to Derbyshire, and the remains they left in them show that these Old Stone Age hunters had reached a considerable degree of advancement. They used fire; they buried their dead with some form of religious rite; they made jewellery of animal teeth and bones; they had axes, spears and arrowheads of finely chipped flint, and harpoons of antler and bone.

The farmers move in

For thousands of years they had all Britain as their preserve; then, about 3500 BC, a new kind of colonist began to arrive from the Continent, probably via Ireland. These were farmers, who brought seed, cattle and agricultural techniques with them. Unlike the wandering hunters, these New Stone Age people led a settled existence, and for the first time, man began to make an impact on the British landscape. Forests were cleared with fire and axe, great causewayed camps – rectangular ditched enclosures – were constructed on the chalk hills from East Devon to the Sussex Downs, and in order to obtain flint to make their splendid chipped and ground tools, they dug mines, most notably at Grimes Graves in Norfolk. They enclosed fields and they buried their dead in the stone-chambered, turf-covered mounds that archaeologists have christened 'long barrows'. It was the New Stone Age folk, too, who established the great trading routes across England, whose lines are now followed by such tracks as the Icknield Way and the Berkshire Ridgeway. They also built the temple of Woodhenge on Salisbury Plain, and, near by, carved the great circular mound and ditch that would later be occupied by the massive pillars of Stonehenge. But their greatest and most enduring monuments are the high grasslands of Salisbury Plain, the Yorkshire Wolds and the South Downs, since to a large extent it was New Stone Age clearances and grazings that created them.

About 2200 BC a new influence began to be felt. For some time in the Low Countries and the Rhineland men had been working in metals – gold, and the copper and tin alloy called bronze – and gradually their products began to filter through to Britain. They were shortly followed by the metalworkers themselves, no doubt attracted by British deposits of tin and copper. The effect of these Bronze Age people was tremendous; due not so much to the influence of their metal tools and weapons as to the great monuments they left behind, from south-west England to the Hebrides.

It would seem that the native population and the new colonists must have mingled freely almost from the start, in an exchange of ideas and technology. Certainly, the first building of Stonehenge, within the Stone Age enclosure on Salisbury Plain, began about 2200 BC, a very early point in what is known as the Bronze Age. The sheer labour requirement alone surely argues the combined efforts of both peoples, especially since the mysterious mound of Silbury and the huge stone circles and avenue at Avebury on the other side of the Plain were also constructed at around the same time. The northern circles and monuments were constructed a little later, as the new influences filtered through the country.

Iron Age warriors

The last great colonising of Britain in what we call prehistory began about 750 BC, as ever-larger bands of Celtic warriors started to cross the Channel. Originating probably somewhere around the Danube, they had gradually overwhelmed large areas of Europe, their course made easier by a naturally pugnacious disposition, the ability to make iron weapons and their skill with the slingshot. In Britain, as elsewhere, they seem to have established a warrior aristocracy, and later, as successive Celtic invaders arrived from the Continent, a number of tribal kingdoms. They were superb craftsmen and farmers too, as the many lynchets, or Iron Age field patterns, bear witness.

But their chief mark upon the landscape was not agricultural, or religious, as their predecessors' had been. It was military – the 3,000-odd hill-forts and other defensive works whose crumbling ramparts would even now, in many cases, present a formidable obstacle to attacking infantry.

The menace of Rome

In the early years of Celtic domination, the forts were built – or adapted from much earlier works – as a defence against fellow Celts of rival tribes. But by the beginning of the 1st century AD, there was a growing and uneasy awareness of a more dangerous foe across the Channel – the everywhere-victorious legions of Rome, and the bastions of some of the hill-forts were strengthened in consequence.

Greatest of these was Maiden Castle in Dorset, the 47 acre stronghold of the Durotriges, whose earliest defences had been raised almost 3,500 years earlier. By AD 43, the year the 2nd Legion Augusta reached it almost straight from the invasion beaches, the palisaded ramparts towered a full 125 ft high. What happened next is not clear. Probably the Romans put down a heavy bombardment of ballista bolts – which far outranged the Celtic slings – and followed up with an infantry assault under shield cover. But they must have had a tough fight of it. As a general rule, the Romans preferred live slaves to dead enemies, yet here, so far as excavation shows, they slaughtered the garrison – men, women and children – and threw their corpses into shallow pits by the defences.

The Pax Romana had arrived.

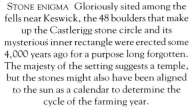

DARTMOOR PASTORAL Grimspound was a Bronze Age settlement of 20-odd huts gathered about a massively walled 4 acre enclosure, presumably used as a corral. Stone hearths and beds can still be seen within some of the 3,000-year-old huts.

STONE ENIGMA Gloriously sited among the fells near Keswick, the 48 boulders that make up the Castlerigg stone circle and its mysterious inner rectangle were erected some 4,000 years ago for a purpose long forgotten. The majesty of the setting suggests a temple, but the stones might also have been aligned to the sun as a calendar to determine the cycle of the farming year.

THE LAYERED PAST Stone Age camp, Bronze Age fort, Iron Age town, a Roman battlefield, perhaps the Camelot of Arthur and Guinevere, a Saxon mint – all these are buried now beneath the hummocky turf of Cadbury Hill in Somerset.

THE BEGINNING Some 250,000 years ago, the first Britons hunted reindeer, bison and mammoth along the edge of the glaciers that reached as far south as the Thames valley. The only mark of their passing is a number of roughly worked flint axes found in caves – such as Kent's Cavern in Devon – which they occupied.

SEMI-DETACHED Best preserved of Iron Age villages is Chysauster in Cornwall, which flourished from the 2nd century BC until perhaps the 3rd century AD. It consists of stone houses, mostly in pairs, each with a courtyard and a garden plot; several possess a drainage system. The inhabitants were farmers who worked nearby fields.

THE NEW FOREST

The hunting ground of kings, where ancient heaths and woodlands sweep down to the sea

Only a king could have devised a playground as grand as the New Forest – 145 sq. miles of woodland, heath and marsh where the deer roamed at will except when a royal huntsman sprang to the chase. William the Conqueror created the New Forest in 1079, planting new woods in a scrub-covered wilderness with scattered farms and home-steads that was the old Saxon hunting ground of Ytene. It has survived 900 years to remain one of the largest stretches of undeveloped land in England, still Crown land but today preserved for public enjoyment and recreation.

The forest lies in a broad, shallow basin between South-ampton in the east and the Hampshire River Avon about 15 miles to the west, and it stretches from the borders of Wiltshire some 20 miles south to the shores of The Solent. The northern part, mainly heath, is a series of ridges and valleys with the highest point, 421 ft, at Pipers Wait in the north near Long Cross. Just under half the area is forested, conifers of the Forestry Commission sharing about equal numbers with deciduous woods of mainly oak and beech. Lyndhurst, the forest 'capital' that 1,000 years ago was a royal manor, stands at the junction of the A35 and A337 that cut through the area together with the A31 to the north.

When William I took over the New Forest, he introduced cruel forest laws to protect the deer for the hunt. 'He made large forests for the deer,' a Saxon chronicler wrote, 'and enacted laws there-with so that whoever killed a hart or hind should be blinded.' In fact, the penalty for killing a deer was death; blinding was for merely disturbing the animals. Local homesteaders and landowners were no longer allowed to fence in their crops against deer, and managed to survive only because they were allowed to exercise five common rights: pannage – the right to feed their pigs on acorns and beech mast; turbary – the right to cut peat and turves; estover – the right to cut firewood; marl – the right to improve the soil; and pasturage – the right to graze their stock. But this valuable grazing right was withdrawn in June and July when the deer were calving, and also in winter if grass was scarce.

It was the need for shipbuilding timber in the 15th century that marked the end of the 400 year reign of the royal deer. The first enclosures to protect young trees from browsing deer were made in 1483. By 1851 the tide had so turned against the deer that the Deer Removal Act initiated a two-year cull in an attempt at extermination. But when the cull was over the deer trickled back, and today there are about 1,000 of them, mostly fallow deer but with a fair number of roe deer, a few red deer and Japanese Sika deer.

A good place for an overall view of the forest is from the high ground in the north, along the B3078 between Godshill in the west and Long Cross in the east. From here the ridges are purple with heather in summer, brushed by shades of green and framed by the dark woods beyond. And when the evening sky reddens, the forest colours take on a sombre hue, black shadows fill the hollows and a wispy mist swirls wraith-like across the darkening road.

*F*OREST MAGIC Tranquil Queen Bower probably takes its name from 'Queneboure', the medieval hunting lodge named after Eleanor, queen of Edward I. Such is its ageless beauty, it would come as no surprise to see Eleanor appear again in this glade by the Lymington river.

Places to visit

Map ref. Ab Ashley Walk

A 'walk' in New Forest parlance is an area which was once the 'beat' of a forest keeper, in the days when deer reigned supreme. There are 15 of them, and Ashley Walk is one of the wildest and most desolate. It lies in the north-west corner of the forest, where windswept heathland rolls away on either side of a road called Deadman Hill. These forest 'highlands' were once likened to the Scottish moors by the novelist Sir Walter Scott, and from any point along the road there are views of treeless ridges and heather-clad valleys laced with brooks and streams. The dense woodlands are away to the south – a distant vista of blue-black and dark green against the sky.

Deadman Hill follows a ridge, and to its north the deep valley of Millersford Bottom opens up like a vast crater with clumps of gorse clinging to its sides. To the south, tracks lead down to Black Gutter Bottom and Stone Quarry Bottom and the rippling Ditchend Brook. The tracks continue over Cockley Hill to Little Cockley Plain, scattered with isolated holly trees – the domain of ponies and grazing cattle.

Where the route begins to descend to Godshill, a road turning off north by the Fighting Cocks public house leads to Castle Hill – an undated Iron Age hill-fort with ramparts and ditches overlooking the Avon valley. The earthworks are overgrown with trees and are hard to make out, but as the road climbs to a ridge a magnificent view begins to unfold in the valley below. Here the Avon snakes across the valley, through water-meadows and passing a red-brick mill by a stone bridge. Then the river makes another turn and disappears from view as it runs close to the western foot of the hill.

Ashley Walk is crossed by the B3078 between Cadnam and Fordingbridge, and includes Deadman Hill which leads to Godshill Ridge as the road descends to Godshill. The road leading to Castle Hill is 1½ miles east of Fordingbridge.

Bb Beaulieu Heath

In the south-east corner of the New Forest the vast, gently undulating vistas of Beaulieu Heath stretch almost from Southampton Water to Lymington. In spring and early summer the eastern part of the heath is ablaze with gorse, massed in great clumps, and westward roll dark seas of heather that turn to purple as autumn approaches. Near the centre of the heath lies the crescent-shaped Hatchet Pond, one of the forest's largest expanses of water. It is close to the junction of the B3055 and B3054, and there are car parks along its banks.

Although little of this sandy heath is more than 100 ft above sea-level, there are often exhilarating views across The Solent to the Isle of Wight. Round barrows scattered over the heath are a reminder that Bronze Age men settled here, when the sea-level was lower than it is now and The Solent was a fertile river valley.

The Beaulieu River cuts a meandering channel across the heath, and widens between grassy banks and mud-flats to become tidal at Beaulieu village. Here, near a broad curve of the river, is Beaulieu Abbey, founded by Cistercian monks in 1204 and now a well-tended ruin. The abbey's massive gateway is part of Lord Montagu's Palace House.

The B3054 Hythe–Lymington road cuts across Beaulieu Heath in a north-east to south-west direction.

Bb Bolderwood Grounds and Mark Ash Wood

There are three walks laid out by the Forestry Commission in these woods, all of which start at Bolderwood Green, south of the A31. The walks take in some of the finest woodland scenery in the forest and provide the best chance to see deer.

The Radnor Walk is a short stroll

THE NEW FOREST

Map labels:
Salisbury 4 A 338 · Salisbury 8 A 36 · Salisbury 11 A 27 · Andover 18 A 3057 · Winchester 7 A 31
WILTSHIRE
Grim's Ditch · Downton · Romsey · Winchester 9 A 33
BREAMORE DOWN · Giant's Grave · Mizmaze
Breamore Wood · Breamore House · Breamore
Millersford Bottom · Deadman Hill · Black Gutter Bottom · Pipers Wait
Castle Hill · Stone Quarry Bottom · Long Cross
ASHLEY WALK · Eyeworth Wood · EYEWORTH POND
Fordingbridge · Godshill · Fritham · CANTERTON GLEN · Cadnam · SOUTHAMPTON
Latchmore Brook · Rufus Stone
HAMPSHIRE · Minstead
Dickens Water · Ocknell Pond
N E W
BOLDERWOOD GROUNDS · Lyndhurst · Hythe
RIDLEY WOOD · MARK ASH WOOD · Knightwood Oak
Picket Post · Knightwood Inclosure · Brock Hill
Ringwood · Vinney Ridge Inclosure · Bolderford Bridge · QUEEN BOWER
Verely Hill · TALL TREES WALK · OBER WATER
Burley · Balmer Lawn · Beaulieu Abbey · Beaulieu Palace House · HEATH · Beaulieu
F O R E S T · Beachern Wood · Whitefield Moor · Brockenhurst · BEAULIEU
Puttles Bridge · Hatchet Pond · BUCKLERS HARD
DORSET · Lymington
Tuckton Bridge · Highcliffe · Chewton Bunny
Christchurch · The Solent
Southbourne · Christchurch Harbour · Christchurch Bay
Warren Hill · HENGISTBURY HEAD · Yarmouth
0 1 2 3 4 5 6 MILES
Wimborne Minster 8 A 31 · Bournemouth 1 A 338 · Fawley 3 A 326

among Douglas firs dating from 1860. There is a flavour of the Canadian timber forests here, with slender trunks climbing ruler-straight to a height of almost 100 ft, and the delicate evergreen foliage contrasting harmoniously with the paler green of the ferns below. In a green glade is the memorial to the 7th Earl of Radnor, who was a Forestry Commissioner from 1942 to 1963. The memorial is carved from Westmorland slate and is sculpted with figures depicting the wildlife of the forest.

Another short walk passes through the lofty avenues of an arboretum, where about 40 different species of trees are numbered and labelled for easy identification. This is a wonderland of greens, reds and browns, with the sweet scent of pine heavy on the air. There are redwoods from California, Japanese cedar, Italian poplar, Norway spruce, Chinese fir and Corsican pine, but pride of place goes to a 140 ft tall Noble fir from Washington State, USA. At one point the walk diverges through tall beeches to an observation platform which overlooks a rough meadow preserved as a deer sanctuary.

The walk through Mark Ash Wood, though no more than a 3 mile circular stroll, plunges deep into one of the oldest parts of the forest, where ancient beeches cast a deep shade and the branches of some old trees are so close that they have actually become joined. This 'inosculation', as it is called, occurs frequently between trees of the same species, but in the Knightwood Inclosure, a mile to the south-east of Mark Ash Wood, a beech and an oak have joined together. Here, too, is the New Forest's oldest pollarded oak, a survivor of the days when trees were lopped – or pollarded – to provide browse for the deer. The Knightwood Oak, 22 ft around at shoulder height, is

LONELY FRINGE Wild, desolate Ashley Walk is on the north-west edge of the forest. Rough heath and scrub with the occasional Scots pine cover this area of forest 'highland'.

one of the New Forest's institutions – like the deer and the ponies.

The start of the Radnor, Arboretum and Mark Ash Wood walks is at the north-western end of the Ornamental Drive which runs north from the A35, 2¼ miles south-west of Lyndhurst, towards the A31. The Knightwood Oak car park is ¼ mile along the Ornamental Drive from the A35.

WILDFOWL AND WATER-LILIES Languid and entrancing in its woodland setting, Eyeworth Pond was not always as peaceful as it is today. In the 19th century it provided power for a gunpowder factory.

Breamore Down

Ac

The Avon valley separates Breamore Down from the New Forest at its north-western edge, and here the scenery changes from woodlands and plains to chalk downland, with small copses of ancient yew trees and paths decked with flowers of the chalk. From behind the Elizabethan manor house half a mile north-west of Breamore village a path climbs steeply north-west through Breamore Wood to the Mizmaze, a turf labyrinth surrounded by yews and set in a small clearing of conifers.

The Mizmaze is one of half a dozen surviving in England. Channels cut in the chalk, with grass strips between, lead tortuously in a complex circular pattern of whorls to a grass-covered podium or hub in the centre, which is said to symbolise Paradise. The design measures 87 ft across, and how it came to be there is an unsolved mystery. It may have been connected with a pagan rite, or devised as a symbol of morality by monks from the priory below. Alternatively, it could have been the setting for a medieval May Day dance. Certainly it has Celtic echoes, and Britons lived on Breamore Down at least until AD 519, when thousands died in a battle with the invading Saxons under their leader Cerdic. A few hundred yards to the south-west is a 180 ft long barrow, called the Giant's Grave, where the Celtic leader King Natan-Leod is said to be buried.

Three-quarters of a mile north-west of the barrow is Grim's Ditch, a double-banked Iron Age earthwork. Although obscured in summer by crops and vegetation, its south-west to north-east course can be traced for about 4 miles. It forms one boundary of what was once a roughly rectangular enclosure containing some 16 sq. miles. It is believed that the enclosed land was once a great stock ranch, dating from about 1000 BC and owned by a single tribe.

Breamore is on the A338, 7 miles south of Salisbury. The path to the Mizmaze runs north from Breamore House.

Bucklers Hard

Ca

A broad, grass-verged street leads down past red-brick cottages then, suddenly, there is a glimpse of water and the tang of the sea. The water is the Beaulieu River, swinging in a great lazy circle around an island of reeds and mud, with dark woods rising behind.

The old rubs shoulders with the new at Bucklers Hard, for close to the marina where sleek-hulled sailing cruisers ride are the remains of slipways where 18th-century warships were built from New Forest oaks. Nelson's 64-gun HMS *Agamemnon* was launched here in 1781.

Boats are still built on the banks of the Beaulieu, in the Agamemnon Boatyard where a delightful 2 mile riverside walk to Beaulieu starts. With the return journey, it takes about two and a half hours at a leisurely pace. The walk is waymarked, and the first section begins at a tall Scots pine known to be about 200 years old. The footpath leads through a copse and then crosses a salt-marsh carpeted with sea lavender and sea purslane.

FLOWERS OF THE FOREST

Heath, woods and streams – the New Forest offers a fine range of plant habitats for the botanist to explore. In the bogs and on river banks the sundew spreads its sticky leaves to trap unwary insects upon which it feeds. At the water's edge, and often well out in a stream, grows the spire-like water horsetail. Damp woodland glades are the home of the rare narrow-leaved lungwort, sometimes known as Joseph and Mary.

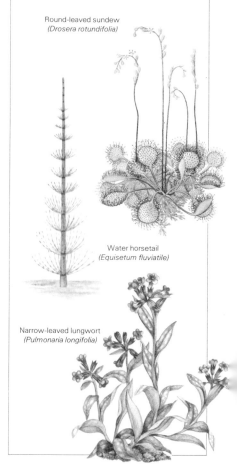

Round-leaved sundew
(Drosera rotundifolia)

Water horsetail
(Equisetum fluviatile)

Narrow-leaved lungwort
(Pulmonaria longifolia)

The walk ends by a 16th-century corn-mill, and beyond the mill-pond stands the gateway which is now part of Beaulieu Palace House.

Bucklers Hard is 2 miles south-east of Beaulieu village and is signposted from the B3054. There is a car park at the top of the village street for visitors.

Bb   Canterton Glen

In this narrow, green valley of oaks and tall beeches the Rufus Stone marks the spot where William II, called Rufus because of his red hair, died in a hunting accident. Or was it an accident? The death of Rufus is one of history's great mysteries, but certainly the arrow fired from Sir William Tirel's bow brought short the reign of a king who had many enemies. Legend has embroidered the tale, and Ocknell Pond, 2 miles to the west, is pointed out as the place where Tirel paused to wash the blood from his hands. The pond is said to redden on each anniversary of the deed, which took place on the morning of August 2, 1100.

The village of Minstead, a mile south-east of Canterton Glen, is a typical New Forest settlement with thatched cottages and a small green. On the western edge of the village stands Castle Malwood, now only an earthwork crowning a wooded knoll but believed to be where William Rufus spent the night before his death. Fittingly, this village bound in with one of history's puzzles is the burial place of the master of mysterious tales, Sir Arthur Conan Doyle. His grave is in Minstead churchyard.

The road through Canterton Glen runs between the A31 and B3079, 2 miles west of Cadnam. The road to Minstead runs south-east from the A31.

Bb   Eyeworth Pond

A narrow lane runs from the tiny hamlet of Fritham and passes through woodland of oaks, beeches and holly before descending to a shallow valley of heath and beechwoods, and the glistening water of Eyeworth Pond. The wedge-shaped stretch of water, about 200 yds long and 75 yds wide at its broadest point, lies half surrounded by the beeches of Eyeworth Wood which spread down to the water's edge. A green apron of reeds covers almost half the pond, at its narrow end, but at the clear end are water-lily pads and small artificial islands for the coots, moorhens and mallard ducks.

Through the valley runs the tiny Latchmore Brook, and it was by damming the brook in the 19th century that Eyeworth Pond was formed. Its purpose was to supply water power for a gunpowder factory, and the pond still brims over a weir, close to where the factory once stood. At the far end of the pond, somewhere beyond the thick reeds, the brook rises from a spring which was once a medicinal 'iron well', and the water is still tinged a rusty red.

Fritham lies 5 miles east of Fordingbridge and to the west of an unclassified road running between the A31 and B3078. Eyeworth Pond is not signposted in Fritham, and the lane to it starts from the end of a No Through Road which runs west from the hamlet.

Aa   Hengistbury Head

Heath, woodland, marsh and meadow are packed into the mile-long Hengistbury Head, a wild and windswept promontory curling like a bent finger around Christchurch Harbour. It is a tiny world in itself, with a history of human activity spanning 11,000 years.

Paths run to Warren Hill, at the

SOLENT VIEWPOINT Beyond Hengistbury Head, across The Solent, the winter sun picks out the white chalk of The Needles.

79

southern side of the Head, passing an Iron Age double dyke with a 12 ft high rampart on the way and then crossing short-grassed meadowland. At the foot of the hill the promontory is almost cut in two by a deep gully, which was an ironstone quarry in the 19th century. Ironstone boulders, called 'doggers', can be seen embedded in the gully sides and floor.

The 118 ft summit of Warren Hill forms a broad plateau ending in tawny sand-cliffs plunging sheer to the sea. A constant wind scything in from the sea keeps the clumps of ling, heather and gorse low-growing, and the turf is thin and patchy. But in the lee of the hill are woodlands, scrub and marshes bordering the harbour, and a lily-pond where dragonflies skim the water in summer.

About 11,000 years ago, when Britain was still joined to the Continent, Stone Age men built a camp on Warren Hill, and flint tools from that period have been found there. During the Iron Age, some 8,500 years later, Hengistbury was a busy port. It remained so under the Romans but was abandoned when they left. It did not attract the invading Saxons, who built their village on the other side of the harbour, and Hengistbury reverted to desolate heathland – until the quarrymen came to dig for ironstone.

Hengistbury Head is one of the finest vantage points on the south coast. Christchurch Harbour, held in the crook of a sand-spit curving round from the Head, is almost a lake, its protected waters sequined with bright-coloured sails and flecked with the dazzling white hulls of motor cruisers. The harbour's outlet to the sea is a 30 yd gap – the Avon Run – between the sand-spit and Mudeford Quay where local fishermen net the running salmon in the spring.

At the back of the harbour lies Christchurch, a greystone jewel set at the water's edge where the River Avon meets the Stour, and the green apron of Stanpit Marsh divides the harbour into muddy channels. To the east of the harbour, across Christchurch Bay, are the bulky outlines of the Isle of Wight, with the gleaming Needles rocks and the coloured cliffs of Alum Bay easily visible on a clear day.

Westward the land curves around the broad sweep of Poole Bay and the misty Purbeck Hills loom above the chalk cliffs of Ballard Down.

Hengistbury Head can be reached by taking the Southbourne road from Christchurch and then following the signposts shortly after crossing Tuckton Bridge. There are also boat trips to the Head from Tuckton Bridge and the Wick Ferry landing-stage at Christchurch.

Bb Ober Water

The Forestry Commission has laid out two walks by the Ober Water which, it says, 'show within a short distance some of the secrets of the New Forest'. Both walks are easy strolls through typical forest scenery, with the added attraction of a peat-stained stream wending its way between the trees.

The walks follow the stream closely for part of the way, along banks thick with bog myrtle and sphagnum moss. In places the stream twists and bends so

FLOODING STREAM After heavy rain, the Ober Water overflows its banks and forms sparkling pools under the trees.

LIFE IN THE FOREST Fallow deer are
shy, but sometimes you may be lucky
enough to see one as it sniffs the air
with ears erect to catch any unfamiliar
sound, for their hearing is keener than
their sight. The whirr of a wood
pigeon's wings overhead is a familiar
forest sound, as is the rapid trilling of
a nuthatch foraging on a
beech tree.

81

tortuously that it has formed loops which became cut off when the ends met, leaving horseshoe-shaped pools called 'ox-bows'. There are small brown trout in the deep water, though they are difficult to spot and much less noticeable than the shoals of minnows darting in the shallows.

At one point the pathway passes briefly through the Aldridge Inclosure of oaks, originally planted in 1775. Here, young oaks are growing beneath the protection of self-sown Scots pine. A dead pine, peppered with the bore-holes of the longhorn beetle, has been left standing because the beetle larvae provide food for woodpeckers whose staccato tattoo is often heard echoing through the forest.

The Ober Water walks start at either Puttles Bridge or Whitefield Moor, both on the Rhinefield road 2 miles west of Brockenhurst. There are car parks at both places.

Bb Queen Bower

The Ober Water flows into the Lymington River at Bolderford Bridge, a narrow wooden bridge which carries a forest track over the river. The track from the Beachern Wood car park winds through oaks and beeches that border the Ober Water. Here and there, openings lead into green glades where the peace is broken only by the hammering of woodpeckers. Fallen trees, dead or uprooted, lie across the stream whose rusty-brown, peat-stained waters are sun-dappled in luminous patterns of brown and grey. After about a mile, the path emerges at Bolderford Bridge. Here, just north-west of the bridge, is Queen Bower, a magical glade where gnarled oaks and beeches dip their bare roots into the water, and the mossy banks are vivid green in the sunlight shafting through the trees.

The queen who loved this place was Eleanor, wife of Edward I, and its majestic beauty is certainly fit for a queen; but after a heavy rainfall Queen Bower is not only beautiful, it is awe-inspiring. Then the swollen Ober Water and Lymington meet in a head-long rush, and their waters become a creamy torrent, racing beneath the bridge, surging over the banks and swirling among the trees. As the water-level rises, seeking out every tiny dell, the glade becomes a swampland of red-brown pools and green islands.

The forest track to Bolderford Bridge and Queen Bower starts at the Beachern Wood car park on the Rhinefield road on the western fringe of Brockenhurst. There is also a footpath to Queen Bower from Balmer Lawn, just north of Brockenhurst beside the A337.

Bb Ridley Wood

From the Verely Hill car park, north-west of Burley on the western edge of the forest, a path leads into Ridley Wood – a path trodden more than 200 years ago by the New Forest smugglers who set up their 'market' beneath the dark canopy of beech trees for the

---

WANDERING PONIES OF THE HEATHLAND

NEW FOREST MARE AND FOAL

THE GRAZING MARE with her fawn-coloured leggy foal has become the symbol of the New Forest. The 3,500 native ponies – thought to be descended from the wild horses that once roamed all over Britain – have taken the place of William the Conqueror's deer as rulers of the forest, and rightly so for they were here even before the Normans came. Though they live in an almost wild state, they are all privately owned by the commoners – people living in the forest entitled to certain privileges.

In the 19th century an attempt to improve the breed was made by setting Arab stallions to run in the forest; this resulted in a cross unfitted to the rigours of the wild. A later experiment with stallions of breeds from Exmoor, Scotland, Dartmoor and Wales introduced a new breed which evolved into the more or less distinctive type seen now. Today, only stallions with local stud-book pedigrees are allowed to roam.

The sturdiness of the New Forest pony comes from being born on a windswept heath. In winter it has a woolly coat, and long protective hair on the back of the fetlock causes the rain to run to the ground. The animal has developed a beard and horny tongue to enable it to cope with the gorse shoots which are its most reliable food.

Every year, there is a 'drift', or round-up, in late summer and autumn when the ponies are brought in – some to be sold and others to be retained for stock.

BIRDS OF THE NEW FOREST

Rare birds of prey, such as the hobby and honey buzzard, may be seen in the New Forest. After smaller fry, spotted flycatchers swoop from the trees to snap up an insect in flight. The musical linnets can sometimes be heard singing in chorus in gorse and bramble where they nest. The perky little firecrest prefers Norway spruce.

Honey buzzard
(Pernis apivorus)

Hobby
(Falco subbuteo)

Linnet
(Acanthis cannabina)

Spotted flycatcher
(Muscicapa striata)

Firecrest
(Regulus ignicapillus)

distribution of tea, brandy, silks and lace brought up from the coast.

The favourite place for the landing of smuggled goods was Chewton Bunny, a small gorge at Highcliffe on Christchurch Bay. From there the packhorses and wagons made their way across moors and along forest tracks to follow the smugglers' road to Ridley Wood and beyond. Still remembered in Burley is a woman smuggler, Lovey Warne. When she became too old to handle the heavy crates and kegs, she became a look-out for the gang and would stroll across Verely Hill wearing a bright red cloak whenever the revenue men were in the area. She could be seen for miles – as anyone similarly dressed would be today.

Verely Hill is 3 miles east of Ringwood and ¼ mile south of Picket Post, on the A31.

Bb Tall Trees Walk

This is possibly the most beautiful and awe-inspiring part of the whole of the New Forest. The conifers here were planted in 1859, and anything less than 60 ft tall is a mere stripling. There are 20 species represented. They form an avenue of timber giants, among which a mighty redwood of 132 ft is outstripped by a pair of Wellingtonias soaring to 160 ft.

The redwood and a white spruce, a red spruce, a Spanish fir and a Lawson cypress are the tallest of their species in England. But it is not only the sheer height of these noble trees that makes the 1¼ mile Tall Trees Walk so enjoyable, for the avenue has been carefully planned so that the trees can be properly admired, and more than 50 of them have been labelled for easy identification. Many need no labels; it is not

difficult to spot the rich red bark of the redwood or the pale needles of silver fir. Nor is it hard to recognise the green pyramid of a Norway spruce, the traditional Christmas tree.

At its northern end, the walk runs through a plantation of sedate oaks, grown for timber production and almost branchless, unlike the traditional English oak of greenwood and village green. Here, too, is Vinney Ridge, the first of the forest's inclosures dating from 1700. Originally it was enclosed by a 5 ft ditch and a 6 ft high bank topped by an oak fence, and a short section has been reconstructed along the walk.

A diversion from Tall Trees Walk leads to Brock Hill, where beeches and oaks stand in a 130-year-old grove crowning a knoll. *Broc* is Old English for 'badger', and on the hill the New Forest's shyest creatures build their setts in the widespreading roots of the beech trees.

Badgers are mostly nocturnal animals, and are unlikely to be seen except possibly at break of day or late evening. The walk in this typically English woodland of shaded glades makes an interesting contrast to the North American-style grandness of the tall timbers.

From the car park at the southern end of Tall Trees Walk, a path leads to the Black Water. The path crosses the stream by a wooden bridge and then follows the bank among plantations of young conifer and broad-leaved trees.

Tall Trees Walk consists of two avenues running parallel to the Rhinefield Ornamental Drive. The drive is a turning south off the A35, 2½ miles south-west of Lyndhurst. There are car parks at Brock Hill, about ¼ mile along the drive, and at Black Water, 1 mile further south.

LONG SHADOWS Some of the tallest trees in Britain cast their shadows over Tall Trees Walk in the New Forest, an avenue of ramrod-straight conifers with ferns and shrubs forming a deep-pile carpet of green at their feet.

—ISLE OF WIGHT—

Coast and downland, formed of the mainland chalk,
provide superb walking country

There are two faces to the Isle of Wight. One, the ever-changing coastline that switches dramatically from wooded shore to sandy bay and then to towering cliffs. The other, the farmlands, woods and rolling downland in the soft centre of the island. Roughly diamond-shaped, the island is believed to have been sliced from the mainland thousands of years ago, when a river, now The Solent, cut through the chalk.

The most attractive scenery lies west of the River Medina and it begins at the island's western tip; there a string of jagged chalk pinnacles, the Needles, stride out into the sea.

Cliffs where a poet walked

Above the Needles, white cliffs rise sheer from the sea to Tennyson Down, named after the poet who loved to walk there. The finest approach starts from west of Freshwater Bay, past a thatched church, and is clearly signposted 'Tennyson Down and the Needles'. The fairly long walk climbs to 500 ft, and provides magnificent views south-east along the foam-fringed coastline curving sinuously away to St Catherine's Point. To the north-west lies the Hampshire coast, while on the north side of the down the white chalk gives way to multi-coloured sandstone cliffs at Alum Bay.

Southern vantage point

At the island's southern end, St Catherine's Hill provides the best vantage point for viewing both south-eastern and south-western coasts. The Needles can be seen in one direction and the Foreland in another. The hill is reached by a short climb from the A3055, just above Black-gang Chine. Crowning the hill are the remains of two former lighthouses. One is St Catherine's Oratory, an octagonal tower built in 1328, the other is a building started in 1785 but never completed. The two ruins are popularly called the Pepper Pot and the Salt Cellar.

The highest point on the island is St Boniface Down. Though cluttered by the aerials of a radar station, the 785 ft summit is a superb vantage point from which to see the whole 6 mile sweep of the south-east coast round to the white face of Culver Cliff.

There are fine walks northwards, over the springy-turfed downs stretching away

FRESHWATER BAY LYING IN THE SHELTER OF TENNYSON DOWN, THE ROCKY FORESHORE EXTENDS WESTWARDS TO THE JAGGED PEAKS OF THE NEEDLES (RIGHT), FORMED BY A PINNACLE OF ROCK WHICH TOPPLED INTO THE SEA IN 1764.

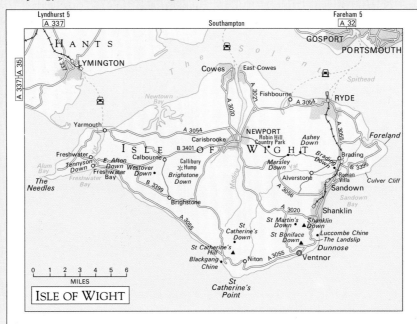

ISLE OF WIGHT

ANCIENT HIGHLANDS BRADING DOWN IS PART OF THE CHALK RIDGE RUNNING EAST TO WEST ACROSS THE ISLAND. THE HILLS WERE 4,000 FT HIGH 20 MILLION YEARS AGO.

POET'S PLEASURE BRIGHSTONE DOWN, ON THE ISLAND'S SOUTH-WESTERN FACE, LOOKS ACROSS TO FRESHWATER BAY AND THE WHITE CLIFFS BELOW TENNYSON DOWN – NAMED IN MEMORY OF THE POET WHO WALKED THERE AND LOVED THE VIEWS.

under huge skies. One starts just north of the approach to the car park on St Boniface Down. Pass through a gate and follow the trail signposted 'Bridle Path to Shanklin'. The walk, over grassy slopes patterned by patches of gorse and starred with cowslips, harebells and dwarf thistles, leads to Shanklin Down and St Martin's Down.

The Landslip

Below St Boniface Down is The Landslip, a wooded wilderness of fallen rocks brought about by landslides in 1810 and 1928. There is an eeriness in this strange twilight world, with the twisted branches of ash, beech and oak intertwining above a path that winds through fallen boulders.

The footpath leads through The Landslip to Luccombe Chine, where huge hydrangeas embower the path in summer in a mass of pink blossom. Small waterfalls gush from the rock face and form streams that run down to the sea – a distant whisper below.

Roman villas

On the same side of the island, about 2 miles north of Sandown, Brading Down ambles inland. Brading, once a Roman harbour, became silted up and was finally cut off from the sea in 1878. A feature of the Roman occupation of the island is the Roman villa at Brading, which contains some of the finest mosaics in Britain. To its north lie ancient field systems that are of the same age as the villa. From Brading Down there is a fine walk westwards across Ashey Down, with its prehistoric tumuli, then over Mersley Down and to the Roman villa at Robin Hill Country Park.

Downland footpaths

Halfway along the minor road between Calbourne and Brighstone is another area of outstanding walking country. To the west of the road lies a forest trail which rises to the bare crest of Westover Down – crowned by five prehistoric burial mounds – from which there are sweeping views of the island's south-western cliffs. To the east of the road, a downland trail leads along a gradually climbing path that slowly yields spectacular views of the island from Culver Cliff to Freshwater. At the summit, a wide path beyond a gate leads through woods to Callibury Hump – the remains of a Bronze Age burial mound. The path continues in the same north-easterly direction to Carisbrooke, 3½ miles further on.

Twelfth-century Carisbrooke Castle is chiefly famed for having been the prison of Charles I in 1647–8, just prior to his trial and execution in London. But having brooded awhile upon the unhappy monarch, climb to the castle's battlements and revel in the view of the green Bowcombe valley.

DOWNLAND AND WEALD

Switchback Downs and towering white cliffs – majestic sentinels at the gateway to the Garden of England

Gilbert White of Selborne, the 18th-century naturalist, described the South Downs as 'that chain of majestic mountains'. Although not mountains – few points exceed 800 ft – they are certainly majestic, reaching the sea at the bold rampart of Beachy Head. Like the towering white cliffs of Dover at the eastern end of the North Downs, these cliffs are, for many seaborne visitors, the first sight of England – Shakespeare's 'earth of majesty'.

Between the great chalk ridges of the North and South Downs, which stretch from Hampshire to the east coast, lies the Weald, a softer, gentler landscape that moved Rudyard Kipling to write of its 'wooded, dim blue goodness'. The Weald extends almost 100 miles from east to west and almost 40 miles from north to south. Romney Marsh at its eastern end, flat and misty, strongly contrasts with the rest of its rolling, wooded landscape.

The central Weald – known as the High Weald or the Forest Ridges – rises to 600 ft. Here is St Leonard's Forest east of Horsham, and the wild heathland of Ashdown Forest further east, its half-plucked appearance due to the felling of oaks for the furnaces of the 16th-century iron industry. The soil is poor, but it is from the sandstone and gravel of this area that many of the rivers arise. Nine rivers carve their way through the chalky Downs – the Cuckmere, Ouse, Adur and Arun to the

Channel in the south, and the Stour, Medway, Darent, Mole and Wey to the north.

The Downs are easy to explore. Paths criss-cross them in all directions, and both ranges are topped by ancient ridge-way tracks worn by primitive man – today preserved as public footpaths. The South Downs Way winds for 80 miles from Buriton near Petersfield eastwards to Eastbourne, with the sea an almost constant companion. The North Downs Way stretches for 140 miles from Farnham in Surrey east to Dover, giving extensive views of pastures and cornfields to the north and the orchards and hop-fields of Kent to the south. Parts follow the route of the old Pilgrims' Way from Winchester to Canterbury.

Looking across the peaceful Weald from the airy heights of the Downs, it is hard to realise that for 200 years, from the 16th century, it was a prosperous industrial area bustling with ironworks fired by charcoal furnaces. Inevitably, the introduction of coke for iron-smelting led the iron industry to move to the northern coalfields, and by 1750 the Wealden industry was dying. The discovery of the East Kent coalfield in 1840 was too late for its recovery, and by that time the Weald of Kent had taken on a new role as the 'Garden of England'.

In the villages where ironworks once prospered, there are still signs of the long-forgotten industry, particularly the hammer-ponds that supplied water power for the mill-wheels and machinery. Now they are tranquil waters where coots and moorhens swim among the reeds.

The bare-topped, turfy Downs support a marvellous range of chalk-loving flowers, including wild thyme, salad burnet, rock-rose and the delicate bee orchid. In the clay area of the western Weald, the oakwoods are thick with wild cherry, wych elm, alder and hornbeam.

SO REMOTE, SO NEAR Standing on the greensand ridge above Westerham in Kent, it is hard to believe that London's southern suburbs lie only a few miles beyond the wooded escarpment of the North Downs that sprawls across the horizon.

Places to visit

Map ref. Ec **Ashdown Forest**

From the ridge at King's Standing, you can look down on one of Britain's most heavily wooded areas – great stretches of heath and woodland that 2,000 years ago were part of the impenetrable forest the Romans called Silva Anderida, 'the Forest of Anderida'. Ashdown Forest in the High Weald stretches for 8 miles, from Maresfield in the south to Forest Row in the north, and covers some 14,000 acres. Although it lacks the thickets, creepers and swamps that once made the Weald impassable, it is still wild and wooded, with a great variety of trees at every stage of growth. Only the Scots pines, planted in the 1800s and allowed to seed, vary the scenery from that seen by the Romans and Saxons.

Ashdown Forest became a medieval hunting ground, and many of the clumps of trees on high ground mark the spot where an English king stood and watched the chase; King's Standing was a vantage point for both Edward II and Edward III. In the 14th century the area was fenced in as a deer preserve for the Dukes of Lancaster. Place names such as Chuck Hatch Gate and Friar's Gate mark the boundaries. In Tudor and Stuart times, hunting declined and the forest was thick

with ironworks, such as at Newbridge and Crowborough Warren.

A drive along the road between Hartfield and Maresfield (B2026) gives some idea of the forest's extent. Paths lead everywhere, and heather and bracken, dappled with the yellow splashes of gorse, line the road edges. Swallows and swifts wheel in the summer sky, and the air is filled with the rich song of woodlarks and linnets. And high above, the hook-beaked

King's Standing is 3¼ miles south of Hartfield on the B2188, close to its junction with the B2026.

Ea   Beachy Head

White cliffs rise sheer from the sea to 534 ft of rugged grandeur at Beachy Head, with a rousing seascape of pounding waves, blown spume, and

hobby soars on long curved wings in pursuit of swallows, swifts and skylarks.

shrieking gulls wheeling on the wind. Offshore, the red-banded lighthouse looks like a tiny toy, but its powerful beam can be seen 16 miles across the English Channel.

The South Downs Way begins its westward route at Eastbourne, less than a mile north-east of Beachy Head. The 3 mile walk along this part of the pathway towards the Seven Sisters takes in magnificent coastal scenery. The views are superb, stretching eastwards as far

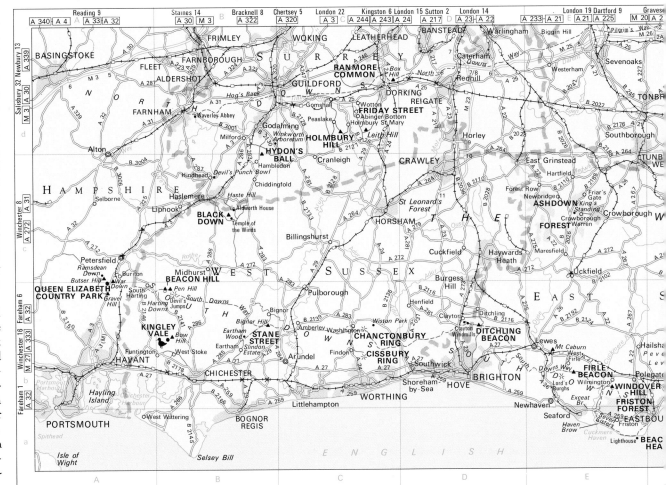

as Dungeness, and west to the Isle of
Wight. West from Beachy Head the
path drops down and passes the remains of the old Belle Tout lighthouse,
built of granite in 1831 by Jack Fuller of
Brightling.

The frowning brows of the Seven
Sisters cliffs soon come into view, rising and falling like a giant roller-
coaster track that ends at Cuckmere
Haven. The dips were once the valleys
of ancient rivers. An additional 3 mile

walk along the switchback path leads
to Haven Brow and views of the Cuckmere River winding through its valley
to the sea, where the shingle bar lies
piled up at its mouth.

Viewed from afar, and even more
obvious to the walker, the Seven Sisters clearly number eight. Their name
owes more to romantic alliteration
than to accuracy.

*Beachy Head is south-west of East-
bourne. The B2103 climbs up southwards*

*from the sea-front and a signposted minor
road leads to Beachy Head.*

Bb   Beacon Hill

Near its western end, the South Downs
Way skirts the southern slopes of
Beacon Hill, at 793 ft one of the highest points along the ridge of the South
Downs. You can join the long-distance
footpath at Harting Downs and follow
it eastwards for about a mile before
leaving it to reach the summit of the
hill.

From the very start of the walk there
are exhilarating views of the Weald to
the north, with the bright green spire
of South Harting Church spiking
through the trees just below the ridge.
As you climb to the summit of Beacon
Hill, the silvery creeks of Chichester
Harbour come into view to the south,
and the slender finger of Chichester
Cathedral's tapering spire probes the
skyline. Around the summit of the hill,
the rectangular ramparts of an Iron
Age hill-fort, over 2,000 years old, are
clearly defined.

South-east from Beacon Hill are the
Devil's Jumps, a line of six rounded
mounds that are Bronze Age bell-
barrows – warriors' graves of some
3,500 years ago. One of the central
barrows is 16 ft high and 140 ft in
diameter, the largest in Britain. To
visit them adds another $1\frac{3}{4}$ miles to the
walk. From Beacon Hill, you can rejoin
the South Downs Way as it dips and
climbs eastwards across Pen Hill, then
turns south-eastwards towards Buriton
Farm.

Here the path is dotted with wild
flowers – yellow cowslips in spring, and
greater hawkbit, common ragwort and
spiky common toadflax continuing the
yellow theme into early autumn; small

BIRDS OF DOWN AND WOOD

The lark-sized wryneck, Britain's
only migratory woodpecker, is
named for its habit of twisting its
neck when disturbed. More often
heard than seen, the shy nightingale
pours out its rich, melodious song by
day and night in early summer. The
summer song of the tree pipit can be
heard as it descends from a steep
flight with wings and tail spread.
The hoopoe is a relative of the kingfisher and is named for its low,
'hoop-hoop' call.

Wryneck
(Jynx torquilla)

Nightingale
(Luscinia megarhynchos)

Tree pipit
(Anthus trivialis)

Hoopoe
(Upupa epops)

DOWNLAND AND WEALD

MILES 0 1 2 3 4 5 10 15

89

LADIES IN WAITING Seven Sisters, the white cliffs edging the South Downs, greet voyagers sailing up the English Channel.

Knob, to the south-east of the Temple of the Winds.

Alfred, Lord Tennyson, the poet, spent his last 20 years at Aldworth House on the eastern slopes of the hill. He wrote of the view from Black Down in his *Prologue to General Hamley*:

'You came, and look'd and loved the view
Long-known and loved by me,
Green Sussex fading into blue
With one gray glimpse of sea;'

The view he loved is little changed – green Sussex sweeping across the Weald to the bare ridge of the South Downs, marked by tree-crowned Chanctonbury Ring, and beyond the silver-grey of the sea fusing with the hazy blue of the sky.

The best view is from the Temple of the Winds, a group of firs at the southern end of Black Down. It can be reached along the 1½ mile nature trail that leads from the upper car park through beechwoods and pine plantations, and by the site of a Stone Age settlement of about 6000 BC. Stopping points along the way give long, lingering views to the west, east and south.

Black Down is 2¼ miles south-east of Haslemere. To reach the National Trust car parks, turn south off the B2131 at Haste Hill to follow Tennyson's Lane, a minor road leading south-east.

scabious and greater knapweed add a touch of lilac and purple in summer. The path to the barrows is a turning east from the South Downs Way up the slopes of Treyford Hill. They lie beyond a beechwood, half hidden in the scrub.

Harting Downs, where the South Downs Way crosses the B2141, lie 5 miles south-east of Petersfield. There is a car park and picnic site close to the road.

Bc   Black Down

The highest point in Sussex, Black Down rears up dramatically from the western Weald to a height of 919 ft – a sandstone ridge clothed mainly in Scots pine, black fir and birch. Rhododendrons burst into flower in early summer, and everywhere there is a golden sea of gorse dappled with the pink and purple of heather. Meadow pipits,

linnets, wrens and yellowhammers are common.

There was already a beacon on Black Down by the 16th century, and it was probably used to pass news of the Armada sailing up the channel. Later, in 1796, the Admiralty installed a telegraph system, using shutters, between Portsmouth and London. The Black Down station was sited on a projecting knob of land, known locally as Tally

Hd   Challock Forest

Hop poles for supporting the climbing hop plants are an inseparable part of the Kentish scenery. Many of them are grown in Challock Forest in the Kentish North Downs, where there are coppices of sweet-chestnut trees. These trees are cut off at ground level, and the new shoots that spring from the stumps grow into sturdy poles after about 15 years, when they can be cut for fencing stakes or props as well as hop poles.

King's Wood, in the heart of Challock Forest, was once part of the vast Eastwell Park, the former estate of the Earls of Winchelsea. Here, sweet-chestnut coppices are intermingled with glades of beech and conifers such as Scots and Corsican pines and Norway spruce – the Christmas tree. The Forestry Commission has laid out a 2½ mile forest walk through King's Wood, where grey squirrels are common and where crossbills can sometimes be seen feeding on the pine cones. There are fallow deer here, too, seldom seen except at dusk, when the silence of the woods may be broken by the churring call of a nightjar.

Park Wood, in the north-east corner of the forest, is another oasis amid the tall conifer plantations. It is light and airy, with sunlight filtering through groves of oaks, beeches and hornbeams, and here in summer you may see blackcaps, chiffchaffs and willow warblers. The wood is managed by the Woodland Trust, an organisation pledged to preserve and maintain woodlands and their wildlife.

Soakham Downs lie to the south of King's Wood, a velvety stretch of sheep-grazed downland overlooking the Great Stour valley. There are fine views south-west to the bare sweep of the South Downs – a hazy line on the horizon.

Challock Forest is 5 miles north of Ashford. King's Wood Forest Walk starts on the A251 about ¾ mile south-east of Challock crossroads (A251/252). There is a car park on the minor road that forks off to Wye, and which also leads to Soakham Downs. Park Wood is on the A252 about 2 miles north-east of Challock crossroads.

Cb Chanctonbury and Cissbury Rings

When Celtic warriors strode the South Downs 2,000 years ago, Chanctonbury Ring was a bare hilltop commanded by the low earthen bank and ditch of an Iron Age hill-fort. Today, a graceful grove of trees, mostly beeches, stands tall and slender within the encircling earthworks, and is a well-loved landmark for miles around. The trees were planted in 1760 by Sir Charles Goring while he was still a boy. In the centre of the ring, among the trees, there are traces of the foundations of a Romano-British temple of the 1st century.

The South Downs at Chanctonbury, 779 ft above sea-level, are wide and open, and on a breezy day the noise of the wind is dramatically magnified as it gusts through the branches. There are superb views from the summit. North-west below the hill lies the charming village of Washington, and to the north-east is wooded Wiston Park and its mansion, once the home of Sir Charles Goring and now a conference centre. Far away to the north, the brown flanks of Leith Hill emerge as a hazy blur.

Cissbury Ring lies just over 2 miles south of Chanctonbury, a far larger Iron Age hill-fort with mile-long double ramparts enclosing some 65 acres. It is one of the largest and most impressive hill-forts in Britain, with probably 60,000 tons of chalk rubble forming its ramparts, which, when originally built about 250 BC, were faced with timber stakes. From the ramparts there are views along the coast to Beachy Head, 30 miles eastwards, and to the south-west beyond the sheen of The Solent, lies the dark line of the Isle of Wight.

At the south-west end of the fort, within and without the ramparts, bushes now overgrow the dips and furrows that mark the site of flint mines worked by men of the New Stone Age over 4,000 years ago. The many mine-shafts through the flint seams, dug out with antler picks, went as deep as 40 ft. Nineteenth-century investigators discovered in one of them the skeleton of a woman who had evidently fallen to her death – or whose body had been thrown down – at a date unknown.

Chanctonbury and Cissbury rings are 6 miles and 4 miles north of Worthing. Chanctonbury Ring can be reached along a footpath south-east from Washington, just off the A24 – a stiff 1½ mile climb. For Cissbury Ring, a well-marked minor road leads 1½ miles east from Findon village, also just off the A24. There are footpaths up to the fort from the minor road. Both rings are linked by a footpath, and Chanctonbury Ring is also on the South Downs Way.

Db Ditchling Beacon

Wonderful downland country surrounds the 813 ft summit of Ditchling Beacon, on the South Downs north of Brighton. The views are magical, with the broad sweep of the Weald extending 31 miles north-west as far as the Hog's Back on a clear day.

A footpath, the South Downs Way, westwards along the ridge, passes the ramparts of an Iron Age fort and then skirts a dew-pond, a reminder of the days when sheep were a familiar sight on the South Downs. Dew-ponds, from which the sheep drank, were built

CISSBURY RING The ramparts of this Iron Age camp were refortified in the 4th century against the Saxons. Excavations have revealed flint mines, ploughing patterns and hut sites within the 750 yd long oval.

by shepherds, who lined a hollow with clay to catch the moisture from the heavy mists sweeping in from the English Channel.

Beyond another dew-pond, the path begins to descend towards the village of Clayton, and the sails of two 19th-century windmills – called Jack and Jill – come into view. Jill is a white post-mill whose entire body could be turned to face the wind, Jack is a brick-built tower-mill with a revolving cap which carries the sails.

Ditchling Beacon is 6 miles north of Brighton. A minor road from Brighton to Ditchling village crosses the Downs just below the summit. From Brighton in the south there is a long, steady climb; from Ditchling to the north the road snakes upwards with sharp bends and steep inclines. Clayton is on the A273 near the B2112 junction.

Eb   Firle Beacon

In the summer of 1588, Firle Beacon was part of England's early warning system, when beacons blazed along the coast to signal the approach of the Spanish Armada. At 713 ft it was a natural choice; the highest point of the eastern South Downs and a prominent landmark even without its crest of fire.

The South Downs Way skirts the hill, but a short detour to the summit is worth the effort. It can also be reached by road from the village of West Firle, followed by a mile walk. Either way the walk is easy, across springy turf and

---

MIST AND MYSTERY The ghost of an ancient Druid is said to haunt Chanctonbury Ring, and, according to legend, anyone who manages to count the trees will raise the ghosts of Julius Caesar and his legionaries.

---

clover and with constantly widening views southwards of the coastline, where the gunmetal glint of the sea changes to peerless blue on a summer's day. To the north-west the River Ouse winds sleekly round the heights on which stands Lewes Castle; and Mount Caburn, with its Iron Age hill-fort, stands out a mile from the river's eastern banks.

The Stone Age custom of burying the dead in high places is evident on the summit of Firle Beacon, where there is a long barrow measuring 100 ft. Bronze Age round barrows are also dotted around the area, and a group of them, called Lord's Burghs, can be seen on a spur to the south-west. Iron Age Celts farmed the southern slopes, where the outlines of their cultivation terraces (lynchets) can still be seen.

West Firle is 3¼ miles south-east of Lewes, south of the A27. The minor road from the village to the Beacon is signposted, and there is a car park at the end.

Cd   Friday Street

Today, Friday Street is a peaceful hamlet hidden in the heart of the Surrey Weald, but 300 years ago it was a stronghold of the flourishing Wealden iron industry. Its hammer-pond, dammed from the Tilling Bourne, is one of the most attractive in the area, with pine trees crowding down to the water's edge. The best way to enjoy this beautiful part of Surrey is to start from the hamlet of Wotton and follow the Tilling Bourne stream south to Friday Street and then go on to Abinger Bottom – a 2½ mile walk through unforgettable scenery.

From the Wotton Hatch Inn the footpath leads across a field into woods, and then over a stream where

dragonflies skim the water and the sandy banks are peppered with the burrows of water voles. At Friday Street the stream widens out to the mirror-flat surface of the hammer-pond, with red-brick cottages reflected in its waters. Coots, moorhens and mallards glide among the vivid green patches of duckweed.

The timber-framed Stephen Lang-

BRIGHT WINGS OF SUMMER

An imperial purple sheen glows from the wings of the male purple emperor, but this woodland butterfly is hard to spot as it keeps to the tops of tall trees, particularly oaks. In August the silver-spotted skipper is on the wing, flying rapidly across the Downs and keeping close to the ground.

Silver-spotted skipper (*Hesperia comma*) on sheep's-fescue

Purple emperor (*Apatura iris*) on English oak

---

ton Inn was named after King John's Archbishop of Canterbury, who was born in Friday Street in 1150. Beyond the inn a footpath heads along a valley shaded by Scots pines; they were planted by John Evelyn, the 17th-century diarist and author on tree culture, on his brother's Wotton estate. The tinkling chatter of tiny streams provides a cheerful accompaniment all the way to the pretty cluster of houses at Abinger Bottom.

Friday Street is 3¼ miles south-west of Dorking, and Wotton is on the A25 north of Friday Street.

Ea   Friston Forest

A few miles inland from Seven Sisters cliffs, beyond the bare, windswept ridge of the South Downs, is Friston Forest, a superb beechwood just under 60 years old. When the Forestry Commission began planting the 1,600 acre forest in 1927, they used fast-growing Scots and Corsican pine as 'nurse trees' to protect the young beeches against the coastal weather until they were fully established.

The pines have done their job, and many have been felled to leave the glorious beeches in full view, with the sun filtering through the leaves in great, golden shafts. The forest is a light and cheerful place, with plenty of space to wander at will, or to follow the two waymarked walks, one nearly 3 miles long, the other about half that distance.

From Exceat Bridge on the Eastbourne–Seaford road (A259), there are fine views of the lovely Cuckmere River as it winds its way through watermeadows to the sea. This peaceful place is part of the Seven Sisters Country Park, where there are nature trails and hides by the river for watching wildlife.

Friston Forest is north of the A259 Eastbourne–Seaford road. The entrance and car park are on a minor road about 2¼ miles west of Friston.

Cd   Holmbury Hill

Wealthy Victorians developed the village of Holmbury St Mary, its houses dotted amid pines on the sandy slopes of a narrow, steep-sided valley about 3 miles south of the North Downs. George Edmund Street, the architect, built the Neo-Gothic church in 1879, at his own expense. Holmbury Hill, 857 ft, guards the western side of the valley where it opens out at its southern end. Leith Hill slopes away on the eastern side. Both hills provide magnificent views across the hills and woods of the Weald, patterned like a chessboard, that stretches southwards to the distant South Downs.

Wild, picturesque country surrounds Holmbury Hill, excellent walking country where foxes may be seen on the hillside and where deer browse among the brambles. Jays and magpies swoop through the trees, woodlarks and whinchats bob among the bushes, and in dry, open spots a poisonous, zigzagged adder may sometimes be seen basking in the sun. Almost hidden among the bracken and brambles are the double ditches and banks of an Iron Age hill-fort, 8 acres in extent, that was in use 2,000 years ago. The remains of 20 stones used for hand-grinding corn were found there in the 1930s.

Leith Hill, 965 ft, is the highest point in south-east England. The 64 ft tower on its summit, built in 1766 by Richard Hull of Leith Hill Place, in-creases its height to more than 1,000 ft, and it is worth climbing to the tower top for the splendour of the view, said to take in 13 counties. South-westwards, Black Down, 919 ft, the highest point in Sussex, juts out into the Weald.

Holmbury Hill, 6 miles south-west of Dorking, can be reached from Peaslake, south of Gomshall on the A25; from the village a minor woodland road opposite the Hurtwood Inn leads to a car park less than 1 mile from the summit. For Leith Hill, follow the A29 south from Dorking, turn west along the B2126 and after about 1 mile turn north; after 1 mile bear left to the car park on the west side of the hill, from where the climb is comparatively easy.

Fd   Horsmonden

In an idyllic setting amid the Kentish orchards, Horsmonden village was once a busy centre of the Wealden iron industry. About half a mile north-west of the village is Furnace Pond, one of the finest of the old hammer-ponds, more than a quarter of a mile long. Its dammed water once turned the wheels that worked bellows for the furnaces and trip-hammers in the forges. The pond glowed from the flames of the furnace fires, and the valley echoed to the thudding of the hammers.

Now the waters reflect only the blue sky and passing clouds, and the stillness is disturbed only by the hunting dive of a kingfisher or the quiet plop of a rising fish. There is a footpath to the pond starting half a mile west of Horsmonden village from Furnace Lane. The village is grouped round a triangular green above the valley of the River Teise, a tributary of the River Medway. With the rise of the 16th-century iron industry, the villagers left the old settlement 1½ miles south to be nearer the scene of their labours. This is why Horsmonden's 14th-century church is so far from the village centre.

Reached along narrow lanes heavy with apple blossom in spring, the sandstone church, with its buttressed and battlemented tower, stands on a hill slope near the hamlet of Elphicks. Eastwards across the Teise valley, with its patchwork of hop-fields, water-meadows and orchards, stands the picturesque hill-top village of Goudhurst, where the squat church tower gives fine views across the Weald.

Horsmonden is 7 miles east of Tunbridge Wells on the B2162.

Bc   Hydon's Ball

Woods, hills and valleys sprawl in a pleasant jumble below Hydon's Ball, 586 ft, a wooded, conical hill on Hydon Heath north-east of Hambledon in the north-west Weald. The views come and go with the mist, sometimes stretching eastwards as far as Leith Hill, or south across the Weald to the South Downs.

The heath is sandy and pitted with rabbit warrens, and early in the morning the musky scent of a fox is easily picked up. In the 13th century the local sand was used for glass-making, an industry introduced by the Normans. Charcoal from the woods fired the furnaces and for four centuries the industry thrived, with the village of Chiddingfold its centre. In 1615, because of the danger of deforestation, the use of wood as fuel for glass-making was banned. The industry moved to coal-producing areas, and the sandy heaths became quiet open stretches of heather and bracken.

Hydon's Ball and 125 acres of the surrounding woods and heaths belong to the National Trust. On the summit of the hill there is a memorial to Octavia Hill (1838–1912), a social reformer who was one of the founders of the Trust, formed in 1894 to preserve places of natural beauty or historical significance. About 1½ miles north-east is Winkworth Arboretum, 99 acres of woods particularly noted for its rare maples and whitebeams. It is thickly carpeted with bluebells in spring, and ablaze with azaleas in summer.

Hydon Heath is 3 miles south of Godalming, reached along minor roads west from the B2130. Winkworth Arboretum is 2 miles south-east of Godalming, east of the B2130.

Bb   Kingley Vale

Yew woods are rare, but on the slopes of Bow Hill – a southern outlier of the South Downs – stands the finest yew wood in Europe. The hill is appropriately named, for until the reign of Elizabeth I the evergreen yew was a protected tree used, because of its suppleness, for making the main military weapon – the longbow. It is said that a yew grove was planted here in AD 859 to commemorate a victorious battle fought by the men of nearby Chichester against marauding Vikings.

Many of the trees at Kingley Vale are at least 500 years old. Today the Vale is a 350 acre National Nature Reserve, and a fascinating 1½ mile nature trail among the haunts of nightingales and blackcaps, rock-roses and bee orchids, takes in the yew groves. The oldest trees are at the foot of the hill in Kingley Bottom; age has gnarled and twisted their huge trunks, and one or two have bowed branches whose tips have rooted in the ground to form

—ROMNEY MARSH—

*History and legend blend to add a touch of mystery
to this land reclaimed from the sea over the centuries*

RECLAIMED FROM THE SEA, Romney Marsh today is a marsh in name only, where longwool sheep graze fertile pastures and reed-lined dykes carve across the flat landscape. Most of the area is barely above sea-level, and village churches, such as the one at St Mary in the Marsh, are conspicuous landmarks. When sea mists drift in, the marsh becomes an eerie place where only the mournful sounds of ships' foghorns in the Channel and the croaking of marsh frogs break the silence. On clear days, however, there are splendid sunrises and sunsets, streaking the sky with fingers of light.

Defences against sea and invader

The first attempts to reclaim the marsh were made in prehistoric times by the Belgic tribes, already skilled in keeping out water from the Low Countries. The Romans built a paved road from Canterbury down on to the marsh at Lympne, and the Saxons built a wall – the Rhee Wall, which is now the line of the road from Old Romney to Appledore – and thereby reclaimed several thousand acres. Most reclamation, however, took place in medieval times and was completed by the 1660s. Local landowners still pay for the upkeep of the dykes.

The other major change to the landscape came in 1840, when the Royal Military Canal was built as a defence line during the Napoleonic Wars. The 23 mile long canal, from Hythe to Rye, makes Romney Marsh virtually an island.

Smugglers' haven

Its closeness to the sea and the Continent made the marsh an ideal haven for smugglers; local men who knew every lane and dyke and who could easily outwit their pursuers. The smugglers, known as 'owlers' because of their nocturnal activities, smuggled wool to the Continent to get a better price, and brought in tobacco and brandy. Sometimes the churches were used to hide the contraband. In the 13th-century St Dunstan's Church at Snargate, a sealed-off part of the south aisle was said to be a smugglers' den, and 18th-century Excisemen recovered tobacco from the belfry and gin from the vestry.

It was at Snargate Church that the Rev. Richard Barham began his ministry in 1817. He later became famous for his *Ingoldsby Legends*, published as one volume in 1840. In it he wrote 'the world is divided into five parts, Europe, Asia, Africa, America and Romney Marsh'.

THE MARSH FROG

The loud croaking of the marsh frogs is a familiar sound on Romney Marsh in the spawning season from April to July. The marsh frog is the largest in Europe, growing to 5 in. long. The frogs came originally from Hungary, imported in 1935 by a zoologist, Percy Smith, who set them free in his garden pond. They escaped and soon spread throughout the marsh. The frogs are timid and usually conceal themselves if disturbed.

Marsh frog
(Rana ridibunda)

DRAINAGE DYKE, ROMNEY MARSH

ST MARY'S CHURCH, ST MARY IN THE MARSH

95

another ring of trees. Younger trees about 70–100 years old – the seeded offspring of the older trees – fan out up the slopes. The dense foliage of these closely growing younger trees blots out sound and most of the light, and in this eerie twilight no other plants can grow. The few birds seen among the branches include robins, blackbirds, great tits and coal tits.

Mixed woods that include oaks, ashes, whitebeams, hawthorns and dogwood also thrive on the chalk soil. On the higher slopes the woods give way to chalk turf where the orchids grow, and the thin clay layer on the summit supports heather in profusion. More than 50 species of birds breed in Kingley Vale, including green woodpeckers and treecreepers. In autumn, flocks of fieldfares and redwings arrive for the winter, and gorge for a month on the red yew berries, scattering the pips and so propagating the trees.

The Devil's Humps – four round Bronze Age burial mounds some 3,000 years old – crown the summit of the hill, two of them half hidden by trees. There are glorious views southwards of the four arms of Chichester Harbour, especially at sunset when the deepening rays turn the waters red.

Kingley Vale is 4 miles north-west of Chichester. The nature-trail car park is at West Stoke, which is on a minor road north from the B2178 to Funtington.

Queen Elizabeth Country Park

Ab

At the western end of the South Downs, Butser Hill, 888 ft, and War Down stand west and east respectively of a deep valley where the Portsmouth road cuts through. In 1953, the coronation year of Elizabeth II, they were

ENGLAND'S ANCIENT TREE

The evergreen yew, prized in the Middle Ages for making longbows, may survive for 1,000 years. Yew woods are rare, found only on chalk or limestone soils, but single trees often grow in churchyards. The reason is obscure, but the yew was sacred in pagan times and may have been planted at places of worship before early Christians built churches on the same sites.

Yew
(Taxus baccata)

combined to become the 1,350 acre Queen Elizabeth Country Park.

The long, curved summit of Butser Hill juts out boldly above a ravine thickly wooded with yew trees. This is fine walking country through some of the most scenic parts of the Downs, with paths radiating in all directions, many of them ancient tracks. On Ramsdean Down to the north, there are three Bronze Age round barrows, and several lynchets – the outlines of Celtic fields. The views stretch eastwards across the Weald and southwards as far as Portsmouth Harbour and the faint outline of the Isle of Wight.

On War Down the scenery changes from the wide open spaces and springy turf of Butser Hill to groves of beeches,

alders and Scots pines in Queen Elizabeth Forest. A waymarked forest walk lasting about an hour and a half leads through sun-splashed glades and leafy avenues, and gives occasional glimpses of Hayling Island, The Solent and the Isle of Wight. There are roe and fallow deer in the forest, but they are less likely to be seen than the brilliantly plumaged golden pheasants that strut across the pathways.

Queen Elizabeth Country Park is 3 miles south of Petersfield on the A3, with the park centre at Gravel Hill near the south end of the forest. There are several car parks. The forest walk starts at Buriton, 1 mile east of the A3. At the southern end of the park, a minor road west from the A3 leads to Butser Hill.

Ranmore Common

Cd

Wooded Ranmore Common, lovely and unspoiled, lies on a ridge of the North Downs that looks eastwards across the River Mole valley as it cuts through the hills below the western slopes of Box Hill. If you climb to the common from the steep southern slopes above Dorking, you can look back on marvellous views across the Tilling Bourne valley south-west and south-east to the woodlands of the Weald, ever-widening as you ascend the slope.

Pleasant walks across the 472 acre common, owned by the National Trust, take you through beech and oak woods where the glades are a mass of bluebells in spring, and where foxgloves stand in purple ranks in summer. Some footpaths are waymarked, and one circular walk through woods and fields includes a spectacular avenue of yews. Wood anemones, red clover, celandines and rosebay willowherb can

be found along the way, and occasionally there are deer to be seen – especially in winter when the trees are bare and views less restricted.

Ranmore Common is 2 miles north-west of Dorking. The circular walk starts from the Stonyrock Road car park, one of several on the common, which can be reached along a minor road west from Dorking.

Stane Street

Bb

A major Roman road stretching 57 miles between London and Chichester – then Noviomagus, capital of the Regni tribe – Stane Street once echoed to the tramping feet of Roman legions and the heavy rumbling of ox-carts. Not much of it remains today, but there is one stretch that can still be followed through a picturesque part of the South Downs on the National Trust's Slindon Estate.

It was the Saxons who gave the road the name of Stane – or stone – Street, for the 30 ft wide embankment, bordered by wide ditching, was surfaced with a 2 ft layer of gravel and flint on top of rammed chalk. Today, the 3½ mile stretch from Eartham Wood north-east to Bignor Hill is a peaceful, tree-lined bridle-path.

Beech trees grow thickly in Eartham Wood, and there are groves of silver birch and sycamore trees where the sun slants through the branches in dusty shafts. Beyond the wood, the road climbs between a line of trees to the 737 ft summit of Bignor Hill to give breathtaking views of the wooded Weald to the north, on a clear day as far as the distant pine-covered slopes of Black Down. At Bignor, below the northern slope, there are remains of one of Britain's largest Roman villas, noted for its fine mosaic floors.

Eartham and Bignor lie 5 miles and 9 miles respectively north-east of Chichester on minor roads between the A285 and A29. Eartham Wood is about ¼ mile north of Eartham village.

Eb ## Windover Hill

On the steep northern slope of Windover Hill in the eastern South Downs, early man has left a lasting but mysterious mark. The 231 ft figure known as the Long Man – holding a stave in each hand – is outlined in the chalk; he towers above the village of Wilmington at the foot of the Downs, from where he is best seen.

His origin, like that of so many other hill figures, is unknown, but his presence was first recorded in 1779 and his outline restored with bricks in 1874. Does he date back some 3,500 years to the Bronze Age, those staves representing the gates of dawn being opened by the god Baldur? Or is he a 1,700-year-old Romano-British figure, like the Cerne Abbas giant in Dorset? Some Roman coins bear the figure of Woden in a similar stance. Could he be a 1,000-year-old Saxon image of a king carrying a spear in each hand? There is a similarity with figures found on the helmet in the 7th-century Saxon ship uncovered at Sutton Hoo, Suffolk, in 1939.

Other relics of early man on the hill are the Bronze Age ditched bowl-barrow, 100 ft in diameter, and the 200 ft Stone Age long barrow on the highest point. Apart from these, the furze-covered crown of Windover Hill is worth visiting for its views. Northwards lie the fields and forests of the Weald, and westwards you can see across the Cuckmere valley to Firle Beacon and in the distant haze the beech-crowned Chanctonbury Ring.

Wilmington is 6 miles north-west of Eastbourne and just south of the A27, 2 miles west of Polegate on the A22. About ¼ mile south-west of Wilmington a path from the minor road leads to Windover Hill, linking up with the South Downs Way.

Hd ## Wye and Crundale Downs

According to medieval superstitions, the Devil shaped much of the English landscape. On the North Downs he is credited with a deep coombe called the Devil's Kneadingtrough, a steep-sided valley that cuts 200 ft deep into the ridge of the Wye and Crundale Downs. Despite its fanciful name it was probably formed by water erosion during a massive thaw about 8000 BC, after the last Ice Age.

The Devil's Kneadingtrough is within the 250 acre Wye National Nature Reserve, and there is a nature trail about three-quarters of a mile long through some of the finest stretches of chalk grassland and woodland on the North Downs. Wonderful views from the crest of the Downs, over 550 ft above sea-level, take in the farmlands of the Great Stour valley to the west and the Weald beyond, stretching some 40 miles away to Ashdown Forest.

Characteristic flowers of the chalk turf include thyme, rock-rose and many kinds of orchids. Blackcaps, willow warblers, yellowhammers and nightingales nest in the scrub at the woodland edges, and in the woods – predominantly ash with hazel scrub – there are nuthatches, treecreepers, chiffchaffs and garden warblers. The laughing call of the green woodpecker echoes among the trees, and at one point there is a badger sett, which can be recognised by the chalky rubble thrown up by their burrowing.

The nature reserve is 4 miles north-east of Ashford between Wye and Hastingleigh, reached by minor roads east from the A28 or north-east from the A20.

WINDOVER HILL The Long Man of Wilmington, one of the most enigmatic of all hill figures, is a familiar landmark at the eastern end of the South Downs.

THE LASTING IMPACT OF ROME

IN THE WAKE OF THE LEGIONS CAME PEACE, AND A NEW WAY OF LIFE THAT CHANGED BRITAIN FOREVER

THE Roman occupation of Britain lasted less than four centuries. It began in AD 43 when the legions landed on the shores of southern Britain, but by the early years of the 5th century the last troops had been withdrawn as the Roman Empire began to crumble. The Romans brought to Britain all the benefits dear to the Roman heart – law and order, fine buildings, roads and towns – and peace for 300 years. Some of this heritage still remains upon the face of the British landscape.

The greatest monuments to the Roman presence are the towns, or at least their sites, which in many cases provided the foundations of present-day cities. They arose in a number of ways. Some, like Canterbury, Colchester, St Albans and Chichester, replaced earlier tribal settlements; others, like Caerleon, Exeter and Dorchester, grew up around forts to cater for the needs of the garrisons, while still others, such as Lincoln, evolved from settlements of army veterans. Richborough in Kent and Sea Mills, near Bristol, were ports; so too was London, though its chief importance was as the administrative capital of the province. There were also industrial estates like Wilderspool in Cheshire, and strings of little towns along the major roads. These grew up about the *mansiones*, the inns that were also staging posts for the Imperial courier service. Chelmsford and Great Chesterford in Essex, Braughing in Hertfordshire and Godmanchester in Cambridgeshire are typical.

Rural splendour

Beyond the towns the countryside was organised in villa estates, with gardens and orchards set out with plants and fruit trees new to Britain, such as vines, walnuts, roses, pansies and poppies. The villas stood at the heart of the estates, some of which extended for 1,000 acres. The earliest villas, built some 20 years after the conquest, were for the most part fairly simple, but by the end of the 2nd century the luxury of the Roman world was being eagerly imitated by the new-rich, Romano-British middle class. Colourful mosaic pavements decorated the spacious living-rooms, and central-heating systems and bath suites added a gracious dimension to life in the villas of merchants and landowners. Two good examples can be seen at Chedworth in the Cotswolds and at Lullingstone in Kent.

In the Lincolnshire and Cambridgeshire Fens the Romans were the first to reclaim the marshes for farming, and it is believed that the area grew corn to supply the garrisons in northern Britain. The course of a Roman canal, Car Dyke, built partly for drainage and partly for transport, can still be traced between Peterborough and Lincoln. From Lincoln another canal, the Foss Dyke, led to the River Trent and provided a water route to the fort at York.

Wealth from the mines

The Roman invasion of Britain was not entirely for territorial gain. Tales of the country's mineral wealth – albeit somewhat exaggerated – had long circulated throughout the known world; no doubt triggered by British exports of tin, and to a much lesser extent of silver and gold, to the Continent. Apart from lead, which the Romans mined in large quantities in the Mendips and used for drain-pipes as far away as Pompeii, the invaders were largely disappointed by the amounts of minerals produced. Nevertheless, throughout the occupation, they continued to mine for tin in Cornwall, for copper in the Parys Mountain in Anglesey, and for gold in Wales.

Many of these mines continued to be exploited until the end of the 19th century, so that most of the original Roman workings have long since disappeared. But at Dolaucothi in central Wales some of the tunnels in a gold-mine are of Roman origin.

Above ground there are extensive remains of a 7 mile long aqueduct, used to bring water for washing and separating the ore.

The roadbuilders

The Romans spun a web of roads across the British countryside, many miles of which are followed by those of more recent centuries. The earliest of all the Roman routes was Watling Street, running across north Kent from the invasion port at Richborough to London: later it was extended northwards through St Albans to Wroxeter and on into Wales. More than 6,000 miles of roads were eventually built by the Romans in Britain, some straight, and some not, depending on the lie of the land. Roman surveyors did tend to work in straight stretches where they could, but would also circumvent hills or use a winding river valley in precisely the manner of their modern counterparts. Perhaps the finest of Roman roads in Britain is Fosse Way, running from Seaton in Devon to Lincoln and never deviating more than 6 miles from the straight in its 200 mile length.

Such directness of line is rivalled only by the motorway builders of the present day, a remarkable achievement considering the simplicity of Roman surveying equipment. Their methods of construction, too, were never to be equalled again in this country until at least the end of the 18th century. Materials varied according to what was locally available; paving, in fact, was rare, but at Blackpool Bridge, deep in the woodlands of the Forest of Dean, a few yards of paved road can be seen that still bears the marks of wheels. Other examples of paved road occur on Wheeldale Moor in North Yorkshire, and part of Stane Street in West Sussex can be traced near Bignor Hill, all still showing the fine Roman camber.

Most regions of Britain, except Ireland and the far north of Scotland, bear some marks of the Roman military presence. It was at Richborough on the Kent coast that the invasion began with the landing of a 40,000 strong army. The only surviving evidence of the event is a massive platform that formed the base of a bronze and marble monument erected towards the end of the 1st century. As the armies advanced north, Richborough remained one of the most important ports in the province; later in the 3rd century, it was fortified as a naval base to counter pirate attacks, and this huge stone stronghold survives still.

Southern and eastern Britain submitted early to Roman rule, and by the end of the 1st century the military occupation was largely replaced by a civil administration. The forts fell into disuse, and in their place rose towns, with market-places, administrative buildings, baths and temples.

But on the western and northern frontiers, the military dominated throughout the occupation. Segontium, a large stone-built fort on the outskirts of Caernarfon, was one of several strongpoints in North Wales and was designed to house a garrison of 1,000 men. The northern frontier, however, needed more than a string of forts to contain the tribes, and in AD 122 the Emperor Hadrian decided to build a wall 'to separate the barbarians from the Romans'. It stretched for 73 miles across Britain, from the Tyne to the Solway, and took only seven years to build.

Hadrian's Wall has become a symbol of the might of the Roman Empire – and of its ending. For 250 years it served its purpose, but its success depended upon a garrison of professional soldiers, and by the 4th century such forces were no longer available. Power struggles in Rome and the external threat to the empire's capital from Huns, Goths and Vandals led to the withdrawal of troops from the wall, and eventually from Britain. By AD 410 the Roman legions had left and the country was at the mercy of new invaders: the Angles and Saxons.

ROME'S WAY Stane Street was the road that joined London with Chichester; much of it has disappeared beneath modern roads, but here, near Bignor, it is a track overlaying the original 30 ft wide foundations.

TRIUMPHAL ENTRY Richborough, Kent, was a vital port throughout the occupation. The great plinth at its centre probably supported a statue celebrating the conquest of Britain.

DISTANT POSTING Mediobogdum, 'the fort in the middle of the bend' of the Esk river, is magnificently sited between Eskdale and Scafell to command Hard Knott Pass. Built about AD 120, it was garrisoned for the next 80 years by a cohort of Dalmatians from Yugoslavia. Their barracks are well preserved.

THE SUFFOLK COAST AND HEATHLANDS

Tranquil landscapes round the River Stour contrast
dramatically with a coast embattled by erosion

Nature herself has held at bay the commercial development of the Suffolk coast. Pierced by estuaries, bordered by acres of marshland and constantly attacked by the sea, the stretch of 40 miles or so from Kessingland south to Felixstowe has defied the road builders – remote and sparsely populated, it remains one of the loveliest coastlines in Britain.

As the North Sea claws at the loose sandy cliffs and high tides flood the marshes, there is continual change in character and contour. Whole villages have disappeared beneath the waves – Slaughden just south of Aldeburgh went during this century, as did All Saints' Church at Dunwich, where the sea has advanced about a quarter of a mile in four centuries. Although many parts of the coast are inaccessible, seen only across shimmering mud-flats or shingle banks, there are long, empty beaches where walkers can wander with only sea-birds for company. And when the east winds drive all but the hardiest from the coast, there are forests and heathland to explore a few miles inland.

This is flat but varied country, saved from the far-reaching sameness of the fens. Along the coast the cliffs hardly qualify for such a name, and the heath behind them barely rises above 80 ft. From the boulder clay of west and central Suffolk, seven rivers wind their way to the sand and gravel of the coast. Perhaps the most dramatic is the Alde, which changes both its course and its name (to the Ore) some 70 yds from

SEA, SAND AND SOLITUDE Suffolk's lonely beaches are part of its enchantment. At Covehithe, even a fresh easterly breeze cannot mar the pleasure of walking for miles along firm sands flecked with grey shingle and backed by low, heather-crowned hills.

the sea, diverted 10 miles south by the long spit of shingle known as Orford Beach. The River Stour, which forms much of the border with Essex, flows through Dedham Vale, birthplace of the landscape painter, John Constable.

Dense forests covered the county in prehistoric times, and the first clearings were made by Stone Age farmers 5,000 years ago. From about 500 BC, Iron Age farmers continued the task. Those who made their home in this area eventually became the Iceni tribe, whose queen Boudicca led a rebellion against the Romans in AD 60. There are many remnants of Roman occupation along the Suffolk coast, which in the 4th century began to come under attack from Anglo-Saxon raiders.

As the coastal defences – such as Burgh Castle near Lowestoft – crumbled under the Anglo-Saxon onslaught, many families buried their valuables for safety. The possessions of one Roman family were discovered near Mildenhall in 1942 – 34 pieces of priceless silverware that are now in the British Museum. Also in the British Museum is the Anglo-Saxon treasure uncovered in 1939 – the accoutrements of a 7th-century Anglo-Saxon king from the great ship-barrow at Sutton Hoo beside the River Deben near Woodbridge.

It was the Anglo-Saxons who made the first real changes in the Suffolk landscape – clearing forests and draining fens to turn the land into arable farmland. When the Domesday Book was compiled for William the Conqueror in 1086, Suffolk was the most densely populated part of England. In medieval times much of the land was turned to sheep-grazing, and a prosperous wool trade grew up. Its legacy can be seen in almost every Suffolk town and village – the large and magnificent churches built by the wealthy farmers and merchants.

Places to visit

Map ref. De Covehithe

A ten-minute walk along a footpath from the village of Covehithe leads to one of the most rewarding views on the entire Suffolk coast. Low cliffs topped with gorse and broom-dappled heathland shelter a beach of pale yellow sand and grey shingle that stretches as far as the eye can see to the point where sand, sea and sky dissolve into a soft, indefinable horizon. There is a feeling of timelessness here; a world apart, where only the gentle hiss of the sea and the plaintive cries of sea-birds break the silence.

A short distance from the end of the footpath, the cliffs slope down among sand-dunes to give easy access to the beach. Here the sands are backed by a lagoon, where shelduck paddle among the reeds and the stately heron stands in wait for its prey, or occasionally rises aloft on slow-beating wings. Buntings swarm and chatter in the reeds, and at low tide oystercatchers, ringed plovers and other waders probe the sands.

Covehithe is a village with a startling landmark – the gaunt ruin of St Andrew's Church that dominates the landscape for miles around. It was originally built in the 15th century, but in 1672 the parishioners found that they could no longer afford the upkeep of

such a huge building. They were given permission to build a new church using the fabric of the old. So they constructed it, with a thatched roof to its nave, inside the shell of the partly demolished building, though the original tower was retained.

Covehithe is 7 miles south of Lowestoft, along a signposted lane leading from Wrentham on the A12. The footpath to the beach starts at an entrance to a field, 100 yds west of the church.

Dd Dunwich Common

An air of mystery hangs over Dunwich Common, especially when viewed from Minsmere Cliffs on its eastern side. From here you can see a mile-long stretch of beach, shingle and sand backed by grassy dunes that separate the ever-encroaching sea from the marshes. These secretive, mysterious marshes, with their reed-beds, streams and patches of dense woodland, are a shelter and breeding ground for many rare birds, some breeding only in this part of Britain.

The marshes bordering the River Minsmere to the south are kept as a nature reserve by the Royal Society for the Protection of Birds. Rare marsh harriers may be found here, gliding above the reed-beds in search of prey, or sparrow-sized bearded reedlings jerking among the reeds after seeds or insects. Little terns and avocets are among the rare visitors.

Entry to Minsmere reserve is restricted to RSPB permit holders, but watchers on the footpath bordering the common and on those parts of the common open to the public may see some of the birds flying over the adjoining heaths and marshes.

Marram grass has been planted along

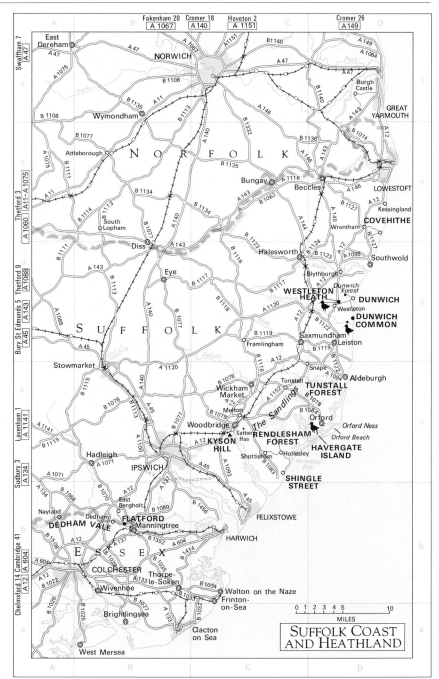

SUFFOLK COAST AND HEATHLAND

the sand-dunes, its fibrous roots helping to hold them as a barrier against the sea. Spiky blue-green sea holly may also be found there, as well as bird's-foot trefoil and restharrow in dry, grassy spots. At low tide the beachcomber may discover amber, a yellow translucent fossil resin, and semi-precious cornelian stones among the pebbles.

Dunwich is 3 miles south-east of Blythburgh on the A12. To reach Dunwich Common, turn off the Westleton–Dunwich road at the Minsmere signpost, or follow signposts from Dunwich village. A footpath leads from Minsmere Cliffs down to the beach and marshes.

Dd Dunwich Village

Nowhere is the Suffolk coast's never-ending battle with the sea more dramatically illustrated than at Dunwich, where a once-proud town vanished beneath the waves. Terror came to Dunwich in January 1326, when a violent storm plucked 400 houses and three of the nine churches from their crumbling foundations and hurled them into the sea. It was the beginning of the end for the town that had been founded in AD 632 by St Felix of Burgundy, who crossed the Channel to convert the heathen East Anglians to Christianity.

With only low, sandy cliffs forming a fragile barrier, Dunwich stood no chance against the remorseless attack of the sea. Year after year, century after century, streets and buildings toppled from the cliffs, and in 1677 the waves were lapping at the doors of the houses in the market-place.

By the 19th century the medieval Church of All Saints, which had probably once stood in the middle of the

WILDLIFE SANCTUARY Marsh and reed-beds by Dunwich Common form part of Minsmere Nature Reserve.

town, was on the cliff-edge. In 1904 part of the church went into the sea, followed by the tower in 1919.

What remains of Dunwich is only a small village. It is said that at times the submerged church bells can be heard, warning of an approaching storm. The legend persists, though there would have been plenty of time to remove the bells before the church was engulfed by the sea. But perhaps by then, nobody cared.

Dunwich is 3 miles south-east of Blythburgh on the A12. It lies along a minor road south-east off the B1125.

Bb Flatford and Dedham Vale

Constable immortalised Flatford in 1817, when he captured forever the beauty of this lovely stretch of the River Stour and its mill. After descending between high, ivy-clad banks, the road leads to the riverside where a thatched, pink-washed 16th-century cottage stands by a small wooden bridge. A left turn beyond the bridge leads past a small lock, and then Flatford Mill comes into view, the waters of its mill-pond tumbling over weirs into a wide expanse of the river

where swans glide and mallard, shelduck and coots dabble among the weeds.

Across the bridge, a footpath winds beside the river, fringed with gnarled willows. It leads about 1½ miles upstream, across shimmering water-meadows, to Dedham Mill, where shady weeping willows bend low over the mill-pond. The meadows are the home of many wild flowers, such as pale yellow oxlips and deep pink marsh-mallows, and in July and August the yellow-brown Essex skipper butterfly, which is rare elsewhere in

103

Britain, may be seen on the wing.

Essex and Suffolk share Dedham Vale, which borders the River Stour from Flatford to Nayland, but it was John Constable who brushed out the county boundary through his landscapes. This part of England has become known simply as 'Constable country'.

Constable was born at East Bergholt in 1776. His father owned both water-mills, at Flatford and at Dedham, and these were the subjects of his earlier works. He also painted many scenes along the banks of the Stour and the surrounding countryside, an area of water-meadows, willow-fringed streams and patchwork fields. He wrote: 'The sound of water escaping from mill dams, willows, old rotten planks, slimy posts and brickwork . . . these scenes made me a painter.'

The countryside that Constable painted is still as English as the man himself, ever-enchanting with its winding lanes, sloping fields and still waters where cattle slake their thirst and waterfowl glide among the reeds. Unchanged and unchanging, Constable country remains much as the painter saw it.

Dedham Vale lies north of Colchester and can be reached by either the A12 or the A134. Dedham is 6 miles north-east of Colchester via the A137 and B1029. Flatford is reached by a signposted lane from East Bergholt, which is on the B1070 about 1 mile south-east of the A12.

NATURE'S MASTERPIECE Downstream from Flatford Mill, the River Stour winds a leisurely course between green and reed-fringed banks – a soul-soothing landscape where river and sky blend together on one giant canvas.

Dc   Havergate Island

A small island in the River Alde (or Ore) estuary, Havergate is owned by the Royal Society for the Protection of Birds. Its 280 acres of salt-marsh are one of the two British breeding grounds of the avocet, which returned here to nest in 1947 after being absent from Britain for 100 years. Fen drainage reduced their numbers in the 18th century, and the birds that were left were shot for their feathers to make fishing flies, and their eggs were stolen for cooking.

Tall, elegant birds with patterned black-and-white plumage and up-turned bills, the avocets arrive early in March and usually leave in June or July for their African wintering grounds. The island is also noted for migratory waders such as the curlew-sandpiper,

which passes through in spring and autumn. The day-flying short-eared owl also breeds here.

Havergate can be visited only with a permit obtained from the RSPB Warden at 30 Mundays Lane, Orford. Visitors are taken to the island by boat from Orford on all-day visits on Saturdays, Sundays and Mondays from April to August.

Orford is 10 miles east of Woodbridge on the B1084. There is a large car park about 100 yds before the quay.

Cc   Kyson Hill

At the ancient town of Woodbridge, the Deben becomes a river worthy of the name – broad and fast-flowing, with the salty tang of the sea borne on the breezes coming up from the estuary 8 miles away. South of the town is Kyson Hill, a finger of land projecting into the Deben where the river makes a brief incursion into Martlesham Creek and then heads for the sea. Four acres of the hill belong to the National Trust.

From the aptly named Broom Heath on the southern slopes of Kyson Hill, ablaze with yellow in the spring, there are fine views across the valley, though the river hides coyly in the tree-clad folds of the land. But a footpath leading down between hedgerows and tall trees soon brings the broad mud-flats and foreshore of the Deben into view. Yachts rest at anchor in the creek, or perch on the mud at low tide, and the stranded pools and river's edge are a meeting place for sea and freshwater birds. Shelduck and oystercatchers probe the mud, black-headed gulls wheel above, and out in the deeper water the surface may be rippled by diving cormorants.

TUNSTALL FOREST Deep coniferous woods provide a home for the rare red squirrel.

At the bottom of Kyson Hill, a footpath follows the river bank back to Woodbridge, skirting a narrow backwater where tall reeds grow. On the quayside at Woodbridge stands a restored 18th-century mill whose wheel was once driven by the tides.

There is a small car park on Broom Heath, reached from Sandy Lane, a turning off the Ipswich road (B1438) in Woodbridge.

Cc   Rendlesham Forest

Though scarcely 2 miles from Tunstall Forest, Rendlesham is subtly different in character. Here the tall pines are thickly set, and the lofty canopy of foliage cuts the light to a misty darkness within a few yards of the forest edge. Its beauty is sinister, underlined by an impressive silence that makes a twig breaking underfoot sound like a pistol shot. There is no undergrowth but only a soft carpet of moss scattered with pine cones and needles. Few birds penetrate the densest part of the forest, although the harsh cries of jays and magpies may be heard, or the echoing tattoo of a woodpecker.

Rendlesham Forest is the oldest and largest of the woodland areas that make up the Forest of Aldewood. It began with the planting of 2,544 acres in 1920 and now covers almost 4,000 acres. Previously most of the land was heath used for sheep grazing, and some patches of heathland have survived, such as Upper and Lower Hollesley commons on the south-western edge.

During the Second World War, Woodbridge airfield was cut out of the forest, and it is still a military air base.

The B1084 Woodbridge–Orford road cuts through the forest, and a large open area on the northern side of the road has been set aside for car parking.

Cc **Shingle Street**

On this astonishing strip of the Suffolk coast the River Ore, having run parallel to the sea for about 10 miles and changed its name from the Alde, finally flows into Hollesley Bay at Orford Haven. A high bank of shingle hides the sea from the road, and from the top of the bank the view is of yet more shingle – to the south, to the north and across the river on Orford Beach. A natural landscape undoubtedly – desolate, featureless and yet with a tranquillity that beguiles the visitor to linger. Many a yachtsman has spent an enforced stay here – stranded through a misjudgment of the tide.

Only the hardiest of wild flowers flourish here: the bright green, low-growing sea pea, bright with purple

flowers in June and July, the yellow horned poppy and the dark green sea beet, its leaves red-tinged. Hollows in the shingle enclose lagoons left by the high tides, sheltered pools for oyster-catchers and black-headed gulls.

Shingle Street is 7 miles south-east of Woodbridge and reached by a signposted lane from Hollesley village, which is off the B1083. The lane ends at the Martello tower, but where it runs parallel to the shingle bank there is a concrete roadway almost to the water's edge.

Cc **Tunstall Forest**

Rendlesham, Dunwich and Tunstall forests are part of the Forest of Aldewood which covers some 14 sq. miles between Woodbridge and Southwold. Each of the three areas of woodland has a distinctive beauty and character; Tunstall's charm is its airiness and diversity. Well-spaced Corsican pines, larches and Scots pines rise from the forest floor and its carpet of pine needles and cones, and on a bright day the sun slants through the branches to bathe the undergrowth in a soft light.

Fire-breaks between the rows of trees make exploration easy, and the lightness of the fern and bracken undergrowth allows the adventurous to penetrate deep into the forest. Red squirrels, rare in most other parts of Britain, make their home here. There are also fallow deer, and red deer are occasional visitors. Most common woodland birds can be seen, as well as typical coniferous-forest birds such as crossbills, which frequent the tree-tops.

At the forest edge, the deep green of the conifers is relieved in spring by brightly flowering trees and shrubs –

From spring through to autumn the Suffolk coast sparkles with the bright hues of wild flowers. In May the white blooms of the sea sandwort appear among the dunes, lasting until July, and the sea campion, common on cliffs as well as shingle, flowers from June to August. Viper's bugloss is in flower from June to September, often growing in masses of glorious colour among the dunes. The sturdy yellow horned poppy that flowers in June can survive on windswept shingle right through to October.

Yellow horned poppy
(*Glaucium flavum*)

Sea campion
(*Silene maritima*)

Sea sandwort
(*Honkenya peploides*)

Viper's bugloss
(*Echium vulgare*)

gorse, hawthorn and flowering currants – which dapple the roadside hedgerows with splashes of yellow, white and red. In some parts of the forest the conifers give way to beech and the occasional oak, and rhododendrons line the roadside verges.

Tunstall is 7 miles north-east of Woodbridge on the A1152. Tunstall Forest straddles the B1078 between Tunstall village and its junction with the B1084.

Dd **Westleton Heath**

In medieval times Suffolk was wool country, and Westleton Heath is one of the last-surviving examples of the east Suffolk heaths where sheep once grazed. Close by is Dunwich Forest, its natural disorder of bracken, heather and stands of silver birch growing in pleasant contrast with the neatly arrayed pine trees of the Forestry Commission plantation.

Today the heath encloses a nature reserve, and the whole area is splendid for walking and exploring. The sandy soil supports gorse, heather and broom as well as rarer wild flowers such as the heath spotted orchid. In summer, yellowhammers, rare red-backed shrike, whitethroats and linnets flit among the bushes, and as evening approaches there is a chance of hearing the rasping song of the nightjar – most common from late May to July. Rabbits are plentiful, and there are a few hares. Westleton Heath is also a home of the adder, Britain's only poisonous snake, which is sometimes found basking on sun-baked footpaths. It is recognisable by its black-and-white markings.

To reach Westleton Heath, take the signposted lane from Westleton village, which is on the B1125, 6 miles south-west of Southwold.

THE LINCOLNSHIRE WOLDS AND MARSHES

Hills where peaceful farmland and lost villages
lie above North Sea marshes rich in wildlife

'Calm and deep peace on this high Wold' was how the poet Tennyson described these hills where he was born and bred. That peace is still reflected in the Wolds today, rich farming country where quiet lanes wind between sloping pastures and wind-rippled cornfields, and where pheasants and partridges wander by the roadside.

Stretching for some 45 miles parallel to the North Sea, the Lincolnshire Wolds are part of the chalk belt that curves from Dorset to East Anglia and then up to Yorkshire. The rounded, chalk-capped hills are only 550 ft at their highest point, and on their steeper western slopes overlook the deep green woods and fields of the Lincolnshire Clay Vale. On their eastern side they slope gently down to the level fields and reed-lined dykes of the marshland that stretches for 10 miles to the sea. The marshland's rich clay soil provides some of the finest grazing and growing land in Britain, an inheritance from the deposits of retreating Ice Age glaciers that left a marshy shoreline several miles inland from the present coast.

Men have lived on the Wolds since prehistoric times, when nomadic New Stone Age farmers tramped out their ancient trackways such as the Bluestone Heath Road well over 4,000 years ago. Later the Romans also made a road through the heart of the Wolds, linking their forts at Caistor and Horncastle; this road is today the unclassified High Street.

AT THE EDGE OF THE WOLDS Red Hill in the western Wolds looks out across the Lincolnshire Clay Vale. Once it was a chalk quarry, but now the grassed-over workings are a nature reserve where chalkland plants and birds such as meadow pipits find sanctuary.

From about AD 870 until 918, much of the Wolds population was Danish, resulting from raiding Norsemen who had settled there. Many village names reveal their Danish origin, such as Ulceby – the ending *by* means a settlement – and Bratoft – where *toft* signifies a homestead. Many marshland villages still have *ings*, or low-lying meadows.

Even before the Norman conquest, villagers had begun to reclaim the marshes. The medieval shoreline followed what is now the minor road through Tetney and North Cotes, and the A1031 through Marsh Chapel and Grainthorpe, where a huge bank was built to hold back the high tide. There were many saltworks here in medieval times. The salt was transported inland along the Salters' Way that ran from Grainthorpe to Lincoln. Ludford village street is on its route.

By the early 14th century, Lincolnshire was one of the most thickly populated parts of Britain. Land was cultivated everywhere it could be made to yield a living, and Wolds villages were often only a mile or two apart. But the story changed after 1348–9, when the Black Death carried off more than one-third of the population. Some of the survivors drifted away, perhaps to the richer soils of the reclaimed marshes. Many Wolds villages were gradually deserted, and by the 17th century had been left to the grazing sheep. Lincolnshire today has over 200 such 'lost' villages, marked only by grassy mounds or the crumbling ruins of churches.

The marshland shoreline is still gradually gaining ground from the sea, as dunes and salt-marshes develop behind sandbanks blown up by the easterly winds. Yet southwards down the coast, by Mablethorpe and Skegness, the cliffs are slowly crumbling under the onslaught of the sea, and stout walls and groynes have been built to hold it back.

Places to visit

Map ref. Bc   The River Bain

Attractive but elusive, the River Bain flows for 20 miles or so below the western edge of the Wolds, dawdling southwards through sloping meadows and fields, and the occasional wood, to meet the River Witham just south of Tattershall. Rising in the Wolds west of Ludford, the river is cradled by hills as far as Donington on Bain.

The banks of the Bain are not easily accessible, except at Donington where there is a picturesque, white-painted old water-mill by the weir. From here you can walk along part of the Viking Way through farm and parkland and the sites of lost villages, following the green banks of the river upstream for part of the way. The Viking Way is a way-marked long-distance footpath between Oakham in Leicestershire and the Humber Bridge, and it runs for some 40 miles through the Wolds.

Biscathorpe House, an early Victorian mansion, stands about a mile north of Donington amid parkland that sweeps down to the Bain, where it has been dammed to form a small lake. North of the A157 are the grounds of Girsby Manor – known locally as the Grange, the house is no more than a ruin. Beyond Girsby the river winds to Wykeham Hall and the sites of the lost

villages of East and West Wykeham.

These two villages were so poor and depleted by 1397 – partly the result of plague – that the parish was joined to nearby Ludford Magna. Today all that remains is a fragment of East Wykeham Church in a private field beside the drive of Wykeham Hall.

Two more lost village sites, at South Cadeby and Calcethorpe, lie a mile or so east; by 1563 they had dwindled to only six families between them, their churches long decayed. Calcethorpe village site can be clearly seen beside the minor road between the A631 and A157, about 5 miles west of Louth. Sheep now graze in the field beside Calcethorpe Manor Farm where grassy mounds and hummocks cover what remains of the village cottages.

To follow the Viking Way through lovely country between Donington on Bain and Girsby Top above Wykeham Hall, a walk of about 5 miles, turn into Welsdale Lane by Donington Mill, just north of the village. A horned-helmet sign marks the route across fields and beside Biscathorpe House, across a minor road and the River Bain, and eventually on to a minor road which joins the A157. Then, across the A157, the Way follows a wide track between cornfields that turns west towards Wykeham Hall and then south and west to Girsby Top.

Donington on Bain lies on a signposted minor road 6 miles west of Louth.

Bc   The Bluestone Heath Road

Sweeping along the crest of the Wolds, the Bluestone Heath Road winds for 14 miles between rolling cornfields and scattered woods that dip away on either side. There are no villages along the road, only wide verges, low hawthorn

hedges and the occasional line of trees. To the west, there are magnificent panoramas of Lincoln Heath.

The downland turf verges that line the road are reminders that once much of the Wolds was rolling grassland that supported thousands of sheep. Today, modern farming methods and fertilisers have turned most of the slopes from pasture to plough.

The finest views can be seen from the southern section of the road. Just east of the turning to the deep and lovely valley that shelters the village of Belchford, there is a lay-by and public viewpoint looking over the River Waring valley and to Nab Hill on its eastern side. During the Napoleonic Wars, Nab Hill was a beacon point, kept in readiness to warn of a French invasion.

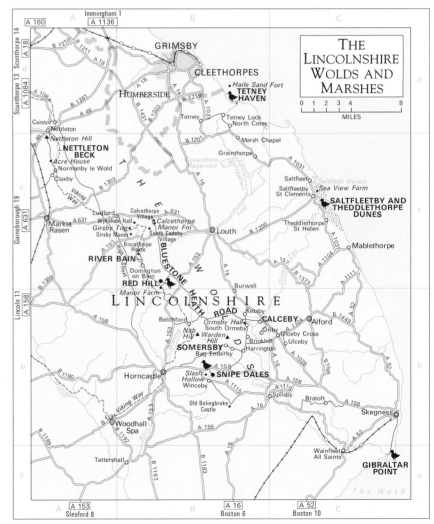

From its summit on a clear day you can see eastwards to the coast at Skegness and westwards 20 miles to Lincoln Cathedral.

The Bluestone Heath Road probably follows the route of a prehistoric ridge-way, worn through the centuries by the tread of countless feet. On this high route, ancient man would have found progress less difficult than in the heavily forested lower slopes or the marshy valleys, and the landmarks that served as signposts would be easier to pick out.

In summer, when the sun is high and drifting clouds cast soft shadows across the gently waving corn, the road is a delightful place. But when the wind is strong there is little protection from its biting force, so trees have been planted on the more exposed parts.

The northern section of the Bluestone Heath Road joins the A157 about 5 miles west of Louth. The southern section joins the A16 east of Calceby.

THE BANKS OF THE BAIN Near Donington the river is at its most attractive, and the Viking Way footpath follows its valley.

Bb   Calceby

Near the south end of the Bluestone Heath Road, an ivy-covered chalkstone ruin on a hilly outcrop springs dramatically into view. This was once the parish church of Calceby, a lost village of the Wolds.

Turn into the road leading north to the A16; from the field gate opposite a red-brick Georgian farmhouse the mounds that mark the village site can be clearly seen. As the -by in its name suggests, Calceby was probably founded by Danish settlers in the 9th or 10th centuries, and in medieval times was a busy community. According to the Domesday Book, it received income, with four other villages, from salt-pan holdings on the coast.

Why the village was deserted is uncertain. It survived for some 200 years after the Black Death. There were still 18 families living there in 1563, but with the death of the last vicar in 1621 the village dwindled to the present farmhouse and a handful of scattered cottages.

A Norman doorway from Calceby Church is now incorporated in the south aisle of the church at South Ormsby village, tucked away in tree-shaded surroundings a mile westwards. Calceby and South Ormsby lie in a lovely, little-known area of secluded villages and wooded parkland. Southwards from Calceby, a field footpath leads to the cul-de-sac hamlet of Driby, and onwards to the south-west there is a bridle-path to Brinkhill.

Northwards from South Ormsby, the wooded parklands of Ormsby Hall (not open to the public) border the west side of the road. The Great Eau (from the Old English ea, 'a stream'), which rises high in the Wolds beyond,

FIELD AND DUNE PLANTS

Common in hedgerows in eastern and southern England, field maples used to be coppiced – cut low to produce staves. Crosswort, a honey-scented hedgerow plant, has cross-like leaves in fours, and the field poppy adds scarlet splashes to road and field verges from June to August. Sea buckthorn forms thorny scrub, taller than a man in places, on old-established sand-dunes.

Field maple
(Acer campestre)

Sea buckthorn
(Hippophaë rhamnoides)

Crosswort
(Galium cruciata)

powered the old water-mill at Ketsby further north. It stands just off the minor road beside a new trout farm, its water-wheel still in position.

All the villages can be reached along minor roads that lead south from the A16 between Burwell and Ulceby Cross.

Ca   Gibraltar Point

Where the North Sea coast turns inwards to form the north side of the 12 mile wide mouth of The Wash, Gibraltar Point looks out across some of the most extensive salt-marshes in Europe. A lonely but peaceful spot, steeped in the salty tang of the sea air and lulled by the constant lap of the tides, it is the southernmost tip of a 1,500 acre nature reserve rich in a variety of wildlife and managed by the Lincolnshire and South Humberside Trust for Nature Conservation.

Gibraltar Point in spring resounds with the warbling songs of skylarks – they are more numerous here than anywhere in Britain – and in summer, little terns and ringed plovers nest on the shingle. In autumn, vast flocks of waders – oystercatchers, knots, dunlins and godwits – visit the reserve on passage or to spend the winter. As the tide comes in, they rise in their thousands to seek higher ground. Common seals bask on the sandbanks about a mile offshore, and in summer, seal pups are often born there, ready to swim off with their mothers at high tide.

Sharp-spined sea buckthorn grows on the East Dunes, its bright orange berries providing autumn and winter food for migrant birds, especially large flocks of fieldfares. Small birds such as yellowhammers and whitethroats nest in the buckthorn and elder scrub, and the older dunes in summer are bright

with flowers such as cowslips and lady's bedstraw, or the deep blue of tall viper's bugloss. From Mill Hill, the sand-dune that is the highest part of the reserve, you can see north-west to the Wolds, and south on a clear day across The Wash to the Hunstanton cliffs on the Norfolk coast.

In the new salt-marsh, covered by the sea at high tide, are marsh samphire, rice grass, sea blite, sea aster, sea purslane and sea meadow-grass – all plants that can survive long periods in sea water. The older salt-marsh is covered with a lilac carpet of sea lavender in summer, and reed buntings nest among the sea couch grass.

Freshwater marshes as well as salt-marshes lie within the reserve, and there is a public hide for watching birds that visit the freshwater Mere, half a mile north of the Visitor Centre. From the hide you may see waders and dabbling and diving ducks, as well as herons and perhaps kingfishers.

Gibraltar Point lies 3 miles south of Skegness along an unclassified road.

Ac   Nettleton Beck

Rising in the Wolds to the south-east of Nettleton village, the deep-channelled Nettleton Beck winds its way down to the foot of the Wolds, and on to the Ancholme valley. Its lower reaches are bordered in summer by breeze-rippled wheatfields fringed with poppies. A grassy footpath – part of the Viking Way – starts from a point half a mile south-east of the village and follows beside the beck to its source about 2 miles upstream.

Near the start of the beckside path, a public bridleway climbs to the east through a cattle meadow, and from the barn on its slope there is a good view of the valley below. Nettleton Hill – known locally as Nettleton Bump because of its modest height (370 ft) – rises above the west side of the valley; and to the north are the red and grey rooftops of the small market town of Caistor, a mile away.

Return from the bridleway to the beckside path, which ascends gradually upstream beside the beck, passing the scars of old mine workings that, until they became uneconomic in 1969, produced Claxby ironstone, named after a village to the south. As you leave the valley and breast the brow of the hill 2 miles from the start of the path, a short distance ahead, some of the most spectacular views in Lincolnshire stretch across the valley to the north-west, where the Ancholme river flows on its way to the Humber.

After it leaves the valley, the path dips and rises to reach the Nettleton–Normanby le Wold road al-most opposite Acre House. The hamlet of Normanby, between 450–500 ft above sea-level, is just below the highest part of the Wolds. It stands on a very steep slope, and from here the plain below is dramatically revealed.

Nettleton is on the A46, 1 mile south-west of Caistor. To reach Nettleton Beck footpath, take the Normanby road south from the village, and just before the end of the village, turn south-east on to the lane marked by a Viking Way sign. The beck is ¼ mile along this lane.

Bc Red Hill

A brick-red gash in the hillside marks the site of the disused chalk quarry on the steep side of Red Hill, now a nature reserve. Like a large cutaway model from a geological museum, the scar reveals the rocks that form the Wolds.

A band of rust-coloured sandstone, called carstone, is topped by a thick layer of red chalk, which lies below a layer of white chalk. Red chalk, its colour resulting from the presence of iron, stretches roughly from South Yorkshire to North Norfolk, under-lying the crown of the Wolds.

Hawthorn bushes line the top of the scar and cluster at its foot. A worn pathway descends beside it, but it is now dangerous to climb the rock face. There is a car park at the top of the steep hill, and from it you can walk across downland to the grassed-over workings behind the scar. Tread carefully in the long grass, however, for this is one of the few places in the Wolds where the meadow pipit breeds, making its nest in grass tussocks.

Because of its steepness, the hillside has never been used for farming, like the gentler slopes near by, so has been undisturbed perhaps for centuries. The result is a profusion of wild flowers: autumn gentians, yellow-wort, kidney vetch, rock rose and the purple-flowered pyramidal orchid. The red and crimson six-spot burnet moth is on the wing here in June and July. It lays its eggs on plants of the pea family, such as kidney vetch.

From the summit of Red Hill, which is on the steeper western edge of the Wolds, the view of the valley below is, on a clear day, like looking at the landscape from a low-flying aircraft – remote, tranquil and astonishing in its clarity and extent.

Red Hill is 2¼ miles south-east of Donington on Bain, east of the road from Donington to the A153. Follow this road to Manor Farm, then turn north-east – the quarry can be clearly seen from the road. The road from Donington passes another Red Hill which lies 1¼ miles north-west of the nature reserve and is topped by radar dishes.

Cc Saltfleetby and Theddlethorpe Dunes

Stretching for nearly 5 miles along the sea-shore, the Saltfleetby–Theddlethorpe Dunes National Nature Reserve is shielded on its landward side by shoulder-high scrub of sea buckthorn, interspersed with elder, blackthorn, hawthorn, dog rose and the occasional willow.

But there are sandy paths to the foreshore, where dunlins and red-shanks feed far out on the sand and mud-flats. Do not attempt the walk to the sea at low tide. These sands can be dangerous, for when the tide turns it comes in fast, and sandbanks soon become islands cut off from the shore.

This is a good place to observe how the eastern coastline is gradually creeping seawards, with marram-clad dunes trapping wind-blown sand. The mature salt-marsh on the foreshore gradually fades to scattered patches of glasswort, or samphire, towards the sea. The samphire is collected in summer and pickled for eating.

Dewberry is abundant on the older dunes, which are some 700 years old and the highest on the Lincolnshire coast; there are also flowers such as bird's-foot trefoil and centaury. Where grazing rabbits clip the turf, the lemon-yellow mouse-ear hawkweed finds a habitat. Apart from the many common brown or blue grassland butterflies that are abundant in summer, you may occasionally see a dark green fritillary; they like to bask and feed on thistles and daisy-like flowers.

Swallows wheel above the scrub and swoop over the saltings; skylarks, linnets, yellowhammers, whitethroats and dunnocks nest in the dense scrub or long grass; and reed buntings and a

---

BIRDS OF FIELD AND MARSH

Flocks of long-crested lapwings are a familiar sight in farming country such as the Lincolnshire Wolds, where they forage for worms, insects and larvae such as leatherjackets. In winter they often feed out on the coastal mud-flats. East Anglia's low rainfall, light soil and culti-vated fields are attractive to red-legged partridges, which are more widespread here than the common partridge. Shy reed warblers are summer visitors that feed mainly on aquatic insects. They build their deep-cupped nests round a number of reed stems.

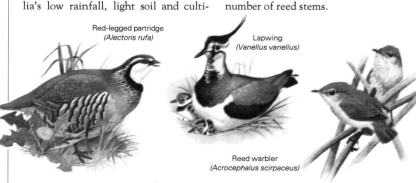

Red-legged partridge
(*Alectoris rufa*)

Lapwing
(*Vanellus vanellus*)

Reed warbler
(*Acrocephalus scirpaceus*)

few sedge warblers favour the fresh-water marshes that stretch between some of the dunes. Britain's rarest toad, the natterjack, also breeds among the sandbanks here. By day it sleeps in a sandy burrow, but at breeding time in spring or early summer you may hear a chorus of males chanting their churring song on warm evenings.

A large section of the reserve lies within RAF firing ranges. Do not enter areas marked by red flags or danger signs. Safety regulations are displayed at entrances.

The dunes lie to the east of the A1031 between Saltfleet Haven and Theddlethorpe St Helen. Cars can be parked at the entrances at Saltfleet Haven, Sea View Farm near Saltfleetby St Clements, and the coastguard cottages near Theddlethorpe All Saints.

Snipe Dales

Stony streams chatter among the steep-sided grassy valleys of Snipe Dales, a 120 acre nature reserve in the southern Wolds. In the damp valley bottoms, below the spring line where the sandstone slopes meet the clay below, marsh marigolds glow yellow among green ferns in spring and early summer, and later meadowsweet and ragged robin stand tall above the grasses. Long-billed snipe and woodcocks couch among the undergrowth by day, coming out mainly at dusk to probe in the mud for food, and herons, kestrels and short-eared owls live here too.

Once, the Snipe Dales area was more wooded. Oak and ash grew on the slopes where today bluebells and primroses still flower in spring. The valleys were thick with willow and alder, as names such as Isaac's Holt – meaning Isaac's wood or copse – recall. Woodland is to be restored to the Dales by the Lincolnshire and South Humberside Trust for Nature Conservation. Oak, ash and beech will be planted on the slopes, and alder carr – a name of Scandinavian origin meaning 'fen woods' – in the valleys.

Little now disturbs the peace of Snipe Dales, but on an autumn day 300 years ago, its valleys were jarred by the rattle of muskets, the clash of steel and the chant of psalms, for Slash Hollow, just to the west where the main roads converge, was a scene of conflict in the Civil War.

Here at the Battle of Winceby on October 11, 1643, Parliament troops led by Sir Thomas Fairfax and Colonel Oliver Cromwell lined up against a Royalist force under the Marquis of Newcastle, on its way to relieve the garrison at Old Bolingbroke Castle 3 miles south-east. The Royalists were routed, and afterwards the castle, once owned by John of Gaunt, was destroyed; only grassy mounds remain.

Snipe Dales is 4½ miles east of Horncastle, north of the A1115 Spilsby road. Cars can be parked at Winceby, in a field on the north side of the road near a telephone box. From the car park a signposted track leads through the old churchyard to the nature-reserve entrance.

Somersby

Narrow, leafy lanes, cool even in strong sunshine, approach the village of Somersby, which lies at the foot of

SECLUSION IN THE WOLDS Snipe Dales Nature Reserve is a haven for snipe and woodcocks, day-flying short-eared owls and sand martins, as well as a profusion of wild flowers.

Warden Hill. South-east from the village, a lane winds between tall trees to Bag Enderby and Harrington.

Peaceful and pastoral, this countryside was the boyhood haunt of the poet Alfred, Lord Tennyson, the 'silent woody places' he mentions in his poem *Maud*. His father was the rector of Somersby and Bag Enderby, and the poet was born in 1809 in Somersby rectory (now Somersby House, not open to the public).

At Bag Enderby, a side lane loops off the main way, passing the greenstone 'Tennyson Church' (the 15th-century St Margaret's) where services in memory of the poet are still held every other year in alternation with St Margaret's in Somersby. Oaks, beeches and other tall trees stand protectively over the sleepy cottages.

The straggling hamlet of Harrington is about a mile east of Bag Enderby. At its western end you pass a neat and whitewashed thatched cottage backed by conifers, with a delightful garden. The manor house of Harrington Hall, built mainly in the reign of Charles II but partly Elizabethan, is at the east end of the hamlet. It is open to the public in summer. The young Tennyson was often a visitor here; it is said that he was inspired to write the poem which opens with the line 'Come into the garden, Maud' while on the terrace overlooking the front gardens.

Somersby is 6 miles east of Horncastle, and can be reached along minor roads north off the A158.

Bd   Tetney Haven

Sea-birds wheel and cry above the lonely expanse of mud-flats and salt-marsh, bright with sea asters in summer, that surrounds Tetney Haven on

A WINDING SOMERSBY LANE

the North Sea coast. Silent oil tankers wait to discharge at the deep-water monobuoy, or pass upriver to Immingham, and Grimsby trawlers pass by in the estuary beyond the Haile Sand Fort – a remnant of First World War defences.

Once, the haven sheltered ships that were waiting for the tide to carry them through the narrow channel leading to the Louth Navigation, a canal extension of the River Lud by which ships of up to 30 tons could go 12 miles inland south-west to the Riverhead warehouses at Louth. They brought in coal and timber and took out wool and corn. Opened in 1770, the canal thrived until the East Coast railway arrived in 1848. It was disused by 1915, and was closed in 1924. Now it is a land drain. The old lock gates have gone and new sluice gates have been built nearer the sea. It also serves as a collector to feed the 218 acre Covenham Reservoir, Lincolnshire's largest lake.

The steep banks of the canal cutting keep the water strangely calm, disturbed only by the floats of the lone anglers strung along the canal side, fishing for pike and perch. From the bridge at Tetney Lock hamlet, 1½ miles south-west of Tetney Haven, a path follows the canal on its southern side for the last mile or so seawards.

A nature reserve managed by the Royal Society for the Protection of Birds occupies the foreshore and saltings near Tetney Haven. Little terns nest there in summer, while later in the year many waders and flocks of Brent geese winter there. It is unwise to wander on to the saltings, for it is dangerous underfoot, with deep channels hidden by undergrowth. The reserve is open from April to August and can be visited by appointment with the Warden of Tetney Marshes Nature Reserve, c/o the Post Office, Tetney, Grimsby, South Humberside.

Tetney Lock is 5 miles south-east of Cleethorpes, and can be reached by a minor road off the A1031 at Tetney.

A POET'S BIRTHPLACE Somersby, where Lord Tennyson was born and spent his boyhood, lies at the foot of the Wolds amid narrow, shady lanes that wind between tall trees and hawthorn hedges. Breaks in the leafy wayside lining reveal open, rolling fields with small woods that curve along the swelling slopes, and here and there a bridle-path leads through woods and fields to link peaceful and secluded villages.

ROLLING FIELDS AROUND SOMERSBY

A DISTANT VIEW OF SOMERSBY CHURCH

NORFOLK AND THE CAMBRIDGE FENS

Water dominates this naturalist's paradise – reed-fringed broads, slow-moving rivers and silent marshes

From Holme, at the tip of The Wash, eastwards to Salthouse there are 25 miles of sand, shingle and salt-marsh where at high tide the sea sweeps unchecked across the flats and through the innumerable salt-marsh channels. At low tide the muddy creeks and lonely saltings shimmer in sunlight or merge into a grey mist with sea and sky. Space and distance seem magnified by the wide horizons and the great arch of the sky. The air of solitary stillness is intensified by the occasional call of a wader or wild duck. For the bird-watcher, there are few more rewarding places than this part of the North Norfolk coastline, host and home to more than 150 species, and much of it made into nature reserves.

East of Salthouse the coastline changes suddenly to long, sandy beaches backed by low cliffs – playgrounds for the holidaymakers at Sheringham and Cromer, and work places for the crab and lobster fishermen who haul their boats on to the open beaches. Behind the cliffs rises the thickly wooded Cromer Ridge.

Man and nature have been wrestling with the North Norfolk coastline for centuries. From Cromer west to Weybourne, the encroaching sea batters at some 8 miles of cliffs, protected at the resorts by concrete promenades or breakwaters. But westwards the land is gaining ground – captured by man from the sea's grasp behind sheltering sea-walls or dunes held fast by pines and marram grass. Some land has

been advanced by the sea itself, where sand and shingle moulded by wind and wave have formed long, curving spits that have caused silting of creeks and harbours.

The tranquil Norfolk Broads lie to the east of Norwich – about 30 calm, mostly shallow lakes fringed with reeds or willow and alder. They are linked by rivers, streams and dykes to form about 200 miles of navigable waterways, many screened by the surrounding landscape.

Most of the broads are freshwater lakes; the largest is Hickling Broad in the north-east. Research in the 1950s has shown that they are man-made, the result of digging for peat in late medieval times.

Typical Breckland scenery is open, sandy heath dotted with meres, brushwood and clumps of Scots pines – wild, mysterious country where the 'vanishing' meres appear and disappear with the fluctuations of the water-level in the underlying chalk.

Breckland 4,000 years ago was probably a vast oak forest, its light sandy soil easily cleared by Stone Age farmers, and rich in flint for making axe-heads. Grime's Graves, near Brandon, is one of the best-known flint mines used by primitive man. Through the centuries, 'brecks' or 'brakes' became the name for cultivated patches of land worked for a while and then abandoned as the soil became exhausted or times were bad. Grazing sheep prevented the growth of new seedlings, and with no tree roots to hold the soil, drifting sand became a hazard.

Heathland was once widespread in the Breckland's 300 sq. miles, shared between Norfolk and Suffolk. Today, although a few fringe areas remain, much of the land is forest again, not of native oak but of conifers planted by the Forestry Commission since 1922. Thetford Forest, covering 83 sq. miles, is the second largest in England.

THE SPACIOUS BROADS Hickling Broad is the largest of Norfolk's unique, shallow freshwater lakes, and although more than half a mile across, is nowhere more than 6 ft deep. Several rare birds, plants and butterflies live in its nature reserve.

Places to visit

Map ref. 1Eb   Bacton Wood

A short way south of the coastal village of Bacton stand the ruins of the 12th-century priory of Broomholm. Today deserted and forgotten, in medieval times it was a popular place of pilgrimage, for one of its relics was believed to be a piece of the true cross. In Chaucer's *Canterbury Tales*, the Reeve tells how the startled miller's wife screamed 'Holy cross of Bromeholme keep Us!'

The ruins stand within sight of the sea beside the B1150 road. South-west along the same road, barely 3 miles inland, lies Bacton Wood, tucked away in a pocket of land that dips into a shallow valley. Part of the Forestry Commission's scattered Wensum Forest, it is also known locally as Witton Wood. Some 30 kinds of trees grow here – old-established species such as sweet chestnut and birch, and others from Japan, northern Europe, Corsica and the north-west coast of America. The imported trees have replaced those felled during the Second World War, so that Bacton Wood is a relatively young forest, although the area was probably wooded in Saxon times.

From the small car park in a dell on the eastern edge of the woods, a 1½ mile forest trail leads first along a ridge and then into a valley. Rosebay willow-herb, gorse and young birch trees border the ridge, softly contrasting with the dark background of closely set conifers, which blot out the light on even the sunniest day. The scene changes on the valley slopes, splashed with many shades of green – the deep green of Scots pines, the light green of larches, the bronze-green of western red cedars and the blue-green of grand firs. Goldcrests and, in summer, warblers can be found in the larch woods, and blue tits are seen everywhere.

Bacton, or Witton, Wood lies about 2½ miles east of North Walsham on a minor road south from the B1150 to Honing.

1Dc   Blakeney Point

A vast spit of shingle and sand, Blakeney Point embraces the villages of Blakeney and Morston like a golden arm reaching across the horizon. Whether shimmering under blue skies or lying dully beneath lead-grey clouds, it has a compelling beauty that whets the appetite for a closer look. Local boatmen are happy to satisfy the curious, and there are regular trips to the Point from Blakeney quay and Morston during the summer.

Blakeney Point's 'spine' is a ridge of shingle running along its entire length on the seaward side. On the landward side there are sand-dunes, salt-marshes and mud-flats. Seals may be seen basking on the sandbanks, and there is also plenty of vegetation and other wildlife.

Marram grass and red fescue grass are common on the dunes, along with such flowering plants as sea bindweed, ragwort, scarlet pimpernel and yellow stonecrop. Two kinds of sea lavender grow on the salt-marshes – common sea lavender and lax-flowered sea lavender, recognisable by their small, blue-purple flowers. Sea asters, very like the garden michaelmas daisy, are also common; their lilac outer petals soon fall, leaving the bright yellow centre.

Because of its extreme northern position on the Norfolk coast, Blakeney makes a good landfall for migrating birds, particularly in autumn. Visitors include various warblers, wheatears, whinchats, bluethroats and pied flycatchers. Perhaps the most delightful visitors are the terns, distinguished from the black-headed gulls by their forked tails and long, swept-back wings that give them the appropriate alternative name of sea swallow.

About 1,435 acres of Blakeney Point are managed as a nature reserve by the National Trust. Part of the reserve can

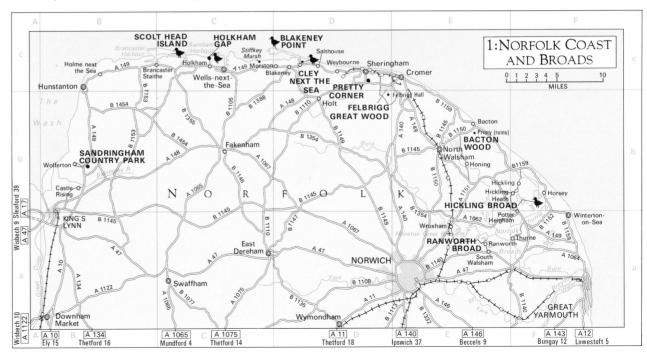

COCKLE HAVEN At Stiffkey Marshes between Wells-next-the-Sea and Blakeney, the sandflats are noted for their fine cockles, known as 'Stewky Blues'.

COASTAL REFUGE Cley Marshes are renowned for their rich and varied bird life, including many rare migrants seeking shelter in spring and autumn.

be reached on foot by following the shoreline westwards from Cley Beach Road car park.

Blakeney lies on the A149, 7 miles east of Wells-next-the-Sea.

1Dc Cley next the Sea

'Not far from the sea' would be a better description of the tiny village of Cley (pronounced 'Cly'), for just over half a mile of open marshland now lies between it and the sea. It was a busy port in medieval times, but the harbour was destroyed when marshland began to be reclaimed for pasture in the 17th century, and meadows now stretch where ships once rode at anchor. An 18th-century windmill (now a private house) stands on what was once a quay. But the magnificent 14th and 15th-century church and the narrow streets of flint houses still give the place something of a medieval air.

In 1926 some of the reclaimed marshes were acquired by the Norfolk Naturalists Trust and established as one of Britain's first nature reserves. Access is by permit only, available from the Warden at Cley.

From the road edging the marshes, there are views across the broad, flat landscape criss-crossed by dykes and dotted with pools and shallows. To the west the River Glaven bends sharply westwards to flow into the channels north of Blakeney. Cattle graze on the marshes in summer, but mostly they are the home of wildfowl and sea-birds. Many rare migrant birds appear each year, and bitterns, bearded reedlings, avocets and black-tailed godwits breed here.

At Salthouse, 2 miles east of Cley, a wide ditch runs close to the roadside, and several species of ducks and geese can be seen at close quarters. Greylag geese and Canada geese lead a parade of tufted ducks, coots, mallards and shelducks in search of tit-bits from passing motorists.

The marshland road at Cley, and another at Salthouse, leads to the shingle beach from where there are good views across the marshes and along the unbroken shoreline.

Cley and Salthouse are on the A149 Cromer–Wells-next-the-Sea road.

2Dc East Wretham Heath

On the eastern edge of Thetford Forest, the regimented rows of pine trees give way to natural woodland, scrub and heath. This is the true Breckland – wild, desolate and mysterious, its reed-fringed meres sometimes gleaming pools, sometimes only dry hollows in the turf.

Wildfowl make their home on the meres. Tufted ducks may be seen feeding in pairs or performing a graceful water ballet as they dive and surface again in perfect rhythm. They are often accompanied by pochards; the drakes can be recognised by their chestnut-red heads. Waders that visit the meres from time to time include common and green sandpipers, greenshanks and ruffs.

Several of the meres are within nature reserves. Ring Mere is on the west side of the A1075 between Thetford and East Wretham and a rough track across the heath a quarter of a mile north passes 150 yds south of Lang Mere, lying in a shallow bowl of emerald-green turf and rimmed with heather and clumps of hawthorn.

In spring and summer the short Breckland turf is flecked with flowers such as yellow and blue forget-me-nots, speedwell and thyme. Many of Breckland's wild flowers are rare in other parts of Britain, and some, like Spanish catchfly and field wormwood,

grow only in this part of East Anglia.

East Wretham Heath is 4 miles north-east of Thetford on the A1075. Visitors to the nature reserve can park near the Warden's Office.

1Dc Felbrigg Great Wood

Mostly natural woodland of sycamores, old beeches, sweet chestnuts, oaks, birches and rowan, Felbrigg Great Wood is part of the great belt of trees that extends along the Cromer Ridge. It is believed that there have been beechwoods on the site since the end of the last Ice Age, and that some of the ground has never been cultivated.

The wood adjoins Felbrigg Hall, a Jacobean mansion owned by the National Trust. The estate dates back to Norman times, and was owned by the Windham, or Wymondham, family from the 15th century until 1969. The present house was built between 1616 and 1627. William Windham I, who inherited the estate in 1665, extended the house and founded the Great Wood that shelters it from the North Sea, planting new trees to unify existing scattered woods into the 500 acre wood. His great-grandson, William Windham III, was an outstanding 18th-century politician who was Secretary at War in William Pitt's government from 1794 until 1801.

A waymarked walk of about a mile takes in much of the Great Wood, and includes a plantation of Douglas firs, Scots pines and Norway spruce, and

---

BARRIER BEACH Blakeney Point, a long spit of sand and shingle, today forms a barrier between the former port of Blakeney and the sea. Dunes shaped by waves and wind are stabilised by marram grass.

---

also a strip of heathland where silver birches and young beeches have been planted along the edge. Stoats may be glimpsed in the undergrowth of brambles and bracken, and there are red squirrels among the conifers. Great spotted woodpeckers, redstarts and nuthatches are also likely to be seen.

The lake, in another part of the grounds, is the home of herons, Canada geese, swans, coots and mallard, and there is a lakeside walk. The lake is fed by small streams spanned by three iron bridges, made by a blacksmith whose smithy and cottage are close by.

Felbrigg Great Wood is 2 miles south-west of Cromer off the A148. From this road, branch south-east on to the B1436. After ½ mile, a signposted west turn leads to Felbrigg Hall. The park is open from April to mid-October, 2–6 p.m. daily, except Mondays and Fridays.

1Fb Hickling Broad

A small sign at the Hickling Heath crossroads reads 'To the Broad' – a modest introduction to the largest and least spoiled of Norfolk's unique waterways. Indeed, this vast expanse of water can easily be missed by the motorist following the sign, for it is hidden behind trees and reed-beds, and comes into view only briefly at Hickling Staithe, where craft are moored at the quay by the Pleasure Boat Inn.

Like most of the broads, Hickling can be fully appreciated only from the water. Boats can be hired at the nearby boatyard, and a water-trail boat runs a 2½ hour, 4 mile trip on Tuesdays, Wednesdays and Thursdays during summer, visiting the most attractive and interesting parts of the broad.

The whole of Hickling Broad is part of a 1,400 acre nature reserve main-

PINE-FRINGED SHORE Holkham Flats stretch seawards from Holkham Gap, with evergreen shrubby seablite abundant above the high-tide line.

tained by the Norfolk Naturalists Trust, and there are wader pools where birds such as spotted redshanks, black terns and sometimes spoonbills can be seen. Among the reeds there are reed and sedge warblers, reed buntings and bearded reedlings – sometimes called reed pheasants because of their long tails and colouring. The broad is also a home of Britain's largest butterfly, the swallowtail, with a 3 in. wingspan.

Hickling Broad, 11 miles north-west of Great Yarmouth, is best approached by the A149. Follow the signposted road 1 mile north of Potter Heigham.

1Cc Holkham Gap

A vast, sweeping cove with a beach so flat it looks as though it has been rolled; grassy dunes of soft, golden sand; pine trees growing almost to the water's edge – yes, this is Norfolk, despite the Mediterranean flavour.

Holkham Gap is as beautiful and unspoiled as anywhere on the Norfolk coast, but its uncharacteristic scenery is not the work of nature alone. About 100 years ago, Corsican pines were planted among the dunes to stabilise the sand, and since 1967 it has been

Found only in the Norfolk Broads, the swallowtail has a 3 in. wingspan and is the largest and most spectacular of Britain's butterflies. It is on the wing in May and June, and sometimes in August. Milk parsley, the main food of its caterpillars, is rare outside the Norfolk fens and marshes. A tall plant that yields a watery white juice when young, milk parsley flowers from July to September.

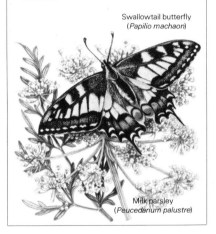

Swallowtail butterfly
(*Papilio machaon*)

Milk parsley
(*Peucedanum palustre*)

part of a nature reserve managed by the Nature Conservancy Council.

The reserve stretches for about 10 miles along the coast, except for a narrow strip at Wells. It is mainly dunes and salt-marshes, some reclaimed for agriculture, but at Holkham there is a driveway from the A149, Lady Ann's Drive, which leads to a point near the beach where a short walk brings the panorama of the cove into view.

At the seaward end of the drive there are evergreen holm oaks, introduced from the Mediterranean, and a few maritime and Monterey pines. In places the pines form a canopy, blotting out the light, and there are large numbers of fungi, a favourite food of the red squirrels which live in these woods. Beneath some of the pines grow creeping lady's tresses – rare plants in the southern half of Britain.

Marram grass and sand sedge are common on the dunes, and there are flowering plants such as common ragwort with its yellow, daisy-like flowers, sea bindweed, creeping thistle and sea holly.

Britain's smallest bird, the goldcrest, nests in the pines, which are also the home of most species of tits, particularly coal tits, blue tits and great tits. Colourful green woodpeckers and occasionally crossbills may also be seen.

Holkham lies on the A149, 1½ miles west of Wells-next-the-Sea.

1Dc   Pretty Corner

Nowhere in Norfolk is there a place more aptly named, and nowhere a place that so thoroughly dispels the widely held notion that Norfolk is flat and featureless. Little more than a mile from the beaches of Cromer and Sheringham, the land rises to a ridge running parallel to the coast and reaching a height of over 300 ft in places.

The ridge is thickly wooded with birch, beech, ash, rowan, pine and fir trees, below which is a tangled undergrowth of brambles and rhododendrons. Wild flowers grow in profusion, including primroses, foxgloves, dog violets and orchids, all thriving in the soft, peaty soil.

At Pretty Corner car park, signposted from the A148 that runs along the ridge, there are several paths leading into the woods. The scenery changes in character every few yards. From glades of gnarled beeches the ground may drop steeply among tall pines into a sunless dell ankle-deep in pine needles. Jays swoop among the trees, tits and finches flit among the lower branches, and squirrels – red and grey – scurry across the paths.

About a quarter of a mile west of the

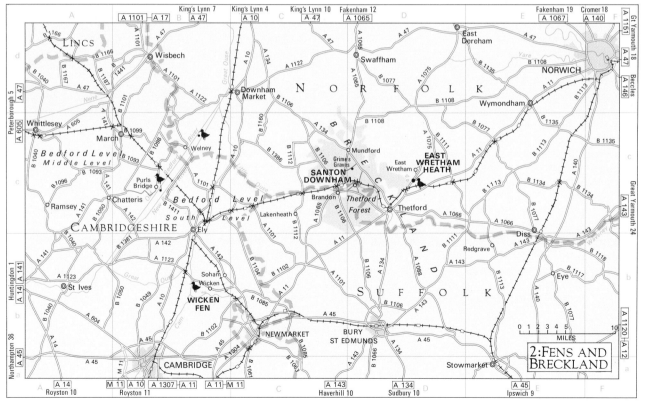

2:FENS AND BRECKLAND

car park, at the top of the hill on the A1082 out of Sheringham, a rough track that can be used by cars leads up into the woods. Side-roads branch off the track and make it possible to drive a considerable distance in all directions among the trees. Along the side-roads are vantage points that give magnificent views across the ridge and out to the North Sea.

About 2 miles east of Pretty Corner car park, a north turn off the A148 signposted 'West Runton' leads to the Roman Camp, another thickly wooded area from which there are splendid walks westwards over Beacon Hill and down to Row Heath and Beeston Regis Heath. The Roman Camp, owned by the National Trust, is the site of an Anglo-Saxon iron-working settlement. At 328 ft it is the highest point in Norfolk.

Pretty Corner lies 1½ miles south of Sheringham, to the east of the A1082 at its junction with the A148.

1Ea   Ranworth Broad

Between Wroxham and Thurne, the River Bure winds a serpentine course eastwards through the heart of Broadland, each twist and turn embracing stretches of marshland, meres and some of the smallest broads. Some, such as Hoveton Great Broad, have nature trails that can be reached only by boat. At Ranworth is the Broadland Conservation Centre – a small area in which all types of typical Broadland vegetation and wildlife can be found. It was established by the Norfolk Naturalists Trust in 1976.

Ranworth Broad nature trail leads through woodland before turning sharply to cross the marshes, where dense shrubs and the smell of rotting

vegetation give an impression of the tropics. The trail here is across raised duck-boards that span the black, almost liquid mud, said to be 30 ft deep beneath its deceptive covering of bog mosses and marsh plants. Later the scene changes to reed-beds, and the trail ends at the water's edge near the Conservation Centre building, a thatched structure floating on a pontoon moored between Ranworth and Malthouse broads.

A permanent exhibition on the ground floor illustrates the natural life of the broads, and above is a viewing gallery with a telescope and binoculars provided. Many kinds of birds can be watched through the windows. Diving ducks, common terns, coots and black-headed gulls approach within a few yards, and often a heron descends on slow-beating wings to land among the reeds close by – there are more herons in Norfolk than in any other English county. The elegant great crested grebe can be seen as it dives for food, and there is always a chance of seeing a rare migrant such as an osprey.

Ranworth is 9 miles north-east of Norwich and lies along a signposted road from the B1140 at South Walsham. The entrance to the Conservation Centre is along the lane leading north past the church, but cars must be parked in the car park opposite the staithe, or quay.

1Bb Sandringham Country Park

The best time to visit Sandringham Country Park is in early summer, when woods and roadsides are swamped with the rich purples, blues and crimsons of rhododendrons in bloom. They pile up in great masses of colour among the pines, cedars and silver birches, almost overpowering in their splendour and

compelling the eye at every turn of the road. There are footpaths through the woods, dipping into steep-banked glens where the rhododendrons cluster 20 ft above and brightly coloured jays swoop among the tree-tops.

Sandringham Country Park is part of the 7,000 acre Sandringham estate, bought by Edward VII when he was Prince of Wales, and since then a favourite royal retreat.

From the large, red-brick house and its grounds the estate spreads westwards in a green apron of well-kept woodland and trim lawns, and the Country Park lies east of the A149, an area of natural woodland and heath which few places can surpass in loveliness.

ETHELDREDA'S ELY

ELY CATHEDRAL has dominated the flat fen country that surrounds it for some 1,300 years, and can be seen for miles around. Ely began as a religious community founded by St Etheldreda, the daughter of a king of the East Angles, who built an abbey there about AD 670. The cathedral was built 400 years later, but its famous octagonal lantern tower, with angle posts carved from 60 ft oak trees, dates from the 14th century.

For most of its history, the 68 ft high mound of Ely was an island surrounded by mile upon mile of swamp and fen, and known as 'Eel Island' because of the abundance of eels. It made an ideal hide-out for Hereward the Wake, the Anglo-Saxon patriot who led resistance to William the Conqueror until 1071.

Ely's marshes were drained in the 17th century, leaving a flat and curious landscape of fertile black-earthed fields and rivers banked higher than the roads. The best time to approach Ely is in an autumn twilight, when the mists are rising and the cathedral is silhouetted against a coppery haze. Then, for an hour, it becomes again the Ely of Hereward and Etheldreda.

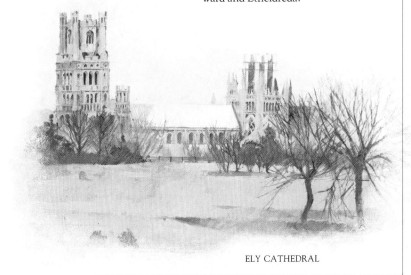

ELY CATHEDRAL

A HAVEN FOR BIRDS AND BIRD-WATCHERS

Farmland and fens, heaths and broads, coastal dunes and mud-flats, make Norfolk a happy hunting-ground for many kinds of birds. The coast is also a refuge on the route of migrants from the north flying to warmer climates in autumn and returning in spring.

Two migrant waders from the northern tundra are the knot and the bar-tailed godwit, which gather in large flocks. Their full, red-breasted, summer plumage is never seen in Britain.

Birds that breed in Norfolk include the fen-dwelling garganey, the night-feeding stone curlew of arable fields, the sand martin, which burrows in sandbanks, and the little tern, which nests in sand or shingle. All winter abroad. The crossbill, a pine-cone feeder of conifer forests, stays all year.

Sand martin
(*Riparia riparia*)

Knot
(*Calidris canutus*)

Little tern
(*Sterna albifrons*)

Crossbill
(*Loxia curvirostra*)

Stone curlew
(*Burhinus oedicnemus*)

Bar-tailed godwit
(*Limosa lapponica*)

Garganey
(*Anas querquedula*)

To the west of the Park lies the village of Wolferton. Its Edwardian railway station was once used by the royal family on their visits to Sandringham, and is now preserved as a railway museum. About 2 miles south of the Park is Castle Rising. It was a port on the Babingley river until the 15th century, when ships became too large to navigate the river. Later, the river silted up and the sea retreated. As a result, the trade went to King's Lynn.

The village is dominated by the Norman castle, built in 1150 by William de Albini. According to legend, the ghostly screams of Queen Isabella echo through the keep where she was banished by her son, Edward III, after her part in the murder of her husband, Edward II. Beyond Wolferton and Castle Rising, reclaimed marshes stretch to the shores of The Wash.

Sandringham Country Park is 6 miles north-east of King's Lynn, to the east of the A149.

2Dc Santon Downham

In 1668 wind-blown sand from the surrounding Breckland wastes swept through the village of Santon Downham, swamping houses and temporarily blocking the Little Ouse river. John Evelyn, the diarist, who visited the area nine years later, described the event as: 'Travelling sands, about ten miles wide and like the sands in the deserts of Libya.'

Today tree roots anchor the light sandy soil, and Santon Downham stands at the heart of Thetford Forest. A pleasant, varied forest trail leads from the Forestry Commission Information Centre, where there is a large car park. Much of the forest is coniferous, with Scots and Corsican pines and Douglas firs planted for commercial use, but there are also oaks, sycamores, beeches, birches, and at one point an avenue of 100-year-old limes. Roe deer live in the forest, shy creatures that stay in the dense undergrowth of snowberry unless disturbed.

If riverside walks are to your liking, there are few to compare with a gentle stroll downstream along the banks of the Little Ouse. It flows through a shallow valley, and steps lead down to the riverside from the far side of the road bridge about 200 yds from the car park. Alders, birches and willows fringe this peaceful stream, which here forms the boundary between Suffolk and Norfolk. The river is crystal clear, with long, trailing weeds on the river-bed combed out like tresses by the slow-moving waters. At the sandy water's edge, wagtails live up to their name with a flicker of white tail feathers, and swallows skim between the banks to scoop up gnats and midges.

A white-painted foot-bridge, arching across the river like a bow, adds tranquillity to the scene. It leads to a footpath on the south bank that links up with the forest trail, which can then be followed back to the car park. There is also a car park and picnic site, St Helen's, on the north bank only a short distance from the river and foot-bridge. Go north-east out of the village, cross the road bridge and after 300 yds turn right just before the level-crossing. St Helen's car park is about three-quarters of a mile along this road.

Santon Downham lies 4 miles north-west of Thetford. It can be reached by three unclassified roads, one from the A134 Thetford–Mundford road 3 miles south-east of Mundford, and the other two from the B1107 Thetford–Brandon road, 1 mile and 2½ miles east of Brandon.

THE WATERY WILDERNESS OF WICKEN FEN

WILD AND LONELY Wicken Fen is one of the few areas of undrained fenland left in Britain – just over 1 sq. mile of the treacherous marshland that once covered some 15,000 sq. miles of East Anglia.

The Romans were the first to try draining the fens, but it was the Dutch engineer Vermuyden who devised a workable drainage scheme in the 17th century. Employed by the 4th Earl of Bedford, Vermuyden dug the Old Bedford River and the New Bedford River, and made a large area of fenland fit for pasture. In the 18th century the landscape was dotted with windmills driving huge pumps, but in time they gave way to the steam-engine, then to today's diesel and electric pumps.

One windmill is still at work in Wicken Fen. Today, however, it is pumping not to drain the fen but to bring water in to keep it a wetland, for the fen is now a nature reserve maintained by the National Trust.

Before the fen became a reserve, it was strip-farmed for sedge and peat by local villagers; they used the sedge for thatching, kindling and animal litter, and the peat for fuel. When this work was abandoned and the surrounding water-level had fallen, scrub began to choke the sedge-beds. Now that much of it has been cleared and the water-level raised, the fen is once again rich in sedge, and supports many kinds of plant and animal life.

Footpaths across the fen start from the National Trust building near to Wicken Lode, one of the old man-made waterways that controlled the water-level and were used as barge roads to fen villages. A walk of about 2 miles gives an opportunity to see many different birds, plants and butterflies, and to take in the tranquil and timeless feeling of the fens.

Wicken Fen is 9 miles north-east of Cambridge, and is signposted from Wicken village on the A1123. There are two other fenland nature reserves. The Wildfowl Trust has a refuge at Welney on the Ouse Washes, a strip of land between the canals known as the Old and New Bedford rivers; waders, ducks, swans and geese can be watched from the fine observatory. The Royal Society for the Protection of Birds also has a reserve on the Ouse Washes at Purls Bridge on the Old Bedford River.

WETLAND RELIC MUCH OF EAST ANGLIA WAS ONCE LIKE WICKEN FEN, THE HAUNT OF WILDFOWL AND MANY UNCOMMON BIRDS AND BUTTERFLIES.

1Cc   Scolt Head Island

Only a narrow tidal creek separates this wild and lonely island from the Norfolk mainland, a creek that winds among salt-marshes where countless tiny channels spread like veins across the desolate mud-flats. The island stretches for 3½ miles from Brancaster Harbour to Burnham Harbour, its sand-dunes, shingle banks, marshes and salt-marshes forming an isolated segment typical of the whole North Norfolk coastline.

Owned jointly by the National Trust and the Norfolk Naturalists Trust, the island is managed by the Nature Conservancy Council whose aim is to ensure that natural development continues with the least possible human interference. Visitors to the island are invited to use a nature trail about three-quarters of a mile long, which takes in some of the most interesting and scenic areas, and gives an opportunity to see the rich variety of plant and wildlife. Boats to the island leave from Brancaster Staithe an hour or two before and after high water.

Near the island landing point is the ternery, where 4 acres of shingle and sand are a breeding ground for common terns and Sandwich terns. Further along the trail, marshland vegetation includes sea asters, sea lavender and sea pinks, bright with flowers in summer. Waders such as oystercatchers, ringed plovers and redshanks can all be seen. There are many shelducks, recognised by their chestnut belts, which often nest in deserted rabbit burrows. The many moths and butterflies include the hummingbird hawk moth, and the sand dart and rosy minor moths.

Brancaster Staithe is on the A149, 7 miles west of Wells-next-the-Sea.

─ INVASION AND SETTLEMENT ─

ANGLE, SAXON, JUTE, DANE, VIKING, NORMAN – OUT OF THESE A NATION CALLED ENGLAND WAS FORGED

THE MOST IMPORTANT DOCUMENT to have survived from the millennium between the withdrawal of the Romans from Britain and the founding of the Tudor dynasty is Domesday Book, compiled at the command of William the Conqueror in 1086. In conception, Domesday Book was a taxation survey. But from its pages, the geography of England in 1086, in all its diversity, can be reconstructed. The great survey was an instrument of the Norman Conquest, a gathering of facts about the economy of the greater part of England.

However incomplete and obscure its information may be, Domesday Book provides a fascinating glimpse of the effects of centuries of Anglo-Saxon and Scandinavian invasion and settlement. It is now known that Anglo-Saxon mercenary soldiers came to Britain during the last half century of Roman rule. They were followed by hordes of Anglo-Saxon migrants, farmers little inclined to the urban way of life, who settled eastern and southern England in the 5th and 6th centuries AD. These cores of settlement developed into a number of independent kingdoms, some of which are still remembered in county names. Sussex is the territory of the South Saxons, while Norfolk and Suffolk recall the settlements of the 'north folk' and the 'south folk' who were Angles by origin from the southern part of the Jutland peninsula.

The sea-wolves gather

The Danes came to Britain as plundering armies in the closing decades of the 9th century, and remained as settlers in the Vale of York, across Lincolnshire and Leicestershire, and in East Anglia. A few years later, Viking colonists from Norway's fjords and from bases in Orkney infiltrated the Lake District and west Lancashire.

Domesday Book looks back across these centuries of foreign invasion and settlement, centuries that all but obliterated the memories of Roman Britain in the lowland south and east. The information is arranged under the headings of the shires, and all the counties are there except Rutland and Lancashire, and those in the north that in 1086 had not yet succumbed to the Norman conqueror – Northumberland, Durham, Cumberland and Westmorland. A glimpse of the size of England's population may be gleaned from the old folios. More than 13,000 places are recorded and the population is assessed at 275,000, though it is important to remember that the surveyors counted only heads of families. There are many other omissions – London, for instance, whose population probably amounted to about 10,000. All in all, it would seem that England might have contained some 1½ million people.

The surviving evidence of the centuries before the Norman Conquest is fragmentary. A few churches, at Deerhurst in Gloucestershire and at Earls Barton and Brixworth in Northamptonshire, for example, have miraculously survived with their pre-Conquest architecture largely intact. In the landscape, however, the Saxon and Viking legacies are less evident, though the sound of those distant centuries can be heard through thousands of place-names. Those whose names contain 'ing', such as Hastings, Ealing or Barking, probably date their beginnings to the 5th century AD. In Lincolnshire and Leicestershire, the scores of villages and hamlets whose names end in 'by' were born at the time of the Danish settlement in the years about AD 900. And in the same period, Viking farmers carved out tiny fields among the boulders of the Lake District. Today, these pioneer settlements are remembered in place-names ending in 'thwaite', meaning 'a clearing'.

The three centuries after the Norman Conquest stand out as a time of growth, both in prosperity and population. By 1300 it has been estimated that the population of England rose to 4½ million, most strikingly reflected in the growth of towns. By the middle of the 14th century the four richest towns in the country were London, Bristol, York and Newcastle upon Tyne, the last being one of the 240 new boroughs and urban settlements that were created in England and Wales between 1066 and 1334. Many of the new towns were ports, such as Harwich, Liverpool and Hull, while others, like Peterborough and Burton upon Trent, rose at the gates of monasteries. But not all the new towns of the Middle Ages were successful; in fact, 23 per cent failed. Some, like Mitchell in Cornwall, are today remembered only in the name of a farm.

In the countryside, the years after the Conquest saw a vastly increased use of building stone for castles, monasteries, new cathedrals and parish churches. In areas where good stone is plentiful, it is still possible to find medieval quarries. From Barnack, near Peterborough, the pale grey limestone was extracted for the great abbeys of eastern England – Bury St Edmunds, Ramsey, Crowland and Peterborough. Today, the Barnack quarries, a maze of grassy holes and hummocks, reveal the source of stone for so many Fenland splendours.

The wilderness retreats

The rise of population in the years up to the middle of the 14th century is apparent not only in the new towns but also in the creation of new arable lands on the edge of long-established villages. Woodlands were cleared and marshes drained for pasture and planting; at Witney in Oxfordshire, for instance, 1,000 acres of woodland were cleared in the early years of the 13th century. Medieval marshland drainage was even more spectacular along the shores of the Humber and in the Somerset Levels. Monasteries played an important part in this new expansion. In Lincolnshire, however, the frontier of farmland was pushed ever seaward by the building of dykes that were often the co-operative undertakings of several villages.

In other parts of England, the picture was very different. The Normans brought their forest laws with them, under which vast tracts of land were set aside as royal hunting preserves. The laws curtailed many old rights of farming, timber-cutting, feeding of livestock and access to game within the preserves, but since they found almost as little favour with the barons as with the peasantry, neither the laws nor their horrendous penalties were as stringently enforced as legend would have it. Nevertheless, the breaking of new ground for arable land was strictly forbidden, and even today the 92,000 acres of the New Forest stand as a unique memorial of Norman England.

Wool and the plague

The later Middle Ages – say from the middle of the 14th century onwards – is generally regarded as a period of decline, or at least of radical change. After 1368 no new towns were founded and many of the earlier boroughs failed. A major cause, of course, was the Black Death, which raged through the country between 1348 and 1350, and carried off perhaps one-third of the population. But the most striking change in the landscape was the desertion of the villages, more than 2,000 in all. In Leicestershire alone 70 villages were abandoned, while in Lincolnshire over 200 lost village sites have been identified. The desertions, which reached their peak in the 15th century, were created by the rise in the demand for wool both for export and for cloth. Arable open fields were converted into pasture and the peasantry were driven on to the roads. The 'green platforms' – the foundations of our deserted villages – are silent reminders of the half a million acres that were enclosed for sheep.

The 14th-century tithe barn at Abbotsbury, Dorset, bears witness to the enormous influence of the Church in the economy of medieval England. The barn's 272 ft length was built to accommodate a tenth – or tithe – of all local produce, exacted to contribute to the upkeep of a Benedictine abbey. The abbey has long vanished, but the barn remains, as do many similar ones up and down the country, to testify to the wealth of the pre-Reformation Church.

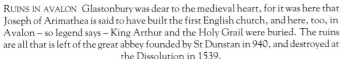

RUINS IN AVALON Glastonbury was dear to the medieval heart, for it was here that Joseph of Arimathea is said to have built the first English church, and here, too, in Avalon – so legend says – King Arthur and the Holy Grail were buried. The ruins are all that is left of the great abbey founded by St Dunstan in 940, and destroyed at the Dissolution in 1539.

WALES DEFINED Offa, Saxon king of Mercia, ordered this great earthwork to be dug in the 8th century to separate his kingdom – most of central England – from Wales. A few gaps excepted, the rampart and ditch of the dyke runs continuously for nearly 170 miles between the rivers Severn and Dee.

RENEGADE'S EYRIE By the end of the Middle Ages, many strategic sites in Britain were crowned with castles, often incorporating fortifications of prehistory. Such was the case with Castell Dinas Bran, built in 1236 on a lofty crag above Llangollen to command the Dee. Its builder, Gruffydd ap Madoc, sided with Henry III against his own countrymen.

THE MALVERN HILLS

A backbone of ancient volcanic rocks, set among
rich pastures, hop-gardens and cider-orchards

Though as English as the composer Elgar, who drew much of his musical inspiration from them, the Malverns are the last encroachment of ancient Welsh rock into England. The bare, sheep-grazed slopes overlook richly wooded foothills, ancient towns with half-timbered black-and-white houses, and gracious spas to which wealthy Victorians flocked for the 'water cure'. Superb and far-reaching views from the solitary summits extend westwards to the Welsh mountains and eastwards across the orchards of Evesham.

From Great Malvern the hills stretch 8 miles southwards in a narrow ridge that until 1974 formed the border between Herefordshire and Worcestershire. They rise steeply and suddenly from the eastern Severn vale, but dip more gently to the rolling fields and orchards around Hereford. There are six major summits, the northern Worcestershire Beacon (1,395 ft) being the highest. Besides Great Malvern there are four other Malverns strung out through the hills – Malvern Link, Malvern Wells, West Malvern and Little Malvern.

The rocks that form the spine of the hills are at least 600 million years old, thrust up through a fault in the earth's surface under tremendous pressure, perhaps volcanic action, some 300 million years ago. Older than the rocks of the Welsh mountains, they compare in age with the ancient rocks of north-west Scotland. The hard, crystalline Malvern

rock has been quarried for roadstone during recent years.

Malvern is a name of Celtic origin, derived from *moel* (bald) and probably *bryn* (hill). In prehistoric times the bare summits were good defensive points, and Herefordshire Beacon (1,115 ft) near Little Malvern served Iron Age Celts as a natural fortress. It overlooks a pass through the hills along a natural fault that now carries the A449. The ramparts of the 32 acre hill-fort, called British Camp, can still be seen; it dates back more than 2,000 years.

During the Middle Ages, the Malvern summits were an island in a wilderness of wood and heath that was an 8,000 acre royal forest. In the 13th century Edward I gave it to his son-in-law, the Earl of Gloucester – red-headed Gilbert de Clare – as a dowry. The Red Earl and his deer shared the chase with Benedictine monks from the priories of Great and Little Malvern, dissolved in 1541. Only the priory churches remain today. Great Malvern Priory was said to have been founded in 1085 on the site of the chapel of the Saxon St Wersten, martyred by the Danes. William Langland, thought to be the author of the 14th-century poem *The Vision of Piers Plowman*, was probably taught by the Malvern monks. 'In a May morning on Malvern Hills,' he wrote, 'A strange thing befell me, a fairy vision methought . . .'

Malvern probably owes its pure spring water to its hard rocks, from which rainwater dissolves very few deposits. The medieval monks used water from Holy Well and St Ann's Well as curatives. The water was bottled and sold, as it still is today at Colwall Stone, in the 18th century. It was not until 1842 that two doctors, James Wilson and James Gully, set up England's first hydrotherapy establishment at Malvern, and it became a fashionable Victorian and Edwardian spa.

ENGLAND'S HEARTLAND Worcestershire Beacon, the highest point in the Malverns, gives views across 15 counties in clear weather. North-west across the wooded and fertile Hereford farmland are the low-lying Suckley Hills, with Shropshire in the blue haze beyond.

Places to visit

Map ref. Ba Broad Down and Castlemorton Common

Below Herefordshire Beacon the Malvern Hills become gentler, and Broad Down immediately to the south-east is, as its name implies, a wide round hill with steep woods owned by the National Trust. There is a 19th-century reservoir at its northern edge, from which Turkey oaks, sweet chestnuts and rowan trees have spread uphill. Nightjars and rare red-backed shrikes were once known to nest here, but have not been recorded since 1969.

On the western side of Broad Down is a small man-made cave cut from the basalt rock called Giant's or Clutter's Cave. It is said that the cave was once occupied by a hermit. Legend also links it with the Welsh prince Owain Glyndwr, who hid in it after fleeing from a battle against the English on Herefordshire Beacon in about 1405. Another story claims that the fugitive Lollard leader, Sir John Oldcastle, sheltered here after plotting against Henry V. Once a boon companion of the king, Sir John was the model for Shakespeare's Falstaff in *Henry IV*. It is more likely that the small hollow — conveniently close to the ancient spring of Walm's Well — was probably carved out as a shelter by one of the

lonely medieval shepherds or swineherds who had to spend weeks on the hills.

East of Broad Down, on the edge of the Severn plain below the Malvern escarpment, is Castlemorton Common. It is one of the many areas of common land in the Malverns saved from enclosure at the turn of the 18th and beginning of the 19th centuries by the stubborn, sometimes riotous, resistance of local people. So valuable are Castlemorton's 600 acres of ancient and unimproved rough-grazing land that 200 acres have been designated by the Nature Conservancy as a Site of Special Scientific Interest.

Marshy, with streams and patches of gorse, Castlemorton Common supports at least 200 species of plants, including marsh marigolds, cowslips, harebells, marsh pennywort, ivy-leaved crowfoot, devil's-bit scabious and ragged-robin. It is well known for fungi, with almost 100 recorded species, and for the 60 pollarded native black poplars which are now rare in Britain.

Yellowhammers, linnets and stonechats flit through the gorse wilderness of Castlemorton, and even the sheep and cattle that graze unfenced along the single minor road that crosses the common have about them a rangy, untamed look.

Broad Down is ½ mile south of Little Malvern on the A449. Castlemorton Common lies south of the A4104 between Little Malvern and Welland.

Ac Bromyard Downs

Bromyard, a small market town 10 miles north-west of Malvern, was recorded in the Domesday Book of 1086 as one of the most important towns in the country, but now it slumbers contentedly among apple orchards and hopfields. Its street pattern remains medieval, and it has several fine black-and-white half-timbered houses.

Above the town to the east are Bromyard Downs, steep sheep-grazed common land with clear views westwards to Wales and south-east to the Malverns. Delicate blue harebells grow there in summer, particularly on the crest of the Downs in Warren Wood, which is owned by the National Trust.

Deep in the heart of a secluded valley on the other side of the Downs is Lower Brockhampton Hall, one of the most perfect medieval manor houses in England. Built in about 1400 for a local squire, it has survived almost untouched, complete with silvery half-timbering, a gatehouse dating from the late 15th century and a moat fringed with pink-flowered water mint. It is also owned by the National Trust.

Near by, in Brockhampton Park, is a nature trail of just over a mile which winds through one of Britain's finest mature oakwoods, planted about 200 years ago and rich in bird and plant life, as well as by ancient yews that are relics of the native woodland. There are fragrant larch and beech plantations, and stands of ash trees grown to make tennis-rackets. Lichens, which grow only where the air is unpolluted, flourish here. In limy soils near the stream grow dog's mercury, yellow archangel and enchanter's nightshade. Around the lakes in summer, noctule bats emerge at dusk: alder wood wasps and dragonflies thrive here and the yellow-and-brown speckled wood butterfly breeds on woodland grasses. Tits, willow warblers and woodpeckers nest in the woods, and sometimes ravens can be seen.

The Downs, Warren Wood and Lower Brockhampton lie just north of the A44, 1 or 2 miles east of Bromyard. About ½ mile further along the A44, opposite Bringsty Post Office, the Woodland Walk in Brockhampton Park is signposted.

Ba Chase End Hill

This is not only the southern tip of the Malvern Hills and the chase, or hunting territory, it also marks the last spot where the Cambrian rocks of Wales appear in England. An Ordnance Survey triangulation stone stands like an isolated full stop on the bare summit of this beautiful bracken-covered hill. To the north the Malverns look like sleep-

ing hounds, hunched against each other for warmth; to the west lie the blue hills of Wales. But south and east a pageant of plump and fruitful fields stretches across the Severn plain to the golden Cotswolds and the Vale of Evesham.

Yet Chase End Hill and the hamlet of Whiteleaved Oak at its foot form one of the most wild and romantic parts of the Malverns. A buzzard, wing-tips curved and spread, can sometimes be seen circling the summit. Here grows the wild daffodil, heather, bracken and purple rosebay willowherb with sudden creamy-yellow spires of toadflax. Slender trefoil, wild mignonette and harebells flourish. In autumn there is a bounty of hazelnuts and elderberries, and a tangle of blackberries. Woodpeckers, skylarks, pipits and warblers sing in its woodlands and over its windy summit, and it is known for its butterflies. The quaintly named dingy and grizzled skippers, green hair-streak and marbled white species have been recorded here.

The tiny hamlet of Whiteleaved Oak, tucked into the narrow lonely pass between the hills of Raggedstone and Chase End, is believed to have acquired its name from a variegated oak which once grew there. Sheltered in a green bowl of the wooded and bracken-covered hillsides, the perfect half-timbered cottages of this secluded place seem to belong to a past century. One has a small vineyard, others working wells. Sheep wander over a tiny green and grassy verges. Just beside the post-box was the meeting place of the old boundaries of the three counties of Herefordshire, Worcestershire and Gloucestershire.

Chase End Hill lies 1 mile south of the A438, 2 miles east of Eastnor.

Bb Herefordshire Beacon

On Herefordshire Beacon stands one of the finest earthworks in Britain, a 32 acre fortified settlement built 1,115 ft above sea-level on this windy summit. The earliest structure dates from about the 3rd century BC. It is reached from the busy hub of the Malvern ridge walk, a car park opposite the Malvern Hills Hotel on the A449. British Camp, as the hill-fort is called, is well marked. Almost too well: so many walkers climb up to it that the Malvern Hill Conservators, who look after the hills, have been obliged to build tarmac paths. Yet the fortification itself, once reached, is so immense, so indifferent to the tramp of human beings upon it,

that it entirely retains its quality of endurance and mysterious pre-history.

It stretches away along the ridge to the south. Its broad level centre is the earliest part, surrounded by a bank and ditch – the ramparts were drystone walled. It is thought that in the 12th century a castle keep was built within this flat summit, and according to legend Owain Glyndwr, prince of Wales, made an unsuccessful attempt to defeat the English somewhere in the vicinity early in the 15th century.

From the centre of the fort the successive banks and ditches, built at later dates, widen like ripples in the great grassy hill. There are several entrances, and an ancient track climbing up from the west. One of a line of such forts extending from the Dorset coast into northern Wales, British Camp is one of the largest and most impressive. Tradition says that the British chief Caractacus made his last, but unsuccessful, stand against the invading Roman army here.

The views from Herefordshire Beacon are magnificent, and in its grasslands grow wild mignonette and harebells, with heather on its southern slopes. Yet the past is most important here. Archaeologists suggest that 1,500 to 2,000 people may once have lived here, although it is strange that there is no natural water supply inside the fort's defensive ramparts. John Masefield, born 3½ miles away in Ledbury, wrote after a childhood visit:

'People there had made the earth their father and protection; and the earth remembered that, and they, as parts of the memory of the earth, could still impress and terrify. Often they have terrified me.'

Herefordshire Beacon is ¼ mile south of the A449 just west of Little Malvern.

Ba Ledbury

Just 7 miles south-west of Malvern, in one of the most fruitful corners of the old county of Herefordshire, is the beautiful and unspoiled little market town of Ledbury. For centuries Ledbury has flourished on the hops, fruit and red-and-white Hereford cattle that have been bred here since the 17th century, and its comfortable citizens have bequeathed it a wealth of black-and-white half-timbered houses. There is a 17th-century market cross supported on 16 chestnut pillars, a cobbled lane with overhanging gables, almshouses and many Elizabethan buildings.

From Ledbury there are several walks. Cobbled Church Lane leads to the charming little woodland of Doghill, and the path continues across a lane up to Frith Wood. A mixed broadleaved woodland on a steep west-facing hillside, Frith Wood is owned by the Forestry Commission. Along its paths and grassy rides are many wild flowers, including the rare violet helleborine and herb paris. It is a good place to see moths and butterflies, including the alder kitten moth.

North of Frith Wood an unmarked path leads across Wellington Heath, east of the village of the same name. The path continues past rising woodland to Oyster Hill, a bare summit giving fine views. Below Oyster Hill is Hope End, the childhood home of the 19th-century poet Elizabeth Barrett Browning. She lived there for about 20 years and wrote lovingly of its beautiful and secluded valley:

'Dappled very close with shade,
Summer-snow of apple-blossoms,
    running up from glade to glade.'

Only the stables – now a hotel – sur-

ANCIENT STRONGHOLD British Camp on Herefordshire Beacon was built over 2,000 years ago by Iron Age Celts.

vive, and still have the minarets that were part of the oriental design of Hope End when it was built in 1809.

East of Frith Wood, across a lane, is the low rise of Kilbury Camp. Not easy to spot but easily reached across a field, it is a thistly coppice of ancient crab-apple and thorn trees, and on its wild little summit the earthworks are clearly visible. From here the hill-fort on Herefordshire Beacon to the east looks startlingly close.

Also within easy walking distance from Ledbury itself, off the Tewkesbury road just past the church, is the beginning of Coneygree Wood – the name probably comes from Coney Garth, meaning rabbit warren. In medieval times rabbits cost almost as much as pigs and were carefully protected by landowners to provide an additional source of meat. Coneygree Wood is natural woodland, with small quarries in which many fossils have been found.

Ledbury is on the A449, at the junction with the A438 and A417. Frith Wood is north of the town, and Kilbury Camp 1 mile north of it.

Bc Leigh Brook

The northern foothills of the Malverns that drop to the valley of the River Teme and its tributary, the Leigh Brook, are wild, wooded and remote. Although the towns of the Malverns are only a few miles away, they are

concealed beyond the lofty summits.

Leigh Brook winds through a secluded valley of which 60 acres are managed as a nature reserve by the Worcestershire Nature Conservation Trust. The Knapp and Papermill Nature Reserve is reached by way of a cottage garden where a meandering lane crosses the brook. Dippers and kingfishers nest along the banks. Further on are old coppiced woodlands and permanent meadows where wild daffodils and early purple orchids grow.

Rising from the valley of the Leigh Brook to the 670 ft peak called The Beck is Old Storridge Common, where ancient tracks – paved in places – lead up through birch woodland, ash trees, oaks and bracken. Here the low evening sun turns the dark slopes into a strangely foreign world: looking back on the climb, the rosebay willowherb is turned to purple fire, and there is neither roof nor chimney-pot visible anywhere.

Local legend says that St Augustine once conferred with the Celtic clergy from Wales on the sparsely wooded cone of The Beck. In Anglo-Saxon times, the spot was called Augustine's Oak. It is a superb viewpoint with unparalleled views of Wales from its summit.

Beyond The Beck is the hamlet of Birch Wood, where the English composer Sir Edward Elgar spent the summer of 1900 and wrote the oratorio *The Dream of Gerontius*. He wrote then: 'I don't like to say a word about these woods for fear you should feel envious, but it is godlike in the shade with the snakes and other cool creatures.'

Snakes do abound here, particularly the grass snake, and Old Storridge Common is noted for bees and butterflies, including the dark green fritillary, the holly blue and the grizzled skipper.

The Leigh Brook valley lies 6 miles west of Worcester, north of the A4103. The nature reserve is 1 mile south of Alfrick, which lies on minor roads between the A4103 and A44.

Ba Midsummer and Hollybush Hills

The southern summits of the Malverns are lower and more densely wooded than those to the north. Here on the twin peaks of Midsummer and Hollybush hills the men of the Iron Age built a great defensive settlement in about 400 BC. Owned by the National Trust, the hill-fort can be reached either along the Malvern ridge or up a long track from Hollybush Pass below, where the A438 curves over the hills from east to west. It is not easy to see from below, but the track turns into a sharp twist of footpath at the top of the ridge and emerges through woodland to the bare turfed summit.

Excavations were made at Midsummer Hill between 1965 and 1970, and revealed pottery and metalwork linking it with a similar massive hill-fort on Bredon Hill, northern outpost of the Cotswolds. Drystone faced ramparts and 17 timber gateways enclosed some 19 acres, including both Midsummer and Hollybush summits. Within the walls is a natural spring and evidence of

---

GRASSLAND SONGSTER

Skylarks are common throughout Britain in open grassland, fields, moors and sand-dunes. They sing regularly from February until July, warbling melodiously for three minutes or more as they fly upwards almost out of sight, and continuing as they hover and descend. The birds usually migrate south in winter.

Skylark
(*Alauda arvensis*)

WOODED SOUTHERN SUMMITS Around Hollybush, the gentler face of the Malverns appears. The view northwards to the more rugged northern ridge emphasises the contrast. Holly trees once grew here profusely.

133

some 250 hut sites: it is believed that as many as 1,500 people lived here before the Romans invaded in about AD 55.

Dusk is a ghostly time here because of the pale green lights of the glow-worms that inhabit the grassy slopes. Midsummer Hill is one of the few places where this dwindling species of beetle can still be found.

Just to the south of the hamlet of Hollybush is a deep ditch and bank, part of the Shire Ditch which runs from north to south along the Malvern ridge. It was built by Gilbert de Clare, red-headed Earl of Gloucester and the owner of Malvern Chase, in the 13th century. After a violent dispute with the Bishop of Hereford about where their common boundary lay, the line was finally agreed. The Red Earl is said to have so constructed the ditch and fence that although the bishop's deer could easily jump downhill on to his land they could not leap back uphill on to the bishop's side.

Midsummer and Hollybush hills lie north of the A438 at Hollybush, 9 miles north-west of Tewkesbury.

Bb North Hill

North Hill is the most northerly of the Malverns, rising to 1,307 ft. Although not the highest, it is wilder and less trodden than its neighbour, Worcestershire Beacon. The path begins from a car park just below the brick Clock Tower in Great Malvern, passing a gaunt quarry face before curving on to the precipitous slopes of the east escarpment. There are other routes, but this gives magnificent views of Great Malvern – from here it is possible to see how closely it clings to the rock face. Through the shrub and woodland the pink and buff stone of Malvern Priory

GRASSLAND FLOWERS

Dry grassy places such as quarry banks or field borders, especially limestone grassland, are the places where burnet-saxifrage and hoary plantain, and the less common bee orchid, are likely to be found. Burnet-saxifrage bears umbrellas of tiny white flowers from July to September; the rounded leaflets of its lower leaves and the narrow ones of its upper leaves help to distinguish it from other parsley-like flowers. The poker-like flower spikes of hoary plantain bloom from May to August, its long, protruding lilac stamens providing a glow of colour. The bee orchid's velvety brown and yellow-marked lower lip looks like a bumble bee visiting a flower, but such an allurement to real bees is unnecessary because the plant is mostly self-pollinated. It blooms in June and July.

Burnet-saxifrage
(Pimpinella saxifraga)

Hoary plantain
(Plantago media)

Bee orchid
(Ophrys apifera)

stands out clear against the Severn plain beyond.

The path winds past Ivy Scar Rock as it levels a little. Younger than the pre-Cambrian rocks which make up most of the Malvern Hills, this great lichen-covered rock face is dark and fine-grained. The succulent wall pennywort grows on its surface, and an ancient oak wrests its way out of a fissure.

After curling round the hill, the path drops into woodland and then climbs the broad track of Green Valley, once part of the old way across the hills from Great Malvern. At some points on the track, the ancient paving stones thrust their way through the turf. The ancient track was planted with an avenue of sycamores 40 years ago.

The summit of North Hill is grazed by sheep and is bare of the bracken, rowan trees and gorse found lower down. Only thin fescue grass and wild thyme grow here. Skylarks nest among the grasses close to the sharp peak. Not far below, the sound of traffic and even human speech or the bark of a dog rise with startling clarity from the town, but up here there is only the sound of the wind. The view encompasses the wooded northern foothills rolling down to Old Storridge Common and then as far as the Shropshire Wrekin. West are the Welsh borders, east the Severn plain and Bredon Hill, and behind, to the south, Worcestershire Beacon and the Malverns.

North Hill lies ½ mile outside Great Malvern, west of the A449.

Ba Raggedstone Hill and Golden Valley

According to legend, this dark double peak of the Malverns – bleak, bare and

jagged from almost any viewpoint – has a menacing shadow. In medieval times a young monk from Little Malvern Priory is said to have fallen in love, and as a penance for breaking his vow of chastity was ordered to crawl each day on his hands and knees the 2½ miles from the priory gate to pray on the summit of Raggedstone Hill. One day, exhausted and bitter, he reached the peak but instead of praying he called down a curse on all those on whom the shadow of Raggedstone might fall. Cardinal Wolsey, the powerful chancellor of Henry VIII, once lived at nearby Birtsmorton Court, and one afternoon fell asleep in the garden: the shadow of Raggedstone passed over him and his downfall began from that moment.

On the marshy eastern levels below Raggedstone Hill is Golden Valley, from where the hill looks sinister enough, but remote. Golden Valley is another stretch of the wild Malvern sheep-grazed common land, covered with yellow gorse, thorn and oaks, turf and bracken. Magnificent sedge, irises and bulrushes fringe its wide old mill-pond. A short drive down a track from the B4208 leads to gentle walks and a picnic spot.

Raggedstone Hill lies south of Hollybush on the A438.

Bc Ravenshill Woodland Reserve

An enchanting survival of the woodland that once stretched from Malvern Chase to the Wyre Forest, Ravenshill Woodland Reserve is managed by the Worcestershire Nature Conservation Trust. Some 30 kinds of native tree, including oak, ash, wild cherry, yew and spindle flourish there. Parts of the

50 acre reserve have been commercially planted with hardwoods, conifers and poplars, and hazel trees are being coppiced in places. Coppicing is an ancient system of woodland management, which involves lopping the main stem of a tree back to a stump. Fresh shoots spring from the stump and provide a crop of poles, which are cut every 7–20 years, depending on the species of tree. Further shoots sprout to provide a new crop.

More than 170 different plants have been recorded in the reserve, including the locally rare herb paris, the bird's-nest orchid, and the creamy-pink spikes of the broad-leaved helleborine. In spring there are bluebells and wild daffodils, primroses and wild violets.

There is at least one badger sett in the wood, and it is not unusual to smell the musky scent of a fox that has just slipped across the path. Grey squirrels build dreys in the tallest birches.

The paths in the reserve are clearly marked, and from the highest point there are fine views of the Malverns, Worcester Cathedral, and the Severn plain. Despite the detailed management, the woods retain an atmosphere of intimacy and hushed seclusion.

Alfrick lies south of the A44 on a minor road 7 miles west of Worcester. The reserve is about 1¼ miles along the road leading north-west out of the village, and is marked by a raven emblem.

Bb Worcestershire Beacon

A clear day is desirable for climbing the 1,395 ft to the summit of the Worcestershire Beacon, the highest point of the Malvern Hills. The views are extraordinary – 15 counties (using the old county boundaries) can be seen from here. A direction indicator, or topo-

RIDGEWAY WALK From Worcestershire Beacon, a broad footpath follows the Malvern ridge south to Herefordshire Beacon.

scope, set on the peak to commemorate the reign of Queen Victoria, clearly confirms that they stretch north from the Wrekin in Shropshire to the Mendips of Somerset in the south, beyond the Severn Estuary, and from Plynlimmon in Wales to Bardon Hill above Leicester to the north-east. From here, too, can be seen vividly the three great cathedrals of Gloucester, Hereford and Worcester, as well as six battlefields of England's warring past – Evesham (1265), where Simon de Montfort was defeated by Prince Edward, later Ed-

ward I; Shrewsbury (1403), the scene of the defeat of Henry Percy by Henry IV; Mortimer's Cross (1461) and Tewkesbury (1471) in the Wars of the Roses; and Edgehill (1642) and Worcester (1651), where Parliamentarians and Royalists clashed in the Civil War.

Evidence of Bronze Age cremations more than 3,500 years ago has been found on the summit, and it has been used as a beacon site for at least 400 years. According to the poet Lord Macaulay, when beacons were lit throughout England to warn of the

approach of the Spanish Armada, 'twelve fair counties saw the blaze from Malvern's lonely height'.

Worcestershire Beacon is much trodden and encircled with paths. Although there is a cafe on the summit, it has acquired a neat respectability by being discreetly sited and having refreshed, since 1878, among others, Edward VII who drove up most of the way – along one of the Victorian gravelled carriage routes – in his Daimler.

Worcestershire Beacon lies ½ mile outside Great Malvern, west of the A449.

THE COTSWOLD HILLS

Green heights and secluded valleys where the wealth of a bygone age is reflected in glorious stone

Few parts of England owe so much of their beauty, character and history to the very stone of which they are made. In the Cotswolds, it is close to the surface – watch a plough turn a furrow in the upland earth and the pale limestone will crumble out of the ground. Cottages and churches of the mellow, honey-coloured stone shelter among the clean-cut Cotswold slopes, in pleasing harmony with the hills on which they stand. The weathered walls, the stone mullions of the windows, and the gabled stone barns, like the drystone walls that fence the hillsides, all glow with the yellows, creams and golden-browns of Cotswold limestone. In the words of the writer J. B. Priestley, they seem to keep 'the lost sunlight of centuries glimmering upon them'.

The Cotswolds, designated an Area of Outstanding Natural Beauty, are the highest and widest part of the belt of limestone that stretches from Dorset north-east to the Humber, much of it known as oolite – from the Greek for egg-stone – because its structure resembles fish roe. From Bath the hills extend some 60 miles north-east almost to Stratford-upon-Avon, reaching their highest point at Cleeve Hill, 1,083 ft, near Cheltenham. On their eastern side they dip gently down to the Oxford clay vale, with cornfields, wooded valleys and innumerable streams and rivers, such as the Windrush, Churn and Evenlode, that flow mostly into the upper reaches of the Thames.

COTSWOLD COLOUR Looking westwards from the yellow-splashed slopes of Hens Cliff, the green pastures of Ozleworth Bottom merge into the blue-green woods on Wortley Hill, over which passes the 95 mile long Cotswold Way between Bath and Chipping Campden.

On their western edge the Cotswolds drop abruptly to the vales of Berkeley, Gloucester and Evesham, with beechwoods clothing many of the slopes below rocky limestone outcrops and exposed cliffs. Bredon Hill, a western outlier, rises to 961 ft just south-west of Evesham. From the windy heights of the Cotswold edge, such as Broadway Tower and Birdlip Hill, you can see beyond the gleam of the Severn to the Welsh mountains, the Malverns and the Shropshire Hills. The Cotswold Way, running 95 miles from Chipping Campden to Bath, traverses much of the edge, which around Stroud is pierced by the deep, winding valleys of the Frome and its tributaries that flow westwards to the Severn.

Cotswold builders in stone have been skilful since prehistoric times, as is proved by the outstanding Stone Age long barrows of Belas Knap near Cheltenham and Hetty Pegler's Tump near Stroud. The Romans kept up the tradition when they built Chedworth Villa in the woods near Cirencester.

It was the Anglo-Saxons who first gave the Cotswolds their reputation as fine sheep-rearing country, as well as their name. 'Cots' is from an old Saxon word for sheepfolds, and 'wolds' describes high open land. Stow-on-the-Wold became a major sheep market, and towns such as Chipping Campden grew up on the wealth of the wool trade.

By the end of the 18th century, the West Country cloth trade had begun to decline, superseded by the coal-powered mills of Lancashire and Yorkshire. Although the great wool age of the Cotswolds has passed, the atmosphere remains – embedded in the very stones of places like the weavers' cottages in the idyllic village of Bibury. There are many such enchanting villages in the Cotswolds – enduring reminders of rural England of the past.

Places to visit

Map ref. Bb **Birdlip Hill and Crickley Hill**

These commanding and ancient peaks overlook the whole of the Vale of Gloucester to the Welsh hills.

Birdlip Hill has cool beechwoods and a windy, bare turf peak with views south-west to the enfolding Witcombe Wood, curving round the escarpment to Buckholt Wood and Cooper's Hill. The woods are private, and visitors should keep to the public footpaths that give access to the wealth of mixed woodland, birds and forest plants. The Roman Ermin Way runs east from the village of Birdlip, perched above its precipitous hill, and from the Iron Age burial mound at Barrow Wake – just north of the village – came the bronze Birdlip Mirror now in Gloucester City Museum.

Crickley Hill, a Country Park, has traces of both a New Stone Age settlement and an Iron Age promontory fort. The site was abandoned early in the Iron Age, but reoccupied during the 6th century AD. The sides of the promontory are steep and rugged, and modern quarrying has exaggerated them. Traces of quarrying can be found all over the hill, which has resulted in fascinating exposed geological formations. There is a nature trail on Crickley, together with geological and archaeological trails, and there are superb views to the Malverns and across nearby Cheltenham.

Both hills can be reached by road off the A417, and there are good footpaths. Not far from the road, a monument in memory of the young geologist Peter Hopkins clearly shows the geological formation so vividly characterised here by the twin escarpments of the Malverns and Cotswolds. Describing 'over 500 million years of Britain's history', the monument is made from sandstone, blue lias limestone, and Malvern gneiss found on the twin escarpments, and the 150-million-year-old pea grit and oolite limestone to be seen virtually underfoot.

The hills lie 6 miles south-east of Gloucester; Birdlip Hill is ¼ mile north-west of Birdlip on the A417 and Crickley Hill is ¼ mile west of the junction of the A417 and A436.

Aa   The Bottoms

These deep combes and valleys that lie along the edge of the Cotswold escarpment, around the suitably named Wotton-under-Edge, include some of the most secret and beautiful landscapes anywhere in England.

Immediately above and north of Wotton-under-Edge is Westridge Wood and the wooded Iron Age fort of Brackenbury Ditches. South of the fort, on the curving ridge of Wotton Hill, owned by the National Trust, are the remains of strip lynchets, ploughed terraces of Anglo-Saxon origin.

North-east of Westridge Wood is Waterley Bottom, high-edged and lonely, in which the motorist may see nothing beyond the immense lane banks. North-east of Wotton, reached by a narrow lane and the drive of a private house, is a footpath up Tyley Bottom into the narrow wooded head of the valley.

Most beautiful of all, and reached only on foot, is the head of Ozleworth Bottom, named after the Anglo-Saxon word for blackbird – and they are among the many birds found here. A narrow lane runs for 2 miles from the hamlet of Wortley to two cottages that span the stream below Ozleworth Park. From this shadowy bridge a muddy track on the south side of the stream climbs under trees to a field gate. There, a pathway climbs through grassy fields, streams, shady glades and warm, silent banks to Boxwell.

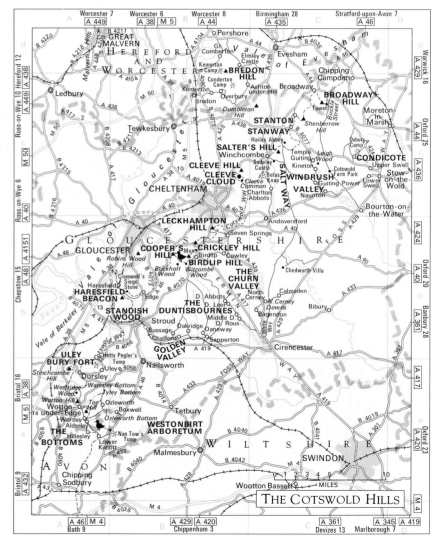

THE COTSWOLD HILLS

Orchids, wild forget-me-nots, pink hedge parsley and honeysuckle grow here and attract numerous butterflies.

Meandering lanes then wind northwards from Ozleworth to footpaths that circle over lonely turf west through Newark Park and Tor Hill, and back south through Wortley to Alderley, Hillesley and Lower Kilcott – all enchanted valleys. Finally, the route emerges through Midger Wood Nature Reserve (managed by the Gloucestershire Trust for Nature Conservation) and up on to the suddenly 20th-century A46 – relieved only by the abrupt sight of Nan Tow's Tump, one of the largest and most mysterious Bronze Age round barrows in the Cotswolds. About 9 ft high and some 100 ft in diameter, crowned with trees, the barrow is believed to contain the skeleton of Nan Tow – a local witch who was buried upright.

The starting point for exploring The Bottoms is Wotton-under-Edge, which is on the B4058, 7 miles south-west of Nailsworth.

Bd   Bredon Hill

At 961 ft, Bredon Hill is not quite the highest point of the Cotswolds, but it seems like it. Massively and abruptly the isolated limestone outcrop rises between the gentle vales of Evesham and Gloucester. From the windy summit, on which Iron Age men built a great fort covering 22 grassy acres, at least eight counties (under the old county names) can be seen – 'the coloured counties', the poet A. E. Housman called them in his poem *Bredon Hill* – a reference to the differing lines of the patchwork countryside. The Malverns, the Welsh hills, the gleam of the Severn estuary and that fruitful lap of

BONES OF THE LAND EXPOSED The limestone that characterises the Cotswolds was once quarried on Crickley Hill.

England, the Vale of Evesham, spread away in an immense cloud-smudged pattern of fields and orchards as if the Industrial Revolution had never happened.

Bredon Hill is like a giant layer cake, with strata of limestone clays topped at the summit by the true Cotswold stone – a hard, creamy-yellow limestone. At the highest point, near the Iron Age

hill-fort known locally as Kemerton Camp, the Cotswold-stone layer is about 100 ft thick. A large chunk of stone, the Banbury Stone, once stood on the edge of a cavity near the outer rim of the hill-fort. About 100 years ago, a landslip brought the stone crashing down into the cavity where it split into large pieces. One piece is known as the Elephant Stone because it resem-

bles a kneeling elephant with its trunk extended.

About 2 miles south-east of the summit hill-fort is Conderton Camp, a much smaller Iron Age earthwork. It was probably built in the 2nd century BC as a cattle enclosure. Some time in the 1st century BC, it was developed as a small settlement. The northern end was enclosed from the rest of the area by a bank and a drystone wall, within which was built a small village of huts and storage pits.

The area is rich in fossils. The remains of a type of oyster with a thick, curved shell, known locally as 'Devil's toenails', are found in the fields on the lower ground below the hill. Also quite common are belemnites – long, cylindrical shells with a pointed end – nicknamed 'bullets'. There are also ammonites – round, flat-coiled shells with prominent ribs. In the Cotswold stone are brachiopods, or 'lamp-shells'; starfish-shaped crinoids known as 'starstones'; and the remains of primitive sea-urchins.

There is a ridge of oak and ash on the eastern escarpment, and dog-roses, hawthorn and elder provide cover for goldfinches on the Iron Age earthworks at Bredon's northern tip.

Bredon Hill is 6 miles south-west of Evesham. Minor roads from the A44, A435, B4080 and B4079 lead to the villages below the hill. Paths from these villages lead to the top of the hill.

Cc Broadway Hill

This is among the highest points in the Cotswolds – 1,024 ft above sea-level – and has a magnificent view across the Vale of Evesham to the great whaleback of Bredon Hill and the Malverns, the Black Mountains in Wales and even the Shropshire Wrekin. In spring, the Vale of Evesham froths with blossom. Footpaths drop down to Broadway and through neighbouring woods of planted beech, larch, spruce and Scots pine. The woods are the haunt of badgers, squirrels, and many birds, moths and butterflies. Among the shrubs there are hawthorns and wild roses. Wild flowers are plentiful,

A CALENDAR OF FLOWERS

Spring on the upland turf of the Cotswolds is heralded by the purple and yellow blooms of the lovely pasque flower. It takes its name from *Pasch* – the Old French for Easter – and flowers in April. May brings the yellow archangel into bloom, and it makes a fine display in woodlands until June. From July to September the purple-crowned flower-heads of the woolly thistle dominate the grasslands. A monarch among wild flowers, it is abundant on limestone and grows up to 5 ft tall.

Woolly thistle
(*Cirsium eriophorum*)

Pasque flower
(*Pulsatilla vulgaris*)

Yellow archangel
(*Lamiastrum galeobdolon*)

and include dog's mercury in spring and rosebay willowherb in late summer.

Broadway Tower is a folly – a mock castle designed by the architect James Wyatt at the end of the 18th century for the Earl of Coventry. It stands on Broadway Hill – known locally as Broadway Beacon – and 13 counties can be seen from its rooftop gallery. Traditionally the hill was used for beacon fires to communicate special happenings to other parts of the country. The land was owned by the earl and legend tells that his wife, wondering whether the summit could be seen from their mansion near Worcester, had a large bonfire lit. This was seen clearly, and she persuaded her husband to build the folly to mark the summit.

Buckle Street, the minor road leading off the main A44 from Broadway to Chipping Norton, which skirts Broadway Hill, is part of the ancient Buggildway along the ridge to Bourton-on-the-Water.

Take the A44 east out of Broadway and after 2 miles turn south on to Buckle Street. The tower is 3/4 mile along the road. Alternatively, park in Broadway and follow any of the footpaths south-east from the village.

Cb The Churn Valley

The River Churn is one of the most westerly tributaries of the Thames, and lays disputed claim to be its source. The Churn rises at the village of Seven Springs near the junction of the A435 and A436, and its springs have never been known to run dry.

Narrow, wooded and winding, the Churn valley is spanned by several interesting villages and fine houses, so that although the main A435 from Cheltenham to Cirencester follows it

south, it has a secret and peaceful air. Turn west off the A435 towards Cowley, with its 17th-century manor and chain of lilied lakes, and cross the Churn at Marsden Manor. Look for dippers here, strange little birds that plunge into the shallow river and run along the bottom searching for food among the pebbles. There are pied and grey wagtails, too, and sometimes herons. Further downstream is North Cerney, with a fine church incorporating Norman and medieval work. To the south-west of North Cerney is the village of Bagendon, where the British tribe of the Dobunni had an important settlement associated with metalworking. Bagendon may have been the forerunner of the Roman town of Cirencester (Corinium), which became the new tribal capital – a new market and administration centre for the Dobunni. Excavations at Bagendon have yielded precious objects such as jewellery, pottery, glass and coins, establishing these pre-Roman people as prosperous and unexpectedly civilised farmers, merchants and manufacturers. Nor is there any evidence of fighting here: Romans and local people seem to have lived together peaceably.

Up on high and windy North Cerney Downs the ancient track called the White Way, an extension of the old Salt Way (p. 145), runs south to Cirencester and the Foss Way. There is a long but lonely walk east from North Cerney up to these downlands and woods. The lane crosses the White Way to the perfect little hamlet of Calmsden with its row of tiny stone cottages with long, narrow gardens.

The Churn valley follows the A435 between Cheltenham and Cirencester. Seven Springs, on the A435, is 4 miles south of Cheltenham.

Bc
Cleeve Hill
and Cleeve Cloud

At 1,083 ft above sea-level, the ridge 1¼ miles south-east of Cleeve Hill is the highest point of the Cotswolds, with Cheltenham spread below. This airy upland remains one of the most breathtaking viewpoints anywhere in England. Herefordshire Beacon is 16 miles north-west, marking the spine of the Malvern Hills. Tewkesbury Abbey, in the same direction, seems close enough to reach out and touch, and the Sugar Loaf mountain 45 miles to the west in the Brecon Beacons is clearly silhouetted against the distant horizon.

Wild flowers carpet the high limestone heath of Cleeve Common: yellow rock-roses, hawkweed and lady's bedstraw gild the turf, while the wild thyme adds a touch of purple.

Just over 2 miles east of Cleeve Cloud, the west-facing ridge below Cleeve Common, is one of the finest of the 30 or more long barrows of the Cotswolds – Belas Knap, a green-turfed hump on the wooded escarpment above the vale of Sudeley. The barrow was built by New Stone Age men about 5,000 years ago, and is some 180 ft long and 60 ft wide. It contains four burial chambers in which the remains of more than 30 people have been found. It is superbly built, in the same manner as Cotswold masons still construct drystone walls today. Its name comes from the Anglo-Saxon words for a beacon on a hill. Brooding, mysterious, Belas Knap symbolises the ancient past of the Cotswolds.

Belas Knap can be reached on foot from Cleeve Hill by following the path south-east over Cleeve Common, past the radio mast, and east to Wontley Farm. From there turn north-east along a track and footpath to the barrow.

The walk from Cleeve Hill to Belas Knap and back takes about three hours. Alternatively, to reach the barrow, drive north on the A46 and just before Winchcombe turn south on to a minor road to Charlton Abbots. A mile beyond the junction a steep lane branches south-west, signposted to Corndean. Either take this lane and join the path from Cleeve Cloud just past a small farmyard, or drive on half a mile to a lay-by and walk up a steep, signposted path through woodland on the west side of the road to Belas Knap above.

Cleeve Hill is 3 miles north-east of Cheltenham. Take the A46 north from Cheltenham to Cleeve Hill Golf Club. There is a car park just beyond the club.

Cc
Condicote

This is upland country where remote stone villages sit snugly in summer and doggedly in winter, following the ancient patterns of settlement that cover the area north-west of Stow-on-the-Wold. From the village of Condicote the Roman Ryknild Street runs southeast and straight across the top of the high downland. It forms a clear track from here to the A436. North-east of Condicote is Eubury Camp, a wide, Iron Age fortification of high bank-and-ditch construction studded with thorn and elder bushes. It is on the north side of the minor road that runs from the village to the A424, and is clearly visible from the road. A closer look at the massive bank can be taken from the path on private land that winds round the valley bottom past a water-tower. There are racehorse gallops here, and the sight of a string of horses at exercise adds to the atmosphere of bygone days that pervades these uplands.

On the same minor road, almost in Condicote itself, a large triangle of grassland on the south side of the road marks the site of a prehistoric henge – an enclosure marked by stone or timber and built for some unknown purpose about 2500 BC.

From a minor road leading southeast from Condicote and then east to join the A424 there is a fine view of the lake by the brewery, from which the River Dikler rises to wind past the villages of Upper and Lower Swell. It is one of the most enchanting valleys in the Cotswolds.

Condicote is 3 miles north-west of Stow-on-the-Wold.

Bb
Cooper's Hill

A celebrated and distinctly dangerous cheese-rolling ceremony is held each Whitsuntide on Cooper's Hill, when those prepared to risk life and limb chase a whole cheese down a precipitous slope below the cockerel-crowned maypole on its northern rim. But for the rest of the year the hill is a peaceful nature reserve of some 137 acres of common land. The reserve is now in the care of Gloucestershire County Council.

Cooper's Hill was once one of the largest Iron Age fortifications in the Cotswolds, probably also known to Bronze Age predecessors, but it has been common land since well before

STONE AGE TOMB The giant earth-bank horns of Belas Knap long barrow near Cleeve Hill enclose a false entrance probably designed to foil tomb robbers.

the 10th century. Local property owners still have commoners' rights such as pannage, the right to let pigs loose to feed on beechmast, or estovers, the right to gather wood for fuel.

The cheese-rolling ceremony is thought to have its origin in ancient prehistoric ceremonies concerning sun worship – it used to be held on Midsummer Day. The cheeses may have represented the sun.

Views from Cooper's Hill are very fine, looking out over the Vale of Gloucester with the Severn Bridge just visible to the south-west and Bredon Hill and the Malverns to the north. There are exposed limestone scarp slopes on the western edge, with some handsome beechwoods.

Nature trails marked on Cooper's Hill indicate such points, including those places where the scarp's soils have been washed away to expose the ancient roots of the beech trees.

Cooper's Hill is 6 miles south-west of Cheltenham. Steep paths lead up the hill from a signposted car park below its western flank on the A46. Alternatively, ¼ mile north, a minor road east off the A46 ends in a grassy car park. From it, a path winds up through ancient beechwoods immediately below the cheese-rolling slope.

Bb The Duntisbournes

This is one of the most enchanting and timelessly gentle valleys anywhere in England. The tiny, unhurried stream of the Duntbrook meanders south-east through two exquisite little villages, two hamlets and four fords in the space of about 2 miles. Eastwards on the ridge above, the Roman Ermin Way takes the A417 arrow-straight to Cirencester: westwards, the valley rises gently to parkland and downs, then falls away

TRANQUIL PASTURES In the gentle uplands around Middle Duntisbourne, farms and outbuildings of cream-coloured Cotswold stone stand amid park-like meadows bounded by ancient, creeper-clad drystone walls.

steeply into the heavily wooded valley of the River Frome.

At Duntisbourne Abbots, the larger of the two villages, the Duntbrook becomes part of the old cobbled road, with high walls and a raised pavement on either side. Carters washed their horses' feet and cleaned their wagons here, and villagers resist all attempts to culvert the sometimes swift-flowing stream. The village water supply still trickles into a stone pool here, though the pool is mossy now and planted in summer with delicate primulas and mimulus.

At Duntisbourne Leer and Middle Duntisbourne, barns and farms drowse in the sun by their fords. The tiny hamlet of Duntisbourne Leer was once

owned by the abbey of Lire in France. Further down the open, green valley the tiny Saxon and Norman church at Duntisbourne Rouse perches on a slope above its own stretch of the Duntbrook.

The Duntisbournes lie west of the A417 and about 4–5 miles north-west of Cirencester.

Bb Golden Valley

Magnificent and solitary woods enfold the River Frome in Golden Valley, which in autumn is gilded by beech, oak and ash to suit the name. Here the old Thames and Severn Canal, now no longer navigable, runs beside the river; ancient backwater villages mark the

canal's hidden path from steep and twisting Chalford itself to golden-stoned Sapperton on its low hillside. At Daneway the canal is dry, and has become a garden of willow, whitebeam and sedge. The old towpath rises to Sapperton Tunnel, almost 2½ miles long, closed and forlorn since 1911.

Chalford and Sapperton are ancient villages, each with a sturdy character of its own. Chalford, with its heritage of mills and fortunes made by the wealthy clothiers, terraces the precipitous hillside of the River Frome and has been nicknamed 'the Alpine village'. Its parish embraces hilltop villages and hamlets such as Bussage and Oakridge. Sapperton was first recorded in Anglo-Saxon times. Its name means 'soapmakers' farmstead' – soap, however, may have meant fullers' earth which was used for 'fulling', or cleaning wool, not for washing.

Chalford is 3 miles south-east of Stroud. Turn north off the A419 in Chalford to follow the course of the River Frome. Follow all the paths and lanes along Golden Valley: all are worth investigating.

Bb Haresfield Beacon and Standish Wood

This area of high, open grassland and mixed woodland owned by the National Trust contains a much-loved local beacon with the finest of all viewpoints on the south-western edge of the Cotswold escarpment. Gloucester lies

WARRIORS' VIEW For hundreds of years, Haresfield Beacon was a military strongpoint used by Iron Age warriors and Roman soldiers. Here, the peaceful scene encompasses the slopes below Standish Wood.

below with its limestone outlier of Robins Wood Hill; the Severn is a wide swathe of often muddy silver to the south-west, and beyond the Forest of Dean are the blue, distant peaks of the Welsh mountains.

Haresfield Beacon is a natural promontory fortification, 700 ft high, and lies secluded above swathes of dark woodland that clothe the slopes on either side of it. Many people have used this perfect military site to their advantage, including the Romans who had a large camp here after the Iron Age settlement. In the last century some 3,000 Roman coins were unearthed on Haresfield Beacon.

The beacon lies on the Cotswold Way, and the National Trust has waymarked the footpaths from the spot. In one direction, the Way leads northeast for three-quarters of a mile to Cromwell's Siege Stone. It is dated 1643 and commemorates the successful defence of Gloucester against Charles I and the Royalists. About a mile further on is an unusual hexagonal-shaped farmhouse.

In the other direction, the Cotswold Way follows the deeply indented ridge southwards, past a topograph (direction finder) overlooking the Severn valley, and then into beautiful Standish Wood.

In summer, local people fly kites and model aeroplanes from the beacon's steep rim, but despite the distant murmur of the M5 motorway far below in the Severn vale the National Trust's 348 acres allow plenty of room for space, peace and solitude. Kestrels hover, treecreepers, nuthatches and woodpeckers frequent the woods, there are primroses and bluebells in spring and dog-roses everywhere in summer.

Haresfield Beacon is 6 miles south of

HELL'S MOUTH There are magnificent views of the Severn valley from the edge of Leckhampton Hill, by the 50 ft rock pillar called the Devil's Chimney. According to legend, it rises straight from Hell.

Gloucester. To reach the beacon there is a narrow and pleasant road from the village of Edge on the A4173.

Bb Leckhampton Hill

Part of Leckhampton Hill's dramatic quality lies in its bare, spectacular limestone cliff and the teetering rock column called the Devil's Chimney which seems to hang in space over the Severn vale below. It was from the cliff quarries on this hill that the beautifully dressed stone for Regency Cheltenham was cut. A steep footpath climbs up from the B4070 at the northern foot of the hill and divides. The route to the west goes round the hill below the summit and provides the most impressive view of the Devil's Chimney set in the cliff below the summit; the other path leads to the summit from which there are views south-west to the Forest of Dean and west to the Black Mountains in Wales.

On the summit, above the Devil's Chimney and its massive, crumbling cliffs, is the grassy site of an Iron Age fortification, where coins have been found revealing later Roman and Saxon occupation.

A flat, metalled path leads east from the hilltop and, initially, takes a wide, meandering course over the plateau of Leckhampton Hill. It eventually turns south-east through cornfields to join a minor road leading west past a quarry on to the B4070. East of the quarry, a path leads north to join the footpath below the summit, and so provides a circular route round the hill. Leckhampton Hill is carpeted with wild flowers – the vivid pink buds and blue petals of viper's bugloss can be found here, also blue tufted vetches, pink sainfoin, moon daisies, rock-roses and woody nightshade. Pink and white dog-roses abound, and in autumn the black sloe berries with their blue bloom appear on the blackthorn bushes.

Flocks of goldfinches and, in winter, long-tailed tits, visit Leckhampton Hill, scourged by cackling magpies. The common blue butterfly and the meadow brown are often seen, and the chalkhill blue can be found where there is horseshoe vetch. Yellow charlock and pink field bindweed grow in the cornfields.

Leckhampton Hill is 2½ miles south of Cheltenham. The path up the hill starts ½ mile south of Leckhampton from a minor road off the B4070.

Cc Salt Way and Salter's Hill

Salt was an essential meat preservative in medieval times, when people had to slaughter their cattle, sheep and pigs in the autumn because there was not enough feed for the animals during winter. Salt became an important commodity and, for centuries, packhorses loaded with it travelled to towns throughout England from coastal saltpans and inland mines such as those at Droitwich in the old county of Worcestershire. One of the 'salt ways' runs across a high ridge of the Cotswolds on what was probably a prehistoric path. Remote, windy and sunny, the airy narrow road that skirts the vale of Sudeley to the west and the gentle Windrush valley to the east is still called the Salt Way. Salter's Hill lies 2 miles east of Winchcombe on the northern section of the Way.

On the west slope of the ridge above the vale of Sudeley there is a planted woodland of conifers. Along the path through the wood the grassy banks are vivid with rock-roses and bright blue

DROWSY SUMMER LAND Across the Vale of Sudeley, the wooded slopes of Salter's Hill doze beneath blue skies.

tufted vetch. The path starts on the west side of the Salt Way 3 miles north of the A436. From it, swallows can be seen swooping and diving in the immensity of air over Winchcombe, the valley of the River Isbourne, wooded Sudeley Castle and the blue reaches of Cleeve Common far beyond.

At its northern end, the Salt Way is a footpath and leads to Salter's Hill. Beyond the hill the path dips down to Salter's Lane and into a precipitous

valley with patterns of fruit blossom covering the orchards on the facing hill in spring. From the path there is a rare view of the ruins of Hailes Abbey, owned by the National Trust and built in the 13th century for the white-robed Cistercian monks.

This section of the Salt Way lies north of the A436, and starts 2½ miles east of Andoversford. It leads north for 7 miles, and ends just beyond Hailes Abbey, where it meets the A46 north of Winchcombe.

Cc Stanton and Stanway

The villages of Stanton and Stanway, tucked under the western escarpment of the Cotswolds, are perhaps at their loveliest in the evening light. A short, easy stroll out from Stanway's avenue of oak trees, called The Liberty and a favourite haunt of nuthatches and owls, leads to a footpath to Stanton, one of the most perfect Cotswold villages. The path heads north across

145

SEASON OF MISTS The soft sunlight of a hazy autumn morning mellows the fields below Shenberrow Hill near Stanton.

open fields at the foot of the steep escarpment. The walk from Stanway passes a fine Tudor country house, with a Jacobean gateway, and a medieval tithe barn. Stanton, which is not on the road to anywhere, is a meandering, many-gabled street of Elizabethan and 17th-century cottages with a wayside cross and a Gothic manor house.

A footpath and bridleway climb steeply out of Stanton up to Shenberrow Hill and its airy, ramparted Iron Age fort standing in the lee of the lofty ash trees on the ridge above. The path crosses farmland as it climbs, following the contours of the curving hill, and views drop away behind to Bredon, Dumbleton Hill and the Malverns, golden in the evening sun. Sheep graze on the hill, and kestrels can sometimes be seen hovering. On the descent from the fort, pink and white dog-roses can be found in bloom in summer, and primroses in spring.

The circuit uphill and down round the fort is not clearly marked and it is easy to stray from the path here, but the descent from the fort is well trodden and the path emerges at the eastern end of the village.

Stanway is on the B4077, 3½ miles north-east of Winchcombe; Stanton is 1½ miles north of Stanway on a minor road.

Aa   ## Uley Bury Fort

Beechwoods flank the hills around the village of Uley, above which stands a massive Iron Age hill-fort enclosing 32 acres of the lofty heights. Only the banked ditches of the outer rim are clear to walkers, the plateau top being used for arable crops. But the views from the summit are immense and give a sense of just how awesome this great fortress must have been when first constructed. Those masons and labourers must have themselves looked out at the dark curve of Stinchcombe Hill to the west and the lowland beside the Severn estuary. The spirit of these ancient Britons lingers on among the ramparts; on a day when the rain marches over that lowland the fort seems to come strangely alive.

Just north of the fort is Hetty Pegler's Tump, a Neolithic long barrow almost as fine as Belas Knap near Cheltenham. The barrow is 120 ft long and 22 ft wide, and its walls and ceiling are made of large stone slabs filled in with areas of drystone work. To enter the barrow the key must be obtained from Crawley Hill Farm, half a mile south on the B4066. Torches are needed to illuminate the burial chambers while crouching inside. Each of the four chambers is reached by a short passage. Some 38 skeletons were discovered in them in the last century. The barrow was named after the wife of a local landowner, but no one knows why; only that there was a Hester Pegler who lived locally in the 17th century.

Hetty Pegler's Tump is signposted and reached by a narrow field path from the B4066, 1 mile north of Uley. Uley is on the B4066, 2 miles east of Dursley.

Ba Westonbirt Arboretum

The owners of Westonbirt House, the Holfords, planted the arboretum in 1829 with hardy native and evergreen species such as oaks, Scots pines, beeches, holm oaks, yews and laurels, giving shelter to subsequent plantings of more exotic species. It is now the best collection of native and exotic trees in Europe. The Cotswold limestone gives way here to deeper, sandy loams – acid enough to grow rhododen-

drons and azaleas – and this sporadic geological deposit is a part of the Hinton Sand found elsewhere in pockets between Bath and Cirencester.

Westonbirt may be artificial, but in 150 years it has become so established that it appears almost natural. Trees simply like growing there. Many are the largest of their species anywhere in Britain, including maples, whitebeams and Caucasian oaks. There is now a Cherry Glade, glorious in spring; a collection of native British species (which number 25 only – Britain's wealth of tree species have almost all been imported); and a collection of willows. In autumn the maples set parts of Westonbirt ablaze with flame-red. In late spring the rhododendrons and azaleas are magnificent.

There is complete freedom to walk anywhere in the woods, which cover some 116 acres, and the rides and paths are clearly marked by the Forestry Commission which owns Westonbirt. The arboretum is open to the public all year round.

Westonbirt is on the north side of the A433 about 3 miles south-west of Tetbury.

Cc The Windrush Valley

In summer the Windrush is a beguiling little stream on its upper reaches, but in winter it has been known to flood, and so gave the name Guiting – from the Anglo-Saxon *gute* meaning 'flood' – to two of the peaceful villages lying in its valley, Temple Guiting and Guiting Power.

South of Temple Guiting lies Leigh Wood – a cool and shady place to explore on the footpaths. The woods are owned by Christchurch College, Oxford, and a Tudor manor at Temple

Guiting was probably built as a summer residence for the Bishops of Oxford.

At Kineton, a mile south of Temple Guiting, a steep lane at the north end of the hamlet leads down eastwards through the cottages, and is marked Not Suitable for Motorists. It leads to a clear, gravelly ford and a narrow, high-hedged lane lying in the shadow of Leigh Wood. Further along the lane a track dips away to the south and crosses the Windrush again at another ford – sun-dappled under ancient trees, with a medieval packhorse bridge to make the crossing easier in flood.

BIRD ON THE UP AND UP

Slightly smaller than a sparrow, the mouse-like treecreeper lives up to its name as it moves spirally up a tree trunk in search of insects. The bird uses its stiff tail as a support as it probes the bark with its slender, curved bill. A woodland bird, the treecreeper has a high-pitched, quavering song, sung as it climbs, and is heard mostly from mid-February to mid-May.

Treecreeper
(*Certhia familiaris*)

A footpath winds south through the lush, wooded water-meadows at this spot, where the hills drop to create a still and sunlit place that feels strangely secret. The footpath is entangled in cow parsley, elder trees, hawthorns and blackthorns. In summer there are creamy curds of elder; in spring cowslips dapple the grassy banks; in autumn there are red hawthorn berries and sloes.

Deep within the watery woodland a narrow foot-bridge – a slab of ancient stone – crosses the chuckling Windrush. Grey wagtails flash their yellow chests as they dance in the air to take insects in flight, and warblers and thrushes nest in the willows, hazels and ash trees.

Guiting Power, 1½ miles south of Kineton, is a classic Cotswold village with a sloping, triangular green and honey-coloured stone houses. A footpath leads southwards past the church and then across open fields. The land is private, so keep to the public footpath. From it there are extensive views down the Windrush valley. Wild flowers and grasses cover the warm slopes where the occasional ancient oak tree stands sentinel.

After crossing a small tributary of the Windrush, the path continues on down the valley, partly by way of a minor road, to Naunton. The river here ambles behind the old stone cottages that line the street through this delightful backwater village.

Further down the valley, across the A436 at Bourton-on-the-Water, the atmosphere becomes more formal and selfconscious – and there are many more visitors.

The Windrush valley is 6 miles west of Stow-on-the-Wold. Temple Guiting is on a minor road south of the B4077.

THE MENDIP HILLS

The hollow, limestone hills that have sheltered and supported man for more than 35,000 years

Since they are numbered in hundreds of thousands annually, perhaps it is fortunate that the majority of visitors to the Mendips are sufficiently sated by the area's subterranean wonders to leave the springy, thymy turf above to kestrels, buzzards and the scattering of hill-walkers who seek the Mendips' high solitudes and sweet winds – in winter, bitter-sweet – that blow endlessly across them from the Bristol Channel. But crowds notwithstanding, it is not a bad idea to begin exploring within the Mendips' water-hollowed ribs, partly because it is rare to see a range of hills from within, and much more so because so much of the district's story has been encapsulated within its chasms, caverns and caves. Long, long ago the River Axe carved Wookey Hole and its extraordinary – and now floodlit – sculptures, one of which is said to be a petrified witch who preyed upon local lovers. Lesser streams, making their way through surface fissures, dissolved the limestone beneath to create caves at Cheddar, Ebbor Gorge and Wookey. In these, an awesome 35,000 years ago, it seems that men and hyenas competed for shelter, both leaving behind the gnawed bones of bear, bison, reindeer and rhinoceros.

By these standards, man's scars on the Mendips' outer hide date from but yesterday. There are a number of long barrows or cairns that belong to the New Stone Age of about 3000 BC, while round barrows, stone

circles and rich artefacts argue a lengthy period of Bronze Age farming prosperity during the 2nd millennium BC. To judge by the rash of hill-fort construction that took place around the time of the Roman invasion – for example, Maesbury Castle and Dolebury Camp – this peaceful era was brought to an abrupt and violent end; though it would seem it was not the legions that the tribesmen feared nearly so much as the westward expansion of the terrible Belgae, with their near-invincible iron weapons.

In time, peace returned to the Mendips – the *Pax Romana*, expressed in large, comfortable villas occupied by gentleman-farmers, and in the area's first taste of industry, the lead mines at Charterhouse, whose product was exported to Gaul and even to far-off Pompeii.

A little mining, a lot of farming and husbandry; this has been the Mendips' story ever since. In the 13th century, the Carthusians of Witham Abbey near Shepton Mallet, who probably developed the Mendip breed of sheep, ran large flocks on the high hills, founding a thriving wool trade. In fact, hilltop sheep fairs had probably been held at the end of lambing since prehistoric times. One such fair is still held at Priddy, the village's right to do so being advertised and maintained by a thatched rick of sheep hurdles on the village green.

Enclosures in the 18th century, and 19th-century imports of cheap wool from Australia, drastically altered the district's economy, at least in the valleys, which are now given over to cattle and root-crops. But climb up into the hills, only a mile or so from the coach and car parks at Cheddar and Wookey, and you are into an older England, stretching all the way to the Bristol Channel and the gaunt battleship-shape of Steep Holm island, itself a part of the same limestone massif.

ENGLAND'S GRAND CANYON Cheddar Gorge, carved by a river that now runs underground, slices through the Mendips for more than a mile. Sheer limestone cliffs tower 450 ft above the road that leads down to Cheddar village, where there are entrances to vast, underground caverns.

Places to visit

Map ref. Ba   Ashen Hill Barrows

A gentle walk of about a quarter of a mile over upland pasture leads to Ashen Hill, a Bronze Age barrow cemetery. Like many prehistoric sites, it is an austere setting. The scattered community of Priddy is situated high up on the limestone plateau, about 800 ft above sea-level, and is exposed to the cruel ravages of the winter winds. Centuries of trampling by human and animal feet – to say nothing of the work of rabbits – has

reduced the barrows to a fraction of their original size. But they and their prehistoric neighbours a short distance south on North Hill, Priddy Nine Barrows, form a landmark which can be recognised for many miles around. In the 19th century some of the Priddy Nine Barrows – there are only seven, in fact – were excavated. They were found to contain burned bones and, in one case, beads similar to those found in Egyptian tombs.

Half a mile to the north, over the B3135, lie the four Priddy Circles. Each of these is 600 ft in diameter – their significance is not known but it is believed they are connected with religious ceremonies associated with the group of barrows to the south.

Stands of beeches and firs dot the hillside, adding colour and variety to the landscape. There is plenty of wildlife, including badgers in the neighbouring woods. Badgers are plentiful in the Mendip woods, but are seen only at dusk.

Priddy is 5 miles east of Cheddar. It is reached by turning south off the B3135 at Townsend, 2 miles from the junction with the B3371. Turn left down Nine Barrows Lane in the village. The barrows lie east, about 1 mile along the lane.

Ca   Babington Wood

A short walk across open fields on a public footpath from the village of Kilmersdon leads to Babington Wood. The wood, with a bubbling stream – a tributary of the Somer – running through the centre of it, is a marvellous retreat, and pleasantly secluded.

There is a wild beauty here which is hard to find elsewhere in the Mendips. The trees – hazels, oaks, Douglas firs, ashes, limes and maples – reach skywards in haphazard fashion, and in autumn, when the sun slants through the dying foliage, the wood is a wonderland of colour, with every shade of green, red and brown. There are riches, too, in the undergrowth, seen at its best in spring. Flowering bluebells, periwinkles and wood anemones provide an early splash of colour before the wild rhododendrons, overhanging the bank of the stream, burst into bloom in May.

The public path threads its way tenuously through the wood, crossing the stream by a simple bridge and then continuing for about 500 yds to Babington Church, a delightful little Georgian building which stands like a private chapel within the grounds of Babington House.

Kilmersdon is 2 miles south of Radstock. Babington Wood can be reached by parking on the B3139, just east of Kilmersdon. The public footpath, which is not marked, leads up from the south side of the road, west of the bridge over the stream.

Ba   Black Down

The highest peak on the Mendip Hills is also, without doubt, the loneliest. This long, seemingly unending hill rises above the limestone plateau like a giant tortoise, gaunt and forbidding against the soft countryside around.

It is not surprising that Black Down presents a different appearance to the rest of the Mendip range, for the 1,067 ft peak is sandstone, not limestone. The different rock structure is apparent in the vegetation: the thin, peaty soil is covered with whortleberries, rough grass, ling and heath which, in the depth of winter, take on a black appearance, believed to be the reason for its name.

The best way up Black Down is to take the footpath that leads from beside Ellick House, which is at the top of

A BEAUTY OF THE GORGE

The sweet-scented Cheddar pink was a favourite souvenir of Victorian tourists. Now it is a rare flower and grows only in Cheddar Gorge, blooming in June and July.

Cheddar pink (*Dianthus gratianopolitanus*)

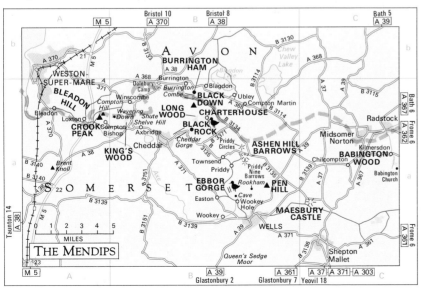

THE MENDIPS

HUMP-BACK HEADLAND The view west from Bleadon Hill takes in distant Brean Down jutting into the Bristol Channel.

hillside above the valley, larches and Scots pines also grow. In spring, before the trees are in full leaf, dog's mercury and bluebells flower, and along the drystone walls there are many lime-loving plants, notably common spleenworts and liverworts.

The valley can be reached by parking at Black Rock Gate, which is on the B3135 at the top end of the Cheddar Gorge. There are one or two parking places on the side of the road.

Aa   Bleadon Hill

The pathway which leads up from the centre of Loxton village to the top of Bleadon Hill offers magnificent views in all directions. To the south is the solitary stack of Brent Knoll, an island of limestone rising 450 ft above the marshes of the Somerset plain; east is the main bulk of the Mendips. Walking along the ridge of the hill opens up a marvellous vista of the Bristol Channel, Brean Down, the islands of Steep Holm and Flat Holm and, on clear days, the hills of South Wales.

In its early stages the path, the West Mendip Way, climbs steeply. Clumps of oak and beech line the pathway before the upper reaches of the hill are reached, where the vegetation becomes more sparse, and bracken and brambles predominate. Beyond Christon Plantation, the scenery becomes well wooded again and here you are likely to startle a pheasant into laborious flight. In wet weather the path at this point is very sticky, so sturdy footwear is recommended.

Loxton is 5 miles south-east of Weston-super-Mare just off the Bleadon–Axbridge road, on the west side of the M5. The path over Bleadon Hill starts from the centre of Loxton, opposite the rectory.

Burrington Combe on the B3134, just a few yards beyond the Burrington Ham parking area. A series of tracks leads to the summit, which can be reached comfortably in less than 30 minutes.

The hill is crowned by the Beacon Batch Bronze Age barrows, and a line of what appear to be molehills – these were wartime defences to prevent aircraft from landing on the summit. On a clear day the views from the top are truly memorable: north over the soft folds of the hills to Bristol and beyond; west to Flat Holm and Steep Holm out in the Bristol Channel; south over the

Somerset Levels to Glastonbury Tor.

Black Down is 1¼ miles south of Burrington just off the A368. Ellick House is 2 miles along the B3134, which heads south from the A368 about 200 yds west of Burrington.

Ba   Black Rock

Less than 2 miles from Cheddar lies Black Rock, a place so quiet, so unspoiled, that it could be miles from any tourist spot. Black Rock was once part of the medieval Mendip Forest, a royal hunting preserve, and is at the north-eastern end of Cheddar Gorge. Here

the gorge opens out into two valleys, one of which runs north-eastwards and then north to Long Wood. Just south of Long Wood, the path splits again, and heads north-east along another valley. This is a historic trail; almost 2,000 years ago it was a track leading to the Roman lead and silver mines at Charterhouse, 2 miles away through Velvet Bottom. In the valley itself, man once quarried the limestone.

Even on the roughest days, Black Rock is a sheltered spot. It has a wide range of trees and plants that are typical of those found in limestone areas – mostly ashes and yews – but on the

Burrington Ham

Ba

In summer and at weekends, Burrington Combe attracts many visitors, but a short drive to the top of this miniature Cheddar Gorge leaves the crowds behind and leads to Burrington Ham, one of the great delights of the Mendips.

From the ridge, only a few yards from the car park, there is a view over much of the county of Avon, providing an inspiring panorama. The view is north-east over Blagdon Lake and Chew Valley Lake to the point where, 7 miles from the Bristol Channel, Bristol nestles comfortably in and around the Avon Gorge. On a clear day, the unmistakable outline of the Welsh hills looms on the north-eastern horizon, on the other side of the murky waters of the Bristol Channel.

Burrington Ham represents the softer face of the Mendips. A broad bridleway drops gently down between brambles and bracken, a marvellous sea of brown in the soft light of autumn, to the village of Burrington, lying in the lee of the steep north-facing edge of the hills. There is an Iron Age oval earthwork, Dolebury Camp, on the hillside above the combe – another excellent vantage point – and close by is the rocky cleft in which the Blagdon curate Augustus Toplady is said to have written the hymn *Rock of Ages* while sheltering from a storm.

The B3134 runs through Burrington Combe, which starts just south of the point where the road joins the A368. The parking area for exploring Burrington Ham is on the north side of the road at the top of the combe.

INDUSTRY THAT SERVED THE ROMAN EMPIRE

WHEN THE ROMANS invaded Britain in AD 43 they lost no time in exploiting the country's natural resources. In Wales they mined for gold, in Cornwall they found tin, and in the Mendips they sought the most useful mineral of all – lead.

Within six years of the invasion, lead was being mined at Charterhouse and a lead ingot now in the British Museum has been dated to AD 49. Lead was used to make coffins, roofing, linings for baths such as the Great Bath at Bath, water-pipes and cisterns. Much of the lead was sent back to Rome, and a cistern in the ruins of Pompeii has been identified as being of Mendip lead.

The lead was mined mainly by slave labour. *Damnatio ad mettala*, 'sentenced to the mines', was one of the punishments for crimes of violence.

Later workings known as 'gruffy grounds' have obliterated the Roman Charterhouse mines. But 3 miles east, between Compton Martin and the Chew Valley Lake, there is part of a Roman road which is believed to have linked Charterhouse to Bath.

ROMAN ROAD NEAR CHEW VALLEY LAKE

Charterhouse

Ba

This lonely village sits high on a hill in a flat, windswept landscape – but it is assured for ever of its place in history. It was here, some 2,000 years ago, that the Romans launched Britain's earliest lead-mining industry. Six-thousand people lived here then; today Charterhouse's population can be counted almost on the fingers of one hand.

Little evidence of the Roman occupation remains, but wildlife thrives. A nature reserve has been established in the 'gruffy ground' – patches of furrowed land containing the overgrown remains of the filled-in mine-shafts and other lead workings. Here alpine penny-cress and spring sandwort are found beside sheep's fescue, sea campions and other wild flowers. There are also many butterflies, such as marbled whites and dark green fritillaries.

There is an almost eerie stillness about Charterhouse, with few sounds apart from the gentle rustle of the wind in the leaves of the trees. Beeches, sycamores, alders, oaks and ash trees grow in isolated stands, alongside the scrub layer of hawthorns, elders and dogwood, just as they must have done before the Romans came.

Charterhouse is 2¾ miles north-east of Cheddar and lies 1 mile from the B3134 from Burrington Combe, along a minor road. Blackmore Educational Nature Reserve is open to the general public. Parking is available at the reserve.

Crook Peak

Aa

A stiff climb up a bridleway from the minor road skirting the western flank of the hill leads to the top of Crook Peak. There is also a more gentle approach from the village of Compton Bishop, three-quarters of a mile southeast of the summit. The limestone

strata slope gently south to the green Somerset plain, across which, 10 miles away, runs the low east-west ridge of the Polden Hills. On clear days, far away to the south-west, the purple-clad slope of Dunkery Hill on Exmoor can be seen.

The peak, which takes its name from the ancient British word *cruc*, meaning 'a pointed hilltop', is well named. It stands 628 ft above sea-level, its limestone head worn to a jagged edge by centuries of erosion by the elements. The limestone contains many marine fossils from the time when the area was covered by the sea.

On the southern slopes, where erosion of the rocks has produced a limestone-pavement effect, there are yellow rock-roses, wild thyme, quaking grass, tormentils and rarer species, such as the spring cinquefoil, the delicate bee orchid, autumn lady's tresses, slender-leaved thistles, and white horehound. Badgers have their underground setts in cracks in the rocks. They appear at dusk to feed on worms, beetles, blackberries and other food found on the hill.

The open downland is a nesting place for stonechats, skylarks and meadow pipits. Although they do not nest there, wheatears can sometimes be seen feeding. Butterflies, notably marbled whites, common blues and dark green fritillaries, are also plentiful.

A walk east along the crest of the ridge, following the drystone wall, leads to Compton Hill, Wavering Down and King's Wood (see p. 154). The wall forms the boundary between Somerset and the comparatively new county of Avon. However, the line it follows is much older – it divides the parishes of Compton Bishop and Winscombe, and was defined in Saxon times

CROOK PEAK VIEW Compton Bishop, starting point for walks up Crook Peak, lies in a secluded valley below Wavering Down.

when it was an important estate boundary.

Crook Peak is 2¼ miles west of Axbridge. A minor road skirts the western foot of the hill, and there is a small parking area close to the start of the bridleway.

Ebbor Gorge

About 270 million years ago, enormous pressure from inside the earth's crust pushed down a strip of Millstone Grit beneath the limestone to form an impermeable floor, over which a river once ran. The result of this transformation of the landscape was Ebbor Gorge, a wooded chasm which is now part of a 116 acre nature reserve managed by the Nature Conservancy Council. It is claimed to be the loveliest and most unspoiled gorge in the Mendips. Here ashes, pedunculate oaks, wych elms and other trees grow in dense and glorious confusion, providing a greenery unmatched elsewhere in this area. The damp woodland is rich in mosses, fungi and ferns; here you will also find dog's mercury, hart's-tongue fern and enchanter's nightshade. Badgers live in the woods, and the entrance to a sett – the badger's underground home – can be seen close to one of the paths through the gorge.

Caves and fissures worn by rainwater provided shelter for New Stone Age man, who lived in the gorge about 3000 BC, and his bones, tools and ornaments have been found there. In Bridged Pot Shelter, at the head of the gorge, a superb axe of highly polished greenstone was found; it is now in the museum at Wells. Remains of animals such as bears, reindeer and lemmings have also been uncovered.

The gorge is situated about 1¼ miles

153

UNSPOILT RAVINE Smaller than its famous neighbour at Cheddar, Ebbor Gorge is also a wilder spot and less trodden. A path leads through the heavily wooded valley and eventually scrambles up on to the lonely Mendip plateau.

north-east of Easton on the A371 between Wells and Cheddar. The property, owned by the National Trust, has a car park, from where two nature trails start.

Ba ## King's Wood

Just below Shute Shelve Hill, and on the eastern side of Wavering Down, lies one of the unexpected pleasures of the Mendips. King's Wood, which stretches for about half a mile, is a marvellous place to be at any time of the year – especially in autumn, when the dying leaves provide a spectacular canopy of colour.

Yet this has not always been a pleasant spot. In the 17th century, Shute Shelve was the site of a gibbet, and travellers on the old Bristol to Exeter road, which passes close to the wood, would have heard the clank of chains as the grisly remains of the unfortunate victims swung in the wind.

The soil in King's Wood is deeper than on the other side of Wavering Down, so a wide range of trees grows here: oaks, ashes, beeches, cherries, sycamores, maples, small-leaved limes and Scots pines.

This beautiful stretch of woodland also has many wild flowers, especially in early spring before the tree foliage blots out the sunlight. Then the wood is a riot of colour with bluebells, primroses, dog's mercury, wild arums and wood anemones growing in large numbers. The rarer herb paris also grows here, as do the hart's-tongue fern and common polypody.

King's Wood is 1 mile north-west of Axbridge. A minor road west from the A38 leads to it. The entrance to the wood is about 150 yds along on the south side of the road, and there is a small parking area. After rain, the paths can be muddy.

Ba ## Long Wood

Subterranean Mendip meets the surface beneath a glorious canopy of green at Long Wood. Shortly after the end of the Second World War a network of water holes – called swallets – was unearthed in the middle of this delightfully unspoiled stretch of woodland, leading to a complicated labyrinth of underground passages and caves. Today the entrances to the swallets are closed because of the dangers they present to inexperienced explorers.

The wood contains much wildlife, which can be seen from the $2\frac{1}{4}$ mile nature trail established by the Somerset Trust for Nature Conservation. Here you can find ancient stands of beech, some of which were planted 140 years ago, along with other trees associated with limestone – such as yews, elders and ashes. Blackberries grow profusely and, in the clearings between the trees, there are rosebay willowherb, hemp

BEAUTY IN THE HEDGEROW

The ringlet butterfly appears in the summer months, and may be seen in lilting, unhurried flight following the line of hedgerows, drystone walls and woodland clearings. It feeds on hedgerow flowers such as marjoram and red campion, and is very fond of blackberry.

Ringlet butterfly (*Aphantopus hyperanthus*) on a blackberry flower (*Rubus fruticosus*)

CELTIC DEFENCES The massive earth ramparts of Maesbury Castle, an Iron Age hill-fort, stand above Castlehill Woods.

commanding position. Today it is rather easier to tackle; by simply walking across a field from the road which runs along the hill. The outline of the original fortifications which encircle the top of the hill can still be seen in the oval-shaped mound, now covered with grass.

Maesbury Castle is 4 miles east of Wells. The road to it is signposted off the B3139, between Wells and Chilcompton.

Ba | Pen Hill

A walk of about 3 miles, from Pen Hill to Rookham, follows the south-western face of a ridge above the Somerset plain. Following the bridle-way down the side of the hill, the view takes in Queen's Sedge Moor and Glastonbury Tor, the steep hill crowned by the 14th-century tower of St Michael, looming above the town. Beyond are the Black Down Hills and the Quantocks. On a clear day, Dartmoor can also be seen, its outline rising darkly on the horizon. Immediately beneath the hill lies the ancient city of Wells, crowned by the delicate square towers of the cathedral and St Cuthbert's Church.

On Pen Hill, the Old Red Sandstone has broken through the limestone layer covering the Mendip plateau, resulting in a landscape that is pastoral and well wooded. Ashes and oaks mingle among the stately stands of conifers, and pheasants scuttle in and out of the woods which line the bridle-path.

Pen Hill is about 3 miles north-east of Wells along the A39. There is a small parking area near the entrance to a television transmitter station which crowns the hill. The bridle-path runs off south-west from the parking area. After about ¼ mile, it bears west beneath Pen Hill Farm.

agrimony and the rarer herb paris. In the moister areas, fungi such as the uncommon amethyst agaric and the deadly yellow deathcap toadstool occur.

At one point along the trail a blow-hole can be seen. This was formed in 1968 when the underground stream burst through to the surface. The thickets are the home of thrushes, wrens and the green and lesser spotted woodpeckers. In spring, the air is filled with the sound of migrant birds – the willow warblers, blackcaps and red-

starts – all competing for territory. Roe deer, badgers, foxes, squirrels, shrews and weasels are common, and adders and grass snakes can also be seen occasionally. Care should be taken when wandering along the paths, particularly during warm weather, so as not to disturb the poisonous adder, recognisable by its zigzag markings.

Long Wood can be reached by following the path from Black Rock Gate, 1½ miles north-east of Cheddar on the B3135. The entrance to the wood is at the northern end of the gorge, ¼ mile from Black Rock Gate.

Ca | Maesbury Castle

For many people, Maesbury Castle is the most exhilarating spot on the whole of the Mendip Hills. This impressive Iron Age fort crowns a hill on the southern side of the plateau, and from it there are compelling views of the Somerset countryside, with the main ridge of the hills rising to the north-west.

Maesbury would have been a difficult place to conquer in those prehistoric days, situated as it was in such a

THE NORTH WESSEX DOWNS

Unsolved prehistoric mysteries surround the ancient
stone circles, burial mounds and hill-forts of the Downs

English civilisation first glimmered into life amid the chalk downland of North Wessex and the rolling slopes of Salisbury Plain. Between about 5,000 and 2,500 years ago, this was the most densely populated part of the country, a Late Stone Age and Bronze Age metropolis centred around the mysterious stone circles of Avebury and Stonehenge, and linked with East Anglia and the Devon coast by the ancient Ridge Way along the crest of the Downs.

It was here in later centuries that the legendary King Arthur, probably a Romano-British general, fought off invading Saxons near the Wansdyke in AD 500, alongside his kinsman Ambrosius. And some 350 years later, Alfred the Great, King of Wessex, was born at Wantage – perhaps in the shadow of the graceful, chalk-cut White Horse of Uffington.

The Berkshire Downs begin where the Chilterns end, as the River Thames cuts through the chalk ridge at Goring Gap. Their rounded, green-clad summits sweep westwards some 25 miles before turning south into Wiltshire to become the Marlborough Downs. To the north these Wessex Downs overlook the flat and fertile farmlands of the Vale of White Horse stretching towards the upper reaches of the Thames, and to the south lie the meadowlands of the Kennet valley. The River Kennet, a tributary of the Thames, is linked westwards via the 19th-century Kennet and Avon Canal to the Bristol Avon at Bath. The

canal flows through the Vale of Pewsey that separates the Marlborough Downs from Salisbury Plain to the south.

This has been farming country since Late Stone Age farmers grew their wheat and barley and herded their sheep and cattle on Windmill Hill. In medieval times sheep dominated the Downs, providing wool for the cloth industry; today numerous wheat fields stretch up the lower slopes. It was a Berkshire farmer and writer, Jethro Tull of Hungerford, who in 1701 invented the seed-drill that was a giant step in the advancement of agriculture. He also introduced horse-drawn hoeing of crops.

You can still walk today along 43 miles of the Ridgeway Path over the top of the Downs from Goring to Overton Hill. In prehistoric times Overton Hill was the site of a circular timber building today known as The Sanctuary. Along with the man-made mound of Silbury Hill to the west, it was part of the religious centre around Avebury that was visited yearly by thousands of people.

It must have been a well-organised community that some 4,000 years ago dug out the circular ditch, almost a mile long, surrounding Avebury henge monument, and that man-handled the heavy sandstone blocks about 5 miles from the Marlborough Downs to set up the largest stone circle in Europe within the earthworks. The 4,000 round barrows scattered throughout the area attest the importance of the society.

Southwards about 20 miles on Salisbury Plain stands Stonehenge, the most dramatic and famous of all prehistoric stone circles. It was begun nearly 5,000 years ago, but the huge bluestones were brought to the site about 1,000 years later from the Prescelly Mountain in Wales, 140 miles away as the crow flies. The circle as it is today, including sarsens brought from near Avebury, dates back about 3,500 years.

NATURAL FORTRESS Iron Age Celts chose the level heights of Westbury Hill, at the north-west tip of Salisbury Plain, to site a 25 acre hill-fort, Bratton Castle. Steep slopes protect three sides of the massive earthwork defences overlooking the plateau edge.

Places to visit

Map ref. Bc   Avebury

On an autumn morning with a light mist rising from the meadows, the great stone circle of Avebury takes on an air of fantasy, almost as if the brooding stones might fade like ghosts in the full light of day. But as the sun rises the stones become real enough, and fantasy gives way to mystery; how did the stones get there, and what was their purpose?

Archaeologists know the answer to the first question. The stones were hauled from the Marlborough Downs in the late Stone Age, about 2000 BC, probably by the Beaker People. This group of settlers from the Low Countries take their name from the sophisticated pottery they made and often buried with their dead. As to the purpose of the stones, no one knows – a temple for sun worship perhaps, or a centre for pagan rituals. It is easy to understand how the circle was built, but less easy to fathom the minds of its creators.

The circle stands inside a great earth bank, 1,400 ft in diameter, and encloses the remains of two smaller circles. Only 27 of the original stones remain, though concrete posts replace the missing stones to show the original layout. Unlike Stonehenge, Avebury's

stones are unhewn. Their natural shapes – some tall and slender, others broad and squat – may represent male and female figures.

Avebury village is a quiet and pleasant place built within the outer ring of stones. There are easy downland walks from the village to other ancient sites, such as Windmill Hill 1½ miles to the north-west. On it stands a fortified camp dating from about 2900 BC, and

a Bronze Age burial site of about 1700–1400 BC. It is believed that the camp served as a rallying point, or fair, where Stone Age farmers gathered at certain seasons for barter and perhaps for worship.

Avebury lies just north of the A4, 6 miles west of Marlborough, and can be reached by the B4003 or by the A361 which crosses the A4, 1 mile south-west of the village.

Bc   Barbury Castle

This Iron Age fort is one of the best known in southern England. Perched on the 850 ft high northern rim of the Marlborough Downs, the fort overlooks the Ridgeway Path and gives sweeping views of the surrounding countryside. To the west lies a vast sprawl of rolling chalkland, a patchwork of green fields and a sprinkling of

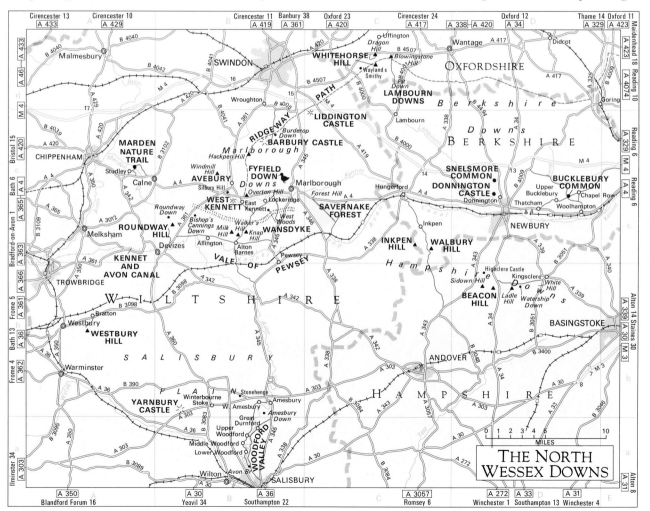

trees with hills rising like smoke in the distance. Half a mile to the north lies the battlefield of Beranburh where the Saxon chief Cynrie and his son Ceawlin defeated the Britons in a bloody massacre. It established the Saxons as overlords of southern England and later, in AD 560, Ceawlin became King of Wessex.

Barbury Castle is a well-defined oval of about 12 acres, with entrances at the eastern and western sides passing through the towering double ramparts. Finds from inside are now in Devizes Museum, and include fittings for chariots. Below the fort on the eastern side can be seen the angular outlines of ancient field systems, probably dating from the Iron Age. They stand out clearly against the softer contours of the surrounding landscape.

The path down from the castle's western entrance joins the Ridge Way, and there is a pleasant 30 minute walk along it eastwards to Burderop Down and back to the car park. The deeply rutted track winds downhill, with pink and white hawthorns lining the path and yellow honeysuckle scenting the air.

Barbury Castle lies 5 miles south of Swindon. Take the A361 out of the town and at Wroughton turn on to the B4005. A mile east, an unclassified road runs south to Burderop Down and ends at a large car park. The fort is ½ mile west along a footpath across a field.

Db ## Beacon Hill

A steep, straight path leads from the A34 to the top of Beacon Hill, a daunting climb but worth the effort for the scenery on the way and for the view from the 858 ft summit. Buttercups and dropwort speckle the green turf on

SACRED SITE The stones of the Bronze Age temple at Avebury were hauled from the Marlborough Downs 4,000 years ago.

the lower slopes, with gorse gilding the crest.

Not surprisingly, there is a superb Iron Age hill-fort on the summit but a modern grave comes as an unusual discovery. It is the burial place of the 5th Earl of Carnarvon, who led the 1922 expedition to open Tutankhamun's tomb in Egypt and died during the course of the excavations in the Valley of the Kings. His death at the age of 57 was due to an infection that developed after he had been bitten on the cheek by a mosquito. This gave rise to the

superstitious fear that he had fallen a victim to a curse associated with the tomb.

It was his wish that he should be buried on Beacon Hill, which overlooks his birthplace, Highclere Castle, to the north-west. The Elizabethan-style mansion is a noble landmark, set in a wooded park ablaze in spring with rhododendrons and azaleas.

To the east beyond the earthworks on Ladle Hill is another landmark, best known for its fictitious family of rabbits – Watership Down of Richard

Adams's novel. Lying between Ladle Hill and the more distant White Hill, Watership Down is one of the high ridges that catch the eye and lead on to the great open scarp of the north Hampshire Downs riding away into the distance.

To the west, the heavily wooded Sidown Hill contrasts sharply with the almost treeless surrounding hills. In the valley between Sidown Hill and Beacon Hill are fields thick with oil-seed rape in summer, their bright yellow standing out vividly against the dark green of meadows and downland.

The Beacon Hill fort, built between 200 and 150 BC, is hour-glass in plan, and encloses about 12 acres. Dotted about within the camp are the outlines of circular huts, which suggest the camp was permanently occupied. Its southern entrance overlooks the outlines of a Celtic field system.

Beacon Hill is ½ mile west of the A34, 6 miles south of Newbury. Watership Down is 2 miles south-west of Kingsclere, which is on the A339, 7 miles south-east of Newbury.

Dc Bucklebury Common

In western Berkshire lies an area of woods and commons that was once part of a royal hunting ground. It was recorded in the Domesday Book as Borgeldeberie Hundred – the land of Burghild's fort; today it is Bucklebury Common, a peaceful backwater of rural Berkshire at its very best.

The common lies between the rivers Pang and Kennet. An unclassified road parallel to the rivers crosses it, running from the village of Upper Bucklebury to the hamlet of Chapel Row and passing between woodlands streaked with the pearly grey of silver birches and darkened here and there with Scots pines. Every 400 yds or so along the road, tracks dive into green tunnels of trees, and there are hard-standings for cars from where paths disappear into the ferns and brambles.

Bucklebury claims to have more footpaths than any other parish in England. More than one leads to the two fishponds, north-east of the crossroads on the common, that were created in the 12th century by the Abbot of Reading to provide fish for his table. Small boys netting newts and tadpoles have

replaced the abbot's monks as fishermen. Apart from the small boys, the still waters, emerald-green with pondweed, are disturbed only by skimming water-boatmen and the occasional leaf falling from overhanging trees.

East of Chapel Row, the road becomes The Avenue, flanked by wide grass verges and rows of stately oaks in the manner of a processional way leading to some great house. The trees give Chapel Row an air of formality, but were planted to commemorate an informal occasion when Elizabeth I visited the home of John Winchcombe, lord of the manor in the 16th century.

Bucklebury Common lies 5 miles east of Newbury. The road across Bucklebury Common is just north of the A4 between Thatcham and Woolhampton. Roads north from either of these two villages lead to the common.

THE SOLITARY SENTINEL

DONNINGTON CASTLE was built in the 14th century by one of the Black Prince's knights, on a hill spur commanding the crossing of the old London–Bath and Oxford–Southampton roads. Still watching over both is the massive gatehouse of 1386 with its two flanking drum towers – all that survives of the castle.

Edward VI gave Donnington to his half-sister Elizabeth in 1551, a legacy that nearly cost her life. Imprisoned in the Tower of London by Queen Mary on suspicion of treason, she was accused of trying to escape to the castle which her servants had stocked for a siege.

In the Civil War of 1642–6, the Royalists dug star-shaped earthworks all round the castle. Cannons sited in arrowhead bastions gave a wide arc of fire with little exposure, and enabled the garrison to hold out for 20 months, although most of the castle was destroyed.

DONNINGTON CASTLE

Dc Donnington Castle

A Royalist stronghold of the Civil War, the castle was one of those that Cromwell 'knocked about a bit', but he left enough to admire on a lofty perch above the River Lambourn. The ruins stand on a grassy hill to the north-west of Donnington village. A path from the small car park at the foot of the hill leads up steeply to the imposing gatehouse with its two round towers. The castle was never large, even before Cromwell's cannons reduced most of it to rubble, but when it was built in the 14th century it commanded a crossing of two main highways, now the A4 and A34. Today it overlooks only a magnificent view across a green, candyfloss countryside with the dark mounds of Beacon Hill and Sidown Hill rising on the distant skyline to the south.

Below the castle can be seen the ridges of earthworks that were dug as defences by Colonel John Boys and his garrison before Cromwell's men besieged the castle in 1644. Admiring the peaceful scene today, sitting on one of the seats by the castle wall, it is hard to imagine the thunder of cannon-fire echoing across the valley, and to feel the desperation of the besieged Royalists who held out for 20 months while their stronghold crumbled around them.

Donnington is 1 mile north of Newbury on the B4494. The castle is signposted west from Donnington village.

Bc Fyfield Down

To reach Fyfield Down, make a diversion eastwards from the Ridgeway Path, about 2 miles north from its start at Overton Hill on the A4.

This pleasant 30 minute walk leads

to a stretch of natural downland which is believed to be the source of the sarsen stones used in the building of Stonehenge. The half-buried boulders of sandstone look, from a distance, like flocks of grazing sheep. For this reason they are known as 'grey wethers', the word 'wether' coming from the Old English for 'sheep'.

Fyfield Down is a nature reserve on which visitors should not wander. Only the paths across it are rights of way. But there is plenty to see without leaving the paths, such as the plants growing close to the lichen-covered stones. Heath bedstraw and sheep's sorrel grow here, living in the pockets of acid soil formed by the sandstone. These plants could never flourish in the surrounding chalk. In autumn a violet haze of gentians softens the cold grey of the stones.

An alternative approach to Fyfield Down is to take the path from Avebury that climbs east over Avebury Down to meet the Ridgeway Path, and join the diversion north of Overton Hill. On old maps it is called a 'herepath', a name that comes from the Old English *here* meaning an army or multitude. It suggests that this may have been a route taken by marauding Saxons as they invaded Wessex.

Fyfield Down is 2½ miles east of Avebury. The Ridgeway Path from Overton Hill starts on the north side of the A4, 4 miles west of Marlborough.

Cc Inkpen Hill and Walbury Hill

A great surge of hills sweeps across the southern border of Berkshire, with Inkpen and Walbury thrusting up to almost 1,000 ft – the highest chalk hills in England. Seen from afar the bare

hills have changing moods; dark and brooding on grey days, green and pleasant under a cloudless sky but always benevolent like lofty guardians of the wide Kennet valley below.

Roads climb steeply up the northern slopes of the hills, and the views from the summits are magnificent. From Walbury, looking back into the Kennet valley, the patchwork of fields and meadows is laced with the dark threads of hedgerows and strewn with the irregular shapes of woods and copses. Looking southwards on a clear day it is possible to see St Catherine's Hill south of Winchester, 23 miles away; to the west are the Wiltshire Downs; to the north-east the slopes of the Berkshire Downs roll away to the valley of the Thames.

Iron Age Celts built an 82 acre fort on the summit of Walbury Hill. About a mile to the west, on Inkpen Hill, there is a grim reminder of more recent times. Here a gibbet looms stark against the skyline. Justice was swift and severe in the days of highwaymen and cut-throats, and after being hanged the miscreant's corpse was strung up on the gibbet as a warning to others. The present gibbet is a replica of one built in 1676, when a man and wife who had murdered two of their children were hung from its two arms.

A path runs along the entire length of the ridge, providing an easy stroll between the two hills with hawthorn, dogwood, wild roses and wild cherry to brighten the way.

Inkpen and Walbury hills are about 5 miles south-east of Hungerford. The road to the top of Walbury Hill starts at the village of Inkpen, on minor roads 3 miles south-east of Hungerford. Follow the signs to Combe. There is a car park on the crest of Walbury Hill.

WHERE THE SCABIOUS BLOOMS

Marsh fritillary butterflies fly in May and June in the south and south-west. The females, larger than the males, lay their eggs on the leaves of devil's-bit scabious, which flowers in damp and marshy places from June to October. Its short rootstock was thought to have been bitten off by the Devil; the name scabious refers to its past use as a cure for itches.

Devil's-bit scabious (*Succisa pratensis*)

Marsh fritillary butterfly (*Euphydryas aurinia*)

Ac Kennet and Avon Canal

West of Devizes the land falls away into a shallow valley, dropping more than 200 ft in 2 miles. But to the Georgian engineer John Rennie, whose Kennet and Avon Canal had to cross the valley, this was no problem. He built locks, 29 of them, and 170 years later they are still there for all but the unimaginative to wonder at.

Four steps down from the main road out of Devizes lead to the canal; wide at this point with deep, dark and still waters. Reeds and water-lilies fringe the banks; ducks, dabchicks and moorhens nibble at the weeds and patient anglers nibble at their sandwiches. To the north-east, the western escarp-

ments of the Marlborough Downs edge the skyline like pale green clouds.

A walk westwards along the gravel towpath brings the first of a series of locks into view, its gates replaced by baulks of timber to dam back the water, and a white bridge a little further on makes a splendid vantage point for looking down into the valley. The locks descend like a giant staircase, with little more than a narrowboat's length between them, and at once the sense of wonderment is tinged with sadness – for the locks are dry except for a muddy trickle, and only the tall-growing reed-mace gives a touch of nobility to the crumbling brickwork.

When the Kennet and Avon Canal was a vital part of Victorian England's waterways, this tranquil scene bustled with activity as the bargees sweated and strained to work their laden craft through the 29 locks – each double-gated. No wonder it took half a day, and no doubt those eastward bound paused at the Black Horse, whose present landlord breeds the Aylesbury ducks which speckle the water where the painted narrowboats once plied.

There is access to the canal from the A361 west of Devizes, about 25 yds west of where it crosses the canal, opposite Avon Road where parking is possible.

Cd Lambourn Downs

The broad shoulder of Lambourn Downs rises to the north of Lambourn, and can be climbed using a path across Pit Down; an easy, ten-minute walk up to downland caressed by a fresh breeze that bends the long grass in rippling swathes. In spring, the rare pasque flower with its purple, bell-shaped head blooms here. And at any time of the year there are horses, not the chalk

ANCIENT PASTURELAND The Lambourn Downs, once a great sheep-rearing area, now grows cereal crops.

figures seen further west but thoroughbreds from the Lambourn stables out for a training gallop. They make a thrilling sight, appearing in a long string from behind a contour of the hills with their tails streaming in the wind.

In the valley west of Pit Down are Lambourn Seven Barrows, a group of 40 ancient burial mounds that include both disc and saucer-shaped mounds (usually built over women's graves), as well as the more common bell-shaped ones. They date from the Wessex Bronze Age, which flourished some 4,000–2,500 years ago, and appear to be contemporary with later building phases of Stonehenge. A little to the north of the group is a chambered long barrow of the New Stone Age.

The Ridge Way skirts the north side of the Lambourn Downs where it crosses Blowingstone Hill. About half a mile north is the strange stone from which the hill takes its name. It is a massive hollow boulder which will produce an eerie, hornlike sound if blown into through one of its holes. It is said that King Alfred used the Blowing Stone to summon his troops to battle, a nice story though an unlikely one. The stone is at the bottom of the hill, just off the B4507, and stands beneath an elm in the garden of a cottage that was once a smithy.

The B4001 runs north from Lambourn across Lambourn Downs; a west fork 1 mile north of Lambourn leads to the Seven Barrows (the start of the Pit Down path) and to Blowingstone Hill and the B4507.

Cc Liddington Castle

In the fading light of evening, the bold outlines of Liddington Castle are dramatic. The earthen ramparts jut out against the sky, and long shadows pick out the faint outlines of wide ditches curling round the southern side. This was an Iron Age hill-fort, a rough and hummocky expanse covering more than 7 acres and sprawling across the brow of a 910 ft high hill.

The path to the castle is lined with aromatic clusters of purple marjoram, and lesser bindweed twines its white and pink cups among the hedgerows. The banks of the castle are clad in lush green grass dotted with yellow carline thistle – a plant that can withstand the attention of grazing cows. A dip in the

bank on its north-western side was probably an entrance to the fort, and the best views of the surrounding countryside are from the top of this bank.

Ignoring the grey swathe of the M4 motorway to the east – it is decently buried in a cutting to the north – the view takes in the western end of the Vale of White Horse and the Cotswold Hills rising mistily beyond the red-brick sprawl of Swindon.

Liddington Castle is 4 miles south-east of Swindon, just south of the Ridge Way – a road at this point – and about ¾ mile west of the A419.

Ac Marden Nature Trail

One of the best ways of appreciating the beauty of the gently flowing River Marden is to walk along the old railway route between Calne and Chippenham that is now a 2 mile long nature trail established in 1970. It follows the course of the River Marden through a shallow valley of woods and meadows.

There is only one entry to the trail, at the old stone bridge half a mile north-east of Studley, where steps lead down to a cutting which has been planted with young larch trees.

The walk westwards leads into Great Bodnage Copse, a small wood of ash, elm, conifers, great sallow, hazel, blackthorn and hawthorn. The trees arching over the track provide an ideal site for such woodland plants as anemones, bluebells, primroses and violets, and wild strawberries grow among the stones that were the ballast for the railway sleepers. Further along the track the river comes into view, moving sluggishly between the meadows where herons fly on slow-beating wings and occasionally there is a flash of blue from a kingfisher. The walk in this direction ends at the remains of Stanley Abbey, a former Cistercian abbey founded by Henry II in the 12th century.

The walk south-eastwards from the bridge ends at Black Dog Hill on the A4. To the left of the trail are water-meadows bright with red campions and ox-eye daisies in late spring, with patches of blue veronica and purple vetch. Some areas of meadow and woodland are marshy, so the plants that thrive here include marsh marigolds, reeds, sedges and mosses. Towards the end of the walk there are laurels, rhododendrons, laburnums and dogwood.

Studley is 2 miles west of Calne, along a minor road north off the A4.

Bc The Ridgeway Path

There is no better way to appreciate the beauty of the Marlborough Downs than to take a stroll along a small section of this prehistoric track, which stretches for 85 miles through the North Wessex Downs and Chilterns. It starts at Overton Hill, and climbs steeply over downland, rising to 663 ft in the first half mile. Sarsen stones litter the fields and the humps of round barrows come into view like small islands – the lonely graves of Bronze Age people who lived here about 3,000 years ago. To the west the great mound of Silbury Hill and the stone circle at Avebury are further reminders that this was the country of ancient races whose culture is still not fully understood.

The path climbs steadily to Hackpen Hill, 892 ft at its highest point, and the view broadens to take in the sweep of rippling hills and downlands. Here and there, copses of beech break up the

otherwise treeless contours. The trees were planted to make windbreaks in the 18th century and are now a natural part of the landscape.

The distance from Overton Hill to Hackpen Hill is about 4 miles; the return journey is along the same route but it provides a chance to see some of the wild flowers which may have been missed on the way – the yellow rockrose, the blue, white or pink flowers of common milkwort and possibly a fragrant or pyramidal orchid.

The start of the Ridgeway Path, at Overton Hill, is on the north side of the A4, 4 miles west of Marlborough.

Bc Roundway Hill

A beechwood crowns Roundway Hill, its majestic trees standing sentinel-like over verdant downland. Clover springs from the long grass, and there are wild flowers such as blue speedwell and yellow goat's beard. Here, the walker can relax beneath the trees or take in the views of the Marlborough Downs to the north-east, where they sweep down to the meandering River Kennet and extend beyond to the Vale of Pewsey.

Roundway was the scene of a Civil War battle on July 13, 1643, when Prince Maurice, brother of Prince Rupert, led a Royalist force to victory against the Roundheads. The battlefield, on Roundway Down, is out of sight from the top of the hill, tucked away in a fold of the Downs about a mile north of the car park at the foot of Roundway Hill. Legend tells that, on the anniversary of the battle, the dead cry out from the nearby ditch where they were buried.

Roundway Hill is about 1 mile northeast of Devizes, along a minor road that forks north from the A361.

Cc Savernake Forest

In the Middle Ages, Savernake was a wilderness of bracken and heathland that had been a royal hunting ground from before the Norman Conquest. In 1540 it was acquired by the Protector, the Duke of Somerset. It thus became an oddity – a forest in private hands. It still remained hunting land with small coppices providing shelter for the deer

BEECH-BORDERED AISLE Splendid beech trees line the Grand Avenue that cuts through the heart of the 2,000 acre Savernake Forest.

and their 'vert', or winter feed. Timber was a by-product but there was no systematic replanting. By 1675, the trees were so decayed that a Navy Surveyor found only three or four fit for use. A few of these ancient trees survive – the big-bellied oak on the A346 Salisbury road is the easiest to see.

Today's forest of stately beeches and oaks was the inspiration of the 18th-century landscape gardener Capability

Brown; he devised a 4 mile long Grand Avenue that ran arrow-straight through the forest, and about halfway along its length he created a 'circus' from which radiated eight walks.

Brown's Grand Avenue may have been as formal as a processional way 200 years ago, but time has given it an air of informality. The road is narrow, and although the great beeches climb like columns in a cathedral nave they have been joined by new trees that crowd the road edge and arch in leafy tunnels. Occasionally the grandeur returns, especially at the circus where tall pines intermingle with the beeches and the young intruders are held at bay. Once again the cathedral-like atmosphere prevails, with the sun filtering through windows mullioned by slender branches.

Informality can be found, too, in the many other walks and drives in the forest, especially in the Postern Hill Walk which is a 2 mile nature trail. Here the venerable beeches give way to a trim, 30-year-old plantation of oaks, young beeches and rowan trees. Bluebells carpet the woods in early summer, when chiffchaffs, willow warblers and whitethroats arrive. Another drive – Long Harry – has trees 90 ft tall, where rooks and jackdaws add their raucous calls to the fluting notes of blackbirds and thrushes.

Primroses, wood anemones and wood sorrel flourish in the woods in spring, and rosebay willowherb and wood sage dapple the glades in warmer weather. Pale bird's-nest orchids grow in the deep shade beneath the beeches.

You may catch a glimpse of a fallow deer, with fan-shaped antlers and spotted summer coat, as it slips silently into a thicket. And a fluster of brightly coloured feathers across a forest path

marks the scurrying retreat of a pheasant.

Savernake Forest is ½ mile south-east of Marlborough, between the A4 and A346. The Grand Avenue starts at Forest Hill, on the A4, and cuts diagonally through the forest in a north-west to south-east direction. The Postern Hill nature trail starts at the picnic site just off the A346 at the western end of the forest.

Dc Snelsmore Common

Few trees are so instantly recognisable or so attractive as birches, with their slender, silver-grey trunks, long whip-like twigs and pale green foliage, turning to orange-yellow in autumn. At Snelsmore they dominate the woodlands, standing in groves like collections of antique silver pieces.

Snelsmore Common Country Park is the largest single tract of open heathland in Berkshire, and the public are free to roam over its 146 acres. There is much to see, apart from the sterling beauty of the birch groves, for the heathland and woodland are full of wildlife. Birds likely to be seen in summer include grasshopper warblers, tree pipits and dusk-flying nightjars, and all-year residents include woodcocks and both great spotted and green woodpeckers. The heathland vegetation is mainly gorse, heather and bracken, providing a retreat for deer, foxes, stoats and weasels as well as common lizards, adders and grass snakes.

The valley bog areas support plants which are rare in many other parts of the country, such as bog bean with its pink and white flowers, and the golden-coloured bog asphodel. Here, too, grows the insect-eating round-leaved sundew, its spoon-shaped leaves and their glistening red tentacles

spread invitingly to entice its victims.

Snelsmore Common Country Park is 2¼ miles north of Newbury and lies to the west of the B4494 between Newbury and Wantage.

Bc Vale of Pewsey

Running between Devizes and Pewsey is the village-dotted Vale of Pewsey. On its northern edge, a ridge of hills lies like a ribbon of fresh green paint, the treeless slopes softly rounded as they sweep down to the valley floor where hamlets and farms are shielded from the north winds by this 900 ft high arm of the Marlborough Downs.

From the road along the north side of the valley there are distant views of Bishop's Cannings Down, then Easton and Horton downs. But at Allington they begin to loom larger – Clifford's Hill, Tan Hill and Milk Hill have their lower slopes close to the road, and footpaths to their summits.

At Alton Barnes crossroads the northbound road climbs almost to the summit of Walker's Hill. A path from the roadside provides a stiffish but short climb to a long barrow called Adam's Grave, from which there are fine views across the valley and along the Downs. On the slopes of Milk Hill there is, inevitably, the figure of a white horse, carved in 1812. Northwards the view takes in Silbury Hill.

Just below the brow of Walker's Hill, on the northern side, a footpath from the road leads to a New Stone Age camp on Knap Hill and to the steep slopes of Golden Ball and Draycot hills.

A minor road leads through the Vale of Pewsey from the A361 in the west, 1¼ miles north-east of Devizes, to the A345 in the east, 1¼ miles north of Pewsey.

Bc The Wansdyke

No journey of discovery into Berkshire and Wiltshire would be complete without a look at this impressive earthwork. It is thought to date from the 5th century AD, and originally ran from the Bristol Channel to the Vale of Pewsey. No one knows who built it, though its function was clearly to keep out invaders from the north. It has been suggested that it was the work of Ambrosius Aurelianus, the last of the Romano-British generals, to keep out invading Saxons who were hard on the heels of the departing Romans.

In places the Wansdyke can be seen much as it was when it was built; a massive bank about 25 ft high with a deep ditch on the northern side. A 2 mile walk along the Ridge Way, south from East Kennett village, leads to the point where the earthwork rides high on the back of Pewsey Downs before plunging into a valley where the ditch becomes lost in a tunnel of thickly woven trees in West Woods. The tangle of trees and undergrowth is almost impenetrable here, and there is an eerie silence save for the sighing of the wind in the tall trees.

East Kennett is 5 miles west of Marlborough, ½ mile south of the A4 at Overton Hill. West Woods lie just south of Lockeridge, south off the A4, 3 miles west of Marlborough. There is also an entrance near Park Farm on a minor road west off the A345, 3 miles south-west of Marlborough. About 400 yds along the wide track skirting the southern edge of the woods, a path branching south follows the Wansdyke westwards.

SHELTERED VALLEY The Vale of Pewsey is protected in the north by the high ridge of the Marlborough Downs.

Ab Westbury Hill

A road leads all the way to the top of Westbury Hill, where Salisbury Plain ends its westward sweep in a climb to 755 ft before falling away dramatically to the Bristol Avon valley. The view here is tremendous, with the steep, chalk slope dropping precipitously into a valley criss-crossed with roads and hedgerows and dotted with farmsteads and villages.

These are commanding heights indeed, which Iron Age men recognised when they built Bratton Castle on the summit. The fort covers 25 acres of the flat plateau, with its ramparts along the edges. Cut into the side of the hill is Wiltshire's oldest and best-known white horse, measuring 175 ft long and 107 ft high with its head just below the castle's upper rampart. The Westbury horse dates from the 18th century, but it replaces an earlier figure said to have been carved to commemorate King Alfred's victory over the Danes at the Battle of Ethandun in AD 878.

The wide downland on the summit provides plenty of space for visitors to roam freely. In spring and summer, harebells and bee orchids strew the grass, and the yellow splash of bird's-foot trefoil attracts the chalkhill blue butterfly to lay its eggs.

Westbury is 4 miles north of Warminster on the A350. Westbury Hill is 2 miles east of Westbury, south-west off the B3098 from Bratton village.

Bc West Kennett

A half-mile walk along a footpath from the A4 leads to the 4,500-year-old West Kennett Long Barrow, the largest chambered tomb in England. The walk to the long barrow is a pleasant stroll

PREHISTORIC TOMB Huge sarsen stones guard the entrance to West Kennett Long Barrow near Avebury.

which crosses the slow-moving River Kennet, passes through a kissing-gate and climbs a gentle hill to a semi-circular forecourt at the entrance to the tomb.

The entrance is startling. Massive standing stones guard the narrow passageway, but it is just possible to sidle past the largest and enter the chamber. Inside are five burial chambers, two on each side and one at the far end, where the remains of some 20 adults, one youth and at least a dozen children were found when the barrow was excavated in 1956. Because of its size – the barrow is 330 ft long, 80 ft wide and 10 ft high – it is thought that it served as a mausoleum for something like 1,000 years.

On the return walk the view of the landscape is dominated by the great, green cone of Silbury Hill. It is the largest man-made prehistoric mound in Europe and stands 130 ft high. Its flat top could comfortably accommodate the giant circle of Stonehenge, and its purpose may have been to serve as a plinth for a similar stone circle. Recent excavations have shown that it was built in four stages, between the period 2145 BC and 95 BC. But that is all that is known for certain, and Silbury Hill remains one of the great archaeological mysteries – and all the more enchanting for it.

There is a path to the top of the mound, a steep and strenuous climb, but the view is marvellous.

WINGS BY THE WAYSIDE

Named for its wing markings that are reminiscent of a peacock's tail, the peacock butterfly comes out from its winter hibernation in March and lays its eggs on stinging nettles in May. It likes to suck nectar from such flowers as red clover and knapweed, a tall, thistle-like plant that blooms in grassy places from June to September. Knapweed is also known as hardhead because of its brownish, knob-like buds.

Peacock butterfly
(*Inachis io*)

Knapweed
(*Centaurea nigra*)

The mystical stones of Avebury lie to the north, with the stone-lined West Kennett Avenue stretching south-east from them, and all around are the green hills and vales of Wiltshire.

There is another long barrow at East Kennett, about 2 miles south-east of Silbury, but this one has not been excavated. It lies in farmland, and its distinctive hump is crested with tall trees. It looks, and is, a lonely place, and whoever sleeps within it, sleeps undisturbed.

Silbury Hill and the start of the footpath to the West Kennett Long Barrow are north and south respectively of the A4, 6 miles west of Marlborough. There is a lay-by for limited parking.

Cd Whitehorse Hill

The white horse of Uffington has been galloping across the Berkshire Downs for centuries; no one knows how many – some say it was carved to celebrate a victory over the Danes by King Alfred, others believe that it dates from the Iron Age and represents the goddess Epona, protector of horses. Whatever its origins, the Uffington horse is impressive and beautiful. From its outstretched head to the tip of its streaming tail it measures 360 ft, and it is the only one of the West Country's chalkhill horses which faces to the right.

Whitehorse Hill is 858 ft high and is crowned by the ditch and bank of Uffington Castle, a circular Iron Age fort covering 8½ acres. The ramparts are constantly windswept, but it is worth the buffeting to climb to the top and look down into the valley with the thatched roofs of farms and cottages embedded among dark green clumps of trees. On a clear day, Wales's distant mountains can be seen like a dark smudge on the western horizon.

Below the white horse is Dragon Hill, a small, almost insignificant mound where St George, the patron saint of England since the 14th century, is said to have killed the dragon. To give credence to the story, a patch of ground on the hill where grass never grows is supposed to have been poisoned by the dragon's blood.

Legends abound in this part of the world, and another concerns Wayland's Smithy, south-west of Whitehorse Hill. There is nothing legendary about its origin; it is a chambered long barrow built in the New Stone Age and dating from about 3000 BC. It has two chambers which can be entered after bending double beneath the massive sandstone lintel. The Saxons believed that Wayland, the smith of the old Saxon gods, lived here, and that if a horse was left by the entrance he would shoe it, provided a coin was left on the lintel stone. Wayland's Smithy is a pleasant 1½ mile walk, south-west along the Ridge Way from Uffington Castle.

Whitehorse Hill is 6 miles west of Wantage, just south of the B4507. Two signposted roads climb from the B4507 to a car park at the top of the hill.

Ba   Woodford Valley

The course of the River Avon, flowing south across Salisbury Plain, is diverted suddenly by the broad shoulder of Amesbury Down. Here the Avon makes a hairpin turn before entering the lovely Woodford valley. From West Amesbury a road winds southwards through the valley, following almost every twist and turn of the west bank of the river and passing through straggling, picturesque villages of thatch and chequered stonework that shelter in the lee of downland slopes.

Sometimes the road climbs the valley side to give glimpses of watermeadows below with rows of weeping willows marking the river's course. Elsewhere, road and river almost touch, as at Middle Woodford where only a few yards of grassy bank divides them. The Avon here is wide, shallow and fast-flowing with green streamers of waterweed fanning out in the rippling current. Watercress grows at the river's edge and rows of willows curve away as the river meanders yet again on its way to Lower Woodford and Avon Bridge.

From Avon Bridge a road leads back up the valley, following the Avon's eastern bank for 4 miles to Great Durnford where there are riverside walks and a restored mill. The Durnford road passes Upper Woodford, which has the only road bridge across the river in the 7 mile stretch between West Amesbury and Avon Bridge. After Great Durnford the east bank road turns northeast, and passes Ogbury Iron Age camp before climbing to Amesbury Down.

The Woodford valley can be explored either by starting at West Amesbury, 1 mile west of Amesbury and just south of the A303, or by leaving Salisbury north on the A345 and turning west at the road signposted Stratford sub Castle.

Bb   Yarnbury Castle

Few Wiltshire guidebooks mention Yarnbury, perhaps because it is overshadowed in renown by its neighbour Stonehenge, 6 miles to the east. But Yarnbury Castle offers a haven of tranquillity, away from the crowds that flock to the great stone circle. It is an

ANCIENT ENCHANTER OF THE DOWNS

THE UFFINGTON WHITE HORSE

THE SPIRIT AND MYSTERY of ancient Wessex is symbolised by the Uffington White Horse, which stands out on the Downs above the Vale of White Horse. G. K. Chesterton wrote in 1911:

*'Before the gods that made the gods
Had seen their sunrise pass,
The White Horse of the White Horse Vale
Was cut out of the grass.'*

Hill-figures cut from the chalk turf are not uncommon in the south of England, but not many are of ancient origin. The Uffington horse is one of the oldest figures, and is the most graceful of the 16 such horses in Britain. Although its presence was first recorded in the 12th century, the Uffington horse may be a tribal symbol dating back to the 1st century BC, for it resembles the stylised horses on coins used by the Celtic Belgae tribe.

Until 1857, the scouring of the horse to keep its outline clear – a task supposed to be carried out every seven years – was turned into a festival or 'pastime', with sports, entertainment and feasting.

Iron Age hill-fort dating from the 2nd century BC, with three grassy banks and three ditches enclosing an area of 28½ acres. In its centre are the just discernible traces of an earlier earthwork built between the 7th and 5th centuries BC, which was overlaid with sheep-pens in the 18th century.

Sheep still graze there, cropping the grass short and pausing only to stare indignantly at intruders who come up the short path from the A303 and climb the steep banks. This is an ideal place to rest awhile; to stretch out on the close-cropped grass and still be able to see the sweeping countryside in all directions. To the south the landscape is soft and gentle, for this is the southern edge of Salisbury Plain where it descends into the Wylye valley. To the north, east and west are the rolling uplands of the plain, the broad cornfields stretching to the horizon reminiscent of the American prairies.

Yarnbury Castle lies north of the A303, 3 miles west of Winterbourne Stoke. The only access path runs from the northern half of the dual-carriageway. There is no break in the central reservation at this point; if approached from the east, it is necessary to travel about 1 mile further on to cross the reservation.

THE CHILTERN HILLS

Gentle, beech-clad hills along which primitive man
once trod the ancient Icknield Way

On their north-west face, the Chiltern Hills rise steeply from the vales of Oxford and Aylesbury to beech-stacked heights such as Aston Hill, or the turf-covered summits of Dunstable Downs. On their southern side they curve and fold into rounded, tree-crowned hills with sloping fields and small, peaceful valleys that are known as 'bottoms'. Beguiling rather than commanding, they beckon the visitor to explore their well-trodden paths and silent woods.

The Chilterns are part of the great chalk belt stretching from Dorset to Yorkshire, with their highest point, 876 ft, in Wendover Woods. From Goring in the south-west, they extend an embracing arm north-west of the London Basin, wooded for some 35 miles as far as Ivinghoe. Beyond, for another 12 miles or so, grassy downland stretches to where the crooked finger of Sharpenhoe Clappers prods into the Midland plain.

Five valleys, or gaps, pierce the chalk ridge – at Goring, Princes Risborough, Wendover, Tring and Dunstable. These gaps were cut by rivers, now long-lost except for the Thames which flows through Goring Gap to separate the Chilterns from the Berkshire Downs. The gaps provide convenient routes for roads to London, two built by the Romans – Akeman Street (now the A41) through Tring Gap, and Watling Street (now the A5) through Dunstable Gap.

But a much older route stretches along the length of the Chilterns

– the prehistoric Icknield Way. Some 4,000 years ago it was part of an ancient ridgeway track from East Anglia to the religious centres at Avebury and Stonehenge in Wiltshire. Another ancient feature of the Chilterns, the biggest of its Iron Age earthworks, is the mysterious Grim's Ditch, or Dyke, which runs right through the hills, appearing sometimes as a deep trench, sometimes as a high bank. It may have been part of Iron Age defences or boundaries. Grim's Ditch can be clearly seen near Great Hampden, at the hamlet of Redland End. In the 17th century, Great Hampden was the home of John Hampden, Member of Parliament for Wendover. His stand against the payment of ship-money, a tax imposed by Charles I in 1635, led to the Civil War of 1642. Hampden died in 1643, from wounds received at Chalgrove Field, and is buried in Great Hampden Church.

Shady beechwoods are typical of Chiltern country, clothing the hill-crests and hanging on the slopes. Their spreading foliage discourages undergrowth, and only in the spring, before the canopy closes, does a filter of sunlight encourage a blaze of bluebells. In high summer the beechwoods are cool, serene and sombre, with a thick brown carpet of dead leaves and the hushed silence of a cathedral.

In past centuries, the beeches were often coppiced or pollarded to grow poles for firewood, but their timber was little valued until the 1700s, when it began to be used for chair-making. Wood-turners known as 'bodgers' set up their pole-lathes in the Chiltern glades, and made legs and spindles for the town furniture factories, particularly those at High Wycombe. To keep up with the demands of the industry, at its peak in the 19th century, the beechwoods were continually replanted. The result is the many beautiful beechwoods of today.

SHADED SPLENDOUR Burnham Beeches is the most famous of the Chiltern beechwoods, where only stray shafts of sunlight can penetrate the dense leafy canopy. The conditions favour plants such as bird's-nest orchids, which require little light and feed on leaf litter.

Places to visit

Map ref. Cc Ashridge and Ivinghoe

The woods at Ashridge are the last of the ridge-top forest at the north-east end of the Chilterns, giving way to grassy downland towards Ivinghoe Beacon, marked as Beacon Hill on Ordnance Survey maps. They are mixed woods, but beeches predominate and some 2 sq. miles of mainly beechwoods sweep up from Aldbury Common. Overlooking the hillside above Aldbury village, the 108 ft high Bridgewater monument peeps over the tree-tops. From it a broad avenue leads through the beechwoods to the Berkhamsted–Dagnall road.

The monument was erected in 1832 in memory of the 3rd Duke of Bridgewater, pioneer of Britain's canal system, who once lived at nearby Ashridge House on the east side of the woods. For those who climb the 172 muscle-dragging steps to the top, there are fine views over the 4,000 acre Ashridge estate, which is owned by the National Trust.

A nature trail of 1½ miles starts from the monument, winding its way northwards at first between a forest of silver-grey trunks that rise to a canopy of delicate foliage. There is little undergrowth where the beeches hold sway, their fallen leaves covering the ground

with a sea of burnished copper for most of the year. Where there are other trees – oaks, birches, silver birches and sycamores – there is enough light to encourage wild flowers such as wood anemones and wood sorrel in spring and early summer.

Tits of all sorts feed on the birch seeds, and these trees also receive attention from grey squirrels which strip the bark and often kill the branches. The beechwoods straddle the Hertfordshire and Buckinghamshire border, and at one point the trail crosses a foot-bridge over a sunken track that was once the county boundary.

Where there is thick undergrowth, particularly bracken, there are fallow deer (about 3 ft to the shoulder) and Chinese muntjac deer (about 18 in. to the shoulder). Deer are best seen at dawn or dusk, when they come out of cover to feed. After mid-August you may see a fallow buck with his full spread of antlers, and at the end of October you may hear his belching snort echoing through the woods as the rutting, or mating, season approaches.

Ivinghoe Beacon lies about 2½ miles north of the Bridgewater monument. The hillside is almost bare of cover, only a few thorn bushes breaking its bold outline. There are paths to the summit – white trails worn in the chalk – and the wild flowers there are lime-lovers such as thyme and rock-roses. From the summit there is a wide-ranging panorama of the vale below, and to the east you can see the hill-figure of a white lion cut in the chalk of Dunstable Downs, advertising the presence of Whipsnade Park Zoo.

Ashridge is on the B4506 between Berkhamsted and Dagnall. It can also be reached from the village of Aldbury, 2½ miles east of Tring. From there, a minor road climbs steeply up the hillside to join the B4506, giving fine views on the way. Ivinghoe Beacon is south of the B489, 1 mile north-east of Ivinghoe.

Bb Aston Rowant National Nature Reserve

Typical Chiltern countryside – grass downland, scrub and beechwoods – is all preserved in the 258 acre Aston Rowant National Nature Reserve, which includes the steep slopes of Beacon Hill, at 800 ft one of the highest points of the Chilterns. Like its sister ridges, it gives fine views over the Vale of Aylesbury below, with the Cotswolds visible on a clear day. The

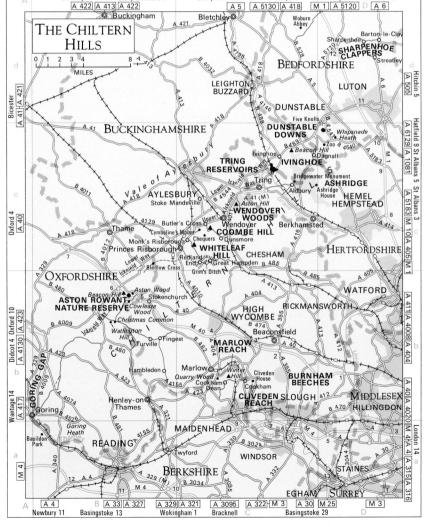

THE CHILTERN HILLS

Beacon Hill nature trail, peaceful and undisturbed despite the hum of motorway traffic below, explains the landscape and wildlife of the area.

This countryside is rich in woods and wildlife. Aston Wood, 104 acres of mixed woods owned by the National Trust, borders the reserve to the north, and south-westwards is Cowleaze Wood, part of the Chiltern Forest managed by the Forestry Commission. There are car parks, a picnic area and waymarked walks in the depths of the conifer and deciduous forest. In summer, willow warblers dart elusively in the branches overhead, easy to hear but difficult to see.

Muntjac and fallow deer may be seen in the woods, and there are foxes and badgers. Jays and magpies swoop among the trees, woodpeckers drum in the woodland depths, and kestrels may be seen hovering above scrub and grassland. Plants include nightshades, wood anemones, woodruffs, bluebells and various kinds of orchid.

South-westwards from the reserve, a minor road leads to Christmas Common. It gained its name in the Civil War, when in 1643 Parliamentarians held the valley and Royalists the ridge above. They called a truce at Christmas and met on the common.

From the road junctions to the east of the common, the north-west road descends Watlington Hill, another National Trust property, with chalk downs, copses and a natural yew wood. The south-east road plunges into a tunnel of beech trees and mossy banks to wind down to Turville, Fingest and Hambleden.

Aston Rowant Nature Reserve is 10 miles north-west of High Wycombe. It can be reached along a minor road off the A40 about 1 mile north-west of Stokenchurch, signposted Christmas Common. Beacon Hill nature trail car park is along a right turn on the minor road, ¼ mile from the A40 junction. Aston Wood straddles the A40, 1½ miles north-west of Stokenchurch.

CHILTERN VIEW From Coombe Hill wooded ridges stretch westwards. Near by is Cymbeline's Mount and its solitary stand of trees.

Cb **Burnham Beeches**

Ancient pollarded beeches of massive girth, their gnarled and stunted trunks bent and twisted into grotesque shapes, are the patriarchs of Burnham Beeches. Their crowns were cut when they were about 6 ft high to produce poles for firewood. Their fascinating misshapenness is the result of regular lopping and re-growth until the early 1800s, when coal became a more

171

common fuel. Now probably about 300 years old, these ancient beeches are gradually dying.

An area of about 500 acres of woods and commons, Burnham Beeches is owned by the City of London Corporation who bought about 400 acres for the benefit of the public in 1879. The name Burnham is after Viscount Burnham, who donated the 88 acres of Fleet Wood in 1921. On the northern fringe are Egypt Woods, once the haunt of gipsies. The woods take their name from the first wandering bands of gipsies who arrived in Britain early in the 16th century and called themselves 'Dukes of Little Egypt' – and so became known as 'gipsies'.

Although beeches abound, there are many other trees scattered among them. Silver birches add a lighter touch among the dark shades of the beeches; holly, pines and firs provide all-year-round greenness; and lovely rhododendrons bloom in some of the dells. Patches of heathland break up the wooded areas – aprons of grass dotted bright yellow with gorse in summer. There are numerous criss-crossing footpaths and bridle-paths, and a number of metalled roads, ramped to restrict speed, give access to various parking areas.

Burnham Beeches lies to the south of Beaconsfield and north of Slough, to the west of the A355.

Cc Coombe Hill

One of the highest points in the Chilterns, Coombe Hill (852 ft) thrusts out into the landscape to give magnificent views of its neighbouring ridges and the Vale of Aylesbury spread out below. A tall granite monument perched on the hillside commemorates the Bucking-

hamshire men who died in the Boer War, and its stepped base makes a good vantage point.

Chequers, the country house of Britain's prime ministers, can be glimpsed among the trees to the south-west, and westwards behind Ellesborough, marked by its church tower, lies Cymbeline's Mount, or Castle. The mound's history is shrouded in the mists of time, but it is said to be the place where the sons of the Celtic King Cunobelinus were killed in a battle with the Romans. The villages of Great and Little Kimble to the west of the mound probably derive their names from it. To the north-east lies Wendover, the tree-clad ridges of

CHILTERN SWEETNESS

Only on the dry, chalky slopes of the Chiltern Hills is the dainty wild candytuft found in abundance. Elsewhere it is rare or unknown. Its white or mauve flowers appear during July and August and, like the cultivated candytufts that originate from it, they have two of their four petals – those pointing towards the middle of the flower cluster – only half as long as the others. Its old name was *Thlaspi candiae* – 'rockplant of Crete'.

Candytuft
(*Iberis amara*)

Wendover Woods climbing behind its rooftops.

Coombe Hill, with 106 acres owned by the National Trust, is on the route of the Ridgeway Path. Heather and gorse are scattered over the summit, and below the northern end of the ridge the steep slopes are thick with lime-loving scrub and trees such as the spindle and the wayfaring tree. There are sometimes sheep on the hill – they help to keep down the scrub. Some of the rams have as many as six horns; these are Joseph's sheep, thought to be the 'sheepe with the little spots and great spots' mentioned in the Book of Genesis in the 1599 edition of the Bible.

Coombe Hill can be reached along a minor road south off the B4010 at Butler's Cross, 1¼ miles west of Wendover. Take the sharp left turn towards Dunsmore that climbs between gnarled beeches to a parking area beneath overhanging trees, where the road bends. A gate leads to the hill, which is only a gentle stroll away. It can also be reached by a fine 1½ mile walk along the ridge from Wendover; the path starts at a sharp bend in the B4010 (Upper Icknield Way), ¼ mile west of the junction with the A413.

Dc Dunstable Downs

The view stretches for miles from the humped, grassy shoulders of Dunstable Downs, which loom over the flatness of the Vale of Aylesbury, fading into a blue haze of distance to the north-west. The feeling of space and distance is almost intoxicating, and the gliders that swoop and hover silently above on a summer's day, climbing on air currents pushed up from the rounded slopes, add to the heady atmosphere.

There are few trees on the downs,

apart from the land owned by the National Trust; the wide stretches of grassland fall quickly away to the valley floor where the centuries-old Icknield Way (now a modern road) starts to pick its course along the Chilterns. At the northern tip of the downs it passes the Five Knolls barrow cemetery, where relics of the New Stone Age and Bronze Age have been found. Southwestwards it continues to Ivinghoe Beacon (also known as Beacon Hill), rising to 756 ft on the skyline and marking the start of the main Chiltern ridge that stretches down to the Thames valley.

From the top of the downs, where the National Trust owns 285 acres, lanes lead south-east to Whipsnade Heath, a grassy expanse in a sheltered dell that lies east of the B4541 and north of the B4540. Here man and nature have combined to shape a Tree Cathedral, the inspiration of a local landowner Edmund Kell Blyth. He planted a variety of trees during the 1930s, setting them out to form a nave, transepts, cloisters and chapels. Now the trees have matured to give the effect of a cathedral, with a dew-pond in the position of the altar.

Dunstable Downs border the western side of the B4541 Whipsnade road 2 miles south of Dunstable.

Ab Goring Gap

At Goring Gap, the River Thames breaks through the chalk hills to separate the Berkshire Downs from the Chiltern Hills. Goring is the meeting place of the ancient Berkshire Ridge Way and the Chiltern Icknield Way. For centuries from prehistoric times, travellers forded the river there on their journey north-east to the farmlands and flint mines of East Anglia, or westwards to the great stone circles of Avebury and Stonehenge.

Today, Goring is a charming Georgian town where pleasure-boats line the towpath and trees slope down to the riverside. Here the gentle waters of the Thames become turbulent for a while as they stream over the weirs close to the double bridge in the town centre. Southwards across the river, on the Berkshire side, lies Basildon Park, where fine parkland surrounds a splendid Georgian mansion owned by the National Trust. From the grounds, open in summer, there are fine views across the river.

Goring is at the south-west tip of the Chilterns, and 4 miles east of the town lies Goring Heath, where the Chiltern beechwoods begin. Cool and spacious with little undergrowth, they are made for easy wandering. But since the woods are deep, and one beech tree looks very much like another, it is as well not to wander too far.

Goring is 8 miles north-west of Reading at the B4526 and B4009 junction.

Cb Marlow Reach and Cliveden Reach

Some of the loveliest Chiltern scenery lies along the winding loop of the River Thames between Marlow and Maidenhead. Winter Hill, high above Marlow on the south side of the river, gives superb views of Marlow Reach and the softly contoured hills to the north. Early in the year when the winds are high, Winter Hill is well named; but in summer, warm breezes temper the air and send hundreds of bright-sailed yachts scudding across the river below. There are fine beechwood walks through Quarry Wood, below the

WOODLAND OF MENACE AND MEMORY

QUARRY WOOD, stretching south-west from the Thames at Marlow, is featured, in different moods, in Jerome K. Jerome's *Three Men in a Boat* published in 1889 and Kenneth Grahame's *The Wind in the Willows* written some 18 years later.

For Grahame, Quarry Wood was the inspiration for the menacing Wild Wood explored by Mole, with its faces, whistlings and mouth-like holes.

Jerome's wood was haunted by the memories of sunny summer days and the ghosts of merry faces: 'Dear old Quarry Wood! With your narrow, climbing paths and little winding glades . . . how from your whispering leaves there softly fall the voices of long ago.'

QUARRY WOOD NEAR MARLOW

west-facing upper slopes of the hill.

Cookham, with its many pleasant Georgian houses, lies within the loop of the river. Footpaths lead from the village to the river bank and beside the backwaters that join the river at Cliveden Reach. From Cookham Lock to Boulter's Lock, beechwoods sweep down to the water's edge on the eastern side – a lovely sight at any time, but glorious in autumn when the woods are

ablaze with tints of russet and gold.

High above the river is Cliveden House. The present mansion in 16th-century Italian style was built in 1850 by Sir Charles Barry for the Duke of Sutherland. Later it was the home of Lord and Lady Astor, and is now owned by the National Trust. Its grounds provide fine views of the Thames.

Marlow is 4 miles south of High

Wycombe on the A404, Cookham 3 miles north of Maidenhead on the A4094. Winter Hill (National Trust) is reached from Cookham Dean, west of Cookham. Cliveden is on the B476, off the A4 about 1 mile east of Maidenhead; the entrance gate is opposite the Feathers Inn.

Dd Sharpenhoe Clappers

A range of low hills shaped like an inverted question-mark stretches from east to west across the Bedfordshire plain for about 3 miles. This is Sharpenhoe Clappers (525 ft), the last remnant of the Chilterns before the landscape levels to the Midland plain.

The most northerly point of the hills, the hooked back of the question-mark, stands above the village of Sharpenhoe, surmounted by Clappers Wood and an Iron Age hill-fort. In summer the leafy beeches cushion the hill crest, but in winter the bare trees stand out like spines along the ridge.

From Sharpenhoe, a minor road climbs south to the small National Trust car park from where footpaths wind east along the ridge. They lead first through a wooded glen, mostly beeches but with some young rowans beneath the larger trees. Beyond, the paths are through hedgerows where just about every species of chalk-loving plant can be found. Musk thistle, with its great purple flowers, is predominant. In addition, there are rock-roses, tall-growing tansies with tiny yellow flowers, and old man's beard.

Suddenly the hedgerows give way to grassy downland, with a full view across a plain plumed with Lombardy poplars. In summer, the downs are speckled with the yellow of bird's-foot trefoil and the purple of self-heal. In spring they are the home of the rare pasque flower, an anemone with large violet flowers.

Where the ridge ends, beeches cling precariously to the steep slope, nevertheless maintaining their stately dignity. These are youngish trees, their smooth bark carved with pierced hearts and the initials of lovers of long ago. What became of KM and LA who walked hand in hand there in 1952?

Sharpenhoe is 6 miles north of Luton, and can be reached along minor roads west off the A6 at Streatley or Barton-le-Clay.

Cc Tring Reservoirs

The sound of rushing water greets you as you leave the car park, and within a few yards you are standing by the tumbling waters of a weir. This is a backwater of the Grand Union Canal, half hidden among overhanging trees, where the shallow, crystal-clear water swarms with minnows and stickle-backs. Beyond the weir is the canal itself, sweeping in a wide arc lined with patient anglers.

To the south of the canal, a bank hides the waters of Startop's End Reservoir, one of the group of three that comprise the Tring Reservoirs National Nature Reserve. Climb the bank and you will see that Startop's End looks the most man-made of the three – angular and featureless – but the bank provides a good view of the canal curving away into the distance and Ivinghoe Beacon jutting on the skyline to the north-east.

RIVER OF REFLECTION Nowhere is the Thames more serene and lovely than on its course through the Chilterns. At Cliveden Reach, beeches crowd the river banks and are mirrored in its tranquil waters.

Beyond the canal bend is the first of a flight of six locks, known as Tring Steps, that lift the canal to a height of almost 400 ft as it cuts through the Chilterns. Each time a boat passes through the lock, about 50,000 gallons of water are lost downhill, and when water traffic is busy the reservoir levels constantly change as water is pumped from them to replenish the canal.

The lock is dated 1865, and its wooden-framed gates are overgrown with grass and nettles. On summer days it is constantly in use as pleasure-boats pass to and fro, but in the quiet of the evening you may see a kingfisher using one of the gates as a diving board.

South of the canal, opposite the lock, lies reed-fringed Marsworth Reservoir, the home of tufted ducks, pochards, mallards, shovelers and noisy, quarrelsome coots. In winter they are joined by teal, wigeon, gadwall, goldeneye and goosander. Among the most fascinating of the birds at Tring are the great crested grebes. Between December and May, watch out for their stately courtship displays, especially the dance when they dive for weeds, surface and swim towards each other, then rise breast to breast with feet paddling and necks swaying.

A bank divides Marsworth and Startop's End reservoirs, and a footpath across the top leads to Tringford Reservoir, passing close to a heronry identified by the bundles of twigs in the branches of dead trees. At the far end of Tringford Reservoir there is a public hide. In autumn, when the water level is low, you may see sandpipers, redshanks, greenshanks, snipe and ringed plovers feeding in the mud.

Tring Reservoirs can be reached from the A41 Aylesbury–Tring road. Turn north on to the B489 towards Ivinghoe. The reservoirs border the east side of the B489, and the car park is on the right-hand side just before the bridge over the canal.

Cc Wendover Woods

Wendover nestles at the mouth of a narrow gap in the Chiltern ridge with Coombe Hill rising to the south-west. To the north-east Wendover Woods, part of the Chiltern Forest, blanket the steep ridges of Boddington Hill, Haddington Hill and Aston Hill. These woods are the highest part of the Chilterns, the summit (876 ft) on the edge of Halton Wood being marked by a cairn.

A minor road winds up from the Upper Icknield Way through overhanging trees to a small car park on Aston Hill, one of the starting points for a number of waymarked walks and trails through the woods. From the hill there is an uninterrupted view across the flat farmlands of the Aylesbury plain, stretching for miles far below. Tring Reservoirs can be picked out to the north-east, the sky mirrored in their shimmering waters.

A forest walk, the quaintly named Daniel's Trudge, starts just below the car park; this name derives from the Old English *denn* (a pasture) and *hol* (a deep place). A trudge it may be, certainly on its second half, for all but the energetic. The path descends the steep ridge through woodlands, then climbs to the top again by a zigzag route, finally leading among ancient cultivation terraces known as lynchets.

There are four other forest walks, all starting from the Cedar Car Park which lies about 2 miles south on the same minor road. Aston Hill Ramble leads through beechwoods and a yew glade; the Beech Hangings is a walk through typical Chiltern hanging beechwoods on the side of a steep slope; Boddington Banks walk follows the line of ancient Iron Age earthworks, and Hale View walk climbs to a viewpoint above the Wendover Gap.

Aston Hill and the Cedar Car Park are 2 miles north-east of Wendover. Turn sharply south from the A4011 (the Upper Icknield Way) north of the Chiltern Forest Office.

Cc Whiteleaf Hill

A huge white cross is cut in the chalk on the side of Whiteleaf Hill, a mile north-east of Princes Risborough. This 80 ft cross overlooks the Upper Icknield Way, and rises from the roadside on a pyramid about 300 ft across at its base.

No one knows who cut the cross or why – theories suggest it to be a Christianised fertility symbol, a signpost at the crossing of ancient trackways, an acclamation of faith by medieval monks or Cromwellian troops, or just a 17th or 18th-century folly. There is a similar cross, but without a pyramidal base, cut in the chalk of Bledlow Ridge a few miles to the south-west.

Remains of some New Stone Age long barrows can be seen on the summit of the hill, from where there are fine views of the Berkshire Downs to the south-west. A car park at the top of the hill is a good starting point for walks through pleasant woods, where helleborines – wild orchids common to beechwoods on lime-rich soil – flower in summer.

To reach Whiteleaf Hill car park, turn south-east off the A4010 Princes Risborough–Stoke Mandeville road on to a minor road at Monks Risborough.

NEW WEALTH, NEW LANDOWNERS

ENCLOSURES AND THE RELEASE OF CHURCH LANDS UTTERLY CHANGED THE FACE OF THE COUNTRYSIDE

HENRY TUDOR'S retrieval of the English crown from a bush on Bosworth Field is generally taken to be a turning point in the history of the realm – the moment when England turned its back upon the medieval past and hurried forward into the modern era. Though a wild generalisation, there is a certain amount of truth in it. Renaissance was in the air and, whatever their faults, the Tudors, between 1485 and 1603, usually supplied a stable governmental climate that encouraged new ideas to take root.

So far as the countryside is concerned, the most striking change effected during the reign of the Tudors was the emergence of a new breed of landowner, no longer so much concerned with soldiering as with the management of his estates and with the improvement of his way of life. How adept he was is apparent in the great houses of the period – houses for the first time, and not castles – that still grace the landscape. Battlements became unfashionable, except in the northern counties, and were replaced by graceful brick, glittering casements and formal gardens.

One of the earliest, and in many ways the loveliest of Tudor houses, is Compton Wynyates, built by Sir William Compton in 1510. Sir William enclosed 2,000 acres of the manor of Compton Superior on the fringe of the Avon valley in Warwickshire to create a deer park; he then built his house, probably on the site of an earlier, fortified structure. Perhaps it was a sign of the times that some of the building materials he used came from a ruined castle.

The new wealth, largely gained from wool, altered the face of England, and many of its effects are with us to this day. In 1506, Sir John Spencer bought the manor of Wormleighton in Warwickshire; the villagers and the occupants of 18 farms had been evicted eight years earlier to make way for sheep. Sir John prospered, bought more land round Althorp in Northamptonshire

and watched his flocks increase to a point where at one time he owned 14,000 sheep. The house he built at Althorp still stands, though much altered in 1790, and it was from there that the lines of two great families sprang – the Earls Spencer of Althorp, and the Spencer-Churchills, whose descendants included the later Dukes of Marlborough, Sir Winston (Spencer) Churchill and HRH the Princess of Wales.

Another road to riches in Tudor England lay through the Court, where services to the State or monarch could be rewarded with gifts of land. Henry VIII was especially generous after the Dissolution of the Monasteries in 1536, granting large tracts of former Church lands to his friends and selling the remainder at knock-down prices. The number of abbeys, priories and granges added to the names of country houses are still a reminder of the great building boom that took place on estates confiscated from various religious orders. In many cases the construction materials were obtained from the source readiest to hand – the abandoned church buildings. Loseley Park in Surrey is built of stone taken from nearby Waverley Abbey, while Longleat in Wiltshire incorporated the ruins of an Augustinian priory, and Lanhydrock House in Cornwall rose from a monastic farm.

Elizabethan extravaganzas

The grand age of Tudor building reached its extravagant peak in Elizabeth I's reign. The dizziest heights were scaled by William Cecil, Lord Burghley, Elizabeth's Lord High Treasurer, with his palatial Burghley House near Stamford, and by 'Bess of Hardwick', Countess of Shrewsbury. This redoubtable lady with a genius for marrying rich husbands – four of them – and a passion for architecture, created Hardwick Hall ('Hardwick Hall, more glass than wall') in Derbyshire. With its formal gardens and

splendid façade, it remains the most exuberant expression of the age.

Exuberance, however, was scarcely the keynote in Scotland, whence James VI emerged in 1603 to become James I of Great Britain. There, the picture was very different – a country torn by religious strife, and where government decrees were as blithely ignored by Border lairds as by Highland chiefs. Though Scotland possessed four universities to England's two, the medieval chill lingered longer in the north, and wise landowners tended to repair the walls of ancestral keeps rather than attempt to emulate the new grandeurs of the south. Few could have afforded such luxuries in any case, and in the Scottish countryside there are almost no great houses of the period to compare with those of England.

Enclosures and reclamations

The new century and the new dynasty were to witness political, religious and economic changes even more far-reaching than those that took place in Elizabeth's reign. Many of these were reflected in the countryside. The land-enclosure movement quickened its pace, and everywhere landlords were turning the ploughed, ridged strips of medieval fields into hedged pastures and gathering scattered smallholdings together into large farms. At the same time, the restrictions of Norman Forest Laws were lifted from many areas, bringing thousands of new acres under the plough.

The 17th century, too, saw the most impressive reclamation of marshland since that undertaken by the monasteries several centuries earlier. In 1630, the Earl of Bedford and his company of 'Adventurers' set out to drain the Cambridgeshire Fens, engaging a Dutch engineer, Cornelius Vermuyden, to manage the project. Vermuyden straightened the wandering Great Ouse by cutting two parallel channels, the Old and New Bedford rivers, for 21 miles

between Earith and Denver Sluice, so hastening the draining of the waters to the North Sea. In the southern Fens, a multitude of cuts, drains and sluices created hundreds of acres of new peat-rich farmlands, and wind-pumps were set up to maintain the rate of drainage at a steady flow. One of these pumps can still be seen at Wicken Fen, which has been left largely undrained in order to provide a glimpse of the wilderness of pre-drainage days.

The age of rebuilding

The years both before and after the Civil War of the 1640s were marked in the countryside by an upsurge of rebuilding, not only of the great houses, but of the farms of yeomen and of entire villages. Stone was often used to replace timber and plaster, an indication perhaps of the growing scarcity of full-grown oaks. The finest examples of the age of rebuilding stretch across the Midlands from Gloucestershire to Lincolnshire, where the rich brown ironstones and luminous limestones provide some of the finest of all building materials. The village of Collyweston in Northamptonshire was entirely rebuilt in stone in the early years of the 17th century, and nearby Rockingham in the decades after the Civil War. Rebuilding spread even to the remote hills of northern England, where Troutbeck, on the fells above Windermere, possesses a score of houses dating from the late 1600s. Low Hartsop, too, a cluster of farmsteads in the secret hills at the head of Ullswater, was completely rebuilt at about this time.

In 1714, Queen Anne, the last Stuart monarch, died, though the House of Stuart was to continue its efforts to regain the throne until the last bloody charge on Culloden Moor 32 years later. But by this time the Georgian Age was firmly established, and already in the British landscape there could be heard the first, faint, far-off thumpings of machinery.

WORSHIP AND WOOL 'By the time of the Dissolution of the Monasteries in the 1530s, Fountains Abbey in North Yorkshire owned a million acres and some 20,000 sheep. Its wealth made it an early target for Henry VIII's commissioners, and its walls and roofs were stripped for materials to build nearby Fountains Hall (inset).

RENAISSANCE, TUDOR STYLE Despite its fragile air, Little Moreton Hall in Cheshire has endured for four centuries. Though built for comfort rather than defence, it is nevertheless moated, partly perhaps to recall military building styles of the past, and more practically to provide a sewer for garderobes on the upper floors.

'MORE GLASS THAN WALL' With its enormous windowed façade, Hardwick Hall in Derbyshire is perhaps the most breathtaking of all great Elizabethan houses – though its style looks both forward to Jacobean and back to the medieval. The famous tapestries in the house include patchworks almost certainly made from copes and altar cloths taken from monasteries and abbeys.

BUILT ON WOOL Arlington Row in Bibury, Gloucestershire, is a terrace of weavers' cottages that has miraculously survived from the 16th and 17th centuries to show that even workers in wool enjoyed a relative degree of prosperity. The old cloth-drying green is near by.

THE YORKSHIRE DALES

Drystone walls and solid farmhouses dominate
the green valleys, watched over by dark, sprawling fells

High moorlands; steep-sided valleys; limestone hills; rivers and streams and plunging waterfalls – mix them together and you have the Yorkshire Dales, a scenic 'lucky dip' which nature seems to have created in a moment of playfulness. That moment, in fact, began some 300 million years ago when great faults in the earth's surface, the Craven Faults and the Dent Fault, up-ended the limestone rocks of the Pennines to the north and east, forming the cliffs and scars of Ribblesdale. To the north, in Wensleydale, the limestone breaks through only occasionally, and further north still, in Swaledale, it lies buried deep beneath the Yoredale Rocks. The final touches were added 10,000 years ago, when the Ice Age glaciers carved the deep valleys with the deftness of a sculptor's blade, and left lakes such as Malham Tarn.

Centuries of erosion of the limestone by rainwater left caves which provided shelter for early man, but it was the invading Norsemen of the 9th and 10th centuries who settled there and first cultivated the upper dales. It is to these Norsemen that the Yorkshire Dales owe much of their character – the word 'dale' is Norse, meaning valley; and it was the Norsemen who called the hills 'fells', the streams 'becks' and a waterfall 'force'. Their farms and settlements are still scattered among the Dales, and carry names often ending in 'thwaite', 'wick' or 'sett'.

There are four large dales in the 680 sq. miles of the Yorkshire Dales

National Park, with a host of smaller dales wandering off into rocky gorges beneath the fells. Each dale has a character of its own. Swaledale in the north is narrow and steepsided, a wild and desolate valley topped by sweeping moorlands. Broad and wooded Wensleydale carves a bold path through the heart of the Dales. Wharfedale in the south-east is long and winding, its valley floor criss-crossed by drystone walls and studded with pretty villages. To the west, Ribblesdale is a valley of rolling countryside below towering moorland peaks.

The fertile soil of the Dales has attracted farmers ever since the Norsemen came. The Angles and Danes settled at the lower ends of the Dales, and in medieval times monastic groups set up their abbeys in the rich pasturelands. Their idyllic days came to an end with the Dissolution of the Monasteries in 1538, and behind them came a new land-owning class – the wealthy farmers whose drystone walls and farm buildings still dominate the Dales.

But the rocky hillsides held other attractions for other men; lead for the manufacturing industries of the Industrial Revolution and limestone for the building of great houses for the men who grew rich on the land. The quarries and lead mines scarred the hills, but many of the scars have now healed, though in some places quarrying still continues. The mines were abandoned in the 19th century, when cheap lead from abroad killed the industry. It was a death mourned only by those who had sought to mercilessly exploit the land – to those who loved the beauty of the Dales, it was a reprieve.

Now the continuing beauty of the Yorkshire Dales is assured, made safe by their designation as a National Park in 1954, and they offer a variety of scenery unmatched in most parts of Britain.

RIBBONS OF STONE In Malhamdale, drystone walling embroiders the hills and fields. This valley in Upper Airedale is typical of many in the Yorkshire Dales, where sheep and cattle graze and a solitary farm stands on the wide, valley floor.

Places to visit

Map ref. Bb Airedale Head

The 5 mile cul-de-sac valley of Upper Airedale is the 18th-century Landscape Movement dream translated into limestone and turf. From the scars along the line of the North Craven Fault, springs and streams leap joyously to combine in the River Aire around Malham, the village which has donated the valley's alternative name of Malhamdale. Less than a mile to the north of Malham are the 240 ft high, bare limestone walls of Malham Cove; to the north-east, crags and gentle hills enfold the savagery of Gordale Scar. From the village, walled roads climb steeply to the north, the only means of escape from the valley's blunt ending.

People have lived here since time immemorial – Stone Age hunters, Bronze and Iron Age farmers and cattlemen. Much later, in the century or so before the Norman Conquest, Scandinavian settlers carved out smallholdings on Malham Moor. After the Conquest, the land was held by the Percys and other great Anglo-Norman families, who, for the good of their souls, presented vast acreages to Fountains Abbey and Bolton Priory. The monks made fine use of the gift, and reared cattle and sheep on a grand

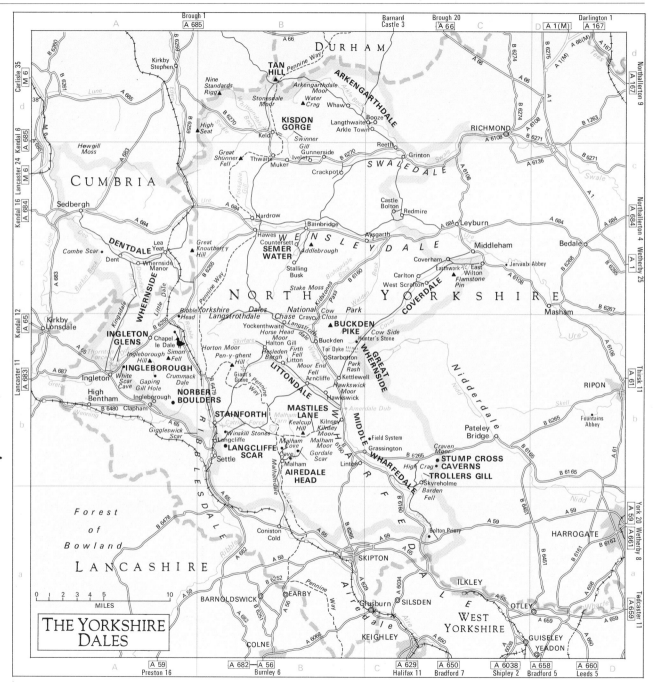

scale. The long-wooled Dalesbred sheep – dark-faced with a splash of white on either side of the nostrils – may well be the monks' legacy.

About half a mile east of Malham, on the twisting road to Gordale Bridge, a footpath to the right leads to Janet's Cave, while a little further upstream is Janet's Foss, a waterfall that drops into a deep pool. Janet is a fairy to whom local people accord respect that is perhaps at least half meant.

On the opposite side of the road, a three-quarters of a mile walk north following the course of the stream leads to the gorge where the Gordale Beck tumbles over the 400 ft cliffs at Gordale Scar.

The scar can be climbed by the sure-footed, though with a final scramble through rocks to reach the top. The path leads north-west for a mile and joins a minor road that returns south to Malham village.

An alternative walk from the village follows the road north out of Malham for half a mile to where the Pennine Way breaks off to the right. The path leads to the greeny-white amphitheatre formed by the cliffs of Malham Cove. The Pennine Way leads up the western side of the cove, skirts round the top and then heads south-east. At the point where the way turns sharply north, a footpath on the right returns the walker to a minor road that heads south to Malham.

Malham lies 5 miles north along a minor road from Coniston Cold on the A65.

Bd   Arkengarthdale

Despite the sparkling clarity of its moorland setting, and its toytown hamlets, there is a touch of harshness about Arkengarthdale. The medieval cattle marauders are still on the edge of memory, and the scars left by centuries of lead-mining are all too apparent. Long ago, this was a famous hunting forest, but now the area's main attraction is the wild, silent moors, where a curlew's cry seems to carry forever.

From the lofty heights of Tan Hill, the moorland sweeps down to the banks of Arkle Beck, a tributary of the River Swale. Beside the sparkling waters of the beck are a string of tiny villages, some of them little more than clusters of farms. Their names –

TOWERING CRAGS In the remote hills above Malham village, Gordale Scar (left) has a wild, almost frightening beauty. Great limestone cliffs tower over the Gordale Beck (above), a dainty stream which becomes a boisterous torrent when it plunges over the rocky face of the gorge.

Whaw, Langthwaite, Arkle Town, Booze, Reeth – are as ancient as the name of the dale itself. Booze, rather disappointingly, is a corruption of the Old English word *bowehouse*, meaning 'house by the curve' – the village stands on a hillside above a bend in the river.

Reeth is the best touring centre for the dale. Starting from the stile by the east end of the bridge in the village, a footpath leads along the east bank of Arkle Beck all the way to Whaw, a distance of some 6 miles.

An easier walk is the short circular route north from Langthwaite, starting on the road up the west side of the

MOORLAND MINING The moors above Arkengarthdale, a secluded valley off Swaledale, were once mined for lead.

There are two routes to the summit of Buckden Pike. A 2½ mile bridle-path known as Walden Wood, running to the pike alongside Cam Gill Beck, begins from Starbotton. A shorter, steeper ascent starts from the centre of Buckden, climbs up through Rakes Wood, along the course of the old Roman road to Bainbridge, forks right after three-quarters of a mile and then leads straight on to the shoulder of the pike. The left-hand fork on this footpath leads to Cow Close, a hillside above the village of Cray with some lovely waterfalls. A track beyond Cray crosses Kidstones Fell and Stake Moss to Bainbridge in Wensleydale, but this is for experienced walkers only, as it is a lonely and exposed 8 mile trek.

The steep, wooded Langstrothdale is a gentle oasis in the wild countryside. It is a quiet and pretty valley at the head of Wharfedale, where rock-roses bloom in summer and the delicate foliage of ash trees lends softness to the hillsides. A minor road leads up the dale from Buckden to Yockenthwaite, with its Bronze Age circle of 20 standing stones.

Buckden is on the B6160, near the head of Wharfedale.

beck. After three-quarters of a mile, turn right at the road junction on to the Barnard Castle road. In the 18th century, packhorses used the road to carry lead from the mines near Langthwaite to Barnard Castle, 10 miles away.

'When Julius Caesar was a king,
Bowes Castle and Arkendale mines
was a famous thing.'

The history is as uncertain as the rhyme, but relics of the old mining days can be seen everywhere. Disused mines are scattered throughout the moors to the north-east of Reeth, while on private ground at the Barnard Castle road junction is an odd, octagonal building with bricked-up windows. This is an old gunpowder store, in which blasting charges for the mines were kept.

The 3 mile circular walk is completed by following the Barnard Castle road across the bridge over the beck, turning right and following the riverside footpath back to Langthwaite.

Reeth is on the B6270, 9 miles west of Richmond. A signposted road from Reeth leads into Arkengarthdale and up the valley to Langthwaite and Whaw.

Bb Buckden Pike

From the 2,302 ft high peaty solitudes of Buckden Pike, magnificent views stretch in every direction. To the west lies the massif of Langstrothdale Chase, the old hunting ground of which Buckden was the centre, and the central wilderness of the Dales, while the proverbial clear day reveals the hills around Morecambe Bay. At the foot of the pike lie the beautiful upland valleys of Langstrothdale and Wharfedale.

Cc Coverdale

Coverdale is a secluded, secret sort of place. Yet from earliest times it was a famous through-route across the country. Drovers, packmen, monks, miners and Yorkist soldiers passed this way, and earlier still, Iron Age men fortified the summits above Park Rash and Red Beck Gill to hold the way against some long-forgotten southern foe.

Even today the ancient winding lanes and steep moorland roads seem to be penetrating an intensely private

BELOW BUCKDEN PIKE Waterfalls and streams score the face of Cow Close.

world. Its secrets, however, together with those of much of the surrounding countryside, are most gloriously revealed from the top of Flamstone Pin. The view from here is a splendid medieval tapestry of castles – Middleham and Bolton – the abbey of Coverham, ancient churches and great estates set against a dark green backdrop. In such a landscape, racehorses at exercise from the stables at the lower end of the dale might easily be taken for the outriders of a medieval army.

Winding lanes lead into Coverdale from Leyburn, but the most dramatic route into the dale is the minor road from Kettlewell in Wharfedale. It climbs steeply out of Kettlewell village, and becomes even steeper at Park Rash, below the Iron Age earthworks at Tor Dyke. On the exposed and frequently misty high moorland of

Cow Side, the road is often gated; but before dropping down into Carlton it passes through more sheltered scenery, often densely wooded and thick with wild roses. The sense of remoteness ends at Carlton, for beyond it lies a string of villages. But a picturesque lane leads from Carlton across the River Cover to West Scrafton.

Kettlewell is on the B6160; Leyburn is at the junction of the A684 and the A6108.

Ac   Dentdale

Bisected by the Dee, at this point a brawling, tumbling infant of a river, Dentdale is the smallest of the Dales and arguably the loveliest. Certainly, the variety of its scenery is extraordinary; west of handsome little Dent town, the geological phenomenon of the Dent Fault slashes through the valley. It could be said that along this line, the Yorkshire Dales come to an end and the Lake District begins, since to the east of the fault the landscape is smoothly swooping limestone fells, while to the west it is the weathered, craggy slate of the Lake District. Barkin Beck, which rises about a mile west of Dent, follows the line of the fault, dividing the slate from the limestone. The change is abruptly emphasised just above the beck by the slate amphitheatre of Combe Scar.

The flat and once-swampy mouth of the valley kept Dentdale in isolation for centuries – so much so that it is said that the southward-raiding Scots never found the place.

Above Dent, the dale narrows into a limestone gorge, and there is a fine hike from Lea Yeat, east of Dent, to Great Knoutberry Hill (2,203 ft) in the Widdale Fell, along part of an old drovers' road. Around Dent itself there are a number of delightful riverside walks, and at the eastern end of the dale a road leads up the gorge under the railway and down to the B6255, giving good views of Dentdale.

Dent is reached by a minor road from the A65, just west of Ingleton. Another minor road enters the dale from Sedbergh, on the A683.

Cb   Great Whernside

From the magnificent, cloud-touching bulk of Great Whernside, above the village of Kettlewell, there are wide views of the northern hills and eastern moorland. There are several approaches to the 2,310 ft high summit. A track leads out of Kettlewell to Hag Dike, or a more southerly footpath strikes across country. The easiest but longest route is by the Coverdale road to the Tor Dyke earthworks – probably constructed by the Brigantes at about the time of the Roman invasion – and then across the upper slopes of the hill.

The area's story is one typical of the Dales. The legions came here, marching along the road that connected the forts at Bainbridge and Ilkley. Later, there was the Norseman, Ketel, who left his name to the village; and later still, land-hungry Norman barons and the monks of Bolton, Coverham and Fountains squabbled over the acres that remained. One of the monks' boundary markers, Hunter's Stone, can still be seen below Great Whernside to the north-west. Forestry, smallholdings, lead-mining and cotton-weaving down the centuries have all left their mark upon the land, telling of prosperous times long gone. A hundred years ago the mines closed, the people departed and the smallholdings fell

into ruin. In our own time, Kettlewell has been saved – or perhaps overwhelmed – by weekending holiday-makers, but Great Whernside itself stands as a lonely, austere summit – hospitable only to those who love its windswept heights.

Kettlewell lies on the B6160.

Ab   Ingleborough

A steep, $2\frac{1}{2}$ mile footpath climbs to the highest point of Ingleborough, which commands extensive views north to the Cumbrian fells and, on a clear day, north-west across to the Lake District fells. Ingleborough is not one peak but

ABOVE THE OPEN MOORS

The loud call of the curlew carries far across the wide, open moors as it flies high on slow-beating wings. It is this plaintive, two-note call that gives the bird its name. Far below the tenacious merlin streaks across the heather in low-level flight, following every twist and turn of its prey which may be a bird as large as itself. It is one of the smallest of the hawks, little bigger than a blackbird.

Merlin
(Falco columbarius)

Curlew
(Numenius arquata)

INGLEBOROUGH HEIGHTS The blue mass of hills sprawling across the skyline above Horton Moor is dominated by flat-topped Ingleborough Hill.

a series of them, a mass of high hills dominating the scenery between Chapel le Dale, Ribblesdale and Ingleton. Ingleborough Hill is the summit of the massif, and at 2,373 ft it is the second highest peak in Yorkshire. A 15 acre Iron Age hill-fort spreads across the square summit, enclosed by a 3,000 ft long rampart containing at least 19 hut circles.

The flanks of the massif are well known to potholers, and Gaping Gill, on the south-eastern slopes, is the largest and one of the best-known potholes in Britain. The waters of Fell Beck plunge 365 ft into its dark depths through a hole near by, and intrepid visitors may be lowered by winch down to the 340 ft deep floor of the hole itself. There, the pothole opens out into the Great Hall, the largest limestone cave in Britain; so large, it is frequently said, that York Minster would fit inside it. At the far end of the

cave, you once again encounter the Fell Beck, falling in a misty torrent from the dim roof high above. Obviously, it is not possible, or would be extremely dangerous, to explore Gaping Gill without expert assistance. This can usually be had at the spring meets of the Bradford or Craven Pothole Clubs, held at the site.

For overland explorers, a hard 2½ mile walk along a badly defined path leads from Ingleborough Hill to Simon Fell and Park Fell, where there is a chance of seeing peregrine falcons and buzzards.

Ingleborough Hill can be reached by footpaths from Ingleton or Chapel le Dale, both on the B6255.

Ab   Ingleton Glens

Two rivers, Kingsdale Beck and the River Doe, drop down through small valleys to Ingleton, where they con-

verge and become the River Greta. Both rivers can be explored from Ingleton on a 4 mile walk, which includes some spectacular waterfalls and fine woodland scenery.

The first half of the walk, beside Kingsdale Beck, involves much clambering over boulders before it reaches Pecca Falls, which are the most dramatic waterfalls on the route. The path then climbs up past the magnificent Thornton Force waterfall, before joining Twisleton Lane, an old drovers' route across the southern tip of Scales Moor.

Around Thornton Force the limestone lies on much older and harder slate. In spite of their closeness, the two kinds of rock are separated by 300 million years of geological history. The river has slowly cut through the limestone, and now drops from the more resistant slate ledges.

From Twisleton Lane, the footpath drops down past Beezley Falls into the wooded valley of the River Doe, and continues back towards Ingleton through the deep gorge which contains the Snow Falls.

A short footpath from Beezley Falls leads across stepping-stones and up to White Scar Cave, which can also be reached from Ingleton by a well-signposted road. It is something of a tourist attraction in the height of summer, but this detracts little from its dramatic impact. The cave reaches for about half a mile under Ingleborough, the major peak in the area, and contains some wonderful stalactite formations, as well as a river and two waterfalls. In persistent wet weather White Scar Cave is liable to flooding and may be closed.

Ingleton and White Scar Cave are both on the B6255, just off the A65.

WOODLAND PHARMACY

The stem of the angular Solomon's seal gives the plant its name, differing from the more common round-stemmed variety. A poultice made from its roots has been used to cure black eyes, a use said to have been approved by King Solomon. It is a woodland plant, as also is the baneberry whose shiny black berries are poisonous. Baneberry roots were once used as a cure for skin diseases and asthma. The dark red helleborine has no such medicinal properties, but the slightly scented flowers of this member of the orchid family are a welcome if rare sight in woods and rocky places on limestone soils.

Angular Solomon's seal
(Polygonatum odoratum)

Dark red helleborine
(Epipactis atrorubens)

Baneberry
(Actaea spicata)

Bd Kisdon Gorge

The steep, narrow and thickly wooded gorge is never silent. Its voice is that of the River Swale that tumbles through the glen from one limestone ledge to another. See it especially on an autumn evening when Kisdon Force, near Keld, is little more than a bass rumble in the darkling gorge, superbly overstating the flaming gold of the bracken above. Only a short distance along the river are Catrake Force, Currack Force, Rainby Force and the wild-swirling Wain Wath Force. Flowing close by are enchanting Stonesdale, Sleddale, Whitsundale and Hind Hole becks; and rearing high above, the lonely moorland expanses of Great Shunner Fell, Rogan's Seat, Nine Standards Rigg and Water Crag.

Keld village – originally Apple-treekeld, 'the spring of the apple tree' – was a lead-mining centre 100 years ago, and the tattered remains of the industry are scattered across the countryside. Nowadays, the village is best known as a stopping-off place on the Pennine Way. The green track of nearby Kisdon Road forms part of it, and is, too, a section of the old Corpse Way, the path along which the dead were carried in wickerwork coffins to the graveyard at Grinton, 11 miles down-river. The lightness of the coffin notwithstanding, the burden was a heavy one; this is why some kindly soul provided a coffin stone at the northern end of the pack-horse bridge at Ivelet, so that the bearers might rest their load on the long journey to Grinton.

A shorter walk from Keld, and one with less melancholy associations, leads along the riverside path, across the Swale, east of Crackpot Hall and then north to Swinner Gill. It is a tour of 2½ miles, and includes the best of both river and moorland scenery.

Keld is on the B6270, 4 miles north-west of Gunnerside.

Bb Langcliffe Scar

Steep, narrow roads enclosed by dry-stone walls lead over the craggy limestone headlands of Langcliffe Scar, part of a Craven Fault above Settle and Langcliffe. The scar is riddled with caves, of which the most famous is the Victoria, which was discovered in the Coronation year of 1838 by one of those rabbiting terriers to whom archaeology owes so much. The floor was excavated layer by layer down to one formed when the cave gave shelter to hyenas who brought home the bones of such creatures as the straight-tusked elephant and the woolly hippo. Above these were the bones of Ice Age animals – arctic fox, reindeer and badgers – and above these again the spearhead of a Stone Age hunter. The uppermost level revealed Roman coins, Celtic weapons and splendid Celtic jewellery in silver and bronze. Presumably the cave had been a place of refuge during the troubled early years of the Roman occupation. Similar stories were unfolded at nearby Attermire and Jubilee caves; a fine collection of relics from all three may be seen in the Pig Yard Museum in Settle.

A 4 mile moorland walk leads from Langcliffe to the scar, south along its foot, past Victoria Cave and Attermire Cave, before turning west towards Settle. About three-quarters of a mile north of the scar lie the Winskill Stones, great masses of slate, which have been transported from the dale floor by Ice Age glaciers and deposited on the limestone. Protected by the slate, the limestone on which they stand eroded more slowly than the surrounding countryside, leaving the stones to stand on limestone pedestals. A further half mile north, Catrigg Beck meets Cowside Beck, and the stream tumbles over Catrigg Force – a favourite spot of the composer Elgar – on its way to join the River Ribble in Stainforth.

Settle is at the junction of the A65 and B6479. Langcliffe and Stainforth are both on the B6479.

THE SWALE BELOW CRACKPOT

ALONG THE UPPER SWALE Not far from its source, near Keld (right), the Swale makes its way over the limestone ledges in Kisdon Gorge. Below Crackpot (above), the river's gentler face appears amid farmland that has been recovered from the heather moors.

WATERFALLS IN KISDON GORGE

Bb Littondale

It is for its short, spectacular walks that the quiet valley of Littondale is chiefly famed. It is separated from Wharfedale by three fells – Firth Fell, Moor End Fell and Hawkswick Moor. At least three paths cross this wedge of land, which is never more than 2 miles wide.

The longest walk – about 3½ miles – starts at the village of Litton, and climbs past waterfalls and across the steep ravine which has Crystal Beck in its depths, to Ackerley Moor and Firth Fell. The bridle-path is clearly marked, and leads to Buckden in Wharfedale. A less obvious bridle-path climbs steeply from Arncliffe and crosses Old Cote Moor before descending through woodlands to Starbotton. A third route follows a rough footpath from Hawkswick, across Hawkswick Moor and down over the scars to Kettlewell. The climb is steep at the start, and further on it provides fine views of Kettlewell and Wharfedale.

Arncliffe village, a dark cluster of roofs in the heart of Littondale, sent its quota of men to Flodden Field in 1513 – their names are recorded on a wall in the church. Yet mining and industry largely passed the valley by, and the marks of human affairs it bears belong to periods earlier than is common in the Dales. There are traces of 1,000-year-old lynchets – terraced cultivated strips – on the fellsides; and high above are the remains of Iron Age farmsteads and enclosures.

Perhaps it is the lack of later development that makes Littondale a naturalist's paradise. At the head of the dale, where valley and woodland meet, there are wagtails, flycatchers, plovers and curlews. In the wooded lower reaches of the dale, snowdrops and

DEEP IN LITTONDALE Above the tiny hamlet of Halton Gill, a tenuous stream struggles along a rocky course on its way down from furrowed Horse Head Moor.

aconites grow beside the river in spring, and later in the year there is a chance to find bloody cranesbill and the rare mountain avens, growing here at the most southerly limit of its range in England.

Kettlewell, Starbotton and Buckden are on the B6160. A minor road runs through Littondale, joining the B6160 at Amerdale Dub.

Bb Mastiles Lane

In the Middle Ages monks used this 5 mile drovers' track across Kilnsey and Malham moors, marking the way with crosses. The bases of some of the crosses still survive. Later, in the 18th and 19th centuries, lead was transported along the track from the moorland mines to Malham and Settle.

The path is well marked. From Malham Tarn it drops down into the valley drained by Gordale Beck, climbs up on to the moorland, then crosses another valley below Kealcup Hill. From High Long Ridge it crosses Kilnsey Moor before descending into Kilnsey itself, passing Kilnsey Crag, a 240 ft high limestone rock overhanging the main road.

Malham Moor is a wide, wild, airy place whose horizons dance in the heat of summer and whose winter winds have an edge like a scalpel. It seems as lonely today as it was in the Middle Ages when the monks' herdsmen used to milk the cattle, with sword or stave lying beside them. The dozen or so farms on the moor are of astonishing age, much older than the farm buildings themselves. Norsemen, monks and dalesmen inhabited them in turn, watching over their wide-ranging herds. Great Close, beside Malham Tarn, was the scene of cattle fairs in the 18th century, with a turnover of up to 5,000 head of cattle, mostly driven down from Scotland.

Malham Tarn is reached by a minor road leading north off the A65 at Coniston Cold. Kilnsey is on the B6160, about 3 miles south of Kettlewell.

Cb Middle Wharfedale

The scenery of Wharfedale is at its loveliest between Ilkley and Grassington. The valley becomes narrower here than it is lower down, more like the perfect picture of a dale; but even so, it is still broader, more gentle and less isolated than the upper reaches above Kettlewell. Homely greystone villages nestle among the fells, crags and waterfalls, and many of them, including Grassington, make ideal bases from which to explore the area.

About a mile north of Grassington lies one of the most outstanding Romano-British field systems in the Dales. The land is privately owned but a footpath skirts the site, where Celtic fields are clearly divided into squares and rectangles by stone banks. Among the fields are indications of a settlement, for circular outlines of hut foundations, perhaps prehistoric farmsteads, have been traced.

South-west from Grassington lies the village of Linton, just across the wide, shallow River Wharfe. Here it is possible to cross the river by clapper bridge, packhorse bridge, ford or stepping-stones. The stepping-stones are particularly adventurous and need a springy stride if the traveller is to have a dry crossing. They are situated behind the church, half a mile north-east of the village. A walk leads back through the fields to Grassington.

Grassington is on the B6265.

Ab Norber Boulders

Ice Age glaciers tore the massive Norber Boulders from Crummack Dale and Ribblesdale, and deposited them on the limestone on the southern flanks of the Ingleborough massif. Aeons of wind and rain eroded the countryside, all except the small portions of it protected by the boulders. The result is that the massive blocks of Silurian slate – some of them weighing 20 tons and more – are now perched on limestone pedestals some 2 ft above their surroundings. These famous curiosities may be visited by walking from the village of Clapham up the scenic bridleway called Thwaite Lane. After 1½ miles, take the footpath that leads north across the fields.

Clapham village is set at the entrance to a small valley in the side of the Ingleborough massif. The stream which flows down the valley, Clapham Beck, feeds The Lake, just north of the village, around which there are several nature trails. Above The Lake, Ingleborough Cave is full of fantastic and fantastically named stalactite formations whose strange images are faithfully repeated in the still waters of the Pool of Reflections.

Clapham is on the B6480, just off the A65, 6 miles north-west of Settle.

Bc Semer Water

Some 10,000 years ago, at the end of the Ice Age, the Yorkshire Dales were a Lake District in miniature – Coverdale was a 6 mile long lake, and there were many other stretches of water, both large and small, especially in Wensleydale around Hawes and Aysgarth. Today, Semer Water and Malham Tarn are the only survivors of the Ice Age lakes, all the rest having long drained away. Semer Water and its 1½ miles of shore are the focal point of many of the Dales' most beautiful views – from Stalling Busk, for example, less than a mile to the south on the slopes below Stake Moss; or in the late afternoon, from the hillside just below the farming hamlet of Countersett, north of the lake.

For more than 2,000 years farmers have worked the countryside around Semer Water. There are Celtic remains in the area, and the traces of Romano-British cattle enclosures on the fell east of Stalling Busk. An Iron Age village looked down over Wensleydale from close to the summit of Addlebrough; and the remains of Iron Age lake villages have been discovered by the shores. Perhaps it was one of these that gave rise to the legend that an ancient city lies drowned in the depths of Semer Water.

The lake gives birth to England's shortest river – the River Bain, which tumbles some 2 miles into Bainbridge where it joins the River Ure. Whatever the season, Semer Water mirrors the Dales' moods. It can seem serene and

---

THE MONASTERIES AND THE LANDSCAPE

FOLLOWING THE NORMAN CONQUEST, monastic orders all over England received gifts of land from the powerful lords. In the Yorkshire Dales the most prominent order was that of the Cistercians, comparative late-comers, who settled in the area in the 12th century.

The Cistercian monks were sheep and cattle rearers, and they managed vast tracts through outlying farms worked by the lay brethren. But the monks of Jervaulx and Fountains also quarried for lead and iron ore, and there were workings in all the dales from Wharfedale to Swaledale. In the 16th century, however, Henry VIII dissolved the monasteries and parcelled out the land to new owners who began to exploit the mines in earnest. Lead-mining became intensive, but died out when cheap lead was imported in the 19th century.

In many of the dales, and notably Swaledale, the scarred hills and spoilheaps can still be seen. Mercifully the wounds have healed and the derelict mines are now part of history.

JERVAULX ABBEY

placid in its deep hollow, with cattle wading far out into the water; or grey and threatening, its waters lashed by blustery winds. In winter it sometimes puts on a sparkling mantle of ice.

Two minor roads lead from Bainbridge, on the A684, to Semer Water.

Bb Stainforth

Steep fells separate Ribblesdale from Littondale, and Stainforth is a good centre from which to explore them. The village itself stands on the River Ribble, which is crossed by a 17th-century packhorse bridge, part of the old route from Lancaster to Ripon. Just outside the village the river rushes over Stainforth Force, a series of cascades where salmon leap.

A minor road called Goat Lane leads north-east out of Stainforth, then

forks left to Halton Gill or right to Arncliffe. Taking the left fork, the road follows part of the Pennine Way to the foot of Pen-y-ghent and Giant's Grave, a New Stone Age round barrow containing the remains of two stone burial chambers and probably dating from about 2000 BC. The barrow and other archaeological finds in the area suggest that by this time some early settlers had begun to leave the uplands and move to the lower slopes and into the river valleys.

From Giant's Grave the moorland road follows Pen-y-ghent Gill down into Halton Gill, with fine views of upper Littondale from Hesleden Bergh. Ring ouzels and golden plovers break from the paths that criss-cross the moor, and there is a seasonal parade of primroses, dog's mercury, wood sorrel and shining cranesbill.

The right-hand fork on Goat Lane skirts Malham Tarn on the way to Arncliffe. The tarn is the largest lake in the National Park, and one of the Dales' most important bird-watching centres. Its fishing has always been famous, as the monks well knew when they acquired it in 1150.

Stainforth is on the B6479, 3 miles north of Settle.

Cb Stump Cross Caverns

Probably the first human beings ever to enter these wonderful caverns were the lead-miners who accidentally discovered them in 1858. But they were by no means the last, for these natural catacombs are among the most popular attractions of the Dales. The entrance is 1,275 ft up on Craven Moor, from which a stairway leads down into the

network of limestone caves. Beneath their low roofs, the caves are lined with formations of stalactites and stalagmites, whose weird shapes have given rise to their names – The Jewel Box, The Sentinel, The Hawk, The Wedding Cake and many others. Part of a reindeer skeleton which was discovered in the caves is on display in the refreshment rooms outside the entrance. How the creature got into the caverns is something of a mystery.

The surrounding moorland is dotted with the spoil-heaps of ancient lead mines from which mineral specimens, such as galena, barytes, fluorspar and calcite, may be picked up. And the gritstone boulders of High Crag immediately behind the cave entrance are well worth climbing for the extensive views from the top.

Stump Cross Caverns are next to the B6265, 4½ miles west of Pateley Bridge.

Bd Tan Hill

One of the loneliest places in the Dales, the 1,758 ft high summit of Tan Hill is often capped with ragged cloud or racked by winds. But it is when the clouds clear that it takes on a wild beauty and the glorious fell scenery stretches out before the eye in every direction. To the south lie the jagged contours of Stonesdale Moor, to the east the bleak uplands of Arkengarthdale Moor, and to the north a vast stretch of empty moorland outside the National Park, which culminates in the massive bulk of Mickle Fell. The 2,591 ft hill lies just in Durham.

Grouse and a few hardy Swaledale sheep are the main inhabitants of the area. The drovers who once used this summit as a stopping place on the way south from the Scottish borders lodged

PEN-Y-GHENT The 2,277 ft peak, seen from near Giant's Grave, dominates the moors north-east of Stainforth.

in the remote Tan Hill Inn. This unassuming 18th-century building, lying on a crossing point of drovers' roads, is the highest inn in England. It was once known as the King's Pit House, and its licensing hours were dictated by need rather than by law – 'Refuse no-one at Tan Hill', the justices ordered one landlord.

Today, however, normal licensing hours apply, though the rigours of the countryside around it remain unchanged. Unmarked mine shafts provide a hazard for walkers, so it is essential to keep to the footpaths.

Tan Hill is reached by a well-signposted minor road off the B6270 just west of Keld, or through Arkengarthdale.

Cb   Trollers Gill

Sir Arthur Conan Doyle is said to have written *The Hound of the Baskervilles* after hearing the story of Trollers Gill, a spectacular limestone ravine below Barden Fell, close to the village of Skyreholme. But this may be Yorkshire patriotism, since similar literary claims are made for Herefordshire, and of course, Dartmoor. Nevertheless, the place is held to be haunted by a barguest, a spectral hound; it is even said to have appeared one night to Troller, the lead-miner after whom the gill is named, on his way home from work. There is certainly a sense of eeriness about the place, and a touch of melancholy added by the disused lead mine at the end of the ravine. But it takes only a few minutes to walk out from Skyreholme, to discover for yourself whether or not Troller's hound is still loose.

Skyreholme is reached by a minor road off the B6265, about 5 miles west of Pateley Bridge.

DROVERS' REST Tan Hill, at a crossing of ancient trackways, was once a stopping point for Scottish cattle drovers.

Ac   Whernside

The craggy bulk of Whernside – at 2,419 ft it is the highest peak in the National Park – separates Dentdale, Kingsdale and Little Dale. A long ridge slopes up from the south, with a drystone wall along the crest, while the northern slopes are more gentle, with newly planted forest land on the lower reaches. A multi-arched, 165 ft high railway viaduct runs along the foot of the hill. Its building in the last century cost the lives of more than 100 navvies, mostly through smallpox and accidents. They lie now in the cemetery at Chapel le Dale. There are outcrops of Millstone Grit to the east, and it is to this rock that the peak owes its name. 'Whernside' derives from the Old English *cweorn* meaning 'millstone', and this was the hillside where the rock for millstones was found.

The area is popular with potholers; indeed, on summer weekends it seems likely there are more people below the ground than above it, exploring the oddly named cave systems of Capnut, Batty Wife and many others. For walkers, there are magnificent views of Pen-y-ghent and Ingleborough – the other two of the so-called Three Peaks of north-west Craven – and of Howgill Moss to the north.

There are several routes up on to the peak, including one from near Ribble Head and another – the easiest – by a well-marked footpath from Chapel le Dale. To reach the top of Whernside, break away from the footpath for the final steep mile to the summit. The footpath itself continues around the hill to Whernside Manor, on the north-western side of the peak.

Peregrine falcons can sometimes be seen hunting over the hills. Dippers haunt the streams, particularly Gastack Beck on the lower, north-west slopes. Wild flowers are abundant along the banks, where rock-roses and milkwort bloom in summer and bird's-eye primroses in late spring.

Chapel le Dale is on the B6255, 4 miles north-east of Ingleton.

189

THE NORTH YORK MOORS

Pierced by lush dales in the south and lapped by the North Sea in the east, the moors are a walker's paradise

Up on the high moors, where the sea roke can drift in faster than a man can walk, swallowing the landscape in a matter of minutes, things are not always what they seem. Cairns that might have been piled up the day before yesterday to help walkers find their bearings may date back 3,000 years or more to the Bronze Age. Natural-looking mounds and ditches may be earthworks built by prehistoric men, speakers of a long-forgotten language, who dug into the rocky soil with picks of antler horn. What looks like a rock will turn out, as you approach nearer, to be a black-faced sheep, bleating through the mist. Then, suddenly, the air will clear, the clouds will scud away, and the west-voyaging sun will once again fill the evening sky with glory. The North York Moors is a region full of surprises.

And the biggest surprise of all is the moor itself – an undulating carpet of heather, stretching into an empurpled distance, laced with streams that look like broken silver threads. It seems unchangeable, timeless, part of the eternal order. Yet this landscape is largely the work of man. Its original vegetation was not heather but trees – scrub oak, alder, birch and hazel. Two major assault waves destroyed this natural cover.

The first started more than 4,000 years ago, when Bronze Age farmers began to settle in a region which had previously supported only

wandering bands of Stone Age hunter-gatherers. They ring-barked and burned trees to clear the land for their sheep, goats and cattle, and for their crops of barley and wheat. The climate was warmer then, and the moors during the Bronze Age supported a larger population of men and animals than they have done before or since. They put their cremated dead in urns, and buried them in circular barrows – raised mounds of earth known as howes. Whether by accident or design, the howes seem always to be sited where there are magnificent views. The second assault wave on the forest came in the Middle Ages and was led by men of God – devout monks and hard-working lay brothers who made sheep runs and cut down trees for charcoal for their iron-smelting furnaces. Great abbeys like Rievaulx and Byland were primarily religious foundations, but also thriving business concerns.

And because of them, the moors were never to be the same again. Without its tree cover, the soil on the top was easily drained of nutrients. It became thin and acid, capable of supporting only tough plants such as heather and bracken, and the hardiest of grasses.

Today, the moors seem made for the walker. There are strenuous walks like the Cleveland Way, a 100 mile horseshoe-shaped track that skirts the moors from Helmsley to Filey, and offers a blend of coastal and bracing moorland scenery; or the Lyke Wake Walk, a 40 mile endurance test from Osmotherley to Ravenscar. There are gentler walks, such as those to be had by taking a train a few miles along the delightful Esk Valley Line and rambling back to the starting point. Or simply take off and explore across the heather – always properly clad and shod, and with map and compass – and perhaps find early Christian crosses, Roman remains, or the sites of old iron or jet workings.

---

*G*ENTLE FACE OF THE MOORS West of Goathland, neatly hedged fields spread to the fringe of the high moors that lie beyond the dark, conifer-fringed horizon. In this part of the North York Moors, grazing land has been snatched from the heather and scrub uplands.

Places to visit

Map ref. Cb The Bridestones

Despite their romantic name and their monolithic shapes, the Bridestones have no connection with prehistoric marriage rituals. The name comes from the Norse word *brinka*, meaning hillside, edge or brink. Weathered into fantastic shapes, these outcrops of massive rocks were once thought to be monuments erected by Stone Age man; and later to have been brought down from the high moorland plateau by glaciers.

It is now known that most of the plateau was never covered by glaciers, and that the Bridestones were shaped by the action of wind, rain and frost.

There are two sets of Bridestones, the upper outcrop in a rough horseshoe shape, the lower stones in a straight line. Some are top-heavy, like gigantic mushrooms, some only half emerge from the surrounding hillside. In one of the upper Bridestones, the unrelenting wind has sculpted a complete tunnel. The reason that these 150-million-year-old rocks have taken on such strange shapes is that they are composed of alternate layers of hard and soft sandstone, which erode at different rates.

The best approach to the Bridestones is from the Staindale car park on the Dalby Forest Drive. Cross the stile and there is a choice of paths, which join up after a mile near the stones. The path west leads fairly gently to the open moor, through woodland that is mainly oak. The path east climbs steeply, along the pretty ravine of Jonathan Gill.

From Low Bridestones the path leads to High Bridestones, dipping to cross Bridestones Griff, a place of refuge from the wind, where birch, aspen and rowan trees have established themselves. 'Griff' is a local word for a ravine cut by a stream, and may be Scandinavian in origin. After leaving High Bridestones the path swings south, in a steep descent down Needle Point to Dovedale Griff. Beside the stream grow pale blue water forget-me-not and the dark blue brooklime.

Staindale car park is on the northern section of the Dalby Forest Drive, which is a toll road. To reach the drive, take the minor road north from Thornton Dale on the A170. After about 1 mile turn east on to the road for Low Dalby and carry on for 3 miles.

Cb Dalby Forest

More than 4,000 years ago, Bronze Age farmers began the first serious assault on the forests of north Yorkshire. They slashed and burned great stands of oak, ash and elm to make grazing runs for their flocks and herds.

Today, man is restoring the forests that he once destroyed, though for the most part with fast-growing conifers instead of the broad-leaved trees of the past. Dalby Forest, near Thornton Dale, proves that just because a forest is

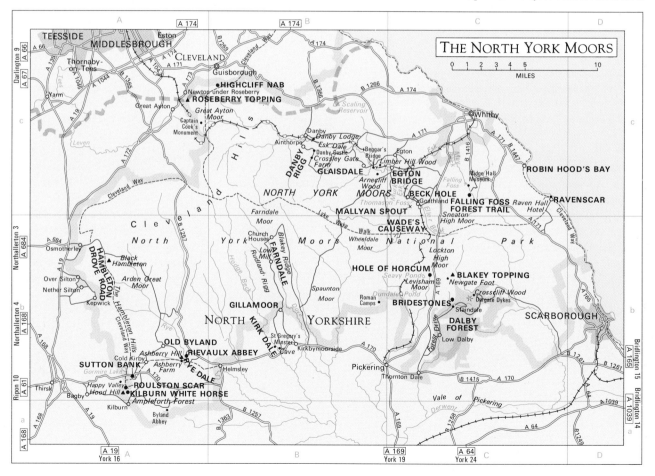

man-made it need not lose its natural look. It is owned by the Forestry Commission.

The forest contains 14 waymarked trails, varying in length from about a mile to 7 miles. On any of them there is the chance of seeing roe deer, grey squirrels, rabbits and foxes, as well as crossbills, goldcrests, siskins, great spotted woodpeckers, pheasants, jays, sparrowhawks and kestrels. Among the pheasants is one that is pure white, but sightings are rare.

Another rare creature has started something of a controversy among naturalists. The forest rangers claim to have identified two distinct races of foxes in Dalby Forest. One is the ordinary red fox, which most naturalists insist is the only fox in Britain; the other is a much longer-legged coyote-like animal, with a coat that is grey rather than red.

The best way to get the general feel of Dalby Forest is to drive through it. A 10 mile forest drive winds through conifer-clad hills that seem more like the foothills of the Canadian Rockies than part of Yorkshire. On the way it passes a Visitor Centre, where there are displays on the history and natural history of the forest, and you can consider which of the waymarked trails best meets your taste.

Just before the forest drive ends, a signposted track to the west leads to the Crosscliff viewpoint, high above Crosscliff Wood. It is only a 250 yd walk from the car park along a woodland path to the viewpoint. The hollows beside the path are Dargate Dykes, the remains of early Saxon or medieval earthworks. At the viewpoint there is an indicator that points out distant landmarks and types of trees. As well as seeing features of the

CARVED BY THE WINDS The weathered Bridestones stand like petrified mushrooms above Dovedale Griff. It was wrongly thought that ancient man had erected the stones. He may, however, have used the site for pagan rituals.

landscape, such as Blakey Topping and the blue bulk of Lockton High Moor, you will see stands of oak, alder, Scots pine, Norway spruce and Sitka spruce.

Dalby Forest lies 4 miles north-east of Pickering. Turn north on to a minor road at Thornton Dale on the A170 and, after 1¼ miles, turn right to Low Dalby. The forest drive is a toll road.

Bc Danby Rigg

More than 1,000 years before the birth of Christ, a race speaking in a long-forgotten tongue left their mark on Danby Rigg, in the form of defensive dykes and some 800 cairns. Nothing has been found beneath any of these piles of stones, so their purpose is a mystery, like so much on the moors. They could have been erected to keep alive the memory of ordinary people of the Bronze Age, just as many of the howes on the moors were built to honour dead chieftains; or they could have been the product of nothing more complicated than a need to clear the ground for grazing and ploughing.

The rigg lies like a long arm of high ground, pointing from the moors to the Esk Valley. The views are so immense that it feels like the roof of the world,

even though you may be hardly more than 1,200 ft above sea-level. To the north-west are Captain Cook's Monument, stabbing the sky from the gentle swell of Easby Moor, and the triangular outline of Roseberry Topping. To the west and south, the moor sweeps round in a great purple arc.

Bronze Age men built a primitive stone circle on the rigg, as well as raising earthworks and cairns. Now only one stone of the 42 ft diameter circle remains, nearly 6 ft high and about 4 ft wide.

A 4½ mile circular walk from the car park at Danby Lodge National Park Centre leads across the rigg. Take the path that leads across a field to a footbridge over the Esk. Take care at the level-crossing, where the path crosses the Esk Valley railway. Turn east at the road and follow it to Danby Castle, now a farm, with only the romantic ruins of the tower as a reminder of its former dominance.

The road runs alongside the rigg past Crossley Gate Farm, reaching a junction about three-quarters of a mile further on. At this point take the steep bridleway north-west up the rigg, following the signpost to Ainthorpe. The first upright stone at the top of the rigg is a marker post. A detour along a footpath to the left near the marker stone leads after about 150 yds to the remains of a Bronze Age dyke. After passing some disused quarries on the left, the path starts to descend. Turn left at the road and carry on through Ainthorpe village, back to Danby and the car park.

Danby is on a minor road south of the A171 from Whitby to Guisborough, signposted 2 miles west of Scaling Reservoir, and 8 miles east of Guisborough. Danby Lodge is ¼ mile east of the village centre.

Cc Falling Foss Forest Trail

The Falling Foss trail provides an opportunity to learn about trees and wildlife of the area in the most pleasureable of all ways – on an easy-paced 3 mile walk along sun-dappled paths. Starting from the May Beck car park, cross the bridge and turn downstream, with the beck on the left. The trail is way-marked with a fox's head.

About half a mile from the start, the path skirts some ponds that were specially created to provide a habitat for frogs, toads, newts and pond plants. Take the left fork at the wild cherry, cross the Falling Foss car park and turn left at a marker stone, down into the woods. Turn right and follow a tumble-down wall that passes a large sycamore.

The path descends to a bridge over the beck, and the soil becomes deeper and damper. This is reflected in the succession of trees – beech, oak and larch near the top; ash, elm and syca-more halfway down; hazel and rowan near the bottom. Near the bridge, ivy and honeysuckle wind their coils around the roots of bankside trees.

As the path begins to climb the other side of the valley it passes meadowsweet, giant horsetail, and wild arum which bears clusters of poisonous yellow berries. Turn right at a large beech and, shortly after crossing a small bridge, head left for the Midge Hall Museum, and for Falling Foss. This is an exhilarating waterfall, where May Beck, after gurgling placidly down from Sneaton High Moor, plunges over mossy rocks into a dark, swirling pool 30 ft below. Return to the path and a short climb brings you into open farmland, with views of the surrounding countryside. A quarter-mile walk leads back to the car park.

The location is 5 miles south of Whitby. Take the A171 Whitby–Scarborough road and turn west along the B1416. After 1½ miles, at crossroads where there is a red gate, turn south-east along the unclassified, gated road to New May Beck Farm. May Beck car park is about ¼ mile beyond the farm.

COAST AND MOOR BIRDS

The long, narrow wings of the fulmar allow it to glide at high speed above the sea and along cliff edges. Conifers, alders and birches are the favourite habitat of the redpoll – the males sometimes perform aerobatic flights above the trees. The golden plover is one of the most strikingly handsome of waders. In summer the male's plaintive 'klew-ee' call may be heard on upland moors where it breeds.

Fulmar
(*Fulmarus glacialis*)

Redpoll
(*Acanthis flammea*)

Golden plover
(*Pluvialis apricaria*)

Bb Gillamoor and Farndale

Nothing about the gentle approach to Gillamoor from the south gives any indication of the village's great treasure – its surprise view.

Turn north-east into the little grey-stone village and park where you can before reaching St Aidan's Church, which was built single-handed by a pious local stonemason in 1802. Just past the church, the road swings north-west, and suddenly the view opens out. It is a tapestry of green farmland dotted with clumps of trees and brave little moorland roads tackling the heights of Spaunton Moor. All is held together by the winding Dove Valley, with every-thing arranged so perfectly, like the backdrop of some gigantic open-air theatre. The surprise view is a bonus on the way to Farndale. This secluded valley, enfolded by the mighty arms of Rudland Rigg, Blakey Ridge and Farndale Moor, puts on a remarkable display of wild daffodils in the spring. A well-marked footpath, beside the eastern bank of the meandering Dove, begins at the Low Mill car park. It leads for about 1½ miles through meadows full of nodding daffodils, past an old abandoned mill then up a short stretch of road to Church Houses. Do not pick the flowers – the area is a nature reserve and the daffodils are protected.

The bridge over the Dove just west of Church Houses was, according to local legend, the setting for a romantic tragedy. The beautiful daughter of a local landowner fell in love with a farmer's boy, and when her parents forbade the match the despairing girl jumped off the bridge to her death. How she managed to do more than get her feet wet in the shallow water is a matter of conjecture.

Gillamoor is about 2¼ miles north-west of Kirkbymoorside on the A170. Carry on north for another 3 miles along a minor road up the valley of the Dove to reach Low Mill car park.

Bc Glaisdale and Egton Bridge

Near the railway arches just to the east of Glaisdale is Beggar's Bridge, an ancient, single-arched stone bridge, much painted by local artists because of its beautiful setting.

Today, Glaisdale is a tranquil village, enfolded by quiet hills. But just over a century ago these same hills were clamorous with the sounds of iron-smelting, and blast furnaces belched their smoke into the air. But, finally, the seam of ironstone that had been worked in the dale since the 13th century started to run out. In 1888 the ironworks, 73 workmen's cottages and the manager's house were sold by auction at a knock-down price, even for those days, of £8,900.

A pleasant 3 mile walk from Glaisdale to Egton Bridge and back leads through the wooded gorge of the River Esk. Cars can be parked beneath the railway arches near Beggar's Bridge. Cross the bridge and climb the steps that lead into Arnecliff Wood. On the far side of the wood the path reaches a minor road; follow the road north-east to the Horseshoe Hotel before Egton Bridge. Just north of the hotel, down a curving flight of steps, the river can be crossed by a set of stepping-stones. If the river is high, it is more sensible to go back to the road and cross by the bridge. When the salmon and sea trout are running, from July to December, it is thrilling to see them leaping the weir near the stepping-stones.

After crossing the river, follow the path west that leads under the railway bridge, then turn left immediately after the stables into Limber Hill Wood. A steep climb through larch trees leads to a bridleway that can be followed back to Glaisdale.

The walk can be started from either Glaisdale or Egton Bridge. Both are reached by a minor road south off the A171, 4½ miles west of Whitby, signposted Egton. For Glaisdale, turn west at Egton; for Egton Bridge, keep on southwards.

Ab The Hambleton Drove Road

In the middle of the last century, one of the busiest roads in Britain ran along the ridge of The Hambleton Hills. Columns of shaggy West Highland cattle and black Galloways stretched back for miles. Collie dogs, ears alert for their masters' whistling, threaded their way through a seeming confusion of pigs, sheep, waddling geese and clacking turkeys.

The Scottish drovers were taking their flocks and herds to market, along an ancient track which crossed the Tees near Yarm, then climbed the moors, avoiding the tolls that were charged on the turnpike roads below.

Parts of this ancient highway are now metalled, making a scenic drive. But there is a 6 mile stretch of rough moorland track, beginning just above the village of Nether Silton, that is ideal for walkers. Take the road east then north from Nether Silton, signposted to Over Silton, but turn right after about 200 yds, along a road that climbs steeply at first. Park beyond the cattle-grid and follow the Forestry Commission track that leads to the

PATCHWORK FIELDS Drystone walls pattern the floor of the placid Dove Valley near Gillamoor.

northern flank of 1,309 ft high Black Hambleton. After about an hour's steady walking, with conifers on either side, the track meets the drove road.

For those who turn right, the promise of the open road – wild, bracing and free – is abundantly fulfilled. The first section of the ancient moorland track leads over the hunched shoulder of Black Hambleton to Arden Great Moor. Once on the rim of the hills, there is a purple sea of heather to the left and glorious views of the Vale of York to the right.

You can retrace your steps at any time, or decide to carry on to complete an 8 mile circular hike. This leads past

some disused quarries, to the east of the track about 1½ miles from the crest of Black Hambleton. About a mile further on is a crossroads, with a white gate on the right, and a track leading west down to Kepwick. Keep west through Kepwick and follow the signs back to Nether Silton. Just beyond Nether Silton, before you reach the parking place, the landscape obligingly stretches out like a panoramic map, to show much of the route you have walked.

Nether Silton lies 6½ miles north of Thirsk. To reach it, take the signposted road east off the A19, 5½ miles north of Thirsk.

Cb Hole of Horcum and Blakey Topping

The Cleveland giant, Wade, was mighty in his rages, as well as in his proportions. One day, his wife, Bel, angered him so much that he scooped up a handful of earth and flung it at her. Bel ducked, and the mountain of soil sailed over her head to land a couple of miles away, where it became known as Blakey Topping. The hollow left behind was the Hole of Horcum.

That, at least, is one legend explaining the origin of this huge natural amphitheatre, just off the main road between Pickering and Whitby. The

GIANT BOWL Rimmed by open moors, the vast cavity of the Hole of Horcum was carved from the limestone by water erosion.

and walk along the bottom of the Hole.

Blakey Topping, an isolated conical hill about 2 miles from the Hole, is a good viewpoint reached by taking the road east from near the car park to Newgate Foot. From there, the walk is mostly on a metalled road, but cars are not allowed beyond the gate at the start. The best view is north towards the giant golf-ball shapes of the Fylingdales Early Warning Station. Follow the track that swings eastwards along the escarpment; below are the remains of a Bronze Age stone circle. Three stones remain in position, and depressions in the ground mark where other stones once stood.

The Hole of Horcum lies west of the A169 Pickering–Whitby road, about 6¼ miles north-east of Pickering.

Ab Kilburn White Horse and Roulston Scar

The Hambleton Hills, above the pretty village of Kilburn, have been noted for their horses since Viking days. It was the Vikings who introduced horse-racing to the area: and still today there are gallops on the hills, where thoroughbreds are brought to racing condition. John Hodgson, a local schoolmaster, clearly had the long association between the hills and horses in mind when, in 1857, he decided to mark out a massive white horse on the slopes above Kilburn. He had 30 helpers for the task, and they used 6 tons of lime to whiten the figure. For, unlike the white horses in southern Britain, Kilburn's is not cut in chalk; it rests on a foundation of gritty limestone that has to be freshened every few years. At 314 ft long and 228 ft high, the horse was meant to be seen from a distance, rather than close up,

top of the Hole commands one of the finest views on the moors – south over the Vale of Pickering and west over the Hole itself, floored with green fields that look flat from above but in fact have a pronounced slope.

This spectacular bowl, curving at its southern end into a narrow valley, is the result of what geologists call spring tapping – the deepening and widening of a natural hollow by the erosive action of springs whose water cannot seep away through the underlying clay.

A short walk from the roadside car park leads to a gate and stile near the

hairpin bend called Devil's Elbow. This is the start of a walk around the Hole. The wind is fierce and persistent at the edge, and the steep northern slopes have become a launching ground for hang-gliders. A track through the heather leads past the lip of the Hole and then, after about 1¼ miles, to Seavy Pond on Levisham Moor. Half a mile beyond the pond, there are Iron Age earthworks across the path and on high ground to the left.

Continue to Dundale Pond and turn left, taking the track down the valley

to Levisham Beck. The rocky ravine beside the track provides shelter after the rigours of the open moor, and mossy oak trees have established themselves along its course.

Turn left at the bottom of the ravine and cross Levisham Beck. Then turn left again, keeping the beck on your left and a drystone wall on the right. The path leads past woodland and a deserted farm, Low Horcum, romantic in its solitude.

Follow the path north-east. Where it forks, you can either go left, up the western side of the Hole or turn right and sightings have been reported from as far off as Leeds, some 30 miles away.

Steps lead to the top of the white horse from a car park at its base, about a mile north of Kilburn village. This is also the start of a pleasant 1½ mile Ampleforth Forest walk, that leads along the edge of cliffs to Roulston Scar, a creamy limestone crag with magnificent views across the chequer-board Vale of York. More than 30 miles away rise the Pennine heights. Just across the valley is cone-shaped Hood Hill, where in pre-Roman times the Druids are said to have practised human sacrifice.

The promontory on which Roulston Scar lies is defended by two prehistoric earthworks, both called the Casten Dike. The southern section is about a quarter of a mile long, while the northern section is about 25 yds wide and some two-thirds of a mile long – a prodigious feat of engineering for people whose main digging tool was probably the antler pick.

The forest walk leads down into Happy Valley below the scar, where rowan trees, elderberries, hazels and hawthorns all struggle for a footing among a profusion of fallen boulders.

Kilburn is 5 miles east of Thirsk. Take the A170 east from Thirsk, then turn south after 2 miles along a minor road to Bagby. Turn east at Bagby and the road leads to Kilburn. Follow the signposts to the White Horse car park, about 1 mile north of the village.

Bb ## Kirk Dale

In 1821, workmen digging for road-stone in a quarry at Kirk Dale made a remarkable discovery. They broke through the mouth of a cave and found its floor littered with thousands of bones – relics of the prehistory of this pastoral valley.

For Kirk Dale was once the home, over a period of many years, of mammoths, cave lions, cave bears, tigers, rhinoceroses, hippopotamuses, bison, Irish elks and giant oxen. The cave was probably the den of many generations of hyenas, and over an immense period of time they dragged in their victims.

About 20,000 years ago, during the last Ice Age, the cave was submerged under the rising waters of an immense meltwater lake, and the cave mouth was sealed, to be discovered only in the last century.

It is easily reached from the road near the ford at the lower end of Kirk Dale. Take the path east of the river into the woods, just beyond the ford, and follow it as it swings right, back to the roadside quarry. The cave openings are little more than slits, through which sightseers must crawl.

Apart from the cave, there are a number of pleasant walks through Kirk Dale. One starts from the ancient church, St Gregory's Minster, where a Saxon sundial above the south door records that the church was rebuilt 'in the days of Edward the King and Tosti the Earl'. The Edward referred to was Edward the Confessor, and Tosti was the Earl of Northumberland. The footpath leads through woods on the eastern bank of the Hodge Beck.

Kirk Dale lies north of the A170 along a signposted minor road 1½ miles west of Kirkbymoorside.

PATIENT MOUNT Kilburn's White Horse has stood on the ridge above the Vale of York since 1857, when it was first cut out.

MOORLAND WATERFALL In the Murk Esk valley the West Beck plunges over the sudden drop of Mallyan Spout. The beck follows a winding course northwards to become the Murk Esk, a tributary of the River Esk.

Cc
Mallyan Spout
and Beck Hole

One of the loveliest parts of Esk Dale is the tributary valley of the Murk Esk, curving round from the south to join the main Esk Valley. An easy-paced three-hour walk from Goathland will take you through woodland, across fields and alongside tumbling becks with picturesque waterfalls.

There are plenty of places for parking in Goathland, an attractive, scattered village whose wide greens are kept close-cropped by sheep.

The walk begins close to the grand edifice of the Mallyan Hotel, at the south end of the village. A footpath just to the east of the hotel leads northwest through larchwoods down to Murk Esk, known this high up as West Beck. Turn upstream and scramble alongside the beck for 200 yds as it tumbles untidily over rocks and boulders. Suddenly, coming in from the left is Mallyan Spout – a spray of water arching over a moss-covered cliff, 70 ft high. The fall can be wispy during spells of dry weather. Retrace your steps alongside the tumbling peat-brown beck, and follow its course beyond the path leading back up to Goathland. Over a stile, the path leads into fields, with a wood on the right. Turn right through a gate, then left after a second gate to reach the delightful little moorland village of Beck Hole, where stone-built cottages cling to a grassy slope.

Climb the slope to cut off a section of road, turn right along the road then right again, on the track that leads past Hill Farm. Follow the track on the right, that goes east and leads past another farm down to Thomason Foss. Here, the Eller Beck plunges over a set of cataracts with a satisfying thunder. Further upstream, spanned by an iron foot-bridge, the beck has cut a straight-sided channel through its bedrock with the precision of a stonemason. Over the foot-bridge, a flight of steps leads to the footpath back to Goathland.

Goathland is 7 miles south-west of Whitby on a minor road west of the A169, signposted about 5 miles south-west of Whitby. The village can be very busy during the peak holiday season.

Cc
Robin Hood's Bay
and Ravenscar

The cliffs between Robin Hood's Bay and Ravenscar are like some gigantic geological textbook, lying with its pages open so that anyone who understands the language can read the history of the last 180 million years.

This is one of the richest stretches of coast in Britain for fossils. Embedded in the shales are cigar-shaped belemnites, oyster-like *Liostrea* and coiled ammonites – known locally as St Hilda's serpents because St Hilda, the Abbess of Whitby, was supposed to have rid the area of snakes by petrifying them.

The oldest rocks date from the Jurassic Period, 180 million years ago, when fine grains of silt were deposited on the bed of an ancient sea, and compressed into shale. Above, like layers in a cake, are sandstone, shales bearing jet and alum, ironstone, more sandstone and then a thick bed of boulder clay, the spoil-heap left 10,000 years ago by an Ice Age glacier.

In the eternal battle between land and sea, the sea is winning handsomely at Robin Hood's Bay, eating away the cliffs at the rate of 2 in. a year. The great bite it has already taken forms the bay itself. And the cliffs are under attack from another direction, too: streams running down from the moors are helping the work of erosion.

The bay is only 3 miles across, but the curve adds another mile. Allow two and a half hours to walk along the beach to Ravenscar, and set off only if the tide is out or on the way out.

At Ravenscar, a stepped path leads up the cliffs, and here the layer-cake structure is plainly revealed. It includes a geological fault, the fracture line left by an earthquake millions of years ago, when the earth's surface sheared sideways along a line of weakness. The fault line today is marked by a valley that comes into view halfway up the cliff path, near the safety fence.

From the Raven Hall Hotel, a two-hour walk along the cliffs leads back to Robin Hood's Bay. The path passes quarries where alum was once mined. To the right of the path is a deep cleft, down which the alum was carried to be loaded on to waiting ships.

Robin Hood's Bay lies 5 miles south-east of Whitby. Take the A171 from Whitby and, after 2¼ miles, take the B1447 signposted to the bay. There is a large car park at the top of the cliffs.

SCARRED BY MAN AND NATURE Roseberry Topping's stern face broods over the National Park's northern border.

Ac Roseberry Topping and Highcliff Nab

Standing apart from the rest of Cleveland like a wary old bull guarding its herd, Roseberry Topping is so dramatic a landmark that in Viking times it was regarded as a sacred hill, the abode of the war-god Odin. No hill in Yorkshire looks out on a prospect more sweeping, or wears a face more battered and scarred by man and time.

From its 1,051 ft summit there are views to the west across the Leven-Tees valley with its pastures, woods, cornfields and towns stretching into misty distance where the Pennines rise. To the south, only a few miles away, there swells the much-quarried scarp face of the Cleveland Hills. Towards the north-east the crags of Highcliff Nab jut forward aggressively from conifer-clad slopes. To the north-west, beneath a perpetual haze, stretches industrial Teesside, an immense and impressive factory landscape.

The scars on Roseberry Topping, and the final touches to its distinctive shape, are the result of man's activities.

Over the centuries the hill has been quarried and mined for sandstone, alum, coal, iron and jet.

Fossilised shells, leaves and ferns have been found high on the slopes of Roseberry, but the commonest fossil of all is jet, formed from the remains of swamp trees that died 180 million years ago.

Another spectacular viewpoint in this lovely tract of country is Highcliff Nab, an outcrop of crags about 2 miles north-east of Roseberry Topping, towering out of the wooded hillside above Guisborough. To reach the crags, follow the path east from the summit of Roseberry. The path follows the edge of woods first, then enters them. As the path winds among the conifers, Highcliff Nab appears and disappears through the trees. A final steep climb leads to the impressive viewpoint, looking out over woods and toytown-like Guisborough at its foot.

Roseberry Topping is 2¼ miles south-west of Guisborough. One of the best starting points for climbing the hill is from the car park on the A173 about 1 mile north-east of Great Ayton, just south of the village of Newton under Roseberry.

Ab Rye Dale, Rievaulx Abbey and Old Byland

It would be hard to find a valley better groomed than Rye Dale. The graceful ruins of Rievaulx Abbey are set perfectly on a shelf of land overlooking a loop of the River Rye. They are overlooked in turn by elegant terraces of verdant lawns, laid out in 1758 at the height of the landscaping craze, complete with Grecian temples. Framing the terraces and the abbey is a huge sweep of wooded hillside, where noble oaks stand side by side with ash and sycamore.

This is marvellous walking country, and one of the best starting points is Old Byland, itself once the site of an abbey. A three-hour circular walk leads to Rye Dale and Rievaulx Abbey. Take the road to Cold Kirby, and after about a quarter of a mile turn off left to Grange Farm. Past the farm, turn south just before a cattle grid, along a path that is ill-defined in places. Swing east, and down through Callister Wood, then cross a wooden bridge, a stile and a plank bridge. Take the track that goes east, passing three large ponds on which mallard duck announce themselves with loud quacking. A metalled road leads east to Ashberry Farm, and to a three-quarter mile detour across the River Rye to the abbey.

A pleasant hour can be spent walking round Ashberry Hill, reached by crossing the stile at the side of Ashberry Farm. The abbey, glimpsed through a tracery of branches, with the terraces above and the river murmuring below, becomes an enchanted place.

To get back to Old Byland from the abbey, return to Ashberry Farm, turn north and follow the road for about a quarter of a mile as it starts to climb, then turn west. This track leads back to Old Byland.

Rievaulx Abbey is ½ mile west of the B1257, 2¼ miles north-west of Helmsley on the A170. Or it can be reached from Old Byland, 2 miles north-west of the abbey. For Old Byland, take the road to Cold Kirby from the Sutton Bank car park on the A170, 6 miles west of Helmsley. Turn left just before Cold Kirby, then right at the T-junction.

Ab Sutton Bank

Like a rousing overture played as the curtain rises on a grand opera, Sutton Bank gives a foretaste of all that is to come in the North York Moors: exhilarating views, prehistoric remains and abundant wildlife. There could be no finer entry point to the National Park. To the west the view stretches out across the broad Yorkshire plain to Swaledale, Wensleydale and the Pennines, with Great Whernside on the horizon more than 30 miles away. The plain is punctuated by such landmarks as Fountains Abbey, 17 miles away, and Knaresborough Castle, 19 miles to the south-west. Roulston Scar juts out assertively along the cliffs to the south, and just below sparkles Gormire Lake, an enchanting (and some say enchanted) lake, whose waters were trapped by a landslip at the end of the last Ice Age. Ahead lies a scenic drive along the southern edge of the moors, passing wooded dales that lead to the high moorland plateau.

The A170 from Thirsk zigzags like an Alpine pass to climb Sutton Bank, and still leaves motorists with a punishing 1 in 4 gradient. Near the elbow of the zigzag, a roadside plaque inside a white fence marks a Bronze Age burial site, dating back to about 1400 BC.

The Bronze Age people of the moors usually sited their graves where there were marvellous views; and this one looks south along the cliffs towards the bluff of Roulston Scar and the conical shape of Hood Hill.

Sutton Bank is on the A170, about 5 miles east of Thirsk. Stopping is prohibited on the road, but there is a car park at the top of the hill.

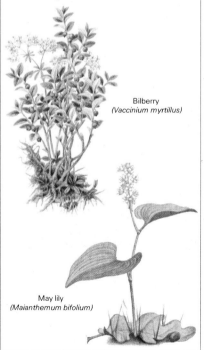

THE SWEET AND THE RARE

Like heather, the bilberry thrives on poor, acid soil and grows abundantly on the moors. Its sweet, black berries are a favourite food of grouse. The may lily is one of England's rarest wild flowers, and is found only in one or two wooded dales in the east. Growing to about 6 in. high, it produces a spike of red berries.

Bilberry
(*Vaccinium myrtillus*)

May lily
(*Maianthemum bifolium*)

Cb Wade's Causeway

One of the best-preserved examples of Roman road-building in Britain marches confidently over Wheeldale Moor. The moor is a bleak, wind-buffeted place today, as it must have been 19 centuries ago when captive British tribesmen sweated to bed the flat, heavy foundation stones into place for their Roman overseers.

The road originally stretched for 25 miles, from near the Roman fort at Derventio (modern Malton) to Lease Rigg, in the Esk Valley. All that can be seen today is a stretch about a mile long on Wheeldale Moor, and another north of the Roman camps at Cawthorne to the south. A notice beside the moor section says that the road was built in the 4th century AD, probably to connect the fort at Malton with signal stations on the east coast, set up to warn of the approach of Saxon pirates. But more recent research suggests that it was built around AD 80 as a highway along which detachments of the Ninth Legion could march to overawe the recently subjugated Brigantes tribe.

The name Wade's Causeway arises from a local legend that the Cleveland giant, Wade, built it as a track along which his wife, Bel, could drive her cattle out to pasture.

Wade's Causeway is 5 miles south of Egton Bridge. It meets the minor road that runs south from the village up to the moor.

HAIL AND FAREWELL The view from Sutton Bank is the North York Moors' great theatre set piece. The sweeping ridge rising from the Vale of York beckons travellers from the west, or provides an impressive farewell to those leaving the moors.

200

THE FOREST OF BOWLAND

A sparsely inhabited tract of moors and fells lying close to the industrial heart of Lancashire

A lonely tract of high, rounded fells broken by gritstone crags and limestone knolls; golden streams rushing down secluded valleys; lonely farmsteads set in networks of dry-stone walls; and quiet villages among lush meadows; these are the qualities of the Forest of Bowland. Yet most people pass by this compact little wilderness without knowing that it is there, often without even having heard of it. And this privacy and solitude are its essence and charm; it is a world apart. You can sometimes drive the 15 miles across it without seeing a single person. Its remoteness is astonishing since the Forest of Bowland lies close to Lancashire's cotton towns.

The fells and moors have always been sparsely inhabited, providing little but game, and grazing for sturdy sheep. Angles settled in the fertile valleys and hardy Norse farmers, descendants of the Viking invaders, established their *thwaites*—'clearings'—on the high moorlands. But once the Normans occupied Britain, almost the whole of Bowland passed into the hands of a single baron, Robert de Lacy, and became a 'forest', not a woodland but a Norman forest—a royal hunting ground—backed up by parks where deer were fattened for the royal table. During the next 500 years, red and fallow deer were the most important and protected inhabitants of the area.

Bowland's isolation made it a place of refuge for those at odds with

the law or the Church. The most prominent outlaw it sheltered was Henry VI, the unwilling principal player in the Wars of the Roses. After his defeat at Hexham in 1465, he hid for a year in Bowland before he was betrayed and led away to captivity.

In the 16th century, Bowland harboured many who remained staunch Catholics when Protestantism became the established faith. A hundred years later it was refugees of the opposite persuasion who came here—the nonconformists, who were forbidden to settle within 5 miles of any town, and many chose the wilderness of Bowland.

Later, the tranquil countryside offered escape of a different kind to workers in the cotton towns, and Pendle Hill especially became a goal for week-end ramblers. Mill-workers would walk all night to reach its summit in time to see the dawn on summer Sundays; Barley villagers rose early, too, in order to sell lavish ham-and-egg breakfasts to the triumphant pilgrims.

The name Bowland comes from the Celtic *buland*—'a cattle pasture'. Large herds of dairy cows are still fed upon the rich grazing in the valley bottoms, where the villages are as tranquil as the gentle surroundings that gave them birth. Streams, peat-tinted to a pale amber, hurry down rills and waterfalls, between banks of rabbit-shorn grass. But this idyll is not really typical of Bowland; rather its true character is to be found on the wild, high moors where the air always has a bite to it, and whose voices are those of the curlew and the plover. The colours are subtle, a mosaic of soft shades that comes to its greatest glory in autumn when bronze and purple are added to the range of greens. Bowland's countryside is not dramatic. But it has a sense of peace that it happily yields to anyone who comes in search of it.

BEACON FELL The height and position of this hill on the southern fringe of the Forest of Bowland made it an ideal place for signal beacons. Whether signalling good news or bad, the flames would have been visible across the Brock valley and in the Bowland villages.

Places to visit

Map ref. Ab   Beacon Fell

In the days when national victories or approaching dangers were proclaimed by lighting fires on hilltops, Beacon Fell was an important link in the chain. Its broad dome is clear of vegetation and commands far, all-round views. Indeed, a view indicator on the summit optimistically points to the Welsh mountains some 80 miles away, but the chance of actually seeing them is rare; 60 in. of rain falls annually on the fell.

For all its impressive views, Beacon Fell is only 873 ft high and it is easily climbed. It consists of Bowland shale capped with gritstone, and the line where the two rocks meet is the birthplace of a myriad springs. One of them feeds the pond by the Fell House car park, from which a delightful walk leads around the thickly wooded hillsides. The trees, mainly Sitka spruce, are crowded with the roosts of thousands of starlings. During spring and summer the birds disperse to nest – some as far away as Russia – before returning to their roosts in early autumn. Tawny owls also haunt the forest. In Bull Coppice, south-west of the summit, 5 ft high stumps have been left during thinning operations to provide night perches for the birds.

Among the predominant spruces there are stands of sycamore, rowan, wild cherry, oak, alder and beech. The open summit is dressed with purple moor-grass – at its colourful best in July and August – and with ling, bell heather, bilberry, crowberry and mat-grass.

Beacon Fell is 9 miles north of Preston. It can be reached by minor roads leading east from Bilsborrow on the A6, 7 miles north of Preston. A one-way, clockwise ring road circles the fell.

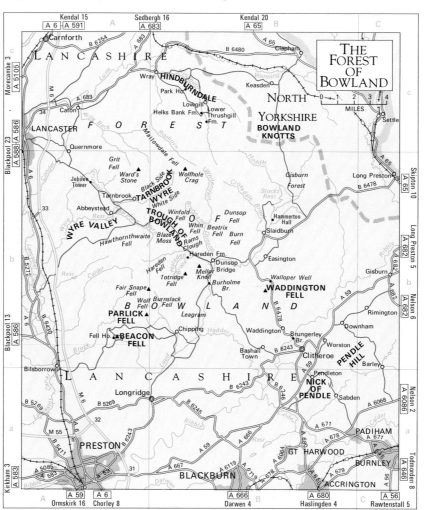

Bc   Bowland Knotts

High stone walls border the road that travels north through the dark conifers of the 3,000 acre Gisburn Forest. As you drive along the road, glimpses of Stocks Reservoir may be seen through the trees. Then suddenly the forest ends, there are no more walls, and ahead high, open windswept moorland spreads out for miles. It is all tremendously exhilarating – the more so in contrast with the dark road behind.

Along the skyline ahead, guarding the watershed and the county boundary, the high gritstone crags of Bowland Knotts face south over the moor. Scramble up to any of the crags and the view to the south takes in mile after mile of open fell, peat, heather and cotton-grass. The only sounds are the call of the curlew, the hollow, lonely whistle of the golden plover, and the 'peewit' of the lapwing. Far below, the waters of Stocks Reservoir glitter in the sun, and from here the plantation around them looks far less gloomy.

The reservoir and its surrounding forest cover the ancient park of one of the great medieval families of Bowland, the Hammertons; Hammerton Hall is just a mile south of the reservoir's dam.

At one time, Hammertons could ride from Slaidburn to York without ever leaving their own land. But in 1536, Sir Stephen Hammerton led out his retainers in support of the Pilgrimage of Grace, a demonstration against the Dissolution of the Monasteries. He was hanged, drawn and quartered, and his estates made forfeit to the Crown.

The vast panorama to the south of the Knotts is only one of the delights they offer, for each summit affords an all-round view. Turn slowly round towards the north and there, shining in the sun, are the three peaks of Ingleborough, Whernside and Pen-y-ghent, great masses of limestone towering

FOREST EDGE Fields enclosed by drystone walls climb to Bowland Knotts, a gritstone ridge marking the northern edge of the Forest of Bowland, and straddling the border between Lancashire and North Yorkshire.

high above the moorland plateau. The contrast between their whiteness and the dark crags of the Knotts is truly startling.

The road to Bowland Knotts, signposted to Clapham and Keasden, turns north from the B6478 between Long Preston and Slaidburn. Long Preston is 12 miles north-east of Clitheroe, and 11 miles north-west of Skipton.

Hindburndale
Bc

The River Hindburn begins as a cluster of little moorland streams rising high on the Bowland fells. The streams drain the moor top, but only after rainstorms are they any more than thin trickles, running down small gullies lightly grooved into the sparse soil. Neither the streams nor their surrounding give any hint of the loveliness that lies downriver.

By Lower Thrushgill Farm, where the gullies have merged into a steep, well-developed valley and the streams have become a river, the first trees lean over the waters or sprinkle shadow on the hillsides. From the double bridges below Helks Bank Farm, a network of footpaths runs down the valley – some close to the river, some higher up the valley side – towards the village of Wray. Which path to take is a matter of on-the-spot choice. It is easy to improvise a circular walk which leads round through Lowgill – where traces of a Roman road can be seen – and back to the bridges.

But perhaps the most attractive part of Hindburndale lies even further down the valley. The road that climbs steeply out of Wray from the bridge leads up on to the flank of fellside which swells between the valleys of the Hindburn and the Roeburn, and then

HINDBURNDALE Down from the high fells, the Hindburn flows through a gentle dale on its way to join the Wenning.

drops down again past Park House towards the Hindburn. Here, sunlight beams through a thick canopy of oak, ash, beech and sycamore, and sparkles on the water. And the water is in full voice, rushing noisily over rapids and tumbling down small waterfalls.

Wray is 2 miles along the B6480, which branches east from the A683, 8 miles north-east of Lancaster. Two narrow, unclassified roads from Wray explore the opposite sides of the Hindburn valley and meet near Helks Bank Farm, about 5 miles upstream from Wray.

Nick of Pendle
Ba

The slumbering-lion shape of Pendle Hill sprawls to the east of Pendleton village, its head pointing north-east, its rump south-west. The rise of the rump – the 'Little End' of Pendle – is grooved by a col called the Nick of Pendle. Pendleton village is stone-built, with a stream running down its street and the green fields of the Ribble Valley spreading about it. But the moment the village is left behind and the first cattle-grid crossed, the scene

changes instantly to one of bleak, sweeping moorland. Clumps of rushes and sedge dot the poor, close-cropped grass, and rocks stick up through the thin soil. Ahead, the road rises up the Nick.

From the top of the pass, where the small quarries just over the crest make convenient car parks, climb the sloping slabs of rock to the west. Enormous views spread in every direction. The cotton towns lie to the south, and to the west stretch the crops on the plain of Fylde with the Irish Sea beyond. The

Pennines dominate the eastern skyline, and to the north is the beautifully wooded valley of the Ribble, planted 200 years ago with more than a million oak trees. Beyond this belt of green, rise the purple crags and moors of the Forest of Bowland, filling the whole horizon.

On the east side of the Nick, a path runs away to the bulk of Pendle Hill. It climbs and climbs, and then suddenly steepens to scramble up the lion's flank. It is a rough track of gritstone fragments, and fairly hard going, but it is a wonderful, exhilarating walk all the way and well worth the effort. The only animals you will see are rabbits, hares and Swaledale sheep, and the common birds are the skylark, meadow pipit and the plaintive lapwing. There are no trees, only the small, erect shrubs that bear the delicious orange-coloured fruits called cloudberries, so named, it is said, because they so often grow on cloud-capped hilltops.

Pendle Hill has always been a natural barometer for local people, 'a vast black mountain which is the morning weather glass of the country people', according to the 18th-century traveller William Stukeley.

At haymaking time the people of Barley, on the eastern side, used to post a sentinel with a flag on the hill. If he saw a storm brewing in the west, he would wave the flag as a warning to the farmers, telling them to bring in the hay as quickly as possible.

Pendleton is on a minor road 2 miles south-east of Clitheroe.

Ab   Parlick Fell

It is a tough climb to the 1,416 ft summit of Parlick Fell, for the hill has convex slopes. The first 800 ft of the climb is the steepest stretch and the most slippery, since it is over shale. But the views from the top make the climb well worth the effort. Parlick is among the southern Bowland fells and, jutting well out from the main mass, it commands tremendous views – over the valleys of the Loud and Ribble rivers, over the wide Lancashire plain, across Morecambe Bay towards the southern hills of the Lake District, and even, when the weather is fine, as far as the Isle of Man and the distant mountains of Snowdonia some 80 miles away. Few other places in Lancashire survey such a wide domain.

Off the road that climbs up to Parlick from Chipping there is a rough farm track, just where the road makes a steep left bend at the foot of the fell. From the gate at the far end of the track, one path, with a gully on the right, climbs straight up the fell. A longer but easier path, to the left of the first, reaches the top of the fell in a series of zigzags.

Sheltering beneath the great rise of the fell is the village of Chipping. It lies in the valley of the River Loud, or rather perches over it, on a shelf about 50 ft above the river. Everywhere the valley is lush. Cattle graze on the rich, green grass between the woods and coppices, and lines of windbreak trees punctuate the landscape. In many parts of Bowland there are bluebells, and Leagram, the area of ancient forest that surrounds Chipping, has one of the finest bluebell woods in England.

In winters long ago, it is said, the wolves that lived above the village on Wolf Fell used to come loping down to search for food in Chipping. But standing in the village today, it is hard to imagine that anything has ever disturbed the peace of the place. Its name,

BOWLAND'S CLOAK OF RED

Woods and hedgerows are enlivened by clumps of red campion, which grows in profusion on rich soils. It can also be found in high places, on rocky slopes and cliff ledges. As its name implies, stone bramble is also a lover of rocky places. Rarer than its close relative, the raspberry, stone bramble is a low-growing plant which bears clusters of two to six scarlet berries. In summer the moors are bright with heather, but the cross-leaved heath thrives only in wet places. It is similar to bell heather, but is easily recognisable by the formation of its leaves, which form a cross when seen from above.

Stone bramble
(*Rubus saxatilis*)

Red campion
(*Silene dioica*)

Cross-leaved heath
(*Erica tetralix*)

recorded in the Domesday Book as Chippenden, derives from the old word for a market, and for centuries the village was the principal meeting-place for farmers in this fertile and prosperous valley.

Three miles north from the centre of Preston along the A6, the B5269 branches off to Longridge 5 miles to the east. From Longridge signposted minor roads lead to Chipping, 5 miles to the north, and beyond it to the foot of Parlick Fell.

Cb   Pendle Hill

There is no denying its domination. Such is its bulk – 7 miles long and covering 25 sq. miles – that it overshadows completely the Ribble Valley and the countryside for miles around. Wherever you are, the commanding presence of Pendle is with you, watching you. The summit reaches 1,827 ft, and is capped by a flat, east-west sloping plateau of gritstone, with patches of bare peat and angular, frost-fractured fragments of grit. There are no trees or walls, either on Pendle's plateau or on its steeply sloping sides. It is a bare hill, and when the mists swirl over it, as they often do, it is easy to imagine that something sinister lingers here – perhaps a last spell cast by the poor women, known as the witches of Pendle, who were tried for sorcery in Lancaster in 1612.

Access to the top of Pendle is easy, in the sense that there are many paths – all of them steep. Perhaps the best approaches, apart from the path that starts at Nick of Pendle, are from the villages of Barley and Downham. Both are at the 'Big End', or eastern end. The paths from Barley are shorter, those from Downham more numerous, but, since Pendle has concave slopes, all paths end with a difficult last 800 ft.

Nevertheless, the climb is worth while for the 270 degree prospect – the view to the south-west is blocked by the hill's own bulk – when the day is clear, with the whole Pennine range wide open to the east. For such a bare-looking hill, Pendle supports an astonishing variety of plants – two kinds of club moss, cotton-grass and its less common relative mare's-tail cotton-grass, butterwort, heather, several mountain grasses, and that unusual orange cousin of the raspberry, the cloudberry.

Pendle Hill lies between Clitheroe and Nelson. From Gisburn on the A59, the A682 runs south and in just under 1 mile a minor road turns off south-west through Rimington to Downham, 4 miles from the turn-off. A road from Downham curves round Pendle Hill to Barley, 4 miles away to the south-east.

Bb Tarnbrook Wyre

A narrow road winds for 1½ miles up the lightly wooded, shallow valley of the Tarnbrook Wyre, one of the two main tributaries which meet at Abbeystead to form the River Wyre. It is an attractive road beneath the canopy of mixed broad-leaved trees, and never strays more than a few yards from water. Then, at the hamlet and farm of Tarnbrook, the road ends and a footpath leads up into the hills, to the highest points in the Forest of Bowland. This is moorland walking at its wildest and most lonely, with sweeping views to distant horizons.

The path leads first across the open moor and then into the narrowing valley and towards the small waterfall at its head. The walk is not difficult, but steepens sharply as it climbs the side of

the valley, known as the Black Side of Tarnbrook Fell – while the other side of the valley is known as the White Side. The names derive from their winter aspects – one is dark, heather moorland; the other is lighter grass moorland. To the south is the broad, dark breast of Hawthornthwaite Fell at 1,568 ft, with Hareden Fell to its east; between them, further south, rises the 1,656 ft summit of Fair Snape Fell. In autumn the hills glow with unexpected colour – the purple of flowering heather, and the gold of dying grass and bracken.

The path, one of the official access routes across private moorland, leads on to the heights of Mallowdale Fell and then, just at the watershed, it makes a T-junction with another concessionary path which runs along at 1,500 ft from Grit Fell in the west to Wolfhole Crag in the east. Only practised long-distance walkers will carry on from here, making the long trudge westwards over the 1,840 ft summit of the moor, and reaching the road again 6 miles west of Tarnbrook. For most people it will suffice to reach the watershed, almost 3 miles from Tarnbrook, and then enjoy the downhill return, having tasted the true wilderness of Bowland and breathed its delightful, most refreshing air.

The Tarnbrook road is signposted off the road through the Trough of Bowland. It heads north-east from this road just after it has crossed the River Grizedale, 7½ miles south-east of Lancaster.

Bb Trough of Bowland

If you want one place that sums up the whole of what the Forest of Bowland has to offer, take the winding road through the Trough of Bowland.

WAYSIDE BOWER For most of its way the road through the Trough of Bowland winds across desolate moors and fells, but the occasional glimpse of a shady glade and sparkling stream brings gentle relief to the wild scenery of the pass.

Mountain, stream and fell combine in one delightful whole. The Trough of Bowland is the wild pass you travel on the switchback road through fells and valleys from Quernmore, near Lancaster, to Dunsop Bridge some 12 miles to the south-east. The name could apply to the whole length of the road, but it is generally given to the stretch between Winfold Fell and Blaze Moss.

From end to end the road is spectacular and full of interest, as much for the motorist as for the walker. In the north-west it climbs steeply out of the Conder Valley then rushes headlong down the Grizedale Valley. It passes the Jubilee Tower, which commemorates the Golden Jubilee of Queen Victoria; the views from the top of the tower are among the most magnificent in the area. The prospect sweeps from the cloud-capped blue heights of the

Lake District in the far north-west, then down the slate-grey line of Morecambe Bay to the ramparts of Blackpool in the south, overtopped by the unmistakable 500 ft spire of Blackpool Tower.

Behind you is the height of Ward's Stone, more than 1,800 ft above sea-level and set off by the crags of Grit Fell. Climb to the top of Ward's Stone, and there you can sink on a cushion of heather and gaze up into the bowl of the sky, trying to pick out the soaring skylarks whose songs fill the air.

After Jubilee Tower the road crosses the upper arms of the River Wyre – a bubbling, infant stream here – and runs in splendour along the Marshaw Wyre, where the river flows through wide stretches of close-cropped grass, shaded by an occasional oak, ash or solitary pine.

Some of the best walks are in the last few miles down to Dunsop Bridge. A path runs up the wide valley of Rams Clough, to the north of the road about 3 miles from Dunsop, leading to Whin Fell and down the Brennand river to the River Dunsop, and so down to Dunsop Bridge – a solid 5 miles in all. The Dunsop is a delightful stream, dropping down rills and miniature waterfalls. Swallows and swifts dart and swoop low over it for evening flies, trout rise for newly hatched midges, and mallards bustle protectively around their chicks on the willow-hung pools.

Another lovely 5 mile walk starts on the south side of the road at the bottom of Hareden Brook, by Hareden Farm, and soon leaves the valley to strike up the side of Mellor Knoll, passing just below its 1,100 ft summit. From there it is an easy descent to the Hodder valley at Burholme Bridge, and the last 2 miles of gentle riverside walking leads to Dunsop Bridge.

The road through Quernmore and the Trough of Bowland is signposted from the A683 at Caton, which is 4½ miles north-east of Lancaster.

Bb Waddington Fell

When the guns open up at the start of the grouse-shooting season on the 'Glorious Twelfth' of August, the footpaths on the moors round Waddington Fell are closed to the public. Red grouse are practically an industry hereabouts, and even out of season their importance is apparent from the number of shooting butts scattered about the moors. But in spring and early summer it is the views, not the birds, that are the fell's main attractions.

A road climbs to the summit of the fell from the village of Waddington, which lies to the south. It was at Waddington that the unfortunate monarch Henry VI was captured after a year spent in hiding, mostly in the fastnesses of the Forest of Bowland. His host at Waddington was Sir John Tempest, and, according to a strong local tradition, it was Sir John's son-in-law Thomas Talbot of Bashall who betrayed him. Sir John's house was surrounded by soldiers as the king was at dinner. He managed to escape into the woods, but was captured as he crossed the River Ribble by the stepping-stones at Brungerley.

Just after the moorland road from Waddington has surmounted the fell and dropped over the other side, it passes a spring bubbling into a stone trough on the left – Walloper Well.

Climb the hill above the well, and at once there is a lovely view of the Bowland fells across the River Hodder. Or park a little downhill from the well and take the path that runs northwards down to the hamlet of Easington. From anywhere along the path, near the plateau edge, there are fine views across the water-meadows of the Hodder to Beatrix and Burn fells, and to Dunsop Fell beyond the valley.

Waddington is 2 miles north-west of Clitheroe along the B6478. This is the road that continues over the summit of Waddington Fell.

Ab Wyre Valley

Green fields grazed by black-and-white cows spread among the broad-leaved woods that shelter the River Wyre's two arms. Marshaw Wyre and Tarnbrook Wyre wriggle down their pastoral valleys to a meeting-place at the hamlet of Abbeystead. The wilderness of Bowland's fells looms on either side of the valleys and across their heads, but the valleys themselves are altogether gentler country.

Where they converge, the woods crowd right across the junction – a domain of green shade in summer and a crisp, golden world in autumn. No sooner have the two Wyres met, than their combined waters swell broadly across the valley, impeded by the dam of Abbeystead Reservoir half a mile below the village. The still water reflects the woods that crowd upon its eastern shores. A path runs along the north bank of the reservoir, first among the trees, and then through the open country beside the river as it emerges from the dam. This is fine strolling country, criss-crossed by a network of easy paths.

Although the district seems prosperous enough today, bad weather and poor harvests were blamed for the failure of the abbey founded at Abbeystead by a community of monks from Furness in the 12th century.

Abbeystead seems to have preserved monastic standards of learning and discipline even when the abbey had gone. In the 17th century the local free school advertised for a schoolmaster. To have any hope of success, a candidate had to be 'a Graduate of one of the Universities . . . skilful in the Greek and Latin Tongues and of a sound religion, of a grave behaviour, of a sober and honest conversation, no Tipler or haunter of Alehouses or Tavernes'.

Abbeystead is 8 miles south-east of Lancaster, and lies ½ mile south of the minor road that runs from Lancaster through the Trough of Bowland.

BIRDS OF WOODLAND, MOOR AND LAKESIDE

Despite its name, the willow warbler has no special preference for willow trees, and its sweet, wistful song may be heard in almost any woodland or scrub. The whinchat gets its name from its habitat – the 'whin', or gorse, of open moorlands where it nests. The male is often seen perching on bracken which it uses as a song post. The common sandpiper is just as likely to be seen on the muddy shore of a lake or river as on a sandy beach. Its dark colouring merges with the background, but in flight its white wing-bars can be seen. On the ground the common sandpiper has a characteristic tail-bobbing walk.

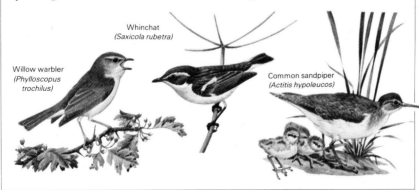

Willow warbler (Phylloscopus trochilus)
Whinchat (Saxicola rubetra)
Common sandpiper (Actitis hypoleucos)

THE LAKE DISTRICT

Like gems embedded in an old and precious metal, Cumbria's lakes lie glistening in an ancient landscape

The mountains of the Lake District were created about 50 million years ago, long before the lakes, when they took on something of their present shape. But the rocks that give the mountains their distinctive character are far older. Skiddaw Slates, the oldest, were formed on an ancient sea-bed some 530 million years ago. They weather evenly and produce smooth-sided, softly rounded mountains, such as Skiddaw itself, in the north, or the unexpected outcrop of Black Combe in the south-west. They are among the oldest rocks in the world.

After the slates came the 500-million-year-old rocks of the central massif – the ash and lava of the Borrowdale Volcanics. These form the sharp-edged crags and cliffs of Helvellyn, Honister, the Langdales, High Street and England's highest peak of Scafell Pikes (3,206 ft).

The youngest Lake District rock – a mere 440-410 million years old – is the Silurian Slate which forms the gentler and sweeter landscape that surrounds Windermere.

The lakes themselves were the product of the last great Ice Age. Countless glacier advances and retreats over a million years carved out the U-shaped valleys and formed the deeply incised lake beds. The lakes and tarns, exquisite late-comers to the mountain scene, may prove comparatively temporary, as they are being filled with sediment

LAKELAND TARN High in the fells, Angle Tarn lies like a sheet of hand-beaten silver on a green-baize setting. Lakeland tarns differ from the lakes in their plant life – common reed is found chiefly in lakes, whereas bottle sedge is common in tarns.

from mountain streams. Already many tarns have turned into peat-bogs, and silting has divided single lakes into smaller ones, notably at Bassenthwaite and Derwent Water, and at Loweswater, Crummock Water and Buttermere.

Little is known of the earliest inhabitants, who settled on the coastal plain but journeyed into the mountains to find stone suitable for fashioning into crude implements. The later Bronze Age people built their settlements on the bare fells and high moorlands, away from the boggy and unworkable valley bottoms and the densely wooded valley slopes. Standing among their cairns by bleak Devoke Water or on the windswept heath at Moor Divock, it is hard to imagine how they survived. But the most perplexing relics of this prehistoric period are the stone circles at Castlerigg near Keswick, and at Swinside below Black Combe.

To the Romans, the Lake District was strategically important because of its proximity to Hadrian's Wall. Their major work in the area was the road from Ambleside to the coast at Ravenglass, with a fort at either end and a great camp built midway along the route at Hardknott.

In the 8th and 9th centuries, a new wave of settlers arrived – Norsemen from Ireland and the Isle of Man – who built farmsteads and cleared the thickly wooded fells for grazing. Unlike their predecessors – the people of the Anglian kingdom of Northumbria – the Norsemen were predominantly pastoralists, rearing cattle, pigs and sheep.

In the early 19th century, William Wordsworth's writing established the Lake District as the foremost tourist area in England. But, whatever the demands on the area, the visitor who is prepared to walk can still find peace and beauty in this 'little, unsuspected paradise', as the poet Gray described the Lake District.

Places to visit

Map ref. Cc Aira Force

The waterfall is one of the Lake District's most romantic spots – a silver stream of water tumbling some 70 ft between gleaming, precipitous walls of rock. Here Aira Beck, which rises high in the wilderness of Matterdale Common, makes its last dramatic gesture before flowing into Ullswater.

Legend tells that Aira Force was once the scene of a tragedy of love. Its heroine, Emma, lived in the nearby Lyulph's Tower, and loved a knight called Sir Eglamore. For some reason he left her, and in despair she took to sleep-walking beside Aira Force, the place where they had first met. One night Sir Eglamore came back and found Emma at the waterfall; but when he called her name she awoke suddenly, tripped, and fell to her death in the foaming waters. The grieving knight became a hermit, and lived out his life near the spot where she had died.

A gate from the car park at the foot of Aira Beck leads into a field, and from the right of the field a stile leads into the woods and over a foot-bridge across the beck. The path follows the beck up through the woods – a delightful mixture of oak, ash, alder, willow, beech and the occasional wych elm. Many orchids can be seen, especially

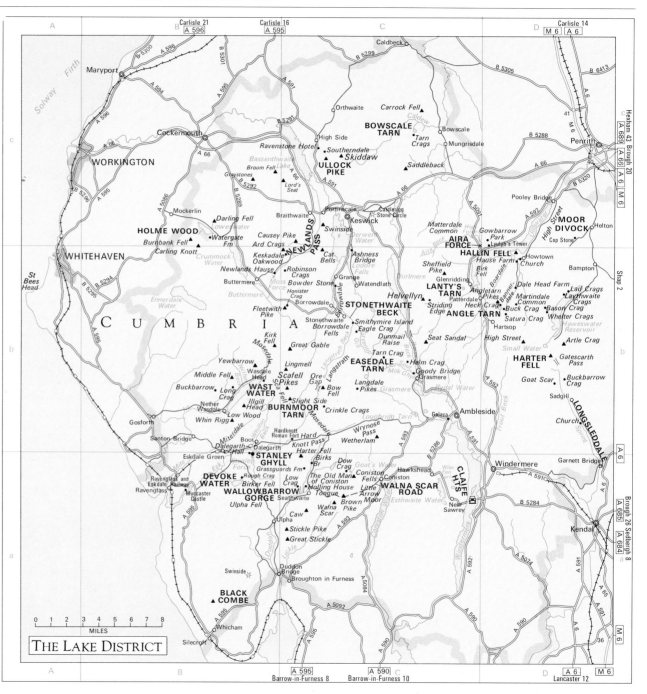

THE LAKE DISTRICT

purple orchids in late spring and spotted orchids in early summer.

Two bridges span the gorge, one above and one below Aira Force; cross the top bridge and follow the beck upstream on its right-hand side to another beautiful waterfall called High Force. The rock slabs around it seem perfectly made for sitting and contemplating for a while, as the water leaps loud and white towards its dark and silent ending in the lake.

The Aira Force car park is near the shore of Ullswater, a few yards north of the A592 and A5091 junction.

Db   Angle Tarn

Many people consider Angle Tarn the loveliest of all lakeland tarns, for it has something more than the wildness, isolation and scenic grandeur common to most tarns. Its shoreline is deeply indented, which gives it a very individual beauty, and two small islands standing far out on its trout-filled waters set off the scenery around them perfectly.

Above the tarn rise the peaks named after it – Angletarn Pikes, a summit with two separate peaks, rocky outcrops with a peat-bog in the depression between them. The views from the summit are not particularly extensive, but the surrounding countryside is glorious. This is part of the Martindale deer forest, and herds of red deer can sometimes be seen watering at the tarn. Fell ponies, almost as wild as the deer, also use the tarn as a watering-place, especially at daybreak and twilight.

There are several routes to the tarn, and one of the loveliest is from Dale Head Farm in Bannerdale. The path climbs diagonally past a stone ruin and a sheep-fold before crossing the screes between Heck Crag and Buck Crag.

Then, quite suddenly, the tarn comes into view in all its glory. Other ascents start at Patterdale and Hartsop, beginning in wooded lowlands and climbing through boulder-strewn, bracken-covered fells to the craggy heights.

From the tarn a path runs half a mile south-east to Satura Crag, from where there is a splendid view back down Bannerdale.

Patterdale is on the A592, ¼ mile from the southern end of Ullswater. Bannerdale can be reached by following the minor road from Pooley Bridge (on the B5320 at the northern end of Ullswater) to Howtown. Beyond the top of the col, or 'hause', the road drops steeply to Hause Farm. From here the left turn leads to Dale Head Farm beside Bannerdale Beck.

Ba   Black Combe

A soft, sweetly scented cushion of heather covers the 1,968 ft summit of Black Combe, and on a clear summer day it is possible to lie there for hours admiring the views all around.

This is a mountain made for views, for it stands alone in the extreme south-western tip of the Lake District, and so commands both land and sea. Snowdon is visible in the far south; the Isle of Man can be seen across the Irish Sea; and to the north the Southern Uplands of Scotland shimmer beyond the Solway Firth. Inland the view swings from the Forest of Bowland right round to the heights of Skiddaw in the distant north-east, with all the majestic summits of Scafell Pikes 15 miles away in front of them. The only sound is the sighing and buffeting of the wind sweeping in from the sea. Birds are the only company – perhaps a kestrel hovering far below in the sun, red grouse starting from the heather or

HIGH AND MIGHTY

Growing at heights of more than 2,000 ft, the alpine lady's mantle is a smaller version of the lady's mantle found in grasslands. The honey-scented grass-of-Parnassus is not a grass but an elegant plant – fit for the mountain which was the home of the Greek god Apollo. The plant is said to have been found growing on Parnassus in the 1st century.

Alpine lady's mantle
(*Alchemilla alpina*)

Grass-of-Parnassus
(*Parnassia palustris*)

meadow pipits on flickering wings darting from one patch of cover to another.

This most undramatic of mountains has attracted more than its share of folklore, possibly because of the Swinside stone circle on its north-eastern flank. The Bronze Age circle, which is 90 ft in diameter, is known locally as Sunken Kirk and was once believed to be a supernatural spot. According to legend, Black Combe bees wake from their winter sleep to hum in unison at midnight on Christmas Eve, and cattle kneel in adoration. Tradition also has

it that the mountain is possessed by a much less Christian spirit by the name of Hob Thross or Hob Thrust, 'a body all over rough'. People believed he could be summoned to do their bidding in the early hours – so long as he was rewarded with a dish of thick porridge with butter in it.

The easiest ascent of Black Combe is from the little church at Whicham, about a mile from the sea. A path between the church and the school leads to a narrow lane lined with brambles and wild roses, foxgloves and harebells. Beyond a white farmhouse, a track leads over a stile and up a valley on the right. The going is always easy; and after about 2 miles of leisurely zigzagging the path arrives at the summit.

Whicham is on the A595, about 6 miles south-west of Broughton in Furness.

Cc   Bowscale Tarn

The surface of Bowscale Tarn is like a black mirror reflecting the bleak, scree-laden cliffs of Tarn Crags. It seems to concentrate in one place all the loneliness of the landscapes around it. Only the occasional croak of a carrion crow, echoing off the rocks, disturbs the deep quiet.

It was this silent and empty wilderness, known as 'Back o' Skidda', that often echoed to the clamour that 'waked men from their beds and the fox from his lair in the morning', as John Peel partook of his favourite pastime. Born at Caldbeck in 1776, John Peel spent most of his 78 years hunting the fox on foot or pony – heedless of the demands of his 13 children.

The climb to the tarn starts low down in the valley of the River Caldew and leads up through rough moorland to the great dam of Ice Age litter which holds back the tarn's dark waters.

The path begins just beyond a row of cottages where the road turns sharply through the hamlet of Bowscale. There a gate leads on to the open fellside and the path climbs steeply to the west for a few yards before levelling out.

Across the valley, the slopes of Carrock Fell sweep down in a cascade of scree, and at the foot of the scree a road runs up to the valley head where a mine working wolfram – tungsten ore – has recently been reopened. Geologically the fell is exceptionally complex, and 23 minerals have been found there.

The path crosses Drycombe Beck, then winds round the next bluff before climbing diagonally up the moraine dam to Bowscale Tarn. The land is littered with boulders, many of them scratched or smoothed by the glacier which deposited them at the end of the last Ice Age. Everywhere Skiddaw Slate breaks through, the rock from which the whole of this area is formed. And then, over the brow of the dam, lies the tarn – black, menacing and to all appearances devoid of life.

A minor road to Mungrisdale turns north about 6 miles north-east from Keswick along the A66. Bowscale is 1 mile further on.

Burnmoor Tarn

Bb

From Eskdale Green to Boot is only a couple of miles along the flat road beside the River Esk; but a delightful 6 mile valley walk connects the two villages, climbing up Miterdale from Eskdale Green, turning round the windswept waters of Burnmoor Tarn, and dropping down again to Boot beside the Whillan Beck.

The first part of the walk north-east up Miterdale leads through Forestry Commission plantations, with many broad-leaved trees mixed in with the usual conifers, a wide variety of wayside and woodland flowers, and the River Mite always close at hand. After about a mile, at Low Place, the forest ends and a foot-bridge leads across the river. On the east side of the valley the fell is bare and stony, with some prehistoric stone circles and cairns up on Low Longrigg. There are impressive views northwards of the backs of Illgill Head and Whin Rigg, the fells which, on their north-west sides, form Wast Water's famous Screes.

The path climbs steadily north-east towards the isolated depression between Tongue Moor and Eskdale Moor, passing a lovely small amphitheatre on the right, with cliffs, waterfalls and a delightful greensward. Soon afterwards it reaches the graceful Burnmoor Tarn, where the view to the north-east is particularly impressive. The ridge ahead is Scafell and, beyond Slight Side, the southernmost summit, the well-named Crinkle Crags can be seen in the distance.

The path south-west down to Boot starts from the north-eastern corner of the tarn, where a complicated maze of tiny streams marks the point where Whillan Beck flows out of the tarn and Hardrigg Gill flows into it. The path is dry and follows the course of Whillan Beck a couple of hundred yards above it on the fellside. This path is the old 'corpse road' from Wasdale.

Bodies had to be brought to the Church of St Catherine, at Boot, because there was no consecrated ground in Wasdale. In the deep winter snows this was a hard journey for a funeral procession, and sometimes ponies took fright, bolting across the fells with their burdens. It was said that one pony was never recaptured, and lone travellers claimed to have met a ghostly, coffin-bearing pony on the moor.

Eskdale Green is 4 miles north-east of Ravenglass. Take the A595 north from Ravenglass and after 2 miles turn northeast on to a minor road to Santon Bridge. Then follow signposted minor roads to Eskdale Green. Alternatively, from Ambleside, take the A593, then the minor road over Wrynose and Hard Knott passes, both with steep gradients and sharp bends.

Claife Heights

Ca

Strange stories are told of the Windermere ferry, where an unbroken succession of ferrymen have plied their trade for a thousand years or more. On a stormy night in the 16th century one of them heard a cry from the Claife shore. He set out to collect the passenger and returned, apparently alone, but he was dumb with fear and died soon after. According to local legend he had brought back a phantom passenger, the Crier of Claife, who was eventually exorcised by a priest and put to rest in an old quarry known now as Crier of Claife Quarry.

On a fine day, such hauntings seem impossible in this lovely place, with its wooded isles reflected in calm water beneath the tree-clad heights of Claife. The gently rolling countryside of Claife, lying between Esthwaite Water and the enclosing curve of Windermere, provided an appropriate background for the stories of Beatrix Potter. Six of her books are set at Hill Top Farm at Near Sawrey, and many others contain her exquisite miniature water-colours of the surrounding woods and fields.

One of the most interesting of the walks on Claife Heights begins just below Hill Top Farm. Take the path north from opposite the Tower Bank Arms in Near Sawrey. The surrounding countryside is typical of the southern lakes – partly woods where roe deer roam and partly fertile grazing land with occasional outcrops of shale.

The path climbs upwards through some very large rock outcrops and soon reaches Moss Eccles Tarn. Here ducks and the occasional diver and grebe dabble on the water, while coots and moorhens dodge among the reeds. Larches, copper beeches and huge rhododendrons fringe the banks of the tarn. Further on lies Wise Een Tarn, wrapped like a silver boomerang around a dark mass of conifers. Ahead there are wonderful views of the central Lake District, stretching from The Old Man of Coniston through Langdale to the shoulder of Skiddaw.

Near Sawrey can be reached by the A593 from Ambleside. After 1 mile, turn south on to the B5286 and then take the B5285 through Hawkshead. Or take the A592 south from Windermere and after 2 miles cross the lake on the ferry.

Easedale Tarn

Cb

The poet Thomas de Quincey said that Easedale in relation to Grasmere was 'a chapel within a cathedral'. Walled round by cliff-like mountainsides, the valley preserves this sense of seclusion. De Quincey also noticed the pathos of

CHURNING WATER Sour Milk Gill hurtles down into Easedale with a force and fury that contrasts savagely with the tranquillity of the valley below. The name is apt for the creamy-white water, and is applied to several other waterfalls in the Lake District.

CORRIE TARN Easedale Tarn lies remote in its rocky, glacier-carved basin below the massive cliffs of Tarn Crag. It can be reached by a scenic walk through the heart of the fells, steep in places but never climbing to more than 950 ft.

the miniature settlement, cut off from the world and dwarfed beneath bleak and unfriendly fells. Even on fine days the dark mountain shadows seem to fall ominously across the tiny green fields, and there is a sinister violence about the stream that rushes past them, aptly named Sour Milk Gill because of the curdling whiteness of its churned water. A mile further up the valley, it issues from Easedale Tarn, rated – by de Quincey again – as 'the most gloomily sublime' of Lake District tarns.

The 2 mile walk to Easedale Tarn, very steep and wet in places, is dominated at first by the immense mass of Helm Crag to the north, with its fantastic rock formation known as The Lion and the Lamb.

The walk starts from Easedale Lane in Grasmere. Follow the lane across Goody Bridge then, ignoring the turn

on the right, cross Easedale Beck by the next bridge. For the rest of the walk the beck remains on the right.

Large boulders litter the valley, the so-called sheep rocks of the Ice Ages, whose shapes, when seen from a distance, resemble those of sheep sleeping on the hillside. Glaciers smoothed the backs of the rocks, and carved out their downhill faces.

The stony path climbs steeply upwards until, suddenly, the tarn lies ahead with Tarn Crag towering some 900 ft above the water. The best time to see it is in the morning or early afternoon, when the sun is still catching its sheer, gleaming precipices.

The easiest way to Easedale Lane is to turn west off the Keswick road as Grasmere village ends. There is a car park at the start of the walk. Grasmere is off the A591, 3 miles north-west of Ambleside.

Db Hallin Fell

It is not always the highest peaks that provide the finest views. Hallin Fell is not much more than 1,260 ft above sea-level, and yet a superb lakeland panorama is visible from its neatly built summit cairn. The mountain is tucked into the inside of Ullswater's 'elbow', and commands views down both stretches of the lake. Across the water are the craggy splendours of Gowbarrow Park. To the north-west lies the Skiddaw massif. The great ridge of Helvellyn dominates the south-west. To the south are the beautiful valleys of Boardale, Bannerdale and Rampsgill, flat-bottomed and U-shaped in perfect lakeland style. The valley bottoms are stone-walled, carefully tended, green and lush; but beyond the walls bracken sweeps over the fell, a dark blanket broken only by the darker outlines of naked crags.

The path to the summit of Hallin Fell starts from opposite Martindale Church. It is said that the fell can be climbed comfortably from the church in bare feet, so velvety is the turf.

Hallin Fell is also a good starting point for a fine walk of about 5 miles along the lake shore, from the hamlet of Howtown, at the foot of the fell, to Patterdale; in parts it is woodland walking at its finest, through oak, beech and sycamore with the shining waters of the lake visible through the trees. The stretch of juniper scrub on Birk Fell is the most extensive in the Lakes. It is possible to return to Howtown by lake steamer.

Howtown is on the minor road running south-west along the eastern side of Ullswater from Pooley Bridge on the B5320. Martindale Church is ¼ mile south-west of Howtown.

Db Harter Fell

The fearsome crags of Harter Fell are impressive on their own; but they become doubly impressive when seen in combination with the man-made wonders of Haweswater Reservoir (which covers the drowned village of Mardale Green) and the jewel-like beauty of Small Water. Every approach to the fell, at the southern tip of Haweswater, celebrates the marriage between rock and water. Climb up the Gatescarth Pass from Longsleddale, with the infant River Sprint tumbling beside the grass-verged track and the enormous masses of Goat Scar and Buckbarrow Crag towering over it, and from the top of the col there is a breathtaking view over Haweswater. In a series of gigantic steps the north face of the fell plunges 1,800 ft to the head of the lake. Continue north-west from the pass along the crag top, and Small Water lies like a sparkling teardrop far below.

A path drops diagonally down Small Water's corrie walls, and continues to the valley of the Small Water Beck. On its way to Haweswater, the stream tumbles down waterfalls, gurgles in deep pools and potholes, and races down long waterslides. From crevices in the rock, rowan trees grow at giddy angles, while the tremendous scatter of drumlins – hummocks of rubble left by melting Ice Age glaciers – makes the landscape wild and strange.

Another approach to Harter Fell is from Bampton by the lakeside road on the south-eastern shore of Haweswater. Beyond the village of Bampton, the rolling countryside, woods and gentle fells are reminiscent of the Yorkshire Dales; but once through the woods at the north-eastern end of the lake, the valley shows its proper face. The crags of Whelter, Bason, Lad and Laythwaite wall in the north-western shore; the great masses of Harter Fell and High Street close in the head of the valley.

Two paths lead on from the car park at the end of the road. The one to the left goes to the Gatescarth Pass, a mile away; the one straight ahead climbs some 700 ft to Small Water. Beyond Small Water the path strikes up the formidable corrie slope at the western end; and the backward views from here are superb. But for many it will be enough just to sit on one of the slabs of rock which surround this lovely lake, and to gaze up at the mighty bulk of Harter Fell above it.

Longsleddale starts 4 miles north of Kendal and is reached by a minor road off the A6. Alternatively, from the south-eastern shore of Haweswater, take the minor road west from Shap on the A6 to Bampton, then turn south following signposts 'Haweswater Reservoir'.

Holme Wood

Bc

Seen from the road along the north-eastern shore of Loweswater, across the lake's gently rippling surface, Holme Wood is a beautiful decoration, a mile-long strip of mixed woodland running from the water's edge up to the 900 ft contour. The rumpled blanket of trees clings close below the crags of Burnbank Fell and Carling Knott and then steals up the shelter of Holme Beck. Its reflection melts into the water. But the real beauty of the wood is in the heart of the woodland, between the conifers on the highest slopes and the delicate alders overhanging the lake. Here mature, broad-leaved trees are seen at their best, a whispering canopy of oak,

ash, sycamore, mountain ash, elm, birch, large-leaved lime and the great, palmate-leaved chestnut.

The best way to savour this beauty is to walk through the woods. Go to the south-east end of the lake and walk through Watergate Farm and along the shoreline. Ford the Holme Beck and turn up along the stream. The roar of water announces one of the hidden wonders of the woods, Holme Force, a series of sparkling cascades tumbling among the trees. Return through the woods to the shore and look out across the water to the gentle, bracken-covered slopes of Darling Fell. Walk on to the northern end of the lake and look back at the views behind. Climb to the terrace on the 900 ft contour and return round the top side of the wood. On a summer's day the scene is one of matchless tranquillity, a perfect blend of woodland, water and hills with the sun and clouds playing hide-and-seek across the sky.

The easiest approach to Holme Wood is along the A5086 south-west from Cockermouth. After 5 miles turn south-east; Loweswater is 3 miles further on.

Lanty's Tarn

Cb

The tarn is tiny, tucked away and unknown to most visitors to the Lake District, and even in the height of summer it offers the determined walker a rare peace and solitude, wrapped in the deep quiet of the mountains. The 1½ mile walk across the fells leads south from the village of Glenridding, at the southern end of Ullswater. Take the road past the shops, keeping the car park on the right, and cross the stream beyond the cottages. Through the gate the path climbs very steeply upwards into typical fell countryside. Outcrops

LAKELAND FLIERS

Though it is a wader, the woodcock is found in damp woodlands rather than open marshes. A superb flier, the bird will take off in swerving flight when disturbed and move adroitly through the trees. A bird of the mountain uplands, the ring ouzel resembles its cousin, the blackbird, but is identified by its distinctive white collar. The female is a paler colour than the male, with a less clearly defined collar. Normally a shy bird, the ring ouzel is likely to become aggressive at nesting time. Above water or below, the remarkable little dipper is at home. In fast-moving streams it walks along the bed in search of food.

Woodcock
(*Scolopax rusticola*)

Ring ouzel
(*Turdus torquatus*)

Dipper
(*Cinclus cinclus*)

of rock stand bare and forbidding among patches of bracken; scattered trees, including oaks, ashes, birches and Scots pines, raise their branches to the sky. In early summer butterworts bloom beside thin streams trickling down towards the lake, and tormentil and sheep's sorrel add a twinkle of colour to the dark undergrowth.

The tarn, ringed with conifers, is wasp-waisted, heavily sedimented and full of fish – though most are very small. It is possible to walk on past its quiet waters, following the path through the bracken. Turn left where the path forks – the right-hand fork leads up to the heights of Striding Edge and then on to Helvellyn, a spectacular but long ascent. To the left the path drops down to Grisedale Beck and then east through the woods to the main road; turn left for Glenridding, half a mile away.

Glenridding is on the A592, at the southern end of Ullswater.

Longsleddale

Db

Among the most charming of the Lake District valleys, Longsleddale is lonely yet well inhabited, intensely private and yet easy to reach. The narrow road into the valley drops steeply away from the A6, winding through the trees to Garnett Bridge. As the road probes deeper into the valley, the impression grows that nothing has changed here for centuries.

The narrow valley, with its string of old stone farms and its pleasant patchwork of fields, forms a passage between the steep fells. Norman Nicholson, the modern poet and topographer of the Lake District, has said that in wet winters 'water pours down gill after gill till the dale looks like a street of terraced

217

NEWLANDS PASS Like a narrow ribbon, the road hems the broad fells that sweep down to the valley floor and Keskadale Beck.

countryside noted for its mountains, lakes and valleys. And yet it is the emptiness of Moor Divock that appeals to the imagination, and the unchecked wind blowing across the blanket of bracken and heather that makes it so refreshing.

The surface of the moor is littered with cairns, standing stones, stone circles, mounds and pits, all of them dating back some 3,000 to 4,000 years. Many of the smaller relics are almost lost in the bracken; but the larger ones, such as the Cop Stone, stand up from the moor like the last, indestructible memorials to an otherwise forgotten people. The relics suggest a purpose, but the purpose remains unknown. Why prehistoric man dug the Wofa Holes, the Pulpit Holes and the Dew-pot Holes is as much a matter of mystery as his reason for raising the Cop Stone or any other of the stones round about it.

The Romans also left their mark on the moor, but they were chiefly concerned with crossing it, not with stopping there. The old Roman road called High Street ran across the moor, on its way south to the Troutbeck valley and the central lakes. To this day the huge mountain over which the road ran is still called High Street. Careful searching of the moor can still reveal traces of the old road.

This is perfect walking country, criss-crossed with green paths of springy turf. Lapwings and curlews call plaintively from above, and skylarks spiral into the sky in full song.

Wild ponies roam the moor. Nothing expresses the spirit of the place better than the sight of a herd of these shy creatures wheeling away from one of the tiny moorland becks, and galloping into the distance.

houses with the roof gutters all burst'. This mighty deluge of waterfalls feeds the aptly named River Sprint and enriches the fields on the narrow valley floor. The church, built in 1712, is in a lovely setting halfway along the valley, with broad-leaved woods closing in on both sides.

Beyond, the fells gradually close in and the landscape becomes starker. In front, visible through the roadside trees, the ferocious mountain masses of Goat Scar and Buckbarrow Crag tower over the valley head. The road ends at Sadgill, the highest farm, but on the east side of the valley a track leads on towards a distant col. This is Gates-carth Pass, between the heights of Harter Fell and Artle Crag. This path linked the valley with Mardale Green, the village drowned beneath Haweswater Reservoir.

Garnett Bridge, at the southern end of Longsleddale, is 4 miles north of Kendal and is reached by a minor road north-west off the A6.

Dc   Moor Divock

From earliest times this wide, windswept plateau off the north-east shore of Ullswater has had a strange fascination for man, which seems curious in a

Moor Divock can be reached by car along a minor road south-west from Helton, which is about 5 miles south of Penrith off the B5320. Alternatively, from Pooley Bridge on the B5320 at the northern end of Ullswater, a footpath runs south-east across the moor.

Cc Newlands Pass

Until the 18th century, no road suitable for wheeled transport led to the village of Buttermere. It was named by the Angles who came this way in the 6th century and made good butter from the cattle they pastured by the lakeside – and farming was to remain the village's chief occupation until the building of the Newlands Pass road in the 1770s.

Father Thomas West, who wrote the first guide to the Lake District, published in 1778, described the pass as 'Alpine views and pastoral scenes in a sublime style'. Even today, the narrow road twisting through the fells, with some stretches steeper than 1 in 4, provides its excitements – sublime perhaps more for the passengers than the driver.

For almost 3 miles from Braithwaite, the road runs along a ledge high above the Newlands valley, with fine views to the east and south-east of wooded Swinside and cosy-looking Cat Bells – the hill where Beatrix Potter's Mrs Tiggy-Winkle lived.

Stretching flat and green below, criss-crossed by stone walls, the Newlands valley is remote and peaceful. Yet 400 years ago in Elizabethan times it was a busy mining centre, with copper and some silver recovered from the local Goldscope Mine. The mine was worked by expert miners brought in from Germany by the Queen's Mines-Royal Company; the name Goldscope

is said to be derived from the German *Gottsgabe* – 'God's gift'. The mining was at its height in the 16th century, and the ores were smelted near Keswick, the local woods being turned to charcoal to feed the furnaces.

GRAND FINALE The sound of tumbling water echoes around the moss-clad granite as Stanley Force tosses a white skein into the beck below. Viewed from a bridge, the lovely waterfall is the climax of a walk along Stanley Ghyll.

After crossing Rigg Beck the road swings westwards from the Newlands valley along the much narrower Keskadale valley, below the steep fells of Ard Crags to the right. It is well worth parking by the hairpin bend over Ill Gill and scrambling up beside the beck for a glimpse of the Keskadale Oakwood. The 14 acre oakwood is now a protected area; in company with the Birkrigg Oakwood, on the slopes of Causey Pike to the north-east, it is thought to be the last surviving remnant of the great oak forests that once covered the lakeland fells. The trees are small and wind-swept sessile oaks, recognised by their stalkless acorns.

The road climbs steeply to Newlands Hause, approaching close to the point where Moss Force cascades spectacularly over a line of crags below the sodden Buttermere Moss.

To reach Newlands Pass, leave Keswick by the A66 towards Cockermouth; 1 mile beyond Portinscale turn left along the B5292 through Braithwaite. From here follow signs to Newlands Pass and Buttermere, a drive of about 7 miles.

Ba Stanley Ghyll and Devoke Water

It is not its height but its spectacular setting in a narrow, thickly wooded gorge that has made Stanley Force, the 60 ft waterfall in Stanley Ghyll, such an attraction. When Ice Age glaciers carved out the lakeland valleys, they cut off many river tributaries and left them hanging in the air – places today where lovely waterfalls tumble to the valley bottoms. Stanley Ghyll was created in this way when the glacier deepening the River Esk valley cut across its course.

A nature trail leads up to the falls by way of Stanley Beck, passing the old farmhouse of Dalegarth Hall, the home of the Stanleys from whom the ghyll takes its name. Attractive woodland that includes oaks, sycamores, rowans and hazels borders the beck,

DEVOKE WATER

with bilberries, wood sage and mats of white-flowered heath bedstraw along the banks.

Pick your way through the boulders brought down by previous floods until the path meets the beck again. Mosses and liverworts, including the light green bog moss, thrive in the damp atmosphere. Rhododendrons bloom among the rocks in June, naturalised from earlier plantings when part of the

---

MOORLAND OASIS Devoke Water is set among wild country high on Birker Fell, with only the gaunt Rough Crag as a landmark (left). From the road that crosses the fell, there are magnificent views across the valley eastwards towards the massive bulk of Harter Fell behind the dark ramparts of Green Crag (below).

TOWARDS HARTER FELL

ghyll was kept as a woodland garden.

All the way to the third wooden bridge across the beck the path remains steep and rocky, and beyond the bridge it becomes very wet and dangerous. But there is no need to go further. You are now standing at the bottom of the waterfall, with fine views from the bridge of the thin wall of water tumbling down its gorge of 400-million-year-old Eskdale granite.

High on Birker Fell above Stanley Ghyll lies the wild and lonely Devoke Water (it is pronounced 'Dev-ock'), surrounded by heather moors. Part of the Muncaster Castle estate, it is noted for its trout and its birds – red-throated and black-throated divers have been seen here. The many cairns around its shores (which are boggy in places) are remains of the Bronze Age settlements of more than 3,000 years ago. The view north-eastwards as you walk back to the road is staggeringly beautiful – most of the major peaks, from nearby Harter Fell swinging northwards round to Great Gable, form a superb backcloth.

Stanley Ghyll and Devoke Water are 6 miles north-east and 5 miles east, respectively, of Ravenglass.

The easiest way to get to Stanley Ghyll is by the Ravenglass and Eskdale Miniature Railway to Beckfoot or Dalegarth stations. By car from Ravenglass, a minor road leads east off the A595 about 2 miles east of the town. Dalegarth station is reached in just over 5 miles; cars can be parked by the railway station and the war memorial, from where the path to the waterfall starts.

For Devoke Water, turn south-east on to the minor road, signposted Ulpha, that leaves Eskdale about 2 miles west of Dalegarth station. There is parking space at the crossroads in about 2 miles; from here a track leads ¼ mile south-west to the lake.

Cb Stonethwaite Beck

Any walk around Stonethwaite is almost bound to be wet, for this was once the eastern limb of a great lake that covered the flat-lands of Borrowdale. The lake was connected by a river to Derwent Water in the north. Over thousands of years the streams rushing down from the ring of high fells around the lake swept more and more debris into it, and eventually filled it. Even today, after a spell of heavy rain, the flat-lands become a lake again and large boulders are carried there by the tumultuous, flooding becks.

On these damp uplands there is a chance of seeing the small mountain ringlet butterfly during June and July. It is found only in lakeland and the Grampians.

Stonethwaite Beck is formed by two streams, Langstrath Beck and Greenup Gill, which meet below the fierce bluff of Eagle Crag. The crag can be reached by turning east out of Stonethwaite village, crossing the bridge, turning right and following the track through the woods. At the meeting of the two becks lies Smithymire Island, where the monks of Furness Abbey, 25 miles to the south, used to smelt iron ore. Beyond, rough, wet beck-side paths lead through wild, lonely country overhung by beetling crags.

By way of old packhorse trails, the Greenup Gill route leads eventually to Grasmere (6 miles away), and from Langstrath, a climb through Ore Gap and down Mosedale and the Duddon valley leads eventually to the distant Furness peninsula.

For Stonethwaite, take the B5289 south from Keswick, and after 7 miles, at Borrowdale, turn south-east along the minor road for ¼ mile.

—THE SOLWAY COAST—

*A tide-washed estuary where the capricious sea
torments and teases an uncertain shore*

THE TIDE CALLS the tune in Solway Firth, the sea-gash between south-west Scotland and north-west England. As the Firth narrows, the currents become faster; and with the sudden arrival and departure of the all-engulfing tide, the inner reaches of the Solway become one of the most dramatic of British estuaries.

The landscape on both sides of the Firth is flat; only the mass of Criffel on the Scottish shore and the distant peaks of the Lake District relieve the endless vistas of mud-flats and marsh.

Silent sands, bare mud-flats

The wide marshes are on the English shore – between Grune Point at the mouth of Moricambe bay and the head of the estuary, near Gretna. At low tide the sands and mud-flats are bare and silent, except for the calls of wading birds searching for food. Then suddenly the tide rushes in, drowning the tawny sand in a gleaming expanse of steel-grey water.

In this endless advance and retreat, the sea is gradually losing its hold. The surrendered territory, bound fast by advancing grasses, becomes salt-marsh; and here, where water and land meet in uneasy alliance, nature is at its most abundant.

Marshes along the estuary

The innermost marsh, Rockliffe, borders Gretna between the English River Eden and Scotland's Esk. From Rockliffe Cross a lane leads to Esk Boathouse, on the very edge of the marsh. From this desolate spot the marshes of the estuary spread to the west. On Burgh Marsh a slender column – man's only intrusion in the emptiness of marsh, sea and sky – is a Victorian monu-

ment to Edward I who died here of dysentery in 1307 while fighting the Scots. Burgh Marsh can be reached by car and then footpath from Burgh by Sands.

Following the coast westwards, through Drumburgh, Port Carlisle and Bowness-on-Solway, there are three other vast marsh-lands: Cardurnock Flatts and Newton and Skinburness Marshes on the south shore of Moricambe bay.

These Moricambe marshes are enclosed by the arm of Grune Point, a shingle spit running north-east from Skinburness village. Mixed woodland and small fields cover the peninsula and a path runs round both shores. The view from the end of the point is unforgettable; acres of sea-washed turf, the tide stealing up narrow creeks and the rippling waters making a world ruled by the ebb and flow of the tide.

TRANQUIL SOLWAY AMONG THE FIRTH'S MANY PEACEFUL SPOTS ARE GRUNE POINT (ABOVE) AND THE REEDY WILDERNESS OF BURGH MARSH (BELOW).

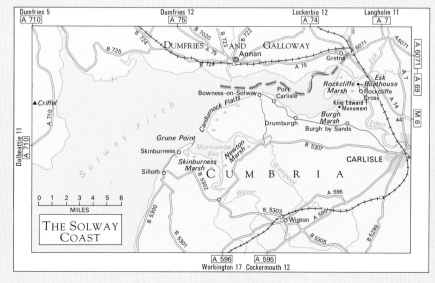

221

Cc   Ullock Pike

The shapely summit of Ullock Pike, 2,230 ft high, offers panoramic views across northern lakeland. Yet, in spite of the mountain's proximity to Keswick, it remains one of the least visited of the Skiddaw and Saddleback mountain group. The final part of the ascent is the most exciting, along the heather-clad ridge, looking steeply down over the wilderness of Southerndale to the north-east, and over the 4 mile long Bassenthwaite Lake to the west – the most northern of all the lakes and the only one to be called a lake, and not a water or mere.

There are two routes up Ullock Pike from the road, both starting from a creosoted gate and stile 30 yds south of the Ravenstone Hotel. The first path climbs to the right through the Forestry Commission plantation – first larch, oak, sycamore and Scots pine, then Sitka spruce and other softwoods – to the tree-line at 600–700 ft. Then follows a steep scramble through bracken and heather and bare outcrops of rock to the ridge about 1,000 ft above. The second path meets the ridge about a mile further north, after climbing behind the hotel and following a wall north-eastwards above the tree-line, then following an old drove road.

The safest way back is to return along the ridge, for the sides are very steep and rocky. But it is possible to drop into Southerndale further down,

THE WONDER OF LAKELAND Viewed from Ullock Pike, Bassenthwaite Lake is turned to polished pewter by a cloud-filtered sun, and the misty heights of Barf, Lord's Seat, Graystones, Broom Fell and Ling Fell lie brooding beyond the water.

MOUNTAIN PEARL Gleaming Goat's Water is cradled in a corrie between the steep flanks of Dow Crag and The Old Man of Coniston. South-eastwards, Coniston Water points its long finger towards the distant sheen of Morecambe Bay.

picking up the path on the east of the valley and following it to the foot-bridge below the natural standing stones known as The Watches. A path leads from the gate below the foot-bridge to the minor road leading from Orthwaite to High Side, a hamlet about half a mile north of the Ravenstone Hotel.

Ullock Pike is 4 miles north-west of Keswick. The Ravenstone Hotel is on the A591, 4½ miles north-west of Keswick.

Ca Wallowbarrow Gorge

Millions of years ago, movements of the earth's crust produced a fault, or break, in the rock to the north-west of Seathwaite. In the last Ice Age, glaciers following the line of the fault scoured out the deep cleft now called Wallowbarrow Gorge.

Here, in its most spectacular stretch, the River Duddon flows straight through a fell instead of round it, walled in to the west by the 950 ft high Wallowbarrow Crag, and to the east by the more than 700 ft high Holling House Tongue. Both sides of the gorge are very steep – in some places vertical – and thickly wooded with oak, ash, beech, birch and rowan. Alder trees and willows overhang the racing water, until the river breaks out of the gorge and begins to meander across the wide flood plain where it is joined by its tributary, the Tarn Beck.

Shortly before the Newfield Inn, in Seathwaite, a signpost marked 'To the Stepping Stones' points the way to the gorge, which leads through a mixed wood with a variety of woodland flowers and fungi. In time of flood the stepping-stones are usually under water and become impassable, but just a little further upstream there is a single-arch bridge.

The path carries on through another wood to the fields of the flood plain, with the southern end of the Wallowbarrow Crags towering above them. From here it is possible to walk up the gorge, although the going is rough.

Another path striking off to the west of Wallowbarrow Crags leads, after about a mile, to Grassguards Farm and through the conifer forest beside it. Then it drops down to more stepping-stones below Fickle Crag, before climbing back south-eastwards through bracken and a scattering of small oaks to the road – about three-quarters of a mile north of Seathwaite. An alternative path leads from Grass-guards Farm through the woods to the famous beauty spot of Birks Bridge, which lies on the same road about 2 miles north of Seathwaite.

About 1 mile west of Broughton in Furness, a turning north off the A595 close to Duddon Bridge leads through Ulpha to Seathwaite 6 miles up the valley. Parking is not easy in the village, but there is a car park at Birks Bridge.

Ca Walna Scar Road

Walking across Coniston Fells by the Walna Scar Road is like travelling back through time, for this is one of the oldest roads in the Lake District. It has been walked or ridden throughout his-tory by shepherds and weavers, pedlars and traders, wool-buyers, merchants and, of course, lovers of landscape.

But for a thousand years or more the chief traffic was provided by pack-ponies, heavily laden with copper ore from the Coniston mines. They are the oldest mines in the Lake District, dat-ing from Roman times. The route from them crossed the Duddon at Seath-waite and led on over Birker Fell to Eskdale and then down to the Roman port of Ravenglass. In the early 19th century, when the mines were at their peak, several hundred men and boys were employed. The boys were trained to wash and sort the ore, using water diverted from mountain streams and tarns. Some of the old waterways can be found above the mine workings on the Coniston Fells. The adult miners were known as 'old men' – perhaps because they were prematurely aged by the appalling working conditions deep inside the mountain. Mine entrances, often no more than about 5 ft high and 18 in. wide, can be found in the area. It is unsafe to enter them.

The road starts at the foot of the Coniston Fells. It can be reached by driving at least part of the way up the steep, rough road signposted from just south of the centre of Coniston. Beyond the second gate there is no choice but to walk. Walna Scar Road leads straight ahead; the track to the right along Church Beck climbs to the top of Wetherlam.

The old road winds steadily upwards beneath the crags of Little Arrow Moor, passing various tiny stretches of water, including Boo Tarn. A path northwards leads to Goat's Water, in a magnificent example of an Ice Age corrie, with Dow Crag soaring 2,555 ft on its western shore.

Once the col between Walna Scar and Brown Pike has been reached, the view ahead is breathtaking. Away in the far south-west is the huge bulk of Black Combe; across the foreground lies the lovely expanse of the Duddon valley. To the north-west is Harter Fell, behind which and further to the north is the mighty jumble of mountains leading to Scafell Pikes, at 3,206 ft the highest peak in England.

The return to Coniston can be made by walking back along the road, or by following the ridge walk north to the summit of Dow Crag, and then swinging round to the top of The Old Man of Coniston. From there the path down is steep but passable, though the area around it is riddled with old mine workings and shafts, and is dangerous.

Coniston is 6 miles south-west of Ambleside, along the A593.

Bb
Wast Water

No other lake is so fierce and austere as Wast Water, at 258 ft the deepest of the lakeland lakes. Sometimes it is as smooth as glass, sheltered by the highest mountains in England and reflecting them on its surface. At other times, when the peaks are lost in cloud and mist and wild south-westerlies squall up the valley, cold spray can be felt hundreds of feet up the slopes and waves race madly up the three dark miles of the lake's length. Above all it is the Screes cliff on the eastern shore that sets the lake apart – nearly 2,000 ft of loose rock fragments spilling into the water. Under bleak, overcast skies, the Screes look black and threatening, but when the skies clear, they are full of colour.

There are many places from which to view the lake, and one of the best is from the south-west end in the area of Wasdale Hall. On the left the crags of Buckbarrow give way to the immense jumble of rocks – Long Crag – which forms the lower slopes of Middle Fell. The valley of Nether Beck slices through the heights, and beyond it are the crag-stepped ridge of Yewbarrow, the Mosedale valley and the great mass of Kirk Fell. To the north-east, at the head of the valley, stands the triumphant shape of Great Gable. On the south-east side are the twin summits of Illgill Head and Whin Rigg, the boundaries of the scree slopes.

The two ends of the lake are totally different. In the south-west, Nether Wasdale is sheltered and thickly wooded, with an abundance of flowers on the forest floor and moss and lichen everywhere. Wasdale Head in the north-east is the very core of the highest part of England, rough and wild above the drystone walls which enclose arable fields on the valley floor.

From the east, Wast Water can be approached from Ambleside by the very steep Wrynose and Hard Knott passes. From the west, the way is from Ravenglass or Gosforth on the A595.

MOUNTAIN WATER Among the peaks clustering at the head of Wast Water are Scafell Pikes and Great Gable.

225

THE PEAK DISTRICT

Rock dominates the landscape – in its limestone pinnacles and
spires, its Millstone Grit crags and its soft, shale valleys

The first-founded of the National Parks reaches deep into
six English counties – Derbyshire, Cheshire, Staffordshire,
South Yorkshire, West Yorkshire and even into Greater
Manchester. But to most people, the Peak means Derbyshire, confirming Lord Byron's opinion that there are things
in that county 'as noble as in Greece or Switzerland'.

To judge by his comparisons, Byron was thinking of the
airy limestone crags that overhang the deep dales, whose
greenness is counterpaned with grey-white drystone walls
and wandering threads of rivers. But there are many other
noble things in Derbyshire, and everyone who comes here
carries away a different memory. There is the Derbyshire
of the great houses such as Chatsworth and Kedleston,
Haddon Hall and Hardwick Hall; the Derbyshire of the villages, whose
never-failing wells are decorated annually with paintings composed of
thousands of flower-petals in honour of water deities whose names are
long forgotten. Then there is the Derbyshire of the quarries, mines and
water-powered mills; of the vast, natural underground caverns; and of
the wild, high moors where people in the various ages of prehistory built
their stone temples and fortifications, and immured their dead in
stone tombs.

Stone – limestone, grit and shale – is everywhere; in the architecture
and the landscape, which in many places consists of little more
than a threadbare blanket of heather or turf with rock
pushing through the holes. Yet in other places near by, the
countryside is gentle, green and lush – a startling contrast
caused by the different kinds of rock that form the bones of
the land.

Seen from a helicopter hovering high above, the Peak
would be a rough oval, some 35 miles north to south and
20 miles east to west. On a clear day the central core of the
southern half would gleam white in the sun, scarred everywhere by the green gorges of the dales; this is the White
Peak, the limestone country, laid down maybe 300 million
years ago. From this height, too, it would be possible to see a
surrounding darker area, a many-decker sandwich of shales
and thin sandstones, through which rivers such as the Noe, the
Derwent and the Goyt have carved their wider, flatter valleys. Finally,
embracing all, is the Dark Peak – the high, brooding Millstone Grit
massifs of Kinder Scout, Bleaklow and Black Hill in the north, the
easterly heights of the Sheffield moors, the airy uplands of Axe Edge in
the west, and the fantastic skyline of The Roaches – last bastion of the
Pennines – in the south-west. Swift-flowing streams provided power for
the cotton-mills of the Industrial Revolution.

On the flanks of the Pennines there are coalfields; lead too has been
dug from the Peak since Roman times and both grit and limestone have
been quarried for centuries. Fortunately, time has smoothed some of
the scars of mining and quarrying to the point where they look almost as
natural as the caves where the Stone Age hunters lived. In several cases
man's activities have rather enhanced the area – these are the great
reservoirs that not only provide the surrounding cities with water, but
have given the Peak a lake district of its own.

NOBLE HILLS AND TORS Lose Hill and Back Tor hunch their
green shoulders above the Derbyshire valleys. There are no
peaks in the Peak District, which probably takes its name from 'Pecsaete',
the name of a tribe that lived in the area in prehistoric times.

Places to visit

Map ref. Bb Arbor Low

This is the Stonehenge of the Peak. Not quite so impressive, perhaps, as its Wiltshire counterpart, since all of its massive limestone slabs save one now lie flat on the ground. But stand among them, at twilight especially, and you can feel the enormous significance this place once possessed.

When Arbor Low was constructed some 4,000 years ago, the 40-odd stones, each weighing 8 tons and more, may have stood on end and the whole formation was surrounded by a rampart and ditch about 250 ft in diameter. Considering the tools of the period – picks and shovels of stone, bone and antler – the labour involved was prodigious, and could only have been inspired by a devotion to some faith long forgotten. Yet the site was regarded as sacred for a very long time, to judge from the numerous burial mounds in the vicinity. One of these is actually built into the bank, and there is another, Gib Hill, about 350 yds to the south-west. These, like the earthwork that leads to the south entrance of Arbor Low, may have been built 1,000 years later than the stone circle.

Arbor Low is about 9 miles south-east of Buxton near a minor road leading east off the A515.

Bb Axe Edge

Two of the loveliest rivers in England, the Dove and the Manifold, are born in the moorlands just below Axe Edge, the highest point on the magnificent road between Leek and Buxton. On the way out of Leek, the road passes the superbly jagged Ramshaw Rocks, and that last breath of the Pennines, The Roaches. It also passes Flash, which at 1,518 ft is said to be the highest village in England. Once, this was the headquarters of a gang of coiners and, in underworld parlance, 'flash' is the name still given to counterfeit money.

The views are splendid throughout the journey, but the real sense of spaciousness comes immediately below Axe Edge itself. The highest point on Edge is a chilly 1,807 ft above sea-level, so providing a prospect as vast as any in Derbyshire. To the south-east, the infant Dove and Manifold begin to carve their separate valleys down to their eventual meeting place near Ashbourne, while to the west and north-west are the conical peaks of Shutlingsloe and Shining Tor. Slightly further to the north is the deep trench of the Goyt valley, and to the north-east, beyond Buxton, is the limestone section of the High Peak.

Axe Edge is west of the A53, 3 miles south-west of Buxton.

Bc Bleaklow

At 2,060 ft, Bleaklow is very nearly the highest point in the Peak District; it is exceeded only by Kinder Scout – and that by a mere 28 ft. But it is a much larger area than Kinder and its dangers are the greater in consequence; therefore traverse it with even more care. Warm clothing, sound boots, and map

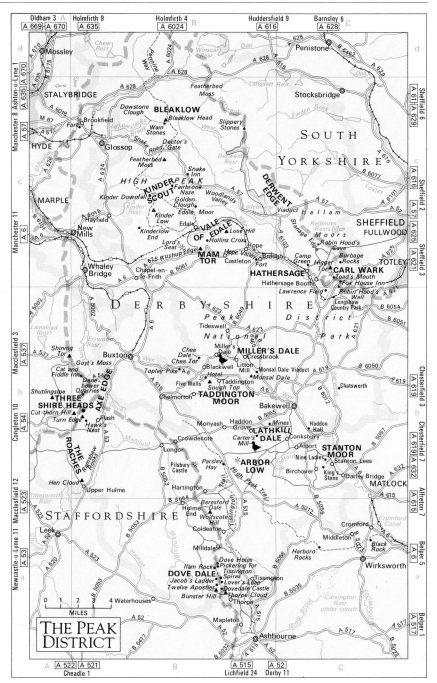

and compass (and the knowledge to use them) are mandatory.

However, for those in whom the pioneering spirit burns less brightly, a fine impression of the place may be gathered from the Snake Road, the name given to the Peak District portion of the A57 which runs from Manchester to Sheffield. At the highest point of the road, just where it is crossed by the Pennine Way on its journey to the Scottish border, Bleaklow can be seen rising to the north. It is a high, almost featureless plateau, but at its western end is the noble gritstone edge of the Wain Stones, looming above the head of Dowstone Clough and the Yellowslacks Brook, which rises just below the crags.

Bleaklow is aptly named. Kinder Scout excepted, it is just about the toughest stretch of the Pennine Way, and offers little comfort to the traveller. Nevertheless, it has a wild, rare beauty. Mile after mile of dark peat hag drops slowly away eastwards from Bleaklow Head, and the only colour in all this is the green of bilberry, the purple of heather and the white feathers of cotton-grass. On bad days, even these disappear in the all-enshrouding mist, but on good ones there is the blue upturned bowl of the sky above you, and for company, a clattering red grouse or a lolloping mountain hare.

Though it may not seem so, you are not the first to pass this way or to see these things. Running off the Snake Road there is a track called Doctor's Gate; in fact, this is the old Roman road that ran from Navio fort at Brough in the Hope valley to Melandra fort at Brookfield, 2 miles north-west of Glossop. It makes a fine, firm path across the moors, as well it might; its foundations were firmly laid by

the Romans nearly 2,000 years ago.

Access to Bleaklow is by the Pennine Way from north or south; from Glossop; or by Doctor's Gate, which starts ¼ mile east of the summit on the A57.

Cc Carl Wark

There is something rather mysterious about Carl Wark, the mighty fortification that darkly glowers from its moorland summit near Hathersage. It was long presumed to be Iron Age work, but recent investigation has suggested that it belongs to a much later period, perhaps the 6th or 7th century AD. In which case, who built it, and why?

Whoever it was had a fine eye for a defensive position. The fort is built on a kind of promontory that juts out south of Higger Tor, so that on three sides its defences are natural rock faces, supplemented by gritstone boulders. The fourth side, the neck of the promontory, is blocked by a great drystone wall, some 9 or 10 ft high and 30 yds long, and backed, on the fort side, by an earthen embankment.

To the north is the high outcrop of Higger Tor, whose summit is a jumble of boulders weathered into fantastic shapes. The view from here is breathtaking – almost as good as that from the hang-gliders launched from the top.

Carl Wark and Higger Tor are best approached from the footpaths leading from the minor road that runs off the A625 at Hathersage Booths, 1 mile southeast of Hathersage.

Bc Derwent Edge

The lakes of the Peak District are highly picturesque, yet the most famous of them are no older than this century. They are, in fact, reservoirs serving

ON THE TRAILS OF THE LONESOME LINES

LIKE ALL THE NURSERIES of the Industrial Revolution, the southern Peak District demanded railways to shift its products – in this case, mainly coal, iron, lime and minerals, with corn, milk and passengers thrown in for good measure. As with most Victorian engineering works, the railways in the Peak were superbly built.

None of the railways survived the various axings of branch lines that have taken place since the Second World War, and most of the rails have now been taken out. However, the track beds, tunnels and other features remain, and many of them have now been taken over by the Peak National Park, or by the County Councils, to create trails of extraordinary interest to railway enthusiasts and long-distance walkers alike. The best-known are the Tissington and High Peak trails, which could

almost be considered as one, since they meet at the charmingly named Parsley Hay. Between them they provide over 30 miles of rambling, cycling and pony-trekking, of panoramic views, a wealth of flowers, and historic sites ranging from the Stone Age to the Industrial Revolution.

The High Peak Trail runs for 17½ miles along the former Cromford and High Peak Railways, one of the world's oldest lines. When it was constructed in 1830, horses pulled the wagons over the level stretches and stationary steam-engines cable-hauled them up the inclines, one of which, Middleton Incline, is 708 yds long, with a continuous gradient of 1 in 8¼.

At the top of this incline, one of the stationary engines has been lovingly restored and can be seen working, though by compressed air, on certain days.

The 13 mile Tissington Trail runs along part of the course of the old L & NWR line from Manchester to Euston. Though not so dramatic as the High Peak Trail, the Tissington Trail still has a number of features to thrill railway lovers – such as the signal box at Hartington Station, still with working signal levers, and Coldeaton Cutting, three-quarters of a mile long and 60 ft deep.

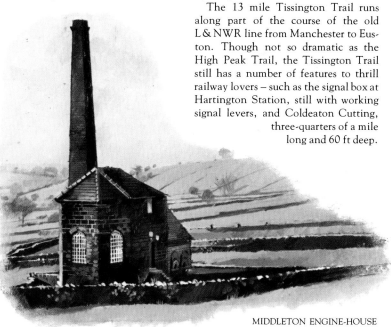

MIDDLETON ENGINE-HOUSE

The damp moors of the Peak District are breeding places for the dunlin, an unobtrusive bird when on the ground but distinctive in flight when it hovers lark-like high in the sky. On moorland edges, the twite builds its nest among heather and scrub, often in colonies. The bird's name is said to derive from its nasal call note, but its song is a pleasant twittering heard during the breeding season. The handsome goshawk is a bird of prey, swooping on long, slow-beating wings above its woodland territory. Larger than its look-alike, the sparrowhawk, it preys on birds and small mammals.

Dunlin
(Calidris alpina)

Twite
(Acanthis flavirostris)

Goshawk
(Accipiter gentilis)

Sheffield, Derby, Leicester and Nottingham, and were created by drowning two valleys – the Woodlands, which separates the Bleaklow massif from Kinder Scout, and the Derwent, which forms the eastern boundary of the Bleaklow moors. The interlinking system of dams and reservoirs was begun in 1912 with the building of the Howden dam across the upper Derwent valley, followed by the Derwent, lower down, in 1916, and finally by the great Ladybower, completed in 1943. Beneath the waters of the last reservoir there lie the remains of two villages, Derwent and Ashopton, and a 17th-century manor house, Derwent Hall. An old packhorse bridge was dismantled before the inundation, and rebuilt at Slippery Stones, at the head of the Derwent Reservoir.

The scars of construction in the valleys have long faded, and apart from the dams, the reservoirs now look entirely natural, making a drive along their wooded shores a perfect delight. Even more exhilarating are the views from the paths that climb Derwent Edge, high up on the east side of the valley. From here you can see the whole 7 miles of the system, the endless conifers planted by the Forestry Commission, and the long arms of water reaching up the side valleys, glittering in the sun. And after rain there is the additional bonus of seeing great cataracts, sliding majestically over the dams.

The top of the edge is decorated with an extraordinary series of sculptures, carved out of the Millstone Grit by aeons of weathering, yet looking for all the world like some outdoor exhibition of modern statuary. Equally impressive from close to, or from far down on the western shore of the reservoir, they have even been given names according to fancied resemblances – the Wheel Stones, the Salt Cellar, the Cakes of Bread.

Derwent Edge can be reached from the northern side of the A57, to the east of the point where it crosses the Ashopton Viaduct, near the Ladybower dam.

Ba
Dove Dale

Correctly – or cartographically, anyway – Dove Dale is that wooded, limestone, highly picturesque part of the valley of the Dove that lies just to the north of Thorpe. But almost every part of the little river's course is extraordinarily pleasant, whatever names its banks are given. And, nearly as important, much of it can be followed by footpath, all the way from its birthplace among the gritstone and shales of Axe Edge down to Burton, where it joins the Trent; from there, the combined waters flow down to the cold North Sea.

Perhaps as good a place as any to introduce yourself to the Dove is at Crowdecote, near Longnor, from which a footpath runs past Pilsbury Castle to Hartington. Incidentally, there are no riverside roads; you can drive down to the Dove, but not along it. Below Hartington, the valley is called Beresford Dale, and it was in Beresford Hall – now sadly demolished – that Izaak Walton stayed with his friend Charles Cotton. Cotton taught him fly-fishing along the Dove, and later added a section on the art to *The Compleat Angler*.

Their gentle, contemplative ghosts still linger along the next stretch of the river, called Wolfscote Dale after the

IN DERWENT DALE The reservoir in the dale is as natural-looking as any lake left by Ice Age glaciers. It is one of three reservoirs formed by damming the River Derwent which rises high in the Dark Peak, on Featherbed Moss.

tumulus-crowned Wolfscote Hill above. Here, the stream's flow is slowed by a number of tiny weirs that create resting pools to encourage trout and grayling to linger in the vicinity. Downstream is Milldale and Viator Bridge, an old packhorse bridge whose narrowness was remarked upon 300 years ago in *The Compleat Angler* – confirmation that it is not passable by modern motor vehicles.

Below Milldale are the Dove Holes, caves carved deep into the limestone long ago before the Dove had worn its way down to its present level. Here, Dove Dale proper begins, a deep gorge heavily clad with ash and alders, out of whose dense cover limestone crags and pinnacles leap skywards. Surely in all England there can be few grander spectacles than the river at this point, guarded by Ilam Rock with its flat, grassy top on one side, and by the multiple spires of Pickering Tor on the other. Further south still is Reynard's Cave, and a natural arch formed by the collapse of part of the cave roof.

Everywhere there are pillars, spurs and outcrops of limestone – Jacob's Ladder, The Twelve Apostles, Tissington Spires, Lovers' Leap. The last is named after an unfortunate Irish dean and his female companion who, with their horses, managed to fall off it in 1761; only the lady survived. The river makes one last great sweep round Dovedale Castle – a crag, not a fortification – and runs on to break through the southerly guardian hills of Bunster and Thorpe Cloud, leaving the limestone behind to hurry on through the shales past Ashbourne to Burton.

Longnor is on the B5053, 6 miles south of Buxton. Crowdecote is 1 mile east of Longnor on minor roads between the B5053 and A515.

VALLEY OF VARIETY The River Dove flows through one of England's loveliest valleys. Though little more than a mile long, Dove Dale has scenery ranging from limestone cliffs to wooded slopes and grassy banks.

Cc Hathersage

Charlotte Brontë stayed at Hathersage vicarage, and incorporated both vicarage and village in *Jane Eyre*. Robin Hood was a frequent visitor, too, to judge from his well near the Fox House Inn, 3 miles along the Sheffield road; his cave, 1½ miles north-east of the village; and the 11 ft grave in the churchyard that is said to contain the bones of Little John. Though what the outlaw band were doing here on the gritstone edge of Hallam Moors, and so far from 'Merrie Sherwode', history does not relate.

But on the moors there is solid evidence of residents that predate even Robin and his men – the mound of a Norman castle at Camp Green, the mighty and mysterious Carl Wark fort and a scattering of tumuli and stone circles. Among these are a number of natural curiosities, such as the Rocking Stone in Lawrence Field, 1½ miles south-east of Hathersage, and the Toad's Mouth rock near the bridge north-west of the Fox House Inn. With a pluck at the imagination, it really does look a bit like a toad. Close by is Longshaw Country Park, with pastures made bright with common dog violets, wood-sorrel, mosses and lesser celandine, and watered by the murmuring Burbage Brook. There is also a disused quarry, where you can see half-finished millstones abandoned by the quarrymen a century and more ago.

From the top of Stanage Edge and the Burbage Rocks there are dramatic views of the moors and Carl Wark, while Millstone Edge, west of Toad's Mouth, has a surprise view of the valley of the Derwent lying to the north-west, and its western tributary, the Noe, which rises in Edale and joins

231

the Peakshole Water at Hope village.

Hathersage is situated on the A625 road, about 5 miles from the outskirts of Sheffield.

Bc

Kinder Scout

The moorland plateau of Kinder Scout is, at 2,088 ft, the highest part of the Peak District National Park. It is flat, bleak, nearly featureless, faintly terrible; and its brooding solitudes are quite unforgettable.

Shaped rather like a starfish, with the legs thrusting out between steep stony valleys, the plateau is a wasteland of peat criss-crossed by hundreds of groughs, or natural drainage channels. These can be deep, for the peat is thick, having been 8,000 years in the forming, and in winter when the groughs are filled with snow, they become traps that can be fatal to the unwary. Also, in hot summers, the peat dries out to produce a dust that creates thirsts of huge proportions.

But if the place still attracts you — and if you are a lover of wild places it will — it might be better to avoid the interior of the plateau and to take instead the well-defined gritty paths that trace its periphery. Here the wind is always fresh, carrying with it the tang of heather and bilberry, and the voices of birds. In May and June it sets the myriad white heads of cotton-grass a-dancing, making it easy to see why so many upland Pennine areas have been named 'Featherbed Moss'.

You can come to the summit of Kinder by many ways; from the A57, where a path about half a mile south-east of the Snake Inn crosses Woodlands Valley and climbs up Fairbrook Naze to the northern edges; or from Edale along the early stretches of the Pennine Way that begins at The Nag's Head. Both are excellent routes among a number of others equally good, but whichever way you approach Kinder, all paths seem in the end to lead to Kinder Downfall on the western edge. Here, the Kinder river makes a spectacular 100 ft plunge – except when a gale blows, and throws back the falling waters in a great cloud of rainbow-tinted spray.

Kinder Scout is a wild and fascinating place, but treat it with respect, especially in winter. The perimeter walk is 17 miles around, and most of it is fairly tough going, requiring proper equipment and a reasonable standard of physical fitness. If you have doubts about either, view the place instead from, say, Mam Tor; better that than find yourself exhausted and stranded at nightfall, miles away from shelter.

Kinder Scout can be approached from the A57; or from Hayfield, Edale and many other points. There is a National Park Information Centre in Edale, where details about routes and weather conditions may be obtained.

Bb

Lathkill Dale

Charles Cotton, Izaak Walton's friend, described the waters of Lathkill Dale as 'the purest and most translucent stream that ever I saw either at home or abroad' – and as author of the fly-fishing section that was added to the fifth edition of *The Compleat Angler*, his opinion carries more weight than most. The appearance of the waters has not changed at all since he wrote of them in the 17th century, and the valley that gives them birth remains quiet and peaceful, smaller than the more famous dales, such as Dove Dale and the Manifold Valley.

The head of the dale lies a little to the east of Monyash, and the Lathkill river, after rain at least, leaps full-fledged to life from a cave about a quarter of a mile below. In dry weather, however, the cave dries up and the river is born piecemeal from a series of springs further down the valley.

The footpath hugs the north bank and runs beside the trout pools that gladdened the hearts of Cotton and Walton, and has delightful views of the woods on the opposite shore. Most of the dale is a National Nature Reserve, and, understandably, admission is restricted to the public footpaths.

Carter's Mill, at the junction with a tiny dale coming down from Haddon Grove direction, was a corn-mill, but now all that remains are its millstones and the weir. Then, a few yards further downstream is another, much larger, pool, now full of trout. Once, this powered the water-wheels that drained the nearby Lathkill and Mandale lead mines, whose derelict buildings add a touch of melancholy to the beauty of the valley.

At Conksbury, the path crosses the river by a medieval bridge on the road from Bakewell, then runs downstream to Alport where the Lathkill marries with the Bradford. From here, their united waters flow on for 2 miles to lose themselves in the Wye, a little below Haddon Hall.

Monyash is 4¼ miles west of Bakewell on the B5055, which joins the A515, about 7 miles south-east of Buxton.

Bc

Mam Tor

The name, in a mixture of Celtic and Old English, means Mother Hill; though whether it is derived from the great bosomy swell of the hill itself, or

from the fact that the 16 acre Iron Age fortification that tops the near 1,700 ft summit is the largest, and maybe the oldest, one of its kind in Derbyshire, is uncertain.

However, there is no doubt about 'Shivering Mountain', the alternative local name for the tor. A few yards to the east of the triangulation point at the summit, there is a tremendous cliff whose face is constantly in movement. It is made up of layers of sandstone and shale, and when water seeps through fissures in the sandstone, it lubricates the surface of the shale beneath, so dispatching great masses of rock into the valley below. From the top of the precipice you can see the evidence of hundreds of such slips which quite often take the Chapel-en-le-Frith to Castleton road with them.

The precipice is appalling, and, edged as it is with slippery, sheep-cropped grass, fairly dangerous. But the views are stupendous, and the ridge that runs from Rushup Edge to the west, then north-east from Mam Tor to Lose Hill by way of Hollins Cross, is easily the best ridge walk in the Peak. On either side the green slopes slide down – into the lovely, U-shaped chequerboard of Edale to the north and into the wide expanse of the Hope Valley to the south. So handsome is the Hope Valley that the huge limestone quarry and cement works in its midst dents its majestic appearance scarcely at all.

The best place to begin the walk

CITY NEIGHBOUR At Hathersage, St Michael's church spire rises above the village in the Hope Valley. Only 5 miles to the east, across Hallam Moors and Burbage Moor, lie the outskirts of Sheffield.

is from a point on the A625 about 2 miles north-east of Chapel-en-le-Frith; though not signposted the beginning is fairly obvious, since it is part of an old, paved packhorse route. The track climbs up Rushup Edge, reaching the highest point, in this first section, at a Bronze Age tumulus on Lord's Seat. Whoever was buried here, with all the countryside laid before him, must have been a great lord indeed.

Now the path drops steadily down to the Edale road, which cuts through Rushup Edge via the Mam Nick Pass, before climbing once more, but not too exhaustingly, to the summit of Mam Tor. The remainder of the high, exhilarating ridge lies before you. It is always windy up here, and skylarks sing perpetually overhead. Below, you can see the brown backs of hovering kestrels, crows flapping their weary way into the wind, and rooks, those aerial comedians, falling and tumbling about in the breeze.

The view is completely splendid. To the south is the gleaming White Peak, the limestone area of Derbyshire, while to the north is the sombre gritstone of the Dark Peak. And the ridge you are standing upon is the place where those two extraordinarily contrasting rock formations meet.

Mam Tor can be reached by the footpath which climbs up from the picnic site at the foot of the Edale road, which runs north from the A625 about 2 miles west of Castleton. This also gives access to the north-eastern portion of Rushup Edge.

DARK PEAK A dark ridge heralds the barren wastes of Kinder Scout. Sombre and forbidding, the gritstone rock rises to a moorland plateau – the lonely domain of red grouse and hardy sheep.

Bb Miller's Dale

The valley of the River Wye has acquired many different names on its long route between Buxton and Bakewell. South of Tideswell village it is called Miller's Dale, a name derived from the two great mills that were built in the valley in the 18th century. The one at Cressbrook was owned by Sir Richard Arkwright and staffed by workhouse boys who were housed in cottages near by. The other was a little further upstream at Litton Mill, and had a reputation, for the treatment of its apprentices, that rivalled that of Dotheboys Hall.

The path from Cressbrook leads through Litton Mill alongside the quiet

BY QUIET WATERS A footpath follows the bank of the River Wye in Miller's Dale. The river once powered two mills, at Litton and at Cressbrook, which gave the dale its name.

236

river, a stretch that is known, quite delightfully, as Water-cum-Jolly-Dale. From Litton Mill, the path becomes a road, but it is little used and is never more than a yard or so from the Wye; just after the hamlet of Miller's Dale, it continues along the north bank.

From now on, the valley is called Chee Dale, and is quite magnificent. Here is Chee Tor, arguably the finest single limestone crag in the Park, around which the river slides in a great curve. The footpath follows the river round on its winding course, in one of the most delightful walks even this area has to offer, until finally it reaches the A6 near Topley Pike, about 3 miles east of Buxton. Deservedly, the dale is now a nature reserve.

All the way from Litton Mill to Chee Tor the cliffs are draped with lime-loving plants – vetches, ferns, even orchids – offering a pleasant contrast to the vigorous plants of the riverside and water-meadows.

The best way to Miller's Dale is by the B6049, which runs north-east from the A6 some 4 miles east of Buxton. A good place to park your car before exploring the area, is at Monsal Head on the B6465.

Ab The Roaches

The Pennines have kept a special triumph to mark the very end of their long march down Britain – the fantastic, battlemented ridge called The Roaches. Like nearby Ramshaw Rocks that overhang the A53, whose base is the old Roman road to Buxton, and the oddly named Hen Cloud, The Roaches are a last outcrop of the Millstone Grit from which the bones of the North Country were formed. Though they never rise to more than 1,700 ft, their weird, weathered shapes and their

GRITSTONE EDGE Looming out of a mist, the stark outlines of The Roaches take on an eerie, unreal appearance. The weather-hewn outcrop marks the southern and western edge of the Dark Peak.

foreign appearance in the landscape make them enormously impressive.

The best side from which to attack The Roaches is the south-west, the way the gritstone edge faces. From Upper Hulme a minor road takes you up the first part of the climb, then just past Hen Cloud there is a path on the right that slopes northwards up the escarpment. Halfway up there is surprising wooded pasture where a bed of shale, sandwiched between the gritstone, results in richer soils and easier slopes. But the final 200 ft or so to the top is something of a scramble.

The views, however, are well worth the breathlessness. Away to the north-east the land dips and rises to the heights of Axe Edge, and to the south-west, shimmering in the haze, is the eccentric shape of Tittesworth Reservoir. Almost due west is The Cloud, the hill that stands over Congleton,

and beyond that the rolling Cheshire Plain.

The path along the top of The Roaches climbs steadily northwards towards the triangulation point marking the summit at 1,658 ft; shortly before you reach it, there is a little pool crouched behind the ramparts of the ridge. Surrounded by flat-topped boulders, it is a perfect place to take a mid-climb breather.

From the triangulation point to the north, can be seen the pyramid cone of Shutlingsloe, the rolling moorlands of Goyt's Moss, and the gritstone country that surrounds the central Peakland core of white limestone.

Access to The Roaches is by Upper Hulme village, which lies west of the A53, 3 miles north-east of Leek.

Cb Stanton Moor

Just south of the point where the Derwent and Wye rivers meet there is a 2 sq. mile stretch of moorland which is never more than 1,060 ft high, yet somehow conveys the exhilarating impression that you have reached the top of the world.

During the Bronze Age, Stanton Moor must have been awarded considerable religious significance, for more than 70 barrows have been identified here, many of which have been excavated. Much of the work was carried out by the late J. P. Heathcote of Birchover, and his finds are now in Sheffield City Museum.

The barrows have been worn down by time, and the heather is deep, so they are not always easy to find. However, there is a little stone circle called the Nine Ladies, with the separate King's Stone standing near by, at the northern end of the plateau. By the

THE PEAK DISTRICT

path running north-eastwards towards the Nine Ladies, the remains of two mounds can be seen, and careful searching will reveal many others all over the moor, but especially in the south and east. Whether you are successful or not, the search gives added interest to a pleasant walk along sandy paths and through heather, among surroundings of great charm.

Stanton Moor can be reached from Stanton Lees, which is 3¼ miles north-west of Matlock on a minor road leading from the B5057 at Darley Bridge.

Bb   Taddington Moor

Moors are unusual hereabouts, since in Derbyshire the term is generally reserved for the dark uplands of the gritstone Peak. But Taddington Moor is a limestone ridge, whose highest point Sough ('Suff') Top reaches up to 1,438 ft above the surrounding windcombed solitudes; so perhaps 'moor' is appropriate here, too, even though it is now mainly pasture, box-patterned with the drystone walls so characteristic of Derbyshire.

The views stretch out to Kinder Scout in the north, the Sheffield moors to the east and due west to Axe Edge; however, Taddington Moor's best-known attribute, the highest Neolithic monument in England, lies within its own compass. It shows on the Ordnance Survey map, a little to the south of the A6, as 'Chambered Cairn', but local people have always known it as Five Wells. Originally, it was a huge oval barrow, some 80 ft by 60 ft, and probably about 20 ft high. When it was built, some 4,500 years ago, a great mound of earth covered its two limestone burial chambers and passages, but this has long eroded

away, leaving them open to the sky and revealing the massive stone slabs of their construction.

Excavations showed that at least 12 people were buried in the barrow, accompanied by pottery, flint tools and other grave goods. These finds are now in Sheffield Museum.

Access to Five Wells is by a track near the hotel that stands on the A6 just west of the Taddington by-pass. Alternatively, there is a path across the moor from Chelmorton to Taddington which forks after a few hundred yards. The left fork leads to the tomb. Though these paths are generally open, they are not public rights-of-way.

Bb   Three Shire Heads

The triangle of high moorland between Leek and Macclesfield in the west and Buxton to the east is the birthplace of five rivers and the meeting place of three counties – Staffordshire, Derbyshire and Cheshire. The actual meeting place, called Three Shire Heads, is in the upper valley of the River Dane where the infant stream divides into two branches; the northerly one is generally taken to be the Dane's source.

The wide, rolling moorland is slashed across by tributaries of the Dane which have eroded through the sandstone and shales of the dip slope to produce attractively named edges such as Cut-thorn Hill and Turn Edge; there is also an eyrie called the Hawk's Nest, which gives a delightful view down the Dane valley towards The Roaches, with Wolf Edge to the east.

About 2 miles north of Three Shire Heads, on the A537, is the Cat and Fiddle Inn which, at 1,690 ft, is one of the highest pubs in England. According to the weather, it provides either a wonderful panoramic view over the

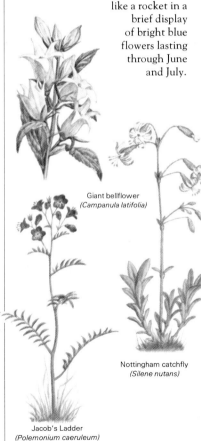

FLOWERS OF THE PEAKS

From July to September the giant bellflower brightens the woods and hedge-banks with its 2 in. long, purplish-blue flowers clustered at the head of a stem growing 3–5 ft high. The Nottingham catchfly is a spring flower of dry, stony places; small insects sometimes become trapped on its sticky stalks, but are not devoured by the plant. In the limestone areas of the Peak, Jacob's Ladder climbs heavenward – but only to about 2 ft – and bursts like a rocket in a brief display of bright blue flowers lasting through June and July.

Giant bellflower
(Campanula latifolia)

Nottingham catchfly
(Silene nutans)

Jacob's Ladder
(Polemonium caeruleum)

moorlands of Macclesfield Forest, or a shelter from the stormy blast.

The easiest access to Three Shire Heads is by the path that runs from the A54 just below Dane Bower quarries, 4 miles south-west of Buxton.

Bc   Vale of Edale

The flat-bottomed valley, threaded by the River Noe, is best appreciated from the heights of Mam Tor or Hollins Cross, from where the full glory of the green chequerboard of the fields is laid out in its entirety. But down on the valley floor there are also pretty hamlets, picnic places by the Noe, and field paths to wander along, surrounded by the high ring of the hills.

The track that starts at The Nag's Head in Edale village is an object lesson in the contrasts of the British landscape – quite remarkable contrasts that may occur within only a few hundred yards or so. The first part of the trail – it is actually the beginning of the Pennine Way – runs through meadows as lush as anyone could wish for, dotted with sycamore, oak and beech. But once across the little stream that runs out of Golden Clough and suddenly the rich pasture changes to poorer, thin grazing, and soon to vegetation so sparse as to be almost non-existent. This is really wild country, where warm clothing and stout boots are essential, and if you are going up as far as Edale Moor, take a map and compass too.

The Vale of Edale is best reached from the east, where a road runs up from Hope on the A625, 4 miles west of Hathersage. Access from the west is more spectacular, since it involves taking a minor road north from the A625, 2 miles west of Castleton, and climbs up to 1,500 ft in the shadow of Mam Tor.

NORTHUMBERLAND'S COAST AND HILLS

Borderland of rolling hills, turbulent rivers and deep
forests, with a past filled with strife and bloodshed

Northumberland is a land of huge sprawling moors, massive rolling hills, turbulent rivers and deep forests. Windy peaks and peat moors, where the wind sighs and curlews' plaintive calls ring out, thrust up through the forests; these are threaded by myriad silvery streams running beneath the shade of towering pines. A fringe of dune-backed sands, rocky cliffs and fishing villages hems the east. Raucous sea-birds in unimaginable numbers scream above them. Between hills and coast lie cornfields and pasture set with sturdy greystone villages and enclosed by drystone walls. And everywhere are reminders of past Border struggles and the primitive hilltop homes of hardier ancient times.

Northumberland is Border country. For centuries it was a kind of no-man's land, since most of it lies north of Hadrian's Wall. The wall remains as a remarkable feature of the countryside. Everywhere there are reminders of the violent past – great castles at Bamburgh, Dunstanburgh and Warkworth, and steep-roofed pele towers where men and beasts took refuge from Border raiders.

But there is evidence of peaceful times, too. When Northumbria was dominant among the seven English kingdoms, it was the centre of learning and religion. Paulinus baptised thousands of Northumbrian converts around AD 625. St Aidan trained missionaries for all over Britain at Lindisfarne, and the monks there wrote out the beautiful

Lindisfarne Gospels – on folios prepared from the skins of more than 1,000 calves.

This Border territory juts boldly into the Scottish Lowlands – a great beak of land bounded by the Tweed and the sea. Down its western side roll the Cheviot Hills. They are low compared to the Pennines – The Cheviot itself rises to only 2,674 ft – but their peaks are more clearly defined, giving a bold uneven look to the western skyline. The Simonside Hills, though rising to only 1,444 ft at Tosson Hill, are more rugged than the Cheviots, with sandstone crags and open moorland above the Coquet valley. The more northerly Cheviots are bare except for purple moor grass, through which wild goats and blue hares run.

The southern hills run into the Border Forest, the largest man-made forest in western Europe. Sixty years ago this was barren moorland, but in 1926 the Forestry Commission began planting millions of trees. Sitka spruce and Norway spruce are the main crop, for these trees are grown for harvesting just as a farmer grows wheat and corn. From these hills Northumberland's turbulent rivers wind through valleys and gorges – the Aln, Coquet, Wansbeck, Blyth and the North Tyne.

Many of the remoter pleasures of Northumberland can be encountered along the Pennine Way, England's longest public footpath, which runs the final stage of its 250 mile course in Northumberland. It strides up from Cumbria, turns along Hadrian's Wall, then skirts the Border Forest and heads for the Cheviots to traverse them until it crosses the Border. The full delights of the Pennine Way are only for experienced and well-equipped walkers, but almost anyone can dip into them here and there and sample the exhilarating and spacious character of Northumberland.

SAILORS' PERIL South of Craster, the Northumberland coast is a knuckled fist of rocky bays and headlands often lashed by relentless seas. Even at Howick Haven there is little respite, and few ships would choose to run for shelter among its jagged rocks and swirling currents.

Places to visit

Map ref. Dd Bamburgh

The red-sandstone castle, seeming to grow out of the massive rock on which it stands, hangs over Bamburgh. Rock and castle are more than 400 yds long and 150 ft high, towering over the village on one side and over windswept sand and rock on the other.

There has been a castle of one kind or another at Bamburgh since almost the dawn of English history. The Saxon Ida the Flamebearer became king of Bernicia, as the area was known, in 547 and founded his capital at the site. His grandson Ethelfrith became king of all Northumbria and named the capital Bebbanburh in honour of Bebba, his wife. Three times it survived ferocious Viking attacks. The Normans took it from Matilda, Countess of Northumberland, who surrendered it to William Rufus rather than have him put out the eyes of her captive husband, Robert.

It was the Normans who built the vast, square keep that still stands. Much of the present building, however, dates from 1894 when the castle was bought, restored, extended and modernised by Lord Armstrong.

Below the castle walls, where the sea once pounded the base of the rock, a wide stretch of sandy beach runs for

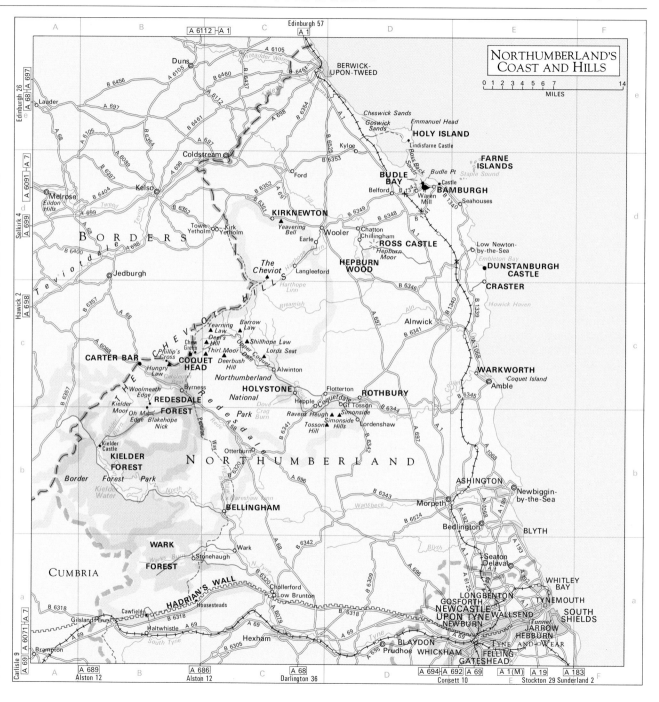

2½ miles to Seahouses, a fishing village with brightly painted cobles – the square-sterned craft designed to operate from open beaches. Such a magnificent beach attracts picnickers and holidaymakers, but there is room for all and a walk along it is invigorating. Sand-dunes roll away inland to the main road that is parallel to the beach, and always in view are the rocky Farne Islands – aloof yet bound closely to the Northumbrian coast's history.

Bamburgh is reached from the B1341 or the B1342, which turn off the A1 midway between Alnwick and Berwick. The B1340 runs behind the beach to Seahouses.

Cb   **Bellingham**

A small market town of less than 1,000 people, Bellingham (pronounced 'bellinjum') lies on the River North Tyne, one of Northumberland's prettiest stretches of water. Its course runs below the bare fells and across the Forest Park, sometimes shaded by wooded banks and sometimes winding through lush grazing lands. Where rushing tributaries have carried stones and silt from above, large islands have formed in the river. There are delightful walks along the banks to east and west. Meadowsweet, greater burnet, figwort, devil's-bit scabious, ladies' bedstraw and the melancholy thistle are among the summer's wild plants. Brown trout flicker in the glinting water, dippers bob above it, and among the trees green woodpeckers laugh and great spotted woodpeckers drum.

Three long walks into the Border Park, all 15–20 miles, start at Bellingham and include fine views, but one of the best sights is close at hand. A footpath running north alongside the

Hareshaw Burn passes the site of an old iron works, enters a wooded valley, criss-crosses the burn, and after about a mile reaches Hareshaw Linn. Here the burn slides more than 30 ft down a sandstone outcrop. After heavy rain it is spectacular – but the path becomes very slippery.

The vigorous men of Bellingham did their share of Border raiding in the stormy past, and also withstood many attacks from the north. Villagers and cattle would then crush together into the squat, sturdy-walled St Cuthbert's Church for safety. Twice the chancel was burned down, and cannonballs that lodged in the building are on display. The risk of fire was ended in the 17th century when a rare type of roof – some claim unique – was put on. Huge stone slabs rest on six-sided stone arches; the walls had to be heavily buttressed to bear the weight.

Bellingham is 13 miles north-west of Hexham. Take the A6079 north from Hexham. At Low Brunton, turn on to the B6320 and follow the signposts to Bellingham.

Dd   **Budle Bay**

Greylag geese use Budle Bay as a winter roosting place, and hosts of gulls and wildfowl come here all the year round to search for food among its mud-flats. The shallow estuary, almost totally enclosed by a finger of Ross Back Sands pointing across to Budle Point, fills with water only at high tide. Then the sea curls in through the narrow entrance – swift, deep and dangerous in the channel below the headland.

The whole of the rectangular bay, a mile wide and 1½ miles long, is within a nature reserve. The road along the southern tip makes an ideal viewpoint

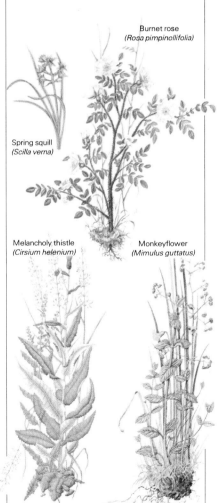

NORTHUMBRIAN FLOWERS

From May until July the burnet rose brightens sand-dunes near the sea. Less common is the spring squill, sometimes found on grassy places along the coast. The happy faces of the monkeyflower smile up from the water's edge by rivers and streams, while the melancholy thistle hangs its head in damp meadows.

Burnet rose
(*Rosa pimpinollifolia*)

Spring squill
(*Scilla verna*)

Melancholy thistle
(*Cirsium helenium*)

Monkeyflower
(*Mimulus guttatus*)

for bird-watchers – and a good parking spot. Only a grass verge and a fence separate the road from the bay. Another good vantage point is the high ground beyond Budle Point, just over a mile from Bamburgh along a footpath that makes its way round the edge of the golf course.

In the 13th century Budle Bay was the port of Bamburgh, and schooners and barges crossed to the creek at its southern tip to reach Waren Mill – more recently a malting-house producing the malted barley used in a local brewery.

Budle Bay is 2½ miles east of Belford on the A1, north of the B1342 from Belford to Bamburgh.

Bc   **Carter Bar**

Up through Redesdale between forests and hills the A68 climbs to Scotland, slowly at first then sharply – 550 ft in a mile – to reach 1,371 ft and Carter Bar, the most dramatic crossing point on the Border. Behind lie the domes and fells of the Cheviots, but spread out ahead are the green fields of the Scottish Lowlands; across them Edinburgh and the Firth of Forth, 50 miles away, are visible on a clear day. The Eildon Hills rise at Melrose, 18 miles away to the north-west.

Four miles south-east of Carter Bar the River Rede has been dammed to form Catcleugh Reservoir. Across its dam, a footpath runs for a mile beside the water then crosses the Chattlehope Burn to join a walk curving north-west through a wood to meet the reservoir again and run with it back to the road 1½ miles above the dam. The water, woods and enclosing hills make a delightful setting for the walk.

On the northern side of the valley,

half a mile after the Rede re-emerges from the reservoir, a path leads from the A68 north-west through the forest to Hungry Law's summit at 1,644 ft. The path leads on from the summit along the Border to Phillip's Cross, where a stone cairn stands on the old drovers' road from Scotland. Ruts worn by the cattle being driven south to the markets still mark the ground.

Redesdale was a fierce place in the 16th century. The Lords of Redesdale were given the lands absolutely by the monarch throughout the Middle Ages, with the right to have their own judges, gallows, prisons and coroners as long as they kept out wolves and robbers. However, the lords themselves consorted with thieves and outlaws, and lawlessness went unchecked.

Border raiding was their sport. The Wardens of the Middle Marches were appointed to settle Border disputes and held several meetings at Carter Bar for the purpose. But the last one, held there in 1575, was as unavailing as previous ones, for soon after it ended fighting broke out and the Scots chased the English 3 miles over the Border and stole 300 cattle. This Redeswire Raid is commemorated by an annual horseride to the Border by riders from both north and south.

Carter Bar is on the main A68, 9 miles south of Jedburgh.

SPARKLING CHEVIOT STREAM The Coquet hurries down from the Cheviots between the rounded hills of Upper Coquet Dale.

Bc Coquet Head

Of all the valleys carved from the great mass of the Cheviots, Upper Coquet Dale is perhaps the most exhilarating. For 12 miles or so, running west from Alwinton, a remote mountain road follows the course of the Coquet to its head, twisting and turning along the sinuous valley floor while the hills close in on either side and all signs of civilisation are left far behind. Along the way streams come to join the main artery of the Coquet, threading their way down through the moors from Shillhope Law, Barrow Law, Yearning Law, Deerbush Hill and Deel's Hill, all more than 1,000 ft high. As it approaches Coquet Head the road dips to skirt Thirl Moor, the highest of all at 1,829 ft.

At the head of the valley the road comes within yards of the Scottish Border at Chew Green. Here are the remains of a group of Roman marching camps which lie on Dere Street, the Roman road from York to Scotland. The earthworks of two superimposed camps are clearly defined – one with ditches defending two enclosures and a labour camp, the other a temporary camp large enough to hold a legion of 5,300 men.

The lines of the camp show up clearly from a distance. There is a dramatic view of the layout from half a mile along Gamel's Path, up which the road swings to the south away from Chew Green. Gamel's Path was one of the meeting places for the Wardens of the Middle Marches, who vainly attempted to settle Border disputes in Tudor times. The track was also used as a smugglers' route.

Gamel's Path now leads through the vast Redesdale artillery range, which also runs all along the south side of the road from Alwinton to Chew Green. Do not stray from the road, and watch out for signs warning of military activity in the area.

The road to Coquet Head is marked from Alwinton, which is 9 miles west of Rothbury along the B6341 and then along a signposted minor road.

Craster and Dunstanburgh Castle
Ed

A tiny harbour set in a cluster of cottages is the heart of Craster, a village named after the family that owned the district even before the Norman Conquest. The Crasters enlarged the harbour in 1906, not for the fishing boats but for the barges and coasters that came to get setts and chippings of the hard whinstone cut from the family's quarries behind the village. The setts were taken to pave the streets of cities as far away as London. Now a disused quarry offers ample parking space.

The few brightly coloured cobles in the harbour are the remnant of a much larger fleet. They fish for salmon, crabs and the sweet-flavoured lobsters that thrive on the limestone rocks protecting the harbour. The coble, the distinctive fishing craft of the north-east coast, has a bow both deep and high to breast the rough seas, and an iron-shod flat-bottomed stern that can be hauled on to the shore for landing.

To the north of the harbour, through the village, a wicket gate marks the start of a 3 mile walk along the coastal path dominated by the spectacular ruin of Dunstanburgh Castle. To the west lie rich meadows and pasturelands; on the east the sea washes the foot of the cliff columns where many fulmars nest. The path is the only way to the 11 acre site of the castle.

This great size had no practical pur-

pose. It was determined by the natural defences of the spot. The castle stands on an outcrop of the Great Whin Sill, with the steep drop and the sea protecting it more than its long curtain walls. Only the south wall was approachable, and here it had towers built about every 30 yds.

After the Wars of the Roses, in the late 15th century, the castle fell into ruin. The main road to the north was developed inland, away from Dunstanburgh; the siege cannon ended its impregnability; and even its harbour silted up behind a shingle bar to form the low-lying pasture that is there now.

From the ruins there is a sweeping view stretching from Coquet Island in the south to the Farne Islands in the north. Sea-birds wheel round the cliffs, wheatears and ringed plovers breed among the boulders, and down on the foreshore 'Dunstanburgh diamonds' – tiny quartz fragments – glint between the rocks.

The path continues north beyond the castle, dipping down to the sandy beach to skirt the golf-course, and crossing Embleton Burn where stonechats nest in the hawthorn bushes. Linnets, yellowhammers and whitethroats love the gorse-covered crag. The path ends at Low Newton-by-the-Sea, beside fields where lapwings make their home.

Craster and Low Newton-by-the-Sea are 6 miles and 8 miles north-east of Alnwick on signposted minor roads leading off the B1339 and B1340 respectively.

Farne Islands
Ed

The sharp, fluted outlines of the Farne Islands stand in the waters off Seahouses like the broken pillars of an ancient ruin, rising vertically to 70 ft

in places. The 15, 20 or 26 islands – for some emerge and submerge with the tides – are scattered like stepping-stones, each with a creamy collar of foam.

The islands, owned by the National Trust, are in two groups divided by the mile-wide water of Staple Sound. Nearest to the shore, about 1½ miles out, are the Inner Farnes with 16 acre Farne Island the largest of the group. The Outer Farnes include Staple Island, Brownsman, Longstone and the North and South Wamses. The rest of the group are mostly barren rocks which hardly qualify as islands since they are underwater most of the time.

Each group has its own lighthouse – on Longstone and on Farne Island. The Farne light is automatic, but the Long-

stone light still has keepers to operate it. The lighthouse-keepers and the bird wardens are the only people living on the islands. But life abounds there – rabbits on Farne, sea-birds everywhere, and a herd of grey seals.

Sea-birds breed and nest on the islands in vast numbers. Puffins come home from their fishing in hordes each evening to their nest-holes in the ground. Ranks of bronze cormorants and green shags stand apparently with arms akimbo as they spread their wings to dry. Chocolate-coloured guillemots are so crowded on the rock ledges that their eggs often get pushed off, despite the pear shape which should make them roll in circles. Razorbills, eider ducks, rock pipits, fulmars, gulls and terns fill the air with raucous cries which resound among the rocks.

The eider ducks are sometimes called St Cuthbert's chickens because the saint tamed and protected them when he lived on Farne Island. Cuthbert had become prior at Lindisfarne, but his contemplative spirit needed a retreat. He came to Farne Island in 676, and lived there in a rough shelter.

A small monastic group lived on Farne from 1255, and the ruins of their buildings remain. The monks sold sea-bird eggs and fish, salvaged wrecks and made a profit on their surplus barley. There are no trees on the islands, but the peaty soil over the hard dolerite rock bears an abundance of wild flowers as well as mosses and lichens.

There are daily boat trips round the islands from Seahouses in spring and summer, weather permitting. Landing is allowed only on Farne Island and Staple Island, and not even there from May 15 to July 15, when the birds are breeding. Seahouses is on the B1340, 3 miles south-east of Bamburgh.

FARNE ISLAND FAMILY

The clumsy creatures that lumber awkwardly over the rocks on the Farne Islands become sleek and graceful in the water – even the 8 ft long, 40 stone bulls. Their alert and appealing gaze inspects boatloads of visitors as they make the crossing to Farne. The islands are the grey seals' only breeding place on the east coast of Britain.

Grey seal
(Halichoerus grypus)

Hadrian's Wall

While the Romans occupied Britain, Hadrian's Wall was their principal deterrent against invasion from the north. Across the entire width of the land, from the Tyne estuary to the Solway Firth, this impregnable barrier ran for 80 Roman miles – a little over 73 miles. It was built between AD 122 and 130 by order of the Emperor Hadrian after he had visited Britain and decided not to attempt to push the empire any further north.

In the absence of a natural frontier the Romans created an artificial one, running from one natural strongpoint to the next until it had spanned the country. Hadrian's Wall, stone-built in the east and turf-built in the west, became the northernmost frontier of the Roman Empire. It was manned by 5,500 cavalry and 13,000 infantry auxiliaries from all parts of the empire.

Some of the best-preserved parts of the wall run through the Northumberland National Park, between Chollerford and Gilsland. Mile after mile the grey line of stones, built to 14 ft high in places, marches across the countryside with the ruins of forts, milecastles and signal turrets set along its length at regular intervals. On the northern side runs a ditch, about 27 ft wide and 9 ft deep – except where cliffs make it unnecessary. A short distance to the south lies the vallum, a flat-bottomed ditch about 10 ft deep and 20 ft wide, flanked on each side by a turf mound originally about 6 ft high. The vallum

IMPRESSIVE RUIN Waves roll into Embleton Bay below ruined Dunstanburgh Castle. Built on an outcrop of rock some 600 years ago, it was abandoned in the 15th century.

245

probably served as a road, and marked the southern boundary of the military zone.

One of the best-preserved of the 17 forts is at Vercovicium, the modern Housesteads; it could garrison 1,000 infantry within its 5 acres and was built to guard the point where the Knag Burn breaches the ridge.

At Cawfields there is a good example of a milecastle. These fortlets for about 30 men were built between the forts at every Roman mile (1,620 yds), with two signal turrets equally spaced between them.

The Romans withdrew from the wall in AD 383, when Rome itself was under threat from invading Goths, Vandals and Huns, and troops were needed to defend the city. Eventually Rome fell, but Hadrian's Wall survived – a monument to the time when Britain was part of that great empire.

Cawfields is on a minor road 2 miles north of Haltwhistle and just north of the B6318. Housesteads is 6 miles north-east of Haltwhistle just off the B6318.

Hepburn Wood and Ross Castle

Dd

Hepburn Wood clothes a steep escarpment of fell sandstone crags below the wild expanse of Hepburn Moor. The crags are part of a fault that curves from Kyloe in the north towards Otterburn in the south-west. The waymarked Woodland Walk, taking about an hour, follows forest roads and grassy rides between the conifer and beech plantations. Green woodpeckers, woodcocks and even peregrine falcons sometimes show themselves. Along the way an optional steep path branches up the crag to give a magnificent view from the edge of the scarp

ROME'S NORTH-WEST FRONTIER Hadrian's Wall, 73 miles long, separated Roman Britain from the wild northern tribes.

across to the Cheviot Hills in the west.

Hepburn Crag Walk turns off the Woodland Walk. The waymarked track takes an hour longer and involves some steep, hard walking. But it rises through the plantations, crosses open moorland and the remains of a 4,000-year-old hill-fort – with Chillingham Park and a ruined 'bastle', or fortified farmhouse, below – and finally leads along the crag top to one of the finest views in Northumberland.

The viewpoint is Ross Castle, the site of a double-rampart hill-fort 3,000 years old, with some traces left of the stone-built camp. The Cheviots roll across to the west; the sea shines in the east. On a clear day the seven castles of Lindisfarne, Bamburgh, Dunstanburgh, Warkworth, Alnwick, Ford and Chillingham show up like tiny models in the vast spread of country. Here, at 1,035 ft, the National Trust and the Forestry Commission have built a viewing platform to reward visitors with the full panorama.

In Napoleonic times, Ross Castle was a beacon point with its fire kept ready for lighting to spread the alarm if Bonaparte and his French forces landed in England. On January 31, 1804, the men on evening watch spotted a fire away to the north and lit their beacon. It started a chain of beacons running for miles before messengers could stop them with the reassuring news that the fire in the north was only gorse alight on the Lammermuir Hills.

Hepburn Wood is 6 miles south-east of Wooler. Take the B6348, turn off at Chatton towards Chillingham, and follow the signs after Chillingham.

De   Holy Island

Across a mile-long causeway, which is impassable for about five hours during high water, lies Holy Island. Its long green spit runs out into the North Sea and thrusts up dramatically at the south-eastern tip into a sharp cone round whose apex Lindisfarne Castle clings in a spiral.

The castle was built from the stones of Lindisfarne Priory, half a mile away. After the Dissolution of the Monasteries, the priory had been abandoned by the Benedictine order who built it in 1093 and lived comfortably on the island by farming. Gaunt, roofless ruins, with sandstone arches framing the sky, are all that remain of the priory. They stand in the village, where now the island's only road leads from the causeway. All exploring is on foot.

The Benedictines were not the first monks to live on Holy Island. It had been Saxon England's greatest centre of religious and intellectual life. St Aidan chose it for his monastery when he came from Iona in 635 to be Bishop of Northumbria. He trained missionaries who went all over Britain, and even to the Low Countries. The sumptuously illuminated manuscript known as the *Lindisfarne Gospels* was created by the monks in the late 7th century. But in 793 the Vikings came raiding and destroyed the abbey. The monks rebuilt it, but in 875 they finally fled as the raiders plagued the area again and again. The island stood desolate until the Benedictines came.

Holy Island's historic stones are now extra adornments on its 3 sq. miles of dunes, rugged cliffs, rocky beaches and, above all, teeming birdlife. The whole east-coast path is a bird-watcher's paradise, with Emmanuel Head at the island's north-east corner the best viewing point. Puffins, cormorants, mute swans, greylag geese in winter, guillemots, gannets, divers, redshanks, oystercatchers, kestrels, short-eared owls, varied ducks and grebes – the variety and vast numbers amaze the eye and stun the ear.

The causeway to Holy Island is reached by a signposted minor road that turns off the A1, 8 miles south-east of Berwick-upon-Tweed. A tide-table is displayed at the approach to the causeway.

Cc   Holystone

An ancient holy well, an enchanted waterfall, an oakwood glen and an Iron Age hill-fort are among the delights to be discovered around the small village of Holystone.

The well was a watering place for the Romans; early Christians were baptised there, so tradition claims, and this sacred association attracted Augustinian nuns to found a priory there soon after 1100. They dedicated it to St Mary the Virgin, and the well soon became known as the Lady's Well. It is still the source of fresh water for the village. A waymarked half-hour walk leads to the well. It is the shortest of three Forestry Commission walks in Holystone Forest, all starting from the car park almost half a mile west of the village.

In a glade among the trees, the smooth surface of the large well, contained within its square wall, reflects the Celtic cross that was placed in the centre 200 years ago when the wall was repaired. At the same time, a medieval statue from Alnwick was set beside the water. The bearded, long-robed man, now half hidden by laurels, has a broken nose that gives him a curiously pugnacious look.

The longest of the walks, taking two and a half hours, follows Dove Crag Burn up to Dove Crag itself. Here the stream tumbles over a mass of rocks – a wonderful sight after a storm, but often dry in summer. There is magic in this place; local folklore tells that on summer evenings fairies, elves and goblins – perhaps the spirits of the ancient Celts – take over this spot for feasting and dancing.

The Farm Walk, which takes about an hour, leads through Campville Farm near to the two concentric earthwork ridges of an Iron Age settlement. Its earlier name was the sweeter-sounding Lanternside. Timber palisades topped the ridges 2,500 years ago, protecting the village of thatched huts.

Oakwoods are rare in Northumbria, but there is one along the Holystone Burn which used to be coppiced: the trunks were cut down to stumps from which a ring of shoots sprouted and, after several years, produced a crop of stout poles. The oak was used to make charcoal, employed as fuel for iron smelting until coke replaced it in the early 18th century. Mines also used the oak poles for pit props.

Holystone is 6 miles west of Rothbury and reached from there by the B6341, then by a minor road forking right 1 mile after Hepple.

PEACEFUL RELIC Built in 1550 to guard Holy Island harbour – a base for troops fighting on the Border – Lindisfarne Castle never fired a shot in anger. In 1903, the architect Edwin Lutyens made it into a private house.

Bb Kielder-Redesdale Forest

From the border of Cumbria to the Cheviot Hills, the Border Forest of spruce, pine and larch throws its dark green blanket over valleys and hills, threadbare only on the highest ground where even hardy conifers will not grow. The Kielder-Redesdale Forest is the largest of the nine man-made forests that make up the Border Forest.

Few forests have so many streams, every one providing beautiful scenery of rock and water among the trees. The Kielder Burn is a spawning ground for salmon and sea trout, and occasionally an otter shows itself. The streams are the haunt of waders, dippers, goosanders, mallards and occasionally herons.

Even a short walk holds the promise of seeing some of the forest's shy wildlife – foxes, perhaps one of the 1,100 roe deer, or possibly a red deer that has strayed over the Border from Scotland. There are blue hares on the high, open moors, and herds of wild goats with magnificent curved horns and long coats. Kestrels and lapwings soar above, and underfoot a variety of mosses, ferns and rushes thrive.

At the heart of the forest is Kielder Castle, once a hunting lodge for the Duke of Northumberland and now a forest information centre. The Duchess Drive waymarked walks of an hour and a half and three hours start here, and also the 12 mile Forest Drive along the toll-road. This links north Tynedale with Redesdale, and crosses some of the remotest country in Northumberland as it climbs to 1,500 ft at Blakehope Nick. It skirts the wild moorland of Oh Me Edge and then re-enters the forest to follow the Blakehope Burn down to the Rede just below Byrness on the A68.

Kielder is 15 miles north-west of Bellingham, and is reached by a minor road which heads west from the B6320.

Cd Kirknewton

History and savage beauty crowd the hills above Kirknewton, a sturdy Border village of thick-walled buildings on the northern edge of the Cheviots. Scarcely a hilltop is without its prehistoric fort or enclosure. The most extensive Iron Age camp in Northumberland sprawls over 13 acres on top of Yeavering Bell, an aptly named dome of a hill a mile to the south-east. Inside the stone rampart are the foundations of some 130 circular or oval huts.

The hill is close to the road, and its 1,182 ft summit, reached with no more than a modest walk, gives a generous reward: a magnificent view over the valleys of the Tweed and the Till in the north, the hills above Chatton to the east, and layer upon layer of hills in the west swirling round to the Cheviots in the south.

Below Yeavering Bell, Edwin, Saxon king of Northumbria, had his summer palace, Gefrin. When it was discovered and excavated in the late 1950s, timber halls and stockades came to light, and also shrines both pagan and Christian. Edwin married a Christian, Ethelberga, who brought with her Paulinus, one of the missionaries who came with Augustine from Rome in 597 to bring their religion to the English. Paulinus converted Edwin in 627. Many of the king's people followed his example. Paulinus spent 36 days at Gefrin teaching and baptising the converts. A plaque marks the site of the palace.

Kirknewton is 5 miles west of Wooler along the A697, then the B6351.

Dc Rothbury

The attractive 'capital' of Coquetdale is Rothbury, a large, elegant, unspoiled village. Old stone houses and wide streets climb from the sloping green, shaded by sycamore trees, up the hill on the north bank of the Coquet.

The Simonside Hills lie south of Rothbury. Their dark, rugged outlines clad with pines, silver birches and rowans on the northern slopes rise like steps to the highest point at Tosson Hill, 1,444 ft above sea-level, and the craggy sandstone bluff of Simonside. The views from Simonside are enormous, an unhindered sweep from Cumbria round to the east coast and including almost all the Coquet from source to mouth.

From the road between Great Tosson and Lordenshaw, waymarked Forestry Commission paths lead through the forest on walks taking half an hour to two and a half hours. Paths lead to Simonside Ridge and Ravens Heugh. A short diversion on Simonside leads to Little Church Rock, a great sandstone boulder cleft from top to bottom as if by a giant sword. Ravens Heugh crags face west, and there is no finer place to be on a late summer afternoon when Coquetdale and the distant Cheviots are bathed in golden sunlight.

Great Tosson was the legendary home of the Duergars, elves who plagued the local folk with their tricks. It was also the scene of many Border raids, and the remains of its pele tower still rise 30 ft above the farm buildings of the tiny hamlet. The stone facings near ground level have been stolen for other buildings, and the rubble masonry within is revealed. When raiders came over the border the villagers

HANDSOME GOOSANDERS

The stately male goosander's dark green head and pink body are its breeding plumage. Later the plumage changes to the same brown head and grey body of the female, but a white forewing distinguishes him from his mate. Goosanders first nested in Scotland in 1871, but are now found in many places south of the Border.

Goosander
(Mergus merganser)

would crowd into the pele tower, first driving their cattle in on the ground floor and then retreating to the floor above up the wooden stairs. As a last resort, the stairs could be burned to prevent the raiders from reaching the villagers.

Just above Lordenshaw there is a Bronze Age camp on a spur of the hillside, at the junction of four ancient tracks. The camp is 40 yds across, with the remains of the rough huts protected by a double circle of banks and ditches. The rocks around the camp bear Britain's largest collection of the strange, unexplained, 'cup-and-ring' markings.

Rothbury is 11 miles south-west of Alnwick on the B6341. Great Tosson is 2 miles away along the marked minor road that leaves Rothbury to the south and then turns west.

Ba   Wark Forest

Wark Forest is the most southerly of the nine great plantations that make up the Border Forest. Together they cover 145,000 acres, the largest man-made forest in western Europe. They have been planted by the Forestry Commission since 1926 to produce timber. Each year a crop is felled and perhaps 1,000 acres replanted in each forest. With trees planted 5 ft apart, 1,500 are needed for each acre – 1½ million for 1,000 acres.

In Wark Forest the Commission has marked three walks of between 2½ and 4 miles, and also the delightful Warksburn Forest Trail – delightful because it offers an easy mile-long stroll alongside a trickling burn, under plantations of young conifers, through mature mixed woodland, and across meadowland with fine views of the North Tyne valley.

The trail starts and finishes near the village of Stonehaugh, which was built for the forest workers. Along much of the way the sound of water, the sweet smell of pine and the chorus of birdsong are welcome companions. Warks Burn winds through the forest, following a stone-strewn course where trout lie in the shallows and water voles scurry in and out of their holes in the bank and splash into the water.

The forest is made up mostly of Scots pine, Norway spruce and Japanese larch. Each species has its own function. Scots pine, a native of Britain, produces the timber known as red deal, while the Norway spruce is felled for traditional Christmas trees as well as for white deal. Japanese larches, deciduous conifers whose dainty, fresh foliage lightens the forest each spring, are planted along the forest roads as

fire-breaks. They grow fast, and quickly suppress grasses which spread fire.

At dawn or dusk you may spot a roe deer emerging cautiously into an open glade with nose twitching and ears erect. These graceful creatures are common in the Border Forest and, although shyness keeps them largely out of sight, there is ample evidence of their presence – frayed bark on the trees where they rub the velvet from their new spring antlers, and stunted trees where they have browsed on the young shoots.

Stonehaugh is 5 miles west of Wark on the B6320, and is reached by signposted minor roads.

Ec   Warkworth

Here the River Coquet makes its final serpentine coil before entering the sea. Emerging from its steep, wooded valley, it winds round the little town of Warkworth in a great horseshoe, slipping past the beautiful Norman church before, overlooked by the stately remains of the castle, it passes unhurriedly beneath a fortified medieval bridge and flows to the sea at Amble.

Warkworth Castle, built early in Norman times on a fortified Saxon site, came into the hands of the Percy family – the Earls of Northumberland – in 1331. They strengthened it, gave it the magnificent cruciform keep, and added some domestic comforts. That straightforward soldier Harry Hotspur was brought up here. He helped Henry Bolingbroke to seize the crown of England from Richard II but later, his loyalty cooled by Henry's autocracy, plotted against him.

Warkworth Castle sits high on its green velvet mount, the grassy slopes running down from it to the water's

edge. A path along the river leads to a 14th-century hermitage half a mile upstream; an even more pleasant approach is by boat. The cell and its tiny, vaulted chapel are cut into the sandstone cliffside. At the entrance the inscription *Fuerunt mihi lacrymae panes nocte et die* sets a sad mood – 'Tears have been my portion night and day'.

Between Warkworth and Amble, the road runs beside Warkworth Harbour. A mile off the harbour lies the flat-topped, rocky Coquet Island. Boat trips give a good view of the island, but landing is forbidden for it is a bird sanctuary and the most southerly breeding ground in eastern Britain of the eider duck.

Warkworth is on the A1068, 6 miles south-east of Alnwick.

EARL'S RETREAT A loop of the Coquet river forms part of the defences of Warkworth Castle. Henry IV battered it with cannon in 1405 to subdue the rebel Earl of Northumberland.

249

PATCHWORK FIELDS AND COACHING ROADS

ENCLOSURES, ROADS AND CANALS – 18TH-CENTURY FEATURES THAT HERALDED A NEW BRITAIN

ENGLAND'S POPULATION in 1700 numbered about 6 million. By the time of the first census in 1801 it had reached 8.9 million – such was the growth of the country during the Georgian century, most dramatically reflected in the immense expansion of towns. London contained 980,000 people, and 13 towns each had more than 20,000 inhabitants when the census was taken, while Lancashire had become the most heavily populated county.

In the countryside, many changes took place during the 18th century, especially in the band of counties stretching from Dorset and through the Midlands to Yorkshire. This was largely lowland country, and at the beginning of the century about half the arable land was open fields. By the end of the century, the farming landscape had changed to the pattern of hedged rectangular fields familiar to us today. The changes came about through Acts of Parliament – the Enclosure Acts of the second half of the century. Some 3,000 parishes were affected by such Acts, of which 1,479 were passed during George III's reign.

The new fields were largely devoted to grazing and might be anything between 5 and 50 acres in size, while the enclosures, too, encouraged the building of farmhouses outside the village and within compact blocks of land acquired by canny farmers. The names of these isolated farmsteads often pin-point the time of their construction. In two neighbouring Leicestershire parishes, Sileby and Seagrave, 'Quebec House' recalls Wolfe's victory of 1759, while 'Bunker Hill' and 'New York' are reminders of the American War of Independence.

Taming the wilderness

The Enclosure Acts led to the improvement of many thousands of acres of waste and heathland. Lincoln Edge, a 40 mile long belt of limestone in Lincolnshire, was a wilderness of gorse in 1770 but by the end of the century it had been converted to farmland. At about the same time, at Flanders Moss in the Scottish Lowlands, hundreds of acres of rich, alluvial soil were obtained by stripping the 6–12 ft thick covering of peat.

As farming in England prospered, and the population increased, so the demand for better roads grew ever more pressing. At first the need was met by the creation of turnpike trusts, bodies that undertook to maintain stretches of road in exchange for tolls collected from traffic passing through the toll-gates. The scheme was started in the previous century, but by 1700 only seven Turnpike Acts had been passed. After 1750, however, there was an average of 40 new turnpike trusts a year.

The turnpike trusts did not create new roads, but simply improved sections of highways that had been in existence in some cases since Roman times. Nevertheless, the turnpikes greatly speeded the transportation of goods and livestock, and towards the end of the century gave rise to a new form of transport – the stage-coach. In their brief heyday, the stage-coach and mail-coach lines provided a superb service, running all over the country to rigid timetables and on beautifully engineered and surfaced roads. But until 1770 at least, many of the turnpikes were quite incapable of carrying such traffic.

Military necessity

Ironically, the best of the early 18th-century roads were built in an area that most emphatically did not want them. They were the military roads of the Highlands, constructed by General Wade and his successors after the Jacobite rising of 1715 to link forts and barracks, and to provide a means of moving troops swiftly to any trouble-spot. In the aftermath of the second rising in 1745, they appeared to increase the desolation of the landscape, where roofless crofts were already marking the beginning of the Clearances that, during the next 100 years, were to empty the Highlands. But many of the roads and bridges remain, a tribute to the skills of the soldiers who built them.

In the more prosperous parts of Britain, the turnpikes were being used by an ever-growing number of packhorses that served the new industries of the North and Midlands. However, an animal carrying no more than 200 lb along rutted roads was hardly an efficient means of transport. The answer was waterways; not just the rivers, but a whole new system of canals.

The great navigators

England's first canal was a modest affair, a 13 mile stretch from the South Lancashire coalfields to the River Mersey, opened in 1757. Both the waterway and its builder, John Eyre, have almost been forgotten, overshadowed by the brilliant James Brindley and his Bridgewater Canal.

It was named after Francis Egerton, 3rd Duke of Bridgewater, who engaged Brindley to build a canal that would carry coal from his mines at Worsley to Manchester. When it was opened in 1761, it was compared to 'the noblest work of the Romans', and hailed as 'the greatest artificial curiosity in the world'. It was Brindley's almost incredible feats of engineering that captured the nation's enthusiasm: the Barton viaduct carrying the canal 40 ft above the River Irwell, the mile-long tunnel reaching underground to wharves at the coal-face, and the barges themselves which Brindley had also designed. They incorporated boxes for transporting the coal and were in fact the forerunners of container vessels.

The canal enabled the Duke of Bridgewater to cut the cost of his coal by half, and it made him a fortune. Others followed his example. In 1772 the Mersey was joined to the Severn and five years later the Grand Trunk Canal was opened to link the Mersey to the Trent. The Grand Trunk crossed the southern flank of the Pennines, and along its 93 miles were 76 locks and five tunnels, including the 2,897 yd long tunnel at Harecastle.

Waterways across Britain

In 1789 a canal was completed between the Severn and the Thames, and in 1810 the Kennet, a tributary of the Thames, was linked with the Avon. The Kennet & Avon Canal, built by John Rennie, features one of the wonders of the canal system – a series of 29 locks in the space of 2 miles to take the canal down Caen Hill.

Altogether, when the Canal Age was at its height, it would have been possible to travel between Littlehampton on the south coast and Kendal in the Lake District entirely by canals and rivers. Similarly, the country could have been crossed from Liverpool to Grimsby.

The centre of the network of canals and rivers was Birmingham, which was linked by water to the ports of London, Bristol, Liverpool and Hull. Coming from the north, south, east and west the canals probed right into Birmingham, which had more miles of waterways than Venice.

The canals created a landscape of their own, a landscape of bridges, viaducts, locks and tunnels representing man's ingenuity in overcoming the barriers set up by nature. A walk along the narrow towpath of Telford's aqueduct at Pont-Cysyllte – 1,000 ft long and 127 ft above the wooded gorge of the River Dee – powerfully illustrates the command that the engineering giants of the 18th century exercised over their environment. The future belonged to them and to the engineers that followed. How they fulfilled their trust became apparent in the next decades.

RE-CREATING ARCADY Inspired by memories of the Grand Tour, and of antiquities set in the sunwashed landscapes of Greece and Italy, many 18th-century landowners swept away the geometric gardens, the parterres, arbours and pleasances so painstakingly established by their forebears. They replaced them instead with contrived 'natural' landscapes that reached to the very windows of their houses. Both they and the 'scenic engineers' they employed – men like William Kent and Lancelot 'Capability' Brown – were utterly ruthless in pursuit of the new ideal. If a hill marred the vista, it was simply removed, and perhaps a lake and a Grecian temple substituted. At Stourhead in Wiltshire (right), Brown transplanted an entire village because it interfered with the view. Yet landowners and gardeners alike possessed a touching faith in the future; the landscapes they planned, including the trees they planted, have reached their full glory only in our own time.

COLLECTOR'S ITEM Turnpikes – named from the pike-like barrier that could be raised or lowered across the way – were a feature of 18th-century roads. So, too, were the toll-houses – like this one by Telford near Holyhead on Anglesey – where the toll-keeper collected tolls from road-users before permitting them to pass.

BARGES OVER THE DEE Telford's Pont-Cysyllte aqueduct – 19 arches long and 127 ft high – shows how even the greatest of canal works could be made to harmonise with – or even enhance – the landscape.

SILENT STEPS Of the 79 locks along the grand sweep of the Kennet & Avon Canal between Reading and Bristol, 29 were built to create the Devizes Flight that carried the canal down the 236 ft descent of Caen Hill. This, the longest flight of broad locks in Britain, is derelict now, but with the entire canal is being gradually restored.

THE BRECON BEACONS

Like a sea frozen in time, the sandstone mountain crests ride above the green heart of Wales

This is a vast and arresting land, out of scale with the rest of South Wales, with mountains rearing up from it like the waves of some gigantic sea, frozen for ever on the point of breaking. The crests face north into the wild heart of Wales, turning away from the murk of the industrial valleys and probing the sky with their highest peaks.

The Brecon Beacons and their neighbours – Black Mountain to the west and the Black Mountains to the east – dominate the 519 sq. miles of the National Park. At 2,906 ft the summit of Pen y Fan is the highest point in Britain south of Snowdonia. Corn Dû is only 43 ft lower, and heights of more than 2,000 ft are commonplace.

In the northern valleys, plump beef and dairy cattle graze a patchwork of lush hedged pastures. On the lower slopes of the hills are great tracts of common land where cattle, sheep and long-maned ponies roam freely as they have done since long before the time when recorded history began.

The long moorlands sloping south from the crests are seamed by amply watered valleys whose streams are captured in many placid reservoirs. Towards the southern edge of the park the headstreams of the Neath race down wooded gorges, vanish into dark caves, and emerge again to thunder over waterfalls. These wild torrents contrast with the placid waters of Llangorse Lake, a paradise for aquatic birds,

and the gentle valley of the Usk, which cuts between the Beacons and the Black Mountains and winds through the northern fringe of the park.

The distinctive landscape of dramatic mountain crests was created by the heaving up and tilting of the Old Red Sandstone rocks; these had been formed from the sediment deposited 345-395 million years ago in the brackish seas that once covered the area. During the Ice Ages, glaciers ground away the northern slopes, scoured out great basins, or cwms, and left lakes such as Llyn-cwm-llwch and Llyn y Fan fach trapped by barriers of debris.

On the thick carpet of peat which covers the uplands, cotton-grass, heather, bilberries, purple moor-grass, fescue and mat-grass blend their subtle colours. Below the moors, huge conifer forests parade stiffly round the reservoirs giving shelter to tree pipits, whinchats and goldcrests. Beautiful woodlands of oak, ash, birch and beech enclose the dimpling streams of the south.

Bitter struggles have been fought for this land. The tribe of the Silures stubbornly resisted the Romans, who never achieved more than a superficial occupation here. The Marcher lords, who held great baronies under the Norman kings, were more successful, although plagued by rebellions of the Welsh heroes fighting for independence – Llywelyn ab Iorwerth, Llywelyn ab Gruffydd, and Owain Glyndwr. There are remnants still of Roman camps and Norman castles. Even older are the solitary Bronze Age megaliths, or standing stones, marking spots such as Maen Llia, whose significance is no longer known. According to local folklore, these ancient guardians of the park uproot themselves and roam the countryside on Midsummer Night, bringing an early death to anyone unlucky enough to see them.

SCULPTED BY ICE East of Pen y Fan, the Brecon Beacons loom above valleys carved by Ice Age glaciers. After the glaciers had retreated, water from the melting ice, lingering in the shaded northern pockets, cut grooves in the land beneath the hills.

Places to visit

Map ref. Aa Black Mountain

Scattered peaks soaring above a wilderness of jagged rocks, bogs, prehistoric burial chambers and long-abandoned quarries are the reality of Black Mountain – for despite its name, it is a range of mountains, triangular and widening from Ammanford at the south-western corner to a long scarp over the Tawe Valley at the eastern end. The whole area is the home of curlews, snipe, ring ouzels and buzzards, and of hardy sheep that are sometimes rounded up by shepherds on horseback for shearing or dipping.

Treeless moorland riven by dark, peaty valleys slopes up from the south to reach the highest summits in the north-east corner. Here the steep, cliff-topped scarp of Fan Foel juts out in an immense tongue. Bannau Brycheiniog, Fan Foel's highest point at 2,630 ft, towers over great banks of scree on the Fan's north-east face with Llyn y Fan fawr, 'Big Lake of the Fan', tucked below. The summit gives an enormous view – south to Exmoor, west to Mynydd Preseli (the Presely Mountain), and north to Cader Idris.

The Fan's north-west face is the dramatic red cliff of Bannau Sir Gaer, 2,460 ft high and curving to enclose the secret, dark water of Llyn y Fan fach, 'Little Lake of the Fan', 500 ft below.

The lake was the legendary home of a beautiful water fairy who fell in love with Rhiwallon, a farmer from the Sawdde Valley, and married him on condition that he would never touch her with iron. Accidentally he broke the pledge after years of marriage and she returned to the lake, taking back her dowry of cattle but leaving behind her three sons. She met the sons later and taught them her secret herbal cures. The sons became physicians at Myddfai, a village 6 miles to the north. Their descendants were still physicians in the 19th century.

A glorious 3 mile walk starts at Llyn y Fan fach, climbs to the top of the scarp, and follows it out to the tip of Fan Foel's tongue and round to the summit of Bannau Brycheiniog.

A 2½ mile track leading east from the village of Llanddeusant leads to Llyn y Fan fach. Llanddeusant is 3 miles along a minor road that branches east from the A4069, 3 miles south-east of Llangadog.

Cb Bwlch

Scanty fragments of purple stone wall, a tumbledown tower and a sycamore-clad mound within a silted ditch are all that remain of the Norman stronghold of Castell Blaenllynfi half a mile north of Bwlch. It was built to command the valleys of the Usk and the Llynfi when Brecon was a Norman lordship.

The village, a borough in Norman times, is set in the high gap between Buckland Hill and the southern tips of Allt yr Esgair and Cefn Moel. Roman soldiers marched through here from their fort at Pen y Gaer, 1½ miles to the east, towards Brecon. The Roman road heaved up over the pass – the Welsh *bwlch* means 'pass' – as the modern road does now.

The castle that is now barely a skeleton was a formidable strongpoint when Llewelyn the Great was fighting for Welsh independence from King John in 1214. It was one of the castles that Llewelyn and his Norman son-in-law Reginald de Braose recaptured for the de Braose family. It had belonged to Reginald's father, William, most powerful of Marcher lords and a friend of King John until a fierce quarrel in 1207. William was declared an outlaw

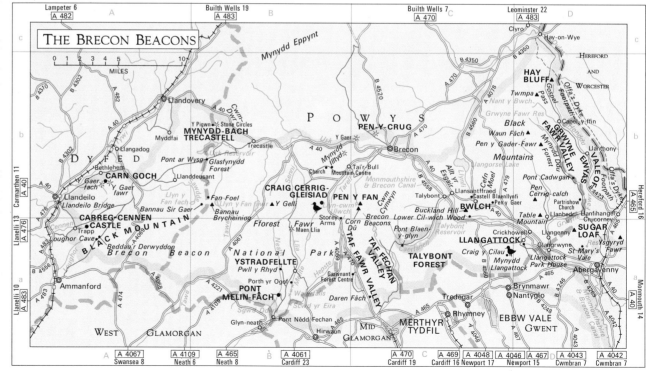

and had to flee to France, losing all his Welsh possessions.

The most delightful of many walks from the village climbs the wooded ridge of Buckland Hill to 1,038 ft, then drops down to the Usk where the slow, gentle water winds beneath the great hills. A lower path returns past the broad-leaved Lower Cil-wich Wood and round the foot of Buckland Hill to complete a 3 mile circuit.

Bwlch is on the A40, 8 miles south-east of Brecon.

Ab Carn Goch

Above ferny lanes sprinkled with fox-gloves stands the long mass of Carn Goch, crowned by the rugged silhouette of its ancient Iron Age hill-fort. The tumbled, pale grey ramparts of loose stones guard the two highest points of the hill. The builders of this largest hill-fort in Wales chose their site well and made the most of its natural defences. Where the hillside is precipitous they built little, and they made their greatest efforts at the most vulnerable points; the walls are still 15-20 ft high in places. The main part of the defences, Y Gaer fawr, 'The Big Fort', was large enough for the whole tribe and their cattle to go to for safety when an attack came. Y Gaer fach, 'The Little Fort', to the west may have been an outer defensive area.

The ridge is 700 ft high and commands sweeping views of the surrounding countryside. Any attackers would have had to advance up the steep slopes under a hail of slingshots from warriors manning the ramparts.

The power of the fort shows best not from within it but from the village of Bethlehem to the north at the foot of the hill. In spring the ramparts stand

Y GELLI

AROUND BLACK MOUNTAIN The flat summit of Y Gelli (above) sits on the cloud-wreathed skyline east of the Black Mountain. Llyn y Fan fach reservoir (right) lies below Bannau Sir Gaer, the Black Mountain's northern face of sandstone cliffs.

out from the green hillside unmasked by the brackens that thrust up later.

Just west of Bethlehem Church a grassy footpath mounts the hill and passes through the fort. The climb is worth it for the views from the summit. Below and to the north-west the winding River Towy loops between the meadows. Llandeilo, set on a hill, is a major landmark to the south-west.

Carn Goch is 3 miles south-west of Llangadog, along a minor road that branches west off the A4069.

LLYN Y FAN FACH

Aa Carreg-Cennen Castle

Perched on the brink of a lofty limestone crag, Carreg-Cennen Castle stands 300 ft above the narrow valley of the River Cennen, which winds its way beneath the bare north-west slopes of the brooding Black Mountain. Ravens and kestrels nest on the cliff-face below the castle, above the green blanket of ash, elm, yew and hawthorn that clothes the lower face. Across the valley, broad-winged buzzards circle high above the mountain slopes.

In the castle courtyard opposite the ruined gatehouse is the entrance to a 230 ft long passage cut through the rock, with valley views from a number of loopholes along its length. It leads to a cave in the cliff – perhaps the first stronghold occupied at the site. Because of its fine defensive position, the cliff-top has probably been fortified for at least 2,000 years; Roman coins of the 1st and 2nd centuries have been found on the site. The first stone defences were built there in the 12th century by Rhys ap Gruffydd, ruler of the South Wales kingdom of Deheubarth.

The crumbling walls and towers of the existing castle date from the 13th and 14th centuries. Their stones last rang to the sound of conflict in 1462 during the Wars of the Roses. The defending Red Rose Lancastrians finally agreed to surrender to the attacking White Rose Yorkists, who later set 500 men to smash the castle foundations.

The best views of the castle, in its spectacular cliff-top setting against a background of high, rolling hills, are from the other side of the Cennen valley. Southwards from the castle, a public footpath leads over the river and across streams and fields to climb to a

AWARD FOR SERVICE Carreg-Cennen Castle was built by Welshmen in the 13th century, but changed hands many times. Henry Tudor gave it to Sir Rhys ap Thomas, who helped to put him on the English throne, as Henry VII, in 1485.

cave that shelters the source of the River Loughor.

Not far north-east of the Loughor cave, near a minor road, there are some long, low, grass-covered 'pillow' mounds. The place is called Beddau'r Derwyddon, or the Druids' Graves. But despite the romantic name, the mounds are really man-made rabbit warrens, built in medieval times for breeding and rearing rabbits to add to the meat supply. From the mounds, a track leads back across fields to the castle. The walk from the castle and back covers about 5 miles.

Carreg-Cennen Castle can be reached from Trapp, which lies 3 miles south-east of Llandeilo along a minor road branching east from the A483 about 600 yds south of Llandeilo Bridge. The castle car park is 1 mile east of Trapp.

Bb Craig Cerrig-gleisiad

The high, brooding crags of Craig Cerrig-gleisiad sweep round in a half-circle of steep smooth walls scattered with rowans and enclosing an empty valley. Ravens soar from their nests on the cliff-face to hang lazily above, dipping and swaying gracefully as unseen currents change their course.

The 2,000 ft crag is awesome evidence of how the Ice Age glaciers carved a hollow into the soft face of the Old Red Sandstone. The whole three-quarter mile crescent swinging west and north is part of a National Nature Reserve, for it marks the southern limit of arctic-alpine plants. On the moist north-facing slopes, which get little sun, are green spleenworts, Dovedale moss, purple saxifrages, globe

flowers and evergreen cowberries.

The grandeur of the crags is best seen from a footpath that leads across the hollow below them. The path continues beyond the hollow, following mountain paths and bridleways for 4 miles until it reaches the National Park's Mountain Centre on the edge of Mynydd Illtyd Common. In a hollow on the common are two huge mossy stones hidden among the bracken. They mark the burial place of Illtyd, who in the 5th century was one of the first great Christian missionaries of Wales. The large circular enclosure round the 19th-century church was probably marked out in Illtyd's time. Beyond the grazing sheep and ponies, in the north-east corner of the common, are the ditch and rampart of an Iron Age hill-fort where tribesmen took refuge during local skirmishes.

On the road south of Craig Cerrig-gleisiad the pass at Storey Arms is only a good mile away. A bridleway starts there and leads north towards Brecon along the east side of the Tarell Valley. Until early in the 19th century, when a turnpike road was built between Brecon and Merthyr Tydfil, this was the main drove route over the mountains. It was etched into the landscape by generations of cattle and sheep as they were driven northwards to graze on the Usk valley pastures.

The footpath to Craig Cerrig-gleisiad leads from the A470 at a point 7 miles south-west of Brecon and just 350 yds south of a marked picnic site.

Db Grwyne Fawr Valley

Cutting through the heart of the Black Mountains is the long, narrow valley of the Grwyne Fawr. The river's head lies at 2,200 ft, above the steep north-west scarp of the mountains. The river rushes through its high moorland valley below the barren summits of the 2,660 ft Waun Fâch and the 2,624 ft Pen y Gader Fawr, the two highest points in the Black Mountains. Their steep slopes are reflected in the small Grwyne Fawr Reservoir, where the river is checked before it rushes on again to enter the shady mixed woodland of Mynydd Ddu Forest. Towards the southern end of the forest, just above Pont Cadwgan, there is a forest trail which takes about one and a half hours to walk. It passes one of several deserted farmsteads in the valley, a poignant reminder of the days when the people moved south to make a living in the coalfields.

It is a long but exhilarating walk to the very source of the river up the 6 mile track that continues beyond the forest trail. Downstream from Pont Cadwgan there is another enjoyable but quite different walk. The river winds through beautiful oakwoods. Hidden in a narrow lane up the hillside west of the river is the valley's greatest treasure, the 11th-century Partrishow Church.

From Glangrwyne on the A40, 4 miles west of Abergavenny, follow the minor road through Llangenny, past the turn-off to Llanbedr, and a further 3 miles to a left turn marked Partrishow and Mynydd Du Forest. The forest trail starts from a car park 3 miles up this road.

Db **Hay Bluff**

Nothing surpasses the breathtaking prospect spreading in all directions from the tip of Hay Bluff. South-west runs the edge of the Black Mountains and the Brecon Beacons – mountains which form the backbone of the

National Park. North-west the crests and valleys roll over the heart of Wales towards Snowdon, northwards lie the hills of Shropshire, and eastwards is the long, hump-backed line of the Malvern Hills.

The 2,220 ft high summit of the Bluff, no more than 300 yds from the border between Wales and England, is one of the most accessible peaks in the Black Mountains. Only a steep half-mile walk is needed up the western slope from the small car park 1,550 ft up on the narrow Gospel Pass road between Hay-on-Wye and the Vale of Ewyas. Even from the road the panorama is almost as vast. Along the eastern side of the long triangle of land mounting to the summit runs the Offa's Dyke long-distance footpath, another magnificent vantage point overlooking the lush farmlands of Hereford and Worcester.

In the foreground down below the Bluff is the town of Hay-on-Wye, with its narrow medieval streets and traces of old wall and castle. Moll Walbee was the best-known inhabitant of the castle. That was the local name for Maud de St Valérie, the stout-hearted wife of the ill-famed William de Braose, the powerful Marcher lord notorious for his murder of 70 Welshmen who were his guests. When William quarrelled with his friend King John and had to flee, Maud remained in charge of Hay Castle. The king tried to make her hand over her sons as guarantee of their father's future compliance, but Maud refused. The king cast her and one of her sons into the dungeons at Corfe Castle in Dorset (though some say it was Windsor), and there they starved to death.

Just a mile north-west of Hay is Clyro, where Francis Kilvert was curate

SCENE FROM HAY BLUFF The view, half masked by the sombre slopes of Twmpa, overlooks the Dulas valley towards the distant peak of Pen y Fan.

from 1870–9. His diaries bring vividly to life the countryside round Hay where he loved to walk.

A good walk of just over 2 miles runs south-westwards from Hay Bluff along the escarpment, crosses the Gospel

Pass road and finally climbs to the 2,263 ft high summit of Twmpa. From this summit a 3½ mile path descends first south-west into the Nant y Bwch valley and then down the steep, stream-cut valley to the tiny hamlet of

Capel-y-ffin on the River Honddu in the upper Vale of Ewyas.

Hay Bluff is 4 miles south of Hay-on-Wye. The minor road leading up to the car park on the hillside leaves the B4350 just west of the town.

Da Llangattock

Behind the village of Llangattock looms the great mountain mass of Mynydd Llangattock, divided from the village below by rugged limestone crags. Old quarries are strung along the cliff-face, linked now by the grassy track that was once a tramway for carrying the stone to the ironworks of Nantyglo. Cottages once occupied by quarrymen still dot the steep slopes.

One stretch of the crag is the 157 acre Craig y Cilau National Nature Reserve. The large and the small-leaved limes grow here, and the lesser whitebeam – a relative of the rowan and unique to the area. Alpine enchanter's nightshade, hawkweeds and angular Solomon's seal cling to the rocky ledges. The scree and rock faces are dangerously loose; binoculars used from the tracks give safe views.

Caves and passages tunnel inside the mountain. The surface is pitted with swallow-holes where the soft rock has collapsed into a cavity beneath. Within the reserve is the entrance to Agen Allwedd, 'The Keyhole', a 12 mile labyrinth of caves and tunnels. Only experienced cavers with permits are allowed to enter.

Down in the attractive village of Llangattock, stone-built weavers' cottages stand beside the lanes, and pretty stone bridges cross the streams and the winding Monmouthshire and Brecon Canal. The Church of St Catwg has the old stocks and whipping-post inside

it – fixtures where drunken weavers and worse were punished.

On the south-western edge of the village the lane forks. The left fork passes Llangattock Park House and joins a path leading to the crags and the old tramway. The right fork connects after 3¼ miles with the B4560, the only road over Mynydd Llangattock. It gives beautiful views back over the Usk valley to the Black Mountains with Table Mountain and Pen Cerrig-calch notable landmarks behind Crickhowell.

Llangattock is ¼ mile across the Usk from Crickhowell, which is on the A40, 6 miles north-west of Abergavenny.

Bb Mynydd-bach Trecastell

Stone circles high on the moorland of Mynydd-bach Trecastell suggest that Bronze Age people pioneered a route along the high ridge between Trecastle and Llandovery almost 4,000 years ago. Generations of travellers followed them on the track – on foot, with carts, in chariots, or in carriages – until the early 19th century, when the road that is now the A40 replaced it.

The old road runs arrow-straight for much of the way, and is tar-sealed for more than 2 miles west of Trecastle. It then becomes a grassy but well-marked track, perfect for easy walking and for pony-trekking. The broad ridge along which it runs rises between the headwaters of the River Usk and the wooded gorge of Cwm-Dwr. The Romans certainly marched along the ridge during the 25 years they campaigned against the obdurate tribe of the Silures from about AD 50. Just north of the track at the highest point on the ridge – 1,353 ft – are the low, grass-covered banks that outline the two superimposed marching camps of

BIRDS OF VALE AND FOREST

Only in the mountains of central Wales can the red kite be seen in Britain today. A common bird in medieval times, 19th-century persecution by gamekeepers and farmers has led almost to its extinction. Its forked tail and white underwing patches help identify the bird as it circles high above wooded valleys hunting for small animals, frogs and fledglings. The goldcrest is a bird of the conifer forests. One of Britain's smallest birds, it is more often heard than seen, as it spends most of its time in the high tree-tops. Its song is a series of high-pitched notes, ending with a squeaky twitter. Both male and female have a distinctive yellow crest, but the male's crest has a deep orange centre.

Red kite
(Milvus milvus)

Goldcrest
(Regulus regulus)

Y Pigwn. These were only temporary camps for use during thrusts into the alien territory, but they could hold 10,000 soldiers encamped in their tents.

Views south-west and south-east of the ridge embrace the Black Mountain and the Brecon Beacons. South of the track, woodlands shelter the Usk Reservoir. The dam is 1,575 ft long, holds back 2,700 million gallons of water, and supplies Swansea. The road to the reservoir swings south through the woods, after running alongside the southern bank, and joins a road that leads to a delightful spot, Pont ar Wysg. Here the Usk is only 3 miles down from its source. The Glasfynydd Forest lines one bank, and from the other rises airy open moorland.

Trecastle is on the A40, 8 miles east of Llandovery. The minor road running west from Trecastle leads to the reservoir, where there is a car park. For Mynydd-bach Trecastell, take the fork to the right 700 yds from the start of the minor road.

Cb Pen-y-crug

Five ramparts and ditches encircle the conical tip of Pen-y-crug. Although worn down by 2,000 years of erosion, the earthworks are still clearly visible. They enclose an area more than 500 yds across at the 1,087 ft summit of the hill.

The warlike Celtic immigrants who came to Britain from northern France about 300 BC were fine judges of a strategic site. Hilltops were their choice. Pen-y-crug commands the valleys radiating from present-day Brecon. Its views reach south over wooded valleys to the Brecon Beacons and north to the upland wilderness of Mynydd Eppynt. It gave the Celts a lookout point and a safe refuge – for themselves and for the cattle and horses they reared – when marauding bands from other tribes came raiding.

The strategic importance of the area attracted the Romans also in their push into Wales about AD 75. Two miles west of Pen-y-crug is the 5 acre site of Y Gaer, the largest in Wales of the forts that were built between the huge legionary fortresses, such as Caerleon, to control the interior of the conquered territory. Y Gaer could accommodate 1,000 auxiliaries drawn from the conquered tribes of the empire. Originally it had a timber-palisaded bank protected by two ditches, and the buildings inside were of wood. During the 2nd century the ramparts were rebuilt in stone. Later that century the fort was badly damaged by the Celts, but it was repaired and occupied on and off until the Romans left Britain about AD 450. Sir Mortimer Wheeler excavated the site in 1924.

Danewort, the rare, wild dwarf elder, grows in the fields round the fort and scents the air of early summer with its creamy flowers.

Pen-y-crug is 1 mile north-west of Brecon along a marked minor road off the B4520. A marked footpath leads to the summit. Y Gaer is signposted from the A40, 4 miles west of Brecon.

Cb   Pen y Fan

The long wave of red sandstone that swells up gradually from the South Wales coalfield reaches its crest at the steep, scalloped rim of crags facing north to Brecon. These are the unmistakable outlines of the Brecon Beacons – five great flat-topped noses jutting out between the four deep round-headed valleys or cwms.

The highest of the jutting noses is Pen y Fan at 2,906 ft; the nearby Corn Dû is 2,863 ft. These two are capped by a hard band of rock called plateau beds which has remained steeper and less weathered than the other summits. Pen y Fan's 600 ft high band is layered so uniformly that it looks as if the rocks were laid on by hand. The slopes and summits are too barren to attract many animals, but buzzards and ravens nest on them.

In the cwms, where the sun could not reach, the Ice Age glaciers became deepest and stayed longest. They bored down at the base and, when they finally retreated, left heaps of rocks and rubble over which the valley streams dimple and bubble. Below Pen y Fan the rubble formed a dam behind which the small lake, Llyn-cwm-llwch, was trapped. The most attractive approach to the mountain is up the 3 mile path that runs upstream to the lake, then climbs the steep crag behind the lake to mount the ridge and turn east along it to Pen y Fan.

From the summit immense views look over Brecon to Cader Idris, over the fields of Hereford to the Malverns, and over the Bristol Channel to the hills of Somerset and Devon beyond.

To reach the summit, turn east from the A470, 3¼ miles south-west of Brecon on to a minor road at Tai'r-Bull; follow this for ¾ mile and, where the road turns sharp left, carry straight on along the track and path.

Ba   Pont Melin-fâch

Smooth natural platforms of grey rock hang over seething misty cauldrons where the upper waters of the River Neath roar over waterfalls into the deep pools beneath. A footpath from

SPECTACULAR PLUNGE Sgwd Ddwli, a mile south of Pont Melin-fâch, is among the finest of the falls along this stretch of the River Neath.

Pont Melin-fâch, 'Bridge by the Little Mill', follows the western side of the river downstream on a marvellous, but not easy, course – now on a ledge where the sheet of water rolls off the edge, now scrambling down a steep ravine to a shelf beside the pool below.

In the cool, damp world under the ash trees, alders, oaks and wych elms are mossy rocks, and among them the vivid green of hartstongue ferns, shield ferns and bladder ferns. Close to the bridge there is a beautiful and secluded picnic place, and running upstream from it is another path which runs a good 2 miles, crossing the river once, to Pwll y Rhyd.

This is near the edge of the soft limestone outcrop into which the river has cut so deeply to make the fairytale cascades and gorges. At Pwll y Rhyd the river has worn a chasm so deep and narrow that the water has disappeared; it rumbles far below the boulder-strewn surface. Caves and tunnels writhe beneath the rocks – but these are accessible only to experienced cavers.

Leave the A465, 10 miles west of Merthyr Tydfil, and take the B4242 to Pont Nêdd Fechan. Take the minor road north towards Ystradfellte and after 2 miles a road branches left to Pont Melin-fâch. There is a car park near the picnic site.

Da   The Sugar Loaf

The unmistakable cone of the Sugar Loaf mountain stands neat and distinct to the north-west of Abergavenny. Its graceful ridge, rising above three great shoulders, makes it by far the most outstanding feature in the landscape, though it possesses little of the steepness usually associated with the sugar-loaf shape. Its green flanks are gashed

with red sandstone, patched with bracken, splashed with gorse, and – in early autumn – covered with the ground-hugging dwarf shrubs that conceal powdered purple bilberries beneath every leaf.

Bulky shoulders buttress the lower slopes of the mountain and ridge tracks surmount them to lead to the 1,995 ft summit. This is surprisingly spacious – not pointed but a tilted sheet of rock and grass. Now the full and varied panorama opens below: Ysgyryd Fawr, the Malverns, and the Cotswolds to the east, the Black Mountains mass to the north, the gentle Usk skirting the Brecon Beacons to the west, and south, beyond the industrial valleys, a glimpse of the Severn.

This view is not gained without effort. The many paths to the summit involve some stiff walking. From the parking place on the southern approach a 2 mile grassy track takes a winding course upwards – and on the way crosses other, steeper ascents. The car park itself is at a magnificent viewpoint 1,132 ft above the Usk.

Lying below the car park, to the east, is St Mary's Vale twisting through a lovely deciduous wood. In the bracken-thick glades are handsome oaks, while alders line the stream and massive beeches make dense pools of shade. The chiffchaff's loud call resounds among the trees. Part of the valley was the site of intensive iron smelting in the 18th and 19th centuries. A nature trail is laid out in the wood and takes about one and a half hours of leisurely walking to complete.

The car park and viewpoint are 1¼ miles off the A40 on the western outskirts of Abergavenny, and reached by a turning marked at Pentre Road. The nature trail starts near Llwyndu Reservoir.

The tall, purple-headed meadow thistle, or marsh plume thistle, is a wild flower of damp or marshy ground, where it may grow to a height of 2 ft. Matching it in height is the greater spearwort, its bright yellow flowers measuring up to 2 in. across. The spear-shaped leaves distinguish the plant from its cousin, the buttercup. On the same damp ground grows the water avens, a member of the rose family. Its nodding flowers are usually orange-pink. The hooked seeds spread by attaching to the fur of passing animals.

Meadow thistle
(*Cirsium dissectum*)

Greater spearwort
(*Ranunculus lingua*)

Water avens
(*Geum rivale*)

Ba   Taf Fawr Valley

Under open skies and bare, smooth moors is the silken sheen of a lake reflecting the dark forests at its fringes or suddenly ruched by a stir of wind. This glorious scene is there to relish three times on the drive south down the Taf Fawr Valley from its head at the 1,400 ft pass over Storey Arms until it narrows at the southern end beneath the crags of Daren Fâch, where sandstone suddenly gives way to limestone. The road over the pass was originally a turnpike road. It was used in the 19th century by carts carrying farm produce to the industrial south.

The three stretches of water and the forests are man-made, but they have added life, variety and beauty to the barren moors. The reservoirs were built between 1892 and 1927 to supply water for Cardiff, and most of the trees have been planted since 1950. It takes 50 years for the trees to reach full size but already some are being felled. This gives the remainder more space to thrive. The thinnings are sent to pulp and paper mills, and to sawmills to make pit props.

The varied golds and ambers of oak, rowan, sycamore, birch and willow enrich the forest in autumn, for these trees have planted themselves in the valley. In spring, too, their fresh leaves – and the new, delicate green fronds of the larches – enliven the darker evergreen conifers.

Just above the head of the southern reservoir, a road branches west to the

SHADOWED WATERS Below the northern slopes of Corn Dû, Llyn-cwm-llwch, a lake said to be the haunt of fairies, has lain trapped in a sunless hollow since the Ice Ages.

Garwnant Forest Centre, housed in a former farm on a wooded slope overlooking the water. Waymarked trails, from 1¼ to 3½ miles long, start from the centre and wind among the glades. The forest, the water and the surrounding moorland give food and shelter to a wide range of creatures, among them foxes, hares, grass snakes, hovering sparrowhawks, and the very small, but pugnacious, goldcrest. Its nest is attached by 'handles' to a branch, usually in a conifer. With yellow-orange blaze vivid on the crown, the birds will dart out to peck at any animal intruder.

The road from Storey Arms is the A470. At the valley's southern end, 8 miles from Storey Arms, it connects with the A465 on the northern outskirts of Merthyr Tydfil.

Ca Taf Fechan Valley

The sylvan beauties of the Taf Fechan Valley as it is today had a miserable start. A cholera epidemic in Merthyr Tydfil in 1854 demonstrated tragically the need for an unpolluted water supply. The town's health authority got permission to make a reservoir in the valley, and work was completed on it by 1859. Three more reservoirs were created between 1884 and 1927, and now the chain of man-made lakes runs down the valley for 5 miles, sheltered beneath the huge conifer forests that protect the hillsides from erosion.

Miles of waymarked woodland trails thread through the forest in the shady green avenues on a soft, silent carpet of amber needles. It is difficult to believe that the forest starts only 4 miles from the industrial hubbub of Merthyr Tydfil. The trails start from the car parks that are on the road running through the woods on the western side of the lower reservoirs. From the furthest car park a track runs north above the eastern side of the upper reservoirs to the very edge of the Beacons crest only 2½ miles away. Here an immense view stretches north over the Usk and Brecon towards Cader Idris. From the crest the track plunges down Cwm Cynwyn in the direction of Brecon, for the track is following the old bridleway that went from Merthyr to Brecon.

The thriving forests of the valley have not become established unopposed. The field vole, waging its private war on them, has often caused damage when its very variable population has reached a peak. There was a plague of the creatures in 1956 that damaged one-third of the valley's four-year-old Lawson cypresses.

The road up the Taf Fechan Valley is marked from the A465 (Heads of the Valleys Road) on the northern outskirts of Merthyr Tydfil.

Ca Talybont Forest

The irresistible music of waterfalls, tumbling down cliffs of dark red sandstone, fills the air in the western crescent of Talybont Forest. Nine cas-

SHELTERED VALLEY The secluded Vale of Ewyas shelters beneath the mighty flanks of the Black Mountains.

cades, some making spectacular leaps, some splashing gently, glint through the trees along the tracks west of Pont Blaen-y-glyn. They are on the course of the Nant Bricfwr and its parent the Caerfanell, which flow from the lofty moors to be caught in Talybont Reservoir before joining the Usk.

Waymarked trails start from Pont Blaen-y-glyn and wind through the forest. High up the southern slope a green strand lies between the vast stretches of pine, larch and spruce, all planted since 1950 between the few stands of native oak, ash and alder. The strand follows the course of the old railway that ran beside the quarries on the hillside and looped round to Merthyr Tydfil. Before the railway was built, ponies used to drag sledges laden with stone down to Merthyr.

The eastern arms of Talybont Forest embrace Talybont Reservoir, keeping its water sheltered and still. Large colonies of wildfowl are attracted to it in winter – coot, teal, pochard, mallard, tufted duck, goldeneye, goosander, wigeon, shoveler, whooper swan, heron, great crested grebe and cormorant all congregate on the waters and the marshy southern shore.

The reservoir was completed in 1938 to provide water for Newport. It has a capacity of 2,567 million gallons and a dam 97 ft high. Rhododendrons bloom at the dam in colourful profusion during early summer.

From the A40, 6 miles south-east of Brecon, a minor road branches south-west at Llansantffraed to cross the Usk to Talybont. From the village the road runs down the western side of the reservoir to Pont Blaen-y-glyn. There are car parks at the reservoir, at Pont Blaen-y-glyn, and at the western edge of the forest, 6 miles beyond Talybont village.

Db Vale of Ewyas

Far beneath the long steep ridges that guard it, runs the beautiful sheltered valley of the Honddu. The ridges are more than 2,000 ft above sea-level for much of their length, thrusting forward to narrow the valley as it twists beneath them. Trees hang above the water in the lower stretches but upstream great purple cliffs rise, and near the source only a few thorns cling to the red-gashed slopes. Wood warblers, redstarts, woodpeckers and pied flycatchers are noisy in the woods while kestrels, ravens and ring ouzels haunt the crags, and red grouse breed up on the moors.

Numerous marked footpaths and bridleways climb the slopes from the valley and make it ideal for walks of different lengths. A minor road also runs north through the valley and over the 1,800 ft Gospel Pass at the head. There are spectacular expanses north from the road into the heart of Wales and west along the crests of the Black Mountains as the road drops down towards Hay-on-Wye. Offa's Dyke long-distance footpath runs along the top of the ridge at the east of the valley, marching along with the boundary of the National Park and the border with England.

Llanthony Priory is 6 miles up the valley; now only lovely fragments of the 12th-century towers, high walls and pointed arches remain. Giraldus, the 12th-century chronicler, wrote after visiting the priory: 'Here the monks, sitting in the cloisters, enjoying the fresh air, when they happen to look up towards the horizon behold the tops of the mountains touching the heavens and herds of wild deer feeding on their summits.'

A much later religious foundation still stands 4 miles upstream from the priory at Capel-y-ffin. The brick pseudo-Gothic monastery was the enterprise of an Anglican deacon, Joseph Leycester Lyne, who called himself Father Ignatius. He attracted passionate adherents by his fiery preaching and repelled equally passionate opponents by his showmanship. His community broke up soon after his death in 1908.

Eric Gill bought the monastery in the 1920s and lived there with a group of other artists and their families. Gill's sculptures, type-face designs and wood engravings displayed his versatility. The monastery is the subject of some of his engravings.

The road through the Vale of Ewyas is the B4423, which branches off the A465 at Llanfihangel Crucorney, 4 miles north of Abergavenny.

Ba Ystradfellte

Romantic wooded gorges and the exciting plunge of foaming cascades make the walk down the Mellte Valley one of rare enchantment. The path starts from Porth yr Ogof, 'Entrance to the Cave', less than a mile south of Ystradfellte, but it does not follow the river for long. The water suddenly vanishes into the wide cavern below a towering cliff into a long stretch of limestone caves – whose exploration is strictly for the experts – to emerge dancing and bubbling from its rocky arch a few hundred yards further on and rush down the valley to its three beautiful waterfalls.

At the horseshoe-shaped middle fall you can stand on the flat shelf beside the wide crescent of water as it rolls over the brink, and see it frothing down the rocks and through the dappled green valley. The path which has scrambled with difficulty alongside the stream cuts across the woodland from the lower fall to the Mellte's main tributary, the Hepste. Here the Sgwd yr Eira, 'Fall of Snow', makes a spectacular leap of 40-50 ft into a deep plunge pool while behind its sparkling, hissing curtain there runs a broad path – so broad that farmers used to drive their stock along it.

Alternate bands of hard sandstone and soft shales have created the falls. The sandstone has resisted erosion but the soft shales have been worn away by the water until they now lie far below the level of the sandstone.

The area is a favourite haunt of dippers, small brown birds with white bibs. They sit bobbing on the rocks or walk in the shallows, often against the stream, with heads below water looking for food.

North of Ystradfellte, a road follows the stream of the Llia towards its source in the wilderness of Fforest Fawr, a tract of open moorland that was a royal hunting ground in medieval times. Near the road's highest point, some 1,400 ft above sea-level, is the huge megalith of Maen Llia. Erected during the Bronze Age, perhaps as a memorial, it has been used through the ensuing centuries as a marker for the routes over the moor. The stone is 12 ft high, 9 ft wide, and almost 3 ft thick. From just north of the stone there are beautiful views down the Senni Valley, where a patchwork of fields nestles among mountains rising to more than 2,000 ft.

Ystradfellte is 6 miles north of Hirwaun, and can be reached by a minor road which leaves the A4059, 4 miles north of Hirwaun.

THE GOWER PENINSULA

A little world whose seclusion and character have
been decreed by geography and history

The first inhabitant of Gower that we know about was a young man whose ochre-smeared skeleton, with a mammoth skull at its feet, was found in Paviland Cave; the latest are the summer campers at Port-Eynon who have come to enjoy, for a week or so, the unrivalled peace of the gentle peninsula. Their dwellings are separated by about a mile and a half and some 30,000 years.

All found the place hospitable, and so, too, have most of the people who have come to Gower in the centuries intervening – farmers and warriors of the Bronze and Iron Ages, Roman soldiers, Celtic saints, Vikings, Saxons, land-hungry Normans, medieval settlers from the West of England, miners of zinc, copper, lead and coal. All have left their marks on the language or landscape, slowly creating a country that is not quite Wales and certainly not England, but a place unique unto itself.

People apart, the mainspring of Gower is the sea. It can be seen from most places on the peninsula, and heard, too, snoring gently at the foot of the great limestone cliffs or, in the aftermath of a westerly gale, roaring in to break upon the vast beaches in clouds of rainbow-hued spray. The sea has provided much of Gower's livelihood since the beginning. Some of its bounty – like cockles and fish – was legitimately acquired, but some of it came by darker means. Though heroic tales of

rescuing men from the sea abound in the peninsula's history, ships that were driven ashore were considered fair game, and many a wreck was stripped to its ribs long before the authorities could reach it. And smuggling here was not just a profitable sideline – it was a full-scale industry.

Much of the natural history, too, has been influenced by the ocean. Thousands of sea-birds nest on the cliffs, and the lonely salt-marshes of the north shore are carpeted with rice-grass, sea lavender and marsh mallow, and populated by geese, teal, oystercatchers and snipe.

The best – indeed, in many places the only – way to explore Gower is on foot. There is a wide network of footpaths that runs round most of the coast, taking you by way of cliffs and wide, empty beaches to caves once inhabited by prehistoric men and beasts, to castles, an ancient wreck or two, strange rock formations, pretty villages and nature reserves. Inland, woods, tracts of common land and hills with views over the entire peninsula are linked together by miles of footpaths and bridleways. One particularly attractive walk starts from Penmaen, high above Threecliff Bay, and runs along Cefn Bryn ridge to the prehistoric burial chamber of Arthur's Stone. From here, the views stretch far beyond Gower to the Brecon Beacons and the West Country.

From here, too, you can appreciate how Gower is cut off from the rest of the world. The roads are few and were, until fairly recent times, atrocious. Great events largely passed the place by, and even its language, an ancient form of West Country English dialect intermixed with a touch of Welsh, has changed little since the Middle Ages. Visitors to this 'Little England Beyond Wales' will find themselves blessing this isolation.

SURF-POUNDED BEACH Rhossili Bay at the western end of the Gower peninsula curves from Worms Head north to Burry Holms, providing a 3 mile sweep of golden sands. Behind the 250 ft cliffs, the land rises to 632 ft on Rhossili Down.

Places to visit

Map ref. Aa **Burry Holms**

Memories of medieval monks cling to this tiny island at the northern end of Rhossili Bay. On the landward side, overlooked by the high dunes of Broughton Burrows and Llangennith Burrows, which must be crossed to reach the island, are the remains of a small religious settlement first mentioned in 1195; later, it was owned by All Souls College, Oxford. It was dedicated to St Cenydd, who founded a monastic community at Llangennith in the 6th century.

Cenydd is said to have been the illegitimate son of one of King Arthur's knights. According to legend he was born with a deformed leg, as a punishment for the sins of his parents, and cast adrift in a cradle on the Loughor estuary. The cradle drifted out beyond Whiteford Point, but the baby was rescued by sea-birds, taken to Worms Head – at the southern end of Rhossili Bay – and looked after by angels.

The limestone island is cut in half by a ditch believed to have been hacked out by Iron Age dwellers about 2,000 years ago. At that time, Burry Holms may well have been a headland rather than an island. Later, this elementary fortification may also have been used as a base by Viking raiders. 'Holms' is

derived from an Old Norse word meaning 'island'. The island is now joined to the mainland for just over two hours on either side of low water. Tide times should be obtained from the coastguard station by the car park at Rhossili.

Although it covers only 15¼ acres, The Holms, as it is known locally, has plenty of atmosphere, and is the haunt of sea-birds and waders. Birds likely to be seen on and near the rock-girt island include oystercatchers, dunlins, cormorants, fulmars, gannets and purple sandpipers.

From Llanrhidian, at the intersection of the B4271 and B4295, follow the signposted minor road to Llangennith. Walk or drive along the lane to Llangennith Burrows (where there is limited parking).

Cefn Bryn

Aa

The Gower peninsula is famed for its spectacular coastal scenery, but visitors who ignore inland Cefn Bryn are missing one of the peninsula's most interesting and attractive features. Formed of Old Red Sandstone, the bracken-clad ridge is the 'backbone' of Gower and runs north-westwards from Penmaen towards Burry Green. It reaches 609 ft – about the highest point on Gower after Rhossili Down – and can be walked from end to end following Talbot's Way, a green road named after a 19th-century occupier of Penrice Castle. Walkers share the ridge with free-roaming sheep and ponies.

There are superb round-the-compass views from the unfenced road that runs eastwards from Reynoldston. The Brecon Beacons, Mynydd Preseli (the Presely Mountain), Lundy island and parts of Somerset and Devon are clearly visible in good conditions. Oxwich Point and Rhossili Down are major

landmarks on Gower itself. There is also a roadside picnic place, complete with a view indicator, just off the A4118 in Penmaen.

From the point where the road from Reynoldston crosses the crest there is a short walk westwards to a remarkable example of prehistoric engineering, Arthur's Stone. This Bronze Age burial chamber is surmounted by a massive capstone that is estimated to weigh more than 25 tons. Despite its name, the chamber dates from about 2500 BC and was old long before the time of the legendary warrior-king.

A mile north-east of Arthur's Stone, near the point where the Reynoldston road joins the B4271, lies Broad Pool. This large expanse of water was formed when glacial clays lined a large hollow, or sink, carved out of Gower's underlying limestone by acidic water. The attractive pool, in which water-lilies grow, has been made a nature reserve which is owned by the Glamorgan Naturalists' Trust. Birds on and around the pool include mute swans, snipe, curlews and herons. Five minutes' walk

to the north-east is another massive sink, 30 ft deep, called Moor Mills. Several streams drain into it and vanish because there is no glacial clay to retain the water.

Penmaen, on the A4118, lies at the eastern end of Cefn Bryn and is a good starting point. Several minor roads off the A4118 west of Penmaen lead north on to the ridge.

Llanmadoc Hill

Aa

Reached by footpaths from Llanmadoc, Cheriton and Llangennith, this steep-sided, flat-topped hill dominates the north-west corner of Gower and is one of the peninsula's most rewarding viewpoints. Weobley Castle (*see Llanrhidian*) is a major landmark, perched on a steep slope above the green wilderness of Llanrhidian Marsh where streams known locally as 'pills' wriggle towards the sea like silver snakes.

The summit of the hill is 609 ft above the nearby sea, and shares with Cefn Bryn the distinction of being the

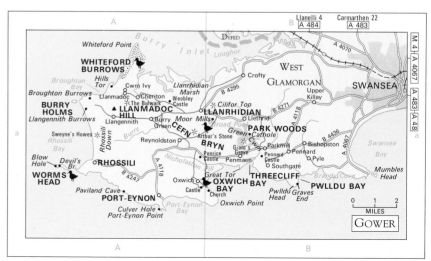

second highest point on the Gower peninsula. The highest, The Beacon on Rhossili Down, is just over 2 miles away to the south.

Sheep and ponies wander over the slopes, grazing on the springy upland turf that grows between thick carpets of bracken and gorse. The top of the hill forms a mile-long ridge whose eastern end is notable for a fine Iron Age earthwork known as The Bulwark. Although not easy to discern from the foot of the hill, the complexity of the enclosure's defences is obvious to walkers. On the western side there are no fewer than six banks and five ditches to protect what was probably a refuge in times of trouble rather than a permanent community. Cairns of tumbled stones elsewhere on the ridge are the remains of Bronze Age burial sites.

Llangennith, Llanmadoc and Cheriton lie on signposted minor roads to the west of Llanrhidian, at the junction of the B4295 and B4271.

Aa Llanrhidian

Built on a steep slope above the Loughor estuary, Llanrhidian overlooks an extensive wilderness of green tidal salt-marsh, beyond which are immense sandbanks where local people have harvested cockles for hundreds of years. Just over 4 miles to the northwest the abandoned lighthouse off Whiteford Point marks the seaward end of the estuary where huge expanses of muddy sand, carved by deep and steep-sided channels, glisten and shimmer at low tide.

For the naturalist, there is nothing quite like Llanrhidian Marsh anywhere else in Wales. The marsh itself is formed from tidal mud that has been trapped and stabilised by plants such as glasswort and rice-grass. On this has spread a sprawling growth of sea manna-grass, sea lavender, creeping fescue and marsh mallow which now provides grazing for sheep and ponies.

During the year, tens of thousands of starlings cross daily from the Pembrey side of the estuary to feed on the marsh and then return to roost. Other birds likely to be seen include mallard, teal, Brent geese, white-fronted geese, oystercatchers, curlews, snipe, dunlins, sanderlings, wigeons, golden, grey and ringed plovers, and flights of knots.

Cars may be parked along the unfenced lane between Llanrhidian and Crofty, but you should take expert advice before venturing on to the marsh. Walkers can easily be trapped by fast-rising tides. Also, it is advisable to keep to the paths as this area was a military firing range during the Second World War and there is still the risk of unexploded missiles off the beaten path. Tall stakes, that make parts of the marsh look like an enormous pincushion, also date from that period; they were placed there to prevent German gliders from landing.

Less than a mile east of Llanrhidian, the 386 ft summit of Cilifor Top is crowned with an extensive Iron Age fort dating from the 1st century BC. It covers about 8 acres and is the largest enclosure of its type on Gower. From within the three great ramparts and ditches that enclose the steep-sided hill, the Silures – the dominant Celtic tribe in Iron Age South Wales – were able to delay the Roman conquest of the area until late in the 1st century AD.

To the west of Llanrhidian, the lane that runs towards Cheriton and Llanmadoc passes Weobley Castle which,

LONG-BILLED MUSSEL-CRACKER

The noisy calling and piping sounds of oystercatchers can be heard round most of Britain's coasts. These duck-sized waders feed mainly on shellfish such as mussels, using their long bills to spear partly opened mussels or to hammer a hole in a closed mussel so that they can force it open. They also eat worms and insects, and some nest inland, particularly in northern Britain. An oystercatcher's nest is a scrape in the ground. Neighbouring birds join forces to mob gulls or other predators near a nest.

Oystercatcher
(*Haematopus ostralegus*)

despite its name, was never much more than a fortified manor house. Between the 13th and 20th centuries, it was only once involved in a battle, and that was in Owain Glyndwr's revolt of 1400. Otherwise, it gently deteriorated to a farm and then to a barn and a store-room; now it is a ruin, and the only warlike notes it hears are the distant bangs of the wildfowlers' guns – in season – from the marshes.

Llanrhidian lies at the junction of the B4295 and B4271 on the north coast of Gower.

Ba Oxwich Bay

One of Gower's best-loved features is Oxwich Bay, which lies halfway along the southern coast. It is best seen from the top of Oxwich Point, which towers 280 ft above the sea; from there, the graceful crescent of sand sweeps round to Great Tor, Threecliff Bay and the battered ramparts of silver-grey limestone that rise to a dramatic climax at Pwlldu Head, 4 miles to the east.

Behind the beach are sand-dunes, a salt-water marsh, a freshwater marsh and reedy pools, some of which are man-made and were stocked with fish in the 19th century. This profusion of greenery is threaded by the Nicholaston Pill stream that flows beneath hanging woodlands to the sea. Much of the area has been a National Nature Reserve since 1963, to which access is limited; however, there are two excellent nature trails. One explores the dunes and possesses a vantage point with views over the wilderness where herons, moorhens, nightjars and many other birds live amid water-lilies and willows.

The woodland walk along the steep flanks of Oxwich Point takes up to three hours to complete. It starts by St Illtyd's Church, whose tiny chancel is thought to have been the cell of a Celtic monk.

At the landward end of the headland, a steep lane climbs through a tunnel of trees to reach ruined Oxwich Castle, a fortified manor house, which dates from the middle of the 16th century. Its first owners were the Mansels, one of whom, Anne, was killed outside the gatehouse in 1557, when her family came to blows with some Swansea men over the ownership of a cargo from a French ship wrecked in Oxwich

Bay. From the castle there are extensive views over the bay towards Pwlldu Head.

Oxwich, a focal point for walks round the bay, is signposted off the A4118, 1¼ miles west of Penmaen.

Ba ## Park Woods

Green Cwm, the valley that runs through the heart of Park Woods, was carved by a stream that now flows beneath the limestone for more than a mile before emerging above Parkmill. Its course is followed by a Forestry Commission road, open only to walkers, which passes the Parc le Breos burial chamber. Known locally as the Giants' Grave, the tomb is covered by a 70 ft long mound of stones, and is one of Gower's best-preserved prehistoric sites. Skeletons dating from about 4,500 years ago were found here when the tomb was opened in 1869.

Cathole, a cave where the remains of prehistoric animals have been found, is on a steep slope about 200 yds higher up the valley. The walk can be continued to Llethrid, on the B4271 between Upper Killay and Llanrhidian, where the stream commences its underground journey. Llethrid Swallet, a limestone cavern near the road bridge, has beautiful stalactites and stalagmites, but should only be explored by experienced cavers.

Parkmill lies just north of the A4118, 2 miles east of Penmaen.

Aa ## Port-Eynon

The road that plunges down into this compact and colourful village passes a poignant reminder that the seas about Gower are not always tranquil. In a corner of a churchyard stands the statue of Billy Gibbs, the coxswain of the local lifeboat, who died with two of his crew while trying to reach a ship in distress off Pwlldu Head in 1916.

The road ends in a car park above the long, dune-backed sweep of Port-Eynon Bay. This is sheltered by a rugged headland where limestone was quarried in the 19th century and shipped out across the Bristol Channel. On

SMUGGLERS' BAY Two limestone headlands shelter Port-Eynon Bay (far right) – Oxwich Point to the east and Port-Eynon Point to the west. Limestone was quarried there in the 19th century. On Port-Eynon Point, a pair of ruined 18th-century cottages stand on the site of a notorious smuggler's house.

OXWICH POINT

PORT-EYNON POINT

the 2¾ mile nature trail climbing the headland there is a chance of seeing ravens, kestrels, shearwaters, gannets and cormorants.

The coves and caves in the rugged coast made Port-Eynon a smuggling base until the end of the 18th century – so much so that at one time no fewer than eight Excisemen were stationed in the village. The most notorious local smuggler and wrecker was John Lucas who, during the 16th century, acquired something of a Robin Hood reputation in the area. He lived in the Salt House on Port-Eynon Point, where its remains can still be seen – or rather, those of two cottages built out of the ruins after the house was destroyed by a storm in 1703.

Just beyond the point, and accessible only at low tide, is Culver Hole, a deep gully fronted by an extraordinary 60 ft high wall, pierced by openings for doors and windows. Who undertook this prodigious building feat, and why, is unknown. Legend says that Culver Hole was a gigantic store-room for John Lucas's loot; or more prosaically, it could have been an elaborate dovecot, built to provide local people with fresh meat in winter.

Port-Eynon is at the end of the A4118, the main road through Gower.

Pwlldu Bay
Ba

A stream bustles southwards from Bishopston, curling through a valley dark with trees, then runs to meet the sea in this lovely little bay. Two isolated, whitewashed cottages overlook a beach where a storm-raised bank of shingle leads to a broad expanse of low-tide sand.

To the west lies Pwlldu Head, 320 ft of craggy limestone – the highest point

on the entire Gower coast. The rocks below the headland are known as Graves End, in memory of some 70 sailors who were buried there after a shipwreck in 1760. The vessel was almost certainly the *Caesar*, an Admiralty tender carrying munitions and a number of recently impressed men battened below hatches. No doubt it was these unfortunates who accounted for the high rate of casualties.

From the headland, and from the lower cliffs on the opposite side of the bay, there are superb views across the Bristol Channel to Somerset and Devon. The cliff-top path east of Pwlldu leads to Brandy Cove, a tiny bay once used by smugglers.

Like many of Gower's most attractive beaches, Pwlldu can be reached only on foot, but lanes and footpaths converge on it from Pennard, Pyle and Bishopston.

Bishopston lies on the B4436, which runs between the A4118 and the A4067.

Rhossili
Aa

Hang-gliders are launched from the steep slopes of Rhossili Down and are often seen wheeling like colourful pterodactyls above Gower's most westerly village. Rhossili, lashed by winter storms, stands on a cliff 250 ft above the sea, and from here a footpath runs down to the vast, surf-pounded beach that sweeps northwards to Burry Holms. At low tide, the oak ribs of the *Helvetia* – a coaster driven ashore by a gale in 1887 – are clearly visible on the sands below the village. All hands were saved, but her cargo, 500 tons of timber, was scattered all over the beach. The villagers 'rescued' it with horse and cart and sold it cheap to South Wales timber merchants.

USEFUL AND ORNAMENTAL

Shoots of butcher's-broom were once used by butchers to brush clean their chopping blocks. An evergreen of the lily family, it grows in dry woods, bearing green flowers from January to April. They grow at the base of the stiff 'leaves' that are really flat shoots. Red berries may appear in winter.

Butcher's-broom
(*Ruscus aculeatus*)

Somewhere near by, Gower's most famous shipwreck lies. No one knows her name, or where she came from, and she is simply known as 'The Dollar Ship', from the gold moidores and doubloons found from time to time in the sand. The coins date from the 17th century, so she had nothing to do with the Armada. One story says that the vessel was carrying a Spanish lady's dowry to her English husband, but this is probably Gower romanticism. Sadly, no coins have been reported for about a century, but it might be worth keeping your eyes open as you walk along the beach.

There is a splendid walk northwards from the village over the whaleback ridge of Rhossili Down, which rises to

632 ft – the highest point on Gower. Neolithic burial chambers near the summit are known as Sweyne's Howes. According to legend, they mark the grave of a Viking chief named Sweyne, who may have given his name to Swansea – 'Sweyne's-ey', or island.

From Rhossili Down, on days when the frequent Welsh hazards of haze, drizzle or mist are absent, it is possible to see Hartland Point, 40 miles away on the Devon coast, and St Govan's Head on the edge of Pembrokeshire.

Rhossili lies at the western end of the B4247, which branches off the A4118 about 2 miles north of Port-Eynon.

Threecliff Bay
Ba

High, sandy slopes clad with bracken form a natural amphitheatre behind this handsome bay whose beach is bisected by the waters of Pennard Pill. The bay is named from the three triangular crags of limestone, pierced by a natural arch, that mark its eastern boundary. To the west, Great Tor overlooks Oxwich Bay.

Reached by footpaths from Southgate, Parkmill and Penmaen, Threecliff Bay embraces considerable, if fading, evidence of early occupation by man. On the high ground behind Great Tor there is a prehistoric tomb, traces of a 12th-century Norman castle, and a few stones marking the site of a medieval church.

On the opposite side of the bay, about half a mile inland, the gaunt remains of Pennard Castle stand upon a steep slope high above the river. It was built in the 13th century and is said to have been the home of the chieftain Rhys ap Iestyn. For his churlish behaviour towards the Little Folk – he refused to let them join in his wedding revels – Lord Rhys, his castle and all his people were overwhelmed by sand on the same night. Whatever the truth of the story, Pennard Castle was described as 'desolate and ruinous' as long ago as 1650.

Parkmill and Penmaen lie on the A4118.

Aa Whiteford Burrows

Sweeping northwards to Whiteford Point, this desert of wind-sculpted sand-dunes overlooks one of Gower's largest and loneliest beaches. Reached on foot from either Llanmadoc or the neighbouring hamlet of Cwm Ivy, the dunes are included within a 3,000 acre nature reserve leased to the Nature Conservancy Council by the National Trust. Rich in lime and relatively undisturbed, the dunes have many damp hollows – known as 'slacks' – where a great variety of insects, including froghoppers and leafhoppers, live among creeping willow, mosses and orchids. Clusters of conifers, planted to help stabilise the dunes, contrast with the huge expanse of slender marram grass.

To the south, beyond the limestone cliffs of Hills Tor, there are walks over the dunes or along the shore to Broughton Bay and Bluepool Corner, accessible only on foot. This part of the coast is scoured by strong tides that sweep in and out of the Loughor estuary. Sixteen ships, outward bound from Llanelli, were wrecked between the Burry Inlet and Broughton Bay in a single night in 1868. The chief cause of the disaster was a heavy onshore swell, resulting from an earlier storm, combined with a lack of wind to fill the sails. Four of the vessels were lost with all hands, and in the morning the sands down the north-west Gower coast were strewn with lost cargoes, shattered wrecks and corpses.

Llanmadoc is signposted along minor roads from the intersection of the B4295 and B4271 at Llanrhidian.

Aa Worms Head

One mile long, but nowhere more than a few hundred yards wide, Worms Head is Gower's most spectacular natural feature. Reached after a walk of 15–20 minutes along the cliff-top from Rhossili, the promontory is joined to the mainland by a rocky causeway that is submerged at high tide and passable only for about two and a half hours on either side of high water. Times when it is safe to cross are posted outside the coastguard station next to the car park in Rhossili. It is essential to heed the notice, and to keep a close eye on the clock: if you do not leave Worm – as it is called locally – at least three and a half hours before high water you will be trapped.

Worms Head is derived from *wurm* – the Old English word for 'dragon' – and the headland does indeed resemble an immense sea monster, particularly from the air and from the Bristol Channel. Near its seaward end is a natural arch known as the Devil's Bridge, while a narrow cleft through which wind and water hiss and thunder is called the Blow Hole.

Worms Head is part of a nature reserve that includes the Limestone Nature Trail, which starts and ends in Rhossili. Along the way you can see the ribs of the *Helvetia*, wrecked in 1887, the remains of an Iron Age fortified village, the Rhossili Vile – a rare Saxon open-field system still in use – and, in spring, the nests of guillemots and razorbills on Worms Head cliffs.

Rhossili lies at the western extremity of the B4247, which branches off the A4118 just north of Port-Eynon.

THREECLIFF BAY Three triangular crags on its eastern side give this bay its name. Where earth movements buckled the rock 280 million years ago, centuries of wave erosion have fashioned a natural archway through them.

271

THE PEMBROKESHIRE COAST

A peninsula of high cliffs, split by coves and creeks –
a reminder of richer seafaring days

Many miles of high cliffs, island sanctuaries for sea-birds, sandy beaches pounded by Atlantic surf, and lonely shingle coves where grey seals bask line Pembrokeshire's coast. Tiny harbours tell of trading days now gone, and just inland, barely beyond the smell of sea water, are reedy creeks and sheep-grazed slopes rich in prehistoric sites.

The entire peninsula is a complicated tribute to nature's relentless energy. Basically it is a rolling plateau about 200 ft high, forced into tortured folds by violent earth movements, then planed smooth by sheets of ice and cut by rivers. The hardest rocks, brewed by volcanoes almost 500 million years ago, resisted erosion and stand up in the north as numerous isolated hills on St David's peninsula, as the rugged Pen Caer on the north coast, and above all as the long westward sweep of Mynydd Preseli (the Presely Mountain). In the limestone crags of the south, the sea has carved caves, arches, blow-holes and isolated stacks.

The sea was Pembrokeshire's main link with the outside world until the railway came in the late 19th century. To the countless little harbours came craft bringing back shop goods in return for farm produce. Crushed rock from the volcanic areas was exported for roadstone, and slates went by sea from the quarries. But the most important cargo was limestone. From the quarries of the south it was

shipped to little havens where it was unloaded on to the beach to be reloaded into horse-drawn carts. All round the coast low, circular kilns are a feature of the landscape, where limestone was burned to produce lime for dressing the land of local farms.

Pembrokeshire's first settlers lived in the limestone caves of the south 10,000 years ago. Bronze Age settlers had a trade route across the county. It started at Whitesand Bay, where traders landed with copper and gold from Ireland, and went east towards Salisbury Plain. Massive stone 'tables' are all that remain now of their burial chambers. The steep hills and precipitous promontories attracted Iron Age dwellers, and traces of their earthworks, farm walls and homes can be seen at the natural strongholds where they settled.

The Romans largely ignored Pembrokeshire, but not so the Normans. They created a division between north and south that is still obvious. The south, like Gower, became 'Little England beyond Wales' – English speaking, with English place-names, and protected by a chain of castles. North of the chain the land remained Welsh. The division is known as the 'landsker', an old legal term for a boundary.

The sea, which shaped the land and played such a large role in its history, has also made the coast a wonderland for wildlife. Sea-birds abound on the cliffs of both mainland and islands. Grey seals breed in remote sea-washed caves, sport in the waters and bask on the rocks. In spring and summer, acres of rock plants drape the cliffs with colour.

The 167 mile long-distance footpath follows the coast almost all the way round Pembrokeshire. Apart from being a great challenge to experienced hikers, it enables visitors to explore the entire coast by short walks from the many points where the roads meet the path.

SEA-GIRT STRONGPOINT Cliffs of gritstone and shale fringe Dinas Island, a headland once cut off by the sea. An Iron Age fort gave Dinas its name – it means 'little fortress' in Welsh. But it was also known as Ynys Fach Llyffan Gawr, 'islet of Llyffan the Giant'.

Places to visit

Map ref. Bc Abercastle

An old lime-kiln and the ruins of two small warehouses are reminders that this rocky inlet – a safe haven on a treacherous coast – flourished as a little port when the sea was Pembrokeshire's main link with the outside world. Records of coastal trading here date back to Tudor times. In the 19th century sloops plied from the harbour to Liverpool and Bristol, carrying out cargoes of corn and butter and bringing back goods from the shops. At least three sailing-ships were built by local craftsmen. Exports of oats and imports of coal did not cease until the 1920s.

Now a few private craft shelter in the narrow harbour, overlooked by cottages and resting on the greyish sand that appears at low tide beyond the pebbles. The harbour is a natural one formed in a 'drowned' valley where the sea-level rose as the glaciers of the Ice Age melted.

A splendid cliff-top walk runs eastwards to the secluded, shingle-backed bays of Aber-mawr and Aber-bach, 2½ and 3 miles away. Beyond, the cliffs of the Pen Caer peninsula rise dramatically to more than 400 ft above coves where seals breed.

A much shorter stroll of only a few hundred yards on the opposite side of

Abercastle's inlet leads to Carreg Samson, an outstanding Neolithic burial chamber 3,000 years old. Its many-sided capstone is 16 ft long and still rests on three of the original seven uprights. The story goes that Samson lifted the capstone into place with his little finger; the finger is supposed to have been buried on the remote and wave-lashed rocky promontory of Ynys y Castell, which shields the harbour from the north. The rocks here are covered with flowers, and you can look back at Abercastle's inlet and the great table of Carreg Samson.

Six miles south-west of Fishguard along the A487 a minor road branches northwest through Mathry to Abercastle, which is 2¼ miles off the main road.

Ba Bosherston

Tens of thousands of white water-lilies flower in summer on the large freshwater pools lying east of the pleasant little village of Bosherston. From the woodland paths beside the pools you can marvel at the sight of the blooms – at their best in June – and watch the hovering dragonflies, the elegant swans, haughty herons and darting kingfishers. At the seaward end of the pools an expanse of 'young' dunes, formed during the last 200 years, leads to the sandy shore of Broad Haven. A lane from the village also leads more directly to the beach.

Fascinating contortions of rocks lie below the 5 mile cliff-path that works westward from Broad Haven to Elegug Stacks – but look for the notice in the village post office indicating when the path is open, for the area is a military training ground. About a mile from Broad Haven is the astonishing St Govan's Chapel. Built in the 13th cen-

tury on the site of a Celtic hermit's cell, the tiny church is wedged deep in a rocky cleft where waves thunder over huge boulders.

A little further along the path is Bosherston Mere, a great cleft from which the sea spouts up 40 ft or more in rough weather. Here is the Huntsman's Leap, where a rider leaped over the narrow gap, but died of shock when he

realised that the chasm was 130 ft deep.

At the end of the cliff-path are Elegug Stacks, standing just off shore. The four huge, sheer pillars of limestone are crowned by tree mallow, and in summer their faces are packed with the chocolate-brown, black and white of guillemots, razorbills, fulmars and kittiwakes nesting in the cracks and on

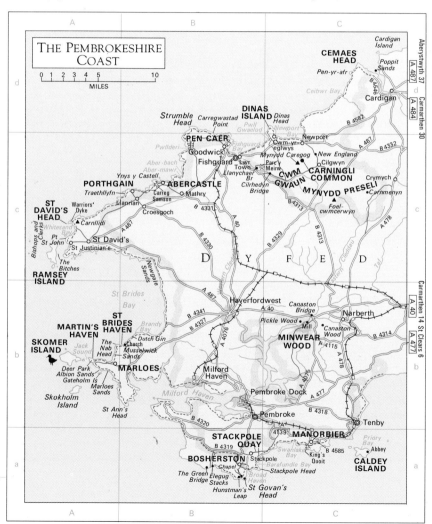

the narrowest of ledges. Elegug is the local name for the guillemot. Opposite the most western stack, the pounding water has worn away a superb arch through the cliff called The Green Bridge of Wales.

Four miles south of Pembroke along the B4319 a minor road branches south to Bosherston, 1¼ miles further on.

Ca   Caldey Island

The dark-robed Cistercian monks who farm Caldey and make perfume from its golden abundance of gorse flowers form a link with the legend-laced Age of Saints, when Celtic holy men sought refuge and solitude on several islands off the Welsh coast. The present community was founded in 1929, but Caldey has been a religious centre since the 6th century.

The smooth, high table of land slopes up gently from the limestone cliffs nearest the mainland to the red-sandstone cliffs at the southern end. Small sandy bays nestle under the cliffs. Quiet lanes thread beneath the trees and between the fields marked out by stone walls. Barley is the main crop raised by the monks, who farm most of the island's 600 acres. They also grow herbs and blooms that are gathered to make perfume.

A footpath from the quay at Priory Bay leads up to the abbey whose white-washed walls, weathered red roofs, arches, turrets and pinnacles create an exotic atmosphere more Mediterranean than Welsh. A leafy lane runs south from the abbey to a lighthouse built in 1829 and standing almost 200 ft above sea-level. From this highest part of the island there is a lovely view, across the neatly chequered island itself, and also across the sweep of Car-

PLACE OF PEACE St Govan's Chapel stands on a rocky ledge above the sea, a mile south of Bosherston. St Govan is a mystery-enshrouded figure, but some say that he was Sir Gawaine, one of the Knights of the Round Table, who became a hermit after the death of King Arthur.

marthen Bay to the Gower Peninsula in the east and St Govan's Head to the west. Beyond the waters of the Bristol Channel the rocky coastline of North Devon rears up.

A few hundred yards from the lighthouse are the old priory buildings on the site of the first monastery. It was set near the spring of fresh water, which is still the island's water source. Farm buildings surround the sturdy-walled priory church which was a place of refuge when the island was attacked by Vikings and other marauders. Now it shelters an ancient stone carved with ogham characters – ancient Celtic script – some 1,400 years ago.

Caldey Island is reached by boat from Tenby throughout the summer months. Tenby is at the southern end of the A478.

Cc   Carningli Common

Local legends maintain that St Brynach, one of St David's contemporaries in the 6th century, used to climb to Carningli's rocky summit to talk with the angels. It is certainly a wonderful vantage point, 1,138 ft above Newport Bay, from which to admire the wide-ranging views north-east over Cemaes Head and across Cardigan Bay, and west over Fishguard to the cliffs of Strumble Head. Just south is the Presely Mountain rising above Cwm Gwaun.

The common, carpeted with heather and gorse, rises steeply to a rough peak whose tumbled rocks are mottled with pale lichens. Iron Age men used the stone to build the defensive wall that encircles the summit. Plain to see inside the wall are the stone foundation circles of the beehive-shaped huts where they lived.

Numerous paths cross the common; the most direct way to the summit starts from the narrow lane that runs south-east from Newport towards Cilgwyn. Short but steep, the path at first follows the arrow-straight line of a tramway, long since vanished, which transported stone from a small quarry. The stone supports for the winding gear that used to haul wagons up the slope are still standing.

Away below the common is the delightful tangle of Newport's narrow streets and colour-washed buildings, huddling round the ruins of the medieval castle. The bay at Newport was once busy with sailing-ships coming to trade or for repair in the shipyard. The yard built square-rigged vessels and schooners during the 19th century. The port was used by trading coasters until the 1930s, but now the harbour has silted up.

From Newport on the A487 a minor road runs south-east to Cilgwyn. The path up Carningli Common starts from this minor road, at New England, just over 1 mile from Newport.

Cd   Cemaes Head

Breathtaking cliffs soaring almost vertically 550 ft from the sea rise from the low promontory of Cemaes Head along its lonely western rim. Layers of sand and mud deposited on the sea-bed 500 million years ago were compressed into rock, then subjected to immense sideways pressure that made them buckle into the present folds. The amazing striped dips and peaks show best in the high cliff and at Pen-yr-afr, 1½ miles south-west of Cemaes Head. The clear but strenuous path along the cliff-top brings them into view as it winds back and forth with the rim. Parts of the path are steep and become slippery in wet weather. From the highest point of the path there are enormous views across Cardigan Bay to Snowdonia and the conical peaks of Yr Eifl, 60 miles away on the Lleyn Peninsula. Hardy walkers can follow the path over the cliffs to Ceibwr Bay, a stream-washed cove where grey seals love to sport.

Below the eastern edge of Cemaes Head lies the broad, sheltered estuary of the River Teifi, widening rapidly once it rounds the elbow from Cardigan. Poppit Sands stretch out into the estuary at low tide. At the northern tip of the estuary is Cardigan Island. Puffins nested there before rats over-ran the island, but now the rats have gone and it is hoped the puffins will return.

Cemaes Head is 4 miles north-west of Cardigan. The B4546 from Cardigan runs beside the estuary for 3 miles to Poppit Sands. From there a narrow lane continues for almost 2 miles to the path.

Cc **Cwm Gwaun**

Carved by a clear river in which swim salmon and sea trout – known as sewin in Wales – the gentle beauty of the deep, wooded valley with its narrow, tree-flanked lanes seems a world apart from the savage grandeur of the nearby coast. Instead of gorse-clad cliffs there are lush groves of oak, sycamore and hazel, thickly carpeted with woodrush, celandines, primroses, bluebells and wood anemones. Instead of the aggressive screams of sea-birds, the sweet sound of warblers, the thin voice of the grey wagtail and the liquid song of the

WILD FLOWERS OF PEMBROKE'S COASTLINE

On sandy, gravelly and rocky beaches the buck's-horn plantain is a tenacious plant which grows in profusion. It is easily distinguished from other plantains by its antler-shaped leaves which give the plant its name. In higher places, on the rocky cliffs and outcrops, cliff spurrey grows, speckling the sandstone with its star-like flowers throughout the summer. Carpets of rose-pink, honey-scented thrift add more colour to the cliffs from May to July. Sometimes called sea pink or rock rose, the thrift stays green – or thrives – throughout the year, hence its name. In pre-decimal coinage days the thrift appeared on the reverse side of the 12-sided threepenny piece. The perennial centaury is Pembrokeshire's floral treasure – the only other place it grows is north Cornwall.

Its smaller leaves and numerous stems distinguish it from the common centaury, which is not perennial. It is said that the centaury was named after the centaur, Chiron – a creature part man, part horse who used the plant to cure a wound.

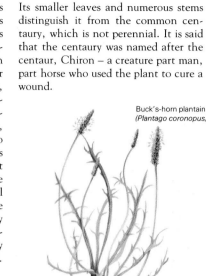

Buck's-horn plantain
(*Plantago coronopus*)

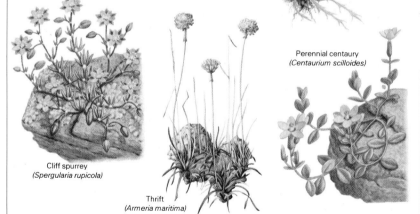

Cliff spurrey
(*Spergularia rupicola*)

Thrift
(*Armeria maritima*)

Perennial centaury
(*Centaurium scilloides*)

dipper are gentle accompaniments to the rippling stream.

Waymarked walks start from two Forestry Commission picnic places in the valley above Cilrhedyn Bridge. The lane that climbs steeply from Llanychaer Bridge swings right on the

valley's rim and passes Parc y Meirw – 'Field of the Dead' – a 140 ft row of eight Bronze Age megaliths, four of the huge stones still upright. A lady dressed in white haunts them on dark nights – according to local belief. People in Cwm Gwaun's scattered hamlets and

farms still celebrate New Year's Eve on January 12, cheerfully ignoring the fact that the Gregorian calendar was changed in 1752 to bring the country into line with the rest of Europe.

Lower Town, where Cwm Gwaun meets the sea, is a picturesque village where *Moby Dick* and *Under Milk Wood* were filmed.

The B4313 running south-east from Fishguard reaches Llanychaer Bridge after 2¼ miles. About 1 mile further on a lane branches left and winds up the valley for 4 miles.

Cd **Dinas Island**

An immense table of rock forms the headland called Dinas Island – not so strangely named. It really was an island about 10,000 years ago – very recently in geological terms – when melt-water from Ice Age glaciers flowed through the flat-bottomed, wooded valley that still marks the 'island's' southern edge.

The table of rock has been set up unevenly, and tilts from the 465 ft cliffs at Dinas Head in the north down to the valley. A path runs across the valley between the two delightful beaches – at Pwll Gwaelod, a former smuggling centre on Fishguard Bay, and Cwm-yr-eglwys, a pretty cove on Newport Bay with a harbour which has sheltered fishing boats and trading vessels since the Middle Ages.

The remains of a small and ancient church stand just above the beach at Cwm-yr-eglwys, a poignant reminder of the sea's awesome power. The church was smashed on October 25, 1859 by a hurricane which also wrecked 114 ships on the coasts of Wales.

A footpath just over 3 miles long runs right round the headland, overlooking cliffs and stacks where black-backed gulls, fulmars, shags, razorbills and guillemots crowd. On the landward slope, sheltered from the full fury of Atlantic storms, thyme and ling, squills and campions, foxgloves and orchids attract peacock butterflies, red admirals and the common blue. From the top of the headland the wide views stretch away over the cliffs fringing Cardigan Bay.

Off the A487, which runs east from Fishguard, there are minor roads after 4, 4¼ and 5 miles. The first two lead to Pwll Gwaelod, the third to Cwm-yr-eglwys, both about 1 mile from the main road.

Ca   Manorbier

A mighty castle dominates the tongue of high ground in the green valley that runs down to Manorbier's sandy beach. Footpaths climb the Old Red Sandstone headlands that flank the bay, and join the track that runs along the clifftop. Only a mile to the west along the cliff, after a walk that surveys the dramatic cliff scenery round to St Govan's Head, you can enjoy the beach at Swanlake Bay. This can be reached only on foot and never becomes crowded.

The King's Quoit rears up on the headland to the south of Manorbier Bay. It is a burial chamber about 5,000 years old, with its massive 15 ft capstone resting on the ground at one end and supported by two upright stones at the other. From the path that leads a few hundred yards to the east you can look across to the beautiful low dome of Caldey Island, resting on its platform of red-sandstone cliffs at the far end and white limestone near the mainland.

Manorbier Castle is impressive enough in itself, but has an extra claim to attention as the place where Gerald de Barri was born about 1146. The son of a Norman knight and a Welsh princess, he went into the Church and became known as Giraldus Cambrensis – 'Gerald of Wales'. Giraldus never achieved his ambition to become Bishop of St David's, but won more enduring fame for his entertaining *Itinerary through Wales*. It is a remarkably vivid picture of his country, written after Giraldus had travelled through the Principality with Archbishop Baldwin of Canterbury in 1188, raising support for the Third Crusade. The castle then was a luxurious domestic setting rather than a fortress, with nut groves, orchards, vineyards and fish-ponds.

Manorbier is 4½ miles west of Tenby on the B4585 road which leads off the A4139.

Ab   Marloes

Pembrokeshire is richly endowed with enticing beaches, but few can rival Marloes Sands. The long stretch of sand is backed by boulders and rock pools. Behind them tower impressive cliffs whose strata were contorted and tilted almost vertical by violent earth movements about 400 million years ago. Constant attacks by the sea have left great mounds of rock on the beach, and worn an arch right through the rock at one point.

A 2 mile nature trail starts from the village car park and runs north-west along the cliffs. Gateholm Island, at the western end of the beach, is a craggy outcrop of Old Red Sandstone cut off from the mainland only at high water. From this outcrop there is a fine view of the sea-birds circling the cliffs of Skomer Island and Skokholm

THE ELITE AND LOWLY ON SEA AND SHORE

As it skims the water in low-level flight, the Manx shearwater seems almost to 'shear' through the wavetops. The bird flies with powerful wing-beats and long glides; it comes to the land only to breed. In contrast, the puffin is a fast-flying diver capable of catching up to ten fish in a single dive. Its distinctive multi-coloured bill has given the bird its popular name 'sea parrot'. On rocky cliffs and islands the portly puffins stand rather like pompous old gentlemen surrounded by excitable waiters – the guillemots. Sleek and dapper-looking in the water, the guillemot resembles a small penguin when standing upright. Like the penguin, guillemots gather in large colonies and often crowd together on narrow cliff ledges.

The herring gull is one of the most common of British gulls. Its yodelling, two-note call, emitted with the head thrown back, is a familiar sound along seafronts, on piers and on the rooftops of seaside towns. Its name is not very apt, because herrings are only a small part of its diet and the bird will eat almost anything edible. Its voracious appetite is shared by the lesser black-backed gull, a bird of similar size, recognised by its black upper wing feathers.

The shag is also a common bird of many coasts. Its quiff-like crest distinguishes it from the cormorant.

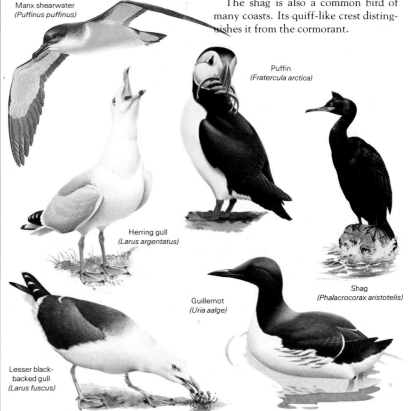

Manx shearwater
(Puffinus puffinus)

Puffin
(Fratercula arctica)

Herring gull
(Larus argentatus)

Shag
(Phalacrocorax aristotelis)

Guillemot
(Uria aalge)

Lesser black-backed gull
(Larus fuscus)

Island. Gateholm, a fine natural fortress, has traces of more than 100 rectangular huts arranged round three sides of a square. Perhaps they were an Iron Age village or an early Christian monastic settlement.

Albion Sands, the beach just on the western side of Gateholm, is named after an early paddle-steamer wrecked there in the 1840s. The gaunt skeleton of the wreck projects from the sands at low tide. Musselwick Sands, reached on foot north from the lane between Marloes and Martin's Haven, is another superb and secluded beach,

sheltered by sheer black cliffs and looking out across St Brides Bay.

Marloes village is 1 mile along a marked minor road that branches west from the B4327, 11 miles south-west of Haverfordwest. There is a car park 1 mile west of the village, and a path leads from there to the beach ¾ mile away.

Ab Martin's Haven

The steep-sided valley between the pebbled cove of Martin's Haven and the sandy little beach at Renny Slip offered a natural basis on which an Iron

Age tribe made a defensive earthwork. This cut off the square promontory to the west of the valley and made it a secure site for their settlement. Now the promontory lies behind a disintegrating stone wall and is known as the Deer Park. It was intended to improve the estate of the great landowning Edwardes family, but no deer were ever introduced.

The 1½ mile walk round the Deer Park has a beauty out of all proportion to its modest length. Over the broad expanse of gorse, heather, bracken and brambles, flickering with butterflies,

there are kestrels and ravens gliding and hovering, stonechats dancing, and the rare choughs, like red-legged, red-billed crows, giving dazzling aerobatic displays. Below in the creaming waters seals play, and in the little bays their round-eyed silvery pups bask in October.

There is a wonderful scene from the highest point of the walk, where a coastguards' lookout stands almost 200 ft above sea-level. Martin's Haven lies below, bustling now and again when a boat sets off for Skomer. The view sweeps round St Brides Bay, past the 2 mile stretch of Newgale Sands to the opposite end of the bay, There, violet-coloured cliffs rise just south of St David's, and at the very tip Ramsey Island lies across its narrow, wicked sound. The Deer Park's furthest spot is Wooltack Point, where the cliffs are high; you can look across the racing waters of Jack Sound to the bright floral carpet laid out on Skomer above its cliffs that quiver with sea-birds.

Martin's Haven is 12 miles south-west of Haverfordwest. It lies 3 miles along a marked minor road that turns west off the B4327. There is a car park.

Cb Minwear Wood

Far up the tidal reaches above Milford Haven are many narrow lanes and footpaths leading to lonely creeks rich in birdlife. Near the tidal limit of the Eastern Cleddau at Canaston Bridge is Minwear Wood, where plantations of American red oaks flash bright green in summer and glow in autumn among the fast-growing conifers. Here, thousands of migratory starlings roost in winter, mallards and swans dip into the river, and badgers roam after dark.

Blackpool Mill stands at the north-

ON MARLOES SANDS Rugged cliffs loom over the beach – a mile of sand broken by rock pools and strewn with boulders.

east corner of the wood, a huge but attractive building in the rural surroundings. Minwear used to provide fuel for an ironworks at Blackpool, but demand eventually exceeded supply and the works was replaced by the flour-mill powered by the tidal water. From the mill, paths lead east through Canaston Wood, north-west into Pickle Wood across the river, and into Minwear Wood, where a mile-long nature trail has been marked by the Forestry Commission.

The Eastern Cleddau flows down to Minwear from the Presely Mountain. It is very likely that the great bluestones used to build Stonehenge passed by Minwear Wood some 4,000 years ago – when it was a natural forest of native oaks. The stones were probably dragged on sledges down the slopes to the tidal creek just above Minwear, and there may have been slung between rafts for a water-borne journey down to the coast and up the Bristol Channel on their way to Salisbury Plain.

The A40 east from Haverfordwest crosses Canaston Bridge after 7 miles. The A4075 runs south from the bridge and in 300 yds a minor road goes to the west towards Blackpool Mill and Minwear Wood. There is a car park at the wood.

Cc   Mynydd Preseli

Smooth but steep, Mynydd Preseli – the Presely Mountain – rises to peaks of shattered rock striding west from Crymych towards the sea. An ancient ridge way rises and dips from one summit to the next, giving marvellous views. Foel-cwmcerwyn, the highest point, lies just south of the ridge way. From its 1,760 ft top, gaudily splashed with gorse and heather, there is virtually an aerial view of Pembrokeshire,

BELOW DEER PARK West of Martin's Haven, the cliffs drop away from the flat promontory to a shoreline of rocky coves.

over its tiny patchwork fields held in a sweep of the sea and probed by the fingers of Milford Haven. Beyond the encircling sea the Lleyn Peninsula rises in the north, and Devon's rocky coast far away in the south.

The ridge track forms part of a prehistoric highway used by men who travelled westwards from Salisbury Plain to Whitesand Bay and then boarded small craft to sail across to Ireland to barter for copper and gold. Bronze Age burial cairns and Iron Age defences and hut circles are scattered over the slopes, recalling ancient ways of life of men in these hills.

Carnmenyn was the source of the massive bluestones that were used to build Stonehenge. Nearly 4,000 years ago, more than 80 huge stones weighing a total of about 250 tons were prised from the hillside. Hewing and transporting such monoliths would have been a formidable task for men with no sophisticated machinery and transport. Our ancestors must have used simple sledges, rollers and rafts to take their precious cargoes down to the tidal waters above Milford Haven, out into the open sea, along the treacherous Bristol Channel, and then presumably up the rivers of south-west England to Salisbury Plain.

Crymych is on the A478, 8¼ miles south of Cardigan. Less than 100 yds south of the village a lane turns west and after a mile reaches the ridge way. Carnmenyn is 1½ miles west along the ridge way and lies just south of it. Foel-cwmcerwyn is a further 3 miles west and lies ¼ mile south of the track; it can also be approached by a 2 mile walk east from the B4329. This road runs south-west from the A487, 5 miles east of Newport and after 5½ miles, at its highest point, crosses the ridge way.

279

MYNYDD CAREGOG The mountain, seen from Mynydd Preseli, overlooks Carningli Common and its many hut circles.

Pen Caer

This rugged, windswept peninsula juts sturdily northwards, sheltering Fishguard Bay which stretches below its eastern slope. Across the bay, a tumble of cliffs running up to Dinas Head makes a gaunt backdrop to the serene waters, ruffled now and then as the ferry boats leave Fishguard harbour for Ireland.

The wild and craggy Strumble Head is the most northerly point of the peninsula. It is a fine viewpoint for surveying the whole of Cardigan Bay, and is reached after an exhilarating walk across a remote stretch of bracken, heather and prostrate broom, where gulls, choughs and ravens wheel above.

Pen Caer is only the tip of an immensely thick layer – over 3,500 ft deep – of hard volcanic rock. Its highest cliffs tower up 400 ft and are at their most impressive at Pwllderi on the western rim of the promontory. Here, seals roll in the water far beneath the summit. Pen Caer is crowned by an Iron Age hill-fort with several rows of stone ramparts linking the natural outcrops of rock.

A solitary stone on Carregwastad Point, east of Strumble Head, commemorates the last invasion of Britain. It took place in February 1797, when more than 1,200 Frenchmen – mainly ex-convicts rather than disciplined troops – landed under the leadership of an American, William Tate. They sacked local farms before surrendering at the end of two days of minor skirmishes. Local folklore claims that the invaders mistook the numerous red shawls of Fishguard's ladies for the red coats of a crack British regiment, and yielded before this superior force. Twenty invaders lost their lives and there were two Welsh casualties.

From Goodwick on the A40 a minor road curves through the hamlet of Llanwnda and round the peninsula about ½ mile from the coast. Tracks lead from the road at various points to Carregwastad Point, Strumble Head and Pwllderi. The coastal-path walk from Carregwastad Point to Pwllderi is about 6 miles. There is a car park at Pwllderi.

Porthgain

Porthgain, a village in a narrow cleft in northern Pembrokeshire's spectacularly wild coast, has an unexpected and individual character. The village is little more than a few 19th-century cottages and a pub – but its snug harbour is overlooked by huge, bramble-wreathed ruins. Here, stone from quarries on the western side of the creek was crushed and stored in bins beside the quay to await loading on to schooners and, later, steamships.

The stone – volcanic, blue-grey and very hard – was used for roadstone from Victorian times until the quarries closed in 1931. In its heyday the village produced 40,000 tons a year to ship to ports as far off as London, Whitstable and Belfast, as well as to local destinations. Tramways linked the quarries, the crushing plant and the quayside loading areas. Old mooring chains and seaweed-draped ladders set into the harbour walls are additional reminders that this was once a bustling, thriving port. The pillars that guided ships into Porthgain's rocky inlet still stand on the embracing headlands.

A path running west along the cliff passes the old quarry workings on its way to the beautiful sandy beach at Traethllyfn. It is a magnificent walk over the empty, gorse-clad headlands with the sea foaming against the adamant fingers of rock and lapping quietly into the sandy inlets.

Nine miles south-west of Fishguard, along the A487, a minor road turns north-west at Croesgoch and runs through Llanrian to Porthgain, which is 2 miles off the main road.

Ac Ramsey Island

Sea-scoured caves and cliff-flanked coves beyond the reach of man make Ramsey one of Britain's breeding grounds for the grey seal. These graceful creatures love the caves and rocky beaches all around the island, and gather there to give birth to their pups from late August to November.

The island's 2 mile length changes from fertile growth in the north and east to heathland on the thin soils that barely cover the hard, volcanic rocks of the south and west. Vast numbers of rabbits graze the land, along with sheep, goats and a herd of red deer imported from the mainland. Choughs, kittiwakes, razorbills and guillemots line the cliffs in summer.

The cliffs rise to 300 ft and are so formidable that there is only one landing point for the boats. It did not exist

until 1935, when, with great difficulty, a wall was built between Ramsey's edge and a vast hump of rock close beside it. This kept out the ferocious waters that had surged between them, and it created a quiet haven in its lee.

St Justinian is credited with making Ramsey an island, in the 6th century. Seeking complete solitude, this stern disciplinarian left his self-indulgent colleagues at St David's monastery and strode off to Ramsey. As he went along he smote with his axe at the narrow neck of rock that linked the mainland and Ramsey. All that he left of it was the cruel reef called The Bitches and Whelps – now usually shortened to The Bitches – through and over which the high tides race at 8 knots. Justinian's austere ways eventually alienated those who had followed him, and they cut off his head. It is said that he

walked back to the mainland carrying his own head, and was buried at the chapel whose ruins still stand near St Justinian's on the mainland.

Ramsey has not been inhabited since the 1960s but it is possible to visit the island, and enquiries regarding boat times should be made at the tourist office in St David's.

Ramsey is reached by boat from St Justinian's, which is 2 miles west of St David's along a marked minor road. Visitors can spend about six hours on the island; a landing fee is charged. There is a car park at St Justinian's.

Bb St Brides Haven

Every bit as beautiful and tranquil as its name suggests, St Brides Haven was a welcome refuge for sailors for many hundreds of years. A few lengths of old

mooring chain and the remains of a red-stone lime-kiln are relics of the coastal trade that flourished until the late 19th century. Limestone was shipped in, burned in the kiln and used to fertilise the fields of local farms.

The ruined kiln now looks out over a snug inlet of red-speckled sand where the tide creams in between tilted tables of purple-red rock. Paths, ploughed fields, beach and cliffs all glow a rich crimson colour – unforgettable when a rosy sunset lights them. From the beach and the neighbouring cliffs there are wide-ranging views across St Brides Bay, which takes its name from the haven, towards St David's peninsula.

The St Bride who is remembered here was the glad-hearted Brigid of Kildare, whose feast day is February 1. She lived about AD 450-525 and was the first abbess to have authority over

WHITESAND BAY In the pale gold of late afternoon, an ebbing tide laps the shore and waders forage at the water's edge.

281

both a nunnery and a monastery. Brigid never left Ireland, but her adherents travelled widely throughout Europe spreading her fame. Churches are dedicated to her in Cornwall, Brittany, Italy and Czechoslovakia.

The church just above the beach at St Brides Haven dates from Norman times, but is only the replacement for a much earlier building which was devoured by the hungry sea. The sea is continually eroding the cliff, and a few yards north of the lime-kiln, a number of small stone coffins from the 6th and 10th centuries have been exposed.

The waters lash below the open, attractive cliff walks on either side of the haven. On the eastern side are remote bays with names such as Dutch Gin and Brandy Bay, recalling the smuggling days of long ago. In the other direction there is wild Nab Head, where skilful Stone Age workers had a flint 'factory' 10,000 years ago to chip tools and weapons from the rocks. Down the western side of the headland the sea has worn a blow-hole through the rock, and bursts through it like a vast fountain in rough weather.

St Brides Haven is 2 miles along a marked minor road that turns right from the B4327, 8 miles south-west of Haverfordwest.

Ac ## St David's Head

This exposed, rocky headland stretches out into the Atlantic, superbly wild crags lining its northern rim and the pretty little cove of Porthmelgan tucked under its southern edge. Thrift, sea campion and heathers smother the rocks in surprising profusion.

From the path above the crags you can see the waves foaming over the treacherous offshore rocks known as the Bishops and Clerks, and then rolling in to break as crashing surf on the long, sandy stretch of Whitesand Bay south of the headland. The best vantage point of all is Carnllidi, the steep-

flanked hill whose rocky summit rises 595 ft above the nearby sea. The hills of Ireland, 85 miles away, are visible on the best days, and there are few better places from which to gaze spellbound at the glory of a summer sunset.

The western tip of St David's Head was used as a fortress during the Iron Age, sealed off by a stone barrier, now tumbled, which later generations dubbed the Warriors' Dyke. Within its protection, boulders embedded in the turf mark the bases of circular huts where Iron Age tribesmen lived almost 2,000 years ago. Near by, on Carnllidi's north-west slopes, the stone walls that enclosed their small fields still show each year before the bracken grows too high.

Whitesand Bay was the western end of a Bronze Age trade route that started at Salisbury Plain. Primitive craft set out from the bay to sail to Ireland in continuation of the trade route. Copper and gold was the lure that made them undertake the voyage. St Patrick is said to have sailed from Whitesand on his last voyage to Ireland, and an inscribed stone marks the site of an ancient chapel dedicated to him.

Signposted lanes lead from the city of St David's to Whitesand Bay, 2 miles to the north-west. There is a car park at the bay, and a path leads from it to St David's Head, 1 mile away.

Ab ## Skomer Island

Birds are the reason for visiting Skomer National Nature Reserve. Hundreds of thousands of them are there to see, crowded clamorously on the cliffs that support the 720 acre island. Razorbills, guillemots, kittiwakes, shags, fulmars, great black-backed gulls and herring gulls flutter and shriek round the

ST DAVID'S HEAD On the head the craggy Carnllidi is part of a volcanic ridge formed more than 400 million years ago.

ledges. About 6,500 pairs of puffins nest on the island.

The puffins' burrows are heavily outnumbered by those of the Manx shearwaters. More than 100,000 pairs of them breed on Skomer, making them the largest group by far on the island. But there is no sign of them. These black-and-white petrels spend the days at sea or in their burrows, emerging only late at night.

Skomer is far from being a bird-thronged wasteland. On the contrary, it is like a vast rock garden in spring and summer. Sea campions, blue squills, pink thrift and yellow samphire drape the hard, dark grey volcanic cliffs and spread on to the island top among the acres of bluebells, red campions and fresh green bracken as it begins to unroll.

Birds, rabbits and the Skomer vole – the only creatures that inhabit the island – have taken complete possession of Skomer now, but 2,000 years ago Iron Age field enclosures and cultivation strips – lynchets – covered the surface. They are still visible, along with the circular hut foundations.

From the cliff-tops you can look down on the grey seals sprawling on the rocks or gliding sinuously through the waters. Two miles to the south is the red-sandstone mass of Skokholm, another island sanctuary for sea-birds, but not one for day visitors. Like Skomer it has a Norse name, not a sign of Norse occupation but of the supremacy of the Norsemen over these seas in the Dark Ages.

Boats cross to Skomer between April and September from Martin's Haven. This is 3 miles beyond a marked turning off the B4327, 11 miles south-west of Haverfordwest. There is a landing fee. A 4 mile marked nature trail circles the island.

Ba ## Stackpole Quay

The Old Red Sandstone cliffs that run west from Manorbier suddenly give way to ramparts of vertical limestone at Stackpole Quay. The division is clearly defined in the rocks immediately east of this enchanting little cove at the mouth of a wooded valley. Grey and flat-topped, the cliffs sweep south to Stackpole Head, while to the northeast the worn and undulating sandstone glows warmly. The cove is artificial, carved from an old limestone quarry and guarded by a short, sturdy breakwater. Stone from the quarry was burned in the rectangular kiln beside the lane above the cove.

A broad expanse of beautiful sand backed by a wilderness of dunes clad with marram grass and shrubs is at Barafundle Bay, only a ten-minute walk away south along the cliff path. Steps cut into the cliff lead down to the beach. A grove of sycamores, sheltered by steep slopes, huddles at the southern end of the beach below the cliffs of Stackpole Head. Here the sea has worn away arches through the jutting rocks. On the far side of the headland, caves carved deep into the cliffs by the persistent sea have collapsed and left blowholes through the rock; water comes bursting up from them when there are heavy seas. From the lonely walk along the cliff path round the headland, miles of the Bristol Channel stretch away uninterrupted as far as the Gower peninsula in the east and Lundy island backed by the Devon coastline in the south.

Stackpole village is signposted from the B4319 along lanes that branch off 2¼ and 3½ miles south of Pembroke. Half a mile east of the village a lane runs to the cliffs above Stackpole Quay; there is a car park.

TEMPERATE ISLE The heather-clad grassland on Deer Park is a good viewpoint for Skomer Island, across the narrow Jack Sound. Skomer bears the full brunt of Atlantic gales, yet its climate is mild with few frosts.

THE CAMBRIAN MOUNTAINS

Wild, bare hills, ancient vales of oak, fast-flowing streams and tranquil lakes lie in the green heart of Wales

A wilderness of lakes, forests, deep valleys and high, windswept moorland makes up the so-called 'Desert of Wales' that lies at the Principality's geographical centre. Its popular name refers to its empty, wild landscapes, not to its vegetation. Green is its colour, and water its element. The green is pale on the moors, emerald in the oak-filled valleys and velvety dark in the conifer forests. Water is everywhere – seeping from the moorland peat, trickling into the gullies, bubbling down the steep valleys, hurling itself over waterfalls, and lying captive in the many reservoirs and lakes.

The population is sparse and thinly spread; people have always been heavily outnumbered by sheep in the area. Small market towns such as Tregaron, Lampeter and Rhayader rank as major centres of importance. There are few main roads. Instead, there are narrow lanes and ancient bridleways which climb beside rushing, rocky streams to cross mountains where red kites, buzzards and kestrels wheel in search of prey. These tracks were pioneered by hardy drovers who, from the Middle Ages until the end of the 19th century, walked their livestock to England's far-off markets. They were replaced by trucks and trains, but little imagination is needed to picture men and beasts moving slowly eastwards, and returning drovers bringing home news of the outside world.

Plynlimon is the highest mountain, a peat-carpeted massif from

whose slopes spring the rivers Severn, Wye and Rheidol. The entire backbone of Wales is within view from the 2,468 ft summit. Unlike Snowdonia or the Brecon Beacons – with their jagged peaks and dramatic crests – central Wales is a landscape of steep but smooth mountains, few of which exceed 2,000 ft. It is country for walkers and pony-trekkers. It is also rewarding country for motorists.

The timeless atmosphere belies the truth – that the scenery has changed since the 1890s. Valleys have been flooded to satisfy the demand for water, and the need for fast-growing timber has spread carpets of conifers on barren hills where the soil had long been considered too thin for cultivation. The new, man-made lakes and forests give an extra dimension to the wild, empty landscape. The foresters' roads have opened up huge tracts of country for visitors.

Men delved for lead and silver in the lonely hills and valleys until about 1900, and a rich fabric of myths and superstitions grew round the industry. The 19th-century author and traveller George Borrow recorded some in his vivid book, *Wild Wales*. Old miners believed that mysterious spirits guided good men to the ore by making knocking noises far underground. Barren slopes were signs of lead beneath, because the metal poisoned the soil.

The history of the area has been essentially the story of ordinary people – of farmers, shepherds and drovers, of miners and of ministers who preached in astonishingly remote chapels. Central Wales never played a significant role in the events that moulded the Wales of today – it was too empty and, natural beauty excepted, its resources were few. The emptiness and the beauty are now the lures that draw visitors to what is still one of the least-known parts of Britain.

HEART OF WALES Deep in the Cambrian Mountains, the scenic mountain road through Dylife to Machynlleth – once a stage-coach route – winds between lonely, grassy hillsides inhabited only by hardy sheep. The distant heights of Cader Idris are always on the skyline.

Places to visit

Map ref. Cd   Dylife

A wild, high tract of uninhabited country lies between Plynlimon and the valley of the Dovey (Dyfi). The drive north-west across it from Staylittle to Machynlleth winds hither and thither through the hills giving an ever-changing view of them, and a distant, unchanging prospect of Cader Idris's towering line of crags and Aran Fawddwy's 2,974 ft peak.

Before the road begins its climb through the hills, it runs beside the infant Afon Twymyn and sees the water plunge 140 ft down Ffrwd Fawr, one of the highest falls in Wales. The river drops over the cliff-edge of Craigy-maes, then turns and runs beneath the cliff through a narrow valley.

Once the road has passed through Dylife, it climbs steeply and soon reaches 1,700 ft. From the highest point a broad track runs south-west. It is a bracing walk along it, passing the small lake of Glaslyn and then on to the foot of the 1,400 ft high crags of Taren Bwlch-gwyn.

Dylife is a sad contrast to its glorious surroundings. Isolated among the mountains, it is a village that has died. It stands 1,200 windswept feet above sea-level and speaks powerfully of the time when hundreds of workers toiled day after day in the lead mines. The mines flourished from the 17th century until the late 1870s, but died when cheaper lead was imported from overseas. In the prosperous years, the mine owners built a chapel and a school for the families who came to live with the miners in the austere dwellings.

Now the Star Inn, a survivor from the days when stage-coaches passed through Dylife, stands almost alone amid crumbling workers' barracks, grey spoil-heaps, ruined mine buildings and the roofless ruin of the school. The rowans in the graveyard round the foundations of a church are the only softening touch in the poignant scene.

The 11 mile minor road through Dylife to Machynlleth leaves the B4518 about 1 mile north of Staylittle. Staylittle is 7 miles north-west of Llanidloes on the B4518.

Bd   Furnace

The short but swift Afon Einion rushes down its wooded valley to join the River Dovey, and when it reaches the hamlet of Furnace it suddenly cascades over mossy, fern-flanked rocks sheltered by a grove of slender trees. The enchanting waterfall is only a few paces from the road. It is overlooked by a picturesque stone building of the 18th century, set back into the hillside high above the river.

The building is large with sturdy, windowless walls sloping inward as they rise. Clinging to one wall is a great wheel that dips into a channel cut to let water from the Einion come racing through. The wheel powered the bellows of an iron-smelting furnace – from which the hamlet got its name. The iron was shipped from Lancashire to Aberdyfi and ferried across to Furnace, where there was abundant woodland to provide the charcoal then needed for smelting.

The once-rampant native woods are less widespread in the district now, but Cwm Einion, the little ravine down which the water hastens, still has a few oakwoods clinging to its steep sides, creating a dappled framework for the silvery falls and bends of the river. A lane climbs steeply alongside the water into Cwm Einion, and from it a waymarked walk of about a mile winds through the woods.

West of the main road through Furnace, fields and heath run down to the shore of the Dovey estuary. The Royal Society for the Protection of Birds has a reserve here, at Ynys-hir. Entry

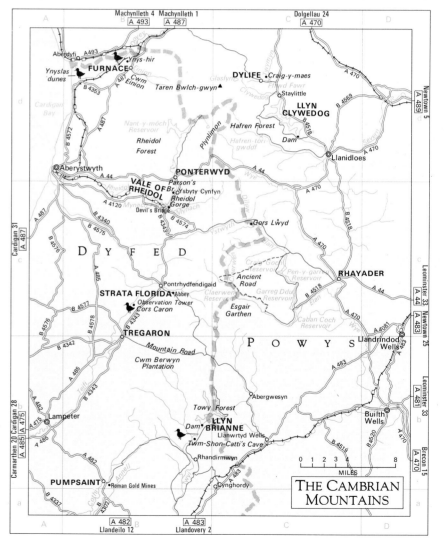

is by permit only, obtainable from the RSPB office in Newtown, Powys. The Ynyslas dunes at the mouth of the estuary are part of the Dyfi National Nature Reserve.

Furnace is 11 miles north-east of Aberystwyth, on the A487.

Cb   Llyn Brianne

One of the wildest and least accessible parts of Wales has been opened up in the last ten years because of an increased demand for water. To supplement Swansea's water supply the reservoir of Llyn Brianne was created by damming the Afon Tywi, a work completed in 1973. Now the long, narrow stretch of water lies beneath steep hills and probes four sinuous tentacles into the conifer spread of the Towy Forest. The narrow lane that once ended at the isolated village of Rhandirmwyn, 4 miles below the dam, now goes on up the Tywi valley and high above the lake's eastern shore.

A mile south of the dam, in the Dinas reserve run by the Royal Society for the Protection of Birds, a nature trail through colourful oakwoods curls round a steep, crag-topped hill. The 2 mile trail first runs beside the Tywi as it races through a spectacular gorge, and then climbs through the trees to Twm-Shon-Catti's Cave. It was a hideout of the 16th-century outlaw and highwayman whom folklore has turned into a Welsh Robin Hood.

The woodland scenery is a delight of unblemished green – and busy with redstarts and pied flycatchers in spring. A bonus for walkers is the occasional sight of a red kite circling effortlessly for hour after hour. The rust-coloured hunter, with its forked tail and wings bent sharply back, was so common in

DYFI DUNES The Ynyslas dunes, at the mouth of the Dovey, are part of the Dyfi National Nature Reserve.

Britain 300 years ago that it scavenged even in the streets of London. Now there are only about 50 of these graceful birds in Britain, and these are all in central Wales.

Llyn Brianne is about 10 miles north of Llandovery and reached from there along the A483, and then by minor roads that branch off it at Cynghordy.

Cd   Llyn Clywedog

Fed by streams hurtling down steep, rocky slopes, the Afon Clywedog used to be one of the main causes of flooding in the Severn valley. Llanidloes, Newtown, Welshpool and Shrewsbury knew that they could expect trouble when heavy rain fell on the hills above the Clywedog.

But the turbulent, troublesome river was tamed when Llyn Clywedog was created. Its 237 ft high dam, the tallest in Britain, was completed in 1968 at the southern end of 6 miles of water winding between the jutting snouts of the hills. The water-level is allowed to fall during the summer to give plenty of spare capacity to absorb the fury of winter storms. Sailing boats scud over

the reservoir, their sails adding bright dashes of colour to the scene of green hills and woodlands.

Now the energetic rivulets tumbling down the dingles of birches, hawthorns, rowans and hazels add to the interest of the shores. From the southern end of the reservoir a long, wooded peninsula curves out across the water. A scenic trail of 2½ miles, which can be cut short to a mile, loops round it. The trail crosses mixed woodland where parties of redpolls dart, and leads through conifer woods and by grassy banks haunted by vivid butterflies

287

NEAR LLYN BRIANNE The Afon Tywi is the longest river within Wales, flowing 65 miles from Esgair Garthen to Carmarthen Bay. It is at its loveliest near the lonely village of Rhandirmwyn, 4 miles south of the Llyn Brianne dam.

and wild thyme, tormentil, harebells and heather sweeten the air in their seasons.

A road that runs to the west of the lake climbs and dives over hills and valleys with the glistening waters almost constantly in view, then skirts the water's edge for a while before curving away into Hafren Forest. The forest, 17 sq. miles of conifers planted by the Forestry Commission since 1937, takes its name from the Afon Hafren – more widely known as the Severn, which rises a few miles to the west and flows through the woodland for 5 miles. On its way, the young river gathers in the water from the streams and rivulets that hurry down from the hills along boulder-strewn gullies and over gushing waterfalls.

Several marked walks explore the cool glades and ferny, damp hollows beside the streams. The longest walk, of 8 miles, follows the Severn back to its source 2,000 ft up on the slopes of Plynlimon. A shorter, but strenuous, walk of 3½ miles leads past the waterfall of Hafren-tori-gwddf – 'Severn-break-its-neck' – and the mile-long Cascades Trail passes a picturesque waterfall that drops into a deep pool once used for sheep-washing.

The minor road that skirts the western side of Llyn Clywedog branches west from the B4518, 2 miles north-west of Llanidloes. The Hafren Forest car park is 9 miles along this minor road.

Bd ## Ponterwyd

The 2,468 ft high bulk of Plynlimon soars majestically to the north of the village of Ponterwyd, gathered around a craggy gorge above the Afon Rheidol. Plynlimon (or Pumlumon Fawr) is a long cluster of smooth-sided hills that merges into one extensive whalebacked mountain. Just north of its highest point, rocky outcrops round a small tarn give it a more conventionally mountainous look.

Plynlimon's moist, peaty slopes are the source of the rivers Severn, Wye and Rheidol. The minor road coming north from Ponterwyd on the western slope, above the Rheidol, is the best start for a climb up the mountain. A track turns north-east from the road 2 miles north of Ponterwyd, mounts a shoulder of hill topped by woodland and joins a path that runs north to the summit. From here you can see the mountains of North and South Wales, and look north-westwards across the dark green expanse of the Rheidol Forest to Cardigan Bay.

One and a half miles south of Ponterwyd is the hamlet of Ysbyty Cynfyn. Its present church, built in 1827, stands on ground where people have worshipped various gods for about 4,000 years. Five prehistoric monoliths – the remains of a stone circle used for pagan religious ceremonies – now form part of the churchyard wall. The first Christian church at Ysbyty Cynfyn was probably built almost 1,500 years ago by Celtic monks. The 'new' religion often took over ancient pagan sites.

From the churchyard there is a walk of a few hundred yards to Parson's Bridge. The path zigzags down the slope beneath the filigree of slender birches and bright oaks – emerald in summer, amber in autumn – to the bridge that spans the most dramatic part of the Rheidol Gorge. Far below it the river, which has raced south from Ponterwyd between crags and steep banks, seethes and roars among the rocks and holes it has sculpted and smoothed. Then it hastens on again through the tree-hung slopes towards Devil's Bridge.

Ponterwyd is on the A44, 12 miles east of Aberystwyth.

Bb ## Pumpsaint

Gold for the coffers of ancient Rome was once mined on the slopes rising steeply above the Afon Cothi. Where the village of Pumpsaint now stands, the Romans built a fort covering

RUSHING TORRENT On its way to meet the Afon Rheidol, the foaming Mynach surges through a rocky gully near Devil's Bridge, south of Ponterwyd. Here the Mynach plunges some 400 ft through a series of scenic waterfalls.

probably brought in specially for the ore-crushing.

Pumpsaint is on the A482, 7 miles south-east of Lampeter. The mines are about ¼ mile east of the village along a marked minor road.

Cc   Rhayader

The Afon Elan threads its way south through a world of heath-topped hills where grouse, skylarks and meadow pipits abound. More than 60 rivulets and streams run down the steep, grassy folds between the hills to mingle in its waters. Four reservoirs are strung along the Elan – Craig Goch, Pen-y-garreg, Garreg Ddu and Caban Coch – all of them long and narrow, and shielded from each other by thrusting shoulders of wooded hills.

Rhayader, the gateway to the valley, stands on the River Wye a mile or two north of the spot where the Elan joins it. It is a small town of colour-washed buildings clustered round a crossroads. In spring and autumn the town is thronged with farmers and sheep at the

5 acres. Iron Age men had already dug there for the yellow metal before the Romans came, but from about AD 75 the Romans exploited the deposits much more methodically than earlier miners. The mine was probably worked by the Romans for some 250 years and reworked at various periods since.

Three waymarked National Trust paths of 1, 3 and 5 miles explore the old workings. The paths climb through groves of mossy-limbed oaks and across sheep-grazed fields that give wide views over a landscape of rounded hills, deep valleys, woodlands and small farms.

The Romans built a 4 mile aqueduct from the Afon Annell, and a 7 mile aqueduct from the Cothi. Holding-tanks and sluice gates were built into the system. About 3 million gallons of water a day could be delivered in powerful streams that washed away the

topsoil and exposed the gold-bearing ore. When all the gold near the surface had been extracted, shafts and tunnels were dug to reach the ore.

Extracted ore was pounded and washed before being sent to the mint. Carreg Pumpsaint, the 3 ft high stone which stands in the grassy clearing where the marked walks start, was almost certainly used for the pounding of ore. But folklore has a more romantic explanation for the hollows that pit its surface. Five saintly brothers are said to have sheltered beside the stone during a blizzard. As the brothers – Gwyn, Gwyno, Gwynoro, Celynin and Ceitho – huddled against the stone, their shoulders made the round depressions in it. The name Pumpsaint recalls the brothers, for it means 'five saints'. The stone is in fact diorite, a hard rock which is not found locally, and was

BETWEEN TWO RIVERS The desolate Gors Lŵyd wetlands are near the head of the Elan valley between the upper reaches of the Elan and the Ystwyth. They lie 8 miles north-west of Rhayader along the old coach road to Devil's Bridge.

stock sales. The road into the Elan valley passes a neat Victorian 'navvy' village built to house the men who created the first of the reservoirs, Caban Coch, completed in 1904. The houses nestle beneath crags, and are reached by a Victorian 'Gothic' suspension-bridge spanning the river.

Beyond the bridge, the road skirts Caban Coch Reservoir, crosses the dam and then follows the Afon Claerwen as it flows beneath lofty crags and thunders over a boulder-strewn waterfall. The countryside around is wild, bracken-clad and bright in autumn with the red berries of mountain ash. The road comes to an end on the top of the Claerwen Reservoir dam, which was completed in 1952.

A drive up the four Elan reservoirs passes through 9 miles of glorious lakeland, with the reflections of trees, crags and sky mirrored in the shining water – viewed first from the east and then the west as the road crosses the head of Garreg Ddu. But the uplands between the Elan valley and the Claerwen Reservoir are for those walkers and pony-trekkers who love to see the bold shapes of the hills in all their grandeur. There is a 6 mile track along the north

bank of the Claerwen Reservoir, and in another mile it joins a track called Ancient Road. This strides north-east across the hills for 7 miles – reaching 1,750 ft at the highest point – until it strikes the road at the head of the Elan reservoirs.

Rhayader is on the A470, 13 miles north-west of Builth Wells. The B4518 runs south-west along the Elan valley from Rhayader for 3 miles, then becomes an unclassified road skirting the reservoirs.

Bc Strata Florida

Hidden away in a green and peaceful valley that gathers the upper waters of the Afon Teifi are the ruins of Strata Florida Abbey. Steep hills patched with stands of trees look down on the abbey that was once a centre of learning, holiness and business. It was in 1164 that Cistercian monks first settled in Ystrad Fflur, the 'vale of flowers'; Strata Florida was their Latin version of the name. A large Norman church and abbey were built for them 2 miles from the first site, on land given by Robert Fitz-Stephen, a Norman baron. Local stone was the main material, but it was clad with sand-

stone, which must have been brought in, for there is none locally.

Many a famous gathering met at the abbey. Llywelyn the Great summoned the Welsh princes there to swear allegiance to his son Dafydd in 1238, and noblemen from far away chose to be buried at Strata Florida. The abbey not only attracted the rich, but also became rich itself by trading in sheep, wool and lead. It owned large areas of land, stretching right to the coast 15 miles away. On the shore at Llanon there are curved stone fish-traps that were first built by the monks.

The contemplative life was interrupted by natural and political disasters, as well as by ceremonies and commerce. Lightning struck the abbey in 1285 and caused great damage. Ten years later, Edward I set fire to it because it was a stronghold of Welsh nationalism. It suffered further damage when it became a garrison for Henry IV's troops early in the 15th century during Owain Glyndwr's fight for Welsh independence.

Almost 450 years have passed since Strata Florida was closed by order of Henry VIII. Only the outline of the ground plan and an arch at the west door remain, but in their tranquil setting the crumbling lines of stonework gently evoke the days when monks toiled and prayed among them.

One mile south of Aberystwyth along the A487, the B4340 branches south-east to reach Pontrhydfendigaid in 13 miles. From there, a minor road leads to Strata Florida 1 mile to the south-east.

Bb Tregaron

Stretching north from the town of Tregaron lies a 4 mile wilderness of wetland. Thousands of years ago a glacier

WELSH WESTMINSTER In the early Middle Ages, Strata Florida Abbey was the ceremonial and religious centre of the Welsh princes.

melting at the end of the Ice Age dropped debris that blocked the course of the Afon Teifi. The river spread behind the barrier and formed a large, shallow lake. Gradually the lake filled with sediments and wetland vegetation, which eventually formed successive layers of peat. The accumulating peat formed a convex shape, with its highest points some 20 ft above the river that meanders across it.

More than 3 sq. miles of Tregaron Bog – Cors Caron or Cors-goch Glan Teifi – now form Cors Caron National Nature Reserve, and a permit from the Nature Conservancy Council office in Aberystwyth is needed to visit most parts. But there is a walk along a disused railway line from the road that

---

ZIGZAG FLYER

Two features make the snipe easy to recognise – its very long bill and its erratic flight. It is found mostly on marshy ground or water-meadows, and uses its sensitive bill tip to probe in the mud for worms. Snipe nest on the ground, usually in grass tussocks near water. When startled, they rise up in zigzag flight, uttering their hoarse alarm call. At breeding time, snipe 'drum' in flight by vibrating their outer tail feathers.

Snipe
(Gallinago gallinago)

skirts the bog's eastern edge to an observation tower a mile away.

The moist, acid soil nurtures sundew, bog rosemary, crowberry and cranberry. In high summer the bog is white with the downy heads of cottonsedge, and in autumn it is rusty red with their dead stalks. Curlews, lapwings, sedge warblers and reed buntings are among the marsh birds that breed there, and among the rare predators that visit the bog are hen harriers, merlins and red kites. It is one of the last refuges of the otter, and a summer hunting ground for polecats.

From Tregaron, the 'Mountain Road' runs south-east some 15 miles to the hamlet of Abergwesyn. The road, narrow and very steep in places, climbs to almost 1,600 ft as it rises and drops across the wild, windswept tracts cut by

---

WOODLAND MOUSE

A yellow collar between its forelegs gives the yellow-necked mouse its name. Found mostly in deciduous woods, its body length is about 4 in. and its tail longer. This makes it larger than the wood mouse, and it also has a redder coat and whiter belly. Yellow-necked mice are found in southern England as well as central and eastern Wales.

Yellow-necked mouse
(Apodemus flavicollis)

---

deep, steep-sided valleys. This was the empty landscape that earned the name 'Desert of Wales'. Now Forestry Commission plantations are changing its appearance, but it still rolls on seemingly for ever.

The wide expanse of the 'desert' was only the beginning of a journey for the drovers who used the mountain track from medieval times until the end of the 19th century. They would set out from Tregaron with cattle, sheep, pigs and even geese and turkeys to walk to markets as far away as Kent and Essex. The fowls had their feet coated with tar to save them from damage on the long trek. The drovers were accompanied by corgi dogs which were trained to keep the livestock together in open country. The dogs often made their own way home, arriving several days before their masters.

Tregaron is 9 miles north-east of Lampeter on the A485. The walk to the observation tower over the bog starts from the B4343, 3 miles north of Tregaron.

Bc
Vale of Rheidol

The Afon Rheidol is one of the most energetic rivers in Wales. It falls 1,750 ft in a 25 mile course from its source on Plynlimon to the sea at Aberystwyth. Some of its energy is now checked in the Nant-y-môch Reservoir and converted to electricity in generating stations, but the river has long ago fashioned the delights of its lower valley. From the lanes that dip into the valley, or from the narrow-gauge steam railway that runs up from Aberystwyth, you might see herons visiting from the Dovey estuary. Blackthorn thickets spread across the ungrazed land, numerous sand martins are attracted to the still backwaters where insects

GREEN DESERT The mountain road south-east from Tregaron to Abergwesyn crosses a once-desolate area known as the 'Desert of Wales'. But today, the Cwm Berwyn forest has softened the outlines of some of the windswept hills.

---

breed, and occasionally you may see the brilliant turquoise flash of a kingfisher darting across the water.

As the valley becomes narrower and steeper, the sides are clothed with sessile oaks, birches, beeches, sycamores and rowans. Pied flycatchers, blue tits, nuthatches and redstarts breed here. Higher still, old lead workings have left their marks on the slopes.

Now the valley becomes even deeper and more confined, until it is a gorge 800 ft deep. The scenic climax comes at a sharp bend where the Rheidol, thundering south from its craggy cleft, is joined by the Mynach flowing from the east on a course higher by 400 ft.

Tumbling down to join the Rheidol, the Mynach produces one frothing silver cascade after another, hissing noisily over the rock walls. Three bridges span the gorge. The medieval arched bridge lies at the lowest point – and is unaccountably named Devil's Bridge, although it was built for the monks from Strata Florida. The 18th-century bridge is much higher, and the 19th-century one is highest of all.

From Aberystwyth the A4120 runs south of the Vale of Rheidol, and the A44 runs north; lanes from them lead down to the valley, but no road runs along its full course. The A4120 reaches Mynach Falls 12 miles east of Aberystwyth.

SNOWDONIA'S PEAKS AND VALLEYS

In the wild mountains, lonely passes and secret lakes of Snowdonia the spirits of great heroes linger still

Snowdon is by no means the highest mountain in Britain – many Scottish peaks exceed its 3,560 ft – but high-rearing cliffs, knife-edged ridges and still lakes, cupped in vast cauldrons of glacier-carved rock, combine to make it one of the most spectacular. As is often pointed out, a line drawn due south from Snowdon on the map does not encounter anything higher until it reaches the Pyrenees, and on the rare clear day the views from the summit are extraordinary – a great airy compass that reaches deep into Scotland, takes in part of Ireland, the Isle of Man, south-west Wales and even the distant Pennines. Legends crowd upon the mountain's tumultuous slopes: Afanc, a water-monster, lives in Glaslyn, a lake near the summit; the ravens of Gwynedd, by the pattern of their wheelings and croakings about the crags, foretell danger or glory for Wales; while the topmost peak's Welsh name, Yr Wyddfa – 'the tomb' – recalls the old story that it is actually a burial mound erected over a giant slain by King Arthur.

The mountain's splendour epitomises the spirit of the 845 sq. mile Snowdonia National Park, whose stern beauty has drawn generations of naturalists and mountaineers, poets and painters, and lovers of lonely places. It is best seen on foot, but for the less energetic there is the sudden revelation of the Snowdon 'horseshoe' breaking through the clouds above the A4086 south-west of Capel Curig; or Glyder Fawr,

MOUNTAIN LAKES The ridge of Y Lliwedd below Snowdon towers some 1,500 ft above the waters of Llyn Llydaw, with the smaller Glaslyn in the foreground. Winding above the far shore of Llyn Llydaw is the Miners' Track, one of the paths to the top of Snowdon.

Glyder Fâch and the mighty ramparts of Tryfan soaring above the A5 as the road climbs Nant Ffrancon.

This is mountaineer's country, where the conquerors of Everest trained. At Pont y Gromlech, an information board points out some of Snowdon's classic ascents; these are strictly for experts with ropes, helmets and ice-axes, but if your object is simply to get to the top of a mountain, there is no need to go to such lengths. Six well-trodden paths climb to the summit of Snowdon, and three ascend the slopes of Cader Idris. But always treat the mountains with respect and adhere to the Hill-walkers' Code (see p. 410). Benevolent weather can change with lethal rapidity; when heavy cloud blankets the upper slopes, sheer drops of 1,000 ft await disorientated wanderers.

For those who wish to take things more easily, there are the National Park's numerous waymarked trails that provide not only ample exercise, but also a splendid insight into the natural history, farming methods and industrial heritage of the region. Snowdonia is the heart and sanctuary of Wales, where people have lived and worked since the Stone Age. It is also a land of heroes, such as Llewelyn the Great and Llewelyn ab Gruffydd, the first and last Welsh Princes of Wales, who fought their wars of independence against the English. The great chain of castles built by Edward I to contain them bears witness to the effectiveness of their threat.

'I love its sea-marsh and its mountains,
And its fortress by its forest and its bright lands,
And its meadows and its water and its valleys,
And its white seagulls and its lovely women.'

This was written 800 years ago by Hywel ap Owain, Prince of Gwynedd.

Places to visit

Map ref. Bd **Aber**

A far-off murmur of falling water swells to a mighty crescendo, drawing the walker along the path that accompanies the busy, swirling Rhaeadr-fawr river on its 2 mile course through the Aber Valley National Nature Reserve. At the head of the valley, the river bursts through a cleft in the high cliffs to fall in a 120 ft white skein to the darkly glistening rocks below.

The falls provide a suitably dramatic ending to a remarkably pleasant walk. The valley's steep sides are clothed with ash, oak, alder and birch, and high above them again are the wooded slopes of Maes y gaer, whose 731 ft summit is crowned by an Iron Age fort. The river, driven on by the impetus of its tumble, swirls and eddies around boulders and fallen trees. But unperturbed by all this activity, a dipper may be seen walking totally submerged on the river bed in search of food.

The village of Aber stands at the valley mouth beside its motte, or mound, which is all that is left of a castle built by the Normans. For centuries, the village was a starting point for travellers to Anglesey, who crossed the Lavan Sands at low tide. At Bont Newydd, about three-quarters of a mile along the valley, the river is crossed by

a stone bridge. Beyond, a rough track which is actually a Roman road leads to the Vale of Conwy.

Aber village is situated on the A55, between Bangor and Llanfairfechan.

Cb **Bala Lake**

Standing on the tiny promenade in Bala village and gazing down the 4 mile length of Llyn Tegid, or Bala Lake, to the ramparts of Aran Benllyn, Aran Fawddwy and Cader Idris at the far end, the valley appears as though it had been created by gigantic hands that had gripped the mountains on either side and torn them apart to form the water-filled gash that is the largest natural lake in Wales.

Though barely a mile wide, its cold, dark waters reach abruptly down to a depth of 150 ft, providing a home for the gwyniad, a trout-like fish found nowhere else in Britain. Less certainly, they also cover a palace, a prince and all his people who were drowned for their wickedness. The only survivor was a harpist, who had been given timely warning of the approaching cataclysm by a small bird.

The A494 from Dolgellau follows the line of a Roman road that ran to Caer Gai fort, about half a mile from the south-west corner of the lake. During the 1st century AD, this was occupied by the First Cohort of Nervii, auxiliary infantry from what is now Belgium. The fortifications they left are still impressive, but permission to see them should be sought from the nearby farm.

Roads run down both sides of the lake, the views are glorious, and there are plenty of paths leading to the pebbled shore. The Afon Dyfrdwy, flowing from its source on the high moors,

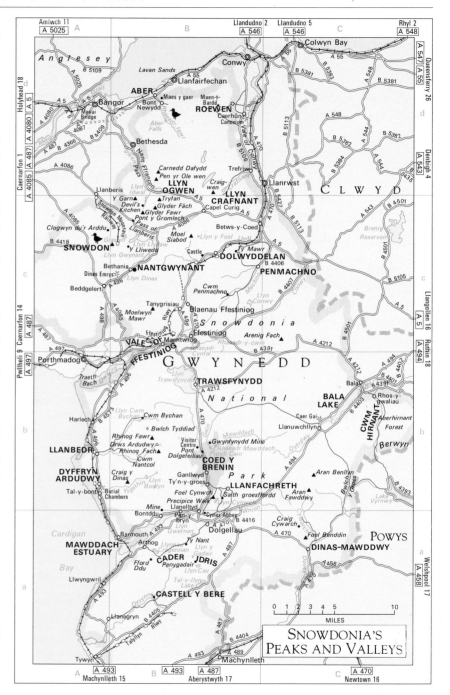

enters Bala Lake at its southern end and exits at the northern end where it becomes the Dee. Local tradition has it that the river waters run straight through those of the lake without mingling.

Bala Lake lies beside the A494, some 15 miles north-east of Dolgellau.

Ba ## Cader Idris

Wherever you go in Snowdonia, Cader Idris is there too. This quiet dominance is due not so much to its height – at its highest point it is only 2,927 ft – as to its extent, a great rolling heave of volcanic rock that runs for some 10 miles across north-west Wales, dividing the old territory of Gwynedd from the land of Powys. It rises sharply above Dolgellau and descends in craggy steps to the sea at Llwyngwril, and everywhere there are the scars of the Ice Age – beetling cliffs 1,000 ft high and deep, stilly, water-filled hollows.

The summit ridge of frost-shattered boulders is called Penygadair, and is best reached by way of the Pony Track which begins at Ty Nant, 3 miles south-west of Dolgellau, along a minor road past Llyn Gwernan. It is a long climb, taking some two or three hours, but the view from the top is among the best in Britain. Far off to the east are the hills of the English border, and to the west, across the Irish Sea, the mountains of Wicklow. Immediately below to the north-west is Llyn y Gadair, like a sheet of blue-grey slate held in a clasp of rock, and to the south-east the reputedly bottomless pool of Llyn Cau, dark and still below its protecting rim of volcanic cliffs. A monster lives here, so it is said, its presence confirmed by a rash youth in the 18th century who, bathing in the

lake for a dare, abruptly disappeared beneath the surface, never to be seen again. Another legend of the same period says that if you sleep by Llyn Cau side, you will awake blind, mad or a poet.

Cader Idris means 'Idris's Chair', but who Idris was is uncertain. Possibly he was a giant or, more likely, a Celtic chieftain who died fighting the Saxon invaders about AD 630. Whatever the truth of the matter, as Charles Darwin said: 'Old Cader is a grand fellow and shows himself superbly with ever-changing light. Do come and see him.'

The best way to follow Darwin's advice is to take the A493 to Dolgellau, with Cader Idris dominating the eastern skyline. Otherwise, come by the A487 from Machynlleth.

Ba ## Castell y Bere

The Dysynni river flows from Tal-y-llyn Lake in the shadow of Cader Idris, then makes a sudden right swerve between the mountain peaks to enter a broad, fertile valley. Here, the fields are lush green and trimly hedged; the mountains no longer crowd in, but are instead misty slopes rising gently from the valley floor.

About half a mile short of the head of the valley there is a rocky headland on which stand the sad remains of Castell y Bere, oddly incongruous in this calm, green place. The last Welsh stronghold to fall in Edward I's conquest of Snowdonia, its garrison of 49 men surrendered to the Earl of Pembroke's army after a ten-day siege in 1283, a year after the death of Prince Llywelyn ab Gruffydd. The castle's custodian was Dafydd, the prince's unruly brother, who managed to escape before the surrender, but only to wan-

der as a fugitive among the crags of Cader Idris. His presence there was betrayed by his own countrymen, and he was captured and taken to Shrewsbury where he was tried on a number of charges ranging from blasphemy and murder to compassing the king's death. Verdict and sentence were a foregone conclusion. He was hanged, drawn and quartered and his head sent to decorate the Tower of London beside that of his brother.

Now the only tangible memory of those last stormy hours of Welsh independence is the jagged grey walls of Castell y Bere that appear almost as one

FLYERS GREAT AND SMALL

For centuries the raven was persecuted for its sinister appearance, as a bird of ill-omen. Measuring about 2 ft from beak to tail, it is the world's largest perching bird. In contrast the dunnock is a wren-like bird, sometimes called the hedge sparrow. Juvenile dunnocks are spotted, but later develop a grey head and breast.

Raven
(*Corvus corax*)

Dunnock
(*Prunella modularis*)

with the lichen-covered rocks of the ridge. Worn and weathered steps lead up to the broken ramparts that look high over the valley to the boulder-strewn hillsides, where kestrels and buzzards fly.

An unclassified road leads up the Dysynni valley from Llanegryn, which is situated just off the A493, 3 miles north of Tywyn.

Bb ## Coed y Brenin

The King's Forest – Coed y Brenin – was so named to commemorate the Diamond Jubilee of King George V in 1935, and a royal place it is indeed, all 22,000 acres of it, embracing farmlands and rapids, mountain views and gold mines, and mile upon mile of forest trails along which there is at least a chance of seeing otters and polecats, buzzards and fallow deer.

Of all these pleasant things, the only one to have passed away is gold, and it is hard to believe now that in the 1840s people dug into the Mawddach valley in search of the metal with a fervour exceeded only by that of the Californian miners of the same period. Results were not comparable, however. During the decade some 24 mines were opened and 150 shafts sunk, but almost all these ventures were abandoned since the value of the gold found did not equal the cost of getting it out of the ground. One mine, the Gwynfynydd, did struggle on until 1938, but now it, too, stands derelict along the 'Gold Road' footpath that starts near Ganllwyd.

The remains of the ore-crushing mill stand on a triangle of land between Pistyll Cain and Rhaeadr Mawddach, two splendid waterfalls flanked by trees that flare into glorious colour during

295

early autumn. The voice of Rhaeadr Mawddach, the falls that powered the mill, can be heard far down the valley, while a bridge at the foot of Pistyll Cain offers a fine duck's-eye view of that tumbling cascade.

The forest's many miles of footpaths include waymarked trails that start from Pont Dolgefeiliau, a bridge where drovers paused to have their cattle shod before beginning the trek over the mountain to the markets of England. One of the trails follows a section of Sarn Helen, a Roman road built to link North and South Wales, while another, between Ty'n-y-groes and Llanfachreth, runs through a pretty little arboretum, the ideal place for a short and not too energetic stroll.

Pont Dolgefeiliau is on the A470, 6 miles to the north of Dolgellau. There is a visitor centre ¼ mile off the road which houses an exhibition of restored gold-mining equipment.

Cb Cwm Hirnant

The tiny village of Rhos-y-gwaliau is the northern gateway to Cwm Hirnant. The narrow road plunges into the valley, dark with the conifers of Aberhirnant Forest, and follows a crystal-clear stream before climbing 1,600 ft into the Berwyn mountains. Keep an eye open for the enchanting picnic place carved out beside the stream.

The summit of the road looks down upon Lake Vyrnwy, a mile across by

---

LLYN CAU The 'shut in lake' is held in an immense crag-enclosed bowl scooped from the slopes of Cader Idris by an Ice Age glacier. Rising above it are the cliffs of Craig Cau and the massive column of Pencoed Pillar.

---

5 miles long and appearing entirely natural in its dark green framing of mature conifers. In fact, it was created in 1881 to supply Liverpool with water, and is a fine example of what Victorian engineers could do when resolved upon a blending of the works of man and nature. The 144 ft high dam, faced with 12 ton blocks of stone, looks like a medieval fortification, while the jaunty little tower on the eastern shore could have been transported straight from the banks of the Rhine or the Loire. Actually, it marks the beginning of the 75 mile pipeline that carries the water to Liverpool.

The road crosses the dam and runs right round the lake. This is a pleasant enough drive, but if you wish for further adventures then take the road that runs off the western shore and climbs up over the desolate moors to Bwlch y Groes, the 'Pass of the Cross'. At 1,790 ft, this is the highest stretch of mountain road in Wales.

Rhos-y-gwaliau lies about 1 mile south-east of Bala on a minor road off the B4391. Bala is on the A494.

Ca Dinas-Mawddwy

It used to be said of Dinas that its earth is blue and its sky is water, emphasising the aloofness of the place from the rest of Wales. True enough, lead and slate have been its industries, and the smooth, steep mountains that ring the village attract more than their fair share of thunderstorms and mist. But what really makes Dinas different is its inhabitants, who for centuries have been aware that they are not quite like the remainder of the Welsh people. In South Wales the population tends to be dark, and in Anglesey fair, but in Dinas there is and always has been a

strong preponderance of red-headed folk, and it has been suggested that they are in fact descendants of long-ago Scots colonists from Ireland or northern Britain.

It is not unknown for red hair and an independence of spirit to go together, and perhaps it was this that led to the formation of the Red Brigands in the 16th century. Whether they were really thieves or a band of red-haired men with a violent dislike of outsiders is uncertain, but at any rate they terrorised the district until they were suppressed with sword and rope in 1554. Their only monument is a pub called The Brigands' Inn, and today Dinas is a peaceful, single-street village of considerable charm and character. Just north of it, a narrow lane curves around the foot of Foel Benddin and into the Cywarch valley to end beneath the spectacular 2,200 ft high crags of Craig Cywarch. The track beyond the lane leads into the heart of the lonely Aran mountains, which reach their climax at the 2,970 ft summit of Aran Fawddwy.

Dinas-Mawddwy lies on the A470, 8 miles east of Dolgellau.

Bc Dolwyddelan

The spectacularly lovely road between Betws-y-Coed and Blaenau Ffestiniog follows the winding Afon Lledr and comes to the village of Dolwyddelan, frowned over by the razor crags of Moel Siabod. The mountain's boulder-strewn slopes and shattered pinnacles, reaching up to 2,860 ft, look like the debris of some titanic explosion at the world's beginning.

Just west of the village, and appearing as though it had grown from the crag on which it stands, is a mighty

castle. Its great rectangular tower dates from the 12th century, and is one of the oldest of its kind in Britain. Here, almost certainly, Llewelyn the Great was born in 1173, and later the castle played an important role in the struggles of Llewelyn ab Gruffydd against Edward I; but it finally fell to the English king in 1283. The savage terrain round about can have changed little since those tumultuous days, and you can see it from a Welsh man-at-arms viewpoint by climbing up to the ramparts.

But should you wish a more intimate glimpse, you should take the path that runs northwards from the village through the woods for about 1½ miles until it breaks into open country just short of Llyn y Foel. There, by the deep, cold lake beneath the tumbled wildness of Moel Siabod, is the loneliness and majesty of Snowdonia in microcosm. A further scramble, up a fairly hard climb to the north-east shoulder of the mountain, gives you the entire National Park – Snowdon itself to the west and, all about, the mountains, forests and lakes of one of the few wildernesses left in Europe.

Dolwyddelan is on the A470, some 5 miles north-east of Blaenau Ffestiniog.

Ab Dyffryn Ardudwy

The golden hem of sand that runs from Barmouth to Harlech is bucket-and-spade country, but behind Dyffryn Ardudwy village, miles of lonely footpaths and ancient tracks run off into the wild hinterland of the Rhinog mountain range. One track leads to Llyn Bodlyn, the remote source of the Afon Ysgethin which on its curling 5 mile course runs around Craig y Dinas, with its Iron Age hill-fort, before coming to the sea beyond Tal-y-bont.

That the area was not always lonely is apparent in the great number of prehistoric remains – cairns, standing stones and stone circles – scattered about the hills. Most impressive perhaps are the Neolithic twin burial chambers near the village. The stones surrounding them are the remains of their covering cairn which, when originally built, was 100 ft long and 50 ft across.

Evidence of the drowned city of Cantref-y-Gwaelod that lies beneath the waters of Cardigan Bay is less tangible. Its story is about the dissolute prince who neglected his sea defences in favour of persistent carousing until, one stormy night, the city and all its inhabitants were overwhelmed by the waves. A causeway called Sarn Badrig can be seen at low tide running out into the sea just north-west of Dyffryn Ardudwy, which is often pointed out as part of the lost city's sea wall. Unimaginative geologists, however, declare it to be a natural reef.

Dyffryn Ardudwy is 5 miles north of Barmouth on the A496.

Ab   Llanbedr

The little village stands between the mountains and the sea, looking west across the salt-marshes and the dunes to Cardigan Bay and east to the mouths of two valleys that run deep into the heart of the lonely Rhinog range. One narrow road, edged by lichen-clad trees, ends at Cwm Bychan, a vast, rocky amphitheatre with a jewel-like lake set at its centre. An easy walk through a magical wood leads to the Roman Steps, a paved route now generally, if reluctantly, conceded to be a medieval packhorse way rather than the work of the legions. But to be fair, such tracks were often constructed on paths already established, and it is not unlikely that the Romans did come this way in search of minerals. Whoever built the track, its fine, sensible course climbs up to the wild pass of Bwlch Tyddiad before curving down again to join the Dolgellau–Ffestiniog road.

The twisting road up neighbouring Cwm Nantcol takes in two nature trails before petering out at a gate overlooked by the tumbled peaks of Rhinog Fawr and Rhinog Fach. They stand at 2,362 ft and 2,333 ft – modest edifices by local standards – but their jagged crags and pinnacles give them a stark dignity all their own.

The pass between them is called Drws Ardudwy – the 'Door of Ardudwy' – and was a gateway to the coastal plain long before today's roads were built.

The roads into the valleys start just east of Llanbedr, which is 3 miles south of Harlech on the A496.

Bb   Llanfachreth

Despite its awesome name, the Precipice Walk near Llanfachreth is an easy 3 mile ramble with little climbing involved since, throughout its circular course, the path sticks fairly constantly to the 800 ft contour, with the steep flank of Foel Cynwch rising a further 268 ft on one side and an airy drop on the other.

The path, which follows the edge of a precipice, was probably an ancient sheep-track before it was widened and opened to the public in 1890. Its winding course, which loops around the elongated summit of Foel Cynwch before dropping gently down to the shores of Llyn Cynwch, is a gallery to all of Snowdonia. To the north are Snowdon and the Moelwyn range, to the north-west the peaks of Rhinog, to the south Cader Idris, and to the east and north-east the high ranges of Aran and Arenig respectively.

In the valley below Foel Cynwch's south-westerly slope, the remains of a 13th-century Cistercian monastery, Cymer Abbey, stand surrounded by sheep-cropped grass. It was never completed, largely because at the time of its building it was in the path of opposing English and Welsh armies, a situation unsympathetic to the contemplative life.

The Precipice Walk begins near Saith groesffordd, about 1 mile south-west of Llanfachreth at the junction with the Ty'n y groes road. Llanfachreth lies 4 miles north-east of Dolgellau and can be reached, eventually, by a number of minor roads running off the A494.

Bd   Llyn Crafnant

This enchanting lake, darkly set among trees and high hills, lies 2 miles south-west of Trefriw, a tiny spa town with a pump-room and baths. The narrow road to the lake climbs steeply at first, following the rushing Afon Crafnant to a Forestry Commission car park, from which a short, steep walk through the trees brings the near-mile-long sweep of water into view. Whether glittering like polished silver under a bright sky, or pewter-grey beneath lowering clouds, Llyn Crafnant is beautiful. The hills all around sweep down from grey crags to tree-clad slopes that tumble down to the shores. Barely a ripple disturbs the still water, and only a few boulders, like stepping-stones, break the untroubled surface.

Away in the distance, the white-washed walls of an isolated farm-house stand bright beneath the 1,818 ft crags of Craig-wen. Serious walkers can take a footpath that skirts the peak and crosses open moorland before dropping down to Capel Curig.

The lake was formerly a reservoir for the little market town of Llanrwst, whose chief claims to fame are a bridge and a chapel attributed to Inigo Jones. The huge stone coffin on the chapel floor is said to be that of Llewelyn the Great, whose remains were brought by the monks of Conwy to nearby Maenan Abbey, of which only a few foundation stones remain.

Trefriw is on the B5106, 9 miles south of Conwy. Llanrwst lies on the opposite side of the Vale of Conwy, on the A470.

Bd   Llyn Ogwen

The great cloud-capped forms of Y Garn, Glyder Fawr, Glyder Fâch, Tryfan and Pen yr Ole Wen stand watch over the mile-long, shallow waters of Llyn Ogwen. Tryfan is said to be the burial place of Sir Bedivere, the last of King Arthur's knights, and Ogwen one of the possible lakes into which he might have thrown Excalibur. From Tryfan, too, many years ago, a great landslide fell into Ogwen, apparently burying a cave containing a fabulous treasure. A phantom coach has occasionally been reported among the tumbled rocks, and a ghostly passenger who

WHEN WINTER COMES High in the Nant Ffrancon Pass, the shallow waters of the glacier-formed Llyn Ogwen once again become a dazzling sheet of ice, spread out beneath the burly mass of Tryfan with the snow-clad Glyders beyond.

NANT FFRANCON VALLEY Below Llyn Ogwen the valley becomes a tapestry of icy green when the spring snows melt to fill the Ogwen river.

descends from it and disappears into a cleft is said to be the Devil himself.

The most glorious approach to Llyn Ogwen is up the Nant Ffrancon Pass from Bethesda, following the road that Thomas Telford drove through the mountains in the early 19th century. Steep screes plunge down to the roadside, and across the valley great ramparts of rock are streaked with the white threads of waterfalls.

The Afon Ogwen throws itself over the head of the pass in a 200 ft cataract that swirls down a boulder-strewn course to cascade beneath the A5 at Roman Bridge. Part of the original bridge – not Roman, but a medieval packhorse bridge – can be seen beneath the modern structure. Beyond the bridge is Llyn Ogwen, with Pen yr Ole

Wen sweeping down to the northern shore, and the Glyders and Tryfan to the south, towering above the valley of Cwm Idwal.

There is a 2 mile nature trail round the floor of the cwm which passes the Devil's Kitchen, an awesome cleft equally well-known among climbers, botanists and geologists, and goes on to encircle the mountain-shadowed Llyn Idwal, which also has its legend. It is said that 800 years ago a prince of Gwynedd was drowned in the lake, and all the birds fled the lake in sorrow, never to return. But they must have recovered their spirits in more recent times, since herons, gulls, cormorants and ducks all visit the shores.

Llyn Ogwen is on the A5, 9 miles south-east of Bangor.

Ba Mawddach Estuary

The Mawddach river rises in the mountains south-west of Bala, and races white-flecked through tree-stepped gorges until it is braked by the tide at Llanelltyd. Here it is joined by the Wnion, a little downstream from Dolgellau, and the united rivers broaden out into a ragged-shored estuary that must surely be one of the loveliest in Britain. Finally, the Mawddach meets the sea at Barmouth.

John Ruskin, the Victorian art critic, said that he knew of only one walk that excelled that from Dolgellau to Barmouth, and that was the one from Barmouth to Dolgellau. A little ponderous, perhaps, but a hint worth taking for all that, even if Ruskin's preferred route along the north shore is now occupied by the A496. However, it is still a most spectacular drive between the peaks of Rhinog to the north and the regal massif of Cader Idris, rearing its 2,927 ft bulk to the south, on the other side of the estuary. The road passes through Bontddu, a pretty little village, behind which lies St David's mine, the last working relic of the gold fever that gripped this part of Wales in the middle of the last century. Finds were on the whole disappointing, but St David's still pays and in the early 1920s produced a nugget from which the wedding rings of HM Queen Elizabeth the Queen Mother, HM The Queen, Princess Margaret and Princess Anne were made. In 1981 there was just sufficient gold remaining to make a wedding ring for the Princess of Wales.

If you prefer to walk, you can cross the river by the Victorian railway bridge at Barmouth, built high over the water to permit passage to sailing ships, or by the bridge at Pen-y-bryn, 2 miles

west of Dolgellau. The southern shore provides walks of sufficient delight to mollify even Ruskin for the loss of his northerly path – sandbanks and pastures, a bird sanctuary and banks of rhododendrons, all embraced between the great arms of the mountains.

From Arthog village, about a mile north-east along the shore from the southern end of the railway bridge, a steep, twisting little lane leads up on to the moors, presenting an ever-widening panorama of the estuary and the mountain bastions to the north. The lane leads to Llynnau Cregennan – 'Cregennan Lakes' – two dark pools set in a rough moorland plateau. There is an ancient trackway here, marked by standing stones, and known as Ffordd Ddu, the 'Black Road'. It is an old drovers' road, but its course may have been first marked out by the Romans.

Access to the estuary is by both the A496 and the A493.

Bc Nantgwynant

Celtic legends mingle with memories of mountaineering heroes in this long and lovely valley overlooked by Snowdon and the rocky peaks of Glyder Fawr and Glyder Fâch. The Pen-y-Gwryd Hotel 6 miles north-east of Beddgelert is so famous among mountaineers that it is practically an extension of the Alpine Club, and here it was that John Hunt – now Lord Hunt – and his team planned their successful 1953 assault upon Everest.

From the upper part of the valley, where noisy streams thrust through groves of trees greyed with lichen, the Snowdon range, known as Erryri in Welsh, or the 'High Lands', stretches ahead. This great horseshoe of naked rock rises to the summit of Snowdon itself – known as Yr Wyddfa, 'the tumulus' or 'tomb', supposedly the grave of a giant slain by King Arthur.

The lower part of the glacier-gouged valley cups two surprisingly tranquil lakes, Llyn Gwynant and Llyn Dinas. You should come to Gwynant at sunset, when the high terraces of Snowdon flare briefly into old gold and ochre; but spare a glance for Dinas, where the ancient throne of Britain is said to be concealed, awaiting a youth who will one day rediscover it and restore the Celtic kingdom. A waymarked walk, which takes about an hour to complete, climbs steeply from the roadside at the southern end of Llyn Gwynant. The Watkin Path, one of the classic routes up Snowdon, starts from Pont Bethania, a bridge on the A498 just east of Llyn Dinas.

Between Beddgelert and Llyn Dinas, a tree-clothed crag overhangs the road. This is Dinas Emrys, to whose summit clings the remains of strongholds dating from the Iron Age to the Middle Ages. Legends link the place with Merlin, and also with Vortigern, the 5th-century British king who, having called in Danish mercenaries to help him in his struggles against the Scots, was unable to pay them. So they took his kingdom instead.

The A498 runs through the Nantgwynant valley, entering it at Beddgelert before running north-east to meet the A4086 at the entrance to the Pass of Llanberis.

Bc Penmachno

This little village on the banks of the Afon Machno is a good starting place from which to sample the contrasts of Snowdonia. South of the village the road follows the river upstream, and a turning to the right loops into Cwm Penmachno, a mile-long shallow valley of pine-covered slopes where the river trickles merrily over grey rocks between banks tufted with ferns and heather. Back on the road from Penmachno, and continuing south, the scenery changes suddenly. The road climbs almost 1,600 ft to wild moorlands that roll away into the distance. On the skyline is Arenig Fach, towering above bogs, streams and small lakes; in a fold of the land, and reached by a three-quarters of a mile long track, is Llyn Conwy, the source of the Afon Conwy.

Two miles to the north-west of Penmachno is the Bishop Morgan Trail, an easy stroll through forest and upland farming country. It concludes at Ty Mawr, the farmhouse birthplace of William Morgan, Bishop of St Asaph, who translated the Bible into Welsh in the 16th century, so laying the foundations of Welsh Protestantism, and of Welsh as a written prose language. The house is open to the public and contains a number of Bibles as well as typical Welsh farmhouse furnishings.

Penmachno is 4 miles south of Betws-y-Coed, and is reached by taking the B4406 from the A5.

Bd Roewen

The Romans came to this part of Britain in the 1st century AD. Undeterred by the inhospitable countryside, they drove their roads across hills, moors and rivers to link settlements with forts

GREAT DIVIDE Nantgwynant valley and the lovely Llyn Gwynant separate the Snowdon and Moelwyn ranges.

301

and forts with mines. One such road joined Deva with Segontium – modern Chester and Caernarfon – and traces of it can still be seen around Roewen, which actually stands on the route.

West of the village, the Roman road climbs to 1,400 ft and crosses mountains scattered with burial chambers and standing stones that were ancient before the legions came. One burial chamber is called Maen-y-Bardd – the 'Bard's Stone' – and consists of a massive capstone resting upon four uprights. After a while, the metalled road peters out into a broad, well-defined track which links up with a lane leading down to the coast at Aber. This is walking country, with views across the Lavan Sands and the Menai Strait to Anglesey.

The Roman road crossed the Conwy south-east of Roewen, at Caerhûn, where the grass-covered outline of a 4 acre fort can still be seen. Called Canovium, it was built about AD 78 to command the ford, and tradition has it that when the Romans left, some 350 years later, it became the palace of Rhun, a ruler of the ancient country of Gwynedd.

Roewen is 4 miles south of Conwy, and lies just to the west of the B5106 which runs down the western side of the Vale of Conwy to Betws-y-Coed.

Bc Snowdon

Given the rare blessing of ideal conditions, large portions of Wales, England, Scotland, Ireland and the Isle of Man can be seen from Snowdon's 3,560 ft stony summit. The earliest recorded person to enjoy the view was Thomas Johnson, an intrepid botanist who made the ascent in 1639. But he could hardly have been the first ever,

FLORA OF VALE AND PEAK

Though a grass rather than a wild flower, wood melick is a graceful and delicate plant often found growing in woods and hedgerows alongside red campion and foxglove. The Welsh poppy is so called because it was first identified in Wales by the 18th-century botanist Linnaeus. Welsh poppy favours rocky places, as does mossy saxifrage which flourishes at high altitudes. Its white flowers on the mountain slopes appear like a magical scattering of summer snow.

Wood melick
(Melica uniflora)

Welsh poppy
(Meconopsis cambrica)

Mossy saxifrage
(Saxifraga hypnoides)

since Welsh folklore abounds with tales of heroes, giants and dragons that cavorted among the uppermost crags when the world was young.

Snowdon is a massif of volcanic and sedimentary rocks, deep-scarred by Ice Age glaciers – the glaciers that carved the appalling 1,500 ft cliffs overhanging Glaslyn, a lake whose waters are stained blue-green by copper seeping from the mines established on its shores in the 19th century. The lake is said to be the grave of a monster that terrorised the Vale of Conwy until it was bound with chains, hauled over the mountains by the two biggest oxen in Wales, and hurled to its death from the top of the cliffs. Another Snowdon legend was Rhita Fawr, a giant who wore a cloak woven from the beards of the kings he had slain. He met his match in King Arthur, however, and now lies beneath the summit, still called Yr Wyddfa – 'the tomb'.

Snowdon's wild beauty can be appreciated from several places along the A498, but if you wish to know it properly then you must walk. There are several classic routes to the summit, none of them really difficult except in bad weather, which can descend with terrifying swiftness. Walkers must be properly equipped (see p. 410); those who are not are risking life and limb – their own, and those of the Mountain Rescue teams. And remember to allow enough time before night falls; it will take at least five hours to the summit and back, whichever route is chosen.

The walk from Llanberis runs roughly parallel to the Snowdon Mountain Railway, Britain's only rack railway, that runs to within 67 ft of the summit. This walk is the longest but easiest, with superb views of Clogwyn du'r Arddu, a sheer wall that presents some

of the most challenging rock climbs in the country.

The Pyg Track starts from the 1,170 ft high Pass of Llanberis, and is therefore the shortest route in terms of vertical effort. It looks down on those two marvellous lakes, Llydaw and Glaslyn, but there is a steep zigzag scramble up a scree slope before you reach the top. Alternatively, the old Miners' Track may be followed all the way to Glaslyn where another steep path reaches up to join the Pyg Track.

Though it involves a climb of about 3,300 ft, the Watkin Path is perhaps the most interesting route. It was opened in 1892 by Sir Edward Watkin, but the actual ceremony was presided over by W. E. Gladstone who, at 83, climbed as far as the Gladstone Stone where a plaque recalls the feat. The Watkin Path, which starts in Nantgwynant, passes waterfalls, old copper mines and slate workings before its final slippery zigzag to Yr Wyddfa.

The Rhyd Ddu and Snowdon Ranger paths climb the mountain's western slopes from the Beddgelert–Caernarfon road. Both offer relatively easy walking but, again, it should be emphasised that no walk up Snowdon should be taken lightly.

Snowdon, a National Nature Reserve, is best reached by the A4085 or A4086 from Caernarfon.

Bb Trawsfynydd

Looking westwards from the churchyard to the Rhinog mountains, the countryside is a splendid wilderness, lightened a little by the placid waters of Llyn Trawsfynydd in the foreground. The shepherd poet, Ellis Humphrey Evans – better known as Hedd Wyn – was born in Trawsfynydd in 1887, and much of his poetry was inspired by what he saw about him. He was awarded the Bardic Chair at the National Eisteddfod in 1917, but never lived to be enthroned since he was killed in Flanders a few days before the ceremony was due to take place. There is a statue to his memory in the village.

He wrote of the surrounding mountains and valleys, but references to Llyn Trawsfynydd are missing from his works since it did not exist before 1930, when it was created to power a hydroelectric scheme. Half a century later, the 3 mile lake looks as though it has been part of the landscape for ever, and now serves a nuclear power station tucked unobtrusively away on the northern shore.

A narrow, gated road signposted Aber-Geirw leaves the A470 just south of Trawsfynydd, then after 2 miles turns eastwards to cross some of the wildest country in Wales. To the south there are glimpses of Cader Idris, framed by the wooded Gain valley; then the road climbs to over 1,700 ft – one of the highest roads in Wales. Just about the point where it joins the A494, there are fine views of the waterfalls above Llanuwchllyn.

Trawsfynydd is just off the A470, 11 miles north of Dolgellau.

NOBLEST OF THEM ALL Snowdon is part of the 'Ring of Fire', a chain of peaks formed by volcanic action 500 million years ago.

Bc   Vale of Ffestiniog

Behind the church at Ffestiniog there is a 700 ft crag from whose easy-to-climb summit you can see all of this lovely valley – its quiet river and rich alluvial pastures; its framing of mountains, whose lower slopes are draped with hanging woods; its distant ending in the broad gleam of the Dwyryd estuary, where it meets the flats of the Traeth Bach – the 'Little Sands'.

South of the church, a path goes down to Rhaeadr Cynfal, a fall whose waters plunge tumultuously into a 200 ft ravine. A pillar of rock above the fall is called Huw Lloyd's Pulpit, Huw Lloyd being a 17th-century poet, warrior and wizard who used to summon up his demons from here.

The churchyard at Maentwrog, in the heart of the valley, contains an enormous boulder, hurled over the hills by St Twrog in the 6th century to destroy a pagan altar. And even if geologists say that it was probably deposited there by a melting glacier, the deed is remembered still in the village name, which means Twrog's Stone.

The road from Maentwrog to Harlech looks across the estuary to the old quays where slate from the quarries at Blaenau Ffestiniog was loaded into sailing ships. In 1836, a narrow-gauge railway was built to transport the slate down to Porthmadog, but it now carries passengers between Porthmadog and Tanygrisiau.

Ffestiniog is on the A470, 3 miles south of Blaenau Ffestiniog, and Maentwrog is 3 miles west, at the junction of the A496 and A487.

THE LLEYN PENINSULA AND ANGLESEY

Remote, modest hills above patchwork fields are set against vast seascapes and the drama of Snowdonia

Here, on the north-western fringes of Wales, the wild mountains of Snowdonia give way to softer landscapes, planed by primeval seas and Ice Age glaciers. Peaks exceeding 3,000 ft are commonplace in Snowdonia, but the highest point on Anglesey is Holyhead Mountain's 720 ft, while Lleyn's loftiest summit – part of the three-pronged Yr Eifl, 'the Fork' – is only 1,850 ft high. However, despite their modest altitudes, the ancient rocky hills of the area are fine vantage points from which to see the green, brown and summer-gold patchwork of the landscape.

The coasts of both Anglesey and Lleyn are extraordinarily varied. In some places, narrow, high-banked lanes, bright with wild flowers for much of the year, wriggle down to sandy beaches and lonely coves where the waves lap against banks of clean, sea-rounded shingle. In other places, such as Newborough Warren on Anglesey, summer breezes rustle the marram grass over acres of dunes that long ago engulfed medieval farms and fields. Then, by way of contrast, on Anglesey's southern shore there are woods and elegant houses bordering the Menai Strait, where a pair of bridges provide the island's only links with the rest of Wales.

Long stretches of the coastline consist of mile after mile of formidable cliffs and reefs upon which, over the centuries, hundreds of ships have been driven to their deaths in the south-westerly gales of winter.

*S*EA DREAM From the golden coves of Llanddwyn Island at Anglesey's southern tip, Lleyn's hilly spine and Snowdonia's dramatic peaks create a misty blue backdrop beyond the broad water of Caernarfon Bay, all blending in a view of dreamlike perfection.

But there is peace here too, as the early Celtic saints discovered when they built their chapels and hermitages on the little offshore islands.

Once, too, Anglesey was sacred to the Druids, until the Romans stamped out their cult in a savage punitive raid in AD 78, leaving a reminder of their passing in the high-walled fort whose remains still stand in the heart of Holyhead. Four centuries later, the legions departed for ever, leaving the sea roads open to the Irish and Norse pirates whose bloody raidings turned this part of Wales into a near-wilderness, until they in their turn were subdued by the Welsh war-lords whose names still ring in legend.

By the 13th century, however, Anglesey had become the granary of Wales, and the principal seat of the Welsh princes who fought so long and bitterly for Welsh independence. Recognising this, Edward I of England blockaded the island, so cutting off supplies from the Welsh army in Snowdonia – a principal factor in its final defeat.

Now, both Anglesey and Lleyn are largely given over to heathland and rough pasture where smallholders rear pigs, black cattle and geese. Their sturdy, low farmhouses of large, rough-hewn stones are white-cemented over all – often over their slate roofs too – as if to anchor them in place against the buffeting Atlantic winds.

In the fields, hardly remarked upon by the people who work them now, stand the monuments of earlier folk – Neolithic burial chambers, Bronze Age stone circles, and the hill-forts built by the Celts just before the Roman invasion. The Celts, of course, never went away: stocky, darkly handsome, fiercely independent, eloquent in both Welsh and English, their characteristics are best summed up in the person of Lleyn's most famous son – David Lloyd George.

Places to visit

Map ref. Bc **Aberffraw, Anglesey**

The village is a gathering of sturdy, greystone cottages set among close-cropped grass by the side of the shallow, tidal Afon Ffraw, which glides beneath the hump-backed packhorse bridge to disappear in the wilderness of sand-dunes that rolls for nearly a mile down to the sea's edge. But even now the Forestry Commission is altering the scene with massive coniferous plantations. Beyond the dunes, the unmistakable prongs of Yr Eifl soar above the Lleyn coastline.

For 700 years, until about 1300, Aberffraw was the home of Welsh princes. No trace of their palace remains, apart, perhaps, from an arch built into the village church.

A footpath from Aberffraw follows the coast westwards along the cliff-tops overlooking Aberffraw Bay and then northwards to Porth Cwyfan, a lonely little bay sheltering an islet on which the 7th-century Church of St Cyfan stands high on a mound. The island is linked to the shore by a cowrie-scattered causeway which is covered by the sea at high tide. When the church was in regular use, the length of services depended to a great extent on the weather. No matter how eloquent the sermon, the congregation would beat a hasty retreat to the mainland if strong westerly winds threatened to maroon them.

Aberffraw is on the A4080, 13 miles west of Menai Bridge.

Cc **Bryncelli Ddu, Anglesey**

Whitewashed cottages, low farm buildings, fields divided by turf walls draped with red and white valerian – that is the smiling face that the present-day Anglesey shows to its visitors. But look closely, and you will see that once it was very different, a place of great religious significance where a people long forgotten worshipped gods now unknown.

One such reminder is Bryncelli Ddu – 'the Mound in the Dark Grove' – though in fact it stands nowadays in an open field. Constructed some 4,000 years ago, it is the finest passage grave in Wales, concealing in its heart an 8 ft wide burial chamber walled and roofed over with enormous slabs. This has remained as its builders left it; and so has most of the 27 ft long stone-lined passage that leads beneath the mound to the chamber.

When the chamber was opened, it was found to contain a slab incised with elaborate wavy patterns, which covered a pit containing cremated human bones. A cast of the slab can still be seen, but the original is now in the National Museum of Wales in Cardiff. Outside the entrance to the passage, in a kind of forecourt, were discovered the bones of an ox, perhaps offered as a sacrifice when the burial chamber was sealed.

The site was sacred long before the tomb was built, since it was originally occupied by a henge monument – a circle of standing stones surrounded by a broad, deep ditch; this ancient temple has now been most lovingly restored.

A signposted path branches west from the A4080, 2¼ miles south-west of Menai Bridge, and leads to Bryncelli Ddu ¼ mile away. A key to the site may be obtained from the farmhouse near by.

Bd **Cemlyn Bay, Anglesey**

A long arm of shingle cast up by storms separates the tidal waters of Cemlyn Bay from a large, brackish lagoon whose level is controlled by a weir. The lagoon is a breeding ground and sanctuary for many water birds, including

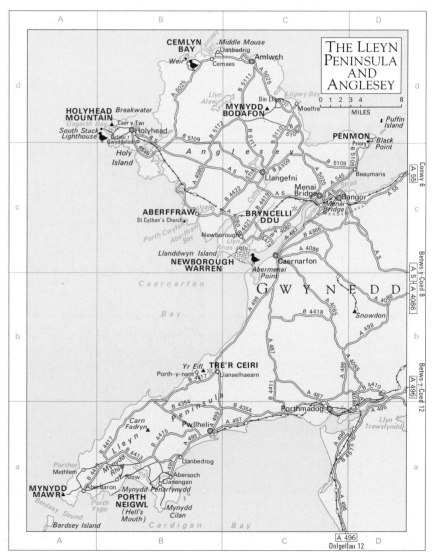

the remarkable Arctic tern, whose migration pattern covers some 10,000 miles a year, from Cemlyn Bay to the Antarctic. The reserve, which is managed by the North Wales Naturalists' Trust for the National Trust, can be seen from the road, and more closely from the bank of sea-smoothed shingle. However, visitors are asked not to walk along the bank between April and July when the birds are breeding. The terns are quite likely to attack anyone who ventures too close to their nests.

A blustery, rugged promontory to the east separates Cemlyn Bay from Cemaes Bay, where three alluring sandy beaches snuggle into the lee of twin headlands. There is fine walking on the promontory, looking across a noble seascape in which there are always large ships in view.

The little fishing village of Cemaes in the deepest recess of the bay has a small tidal harbour that was an important port before Amlwch was developed. Shipbuilding and trading thrived there in the 19th century – and smuggling too, in the hidden coves.

Towards the eastern tip of Cemaes Bay is Llanbadrig, where an ancient church teeters on the brink of a precipitous cliff. It is said to have been founded in the 5th century by St Patrick in thanksgiving for having survived a shipwreck on the Middle Mouse, a wicked reef a mile offshore. The church's simple rendered walls give no hint of its astonishing interior, where tiles and cusped arches gleam in the blue light filtering through the stained-glass window.

The church was restored in 1884 by the 3rd Lord Stanley, a local landowner who had embraced the Islamic faith. He financed the restoration on condition that the new interior

ISLAND LIGHTHOUSE Across a chasm from the cliffs west of Holyhead Mountain lies South Stack, its lighthouse towering 197 ft above the sea. Though tranquil in summer, the cliffs in spring are a shrieking mass of nesting sea-birds.

should resemble that of a mosque. *The A5025, which circles northern Anglesey, reaches Cemaes 22 miles northwest of Menai Bridge. A marked minor road 1 mile further on branches right to Cemlyn Bay, which is 1¼ miles away.*

Bd **Holyhead Mountain, Anglesey**

A craggy fist of rock rising 720 ft above the sea, Holyhead Mountain is the highest point in Anglesey. On a clear day the views are tremendous, taking in the Wicklow Mountains and the Mountains of Mourne in Ireland; the Isle of Man; Snowdon in the southeast; and, to the south across Caernarfon Bay, a glimpse of Bardsey Island at the tip of the Lleyn Peninsula. Dwarfed to toytown proportions below is Holyhead, protected by its 1¾ mile breakwater – the longest in Britain.

Snaking round the summit are the stone ramparts of an Iron Age fort, magnificently engineered to take the best advantage of the natural cliff defences on the western side. Beside the main entrance to the fort, which occupies some 17 acres, ramparts still carry the walk used by lookouts and defenders. Caer y Twr, 'the Fortress of the Tower', was probably a refuge for people of the coastal villages when they were threatened by raiders from across the Irish Sea. The fort was abandoned in the 4th century AD.

But 1,500 years later, Liverpool ship-owners – reacting, perhaps, to some ancestral memory – established a signal station in the old fort in order to capture the earliest possible intelligence of ships inward bound from the New World.

Paths from Holyhead lead up and over the mountain – a rough, breezy walk above the rocky slopes plummeting down to Gogarth Bay. Grey seals breed in the sea caves here, and can often be seen sticking their inquisitive heads out of the surf.

At the southern end of the bay a long flight of steps leads down to South Stack lighthouse, whose single white beam, flashing every ten seconds, can be seen 20 miles away. Between 1809, when the lighthouse was built, and 1827, when the present little suspension bridge was constructed, the lighthouse-keepers used to cross the truly awful ravine between South Stack and the mainland cliffs in a box slung from a cable.

Look back from South Stack to the cliffs, a marvellous tenement of ledges crowded with guillemots, razorbills, ravens, choughs, fulmars and puffins. There, the birds live, breed, feed and eternally yell abuse at each other in a cacophony that drowns even the boom of the sea. South Stack and the cliffs are managed by the RSPB as a bird reserve.

Half a mile inland from South Stack are the remains of a 2nd-century settle-ment called Cytiau'r Gwyddelod, 'the Huts of the Irish'. Perhaps, as legend says, the little houses, once thatched, were occupied by Irish metal-workers. At any rate, though their roofs have gone, the lower parts of the houses still contain hearths and stone seats or beds, reminders of the simple life-style of the folk who once lived here.

Holyhead town lies at the western end of the A5. From here, a minor road skirts Holyhead Mountain, giving access to footpaths to the summit.

Cd Mynydd Bodafon, Anglesey

Heather, bracken, gorse and springy turf carpet the rocky ridge of Mynydd Bodafon, whose numerous paths and tracks make it a delightful place for gentle strolls and long, lazy summer picnics. Rising steeply to 548 ft from a patchwork of fields and woods, the hill commands a superb panorama which takes in the whole of Anglesey, mile after mile of the mainland coast – with ships like toys riding at anchor in Conwy Bay – and behind the coast the serried summits of Snowdonia. The narrow road crossing the hill skirts a small, tranquil pool overlooked by cot-tages and farm buildings, before climb-ing to the summit.

Below to the east is the coastal vil-lage of Moelfre, looking more Cornish than Welsh. Across its pebbly beach there is a magnificent prospect of sea, cliffs and distant mountains which can be seen even better from the mile-long walk along the top of the low cliffs to sandy Lligwy Bay. There is a seaweed-draped wreck lying among the rocks near the coastguard station; this is the coaster *Hindlea*, driven ashore by 100 mph winds in 1959. Another reminder of the savagery this smiling coast can produce is the monument to the 452 people who lost their lives when the *Royal Charter* was wrecked off Moelfre in 1859. Homeward bound from Mel-bourne to Liverpool, she had almost reached port when she encountered a great storm and was pounded to pieces on the rocks within a few yards of the shore. As well as passengers, she was carrying gold – at least £450,000 worth in the prices of the time. Much of it was recovered, but some still remains among the tangle of boilers and barnacle-clad plates of the wreck.

A stretch of beautiful golden sand lies below the path at Lligwy Bay. A few hundred yards along the minor road leading south-east from the beach, a waymarked footpath crosses an open field and runs through a grove of ivy-clad trees to reach Din Lligwy, the well-preserved remains of a for-tified village. A 5 ft thick wall sur-rounds the ruins of nine substantial stone buildings. Almost certainly, this was the palace of Celtic chiefs or lords. To judge by coins and a silver ingot discovered when the site was excavated in 1905, it was abandoned in the 4th century.

Mynydd Bodafon is 1 mile along minor roads leading west from the A5025, 10 and 11 miles north of Menai Bridge.

Aa Mynydd Mawr, Lleyn

Standing guard at the very tip of the Lleyn Peninsula is Mynydd Mawr, a steep, heathery, bracken-clothed hill sitting on top of sheer, black cliffs. A number of charming tracks and lanes, bright with celandines, violets or fox-gloves, climb over and spread out from the hill to explore the craggy shore, with its secret bays and rocky coves. One of them, Porthor, is known as

BUILT TO LAST The massive foundations of the 4th-century dwellings at Din Lligwy, near Mynydd Bodafon, cover half an acre.

Whistling Sands; and in warm, dry weather the sands do at least squeak as you walk over them. The cause is said to lie in the unusual shape of the parti-cles, which make a noise when rubbed together.

Mynydd Mawr is only 524 ft high, but because it sits right on the rim of the land, it makes a magnificent van-tage point. The huge, graceful curve of Cardigan Bay stretches away to the south, and to the north-east are the blue peaks of Snowdonia. Closer at hand Aberdaron sits on its pale, windy beach, and south-west across the choppy water is Bardsey Island.

A desolate strip of land with little rock-strewn fields and a green hump rising to 548 ft at one end – this is how the island looks from the mainland.

LIVING ON A CLIFF EDGE

After diving to fill their gullets with fish for their young, cormorants stand on rocks to dry, often with wings outspread. Their feathers get waterlogged, and this reduces buoyancy and so aids diving. After breeding, cormorants may roam in-land, but kittiwakes are true seabirds. They follow fish shoals over the seas, and come to land only to breed. They cement their cup-shaped nests to the cliff ledge with mud.

Cormorant
(*Phalacrocorax carbo*)

Kittiwake
(*Rissa tridactyla*)

This bleak impression is only slightly modified by a visit, which is not always easily made. There is a fearsome tide-race through Bardsey Sound, and quite often the island is cut off for several days at a time. Nevertheless, in the early Middle Ages, Bardsey was thought to be 'the gate of Paradise', and three pilgrimages to its abbey – now a ruin – were considered, for the soul's health, to be the equivalent of one journey to Rome. The dust of 20,000 Celtic saints is said to mingle with the island's soil.

Now only a handful of people reside among the thousands of birds that attract ornithologists to Bardsey between April and October. Choughs wheel overhead, huge colonies of razorbills, guillemots and kittiwakes clamour on the cliffs, and young Manx shearwaters wait silently in their burrows until dead of night when their parents return to them with food from the sea.

At Llanbedrog, almost 4 miles south-west of Pwllheli along the A499, the B4413 branches right to Aberdaron which is 12 miles further west. A marked minor road from Aberdaron continues west to within ¼ mile of the summit of Mynydd Mawr. Porthor is 2¼ miles north of Aberdaron, near Methlem. Boats for Bardsey Island sail from Aberdaron.

Cc Newborough Warren, Anglesey

Medieval farms and the lost village of Rhosyr lie beneath this wilderness of dunes and the damp hollows known as slacks. Possession of this, the south-west corner of Anglesey, has been contended between man and nature ever since Newborough itself was founded by order of Edward I at the end of the 13th century. Trees were felled then to create farmland, but their removal permitted vast quantities of sand to be swept inland by storms, engulfing houses and choking the anchorage at Abermenai Point. During Elizabeth I's reign, a law was passed forbidding the cutting of marram grass, whose roots help to stabilise sand-dunes. All the same, Newborough later became a centre for marram-weaving. The dunes were a breeding ground for rabbits: as many as 100,000 were trapped every year until their numbers were reduced drastically by myxomatosis in 1954.

Tree planting by the Forestry Commission began in 1948, and now a waymarked trail and six public foot-paths wind through both the new pine forest and the warren. Herring gulls, oystercatchers, curlews, skylarks, swans and many other birds feed among the dunes and on the Cefni estuary's salt-marsh. A bird-watchers' hide is tucked away at the edge of Llyn Rhos-ddu, a small, reed-fringed lake on the back edge of the warren. The warren is a National Nature Reserve managed by the Nature Conservancy Council, and permits are required to visit some parts of it.

A narrow isthmus juts out from the forest, connecting it to the lovely little island of Llanddwyn. As you walk south down the island there is a magnificent prospect of the three cones of Yr Eifl rising straight from the sea, and to the east of them the blue mass of Snowdonia. At the tip of the island a 200-year-old tower, built as a landmark for sailors, overlooks rocks where shags and cormorants breed.

Half a mile after the A5 crosses to Anglesey, the A4080 strikes west from it to reach Newborough after 11 miles. It is a 3 mile walk from Newborough to the very tip of Llanddwyn Island.

SILVER SYMPHONY Pale as if in a perpetual dawn, Aberdaron's beach lies sheltered by the south-western tip of the Lleyn Peninsula. The pewter shallows spill over fine sand, and silver breakers curl in from the deep sea.

Dd   Penmon, Anglesey

Superb views reward walkers who take any one of the routes radiating from the pretty village of Penmon, set on its rocky spur at Anglesey's eastern tip. Across the Menai Strait are the great bastions of Snowdonia; to the east over Conwy Bay is Great Ormes Head, a massive limestone headland above Llandudno; and less than a mile offshore is the craggy lozenge of Puffin Island. A toll-road, free to walkers, runs for three-quarters of a mile to Black Point, where a coastguard station overlooks the island, whose only inhabitants are the birds that gave the place its name. They are less numerous now than they used to be. A main cause of the decline in population was a

NEAR PENMON Beyond the surging waters where Black Point lighthouse stands is Puffin Island. Great Ormes Head juts from the distant mainland.

310

taste – now fortunately abandoned – among French and English gourmets for pickled puffins; to satisfy it, thousands of boned carcases were exported annually in barrels of spiced vinegar. Among the birds' other enemies are rats, which live on the island, robbing the puffin burrows of eggs and young.

Penmon's saint was Seiriol, who in the 6th century established a community here. The remains of his beehive cell, and the well that he used for baptisms, can still be seen among the ruins of the 12th-century Augustinian priory dedicated to him. So, too, was the early medieval monastic settlement on Puffin Island; here the Augustinians were buried, and there are fragments remaining of a Norman tower.

If you walk towards Holyhead, you are treading where the saints have trod. St Seiriol the White, as he was called, and his friend, St Cybi the Yellow, who had established a monastery at Holyhead, used to walk daily the 25 miles between the opposite tips of Anglesey to meet and discuss matters spiritual. Seiriol, who had to walk west in the morning and east in the afternoon, always had his back to the sun and so remained pale. Cybi, on the other hand, was always facing the sun and so acquired a tan.

Penmon is 7 miles north-east of Menai Bridge, and is reached by the A545 to Beaumaris, then by the B5109 and marked minor roads.

Ba   Porth Neigwl, Lleyn

Lofty headlands frame Porth Neigwl's 3½ miles of sandy beach, idyllic on a calm, sunny day, but when south-westerly gales drive snarling waves on to the shore it is easy to understand

why, in the days of sail, the bay acquired its alternative name of Hell's Mouth. Many ships were devoured by its relentless breakers.

Less than a mile behind the beach, near its eastern end, is the tiny village of Llanengan, gathered about the twin-naved church that St Einion, King of Lleyn, founded in the 6th century. The lane south of the village loops round to the beach, while north it runs beside the slow, winding River Soch. Swans live by the quiet pools, herons stalk beside the stream, and ponies run free over the flat, wet lands of the valley. A lane swings 3 miles east and south from the village to mount the grassy promontory of Mynydd Cilan which forms the lower jaw of Hell's Mouth. Beyond the bright gorse and the deep pink valerian that spills from every cranny in the rocks, all Cardigan Bay stretches away to the south.

The upper jaw of Hell's Mouth, Mynydd Penarfynydd, is much steeper and craggier. On its other side is Porth Ysgo, a cliff-backed bay whose sandy beach is generally ignored by the crowds. A stream cascades down to the sea in a series of small waterfalls, through a valley of ferns, gorse and foxgloves. But Porth Ysgo, like its notorious eastern neighbour, becomes a boiling cauldron when gales lash the seas in from the south-west. Behind the headland rises the whaleback ridge of Mynydd Rhiw. There is an exhilarating 2 mile walk along the ridge path that rises to almost 1,000 ft, with the rocky slopes of 1,200 ft Carn Fadryn dominating the view ahead and the long stretch of Hell's Mouth below.

Llanengan is on a minor road 1¼ miles south-west of Abersoch, which is on the A499, 6 miles south-west of Pwllheli. Porth Ysgo, Mynydd Penarfynydd and

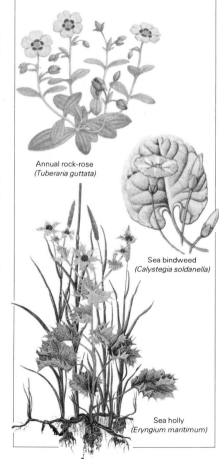

ADORNING THE DUNES

Only among dry turf on Lleyn and South Stack can you hope to find the rare little annual rock-rose. Look for it early in the day, or it will have dropped its petals. Sea bindweed and sea holly are much less choosy about their habitat, in Wales or elsewhere, as long as it encompasses sand-dunes or shingle. The bindweed lies prostrate, with inch-wide trumpets resting among fleshy, round leaves. But sea holly is stiff and erect, 6–12 in. of greyish-green prickliness.

Annual rock-rose
(Tuberaria guttata)

Sea bindweed
(Calystegia soldanella)

Sea holly
(Eryngium maritimum)

VIEW FROM THE PAST From the ancient walls of Tre'r Ceiri hill-fort on Yr Eifl, the Lleyn's backbone of hills stretches away to merge with Snowdonia. Sheltering below Yr Eifl is Porth-y-nant. The 5th-century British king Vortigern fled to this place after losing his kingdom to the Saxons.

LOOKING NORTH-EAST FROM TRE'R CEIRI

Mynydd Rhiw are reached by lanes from Y Rhiw, which is on a minor road at the western end of Porth Neigwl, 7 miles south-west of Llanbedrog.

THE DISUSED QUARRIES OF PORTH-Y-NANT BELOW YR EIFL

Bb Tre'r Ceiri, Lleyn

A sturdy trident thrusting up from the sea dominates the skyline of the Lleyn Peninsula. Yr Eifl, 'the Fork', is the apt Welsh name for the three sharply pointed summits. Their English name, for once more poetic, is The Rivals.

All three cones are scattered with boulders and rocky outcrops, in harsh contrast with the gentle green lands below. It is only on climbing the steep path up the most easterly prong of the fork that you can see that people once lived here, turning inaccessibility into safety. At almost 1,600 ft on the windswept hilltop is Tre'r Ceiri, 'the Giants' Town'. Massive stone walls, 15 ft thick and almost as high in some places, link up natural rocky heights to encircle the remains of an Iron Age settlement of some 150 circular, stone-walled dwellings.

The view is tremendous. On the best days it covers parts of the Isle of Man and Ireland, the whole of Anglesey, Snowdonia's peaks, Cader Idris, the mountains of central Wales, and part of the Pembrokeshire coast, almost 70 miles away across Cardigan Bay. Cer-tainly, the 300 or 400 people who lived in Giants' Town could never have been caught unawares – and perhaps this is why the settlement flourished during most of the Roman occupation.

Tre'r Ceiri is 1 mile west of Llanaelhaearn, which is near the junction of the A499 and B4417. Paths climb Tre'r Ceiri from 1, 2 and 3 miles along the B4417 from Llanaelhaearn.

THE WYE VALLEY AND WELSH BORDERS

Full-scale border wars once raged through today's tranquil pastures and valleys along the course of the Wye

Rising on the barren slopes of Plynlimon, close to the source of the River Severn, the Wye sweeps through a medley of landscapes – now dramatic, now dreamily pastoral, but consistently beautiful – during its 130 mile journey between rich farmlands and thrilling gorges to the Severn estuary. Apart from the city of Hereford, its course takes it past nothing larger than the market towns of Builth Wells, Ross-on-Wye, Monmouth and Chepstow.

The lusty young river races down through the wild heart of Wales to Hay-on-Wye, then undergoes a change of character and meanders towards Hereford in a series of long lazy loops. High hills grazed by sheep give way to lush meadows cropped by plump cattle, and old orchards whose apples go to make Hereford's renowned cider. The Wye's character changes abruptly again near Goodrich. Hills close in on either bank, and the fields of dark red soil give way to a series of spectacular gorges cut deep into the soluble limestone as the river swirls back towards Wales. Trees cling to the steep slopes whose grandeur is punctuated by barren cliffs and pinnacles of pale rock.

The whole valley and the borderland to its north seem to speak of gentle rural life and natural beauties unspoiled for centuries – but the truth is very different. Skirmishes and full-scale battles raged over the region while English and Welsh contested the frontier. The river itself

was not chosen as the border. Offa, ruler of Mercia, the most powerful of Britain's 8th-century kingdoms, had a vast dyke built on the high ground just east of the river so that his men could have a clear view of intruders as they crossed the open water. Twelve-hundred years later, long stretches still survive of the 30 ft high earthwork striding north from the Wye's mouth towards the Dee.

Even when the Normans had occupied Britain and planted their barons in castles at Chepstow, Monmouth, Goodrich and New Radnor, the Welsh were not subdued. Owain Glyndwr, fighting for Welsh independence, destroyed New Radnor Castle in 1402 and slaughtered 1,100 English soldiers in the nearby woods. When his rebellion petered out, he sought refuge in the Golden Valley.

It was not all warfare in the region. Tranquil meadows and secluded valleys among the tree-clad hills attracted communities of Cistercian monks. At Abbey Dore and, above all, at Tintern Abbey – though ruined – you can still appreciate the skill and eye for beauty of their master masons. The surrounding heaths and woods where deer and other game roamed became the private hunting grounds of the Norman lords.

But alongside fighting, religious contemplation and hunting a quite different life went on – that of industry and trade. The river was a trade route – despite its shallows, rapids and variable tides – until the railways came in the 1870s; the Forest of Dean provided the wealth. Timber-felling, quarrying and mining on the lands between the Wye and the Severn made this a principal industrial area until the 1930s.

Now the scars have mainly healed, and there are few signs of this past life. Myriad paths thread the forests, and tracks and roads lead through a valley unsurpassed for breathtaking vistas and rural beauty.

*O*SYLVAN WYE' At this point, just east of Llandogo, the river beloved of Wordsworth and many fellow-Romantics has passed the high drama of Symonds Yat, and gentle wooded hills and peaceful water-meadows contain its wide, meandering course.

Places to visit

Map ref. Cb **Forest of Dean**

A sense of life as it was hundreds of years ago pervades the Forest of Dean. Secret and wild it seems, stretching on and on whichever way you turn. But then the green glade widens and you can see out over undulating blue-green tree-tops to cultivated fields, distant hills and shimmering curves of river.

In reality the forest is far from wild. Replanting has gone on over the centuries and does today, making the mixture of trees very different from what it was in the forest the Normans knew. Now the oaks mingle with beech, birch, ash and chestnut – and foreign softwoods outnumber these. Spruce, larch and fir are the fast-growing crop of the modern working forest. All the 22,000 planted acres of trees are nursed and thinned over the great triangular spread of forest that lies between the Wye and the Severn.

Ferns and mosses, lichens and liverworts carpet the ground. You can glimpse shy deer and swift squirrels, and hear the busy drilling of woodpeckers. Deer were the quarry of the royal huntsmen who held this vast domain as their preserve from the 11th century. King Canute set up the Court of Verderers to be responsible for anything that grew or lived in the forest. The court still meets at the 11th-century Speech House deep in the heart of the woodlands.

Except for the Forestry Commission workers, most people come to the Forest of Dean now for leisure and quiet enjoyment. It was very different in previous centuries, for the forest, with its natural resources of coal and iron ore as well as timber, played an important role in England's economy for hundreds of years. The iron was mined from before Roman times until the Industrial Revolution. In medieval times the forest supplied timber for shipbuilding, and was so vital to British naval power that its destruction is said to have been an objective of the Spanish would-be invaders in 1588.

During the Victorian era, the forest was a coalfield producing a million tons of coal each year. After a decline in the 1930s, open-cast mining has been resumed in some areas. A few seams are exploited by 'free' miners. Their rights are a reward dating back to 1296, when the city of Berwick-upon-Tweed was under siege. Miners from the Forest of Dean were enlisted by Edward I, and won his gratitude by tunnelling under the city walls.

There are 37 miles of forest walks laid out by the Forestry Commission, and numerous marked nature trails. The forest also has a maze of leafy lanes, and the Forestry Commission has route-marked a scenic drive starting near Coleford.

The A4136 east from Monmouth crosses the northern part of the Forest of Dean. The B4431 branches from it across the southern forest, and the B4226 branches from this across the central area. There are car parks within the forest on all the roads.

Bb **Golden Valley**

Rich, fat and fertile, the Golden Valley lies between Hereford and the dark line of the Black Mountains. Red-gold with Herefordshire cattle, ripening apples and fields of corn it seems aptly named, but the name probably arose only from a confusion of languages. The Welsh referred to the valley's river as *dŵr*, meaning 'water', but the Normans mistook this for *d'or*, the French for 'golden', and so the River Dore flows through the Golden Valley.

Standing sentinel at the northern

THE WYE VALLEY AND WELSH BORDERS

end of the valley is Merbach Hill, swelling steeply to 1,044 ft. The river rises on its southern slope and slides gently through the tranquil charm of Dorstone, Peterchurch, Vowchurch and Abbey Dore. It mingles with the Monnow at Pontrilas. All the way down, the dramatic natural rampart of the Black Mountains dominates the western view, its rim towering above the mosaic of fields at its feet. Wooded slopes make a softer horizon to the east.

During the long years of border warfare, the valley was a favoured route for Welsh raiders coming in to harry Norman estates. A castle was built to command the valley and deny the raiders entry. Now only scanty remains of the stronghold are left on the isolated little hill, Snodhill, south of Dorstone. Just over half a mile to the north of the village is Arthur's Stone, one of the few Neolithic tombs in the area. The enormous capstone on ten uprights covers a chamber 20 ft long.

Down the valley at Abbey Dore there is a fine, large, Early English church, too large for such a village one would think. It is part of the great Cistercian abbey of the 12th century, restored and re-roofed as a parish church by Viscount Scudamore in the 17th century. His family had become wealthy and powerful on spoils from monasteries after the Dissolution – a deed that lay heavy on the viscount's conscience. He compensated for it by endowing half-a-dozen churches, supporting unemployed clergy, and leaving sums of money to maintain schools for Hereford's poor.

Dorstone is on the B4348, 6 miles east of Hay-on-Wye. Pontrilas is on the A465, 11 miles south-west of Hereford.

IN WYE WOODLANDS

The bushy, red-stemmed Tintern spurge is confined almost exclusively to clearings in limestone woods along the lower Wye valley. The perforate, or common, St John's-wort is much more widely distributed, but appears to be particularly well-suited to hedgebanks and other woody sites along the Welsh borders.

Tintern spurge
(Euphorbia stricta)

Perforate St John's-wort
(Hypericum perforatum)

BATTLE HONOUR High on its spur above the Wye, Goodrich Castle commanded the road from Gloucester to Caerleon. Built in the 13th century, it fell to the forces of Parliament after a long siege in 1646, and was rendered indefensible.

Bb Goodrich Castle

Towers and walls of rich red sandstone, springing from a dry moat cut deep into solid rock, create the impression that Goodrich Castle grew magically from its rock foundations rather than being built upon them.

The castle, whose name originated as Godric's Castle, stands high above the meandering Wye on a beautifully wooded spur. The oldest part, the three-storey keep, was built about 1160 for Godric Mappestone. Its purpose was to guard a river crossing during the turbulent period when the Wye was a river of considerable military importance. No better position could have been chosen, for the view over the river and the surrounding countryside is superb – a military advantage in the 12th century and a scenic one now.

Corner towers braced by spurs and triangular buttresses strengthened the castle's outer wall, and complicated traps were devised to deter invaders. The long tunnel under the gate tower, for example, was blocked by a portcullis, and while intruders were held up there hot lead or water could be poured on them from openings above.

Goodrich Castle was impregnable during border warfare, and in the Civil War in the 17th century it was the last Herefordshire castle to fall to the Parliamentarians. The commander, Sir Henry Lingen, surrendered in 1646 after Colonel John Birch's artillery had battered the defences with 'Roaring Meg', a huge siege gun which could hurl a 200 lb ball. 'Roaring Meg' now stands on Castle Green in Hereford.

During the fighting, the colonel's niece Alice ran away with her lover, Charles Clifford, but the pair were drowned when they attempted to cross the Wye. Their ghosts are supposed to haunt the river, trying to cross it on a phantom horse.

Goodrich is 4 miles south-west of Ross-on-Wye, just off the B4229, which connects the A40 and B4228. The castle is 500 yds along a path from the village.

315

Bb Highmeadow Woods

Oak and larch, beech and cedar, ash and elder, chestnut and spruce mingle gloriously in the vast woodland that sprawls over high ground across the river from Monmouth. Beneath the varied canopy, in light constantly changing as it filters between needles and broad leaves, you can wind through the glades and up and down the slopes, following the waymarked trail northwards for almost 2 miles from the Staunton road to the Wye.

On the way, the path passes the enormous sandstone Suck Stone – 60 ft long and 40 ft wide – broken off from the hill above and thought to be the largest boulder in the country.

Where the path reaches the Wye, a suspension bridge for walkers spans the water, and on the other side you can take leisurely strolls either way along the towpath that was used in the days when the Wye was a busy commercial route. The path leading west runs below the Seven Sisters Rocks – tall spurs jutting from the trees – and mounts one of them to give a wonderful view down the river. Then it climbs to King Arthur's Cave, occupied by human and animal hunters in prehistory; bones of mammoth, bear, rhinoceros and bison have been found in it. Instead of crossing the footbridge you can follow the path eastwards above the river for 1½ miles, to an unsurpassed view from the most impressive vantage point on the Wye's 130 mile course. Symond's Yat Rock stands 504 ft above sea-level on a narrow neck of land almost cut off by a great ox-bow loop in the river. The patchwork of fields far below rolls away to the north, while trees tenaciously cling to the steep slopes falling away at either side of the viewpoint.

On the south side of the Staunton road the waymarked path leads to the Buck Stone, which may have been a pagan sacrificial altar. It used to be a rocking stone until a band of itinerant actors rolled its massive weight down the hill in 1885. It was replaced with great difficulty, but could not be made to balance again and is now pinned and cemented in place. The stone tops a steep hill, which is worth the climb for the wide view it gives over the woods.

Further west from Staunton another path strikes west up the Kymin, a steep 800 ft hill that looks over Monmouth, the Wye and the Monnow valley, and across the border lands to the Black Mountains. The days when delightful follies were created to 'improve' Britain's scenery are recalled on its crest. The Round House was built in 1794 by Monmouth's leading gentry so that they could admire their surroundings through a telescope presented by the local MP. In 1800 the folly was joined by the pagoda-like Naval Temple, with its trident-clutching Britannia and coloured plaques commemorating the victories of Nelson, Rodney, Hawke, Howe, Duncan and other contemporary naval heroes.

The waymarked path leading north into Highmeadow Woods and south to the Buck Stone crosses the A4136 Monmouth–Staunton road just over 2 miles east of the bridge at Monmouth. The path up the Kymin starts 1 mile west.

Bc Kington

High, rounded hills encircle the ancient market town of Kington, giving it a backdrop of great beauty whichever way you look. From their summits the hills survey glorious scenes. Kingswood Common, 2 miles south of the town, looks down to the Wye meandering gently to and fro across a wide, fertile valley, with wooded slopes beyond it. Smooth, small hills lie to the east, but in the south the Black Mountains loom dark and bold. On the other side of the town, Bradnor Hill rises sharply. A strenuous 2 mile walk from Kington Church climbs the hill to a magnificent 1,282 ft viewpoint which scans line upon line of hills as far as the majestic peaks of the Brecon Beacons. Just to the north are well-preserved sections of Offa's Dyke.

From Kington Church a lane climbs west up the shoulder of Hergest Ridge to a lofty, turf track that marches for 2 miles along the crest at almost 1,400 ft – a heady, open walk between patches of gorse and bracken. All this territory was once in the possession of the Vaughan family, the great landowners of the region. Their house, Hergest Court, lies on the south side of the ridge. The most notorious of its residents were Thomas Vaughan, known as Black Vaughan, and his wife Ellin, who for some unknown reason was known as Gethin the Terrible.

This vengeful lady dressed as a man to attend an archery contest where one of the competitors was a relative who had killed her brother. When her turn came, she shot her arrow at the assassin and killed him, escaping in the resulting confusion. Thomas was killed in the Wars of the Roses, but his ghost haunted the lanes until 12 parsons armed with 12 candles lured the ghost into a silver snuff-box and cast it into Hergest Pool. Effigies of the wicked couple lie with deceptively placid faces on their tomb in Kington Church.

Kington is 14 miles west of Leominster along the A44.

Bb Llandogo

The tides that surge up the Wye as far as Bigsweir Bridge enabled Llandogo to develop as a busy inland port. When timber, coal and iron ore made this lovely valley one of the most valuable industrial areas in Britain, ships sailed from Llandogo to Bristol and to the far corners of the world – voyages recalled by such exotic local place-names as Botany Bay and Barbadoes Hill. Its shipping trade died when the railway came in the 1870s. Llandogo became a beautiful, sleepy village, but the remains of old quays are still to be seen along the river bank.

You can walk beside the water to Bigsweir Bridge, a mile upstream – and if it is a spring evening the water may be alive with thousands upon thousands of young eels. Beyond the bridge you can walk as far as you like up towards Monmouth with green woodlands tumbling down the western banks and, across the water, steep banks topped by Offa's Dyke. The mounted Saxons who patrolled the top of the dyke must have been a daunting sight for anyone planning to encroach into Mercia.

Behind the village, paths on the wooded slopes climb north to just over 1,000 ft on Beacon Hill, which looks westwards over Trelleck towards the Brecon Beacons. Another lane from the village climbs south into the heart of Bargain Wood, where there are marked walks from the car park leading

MORNING MIRROR Stilled under a windless sky, the Wye above Bigsweir Bridge, north-east of Llandogo, reflects the mist-enshrouded landscape. Offa's Dyke follows the ridge above the distant woods.

to superb, sweeping views of the river.

Llandogo is named after St Oudoceus, a 6th-century saint who was given the land by the Welsh Prince Ennion to build a monastery – though at a price. The tale is that the two men met when hunting, and argued about the stag they were pursuing. Finally they agreed that Oudoceus could have all the ground that the stag had covered that day in return for ensuring Ennion a place in Heaven.

Llandogo is on the A466, 7 miles south of Monmouth.

May Hill

Cb

The breezy summit of May Hill is a perfect spot for short but rewarding walks. For miles around, the topknot of dark trees on its broad dome is an easily spotted landmark. Tracks criss-cross the hill, mounting gradually up the springy turf between the bright splashes of gorse and the bracken fronds towards the crowning cluster of tall pines. The trees were planted to commemorate Queen Victoria's Golden Jubilee in 1887. In 1977, and again in 1980, there were further plantings to commemorate the Silver Jubilee of HM The Queen, and the 80th birthday of HM The Queen Mother.

The hilltop, at almost 1,000 ft, is a superb viewpoint offering glimpses into ten counties on the best days. Green waves of wooded hills roll westwards to merge with the mountains of Wales. To the east, the long line of the Cotswolds rises suddenly from the broad Vale of Gloucester, where the Severn meanders seaward through a fertile landscape of farms and villages. The Forest of Dean lies to the south-west, but what catches the eye most is a huge loop of water where the Severn

curls and, at low tide, the silvery sheen of silt.

Newent Woods cover the north-east side of the hill. They are sunny with drifts of daffodils in spring and then sweet with perfume from the thick carpet of bluebells in early summer. By ancient custom, rival parties of young folk from Newent village used to walk up through the woods to the top of the hill on May Day and there do battle, summer's supporters against winter's. Summer's friends were always victorious, and triumphantly took fresh summer greenery back to the village.

May Hill is 1 mile along a marked minor road that turns north off the A40, 7 miles east of Ross-on-Wye.

HUNTERS AND FISHERS

The great spotted woodpecker is seldom seen in the valley, but the drumming of its beak is frequently heard as it drills into dead branches in search of insects. Look for the electric blue flash of the kingfisher along the Wye in the early morning or evening. This bird dives to catch small fish, which it carries to a perch to eat.

Great spotted woodpecker
(Dendrocopos major)

Kingfisher
(Alcedo atthis)

Mordiford

Bb

The wooded hills that spread east from Mordiford are laced with a tangled skein of narrow lanes, delightful and bewildering to the stranger. The lanes in turn are interwoven with many miles of footpaths and bridleways.

Mordiford stands on the River Lugg – a fine river for grayling – just above its junction with the Wye. Despite its plain name, the Lugg is a beautiful river, winding as sinuously as the Wye through rich farmland and orchards, and between lush water-meadows dotted with pale willows. At Mordiford the river glides beneath the nine arches of the 600-year-old bridge. Each time the king rode over this bridge in medieval times the lords of Hereford had to give him a pair of silver spurs; that was their payment in return for the manor of Mordiford. From Backbury Hill, reached by a path leading north-east from the town, you can look down on the river, the town, and beyond to Hereford's sandstone cathedral and even the distant mountains of Wales.

Haugh Wood flanks the lane between Mordiford and Woolhope, and has a 3 mile waymarked Forestry Commission trail circling within it. It makes a tranquil interlude to wind among the dappled glades, with glimpses through the oaks from the high ground to the fat land outside the woods. A winter and early spring visitor, attracted by the conifers, is the vivid little siskin, yellowy-green with a black bib, creaking and twittering in its jerky, bounding flight. This finch is still uncommon

in England as a breeding bird.

A delightful drive south from Mordiford towards Ross-on-Wye passes through some of the Wye valley's most attractive scenery. The road from Fownhope to Brockhampton is particularly lovely as it climbs through Capler Wood, where trees frame vistas of the river's graceful curves.

Mordiford is 4 miles south-east of Hereford on the B4224.

Radnor Forest

Ac

Despite its name and its closeness to the woods of western Hereford, this is not a forest in the modern sense. It was a Norman forest – an extensive tract of country with or without trees set aside for hunting. Though many trees have been planted on the 30 sq. miles by the Forestry Commission in recent years, most of the land is still open grazing roamed by huge flocks of hardy mountain sheep.

From a haphazard framework of valleys the forest plateau rises on steep, smooth flanks seamed by many rivulets. One dashing stream suddenly plunges 75 ft into a wooded gorge. After a wet spell of weather this waterfall vividly fulfils its name, Water-break-its-neck. From here a walk follows the plateau's western rim and gives fine views over the Ithon valley to the heart of Wales.

No roads suitable for cars cross the forest, but its footpaths, ancient trackways and open spaces make it ideal country for pony-trekkers and determined walkers – but not when clouds come down and conceal the landmarks. The highest point in the forest is 2,165 ft – high enough to be very bleak in bad weather – and much of the land is above 1,600 ft. The quaintly named conical peak of the Whimble, near the forest's southern edge, is almost 2,000 ft. It is a brisk but rewarding walk from New Radnor up the zigzagging path through woodland to the summit, which looks south over the layers of hills towards Hay Bluff, 15 miles away.

New Radnor fits neatly into the landscape. Grassy, hedge-topped banks mark the line of medieval town walls and partially enclose the village, whose rectangular street pattern has survived since the 13th century. The layout is seen best from the steep hill above the church. Hummocks on the grassy hill are all that remain of New Radnor's once mighty castle.

New Radnor is on the A44, 6¼ miles north-west of Kington. The path to Water-break-its-neck leaves the A44 1½ miles south-west of New Radnor, and continues round Radnor Forest's western edge. The A488, 5 miles south-west of Knighton, runs along the forest's northern edge.

Ba ## Tidenham Chase

Sprawling along the top of the eastern bank of the Wye are the former hunting grounds of the lords of Chepstow. Just 4 miles north of the town of Chepstow, where the lords had their castle, well over 1,000 acres of land were their exclusive preserve for hunting deer over the stretches of open land and through the thickets where birch, larch and yew are mixed now. The limestone table that supports the Chase thrusts through in places, giving pale grey vantage points for looking over the landscape. But these are eclipsed by three breathtaking viewpoints reached from the road that runs through the Chase from Chepstow.

NEAR TIDENHAM CHASE West of Wintour's Leap, a spit has formed where the Wye swings slowly through a huge bend.

Wintour's Leap towers 200 ft above the Wye, a massive grey crag over water that sweeps sharply round in a hairpin bend after encircling the Lancaut peninsula. The backwash as the water rounds the hairpin has worn away the tongue of land and made a pronounced hook at its tip. The leap is named after Sir John Wintour (or Winter), a Civil War hero who is said to have galloped his horse over the edge and swum across the river to escape from the Roundheads.

At the northern end of Ban-y-gor Rocks, three-quarters of a mile further up the road, is a double view – down the almost vertical wall of rock to the Wye, and in the other direction over the sloping fields to the Severn's broad estuary with the Vale of Berkeley and the Cotswolds beyond.

Offa's Dyke Path turns west from the road after a further half mile and follows the original Offa's Dyke. Striding along above the steep, wooded slope you can admire the line chosen for the 8th-century boundary between Mercia and Wales. The view of the river, and of the Welsh borders beyond it, is superb. The Devil's Pulpit is 2 miles along the path. Below this natural rock platform and across the river lies a low green meadow bearing the elegant, soaring, grey ruins of Tintern Abbey. According to legend, the Devil used to visit the platform to shout insults at the Cistercian monks.

The B4228 turns off the A48 just east of Chepstow and runs past Wintour's Leap and across Tidenham Chase towards St Briavel's. Wintour's Leap is ¼ mile north of the turn-off.

THE SHROPSHIRE HILLS

Iron Age hill-forts, Saxon earthworks and Norman castles are a reminder of border battles of long ago

In his London exile 80 years ago, the poet A. E. Housman, recalling the land about the rivers of Onny, Teme and Clun, remembered it as 'The country for easy livers, the quietest under the sun'. People do not hurry in Shropshire. Mindful of a turbulent past when their ancestors held the gate between the wild Welsh borders and the orchards of England, they are now content to let the future take care of itself. The chequerboard landscape of field and forest in which they live is a timeless one, symbolised perhaps by the mighty 900-million-year-old rocks of The Wrekin, rearing abruptly from the Severn plain.

Shropshire roots run deep. The low hills, forests and streams around Clun were occupied 5,000 years ago by Stone Age peoples, and by the beginning of the Bronze Age a great trade route ran across the Clee Hills to the Severn and on into south-east England. Long before the Romans came, the Celtic Cornovii had established the network of forts whose lines still show upon almost every Shropshire hilltop. From these bastions the chieftain Caradoc (Caratacus) fought his valiant, if unavailing, battles against the legions. After his defeat, Romanised Celts helped to create Viroconium, near present-day Wroxeter, the fourth-largest town in Roman Britain. Perhaps, too, it was Celtic prisoners-of-war, working under Roman taskmasters, who were the first to dig lead from around

the Stiperstones. If it was, then it was these long-forgotten men who established a Shropshire mining industry that was to endure for the best part of 2,000 years.

In time, the Romans departed, and during the sombre and bloody centuries that followed, Shropshire was forged as a kind of buffer area between Celtic Wales and Saxon England, whose Marches were defined by the prodigious dyke built by King Offa of Mercia in about 790.

But it was in Norman and early medieval times that the Shropshire landscape acquired much of its present shape and feel. Castles were built at Clun, Ludlow and Shrewsbury, and towns grew up around them. Monasteries such as Buildwas were established, and villagers gradually pushed their strip fields further and further into the heaths, woodlands and old royal hunting grounds. In fact, at this time, the hill country was probably far more populous than it is now; in the later Middle Ages, enclosures and the Black Death caused a decline in peasant communities. More than 100 'lost village' sites have been identified in Shropshire. One such is Cold Weston, in the lee of Brown Clee Hill.

Other half-healed scars on the countryside are those bequeathed by the old lead, coal, iron and stone workings, and by the great iron foundries. Most famous of these was at Coalbrookdale where, in the early 18th century, Abraham Darby discovered the means of smelting iron with coke, so laying the foundations of the Industrial Revolution.

The wild quality of the Shropshire hills has survived the centuries of border warfare and indiscriminate industrial exploitation. On the high moors of The Long Mynd, bilberries and heather tint the hills rose or purple according to the season, and brown trout quiver in the swift streams in the deep-carved 'batches' or valleys.

BORDER BASTION The Long Mynd takes its name from the Welsh *mynydd*, 'mountain'; the ridge is cut by deep valleys, known as hollows or batches, running from north-west to south-east. From the Burway track, Caer Caradoc can be seen to the north-east.

Places to visit

Map ref. Ca Bircher Common

This high open grassland, rising to 900 ft, is part of the 1,300 acre Croft Castle estate just over the Hereford and Worcester border. The castle is National Trust property and includes not only the common, with its bracken, gorse and small woodlands, but also a landscaped stream valley, parkland and an Iron Age hill-fort on the crest of a steep limestone ridge.

The Croft family are thought to have come to England from Normandy even before the Norman Conquest, and still occupy the castle, forming one of the oldest territorial links in Britain. Their castle combines the square strength of a medieval Marcher castle with later 18th-century additions. It is set in classic parkland with huge oaks and avenues of Spanish chestnuts thought to be some 350 years old.

There is a walk up past the Spanish chestnuts through Forestry Commission woodland to the windy and bracken-covered summit of Croft Ambrey, a hill-fort with views to Wales and south-east to the Cotswolds. Fourteen counties, it is said, can be seen on a clear day. The hill-fort is impressive, with 38 acres enclosed behind massive ramparts and a precipitous natural drop on the north side.

It is known to have been occupied from about 400 BC until the defeat of Caratacus in AD 50.

There are fine trees on the Croft estate, including giant Wellingtonias. Wild flowers include herb robert and dove's-foot cranesbill with its tiny purple flowers, and in spring there are holly blue and pearl-bordered fritillary butterflies, followed by ringlets, commas and small tortoiseshells.

Bircher Common is 6¼ miles south-west of Ludlow. Take the A49 from Ludlow, and at Woofferton turn west on to the B4362. The common and Croft Castle are on minor roads north after Bircher.

Ca Bringewood Forge

Although only a few miles west of Ludlow as the crow flies, this stretch of the River Teme is one of the wildest and most secluded in the area. It twists north through a steep-sided valley at the village of Downton on the Rock, then winds north-east to Bromfield, whose history goes back to the Bronze Age. In places the valley is a narrow gorge, and rock strata are clearly visible along its sides.

At Bringewood Forge, reached down a narrow, little-used lane that heads east beyond the main entrance to Downton Castle, great charcoal furnaces once smelted over 500 tons of iron a year. In the 17th century the people of Ludlow protested that it was not lawful to fell the wood on Bringewood Chase, for it was common land. But in the 18th century much old woodland had gone, and new coppices were being planted to provide fuel for the furnaces. Yet by the end of the 18th century, Bringewood was shut down for the last time; coal had supplanted timber. Now Bringewood Forge is a forgotten wilderness. All that remains are ancient crumbling buildings – and a magnificent, lonely 18th-century stone span of bridge, a great high arch over the Teme, standing as a monument to those early ironmasters.

Footpaths lead west through the wild parkland of Downton Castle, built in the 19th century by the Knight family whose wealth came from the iron. Northwards, through tangled woods, past overgrown streams and lakes crowded with wildfowl, the paths lead to Bromfield. Tucked just off the main A49, Bromfield is almost on the site of one of the biggest Bronze Age settlements in the west of England. North of the village is the site of a Roman fort that once stood guard at this junction of the rivers Teme and Onny. The village has one of the finest medieval timber-framed gatehouses in England and a picturesque bridge.

The hedges around are full of thorn, ash, oak, briar and alder. Herons, grey wagtails and dippers can be seen on the Teme, and the lakes attract many wild ducks in winter.

Downton on the Rock is 5¼ miles west of Ludlow. Take the A49 north to Bromfield, then turn west on to the A4113. After 2 miles a signposted minor road leads south-west to Downton on the Rock.

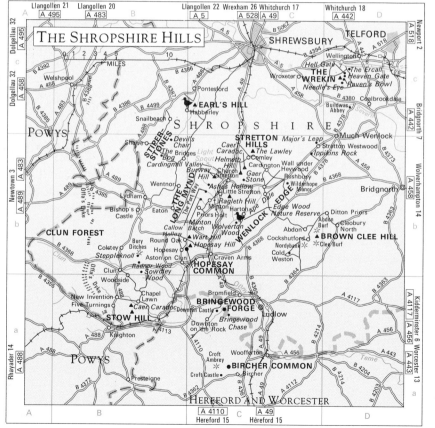

Cb Brown Clee Hill

Highest of the Shropshire hills is Brown Clee Hill at almost 1,800 ft. The rocks that make up the Clee Hills are much younger than most of Shropshire's uplands, and were formed less than 400 million years ago of Old Red Sandstone. Like its neighbours, Brown Clee is capped with a layer of volcanic rock called dolerite (locally 'dhustone'). This protects the underlying Coal Measures, from which coal and ironstone were once mined. The old shallow-shaft workings have left a hillocky summit now invaded by bracken.

Many people around the slopes of Brown Clee had common rights for grazing and gathering wood on the hill, and those who lived further away, 'the out-commoners', used old tracks called 'driftways', 'straker ways' or 'outracks' to climb to the grazing areas on the hillsides or carry iron ore and coal down. Many of the driftways still exist as sunken tracks, and the name Outrack is still given to a sunken road in Ditton Priors leading to Brown Clee. The commoners were granted these rights when Brown Clee was part of the great Clee Forest stretching to The Wrekin in the north and Wyre Forest in the south-east – a royal hunting preserve until medieval times. By the 16th century, the local people had encroached into the forest, their villages and fields eating into the wild land.

Just above one of these 'squatter' villages, the hamlet of Cockshutford on the western slopes of Brown Clee, is Nordybank Iron Age hill-fort, one of three. The other two are on Abdon Burf and Clee Burf summits on Brown Clee, but they have been much destroyed by quarrying. Nordybank is well preserved with clear ramparts and

IN RUSSET MANTLE The highest hill in Shropshire, Brown Clee Hill rears its bracken-clad slopes to almost 1,800 ft.

ditches, and provides a fine vantage point amid wide grass rides and bracken-covered slopes.

On the eastern side of Brown Clee, just out of the village of Cleobury North, lies Brown Clee Forest Trail climbing up open sunny hillsides to private woodlands. Managed by the owner in conjunction with the Shropshire Conservation Trust, this trail winds through woodlands of Norway and Sitka spruce and pine, although there are some fine deciduous trees including sweet chestnuts, sycamore

and birch. The trail diverges from the public footpath in the woods, but if the footpath is followed to Abdon Burf on Brown Clee, there are immense views. The tower blocks of flats in Dudley, not far from Birmingham in the West Midlands, are clearly and incongruously visible across an otherwise richly pastoral landscape, and make the watcher aware of how precious is this wild hill, now left to recover from its own industrial scars.

Brown Clee Hill is 9 miles south-west of Bridgnorth. Cleobury North lies on the B4364 from Bridgnorth. A minor road from the village circles northwards round the hill to Cockshutford.

Bb Clun Forest

This great border landscape was once a royal hunting forest, although probably never heavily wooded. Many of the woods that stand here now have been recently planted, and most of them lie to the east of the slumbering little town of Clun at the centre of the peaceful River Clun valley.

OLD WARS, NEW PEACE Veiled in misty sunlight, Sowdley Wood near Clun Forest is one of the most tranquil places on earth. Yet in the Middle Ages it was a scene of bloody battles between the English Marcher barons and the Welsh.

Today the area is one of the most remote in Shropshire. Studded with lonely farms and bracken-covered uplands where buzzards and ravens sweep, it has a turbulent history. The hills are full of Bronze and Iron Age remains – stone circles, forts, hilltop settlements and buried weapons and tools. Offa's Dyke strides north and south, marking that Saxon king's boundary. Another Saxon chief, Edric the Wild, struggled against the Normans here, and a Norman fortress still stands in Clun. The town was continually fought over and sacked by both Welsh and English for centuries, until one day, caught up in yet another war – this time the English Civil War – the men of Clun fought against both sides in order to keep their own private peace. Now Clun sheep, a famous breed, safely graze these once violent Welsh Marches.

East of Clun and south of the gently meandering river stands Sowdley Wood. A narrow lane signposted Woodside, just past Clun parish church, leads to an unmarked track which hugs the edge of Sowdley Wood. The first part of the path skirts a planted oakwood, young and airy still, full of mosses, ferns, lichens and sunshine. In autumn, puffballs and scarlet-lacquered toadstools sprout from its moist turf.

Between Clun and Bishop's Castle are wood-capped hills and swathes of valleys, golden with corn in late summer. A solitary and beautiful walk over these upland fields starts from Clun, near the youth hostel on a minor road north-east of the town. The path heads north-east between Radnor Wood and Steppleknoll to skirt the earthen ramparts of Bury Ditches, an Iron Age hill-fort. This is Forestry Commission land, and several tracks lead to the fort. The conifers that once surrounded it were blown down in 1976.

At Colstey, on the A488 south from Bishop's Castle, there is a picnic place which marks the beginning of woodland trails through what was once part of the great Mortimer Forest stretching west from Ludlow. Here the visitor can find remote and lengthy walking among gently flowing streams and high, wooded uplands.

Clun lies on the A488, 6 miles north of Knighton and 5 miles south of Bishop's Castle.

Earl's Hill

Cc

A narrow lane off the A488 leads to one of the most enchantingly varied fragments of wild countryside in Shropshire. Iron Age settlers built a ramparted fort on the craggy summit of Earl's Hill, 1,049 ft high; perhaps they, too, appreciated the beautiful lap of the Habberley valley to the south. Buzzards circle, swifts dart and dive; delicate blue harebells quiver in the grass and dwarf dandelions, wild thyme and gorse grow on the thin soil.

Earl's Hill is in the care of the Shropshire Conservation Trust, which has laid out a delightful nature trail that leads to the summit of the hill. Along its course, the trail runs through ash and oak woods, across upland meadows and along a stream in a deep valley. A walk through the reserve reveals places where ash saplings grow out of tumbled scree from the crags above; where mosses and yellow stonecrop thrive; where the hummocks built by yellow ants provide tiny gardens of clover, speedwell and forget-me-not; and where cowslips grow in the long grass.

Pied flycatchers can be found down by the brook and, more commonly, dippers and grey wagtails. Woodpeckers, tree pipits, tits and warblers live in the woods. Butterflies are abundant: peacocks and commas emerge from winter hibernation in late March, and in spring and summer the grizzled and dingy skippers, the green hairstreak, the common blue and the pearl-bordered fritillary can also be seen.

The paths on and around Earl's Hill sometimes call for a breathless scramble, but so much is seen and learned along the way that the two or three hours needed for a fairly brisk exploration are worth while. On the way to the nature reserve, as the path climbs through woods and fields, there is an information centre at Earl's Hill Barn.

Earl's Hill lies 7 miles south-west of Shrewsbury along the A488. Just after Pontesford a lane leads south to the reserve. Cars can be parked behind the filling station near the lane.

Bb Hopesay Common

Two miles to the west of Craven Arms lies Hopesay Common, owned by the National Trust. From its hedged and narrow-laned western foot, just north of the village of Hopesay, a path climbs steeply up to the sparse pines on the crest of Hopesay Hill. Another track east of the hamlet of Round Oak makes a wide grassy swathe southwards through bracken along the lofty summit of Hopesay Hill, with its grazing sheep and ponies, and its crystalline views on a clear day.

Nowhere is so airy and peaceful as Hopesay in the early morning in late summer, when mists hang in the valleys all the way to The Wrekin in the north-east. Yet this is the edge of the border country, with Wales only 7 miles away. It has been fought over for

centuries. To the north the bare peak of Wart Hill rises above dark Forestry Commission conifers. It is capped by an Iron Age hill-fort. So, too, is the green cone of Burrow, 2 miles to the south-west, its centuries-old fortifications sharply defined in the morning sun. On Hopesay it is possible to see how these hill-forts mark a clear line across Shropshire, each one backed up by the next. Caer Caradoc's ramparts stand out crisp against the sky. There is a sense of watchfulness here, and of great age. Below, sheltered farms waken for the day, to follow the age-old pattern of the harvest. Even the trees that brood over the scene are old: ancient hollies, hawthorn, ash and thin Scots pine.

Hopesay Common is 2 miles to the west of Craven Arms. Take the B4368 westwards, and at Aston on Clun turn north along a minor road to Hopesay. A turning east in the village leads to the common and Round Oak. Long Lane, a minor road west off the A49 at Craven Arms, leads direct to Round Oak.

Bb The Long Mynd

The great 6 mile range of hills known as The Long Mynd, rising to 1,700 ft, is a world of its own. It encompasses wild moorland where red grouse whirr out of the heather, waterfalls that cascade into half-hidden narrow valleys, springs that rise icy clear through bog moss and pink bog pimpernel, bracken-covered hillsides and sunlit streams. During the last Ice Age, between 10,000 and 26,000 years ago, frost broke up the 800-million-year-old pre-Cambrian rocks of The Long Mynd to form a stony deposit blanketing the surface. This has given it its characteristic rounded outline, so unlike

the jagged Stiperstones to the west.

The Burway, a single track climbing steeply up out of the snug little town of Church Stretton which is tucked into The Long Mynd's eastern side, gives spectacular views of the surrounding diversity of the Shropshire hills. There are more intimate glimpses, too, of the deep valleys that cut through this high moorland. A track called The Port

HEDGEROW WITCHERY

The bruised, slightly poisonous red autumn berries of bittersweet (or woody nightshade) were long used as a protection against witchcraft and to drive away criminals. A remedy for jaundice and dizziness was prepared from the dried stems. Bittersweet flowers all summer, like sprawling yellow pimpernel, once thought to lessen pain. Both may be found in hedgerows and woods.

Bittersweet
(Solanum dulcamara)

Yellow pimpernel
(Lysimachia nemorum)

Way has run along the ridge for more than 3,500 years, and the Burway joins its course there.

Much of The Long Mynd belongs to the National Trust and parts are leased as grouse moors, with commoners having rights to graze their sheep and ponies.

The best way to explore The Long Mynd is on foot, from one of the villages along its eastern flanks. The springs that rise on The Long Mynd have carved deep valleys known as 'hollows', or 'batches', the most famous being Cardingmill Valley with the Light Spout waterfall at its head. Much less frequented and almost equally lovely is Ashes Hollow, reached from the black-and-white village of Little Stretton where a brook chuckles down between the houses. From here, too, can be found Callow Hollow, over an intervening hillside. Further south is Minton Batch. Minton village is secluded and charming, and from Priors Holt in the lee of woodland there is a walk north through the trees and up The Long Mynd slopes to the Port Way that runs along the top.

In the valleys there are many butterflies and birds, including the grey wagtail. On the high moor, where heather, gorse, sundew and bilberries grow wirily against the wind, ravens and buzzards fly; sometimes a white-rumped wheatear can be seen, and, more rarely, the ring ouzel, a mountain blackbird with a white bib.

Almost in Church Stretton itself is Old Rectory Wood, 17½ acres of mixed woodland with a yew-shadowed pool, fine views of the Stretton Valley and delightful meandering paths. Native and exotic trees mingle here, and are cared for by the Shropshire Conservation Trust. It is not easy to find: the

325

DEEP SECRET Cardingmill Valley is typical of the deep-cut, unexpected valleys slashed through The Long Mynd. At its steep, bracken-clad head is the Light Spout waterfall.

stile entrance is along a path that leads away south from the cattle-grid start of the Burway, west out of Church Stretton.

The Long Mynd ridge is about 3 miles west of Church Stretton on the A49. Minor roads from the B4370 lead west to footpaths that climb to the moorland on The Long Mynd.

Bb The Stiperstones

When all around is sunshine, the chances are that there will be a dark cloud smudging the bleak and ragged ridge of the Stiperstones, at 1,762 ft the second highest hills in Shropshire. Even the most unimaginative feel a sense of desolation and unease when in the shadow of the Stiperstones, or on their grim, rock-strewn summit. One of the curious rock formations is called the Devil's Chair, and it is said that when cloud hides the Stiperstones, the Devil has taken his seat. According to legend, witches and demons have met here for centuries.

The Stiperstones lie 5 miles north-west of the great moorland back of The Long Mynd. The rocks were formed about 500 million years ago, when shales and sandstones were laid down under a shallow sea. Later folding of the rock brought the Stiperstones quartzite, hard white sandstone, to outcrop at a steep angle. During and after the last Ice Age, frost shattered the quartzite into the jagged tors and tumbled screes that cover the summit today. Because of their geological interest and vegetation – a transition between the southern heaths and the northern moors – the Stiperstones were bought by the Nature Conservancy Council in 1981 to become a 1,015 acre National Nature Reserve.

The Romans found lead on these hills and started a tradition of thriving independent mines which continued through medieval times until, in 1835, at the height of the industry, 3,500 tons a year were being produced. The centre of the area was the village of Shelve, west of the Stiperstones, the mines running eastwards to The Bog and north to Snailbeach. At Snailbeach, waste tips of white calcite, like some strange lunar landscape, still remain. The miners were part-time farmers and a tradition of smallholdings grew up in the area, the fields marked out by drystone walls. But by the beginning of this century the lead industry had collapsed.

There are several paths up to the Stiperstones, and the views, should the day be clear, are magnificent, looking west into Wales and south-east to The Long Mynd. The easiest path leads off the single track road that leads northwest from the village of Bridges, on the eastern side up to The Bog.

The Stiperstones are about 7 miles north-east of Bishop's Castle. Take the A488 to Lydham, turn east on to the A489 and at Eaton take the minor road north through Wentnor to Bridges.

Ba — Stow Hill

Two miles north-east of the Welsh town of Knighton, the great curved upland of Stow Hill guards the valley of the Teme. It is 1,391 ft high and an ancient 'green lane', a track that may have been used as long ago as the Bronze Age, spans the length of it.

There are few signposts in this remote country. On the main A488 south from Clun there is nothing to say that a tiny hamlet is quaintly named New Invention – legend has it that it

was so called because Dick Turpin stopped here and had his horse shod back to front, so confusing his pursuers. South up the hill from New Invention is Five Turnings, aptly named because here the green lane crosses the road, and another way turns north-east to skirt Caer Caradoc. The green lane passes through Five Turnings Farm and begins

a long and gentle climb to the east up Stow Hill. Vetches, hawkweed, hedge parsley, thistles and celandines grow in the sunny ditches. Further on the lane is overgrown, a green dim tunnel of overhanging trees, full of blackberry brambles and nettles, but it is passable, and opens on to high pasture. From here it is possible to look north and see,

just across a deep stream valley, the bracken-covered summit of Caer Caradoc – and beyond it, in the far distance, the other Caer Caradoc of the Stretton Hills. Both bear the ramparts of Iron Age hill-forts, and both are associated with the story of the British chief Caratacus making his last stand on their summits against the invading Romans.

Higher still, the views grow broader at every step: south into Hereford and Worcester to the Welsh borders, west into Wales, east to the Clee Hills, north to The Long Mynd. The lane drops down north-eastwards between stands of conifers on high grasslands. There are dew-ponds here, with buzzards and ravens circling in the sky above. Over the southern edge of the hill, steep rocky slopes fall away to the Teme winding below. At the end of the trackway is the River Redlake, meandering cheerfully over pebbles through a charming valley and under a small wooden bridge. The lane here winds round to Chapel Lawn from which a footpath leads to the imposing summit of Caer Caradoc. It is a high, remote, delightful three-hour walk.

Five Turnings, from where the walk across Stow Hill starts, is 4 miles south of Clun and 2 miles north of Knighton along the A488.

Cb — The Stretton Hills

Across the narrow Stretton Valley, to the east of The Long Mynd, is the miniature mountain range of the Stretton Hills. The valley itself follows an enormous fault, a break in the earth's crust, and separates the rounded whaleback of the pre-Cambrian Long Mynd from the even older and craggier summits of Caer Caradoc, The Lawley

---

BETRAYAL AT A BORDER CASTLE

PEOPLE say that you can still hear the screams of Marion de la Bruere echoing from Ludlow Castle on winter nights. A 12th-century minstrel's song tells how she let her lover into the castle one night in 1139, realising too late that she had also opened the door to enemies. So she killed her lover with his own sword and then leaped to her death from the Pendower Tower.

The 11th-century castle stands on a low cliff above the River Teme. One of 32 castles built to guard the Welsh border, it had a stormy early history. In 1475 it became the seat of the Council of the Marches, set up to govern Wales.

It was at Ludlow Castle that the two sons of Edward IV, better known as the little princes in the Tower, spent most of their brief lives before leaving for London and death in 1483. Prince Edward became Edward V there, but reigned for only three months before being deposed and probably murdered by his uncle, who became Richard III.

Another unfortunate Prince of Wales to live at Ludlow was Arthur, sickly eldest son of Henry VII. He was married at 14 to Catherine of Aragon, and the couple spent six months there after the wedding, until Arthur died in 1502.

LUDLOW CASTLE

and Ragleth Hill. Unlike The Long Mynd, the Stretton Hills were not formed from ancient sea-bed sediments but by the lava and ash spilled from volcanoes some 900 million years ago. Like The Wrekin, their rocks are among the oldest in Britain.

The Stretton Hills are also among the most beautiful, and within about 10 miles encompass shady trackways, pebbled streams, bracken-covered slopes and high, invigorating summits. Caer Caradoc is the highest peak at more than 1,500 ft. It can be reached either from the crossroads in the hamlet of Comley at its northern foot – a steep and breathless clamber up through bracken, past a blue dew-pond and over grassy turf and wiry bilberry – or by way of a lane and track that leads from the village of Cardington. These ancient tracks and paths link Cardington with Church Stretton, winding through cushiony farmland and wild moorland under the crags of Caer Caradoc and the Gaer Stone. The climbs up to the windy summits are not difficult, and yield immense views.

Harebells quiver in the grass on Caer Caradoc, and in early summer the bilberry – sometimes known as whortleberry – flowers pink over the hills. In spring and autumn its tough, small leaves have a rose tint; the tasty blueblack berries can be picked in July and August. Heather and bracken grow on the hills, too, and larks abound, so that on the final scramble up to the crags of Caer Caradoc the thin turf seems alive with them.

On the summit of Caer Caradoc is a high and precipitous Iron Age hill-fort, enclosing some 6 acres with well-defined double ramparts. It is said that the British chief Caratacus made a stand here against the invading Roman

YELLOW BIRD OF SUMMER

Water-meadows and marshy areas are the haunt of the shy and cautious yellow wagtail, which nests in a hollow in the long grass and feeds mainly on insects. Its all-yellow head and breast distinguish it from the grey wagtail, a bird of fast-running streams. Slim, long-tailed yellow wagtails are summer visitors; they winter in tropical Africa.

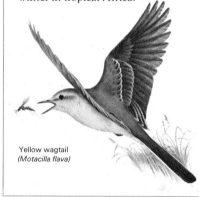

Yellow wagtail
(Motacilla flava)

army – although such claims are made for several other parts of England.

Beyond Caer Caradoc is the gentler Lawley to the north, and the more wooded hills of Helmeth and Ragleth to the south above Church Stretton.

From Church Stretton on the A49, the B4371 heads eastwards across the Stretton Hills. Tracks lead north and south from the road into the hills, and a minor road from Wall under Heywood leads north to Cardington and Comley.

Cb Wenlock Edge

Wenlock Edge runs ruler-straight for 16 miles across Shropshire from northeast to south-west; its steep limestone edge faces west, the eastern side has a gentler slope. It is hard to believe that

it was formed as a coral reef some 420 million years ago in a tropical sea.

Although distinct from a distance, Wenlock Edge is strangely elusive when approached. The only main road to cross it is the A458 at the north-east end, but a good secondary road runs along the northern half. From remote black-and-white half-timbered villages along its dip slope, many tracks and paths across open farmland and through deep woods climb up to its unexpectedly level plateau. At Rushbury the Romans had an outpost, commemorated in the hill lane called Roman Bank. In many places, almost forgotten, are the mounds of an early medieval motte-and-bailey castle or an Iron Age earthwork.

In the northern half of the Edge lie many quarries, for the limestone was once used as a building material and is today used as aggregate. Ippikin's Rock is opposite Lilleshall Quarry, now disused, beside the B4371 north-east of Easthope. A projecting crag of hard, weathered rock, it gives an airy view across Ape Dale towards the Stretton Hills. Legend tells that the crag was named after a notorious robber who lived in a cave in the cliff. Ippikin's stolen hoard was buried by a landslide and his ghost still stands guard, ready to push over the cliff anyone nearing the treasure.

Major's Leap on the precipitous Edge near Stretton Westwood, on the B4371, owes its name to a Royalist officer called Major Thomas Smallman, who rode his horse over the cliff to evade Parliamentarian pursuers. His horse was killed, but his fall was broken by a tree and he escaped safely to Shrewsbury. His family home, the 16th-century Wilderhope Manor, now belonging to the National Trust, is a

perfectly unspoiled and lonely house further south on the dip slope.

Wolverton Wood, west of the point where the minor road from Harton crosses the Edge, contains a secluded nature reserve with a shadowy entrance in the woods that lie in folds down the escarpment. Edge Wood Nature Reserve, managed by the owner in conjunction with the Shropshire Conservation Trust, is a deep, enchanting, rustling wood, with a mile-long nature trail. Much of it is of planted conifers, but visitors can see ancient oaks, great holly trees, hazel coppices, a marshland area, and a wood consisting almost entirely of birches.

At another point on the trail, there is an old quarry and lime-kiln. This is one of the places where farmers dug limestone and burned it to produce lime, which they used as a dressing for their fields around the Edge. Near the kilns there are lime-loving plants such as common spotted orchids and spindle trees – bright with rose-red seed-pods in autumn. The wood from the trees was once used for making spindles for spinning wool.

Wenlock Edge can be reached along minor roads north-west from the B4368 and B4378 between Craven Arms and Much Wenlock, or from the B4371 between Church Stretton and Much Wenlock.

Dc The Wrekin

The sombre 1,334 ft hump of The Wrekin stands out like some giant geological pimple on the smooth face of the Severn Plain. It rises abruptly between the wild Shropshire hills to the south and the flat, northern lands. Visible for miles around, The Wrekin is formed from some of the oldest rocks in Britain – lava, ashes and debris disgorged from a volcanic cleft 900 million years ago. Though it has the appearance of an extinct volcano, it is not one. According to legend, however, its formation was quite different. Two giants are supposed to have fashioned the mound from mud dug from the Severn. But during a quarrel, one struck at the other with his spade, missed, and cleft the rock now called the Needle's Eye. His next blow was thwarted by a raven pecking at his eyes, and the tears he shed formed the pool known as the Raven's Bowl, which has never run dry since. The aggressor's third blow was successful, and he buried his unconscious adversary beneath the nearby hill, called The Ercall, from where his groans can still be heard at dead of night.

Although much trodden in summer and at weekends, The Wrekin still retains a special magic. Two-thousand years ago, the earthworks on the summit were the ramparts of the tribal capital of the Cornovii. Now almost obliterated by time and weather, the remains stand as a reminder of the fiercely fought resistance of the British tribes to the Roman expansion from the east. The fort is elongated and takes in most of the hill. It consists of a large central area of about 7 acres surrounded by a series of outer earthworks which enclose a total of $10\frac{1}{2}$ acres. Excavations have shown that the central area was probably a settlement before the 5th or 4th centuries BC. Hut floors, post holes, gutters and storage pits have been found inside the main fort, which was probably built later when local wars and land-hunger among neighbouring tribes made it necessary to fortify the site.

To tread the broad tracks and paths that wind up to the summit through oak, birch, holly, yew and upland bracken is to tread the paths that our ancestors followed. Nature's gently changing seasons add to the timeless character. Bluebells carpet the woods in spring, and on the lonelier southern slopes there are primroses; in summer, foxgloves and rosebay willowherb flourish. Green woodpeckers cackle in the woods and may be seen searching for ants on the ground, treecreepers dart up the oak trunks and tits flock among the branches.

Though now crowned by a television transmission mast, the wild and windy summit is magnificent. The inner and outer entrances to the hill-fort are known as Heaven Gate and Hell Gate. A topographic stone map identifies the surrounding heights: west to Wales; north to the flat plains; east to Staffordshire and the Black Country; and south into the main mass of the Shropshire hills – a remote and misty landscape of crags, sharp peaks and whaleback ridges.

The Wrekin is $2\frac{1}{4}$ miles south-west of Wellington. The path to the summit via Hell Gate and Heaven Gate starts on the east side of the hill, near the Forest Glen cafe on the minor road from Wellington to Little Wenlock.

WENLOCK EDGE The great tree-covered escarpment that the poet A. E. Housman loved and often refers to in his verse cycle 'A Shropshire Lad' was a coral reef in a tropical sea millions of years ago.

LEGACY OF A REVOLUTION

DARK SATANIC MILLS – BUT WORKS OF MAJESTY TOO, THAT ADDED AN ODD GRANDEUR TO THE LANDSCAPE

BY THE MID-19TH CENTURY, Britain was the workshop of the world. From its modest beginnings in the late 18th century, the Industrial Revolution had become an unstoppable juggernaut that transformed the country and the lives of its people. As early as 1851 the most significant change was already apparent; for the first time in British history, more people lived in towns than in the country. The legacy of those days is still with us, whether in squalid miles of jerry-buildings or honest attempts to improve the workers' lot, such as that made by Robert Owen in his model mill-town of New Lanark.

The Industrial Age began by swift-flowing rivers where textile mills, powered by water-wheels, were set up along the banks. Even after the advent of steam, the free energy provided by water remained a major power source for many years. The River Kent, in Cumbria, had 90 mills along its course by 1850, and at that time the river and its tributaries provided more power than all the steam-engines in the factories of Birmingham. Hamlets grew up around the mills, such as Meal Bank on the Mint, a tributary of the Kent. Meal Bank had three mills that not only produced woollens, but also ground snuff and corn.

Former mill settlements can be found in the Pennines and in the Welsh Marches. Mostly the mills are gaunt, overgrown ruins, their great wheels long-since vanished and the mill-ponds choked with weeds. But some of the settlements have survived. Cromford, in a deep wooded gorge of the Derbyshire Derwent, is an example, and something of a milestone in the history of the Industrial Revolution. Here, in 1771, Richard Arkwright set up the world's first water-powered cotton-mill, incorporating his own invention, the water frame.

Always an innovator, Richard Arkwright installed the first steam-engine for cotton-spinning at his Manchester mill in 1783. Other factory-owners followed suit, and by 1800 there were a further 42 engines helping to power the Lancashire cotton industry. About the same time, steam-engines began to be used to pump water from the tin mines; many of the granite-built engine-houses and chimneys remain as familiar landmarks in the Cornish countryside.

One of the earliest marriages between steam and transport resulted in the launching of the 38 ft *Comet* on the Clyde in 1812. Though her inventor and owner, Henry Bell, made little out of the venture, the little paddle-steamer's effect was momentous. Her descendants were the steam tugs that towed ocean-going sailing ships into the heart of Glasgow, by the straightened and deepened Clyde. This gave rise to the two great Clydeside industries – ship and engine-building. Similar changes took place along the Thames, the Medway, the Mersey and several other British rivers, where miles upon miles of docks were built, mostly now falling into desperate decay.

The railway kings

But perhaps the most lasting impression made by the Industrial Revolution upon the countryside was that of the railways, whose impact may be dated from 1830 and the opening of the Manchester–Liverpool line, the world's first commercially successful railway. Its building posed some enormous problems for the designer, George Stephenson. On the outskirts of Manchester the track had to be supported on bundles of heather and wooden hurdles in order to cross the peaty morass of Chat Moss. And later, when taking the line into the heart of Liverpool, a 2 mile cutting had to be dug, 80 ft deep, into the red sandstone.

Other railway engineers faced similar problems, and they overcame them with a flair that still excites our admiration today –

Brunel's 1½ mile cutting at Sonning, Berkshire, Robert Stephenson's 70 ft high Britannia Bridge that carried the railway over the Menai Strait, and his 160 ft deep Kilsby tunnel in Northamptonshire.

The railway networks spread throughout Britain with astonishing rapidity. By 1844, 240 miles of track ran from London to Lancaster; Brunel's Great Western Railway linked the capital to Exeter, and there were lines to the Channel ports of Dover, Folkestone and Southampton. Altogether, nearly 5,000 miles of track were in use at the mid-century.

This, of course, rang the death-knell of the stage-coaches which, since the middle of the 18th century, had provided the principal means of passenger transport between towns. At best they could travel 100 miles in 24 hours; but now such journeys could be done in a fraction of the time, in greater comfort and without the frequent stops to change horses. The stage-coaches left a legacy of coaching inns with their arched entrances and cobbled courtyards, and a myriad memories recalled in pub names, prints and Christmas cards. They also left a nationwide network of roads which, until the coming of the motor car, were occupied solely by farm carts, village carriers and local horse-drawn transport.

The canal age created only one new town, Stourport, at the point where the Staffordshire and Worcestershire Canal joined the River Severn. The railways, however, gave birth to several townships and brought new importance to others. Crewe obliterated the obscure hamlet of Church Coppenhall, and New Swindon soon overshadowed Old Swindon when the Great Western Railway Company set up its engineering works there.

As the railways expanded, so the canals declined. Though they did not suffer the total obliteration of the stage-coaches – some of the routes were still essential for the

transport of heavy bulk cargoes – many of the minor systems fell into disuse, their waterways gradually filling up with weeds. But in recent years the canals have undergone a rebirth as recreational waters. Teams of voluntary workers have made many miles of canals navigable again, and canal cruising has become a popular pastime.

Full circle

In time, a similar fate overtook some 500 of the branch lines of the railway system. The wheel had gone full circle and once more it was the roads that were capturing the bulk of transport. In the 1960s, the British Railways Board trimmed back the railway network with massive cuts. Tracks were torn up, signalling systems were dismantled and wayside stations were left to crumble. Cuttings and embankments were repossessed by nature – and just as the hill-forts and ramparts of prehistory vanished under grass and scrub, so the outlines of man's more recent works were softened into valleys and hillocks, covered with wild flowers and providing new habitats for wildlife. In some areas these have been adopted as nature trails. In Derbyshire, the old railway line between Buxton and Ashbourne is now the Tissington Trail, and a mile of track along the southern shore of the Mawddach estuary in Wales is now a footpath, while a signal box has been converted into a wildlife centre.

The legacy of the Industrial Revolution has left a wealth of splendid buildings and machinery. But the inheritance also includes acres of industrial waste from coal mines, iron works and chemical plants, miles of rotting docks and of ravaged countryside. Mercifully some of the wounds are healing as nature reclaims its own. Nowhere can this be better seen than in South Wales where the slag-heaps piled high in the valley coalfields are returned to grass to blend with the majestic hills around.

WIPED CLEAN Roofless now itself, Cwmystradllyn slate factory in Gwynedd supplied roofing materials to the factory towns that sprang up all over Britain in the early years of Queen Victoria's reign.

WIGMAKER'S CASTLE Richard Arkwright, founding father of the Industrial Revolution and ex-wigmaker, built his Masson Mill at Cromford, Derbyshire, in 1783. He chose this site by the River Derwent partly for its readily available water power, and partly to escape the wrath of the Nottingham hand-spinners, driven into unemployment by his machines. The cotton-mill was operated largely by workhouse 'apprentices' working night and day in 13 hour shifts.

'THE LONG DRAG' This is the name that railwaymen gave to the 72 mile Settle to Carlisle stretch on the Midland line to Scotland. Completed in 1876 at the cost of more than 100 lives, it climbs by 20 viaducts and 14 tunnels to over 1,100 ft.

WATER BRIGHT The pumping station at Papplewick was built in 1884 to provide Nottingham with water. Its two beam-engines and wrought-iron decorations are in perfect order.

HEIGHTS AND DEPTHS The stilled engine-house and headstock gear of a derelict colliery near Pontypridd stand as a monument to the old way of life in the Rhondda. Work was hard and dangerous, but the community was close-knit and there was the sense of the hills not far away.

THE SCOTTISH LOWLANDS

Superb hill-walking country that provides a setting for the Border ballads of love, war and treachery

Eskdale, Liddesdale, Teviotdale, Jedburgh, Kelso, Solway . . . the names on the signposts click in the mind like the echo of a half-forgotten song. And well they might, since this is the land of the steel bonnets, the 'Debatable Land' of the English-Scottish Borders and Lowlands, the country of Johnnie Armstrong, Kinmont Willie and their like. Their doings were recorded by contemporaneous 'makkars' or balladeers, and later by Sir Walter Scott, who between them turned the often appalling villainies of the Border raiders into epic poetry.

Even by Scott's day, the reivings – the cattle raids – were an ancient memory. One of the first things James I did on ascending the throne of the United Kingdom in 1603 was to hang a few dozen reivers to dissuade the remainder from their lives of 'theft, spoyle and bloode'. Yet the land has changed little. Take one of the roads across the Lammermuirs when the moon is silvering the heather and the wind is blowing thinly over the wide, low hills, and it is not too difficult to picture Armstrongs, Johnsons or Hepburns riding by on their way to extract 'black-mail' – black-rent, or protection money – from some feebler neighbour.

So perhaps it is some ancestral fear that leaves the Lowland and Border country so unjustly neglected. Otherwise it is inexplicable, for it is land of great charm and variety 'from Solway Sand tae where Tweed rins tae the ocean', as an old ballad puts it. There are slow, serpentine rivers winding between tree-draped banks, mighty torrents like the Grey Mare's Tail that plunges 200 ft and more from the head of the Birkhill Pass, and odd land forms such as the Devil's Beef Tub, a vast natural amphitheatre near Moffat, in which the raiders hid their rustled cattle. There are great houses – Abbotsford, built by Sir Walter Scott; Traquair, the oldest inhabited house in Scotland; and Maxwelton House, once the home of Annie Laurie. Everywhere there are the Border keeps and castles, almost all in lovely settings, and none without its tale of love, war or treachery.

But the joy of the Lowlands is its ranges of hills, criss-crossed by old drove roads that make fine walking routes; each range possesses its own particular character and associations. The triple-peaked Eildon Hills for example, called Trimontium by the Romans when they built a signal station there, are said to cover a great cave where King Arthur and his knights lie sleeping. The Lammermuirs are wide, wild moorland, peopled mostly by ghosts and sheep, while the Ettrick hills, whose romantic beauty excited the admiration of both Scott and Wordsworth, enshrine the tranquil St Mary's Loch, perhaps the loveliest stretch of water in southern Scotland. The grassy Ochils, on the other hand, are pierced by tiny glens, each with a busy little burn in its depths.

The Lowland hills should be seen in all seasons – silent under snow, vivid in the youthful green of spring, royal in the golds and purples of autumn. And when you go, take a collection of ballads with you. They will people again the empty dales and ruined keeps with the jingle and tramp of the armoured moss-troopers.

CLYDE FEED-WATER High in the smooth, green Lowther Hills, Shortcleuch Water meanders lazily between sheep-grazed slopes. A few miles on, it joins Elvan Water and then the Clyde, Scotland's best-known river, which flows north-west to meet the Atlantic.

Places to visit

Map ref. Fe Abbey St Bathans

Spreadeagled across the boundary of the former counties of Berwickshire and East Lothian are the Lammermuir Hills. There is no drama in their gentle summits but they have their own almost secret and rarely visited corners.

One substantial river valley cuts through the hills, where the Whiteadder Water gathers the burns on the old Dunbar Common and then sidles down to the rich farmlands of the Merse of Berwickshire.

The Whiteadder's main tributaries – the Bothwell, the Faseny, the Monynut and the Dye – provide their own lonelier valleys. Before the days of fenced-off grazing lands, 'gathering folds' used to be held twice a year in a great grassy hollow at the headwaters of the Dye. All the strayed sheep on the Lammermuirs were gathered together and returned to their rightful owners.

Down the Faseny Water runs the course of an old 'herring road', which the people of Lauderdale followed on their way to buy winter supplies of salt herring from the Dunbar fishermen.

Villages in this predominantly sheep-rearing landscape are few and far between. Most are on sites originally chosen to be out of sight of wandering marauders. One such village is Abbey

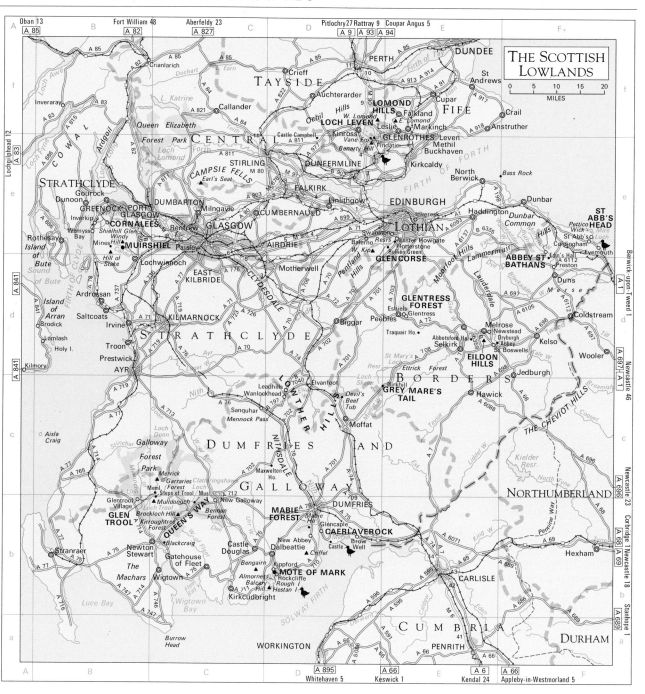

St Bathans on the Whiteadder, downstream of the point where it is joined by the Monynut Water. Nobody knows which of the three saints of the Celtic Church with almost identical names is commemorated – Bathan, Baithon or Bothanus. Nor was there an abbey here, although you can still see one wall of a 12th-century priory built into the present-day parish church.

A foot-bridge over the Whiteadder leads up through birchwoods to an open hillside beyond. To the southeast, a fine walking route goes past Edin's Hall – the remains of a 1st-century Iron Age broch. It stands above the birch and oakwoods of the Whiteadder valley, a partly reconstructed circular building, of a style more often seen in the north. In its double walls, up to 18 ft thick, can still be seen the pattern of rooms and storage spaces of a family stronghold and dwelling-house. From the traces of earlier ditches and earthen ramparts that surround the site, this was a fortress in even more remote times than the broch-builders knew.

Abbey St Bathans is 5¼ miles north of Duns. A minor road leads to the village from the B6355, which runs westwards from the A6112 at the village of Preston.

Db   Caerlaverock

The parish of Caerlaverock is off the beaten track to the south-east of Dumfries. On the west it is bounded by the River Nith, where, near the one-time port and boat-building village of Glencaple, salmon-fishing is still carried on by haaf-netters. They wade out carrying rectangular nets on long poles, stand in line and whip the nets out of the water as salmon tumble in.

Between Glencaple and Brow Well

is a curious and individual coastline – the Merse of Caerlaverock, an expanse of tidal salt-marsh. In 1957, 6 miles of it were declared a National Nature Reserve, together with some farmland and the extensive foreshore covered and uncovered by the fast-moving, treacherous Solway tides.

A sanctuary area, administered by the Wildfowl Trust, it is one of the finest refuges in Britain for wintering wildfowl. All the barnacle geese which spend the summer on the Norwegian Arctic island of Spitsbergen have their traditional wintering ground at Caerlaverock. Around 10,000 pink-footed geese roost on the reserve, flying inland during the day. Hundreds of greylags also roost here.

On the lands of Eastpark Farm, the Wildfowl Trust has erected a series of

HUMBLED PRIDE Ruined Caerlaverock Castle stands near tidal marshes where the River Nith meets the Solway Firth. It was sacked by Covenanters in 1640, after a three-month siege.

watchtowers and hides. Many of the hides are approached along roads that are bounded by high banks, so that the birds will not notice the human observers.

To the west is one of the great castles of southern Scotland. Caerlaverock Castle was built of red sandstone towards the end of the 13th century using a curious triangular ground plan. For several hundred years, its Maxwell lairds were the most powerful family in the county of Dumfries. But it was never lived in again after a siege by Covenanters in 1640.

The Caerlaverock district lies about 6 miles to the south-east of Dumfries and is reached by the B725 which skirts the east bank of the River Nith. The castle and nature reserve are south of the B725 where it turns inland.

Be   Cornalees

As the Industrial Revolution made progress on Clydeside, the towns of Greenock, Port Glasgow and Gourock began to run short of water for their factories, mills, ropeworks and increasing numbers of houses. A brilliant civil engineer, Robert Thom, devised a water system based on a series of new reservoirs near Cornalees on the hilly plateau above Greenock, well out of sight of the town itself.

This was a little-visited moorland, as is shown by the fact that a map drawn in 1827, the year Thom's scheme was opened, marked one hillside south of Cornalees as 'Back of the World'.

The heart of the scheme was the Great Reservoir. Local people from the towns, drawn at last to wander on the

WOODED OASIS Kip Water winds its way between banks green with ash, rowan and birch, and golden with gorse. It lies deep in Shielhill Glen – an island amid the farmland and heather moors at Cornalees.

moorland as they viewed the new working landscape, called it the Little Caspian. Finally, and fittingly, it was officially named Loch Thom.

But Robert Thom's ambitious and successful plan involved more than the creation of what now looks like a Highland loch. He built the Greenock Cut, a channel contouring the hillside, to lead the water to the top of the town, and he constructed the Kelly Cut, which approached Loch Thom from the south, to bring supplies from another reservoir above Wemyss Bay. Pathways, which still survive, were built along the sides of the cuts.

It was only in 1971 that the original channels were replaced by modern tunnels. A year later, the older system was declared an ancient monument, and in 1973 a visitor centre was opened at Cornalees Bridge.

This is fresh, airy walking country, with extensive views across the Firth of Clyde to the mountains of Cowal, Ardgoil and Loch Lomond. Herons stalk the shallows of Loch Thom, whooper swans winter there, and kestrels patrol the moors. But the real fascination is to walk alongside the cuts, now with slow-moving shallow water instead of the bustling currents of their busiest days. After heavy rain, the sluice-gates are opened at Cornalees Bridge, and great foaming falls pour out into the narrow valley of the Kip Water.

A nature trail wanders deep into the heart of Shielhill Glen, where the Kip Water suddenly plunges out of the bare moorland above into a chasm of birches, ashes, oaks and rowans, one of the last remaining deciduous woodlands in this corner of Strathclyde.

Cornalees is 2¼ miles south of Greenock. Minor roads lead to it from Greenock, and also from the A78 at Inverkip.

Ed
Eildon Hills

The most famous Borderer of them all, Sir Walter Scott, had a favourite viewpoint, above Dryburgh Abbey, looking west across the windings of the Tweed to the Eildon Hills. But the Eildons had attracted man's attention long before his time.

More than 2,000 years ago, the 1,327 ft summit of North Eildon Hill was a settlement of one of the shadowy tribes who lived in Tweeddale. Round the summit they built a circular fort, with banks and ditches which can still be followed today. And inside that protecting circle the foundations of more than 300 stone buildings have been traced.

Then came the Romans. On the same summit they built a signal station for their great military road, now known as Dere Street, which ran almost dead straight from the Cheviots to the east side of the Eildons, and on to Inveresk on the Forth.

Their main fort in the Borders was on the north-east side of the Eildons. They called it Trimontium, after the triple peaks of the Eildon Hills. The site is marked, but nothing remains above ground. However, the village of Newstead alongside claims to be the oldest continuously inhabited settlement in Scotland.

There are footpaths to the Eildon summits, past farmlands on the lower slopes, but then more steeply over a grassy moorland with gorse, bracken and heather. The views, especially from the northern summit, are superb. Down below is the town of Melrose, with its ruined abbey where the heart of Robert Bruce is said to be buried. The Tweed winds its way by Dryburgh and St Boswells to the hazy farmlands of the Berwickshire Merse. And on the southern horizon, just as it was when Roman lookouts scanned it almost 20 centuries ago, is the line of the faraway Cheviot Hills.

The Eildon Hills rise on the southern outskirts of Melrose. The path to the summits, the Eildon Walk, starts near the old station car park on the B6359.

Bb
Glen Trool

More than 240 sq. miles of south-west Scotland make up the Galloway Forest Park. As so often in Scotland, 'park' is a very mild word for the wild and rugged landscape within its boundaries. There are mountain ranges, not simply single peaks; harsh upland lochs; and, above the tree-line, a wilderness fit only for minor expeditions, not casual strolls.

In the heart of the forest park is the almost Highland scenery of Glen Trool. Its entrance is spectacular, at the Black Linn on the Water of Minnoch. There are rapids above a bridge, and tumbling falls that foam down a winding gorge of granite below, as the Minnoch battles through plantations of larch and pine to join the Water of Trool. The park is the only place in the Lowlands where there are red deer.

Forest walks spread north and south from Glen Trool, but the public road heads eastwards up the glen until it stops high above the north shore of Loch Trool. A granite memorial, the Bruce Stone, stands on a hilltop – a magnificent viewpoint over the curving shores of the loch. Below it lie the beautifully preserved Buchan oakwoods which in past years were coppiced for commercial use. The woods are quiet now, and the only sound is of the falls of the Buchan Burn, crashing down a granite ravine among the woodlands. Opposite, forest plantations climb the steep flanks of Mulldonoch.

The Bruce Stone stands where Robert Bruce is traditionally believed to have stood one spring day in 1307, directing his men in a guerrilla action against the English at the Steps of Trool on the slopes of Mulldonoch on the far bank. This was at the start of his seven-year campaign to assert his position as King of Scotland, which ended with his victory over Edward II's army at Bannockburn in 1314.

The Steps of Trool can still be seen today, where a mountain burn tumbles

THE BRUCE STONE, LOCH TROOL

GAIRLAND BURN, GLEN TROOL

LOWLAND HEIGHTS Loch Trool shines sapphire blue amid the rugged hills of Galloway, and boulder-strewn burns tumble down its surrounding slopes. Highlands within the Lowlands, the hills are studded with lochs and glens, and are part of the 240 sq. mile Galloway Forest Park.

down the steep hillside to the loch. As an English force made its way across the face of the hill, Bruce's men hurled boulders down on them, then swept down to finish the fight man to man.

North-west of the viewpoint rise the rugged crags of the Fell of Eschoncan: rock faces, scree runs and heather ledges. A footpath heads beyond it into even wilder country, towards the summit of the Merrick, at 2,765 ft the highest point in Galloway.

The names of the mountain features are as intriguing as the landscape: the Rig of the Jarkness, Mullwharchar, the Round Loch of the Dungeon, the Murder Hole of Loch Neldricken, Curley-

wee and the Range of the Awful Hand.

Glen Trool is 9 miles north of Newton Stewart. The road leading into the glen starts at Glentrool Village, on a minor road 1 mile east of the A714.

Ee Glencorse

Sweeping south-westwards beyond the boundaries of the city of Edinburgh are the Pentland Hills, aeons away in spirit from the main roads and busy streets for which they form the skyline. From the hamlet of Swanston, boyhood home of Robert Louis Stevenson, by the battlefield of Rullion Green and the Roman road along the eastern edge, to the hill burns and wooded reservoirs, the Pentlands are a carefully preserved natural world apart.

The hills are criss-crossed by walking routes, on pathways signposted for 100 years by the Scottish Rights of Way Society. And this is genuine walking country. No public roads penetrate the lonely passes of the Maiden's Cleuch and the Cauldstane Slap, among the grassy, heathery hills with names like Allermuir, Carnethy and Caerketton.

Flotterstone, a stone inn off the Edinburgh–Biggar road, is a favourite access point to the hills. A mile from it is Glencorse Reservoir, opened in 1822 and the first one in the Pentlands to supply water to Edinburgh. But this is no tame Lowland waterway. Curving through a steep-sided valley, it is uncompromisingly Highland in aspect, an impression helped by the windswept pines along its north-eastern shore, a wooded island and the conical peak of West Kip hill above the more rounded slopes on the south-western skyline.

Where the reservoir bends, a path goes uphill across the Maiden's Cleuch, on the line of an old drovers'

road, leading to Balerno village and the reservoir at Threipmuir.

Near the Flotterstone Inn, a memorial service is held every year for the Covenanters killed at the Battle of Rullion Green, fought in 1666 on the slopes of Turnhouse Hill, which rises south of Glencorse. And the peaceful track across the Maiden's Cleuch was the route by which General Dalyell of the Binns marched his Royalist troops to crush the rebels on that grim November morning.

Glencorse lies about 3 miles from the southernmost outskirts of Edinburgh; Flotterstone is east off the A702, 1 mile south of Easter Howgate.

Ed Glentress Forest

In 1919, when the Forestry Commission came into being, one of the Commissioners' first acquisitions was 1,000 acres of land on the Haystoun estate near Peebles. This was the beginning of Glentress Forest, which today extends to more than ten times the original area on the hills around the Tweed Valley.

Glentress is made up of nearly 30 separate plantation areas. The centre of the forest is a fine sweep of hillside east of the town of Peebles, with forest walks and trails extending to a height of almost 1,500 ft, rising on both sides of the Glentress Burn. The higher the road or pathway, the more widely does the view open out over the rich landscape of Tweeddale.

Names such as Eshiels suggest that, long before afforestation was ever thought of, people from the valley used to bring their livestock here to the shielings – the upland grazings – to take advantage of the sweet summer grass. Early this century, private landowners began to introduce trees on the poor hillside ground. They chose the wrong species, and timber yields were low. The modern forest is made up largely of Norway and Sitka spruce, Douglas and silver firs, Scots pines, Japanese and European larch. Beech and sycamore have been planted to give variety and add to the attractions of these hillside plantations.

With its variety of tree cover, Glentress attracts many kinds of wildlife. Birds range from crossbills and woodpeckers to sparrowhawks and hen harriers. There are red squirrels here, and groups of delicate roe deer can often be seen browsing in the early morning and at dusk.

Glentress Forest lies to the east of Peebles. The entrance is at Glentress village, off the A 72, 2 miles from Peebles.

Dc   The Grey Mare's Tail

There are several waterfalls in southwest Scotland called the Grey Mare's Tail. But by far the most impressive of them is high up the valley of the Moffat Water, near the head of the pass which leads north-east towards St Mary's Loch and Selkirk. The summit of the pass is at the lonely house of Birkhill, once a welcome sign to drivers of horse-drawn coaches that the long hard haul up from Moffat was coming to an end.

Near the summit of the road the Tail Burn plunges down from Loch Skeen, far out of sight in its craggy and ice-scooped hollow to the north-west. The spurs of the eroded hillside interlock among each other, from the left bank and then from the right of the Tail Burn. And a nick on the skyline marks the point where the burn begins its precipitous descent in the 200 ft fall.

In the wild and lonely hill country of rough grassland, heather, bracken, rock and scree which marks the head of the Moffat Water, the Grey Mare's Tail is a suitable climax. In 1962 the fall itself, Loch Skeen and the crags which circle it passed into the possession of the National Trust for Scotland, when they bought 2,380 acres of Birkhill Farm.

A pathway to the left of the Tail Burn leads to the foot of the waterfall. Another on the far bank rises steeply to the outflow of Loch Skeen. This is very difficult country, and great care is needed on the higher reaches because of the steep and slippery slopes.

The Grey Mare's Tail is 8 miles northeast of Moffat, on the A 708.

Df   Loch Leven

Many of Scotland's inland lochs have been deepened and increased in size to provide extra water supplies. But at Loch Leven, east of the old county town of Kinross in the angle between Benarty Hill and the Lomonds, exactly the opposite was done. In 1830 the course of the River Leven, which runs from the south-east corner of the loch, was deepened and straightened, partly to regulate the essential water supplies to the paper and textile mills of towns like Leslie and Markinch. In lowering the level of the loch by 4½ ft, many acres of the rich alluvial soil at the edges could be drained and ploughed.

From Findatie, near the outlet from the loch, the 'new cut' of 1830 can still be seen, running dead straight from the sluices for more than 3 miles across the almost level farmlands to Auchmuirbridge, where the original course of the river takes over.

The lowering of the water level in

the loch also increased the size of its six islands. St Serf's is the biggest of them, with the ruined tower of a 9th-century priory on a rise of ground above the scrubby woodland. Castle Island is known for the remains of the castle where Mary, Queen of Scots was imprisoned in 1567, and from which she made a daring escape in May, 1568.

The whole loch, with its 11 miles of shore, was declared a National Nature Reserve in 1964. It is one of the finest places in Scotland to see wintering ducks, geese and swans. In the autumn, thousands of pink-footed geese gather on St Serf's and the lochside farmlands. Vane Farm, near Findatie, is an RSPB (Royal Society for the Protection of Birds) reserve, with an information centre and nature trail.

Kinross, at the western end of Loch Leven, is at the A977/A922 junction. Access to the loch shore is restricted to three places – car parks near Findatie beside the B9097 on the south side, at Burleigh Sands on the north side, and at Kirkgate Park in Kinross, from where a summertime ferry runs to Castle Island.

Ef   The Lomond Hills

East of Loch Leven, above the plain of Kinross, rises the escarpment of the Lomond Hills. The lie of the land here is evidence of the west–east movement of the last of the Ice Age glaciers which scoured across Fife. On the side which took the brunt of the glacier's advance, the map shows the contour lines packed together. On the other side, the gradients are gentler.

The escarpment above Loch Leven, and the long hill of Benarty south of the loch, make the Lomonds, with their thermal currents and upward-sweeping winds, the finest site in Scotland for gliding. Walkers on the

GOLDEN HILLS Only sheep and grouse and the occasional hiker roam the Lowther Hills today. For centuries, however, they attracted miners in search of gold and lead ore, and there are many old workings in the area.

BIRDS OF LOCH AND PINE

The rich feeding grounds of the Solway estuary and large inland waters such as Loch Leven provide a winter haven for thousands of wildfowl. They include goldeneyes, distinctive diving ducks from the far north, and native greylags – largest of the geese – that like to nest among the heather in spring. It is the pine forests that attract siskins, tiny resident finches that feed on pine and spruce seeds.

Goldeneye
(*Bucephala clangula*)

Greylag goose
(*Anser anser*)

Siskin
(*Carduelis spinus*)

Lomonds should be prepared for the sudden, silent approach of a glider as it searches for height from the launching ground at Portmoak below.

Falkland and its palace, a favourite home of the Stuart kings of Scotland, lies at the foot of the northern slopes, separated from the upland moors and summits by a bank of conifer plantations where roe deer roam. This is not the same Forest of Falkland where the Scottish kings used to hunt deer and wild boar – brought over from France – and to fly their falcons. That was north of the little town, on the level ground seen from East Lomond Hill, towards the course of the River Eden.

The original oak forest was felled by Cromwell's troops in 1652. The year before, Charles II was the last king to stay in the palace.

The Lomond Hills are well served by footpaths. They go to both the main summits, West Lomond and East Lomond. On the rounded top of East Lomond, 1,471 ft, is the site of an Iron Age fort. The view is superb, as from so many points on the hills. It takes in not only the North Sea coast and the mountains of the Highland Line, the Moorfoots and the Lammermuirs away to the south but also, on a clear day, the 4,241 ft plateau of Cairn Toul in the distant Cairngorms.

From West Lomond, all the rich farmlands around Kinross come into view. But the most spectacular sight is on the hills themselves. Almost 1,000 ft lower than the summit of West Lomond is the curious Bannet Stane. Balanced on an outcrop, it seems to defy the force of gravity – a mushroom of sandstone with a slim supporting pillar. Whether caused by erosion or by some long-ago action of the glaciers is a matter of continuing debate.

ROUGH ISLAND Viewed from the Mote of Mark, the island bird sanctuary lies serene in the tranquil waters of Rough Firth.

The Lomond Hills lie to the south-west of Falkland, from where a minor road leads across them to Leslie. Near the summit, there is a car park, signposted Craigmead. From it, walks lead to the East and West Lomond Hills.

Dc The Lowther Hills

In the heart of the Lowther Hills stand two remote villages, Leadhills and Wanlockhead, at more than 1,300 ft the highest in Scotland. The approaches to them are long and winding, climbing up from Clydesdale and Nithsdale by valleys among grassy, heathery hills managed for sheep and grouse.

In these quiet hills above the Elvan Water, the Glengonnar, the Wanlock and the Mennock, there used to be such a concentration of mineral wealth that the Lowthers were known as 'God's Treasure House in Scotland'.

Once, while on a hunting trip, James V wagered with a French envoy, who had made disparaging remarks about the bare and unproductive country they were in, that these hills could provide richer fruit than any in France – and had him served at the next meal with dishes full of coins made from Lowther gold. But from the 18th century onwards it was lead that made the fortunes of the great Lowther landlords. That is why there are two separate villages: Leadhills lying on the estates of the Earl of Hopetoun, and Wanlockhead on the lands of the Duke of Buccleuch.

Lead-mining has finished now. But at Leadhills the library founded by the miners in 1741 is still open, with extensive records and maps of the lead-mining ventures from 1739 to 1854. The miners named the library after Allan Ramsay, who was born in Leadhills in 1686; he was a poet and the author of *The Gentle Shepherd.*

At Wanlockhead there is an open-air mining museum. But disregarding industrial archaeology, the Lowthers are invigorating. There are fine footpaths over the hills and through the glens, especially around the Mennock Pass. And take heart from John Taylor's memorial in the hilltop graveyard at Leadhills. After a century of working in the mines, he died at the age of 137. His longevity is attributed to the fresh, clean air of the uplands.

Leadhills and Wanlockhead are 7 and 6 miles east of Sanquhar on the B797, which runs across the Lowther Hills between the A76 and A74. The B7040 from Elvanfoot on the A702 also leads to Leadhills.

Db Mabie Forest

South-west of Dumfries, on high ground that was once open grazing, are the conifer plantations of the Forestry Commission's Mabie Forest. On the lower slopes, around Mabie House, there were 'policy' woodlands – the Scots name for ornamental grounds.

Samples of the more exotic trees are preserved in an arboretum, including cypresses from Japan and a giant redwood from California. Around them, and away into the highest reaches of the forest, walks and trails fan out to reach a series of panoramic viewpoints.

In spring, rides among the trees are deep in bluebells. On the lower slopes there are mixed woodlands of beeches and oaks, and by the side of tumbling burns there are alders and elms.

The main plantations are spruce and larch, pine and Douglas fir. They are saved from monotony by the contours of the forest, which rises in a series of hills and glens where, on heavy days, wisps of mist trail through the trees.

A water system built to drive a Victorian sawmill can still be traced. And a tiny reservoir beside one of the walks, high up on the Mabie Burn, once topped up the water tanks of Mabie House.

Five major viewpoints have been cleared along the forest trails. One is over the narrow tidal channel of the River Nith, another looks down to Mabie House, a third to the marshy coastline of the Caerlaverock Nature Reserve and a fourth south to Criffel peak. The fifth looks inland, to the long valley of Nithsdale and the northern horizon of the Lowther Hills.

Mabie Forest is 3 miles south-west of Dumfries. The road to the start of the forest walks, signposted 'Solway Forest', runs from the A710, 3 miles north of New Abbey.

Db Mote of Mark

Excavations in 1913 and 1973 revealed an early settlement on the Mote of Mark, a hilltop site in one of the most beautiful areas of the Solway coast, now in the care of the National Trust for Scotland.

The Mote of Mark lies between the villages of Rockcliffe and Kippford on the estuary of the Urr Water, and was probably first settled in the 5th or 6th century. There are remains of ditched fortifications here, and at one time the defences included heaped-up stones supported by timber frames. As with so many similar sites, the timber was burned, perhaps in some 7th-century attack by invading Angles, and in the intense heat the stonework vitrified.

Signs of a gateway and metalworking areas have been discovered, and excavations have brought to light examples of Celtic craftsmanship – decorated clay moulds, and bronze and iron implements. Evidence has also been found of the international trade of those early years. There were pieces of Bordeaux pottery, glass from the Rhineland, ornaments of Yorkshire

MABIE FOREST From a forest trail, fields and woods stretch southwards to the distant peak of Criffel, overlooking the Solway shore.

LONELY GLEN Green slopes and grazing sheep overlook the Calder valley near Muirshiel Country Park in the Renfrew hills.

Mote of Mark, is on a minor road which leads west from the A710, 4½ miles south of Dalbeattie.

Be ## Muirshiel

Only a few miles from the great conurbation of Glasgow, Paisley and Greenock is the Muirshiel Country Park, a superb blending of moorland and woods near a steep-sided glen enclosing the tumbling waters of the River Calder. There is also a path from the park leading up to the high moors and Windy Hill where there are fine views of the Firth of Clyde. The rhododendrons growing among the trees are all that is left of the policies – landscaped gardens – of an 18th-century house pulled down in 1954.

The Renfrew valleys have a hard climate, especially in winter. Although the hilltops are modest in altitude – 1,712 ft at the Hill of Stake, the highest summit in this part of Strathclyde – this is a rough and rumpled landscape of grassland, heather and bracken, grazed by hardy sheep and noted as a grouse moor. Every spring, patches of heather on the hillside across the valley from Muirshiel are burned to make way for new growth.

Beech, birch and sycamore are the older Muirshiel trees, but there are conifer plantations, too, with Norway and Sitka spruce, larch and an occasional relic of a former pinewood.

Nearer the head of the valley, above the woodland cover, is an old barytes mine. It was a source of barium, used in paint and paper-making, but closed down in the late 1960s.

Muirshiel Country Park is 4 miles north-west of Lochwinnoch. A road to the park branches north-west from the B786, ½ mile north of the town.

jet, and iron tools forged from Lake District ore.

The splendid outlook from Mote of Mark is over a rugged coast of bays and rocky islands, plantations and natural woods, with the stately heights of Bengairn and Screel Hill across the estuary. This was once smugglers' country. In the days when French brandy, wine and lace were shipped openly to the Isle of Man, then brought by night to secret creeks and inlets on the Solway shore, White Horse Bay on the Almorness peninsula was a favourite landing place. So was Hestan Island, off the southern tip. Beyond Almorness, the view from Mote of Mark takes in the promontory of Balcary Hill, where the smugglers were so confident and so well organised that they built a mansion for their headquarters – all that remains is a ruined tower below the hill.

Between the two villages of Rockcliffe and Kippford, a maze of footpaths leads across the hillside and along the shore. On the ebb tide, if you are careful, you can cross the causeway known as The Rack to the bird sanctuary on Rough Island.

Rockcliffe, the nearest village to the

Cb   The Queen's Way

At the time of the Silver Jubilee in 1977, the Forestry Commission gave the title of the Queen's Way to the stretch of the A712 that runs through Bennan, Clatteringshaws and Kirroughtree forests.

This is far more than a landscape simply engulfed in trees. One stroll through the forest fringe beside Clatteringshaws Loch, for example, leads to the battlefield of Raploch Moss. In 1307 this was the site of one of Robert Bruce's earliest victories.

The loch was created by a dam on the Black Water of Dee. The rocky course of the river below Clatteringshaws is low in water because most of the outflow is tunnelled eastwards to feed the great Kendoon hydroelectric scheme.

Among the sheltering pines by the lochside, the white house of Clatteringshaws has been turned into the Galloway Deer Museum. West of the loch, a dead-end public road heads northwards through a lonely landscape to a forest road which walkers may use to hike up through the plantations of Garraries Forest to the desolate country of the Merrick range.

Nearer at hand, off the lochside road, lower-level walking routes lead to Lilie's Loch, and along the course of the old Edinburgh–Wigtown road, used by honest travellers and smugglers alike hundreds of years ago.

A forest road which turns south off the Queen's Way is used in summer as a public forest drive. Called the Raiders' Road, this was a route used by the tough and troublesome cattle thieves of the 18th century – the Faas and the Marshalls.

Natural history takes over again at Brockloch Hill on the north side of the Queen's Way, where there is a red-deer range. And among the bracken and heathery crags of Craigdews Hill is a wild-goat park.

Beyond Craigdews, at Talnotry, there is a fine waterfall and the start of a network of hill and forest walks which include part of the old Edinburgh road. Relics of lead and nickel mines can be seen on the way. From the summit of Blackcraig, south by the A75, a panoramic view extends over forests and sturdy hills to Wigtown Bay and the farmlands of the Machars on the southern horizon.

The Queen's Way is part of the A712, between New Galloway and Newton Stewart. The scenic road starts about 2 miles west of New Galloway.

Fe   St Abb's Head

The highest cliffs on the east side of Scotland, rising to little over 300 ft, are on the Borders coastline near the little fishing village of St Abb's, clustering round its harbour pounded by the North Sea waves. North of the village, the wild coastline and the gentler landscape above the cliffs together make up the St Abb's Head Wildlife Reserve, owned by the National Trust for Scotland.

Fishermen founded the village as recently as 1832, calling it first of all Northfield, and then Coldingham Shore. Its modern name is taken from St Abba, or Ebba, a daughter of the royal house of Northumbria who established a religious settlement here 13 centuries ago.

St Abb's Head is the highest point of the reserve, marked by a lighthouse built in 1862. The all but inaccessible cliffs, rock stacks and inlets around it are the home, at all levels, of thousands of sea-birds. There are kittiwakes and guillemots, razorbills, fulmars and herring gulls.

A few puffins settle here. There are fleeting visits from terns, skuas and shearwaters, and gannets can often be seen, cruising by on their way to and from their great nesting ground on the Bass Rock.

Perhaps the best view of the underlying structure of this coastline is from Pettico Wick, a precipitous bay on the northern edge of the reserve. Until the lighthouse road was built, the keepers' supplies had to be landed here. It marks the fault-line between the volcanic rocks of the headland and the shales and greywackes to the north.

The fault-line south-east from Pettico Wick provided a route for the melting waters of an Ice Age glacier. The narrow valley, once bog-land, was dammed in 1900 to create the Mire Loch. Tree planting was tried, but the winds sweeping down the valley made the project wellnigh impossible.

Mire Loch provides the reserve with a home for other than coastal birds. Grebes and moorhens nest here, and the grazing and arable lands around it attract wheatears and skylarks, stonechats and yellowhammers.

Sheep grazing on the grasslands of the reserve keep much of the vegetation trimmed. But on the cliffs, well out of reach, there are sea campion and rose-root, vetches and lovage.

The village of St Abb's is on the B6438, 1¼ miles north-east of Coldingham. Footpaths to St Abb's Head start near the church in the village.

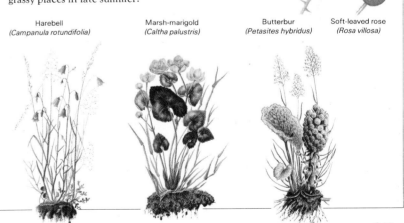

GOLDEN SPRING AND SUMMER BLUES

Golden-yellow marsh-marigolds, or kingcups, brighten marshes and wet woods or meadows in spring and early summer, and strange butterburs, whose large leaves were once used to wrap butter, flower also in damp places at the same time. Midsummer is the time to see soft-leaved roses in scrub and hedgerow, and delicate harebells, called bluebells in Scotland, nod in the breeze in dry, grassy places in late summer.

Harebell
(*Campanula rotundifolia*)

Marsh-marigold
(*Caltha palustris*)

Butterbur
(*Petasites hybridus*)

Soft-leaved rose
(*Rosa villosa*)

LOCH LOMOND AND ARRAN

Where the rolling hills and pastures of the south meet the wild mountains and lochs of the Highlands

It is as if Loch Lomond had been made from odd, unmatching halves. The long, narrow north end cuts like a knife-blade deep into the Highland mountains, which soar to more than 3,000 ft above it. The south end is broad and shallow, fanning out to include a scattering of lovely wooded islands, tidy oakwoods and gentle farming country around its shores. Similarly, on the wild, mysterious island of Arran, the stern, granite heights of the north seem a world away from the rolling hills and quiet pastureland of the south. On Arran, as on Loch Lomond, the Scottish Lowlands come face to face with the Highlands. The line where they meet, the geological boundary between them, is known as the Highland Boundary Fault.

As remarkable as the abrupt change from pastoral to mountain scenery is the skewed angle of so much of the land, the way so many hills, ridges, lochs, valleys and inlets from the sea run parallel from north-east to south-west, as if a giant comb had been dragged across them. Again, geologists explain this phenomenon as a consequence of faulting – the dislocation of rock layers under intense pressure.

Inland there are lochs and mountains, narrow glens and immense forests – this is the country that Sir Walter Scott made famous in works such as *The Lady of the Lake* and *Rob Roy*. These are the hills and shores where the real Rob Roy lived, a cattle-stealer and bankrupt freebooter,

by no means such a genial outlaw in fact as Scott made him in fiction. On the coast there is a seemingly endless, meandering shore, a jagged interlocking of sea and mountains, a maze of peninsulas and sea lochs. And offshore lies an immense variety of islands, including pinnacled and shapely Arran.

The coast and the islands offer some of the area's loveliest scenery; they also have a fascinating history. The first Scots arrived on this coast from Ireland between the end of the 2nd century and early 3rd century. In the 6th century they established the kingdom of Dalriada. Their kings were crowned at the hilltop fort on Dunadd, on Mòine Mhór; rock carvings used in coronation rituals survive on the summit. By the 9th century they had driven out the Picts, and in 843 Kenneth MacAlpin was crowned first king of a united Scotland. At about the same time the Vikings were invading the Western Isles, and in 1093 the Scots officially granted all islands off the west coast to Magnus Barefoot, king of Norway. Curiously, this included the Kintyre peninsula – for Magnus defined an island as any piece of land round which a boat could sail, and he had his galley towed overland with sails set from East Loch Tarbert to West Loch Tarbert. Tradition claims that the king himself took the tiller. The islands, and Kintyre, remained under Norse control until 1263, when Alexander III of Scotland defeated King Haco of Norway in a sea battle off Largs.

And at the heart of this geological and historical wonderland lies Britain's largest lake – 23 miles long and 5 miles wide at its broadest point – and one of Scotland's loveliest. Its 'bonnie banks' immortalised in song, Loch Lomond is the Scotsman's Scotland – shared and loved by both Highlander and Lowlander alike.

'THE BONNIE BANKS' The bitter-sweet ballad of Loch Lomond is sung by Scotsmen everywhere. It is said to have been written by one of Prince Charlie's supporters awaiting execution in Carlisle gaol. The 'low road' was the path his spirit would take to his native land.

Places to visit

Map ref. Cd Achray Forest

At the village of Aberfoyle there is a sudden and dramatic change in the landscape, because this is one of the gateways to the Highlands, built exactly on the geological dividing line known as the Highland Boundary Fault. The approach from the south is through undulating farmland, but immediately behind the village rise the steep, wooded slopes of the Menteith Hills and the rugged outliers of Ben Venue. Here, in the hills, the finest viewpoints, woodlands, rivers and lochs fall within the bounds of Achray Forest, part of the Queen Elizabeth Forest Park.

Waymarked forest trails start from the David Marshall Lodge, the park information centre on a summit directly above Aberfoyle. The lodge itself is a splendid viewpoint, with an outlook extending for miles to the south, across the lower-lying Loch Ard Forest. The view also takes in the scattered plantations on the former bogland of Flanders Moss, around the winding course of the River Forth. Looking at the landscape, mostly rich, black farming country, it is hard to believe that only 200 years ago it was a vast wilderness of peat bog.

A spectacular route over the Duke's Pass, called the Duke's Road, splits Achray Forest from north to south. The original toll-road was built in 1820 by the Duke of Montrose, partly to cope with the flood of visitors attracted to the district where Sir Walter Scott's novel *Rob Roy* and his epic poem *The Lady of the Lake* were set. The Forestry Commission bought the lands of what is now Achray Forest in 1931, and only then was the road transferred to public ownership. Now it is the twisting, swooping A821, which leads past picnic areas and forest trails.

It passes the entrance to the old Aberfoyle slate quarry, closed in 1958 and now a fascinating relic of the area's industrial past. It also leads to a forest drive, open from March to October. The drive winds for 7 miles through the plantations, to information areas, walks and viewpoints, including Larch Point, Pine Ridge, Spruce Glen and Birch Bay. Some of these are above the shore of Loch Drunkie which, before the drive was opened, was only visible to motorists as a glint of water in the heart of the forest. A nearby mansion used to have the same name as the loch, until just before Queen Victoria was due to visit it, when it was discreetly re-christened Invertrossachs House.

The A81 north from Glasgow runs to the east of Aberfoyle, and a turn on to the A821 leads into the village. Follow this road through the village for the start of the climb up the Duke's Road. The David Marshall Lodge, where there is parking, is ¼ mile up this road.

Bc Ardgoil

Once this mountainous triangle of land lying between Loch Long and Loch Goil was on the route used by the Earls and Dukes of Argyll, when they needed to move quickly from their

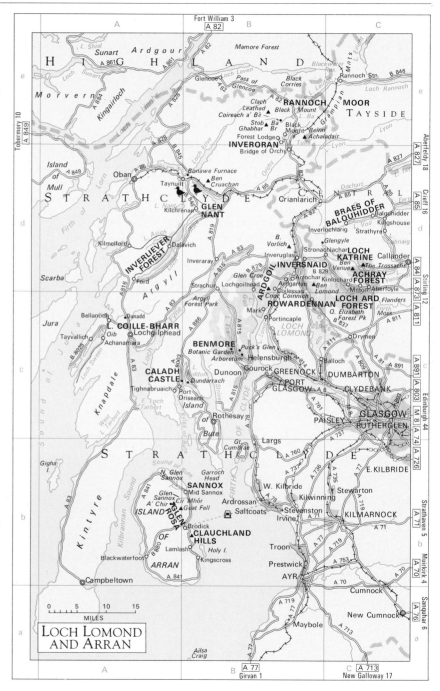

LOCH LOMOND AND ARRAN

stronghold at Inveraray to the Low-lands without crossing hostile clan ter-ritory. They would be ferried across Loch Fyne, then ride to Lochgoilhead and hurry along a half-secret track, much of which can still be traced, to Mark on the west shore of Loch Long. A ferry across to Portincaple brought the Lowlands safely within reach.

The Helensburgh to Arrochar road above Portincaple still offers one of the most striking views of this wild region; across the shimmering waters of the loch the mountains climb towards the sky, reaching 2,497 ft at the summit of Cnoc Coinnich – evidence that the rugged Highlands are at hand. Many of the hillsides are forested, for the estate has belonged to the Forestry Commis-sion for many years and is now part of the Argyll Forest Park. Some of the oldest woods stand along the shore of Loch Long, from Coilessan to Mark. There are oaks and birches, hazels and rowans, with the conifer plantations soaring above. Off the rugged shore, wild duck gather in winter, and herons patrol all year.

Although several of the gravelled forest tracks head southwards, there is no reasonable route round the tip of the peninsula. But the main forest track from Coilessan ends at a splendid viewpoint, backed by rock and over-looking the meeting of the two lochs. At this point, the track has already passed the bare hillside below Corran Lochan, about 850 ft above the sea. Experienced hill walkers leave the path here to head north through a pass lead-ing to the head of Loch Goil – the pass once used by the Dukes of Argyll.

Walking routes in Ardgoil start at Ard-gartan on the A83; near the western end of the B828 near Lochgoilhead; at the foot of Glen Croe; and at Lochgoilhead itself.

IN ACHRAY FOREST Scott's poem *The Lady of the Lake* describes the 'copsewood grey that waved and wept on Loch Achray'.

Bc   Benmore

Some of the finest mountain and loch-side scenery in Scotland, and some of the finest trees, can be found on the Benmore estate at the foot of Loch Eck. This is part of the Argyll Forest Park created in 1935, the first of its kind in Britain. Almost all of the park is now open to the public, from the riverside stretches to the rugged hill-sides above.

The grounds of Benmore House form the Younger Botanic Garden, an annexe of the Royal Botanic Garden in Edinburgh. The entrance is through a spectacular avenue of Wellingtonias reaching more than 130 ft high. Other trees in the collection include deodars, maples, cypresses, spruce, pines and beeches. There are many examples of more exotic species, and more than 200 varieties of rhododendrons, mostly from China and the Himalayas, flowering red, yellow and delicate pink from January to September.

A network of forest paths sweeps up the steep hillsides on the east side of the valley. Puck's Glen is the name of one famous walk through the conifer plantations. Another walk leads into the upper reaches of the Kilmun Ar-boretum on the hillside above Holy Loch. Here, since 1930, the Forestry Commission has transformed what used to be rough sheep-grazing country into extensive plantations of mixed woodland which include almost 30 var-ieties of eucalyptus. Perhaps the pride

347

of the arboretum is the collection of dawn redwoods, established in 1951. The species was rediscovered in China in 1941 – until then it was thought to be extinct, and to be in existence only in fossil form.

Benmore is reached by the A815 from Strachur to Dunoon. About 1 mile beyond the southern end of Loch Eck, on the west of the road, is the Younger Botanic Garden (usually open from April to October). The main forest walks are on the opposite side of the road. Puck's Glen walk is about 1 mile further south.

Cd Braes of Balquhidder

It was to the wild, roadless country around Inverlochlarig that the red-haired outlaw Rob Roy came to farm in peace after he had been pardoned in 1727; and when he died quietly in his bed seven years later, it was in the nearby churchyard of Balquhidder that he was buried. Here, too, other members of his family found their last resting place, including his son Robin, who inherited the old MacGregor temper and was hanged in 1754 after killing one of his neighbours to settle an argument about some land.

The narrow glen road beneath the soaring heights of the Braes of Balquhidder leads to some of the most striking scenery in the Central Highlands. West of Balquhidder village the road climbs high above Loch Voil, then darts down to the water's edge. Conifer plantations cover the hillsides on both banks of the loch, and there are many acres of recently planted land. But by the waterside the old natural woodland survives round little bays and curving inlets.

Separated by a narrow spit of land from Loch Voil is Loch Doine. Once the two lochs were joined together, but earth and stones washed down from the braes by the Monachyle Burn, which still forms a fine roadside waterfall, finally divided them. It is probable that at one time they were also joined to Loch Lubnaig, which lies south-east of Balquhidder village.

The public road ends before the farm of Inverlochlarig. The view ahead is magnificent, into the heart of the mountain country north of Loch Katrine and east of Loch Lomond. A lovely panorama of shapely peaks and steep-sided glens spreads out before the eye – a delight in summer, but bitterly cold and inhospitable in winter when only red deer and the hardy Blackface sheep can survive there.

The road to Balquhidder turns west from the A84 at Kingshouse, north of Strathyre. There is a car park and information point at Inverlochlarig.

Ac Caladh Castle

A century and a half ago, Tighnabruaich would not have rated even the briefest of entries in a travellers' guide to Scotland. But then Victorian Glasgow woke up to the magnificent coastal scenery of the Firth of Clyde, and Tighnabruaich became a favourite resort. It grew up as a hilltop village of holiday homes magnificently situated on the edge of the western of the two Kyles of Bute, looking out directly to the wild north-west corner of the Isle of Bute. The Gaelic name that the Victorians gave the village sums up its situation – Tighnabruaich means 'The House on the Hill'.

North of the village is the Caladh Castle forest trail. Steep pathways lead down from a viewpoint on the exhilarating road above Loch Riddon.

Mountains, lochs and islands spread out all around. In the narrow entrance to Loch Riddon is Eilean Dearg – the Red Island – where there was a Campbell stronghold until 1685. It was blown up by an English fleet because the Campbell Earl of Argyll was plotting to join Monmouth's rebellion. More than a century later, defences were raised in the narrow Kyles against possible invasion by Napoleon's fleet. Dundarrach, on the far mainland shore beyond the Burnt Islands, was the site of a coastal gun battery.

Today it is the landscape and the wildlife that catch the attention – even Caladh Castle itself was demolished in 1959. The trees of the forest trail are Noble fir, European and Japanese larch, Western hemlock, Norway spruce, pine and oak. The mixed woodland attracts a fine variety of birds and animals – the half-light of dawn and dusk are the best times to see roe deer, foxes, badgers, stoats and perhaps even a wildcat. Waterfowl gather at a small loch in the woods, and the Forestry Commission has built carefully camouflaged hides beside it.

The A8003 enters Tighnabruaich from the north. The forest trail starts from the viewpoint above Loch Riddon or, to avoid the steep paths, from Port Driseach north of the village.

Bb Clauchland Hills

No view shows better the two contrasting faces of Arran than that from the Thomson Memorial Seat, the highest point of the road from Brodick to Lamlash. The memorial is named after a much-respected member of the Glasgow Arran Society. To the north lie great granite mountains, rising to more than 2,800 ft. A gentle panorama of rolling hills, moorland and forest spreads out to the south.

East of the road are the Clauchland Hills, with footpaths and rights of way threading through the forests. One route, which starts from near the seat, leads through dark conifers and over bracken-covered hillside to another fine viewpoint overlooking Lamlash village. Backed by sweeping forest, Lamlash and its surrounding farmlands fringe the shore of a great semicircular bay, which is separated from the open waters of the Firth of Clyde by the impressive bulk of Holy Island. This is no gentle offshore islet, but a 2 mile range of cliffs, jagged rocks and rugged moorland, rising at its summit to 1,030 ft – higher than any mainland Arran hill for nearly 3 miles around.

Holy Island is named in honour of the 7th-century St Molaise, who is said to have lived to be 120. His cell is on the western shore and can still be visited. There are graffiti on the walls in runic – the old Norse alphabet – carved by Norwegian sailors who gathered in Lamlash Bay before the Battle of Largs in 1263. Their defeat ended the centuries of Norse control of the Western Isles. It was also from Lamlash Bay – from Kingscross at the southern end – that Robert Bruce set sail for the Ayrshire coast in 1307, at the start of his seven-year campaign against the English that ended with his triumph at Bannockburn.

Holy Island today is a field study centre, with Highland cattle, Soay sheep, wild goats and more than 50 species of nesting and migrant birds.

The highest point of the A841 between Brodick and Lamlash is marked by the Thomson Memorial Seat. A ferry runs from Lamlash to Holy Island, from May to September.

Glen Nant

Bd

In the narrow, rocky valley of the River Nant, south of Taynuilt in Argyll, two nature reserves face each other. On the east bank is a National Nature Reserve and on the other side of the river is a Forest Nature Reserve.

From 1753 to 1870 the woodlands of the forest reserve were exploited to provide charcoal for the Lorn Furnace at Bonawe, on the shore of Loch Etive. The furnace was established by a firm of ironmasters from the Furness district of Lancashire, where fuel was growing scarce. Something like 75 acres of woodland had to be felled each year to keep it burning, but fortunately for Glen Nant the felling was carefully controlled, with woods being coppiced so that after 20 years or so there was a new crop of poles ready to be thinned once again.

Since 1870 the mixed, broad-leaved woodlands of Glen Nant have been left to develop naturally, and a walk along the nature trail laid out through them shows how well they have recovered. But there are still signs of the old industry – the sites of the hearths where the charcoal was made, for instance, before being taken by packhorse to Bonawe.

At Bonawe itself the furnace has been rebuilt as an industrial monument. Standing on a rise of ground between the River Nant and the River Awe, the furnace, the casting house and the storage sheds look exactly as they did in 1753. Kelly's Pier, by contrast, where pig-iron was shipped in and cast-iron out, is in ruins. And its old, unofficial importance to smugglers – Excise men once snatched 34 casks of brandy hidden there – is no more than a memory.

LOCHSIDE BRAES Soaring above Loch Voil, the majestic slopes of the Braes of Balquhidder rise to more than 2,000 ft.

A different industry exploits the natural resources of the district today – the hidden hydroelectric scheme buried deep in the heart of Ben Cruachan. It causes sudden fluctuations in the level of the River Awe. But herons still hunt their prey along the river mouth, and the mountain and lochside scenery is still as marvellous as it has always been, and so far remains untroubled by industry.

Glen Nant is reached by the B845, which turns south off the A85 on the east side of Taynuilt. A bridge on the west side of the B845, about 2 miles from Taynuilt, leads to the forest trail. To reach Bonawe Furnace, follow the signposts from the crossroads in Taynuilt.

Ab   Glen Rosa

For travellers arriving on Arran by the ferry to Brodick, the first impression of the island is created by the soaring, conical peak of Goat Fell. The mountain towers 2,866 ft above Brodick Bay, making it the highest point on the island. Just to the west of it is another of Arran's wonders, sandwiched between immense mountain walls. This is Glen Rosa, which starts from sea-level at a winding river mouth cruised by swans and climbs into the heart of the great, granite mountain range.

Lower Glen Rosa has cottages and farmland between the forestry plantations which sweep up its sides. Between the two main blocks of woodland on the north side, a path climbs towards the summit of Goat Fell alongside the Cnocan Burn. Higher up the glen, the landscape becomes more obviously glacial. The Glenrosa Water curls down a U-shaped valley cut through mounds of glacial moraine – the debris left behind by retreating glaciers some 10,000 years ago.

Near a foot-bridge where a tributary burn tumbles down from the west side of the glen, the underlying rock structure changes. Here Glen Rosa crosses into the heart of the granite country. Even the name of the stream is a clue to this – Garbh Allt means 'the Rough Burn', a name which accurately describes the obstacle course of massive granite boulders through which the stream drops.

From here the peak of Cir Mhór dominates the northward view, rising above The Saddle – the col which links Cir Mhór with Goat Fell. To one side is the bristling A'Chir ridge; ranged along the other is a wild series of rock pinnacles and gullies. Between two of these pinnacles is one of the most famous features of Arran's mountain scenery – the Witch's Step, formed by the weathering away of a dyke of soft rock intruded into the harder granite. In fact there are so many of these intrusive rocks on the island that they are known collectively as the Arran Dyke Swarm. For years they have made Arran a geologists' paradise, and the local people are no longer surprised to find 'jolly-boys', as the geologists are sometimes called, tapping away at the rock in the most remote corners of the island.

From Brodick Pier, turn west and take the B880 Blackwaterfoot road. After 200 yds, a road signposted 'Cart Track Glen Rosa' leads north. The tarmac gives way to an unsurfaced road, and after the foot-bridge this becomes a path.

THE ROMANCE AND REALITY OF ROB ROY MACGREGOR

As DESCRIBED in Sir Walter Scott's novel, Rob Roy was an outlaw hero in the same mould as England's Robin Hood. A legend has built up around the fiery MacGregor who lived in the turbulent days of the early 18th century, with stories of how he robbed the rich and gave to the poor.

Rob the rich he certainly did – in particular his former employer the Duke of Montrose from whom he stole cattle. The Duke's sworn enemy, the Duke of Argyll, gave Rob Roy refuge, and with such patronage it is little wonder that he was able to carry out his unlawful activities unchecked.

Among his sidelines, Rob Roy ran a protection racket that would have been the envy of Al Capone. His 'clients' were the Duke of Montrose's tenants, who paid 5 per cent of their annual rent as 'insurance' against their cattle being stolen.

The MacGregors, led by Rob Roy, terrorised the district around Loch Lomond. Near Inversnaid is Rob Roy's Cave which the gang used as a meeting place and hide-out.

Rob Roy MacGregor died in 1734 and is buried in the churchyard at Balquhidder with his wife and two sons, James and Robert the Younger.

BALQUHIDDER CHURCHYARD

Ad   Inverliever Forest

The 78 sq. miles of Inverliever Forest are the oldest state-owned forest in Argyll; planting was begun by the Office of Woods in 1908, before the Forestry Commission had been established. Some 36 sq. miles are tree-covered. In the forest there are many lochans, or small lochs, burns, glens, forest roads and tracks; there are Loch Avich and Loch Nant and 17 miles of the shore of Loch Awe; there is a crannog, a long-ago loch dwelling linked by a causeway to the shore; there is the River Avich, draining Loch Avich to Loch Awe and one of the shortest rivers in Scotland; and there is a ruined settlement called New York, a relic of the York Timber Company of London, which took over many forfeited estates after the Jacobite rising of 1715. There are also ten forest walks and trails, most of them in the plantations rising high on the western hills, or down by the loch shore. In places the trees have been cleared to provide breathtaking views along the meandering course of Loch Awe.

The most common trees are Norway and Sitka spruces, Scots, Lodgepole and Corsican pines, Japanese larches and Douglas firs; but there are also older woods of oak, birch and alder, patches of woodland flowers and the bog plants and heathers that covered the mossy hills before the foresters came. Lurking among the shadows of the woods there are red deer and roe deer, badgers and occasional wildcats.

Buzzards, kestrels, sparrowhawks and even golden eagles circle overhead, and in the forest jays, martins, crossbills and woodpeckers are common. Probably the strangest sight on the open moorland is the 'lek' – the spring courtship display of black grouse.

The minor road from Ford to Kilchrenan along the west side of Loch Awe gives access to all the Inverliever Forest walks. The forest office is in Dalavich, 1 mile south of the junction of the Kilchrenan and Kilmelford roads.

Be   Inveroran

For hundreds of years, one of the great problems facing road-builders in the Highlands was how to tackle the unrelenting country of the Black Mount and the western edge of Rannoch Moor. Two of the early routes converge at Inveroran, once an overnight stopping-place for drovers bringing cattle and sheep south to the Lowland markets. From Bridge of Orchy on the modern main road, the old military route of the 1750s – now a narrow track for walkers only – heads direct for Inveroran, over the pass of Mam Carraigh, with splendid views of mountains all around. Inveroran can also be reached by car, along a lower road by the southern shore of Loch Tulla.

Above the lochside, facing the Victorian shooting lodge of Black Mount across the water, the Inveroran road passes through the wood of Doire Darach. In Gaelic *darach* means 'oak', but curiously the wood is a protected remnant of the old Caledonian pine forest, fenced off against red deer. Inveroran itself is simply a whitewashed hotel, built about 1820 to replace the older inn that was visited by William Wordsworth and his sister Dorothy

during their Highland tour of 1803.

The main road to Glencoe came this way until the 1930s, when the present A82 was opened up to the east of Loch Tulla. Beyond Inveroran, a mile or so of the former road remains public, leading to the gate at Forest Lodge; beyond this it is a right of way for walkers only, through some superb mountain scenery. The ridges and corries of the Black Mount, all deer-stalking country, provide a striking background to the wooded areas around Loch Tulla. It is an exhilarating 9 mile hike north along the old road which eventually meets the A82, 5½ miles east of the Pass of Glencoe. There are wide-ranging views from Bà Bridge on the way – eastwards over the vast expanse of Rannoch Moor, and west to the huge scoop of Coireach a' Bà in the heart of the Black Mount.

To reach Inveroran and Forest Lodge, turn off the A82 at Bridge of Orchy on to the A8005.

Bd   Inversnaid

The lonely farm called Garrison of Inversnaid, which looks down on Loch Lomond, once belonged to Rob Roy; but his house there was destroyed in 1712, and the government built a garrison fort instead, to keep the MacGregors in check after the first Jacobite rising. Across a bridge beyond the church, above the ravine of the Snaid Burn, there is a splendid viewpoint looking out to the shapely peaks of the 'Arrochar Alps' – Narnain, Beinn Ime, Ben Vorlich and Ben Vane – across the narrows of Loch Lomond.

From the hilltop the road plunges towards the loch, to the Victorian hotel, the tiny harbour and the steamer pier. In Victorian times, parties of

FLOWERS OF THE LOCHSIDES

So localised is the Scottish dock – it is known to grow only on the gravelly eastern shore of Loch Lomond – that it is sometimes called Trossachs dock. Bog myrtle is a small shrub, widespread in wet places in Scotland, with a eucalyptus-like aromatic smell. The plant is said to repel fleas, and Highlanders once put it in their mattresses. It also has more pleasant associations – it was used for flavouring beer before hops were cultivated for the purpose. The bogbean was also used for adding a bitter taste to beer, and in the Middle Ages it was considered a cure for scurvy. Nowadays it has only one function – to grace lakes and ponds with its feathery flowers.

Scottish dock
(*Rumex aquaticus*)

Bog myrtle
(*Myrica gale*)

Bogbean
(*Menyanthes trifoliata*)

tourists used to come here in coaches-and-four, keeping the brake hard on down the steep and winding hill. Above the toy-like harbour a lovely waterfall pounds over a rock step to a dark pool below. A foot-bridge across the fall leads on to the West Highland Way to Rowardennan, seven hard but beautiful miles south beside the loch.

Inversnaid can be reached along the B829 from Aberfoyle, taking the left turn at the T-junction at the east end of Loch Arklet. Walkers can come from north or south along the West Highland Way. In summer Inversnaid is also one of the stopping-places of the steamer Maid of the Loch *from Balloch; and there is a regular ferry across the loch from Inveruglas.*

Cc   Loch Ard Forest

Since the 18th century, commercial woodlands have covered the lower slopes of this splendid sweep of country from the shores of Loch Lomond to the heart of the Trossachs. In the early days the trees were mostly oak, ash, alder and birch. One lucrative product was oak bark, refined to make tannin and used in the leather industry. The Duke of Montrose's estates had a firm forestry policy – thinning, felling and replanting on a 24 year cycle. In 1928, the Forestry Commission started buying land in this area; now commercial plantations of spruce, pine and larch have largely taken the place of the older woodlands. In 1953, at the time of the Coronation, the Queen Elizabeth Forest Park was created, with Loch Ard as part of it.

There are walks and trails on forest paths and roads, and some exhilarating longer routes lead westwards to Ben Lomond and Rowardennan. There are intimate corners of the forest: a foot-bridge makes the mighty leap from the Lowlands to the Highlands, for the burn it crosses marks the line of the Highland Boundary Fault. By the sparkling Duchray Water are the ruins of the township of Daldannet, deserted two centuries ago when the land was taken from the crofters to make way for large-scale sheep farming.

Wildlife is abundant in the forest. At Lochan Spling, near the forest's northern edge, there are goosanders, mergansers, moorhens, coots, swans and grebes; elsewhere roe deer and red deer may be seen, as well as stoats, foxes, weasels, otters and possibly a solitary hunting wildcat.

Sir Walter Scott often stayed in the old manse at the Kirkton of Aberfoyle, at the edge of the modern forest; and the Reverend Robert Kirk, minister here at the end of the 17th century, used to preach in the now-ruined church. He wrote a scholarly work – *The Secret Commonwealth of Elves, Fauns and Faeries* – and at the end of his life it was widely believed that the fairies had spirited him away.

One of the best approaches to Loch Ard Forest is by walking from Aberfoyle. Other access points are at Milton and Kinlochard, on the south side of the B829.

Ac Loch Coille-Bharr

Nowhere in the West Highlands displays so clearly the north-east to south-west lie of the land as North Knapdale in Argyll. There are long hill ridges, given over to forestry or to sheep-grazing, separated by deep, loch-filled troughs. Cutting deep into this landscape is Loch Sween, an inlet of the Sound of Jura; and in the heart of the Knapdale Forest, where the dead-end

roads down either side of Loch Sween diverge, is Loch Coille-Bharr.

Loch Coille-Bharr is a freshwater loch. Commercial spruce plantations grow all around it, though there are many trees of the old natural woodland – oaks, hazels, ashes, alders, rowans and willows. Forest roads and paths lead all round the loch. On the east side, one route crosses a carpet of bilberries, a favourite food of roe deer, which can often be seen here. There are also red deer and the introduced sika deer, together with foxes, badgers and, more rarely, wildcats. A burn drains a smaller lochan into Coille-Bharr, and this is a perfect place to see otters.

Running south-westwards from Loch Coille-Bharr is the Oib peninsula, which has been uninhabited for more than 100 years but is still criss-crossed with old stone walls and dotted with ruined farms, tiny townships and even a corn-mill. In a clearing by the lonely forest road on the west side of the loch are the few remaining walls of the old township of Kilmory Oib. This was the last of the peninsula settlements to be abandoned. All the others had been deserted in hard times around 1740 or some 90 years later, when the crofters had emigrated to North Carolina and to Canada. But, because it was the largest settlement, Kilmory Oib survived until after the middle of the last century. Then, in the 1840s, potato blight ruined the staple crop. Among the ruins there still remains the carved upright stone which marked the hamlet's holy well.

Further along the lightly forested ridge, dappled with sunlight and with buzzards soaring high overhead, there is suddenly a marvellous view over a secret bay, out of sight of any public

TROSSACH PEAK Ben An above Loch Katrine is one of the sharp little peaks that gave the Trossachs their name, which in Gaelic means 'the bristly country'. A 2 mile walk leads to the 1,520 ft summit.

road. This is a tidal arm of Loch Sween, whose wooded islets, known locally as the Fairy Isles, reflect in miniature the familiar alignment of Knapdale, dramatically demonstrated by the ridges on the skyline.

From Bellanoch take the B8025 towards Tayvallich. At the next junction bear left on the Achanamara road. The Loch Coille-Bharr walks start from a wooden chalet 100 yds along this road.

Cd Loch Katrine

The Trossachs is the name now used to describe most of the splendid landscape of mountains, lochs and forests west of Callander and north of Aberfoyle. But to Sir Walter Scott, whose poem *The Lady of the Lake* made the district famous, it meant the tangle of hills and woodlands, mostly oak and birch, around the pass between Loch Achray and Loch Katrine. Here Scott walked and rode, and other writers, including Dorothy Wordsworth, came here too. It was also the country of the outlaw Rob Roy, who was born at Glengyle, a farm on the far north-west corner of Loch Katrine.

The rustic Trossachs Pier is the most accessible point on the beautifully wooded lochside. This is the base for the turn-of-the-century steamer *Sir Walter Scott*, which makes summer cruises on the loch.

The road beyond Trossachs Pier, which follows the north side of the loch, is restricted to pedestrians and cyclists. Beyond Glengyle it curves round the head of the loch and turns back along the south side to Stronachlachar. Motorists can reach there by a much more roundabout route, which doubles back by Aberfoyle, Loch Ard and Loch Chon.

In spite of its remoteness, Stronachlachar is no quaint Highland clachan, but a flamboyant display of Victorian architecture set among wooded headlands, pines and rhododendrons. It was built by the Corporation of the City of Glasgow, when the loch was made the city's main reservoir. Royal Cottage, to the east of Stronachlachar, is where Queen Victoria stayed when she came to open the mighty water scheme in 1859. Ornamental milestones can still be seen along the Stronachlachar road, marking the royal route.

A fine summer excursion is to walk or cycle from Trossachs Pier along the private road by Glengyle to Stronachlachar, and then take the *Sir Walter Scott* for the return journey.

Trossachs Pier lies on the A821, 9 miles west from Callander or 4 miles north from Aberfoyle.

Be Rannoch Moor

A jigsaw of lochs, pools and meandering burns in some 60 sq. miles of soggy peat bog with knolls and hummocks of glacial debris, pine-tree roots from the original Caledonian Forest, and a surrounding ring of mountains. This is Rannoch Moor, the most famous and perhaps the wildest extent of moorland in the whole of Scotland. One of the last great Ice Age glaciers spread over Rannoch and its granite underlay, with ice flows running in all directions down the valleys and channels of pre-glacial times. The ice created the moor as it is today; the watery, jumbled wasteland draining through Loch Ba and Loch Laidon east into the River Gaur and Loch Rannoch, and eventually to the North Sea.

Roads touch only the fringes of the moor, and the railway that runs across

it was built by Victorian navvies with immense difficulty, laying piles of brushwood across the bog to support the causeway. The surrounding mountains seem to emphasise the isolation. From the road between Loch Ba and Lochan na h-Achlaise, the view westwards is to the deer-forest peaks of Clach Leathad and Stob Ghabhar, separated by one of the most striking corries in Britain, Coireach a' Bà. To the south lie the ridges of Beinn Achaladair, and to the north the bleak hills of Black Corries. And away to the east is the long vista of the heart of the moor, with the cone of Schiehallion on the horizon.

In wet and misty weather the moor is eerie, forbidding and dangerous, a

misery of peat bogs and treacherous spongy ground. On a fine day it presents quite another aspect – a desolate, lonely place, but beautifully wild, where the tangled waterways are thronged with ducks, divers, dunlin, plovers, greenshank and swans, the sky rings with the singing of skylarks and the damp places twinkle with bog cotton, asphodel and tiny orchids.

The A82 between Bridge of Orchy and Glencoe crosses the western fringe of Rannoch Moor: parking near Loch Ba and picking out a short route along its southern bays is a pleasant introduction to the moor. The B846 from Tummel Bridge to Rannoch Station along the northern shore of Loch Rannoch ends on the north-eastern edge of the moor.

A MOORLAND MARAUDER

Domestic poultry were reputed to be the main prey of the hen harrier – hence its name – but in fact the bird will pounce on anything from a lizard to a hare. The adult male is distinctive, with pale grey body, black-tipped wings and a white rump revealed in flight.

Hen harrier
(*Circus cyaneus*)

Bc Rowardennan

The road from Drymen, along the eastern shore of Loch Lomond, ends at Rowardennan. The village is no more than a whitewashed hotel beside a bay, two former shooting lodges, occasional cottages tucked discreetly away and a steamer pier. It is the mountains all around that make it so spectacular. To the north, woods of oak, birch, alder and hazel climb steeply up the flanks of Ben Lomond from the water's edge. Beyond them are the peaks around the head of the loch, with the cone of Ben Vorlich crowning the northern skyline. Opposite Rowardennan, across the narrows of the loch, the gash of Glen Douglas cuts deeply into the hills that rise from the western shore.

The land around Rowardennan was part of the Duke of Montrose's estates. The Forestry Commission eventually acquired it after 1945. Back from the rocky shore is the Forestry Commission car park, set in woodland, and the starting point for many magnificent walks. One of the most strenuous is the long haul up the track to the summit of Ben Lomond, 3,194 ft high. The walk takes at least half a day, and should be attempted only in good weather. Then, the view from the summit is superb, looking out over range upon range of mountains, with the fjord-like sea lochs in the west and the heights of Ben Nevis in the far north-west.

There are gentler walks through the lochside oakwoods. One footpath is said to have been used by Rob Roy's two sons, James and Robert, on a December evening in 1750 when they abducted a young woman widowed six weeks earlier and forcibly married her to Robert. The brothers were caught, but the girl died before the trial.

Drymen, from which the road to Row-ardennan is signposted, lies on the A811, 10 miles north-east of Dumbarton.

Bb Sannox

Until the early 19th century the moor-land around North Glen Sannox was one of the most heavily populated parts of Arran – around 500 people lived here, earning their living by farming and fishing. But they were evicted in 1832 to make way for sheep, and most of them emigrated to Canada, where they settled in New Brunswick. Today, in their home glen in Arran, only some scattered ruins remain.

It was not only sheep that replaced the people. Around North Glen San-nox the fields are enclosed by high fences, to keep out the red deer which roam the island's northern glens and corries. Towards the end of the 1970s it was estimated that some 4,000 red deer lived on the island, but there have since been heavy culls to reduce the

numbers to a more reasonable level.

Where the North Sannox Burn reaches the sea, conifer plantations stand back from the shore, above the steep north-eastern crags. A path through the forest leads to one of the geological showpieces of Arran – the Fallen Rocks, huge boulders which tumbled down the cliffs in an im-mense, primeval landslide. To reach the start of the path, turn east beyond Mid Sannox by the road signposted 'North Sannox Picnic Area'. Also along this forest walk, tall pylons mark one end of the famous Measured Mile – the stretch of water between Arran and Garroch Head at the south end of Bute – where generations of Clyde-built ships, including the *Queen Mary* and both *Queen Elizabeths*, have come for speed trials.

The most spectacular part of north-east Arran is Glen Sannox itself, which can be seen from the village, ringed by magnificent mountains. There are splendid summit peaks and ridges of weathered granite, and numerous rock climbs and scrambling routes. A road signposted 'Cart Track Glen Sannox' leads out of the village and up the glen, passing the ruins of an old mine that once produced barytes, a mineral used in paint manufacture. After a scramble, the track eventually reaches the Saddle, the coll between Goat Fell and Cir Mhór.

Mid Sannox is 6 miles north of Brodick on the A841.

RANNOCH MOOR This 60 sq. mile wilderness of peat and rock has so much water that – so it is said – you can swim across it in June or skate across in January. Mere walkers on the moor are rewarded by outstanding views of the surrounding mountains.

THE GRAMPIAN MOUNTAINS

The land of the ancient Caledonians, savage tribesmen whom the might of Rome ruthlessly crushed

Here is a land of mighty, wind-blown granite heights slashed through with deep, forest-lined glens, corries which are snow-filled in winter, dark scree-runs and towering cliffs above lonely lochs, and the ever-present sight and sound of tumbling mountain burns. The landscape has immense drama and grandeur, as if it were a stage set awaiting the arrival of gods and titans as players. Even the birds, animals and flowers are outside the commonplace – the golden eagles, the leaping salmon, the ospreys of Loch Garten, the reindeer of Glen More, and the rare and lovely alpine plants which grow on the topmost plateau of the Cairngorms.

The underlying structure of the land – the great valleys running diagonally from north-east to south-west, the extraordinary fracture in the rock known as the Highland Boundary Fault – was laid down millions of years ago. But the superb pattern on the surface was set by the immense glaciers of the last Ice Age, retreating yard by yard across the Central Highlands some 10,000 years ago. Sure signs of the passage of the Highland glaciers are the U-shaped valleys with tiny rivers running through them – the rivers alone could never have created such giant landscape features – and the hanging valleys stranded high in the mountain walls. The lush valleys of the Tay and the Garry are among many classic examples of landscapes created by melting glaciers.

For most of the 6,000 or so years since men first ventured into the Grampians, one feature above all has dominated the scenery. Up to 2,500 ft there once spread the millions of pine trees of the original Caledonian Forest. Only a few scattered remnants are there still – the ancient pine forests at Glen More and Rannoch for instance – but they are among the most beautiful parts of the Highlands, especially when they are threaded through by the sparkling rapids of some mountain-fed river. The destruction of the old forest was at the hands of man, either to flush out human enemies and hunted men; to create upland grazing for cattle and sheep; or to clear the wolves which once terrorised the scattered and superstitious population of these hills and valleys, as they huddled round their glowing peat fires.

It was among these wild hills that the Romans won their most northerly battle. Led by Agricola, they pushed north from their bases in south Scotland, and in AD 84 they routed a force of more than 30,000 Caledonians at Mons Graupius, a little north-west of Inverurie, possibly near the Roman camp at Durno. The tribesmen fled, melting into the hills, leaving 10,000 dead. However, Roman triumph was short-lived; the legions retreated south two years later, and were never to venture so far north again. It is said that the name Grampian derives from Graupius.

There are many tangible relics of history in the mountains, from mist-shrouded standing stones and Roman signal stations to the old military roads driven through the mountains after the Jacobite risings in the 18th century. In fact, modern Highland roads mostly follow the routes pioneered then by military engineers such as General Wade and General Caulfield, or in the 19th century by Thomas Telford.

L AND OF GRANITE The Grampians are the highest mountain chain in Britain, with the granite domes of the Cairngorms pushing up to more than 4,000 ft. Here, in the north-east corner of the range, winter snow lingers into summer and the vegetation is alpine.

Places to visit

Map ref. Ba **Ben Lawers**

The highest mountain in Scotland south of Ben Nevis is Ben Lawers, sweeping up to 3,984 ft on the north side of Loch Tay. Almost all the south side of the mountain, up to the summit ridge, belongs to the National Trust for Scotland. It is open to the public even during the deer-stalking season, when other parts of the hill can be hazardous for thoughtless wanderers.

A visitor centre has been built beside the public road over the Pass of Lochan na Lairige, which separates Ben Lawers from the Tarmachan range to the west. The view takes in the sweep of mountain country west and south.

At Ben Lawers the hillside is grassy, in contrast to the heather-covered slopes of less-fertile hills. At one time there was a forest on the middle slopes, but burning and overgrazing through the centuries left the hillside bare. Below the Trust property, conifers have been replanted. Above them, right to the summit, grows a profusion of alpine flowers. This is a National Nature Reserve, and its catalogue of plants includes alpine lady's mantle and alpine meadow rue, yellow mountain saxifrage and mountain fern.

At different levels and in different habitats – gorges, exposed grasslands,

springs, cliffs and bogs – Ben Lawers has a bewildering mixture of plants. There is a Ranger/Naturalist service which offers walks on certain days.

One memory of the days before the sheep lies in a fold of the hill, away from the strong prevailing winds. It is a lonely and long-since deserted shieling, where the crofters of Tayside used to bring their cattle for a taste of the sweet summer grass.

The south side of Ben Lawers is traversed by the A827, and 4 miles north-east of Killin a minor road leads from Edramucky to the Ben Lawers Visitor Centre.

Dc **Bennachie**

Far from the main part of the range, Bennachie is the last throw of the Cairngorms before they admit defeat at the edge of the lowlands of Garioch and Formartine.

Several tops are gathered together under the general name of Bennachie: Watch Craig and Hermit Seat, Oxen Craig, Craigshannoch and the most spectacular summit, Mither Tap. The lower slopes of Bennachie are clothed in pine, spruce and larch planted in 1951. And from four starting points on that forest fringe, pathways wind up to the summit ridge.

One of them starts near the carved Pictish Maiden Stone, an early Christian monument to the north-east, and goes up an ancient road known as the Maiden Causeway. Others start from Puttingstone in the north and the Donview Visitor Centre at the south. Each pathway is about 3 miles in length. They rise from the forested area to wander as heathery tracks over the main ridge, sometimes exposed to raking winds sweeping unhindered from

the icy wastes above the Arctic Circle.

The shortest track – about a mile – is also the steepest, and reaches Mither Tap from Esson's car park on the east side of the range. The name Esson commemorates the last survivor of a community of smallholders who wrested a bare living from the harsh slopes of Mither Tap. George Esson, who was a descendant of the original

settler, kept his croft here until 1939.

From Esson's car park, the steep heathery ridge with its scattered rocks gives no warning of the sudden and unexpected sight of Mither Tap, a rugged granite tor weathered into shattered cliff-faces and bare boulders. And ringing the summit are the tumbled walls of an Iron Age fort, to which the Maiden Causeway still gives the clearest access.

A view indicator on the 1,698 ft summit shows the peaks on the horizon. To the south-west, Lochnagar can be seen and – almost unbelievably – the Caithness hills, 80 miles to the north-west across the Moray Firth.

Bennachie is 7 miles west of Inverurie, which is on the A96. Maiden Stone and Puttingstone are reached by minor roads from the A96 and B9002. Esson's car park is on a minor road 2 miles south-west of Chapel of Garioch. The Donview Visitor Centre is 5 miles east of Keig on a minor road that follows the northern bank of the River Don.

Ba **Birks of Aberfeldy**

The depths and heights of this narrow and heavily wooded ravine, with its interconnecting falls, are startling.

There are steepish pathways on both sides of the Urlar Burn. Tackle them in the direction suggested by a nature trail laid out up the northern side of the ravine and down the other side.

The uphill path leads through beech, birch, hazel, oak and alder. On the hillside to the right you may catch a glimpse of roe deer. Red squirrels dart among the trees, which provide food and nesting sites for finches, pigeons, tits and warblers.

The falls themselves are little more than a muffled rumble until a point

GRAMPIAN WILD FLOWERS

At high altitudes, only a few plants survive the severe weather. Among them is the alpine gentian, one of Britain's rarest mountain plants. On the moorlands the Scottish lupin thrives, and so does the crowberry, its fruit providing an autumn feast for grouse and ptarmigan.

Alpine gentian
(Gentiana nivalis)

Scottish lupin
(Lupinus nootkatensis)

Crowberry
(Empetrum nigrum)

high up the ravine where the pathway turns to the other bank. The footbridge is directly above the upper falls; there the river pours over rock slabs, then hurtles over the dizzy drop into deep pools far below.

All the way down the other side of the ravine, the sound of crashing waters is ever present. It disguises until the last possible moment one of the surprises of the eastern wall of the Moness glen – a series of tributary burns with their own smaller falls, pouring down in lacy patterns, or over natural steps of rock, down to the hidden depths of the ravine.

Robert Burns came here in August 1787. He sat on a stone seat, still at the side of the downward path today, and afterwards composed the lilting verse of *The Birks o' Aberfeldy*. Captious critics, perhaps misled by the varied woodland cover here, have sometimes claimed that he made a mistake; there were no birks, or birches, at Aberfeldy. Did he mix it up with Abergeldie on Deeside? But a farmer-poet, son of the gardener on a wooded estate, would know his trees. And there are birks at Aberfeldy yet.

Aberfeldy is at the A826/A827 junction, 20 miles north of Crieff. The car park for the nature trail is by the river bridge on the A826, south of the town.

Aa Black Wood of Rannoch

In the Black Wood of Rannoch, 'black' means dark, for this is a pinewood rather than one of oak or birch. It is one of the original stretches of the great Caledonian Forest which once smothered most of the Highlands.

It sweeps up from the south shore of Loch Rannoch, a defiant survivor of centuries of exploitation. Once it was

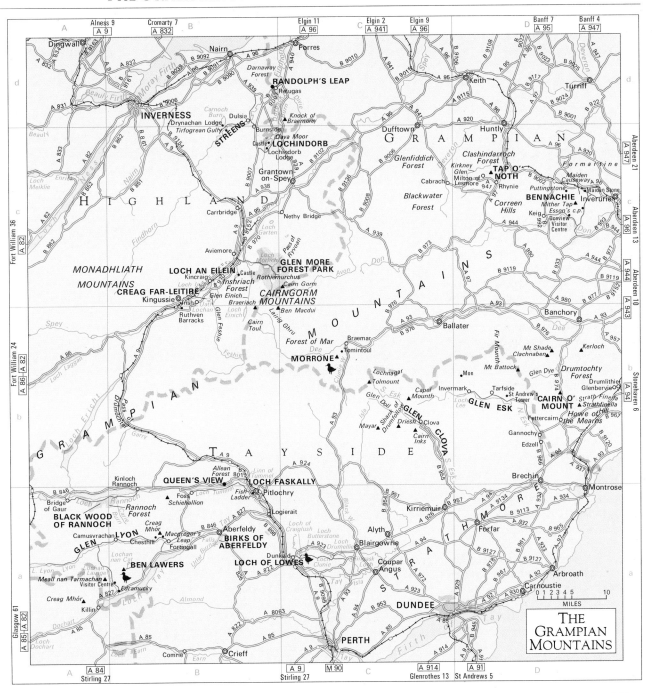

the home of hunted outlaws and desperadoes. Then, burning and cutting and overgrazing reduced it relentlessly in size.

The wood was used by many: there were illicit whisky stills far out of reach of the Revenue men; there were charcoal burners; and splinters of Rannoch pine had a vogue as torches. Deer browsed off the young shoots, and crofters put their cattle and sheep to graze here in summer, having burned off old growth in the spring to bring on fresh green grass.

Early last century the owners sold the trees of the Black Wood to a timber company. Canals and sluices were built in the higher reaches. Stacked behind dams, logs would be released to plunge down wooden ramps, up to a mile long, into the waters of the loch. Only the financial failure of the company stopped the entire Black Wood from being felled.

In the First World War, it again narrowly escaped being obliterated. And in the Second World War, the Canadian Forestry Corps felled the central and southern parts of the wood. When bought by the Forestry Commission in 1947, the old and almost exhausted woodland harboured a miserable stock.

The square-mile heart of the original Black Wood is now a forest reserve, fenced off and being rejuvenated. To the east of it, in the modern Rannoch Forest, a series of low and high-level walks head into the hills from the rocks and falls of the Carie Burn.

There are fine views of the Black Wood and over the loch. Old stands of pine and birch mingle with more recent spruce and larch, Scots and Lodgepole pine. In the heart of the forest, treecreepers and crossbills,

black grouse and owls, and birds as different in size as the tiny goldcrest and the blundering capercaillie find their food. Jays and woodpeckers, wrens and chaffinches throng the woodland edge.

Deer are not encouraged, but foxes prowl the area, red squirrels race up and down the pines, and in remote corners wildcats still have their dens.

The Black Wood of Rannoch is beside the minor road on the south side of Loch Rannoch, between Kinloch Rannoch and Bridge of Gaur. There is a Forestry Commission car park, with access to the forest, about 3¼ miles west of Kinloch Rannoch.

Db   Cairn o' Mount

One of the all-but-forgotten placenames of Scotland is The Mounth, denoting the great hill-mass running eastwards from the Pass of Drumochter to the plains of Strathmore. Ancient rights of way like the Fir Mounth and the Tolmounth preserve the name. But the most familiar to modern travellers is the Cairnamounth, which appears on today's maps as Cairn o' Mount.

This is the only one of the old routes which has become a modern through road, sweeping steeply up from Fettercairn to a summit at 1,488 ft, before continuing its hard-fought way north to Deeside.

At the summit, a rocky cairn is a splendid viewpoint over two entirely different landscapes: two entirely different Scotlands. To the north and west is the genuine Mounth, a land of empty hills and secret glens.

But in other directions there is much softer country. To the north-east lie the rounded heather moors of Kerloch. Eastwards, Drumtochty Forest sweeps down to Strath Finella, and beyond

spread the fields around Drumlithie and Glenbervie, the country of Lewis Grassic Gibbon's classic novel of Kincardine folk, *Sunset Song.* South-east of the summit is the grassy ridge of Strathfinella Hill, while to the south stretches the rich arable land of the Howe of the Mearns.

Despite names like Mount Battock and Mount Shade, the Mounth hills are mainly rounded. One sturdy exception, to the north-west, is Clachnaben – literally, 'the Stone on the Mountain' – whose summit is a sudden granite tor. It can be identified by the curious notch in the ridge, as it falls away to the east.

There are deer fences at the summit of Cairn o' Mount, but this is grouse moor rather than stalking ground. And like most grouse country, Cairn o' Mount can suffer from savage weather. Snow poles along the roadside, and fences above it to catch the drifting snow, show that this is a far harder landscape than the settled farmlands in the plains below.

Outside the grouse-shooting season, from August 12 to December 10, Clachnaben may be climbed from Glen Dye, the first main valley north of Cairn o' Mount.

Cairn o' Mount is 10 miles south of Banchory, and lies on the western side of the B974.

Bc   Creag Far-leitire

Pine and birch, heather moors and lochs, rocky crags and distant mountains are at the heart of many memorable Highland views. But they are rarely gathered together in so small a compass as at Creag Far-leitire (Craig Farletter), which lies in the heart of Inshriach Forest.

Creag Far-leitire is a little ridge pointing north-west and south-east, against the usual run of landforms in this area. The ridge rises from woods of pine and birch, and luxuriant purple carpets of heather. There are old Scots pine trees, well spaced out, as well as denser, younger woods. From the summit, all the plantations of Inshriach Forest lie spread out, and there is a long view north-east down the Spey Valley.

Just to the north is Loch Insh, marking the end of the marshy country down which the Spey meanders through embankments on its way over the flood plain from Kingussie to Kincraig. East and south-east the view is to the mountain wall on the far side of Glen Feshie, marking the start of the main Cairngorm range.

Glen Feshie is fine country for walkers and climbers, with farmland on the valley floor, forests rising on either side, and deer-stalking grounds in the wild and lonely corries above.

A far different landscape from this nestles at the south-east end of the Creag Far-leitire ridge. Set among open heather moors, ringed by pines and birches, lie Uath Lochan and the three smaller Rock Wood Ponds.

Crossbills, goldcrests and treecreepers nest in the deeper woodland. The heather moors attract grouse, curlews and meadow pipits. The woodland edges are the home of blackcocks, chaffinches and sparrowhawks. And the moorland with scattered trees is

ROAD THROUGH HISTORY Cairn o' Mount's summit is marked by the cairn from which its name is derived. The modern road linking Banchory with Fettercairn follows a 17th-century toll road and a medieval route used by the 11th-century king Macbeth.

One road, the Tolmounth, goes north-west over the hills to Braemar; the other, Capel Mounth, heads northwards, passing through Glen Muick, to Ballater.

There are low and high-level ways to explore the head of the glen. Walks along the drove roads give an idea of the wild hill country, which is not to be tackled lightly. Forest walks in Glen Doll, towered over by cliffs and scree-runs, amble through Scots pine and Japanese larch.

For botanists, the hillsides of Glen Clova and Glen Doll are most reward-ing research grounds. One of the first to realise this was a Forfar gardener, George Don, the author of *Herbarium Britannicum*, published in 1804. For 30 years at the turn of the 18th and 19th centuries Don combed the Clova area and other Scottish mountains, record-ing rarity after rarity, from hawkweeds and saxifrages to tiny mountain bog sedge and russet sedge.

In 1650 the glen was the scene of the so-called 'Start' – an abortive attempt by Charles II to escape from the Pres-byterians who were demanding too many concessions from him in return for their support. He arranged a ren-dezvous with Royalist chiefs at Glen Clova, but they failed to appear; in their stead there arrived a troop of Presbyterian horse who returned him to their headquarters at Perth.

The mountain tops above Glen Clova, despite their often spiky ap-pearance, lead on to a high grassy tableland well out of sight of travellers in the valley below – the country of red deer, wildcat and ptarmigan.

The southern end of Glen Clova lies 7 miles north of Kirriemuir. The B955 runs on both sides of the glen, following the River South Esk, as far as Clova.

GLEN OF ROYAL DESPAIR Having failed to rally the clans, in 1650 Charles II surrendered to the Presbyterians in Glen Clova.

where whinchats, redpolls and willow warblers live. Above the crags, kestrels and buzzards hunt.

To complete the amazing variety of landscape, a half-hidden alleyway through the woodland leads to a hide where wigeon, teal and goldeneye can be seen on Uath Lochan, with tufted duck on the reed-beds.

Creag Far-leitire is on the B970, 5 miles east of Kingussie. A road signposted to Glen Feshie leaves the B970 southwards at Farr, and just over 1 mile along this road is the entrance to the Forestry Commission's car park for Rock Wood Ponds.

Cb Glen Clova

With seemingly outlandish names like Mayar and Driesh, Cairn Inks and the Shank of Drumfollow, the mountains at the head of Glen Clova lose none of their remote wildness by being clothed with man-made forest on their lower slopes. As the glen marches into the heart of the mountains, so it narrows, steepens and becomes a far different place from the lushly wooded arable country in which it leaves the fertile plain of Strathmore.

Beyond Clova, the village of the glen, the hillsides begin to close in. Bare rocky crags and fallen boulders loom over the road, and individual peaks dominate the skyline ahead.

At its head, the glen splits into two much narrower valleys, each of them containing an old drove road – today these tracks are open only to walkers.

Db Glen Esk

Of all the valleys which slice into the south-eastern Grampians, the one with the grandest yet most unexpected entrance is Glen Esk. Let into a wall beside Gannochy Bridge on the road from Edzell to Fettercairn there is a wooden door. Open it, and from the neatly farmed and forested country around Edzell you are suddenly plunged into a landscape of cliffs, whirlpools, cascades and weird rock formations.

This is where the North Esk has gouged its way through the sandstone along the Highland Boundary Fault. For just over a mile a dramatic pathway above the east bank, planted with trees 200 years ago to relieve the harsh rock formations, keeps pace with the natural sculpture of the Loups of Esk and the Rocks of Solitude.

Eventually, this pathway joins the public road which matches the river's windings mile by mile until it ends at remote Loch Lee and the ruined 16th-century tower of Invermark. The centre of activity in the glen is a little hamlet called Tarfside, with a remarkable and detailed folk museum devoted entirely to Glen Esk, its people, its way of life and its history.

Here you will find there have been busier times in the glen Towards the end of the 16th century, Sir David Lindsay, the local laird, tried to bolster his failing fortunes with mining speculations. Gold and silver, lead, iron and copper were all discovered. But within 150 years, mining was only a memory.

There was a later, lucrative and more secret trade. In little settlements, now all but disappeared, whisky was produced in illicit stills. Glen Esk is still crossed by the route of an old whisky road, along which smugglers took the tax-free spirit to moisten many a Lowland throat.

North-west of Invermark stands an unexpected monument in the shape of an imperial crown, almost 20 ft high and made of local stone. It marks a spring where Queen Victoria paused during a pony expedition in 1861.

More sombre is St Andrew's Tower, 2½ miles south-east of Tarfside on a hidden stretch of the old Glen Esk road out of sight of the modern route. It was set up in 1826 as a shelter for travellers benighted by winter storms.

Gannochy Bridge is 1 mile north of Edzell on the B966. The doorway to the riverside path is on the north side of the bridge, and just beyond it a minor road leads north-westwards and follows the river to Invermark and Loch Lee.

Ba Glen Lyon

The longest glen in Scotland – more than 30 miles of it – is Glen Lyon. And yet from the village of Fortingall at its entrance it is invisible. Fortingall itself is a curious place. Many of its houses are thatched, to an English pattern. In the churchyard is a gnarled and twisted yew, thought to be little less than 1,500 years old and one of the oldest living trees in Britain.

A persistent legend claims that Fortingall was the birthplace of Pontius Pilate, when his father was a Roman emissary to one of the Pictish kings.

West of the village, Glen Lyon sneaks into the mountains by a narrow pass, curling through what looks like an impossible gap between the bulk of the Culdares Hills and the steep slopes of Creag Mhór. At one point in the rocky ravine is MacGregor's Leap, recalling an incident in the fierce days of the 16th century when the rebellious young Gregor MacGregor, an ancestor of Rob Roy, flung himself to safety on the far bank with his pursuers' bloodhounds baying at his heels.

Stories like this, and from a much earlier time, stalk you through Glen Lyon. There are ruined castles, standing stones and weird relics of the past, with Gaelic legends spun around them. It was the heart of the land of the Picts, and later a hunting ground of the Scottish kings.

Chesthill, in the lower part of the glen looking across at a fine waterfall, was the last property on his ancestral estates occupied by Robert Campbell of Glenlyon, the feckless and drunken 17th-century laird who led his clansmen at the massacre of Glencoe.

There are memories, too, of a gentler soul – St Adamnan, who had a chapel here. In 664, so the story goes, he stopped a plague by enticing it into a stone. The stone is still to be seen, although, like so many features of Glen Lyon's shadowy past, it lies little regarded by the roadside near Camusvrachan.

Fortingall is 8 miles west of Aberfeldy. It is reached by minor roads from the A827 or the B846. A minor road to the west of Fortingall leads north then west into Glen Lyon and follows the River Lyon to Loch Lyon at the end of the glen.

Bc Glen More Forest Park

Despite its name, much more than half of the Glen More Forest Park is treeless, for it is too high for trees to thrive. In the north-west corner of the Cairngorms, it starts in the woods around Loch Morlich, then sweeps up the mountain wall right to the 4,084 ft summit of Cairn Gorm itself.

These alpine northern slopes in the south-east of the park are Britain's finest skiing area. But around the loch and in the forests are dozens of pathways through Scots pine, Sitka spruce, Douglas fir, larch and alder.

Three walking routes waymarked by the Forestry Commission concentrate on the shoreline, the pinewoods and the rivers which, quiet enough in summer, show by the many boulders in them how wild the spates are as the snows above melt in spring.

There are enough miles of pathway at Glen More to let the observant visitor catch a glimpse of roe deer, red

BIRDS OF HIGH PLACES

Bleak mountain tops are home for the ptarmigan, which in the Grampians lives only above about 2,500 ft. The ptarmigan is the only British bird that changes colour with the seasons – white in winter, brown in summer. Another bird of the high regions is the snow bunting, which breeds in the Arctic and visits Britain between September and April. The male's almost entirely white wings are an unmistakable feature when the bird is in flight.

Snow bunting
(*Plectrophenax nivalis*)

Ptarmigan
(*Lagopus mutus*)

363

squirrels and perhaps even the elusive wildcat. Golden eagles soar effortlessly over their hunting grounds in the high corries. There are grouse on the moorlands, capercaillies, crossbills and woodpeckers in the forest.

Wildfowl hides have been set up around Loch Morlich, fringed by birch and willow, alder and rowan. The water itself, at 1,070 ft above the sea and fed by mountain burns, can be bitterly cold even on a summer's day.

Glen More is also the home of Britain's only herd of reindeer, introduced from Lapland in 1952, browsing on the lichen thousands of feet higher up.

For hill-walkers, Glen More is a paradise. They can follow the tracks on which old-time cattle thieves hustled their stolen herds through the Pass of Ryvoan to Nethy Bridge. Or hike to Glen Einich and its loch in a scooped-out glacial hollow. Or start off on expeditions through the classic mountain passes such as the Lairig Ghru, 25 hard miles through the Cairngorms to Braemar.

Loch Morlich, in the heart of Glen More Forest Park, is 5 miles east of Aviemore. The road into the forest starts from the B970, 2 miles east of Aviemore.

Bc   Loch an Eilein

In the heart of Rothiemurchus, a district once completely covered by the Caledonian pine forest, lies Loch an Eilein. Although most of the ancient

FINGAL'S GLEN The River Lyon follows a winding course through Glen Lyon, whose Gaelic name is *Cromghlearn nan clach* – 'the Crooked Glen of the Stones'. Here, Fingal, a hero of Celtic mythology, is said to have had 12 castles.

REMAINS OF A FOREST Loch Morlich in Glen More is a bleak stretch of water high in the Cairngorms. The Scots pines at the water's edge are a remnant of the ancient Caledonian Forest that once covered the area.

forest has long since been felled, natural woodland of tall Scots pines surrounds the loch, with the wall of the Cairngorm plateau soaring up beyond.

Milton Burn, which drains the loch, still has the remains of a stone dam across it. This was once used to control the level of the water as felled pine logs were floated downstream to saw-mills closer to the Spey. One aspect of the timber trade here was the 18th-century manufacture of water pipes from the straight trunks of the pines. Hundreds were sent to London, and the site of the old boring-mill can still be seen near by.

Many of the trees were cut down during the two World Wars, but now the Nature Conservancy Council is trying to preserve the beautiful pine and juniper woods round Loch an Eilein. The conifers provide food for a varied wildlife: both red squirrels and crossbills feed on the seeds.

In this natural woodland, roe deer, foxes and wildcats may be seen by early morning visitors. Goldcrests, the smallest of British birds, are often seen among the trees on the northern shore.

Herons fish on the margins of the loch, standing motionless for long minutes, observing the water and their selected prey before that final downward dart. Mallards, wigeons, tufted

ducks, goldeneyes, mergansers and whooper swans are here in their season. Ospreys sometimes swoop over the loch, snatching up fish with their vicious talons.

Until 1899 ospreys nested at Loch an Eilein, on the ruined 15th-century castle on the island which gives the loch its Gaelic name. But the nest was repeatedly plundered, and the birds were hunted out of the district. Those seen at Loch an Eilein nowadays come from nesting places elsewhere, and the ruin of the castle now provides a haunt for jackdaws.

Loch an Eilein is 2 miles south of Aviemore, and is reached by a minor road running south-east from the B970.

Bb   Loch Faskally

One of Scotland's newest lochs is Loch Faskally, formed in 1950 when a dam was built across the narrow gorge of the River Tummel at Pitlochry for a hydroelectric power station. The loch winds between wooded banks, each curving section hidden from the next, with pathways for most of its length.

Faskally Woods on the eastern shore are a blaze of varied colours in autumn, and throughout the year the woodland paths are full of interest. Lime, elm, ash and sycamore, beech and gean – wild cherry – Douglas fir and Silver fir, rhododendron, pine and birch have all been preserved by the Forestry Commission, some of them more than 200 years old. In the heart of the woods lies little Loch Dunmore, its surface dappled with water-lilies. The loch was created as part of a woodland garden more than a century ago.

On the west shore, beside the road from Logierait to Foss, there are birchwoods along the winding banks.

And at the northern end, where the River Garry joins the Tummel and their combined waters feed the loch, is a forest nature trail. Part of the trail crosses the Bonskeid estate, where there is a fine specimen of Douglas fir – the species introduced into Britain in 1828 by David Douglas of Perth.

Once called the Falls, this place has been known as the Linn of Tummel since construction of the hydroelectric complex. Dippers and wagtails are common, and there are roe deer and capercaillies in the higher woodlands.

Greylag geese both breed and winter on the loch, and Faskally is a noted place for salmon and trout. A special fish ladder, with 34 pools, allows salmon to fight upwards to their ancient spawning grounds past the dam which closes the southern end.

Pitlochry is 24 miles north-west of Perth. The A9 bypasses the town and crosses Loch Faskally.

Bc Lochindorb

To the farmers, villagers and towns-folk of the settled Moray lowlands 600 years ago, the very name of Lochindorb was a prelude to terror. For it was from an island fortress there that ruthless raiders swept down to plunder and destroy.

Lochindorb is the largest of a scattered collection of lochs and ponds left behind by the last retreating ice-sheet on what is now the undulating and heathery Dava Moor. The whole area is covered with moraine debris from the Ice Age; through it the Dorback Burn drains Lochindorb to the Divie, the Findhorn and, eventually, the Moray Firth.

Around the Dorback basin are pudding-shaped hills such as the Knock

LAIRS OF THE WOLF

OF ALL THE LEGENDARY VILLAINS in the Highlands, the most infamous is Alexander Stewart, Lord of Badenoch and Earl of Buchan, who in the 1380s assumed governorship of the North under his father, King Robert II; his misdeeds in that office ring clear in folk memory to this day. Operating from an island fortress in Lochindorb and a castle at Ruthven, he terrorised the Moray district, swiftly earning himself the title of 'Wolf of Badenoch'. To this day it is remembered how, on being chided by the Bishop of Moray for deserting his wife, he riposted by sacking Elgin, and leaving its churches, hospices and cathedral in flames.

The grim ruins of Lochindorb still stand as his monument, but Ruthven Castle on Speyside was replaced by a barracks in 1716. The Jacobite army disbanded here after Culloden in 1746.

RUTHVEN BARRACKS ON SPEYSIDE

of Braemoray, whose name betrays its silhouette, since *cnoc* is the Gaelic for 'rounded hill'. South and west is a range of rugged-looking ridges rising up from the empty grouse moors. But they are much lower than their appearance from a distance suggests.

This is a rolling landscape of heather, peat-stacks and boggy grassland. On the north side of the loch is an isolated sheep farm, and the only other buildings in view are at Lochindorb Lodge, half-hidden among pines on the eastern shore.

On an island in the middle of the loch stands the shell of the castle that was once the stronghold of Alexander Stewart, Earl of Buchan, who terrorised the district until his death in 1405.

Lochindorb is 7 miles north-west of Grantown-on-Spey. A minor road leads to it, branching west from the A939.

Ca Loch of Lowes

Between Dunkeld and Coupar Angus, there lies a string of little lochs unsuspected by casual passers-by. Even the names are unfamiliar: Butterstone and Clunie, Drumellie and Fingask. They stand mostly behind a screen of trees or just far enough away from the public roads not to be noticed.

But one of them, the Loch of Lowes, is a reserve of the Scottish Wildlife Trust. Lowes is an unobtrusive loch, for all its fascination to naturalists. Its southern shore is fringed by oak and beech, sycamore and alder, pine and birch. The reserve includes the whole of the loch, this screen of woodland, and the reed-beds in the western bay.

Outside the reserve area, but just to the north-west behind more woodlands, is the Loch of Craiglush. A small canal was dug between the two lochs early last century, in a miscalculated attempt to drain the marshy land for cultivation. But there is no fall of water, and so the marshland remains.

Bought by the Scottish Wildlife Trust in 1969, Lowes provided its first surprise very soon after that when ospreys nested near the west bay. An observation hide and visitors' centre were set up there, but perhaps the greatest attraction of the reserve is its opportunity for informal viewing. Lay-bys along the public road on the southern shore lead to several splendid viewing areas by the water's edge. One especially beautiful time is on a calm morning with early mist clearing slowly from the loch.

The reed-beds are favourite nesting places for grebes, coots and dabchicks. Tufted duck, mallard and teal are there all the year round, and great flocks of greylags roost in the winter.

The Grampian Mountains

Among the woods, siskins and redpolls feed on the birch and alder seeds in autumn and winter. Willow warblers, spotted flycatchers, wrens and treecreepers prey on the rich insect life of the woodland fringe.

Loch of Lowes is 1 mile north-east of Dunkeld, and is reached by a minor road branching east from the A923.

Cb Morrone

On Upper Deeside, the forest cover is mostly woods of old Scots pine. But at Morrone, the hill rising above Braemar in the angle between the River Dee and the Clunie Water, is one of the most fascinating birkwoods, or birchwoods, in Scotland.

The trees are not the tall, upstanding birches of lower ground. Close to the upper limit of tree growth in the Highlands, they are gnarled and twisted, scattered over the hillside so that they add to, rather than obscure, the view. Under their shelter is a carpet of juniper, which in its turn protects a great variety of tiny alpine plants.

Constant heavy grazing by deer and sheep reduced the birkwood in quality and extent until it was declared a National Nature Reserve in 1972. In 1978 the Nature Conservancy fenced off large areas to protect them from the depredations of red and roe deer. Once the natural processes of regeneration are well under way, the fences will be taken down.

There are still many tracks and pathways open. One of them winds easily up to a view indicator set in place by the Deeside Field Club. Although it is on the lower slopes of the hill, it identifies the dramatic view towards the main range of the Cairngorms. Three of Britain's loftiest peaks, which reach more than 4,000 ft, are visible from here: Ben Macdui, Braeriach and Cairn Toul. In the quadrant of the compass from west to north there are ten mountains of more than 3,000 ft to be seen.

Morrone itself is a 2,819 ft hill, and a stiff walk leads all the way to its summit. Clouds and mist can descend suddenly, so do not start the walk in doubtful weather. Avoid it also during the grouse-shooting season, from August 12 to December 10.

Eastwards from the view indicator the track passes behind one of the buildings of the farm of Tomintoul, some of whose fields at over 1,400 ft are reckoned to be the highest cultivated land in Britain. On the right, a pathway marked by cairns heads uphill over grass and heather moors to the summit of Morrone and its ever-widening panorama of the Cairngorms and the Forest of Mar.

Braemar is on the A93, 15 miles west of Ballater. Morrone is to the south-west of Braemar, and the path to the summit starts from a car park in Chapel Brae.

Bb Queen's View

In her travels around the Highlands, Queen Victoria stopped to admire many a splendid view. The most famous Queen's View is above Loch Tummel, on a knoll looking westwards to the cone of Schiehallion, 3,553 ft high but not at all a mountain in the rockclimber's sense of the word. Beyond it

CLEAR AND COOL The Clunie Water cuts a broad valley through the Grampians on its way to join the Dee near Braemar.

367

the view extends to the wild land of Rannoch.

The modern view is not the same as the one the Queen admired. She looked down on a Loch Tummel only half the size it is today. The valley was flooded in 1950 as part of a hydroelectric scheme, and the loch extended by some 4 miles, so the little wooded islands below the viewpoint are actually the tops of former hills.

Above the Queen's View, the bare hillside was planted with trees in 1948.

And that view is repeated, from higher levels, at several places on the Allean Forest walks. The walks curl upwards through plantations mainly of pine and spruce trees, but there are stands of larch, as well, brightening up the autumn forest.

One forest road cuts through a partly restored clachan, or hamlet, whose inhabitants used to eke out a bare living on this windy hillside long before the forest came. So remote and tiny was this place, with only three houses, that there is no definite record of its occupants or even of its name. It may have been Tombuie.

Whatever it was called, and whoever originally lived here, in one of the periods of occupation the thick-walled stone cottage now known as House I was used for carding fleeces and dyeing wool. An old corn-drying kiln alongside was converted to burn limestone for fertiliser. The clachan was probably lived in, and crops were grown in its tiny walled-off fields in the early 18th century.

This miniature but self-contained and self-sufficient community has been deserted for at least 150 years. At another site beside one of the forest roads stand the ruins of a far more ancient building – a ring-fort used for defence by even more remote Highlanders 1,000 years ago.

Queen's View is on the B8019, 6 miles west of Pitlochry. The car park for the Allean Forest walks is about 1 mile further west along the B8019.

Bd Randolph's Leap

The River Findhorn, intimate and reserved, keeps its finest reaches out of sight of casual passers-by.

One of its most dramatic stretches is at Randolph's Leap, a spectacular chasm where the brown peaty water swings round a bend to be confronted by a narrow rocky throat. It rages its way through in a series of falls and whirlpools, sweeps and swirls, meets the waters of the Divie coming down a tributary glen, and then races off on winding miles by Darnaway Forest towards the sea.

The name is a strange mistake. It was not the 14th-century Thomas Randolph, Earl of Moray and companion of Robert Bruce, who made the desperate leap across the rocky gorge, but a man whom Randolph's troops were pursuing after a battle.

The wooded surroundings of the Leap are superb. Footpaths lead high above the river, wandering through beech and larch, oak and elm, ash and silver birch towards the triangle of rocky land where the Findhorn and the Divie unite.

High above the modern river level are two flood stones. They commemorate the ferocious Moray floods of August 1829. Cloudbursts in the headwaters of the Findhorn turned it suddenly into a torrent. It rose so imperiously high that the whole headland at the junction of the Findhorn and the Divie was inundated. Marking the highest point lashed by the raging waters, the flood stones are almost 50 ft above the normal level.

Randolph's Leap and the wooded pathways above it are on the Relugas estate. In 1829 this was the property of Sir Thomas Dick Lauder, the historian of the Moray floods. He knew about the disaster at first hand, for the rampaging Findhorn and Divie were within yards of his own home.

Randolph's Leap is 7 miles south of Forres and is reached by the B9007, which leaves the A940, 6 miles south of Forres.

Bc The Streens

Gaelic place-names, even in mutilated Anglicised forms, unerringly pinpoint the essential character of a place. In the middle reaches of the River Findhorn are the Streens, which take their name from the Gaelic *srian*, meaning 'bridle'.

The implication is clear. As the Findhorn cuts through the high moor-

BY APPOINTMENT Queen Victoria was deeply impressed by Loch Tummel when she came here in 1866. The loch is larger now, but the view is still superb, with the snowy cone of Schiehallion a dramatic centre-piece.

land country from its headwaters in the remote Monadhliaths, it comes here into a stretch of steeply angled hillsides which hold it in check, like a bridle controlling a mettlesome horse.

But not always. A casual look at a tributary like the Carnoch Burn at the exit from the Streens, its steep and final descent to the main river littered with boulders hurled down in times of spate, gives ample evidence of the Findhorn's escapes from restraint.

In August 1829 there was torrential rain around its headwaters. Millions of gallons of extra river water poured from the Monadhliaths, and as the Findhorn careered towards the constricted throat of the Streens, the 'bridle' could no longer cope.

As the river rose higher and higher, it burst over the banks of the meanders that guide it through the Streens. Hundreds of acres of riverside farmland disappeared, and the cottages of the smallholders were destroyed by the uncontrollable floods. There has never been such flooding since, but the riverside farms are fewer now.

On both banks, the ground rises out of the Streens to grouse moors on the level above. Opposite the end of the public road, on the south bank, is Tirfogrean Gully, scene of one of the classic erosion developments of recent years. Sixty years ago, the gully did not exist. Since then it has been ripped relentlessly out of the soil, showing that the Streens are still a force to be reckoned with.

The Streens lie 11 miles north of Carrbridge via the A938 and B9007. Take the minor road west from Burnside on the B9007, and just beyond Dulsie turn south-west into the Streens. Follow the road to Drynachan Lodge where a footpath begins.

FEARSOME CHOICE Randolph's Leap, on the Findhorn, recalls a soldier's desperate escape bid in the 14th century.

Dc ## Tap o' Noth

High above the village of Rhynie, soaring up from farmlands and forest, stands the landmark hill of Tap o' Noth. A stunning viewpoint, reached by steep tracks through heather and grasslands, the 1,847 ft summit comes as a complete surprise, for it is not level or pointed – but hollow.

Around the top of the hill, like the remains of a pie-crust, are the rocky walls of a vitrified fort. This Iron Age defence work, perhaps 2,000 years old, is one of those still-mysterious fortifications once laced with internal timbers which, by accident or by cunning design, caught fire and fused the rocks together.

From the fort on the summit of Tap o' Noth there are magnificent views. To the west is the road from Rhynie over to Cabrach and Dufftown, notoriously one of the earliest in Scotland to be blocked by winter snows. Beyond it are the remote hills of the Blackwater and Glenfiddich deer forests. To the south-east, above a glimpse of Rhynie village deep in the valley, are the Correen Hills and range upon range stretching to The Mounth.

Even here, where winters are harsh, dogged Grampian farmers have cultivated miles of land sweeping up the valley sides. What does not support crops or grazing for animals is given over to timber.

On its northern side, Tap o' Noth falls down into Kirkney Glen. Here, in 1929, the Forestry Commission first bought land to create its massive Clashindarroch Forest.

Rhynie is at the junction of the A97 and A941, 8 miles south of Huntly. The most direct path to the summit of Tap o' Noth starts from near Milton of Lesmore, 2 miles west of Rhynie and just to the north of the A941.

THE GREAT GLEN

Memories of the Jacobite risings haunt Glen Mor, the huge
landslip that isolates northern Scotland

The far north and west of Scotland is, in effect, an island, cut off from the remainder of the country by the waters of Ness, Oich, Lochy and Linnhe, all four being linked from sea to sea by the Caledonian Canal. All are contained within Glen Mor, the Great Glen (or Glen Albyn to the poetically inclined), the most stupendous geological feature in Britain. It was formed, it seems, about 350 million years ago when, in some cataclysm, the land tore straight across, leaving the upper portion to slip more than 60 miles to the south-west. Our legacy from this upheaval is some of the wildest and loveliest landscapes in Europe.

A journey through the glen might begin at Port Appin, an unexpectedly peaceful corner of the craggy Argyll coast that looks over to Lismore island and the cloud-girt bastions of Mull. From there, close by the impossibly romantic Castle Stalker, the A828 runs up the south shore of Loch Linnhe to Ballachulish; this is the country that Stevenson introduced to the world in *Kidnapped*.

At the Ballachulish bridge, the road joins with the A82 and then continues on to Fort William, an oddly foreign, frontier name among the soft Gaelic. The original fort, about which the present town developed, was built in 1655, the first of the fortress chain built along the glen to contain the clans to the north. It was later reinforced by Fort Augustus at the western end of Loch Ness and by Fort George on the Moray Firth. But over bustling Fort William there looms the stolid bulk of Ben Nevis, indifferent equally to the rival claims of Royal Houses and to the new factories.

The road runs on north and east to Spean Bridge where the first skirmish of the '45 rising was fought, and much later warriors, the Commandos, trained during the Second World War; there is a fine monument to them there. The A82 then continues up the sides of Loch Lochy and Loch Oich to Fort Augustus at the foot of Loch Ness, from which General Wade's military road goes over the Corrieyairack Pass, no longer driveable, but providing some magnificent walking.

From Fort Augustus, all Loch Ness stretches before you, 24 miles long and more than 900 ft deep in places. Overshadowed by the high hills, its dark, slaty waters seem a suitable hideaway for giant molluscs, prehistoric reptiles, or whatever. The best chance of seeing one, it is said, is early on a sunny morning from ruined Urquhart Castle about halfway along the loch. Even if nothing appears, the view is breathtaking anyway.

The entire glen is full of old memories of the clans. Prince Charles Edward slept in the now-ruined Invergarry Castle by Loch Oich before and after the Battle of Culloden, and by Loch Oich, too, the ghoulish monument of the Well of the Seven Heads tells how the heads of seven executed criminals were washed at this spot before being presented to the Macdonnel chieftain. And everywhere there are the reminders of the Jacobite risings and their aftermath, most poignant, perhaps, being the lonely roads and bridges that General Wade and his successors built in order to police the truculent clans and bring Government control to the wild hills.

ISLAND CASTLE Long the stronghold of the Stewarts of Appin, Castle Stalker stands as if enchanted on a turf-capped islet in Loch Laich. There is little to enchant in its history, however – a saga of murder and treachery between the Stewarts and the Campbells.

Places to visit

Map ref. Cb **Achnacarry**

Lying as it does within the walled estates of Cameron of Lochiel, the tiny village of Achnacarry, between the shores of Loch Arkaig and Loch Lochy, must be one of the best-hidden places in the whole of Britain. The sign 'Private Road', however, does not deny access to the village, and visitors may pass through the open gates and along the estate road between a rich variety of magnificent old trees.

The village lies beneath a wooded rocky outcrop, and consists of a farm, a few estate cottages, the fine building of Achnacarry House and a small post office. This enchanting scene is completed by a small village green and the sight of Highland cattle grazing in the surrounding fields. Under the boughs of an oak tree an old cannon sits peacefully, and behind are the moss-covered ruins of a castle destroyed by the Duke of Cumberland in 1746.

A walk from the village leads through the estate and across a bridge over the River Arkaig. Turn right and you will pass a magnificent waterfall down which tumble the waters of the Chia-aig. The road continues along the 'dark mile', a straight, tree-lined avenue alongside the moss-covered estate wall. The wooden forestry houses at Clunes mark the start of the Loch Lochy section of the walk that follows the shoreline past superb old pine trees and into Bunarkaig. Just a little further round this sheltered bay is the entrance to the Achnacarry estate. The whole circuit is among the best 5 miles of easy walking anywhere.

The entrance to the Achnacarry estate is from the B8005 from Gairlochy, just before the first houses of Bunarkaig.

Bb **Ardgour**

At the foot of the steep mountains on the western shore of Loch Linnhe lies the small community of Ardgour. It can be reached only by ferry across the Corran Narrows, or by a long detour by road; thus Ardgour has kept its unspoiled character down the years.

A delightful and easy walk begins just after the old post office at the end of the village street. Almost at its start the path disappears into a tunnel of rhododendrons and leads past a magnificent row of old overhanging beech trees to two well-hidden small lochs. Here, the still waters, greenly reflecting the wooded mountainside, are disturbed only by the sudden flight of waterfowl or the swift movement of fish from beneath the surface.

The wooded glades – home of deer, badgers, squirrels, wildcats and rabbits – give way to the shore of the loch and the widening view south-west towards Mull and the open sea. A walk along the pebbly shore, accompanied only by the sounds of gulls and the piping call of the oystercatcher, can be rewarded by the sight of seals and their pups at play in a small bay that lies just behind Sallachan Point.

The walks around the inland lochs of Ardgour can be completed within an hour. But such is the beauty of the place, they may take very much longer.

The best way of getting to Ardgour is by the car ferry, 2 miles north of Onich on the Fort William road (A82). Or park just below the Netherlochaber Hotel by the landing-stage and travel across as a foot passenger.

Bb **Ben Nevis**

The massive bulk of Ben Nevis looms above the bustling town of Fort William. It is not a particularly handsome mountain and, as often as not, clouds obscure its 4,406 ft summit. This,

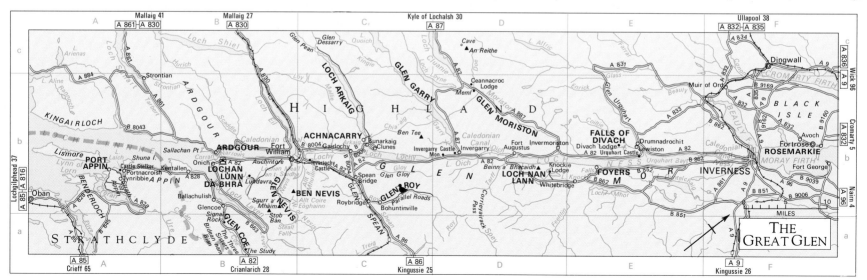

together with the absence of a crowning peak, sometimes leads to Ben Nevis being dismissed as a huge but uninteresting lump on the landscape. However, a cautious glance down the precipitous North-east Buttress, or Tower Ridge, will quickly convince any doubters that in fact it possesses an awesome grandeur all its own.

These North Face cliffs must be left to the most experienced rock climbers, but splendid views of the towering rock faces may be had by following either the Allt a' Mhuilinn footpath from a point a couple of miles along the Inverness road opposite the grounds of Inverlochy Castle, or from the branch of the path that skirts the marshy edge of Lochan Meall an t-Suidhe. But, for most people, the way to the top is by the well-trodden 'tourist' path.

Do not be put off by the fairly strenuous start. Higher up, the climb is easier, particularly after about 2,500 ft where heather and tufted hair grass give way to rocky scree among which alpine flowers, lichens and mosses grow. Those who get to the top will find their efforts amply rewarded.

From here, among the shattered lava and the multitude of cairns commemorating various people and events, you can see the superb Aonach Eagach ridge high above Glen Coe, while further off are the distant peaks of Ben Lomond, Ben Lawers and the three peaks of the Paps of Jura, 77 miles away. To the west are Rhum, Eigg and, in the distance, 92 miles off, South Uist, as well as the Cuillins on Skye. Below Ben Nevis, the mighty rift of the Great Glen can be seen, cutting its way through the mountains from Loch Linnhe towards Inverness. In very clear weather, it is even possible to see the Antrim mountains in Northern

LOCHSIDE LOCHS The quiet and secluded waters behind Ardgour are only yards away from the great stretch of Loch Linnhe.

Ireland, more than 120 miles south.

Fort William is on the A82: the summit path runs from the bridge opposite the Glen Nevis Youth Hostel, 2 miles along a minor road signposted from the north side of Fort William. There is a car park.

Eb   Falls of Divach

A rewarding walk through delightful countryside will take you to the Falls of Divach on a tributary of the River Coiltie. Start from the small village of Lewiston – a straight row of neat and brightly painted houses that is not far from Urquhart Castle and the shore of Loch Ness. A sign to the falls, which lie south of the village, points past a farm with slatted wooden deer larders. The hooks and chains that were once used to hang the day's bag can still be seen. This farm and the partly ruined, but still splendid, buildings around were once part of a great estate. The old mill, now almost hidden in trees, was actually a miniature gasworks supplying piped gas up to the now demolished hall.

The land climbs steeply to a point where fine views of Loch Ness and Urquhart Bay open out. This is splendid scenery, a perfect blend of wooded hillsides, green fields and the reflecting waters of the loch below. As the land levels out a little, the thunder of falling water can be heard. On the right-hand side of the road there is a small car park from which a path cuts through woods of birch and oak to the falls.

Less impressive than those at Foyers across the loch, the Falls of Divach are majestic enough nevertheless. The natural amphitheatre set in dark woods offers the photographer magnificent opportunities, especially from the viewing point. At the end of the lane, a lovely old house overlooks the falls. This is Divach Lodge, once owned by the actress Ellen Terry. It was here, in 1904, that J. M. Barrie sat in the garden and wrote *Peter Pan*.

Lewiston is 14 miles south-west of Inverness, on the A82, at the entrance to Glen Urquhart.

Eb   Foyers

The Falls of Foyers, on the eastern shore of Loch Ness, are one of the most famous sights in Scotland. The enormous force of water crashing through the thickly wooded gorge is best seen in full spate after heavy rain, when the peat-stained river foams and thunders through the tortuous passages of the ravine, flinging up clouds of misty spray that sparkle among the tree-tops.

The best places to see this splendid spectacle are from the vantage points along the well-protected path through the trees. This starts opposite the shop in Upper Foyers and leads down the ravine to where the river, its energy spent, flows into the broad waters of Loch Ness. It is advisable to return by the same path, since this avoids a much longer walk along the road.

Foyers is also of special interest to geologists for its long-severed connection with Strontian, away to the south-west. Both Foyers and Strontian have an identical and isolated granite composition, proving that they were once part of the same mass. These geological clues clearly show the tremendous distance the Northern and Western Highlands have slipped along the Great Glen fault; Foyers and Strontian, for example, now lie 55 miles apart.

Foyers is on the B852, off the old military road from Fort Augustus to Inverness (B862) on the east side of Loch Ness.

Ba   Glen Coe

Had the infamous massacre of 1692 been a play, and its stage-manager some Victorian master of the Gothic setting, then he could not have chosen better than the towering and sombre wilderness of Glen Coe. The dark peaks and the high, bleak corries seem still to brood upon that February night when Campbell militia, on secret government orders, slaughtered some 40 MacDonalds of Glen Coe, leaving many others to die of exposure in the frozen hills. What made the crime particularly abominable in Highland eyes was that it was 'murder under trust' – the soldiers were guests of the MacDonalds at the time. That, and the connivance of the king, William III, who had determined to make an example of the clan for its tardiness in swearing allegiance to him.

Nothing tangible remains of that terrible night except a monument to the MacDonald chief and his people – the stones of their houses are long scattered – and Signal Rock, now deep in woods, from which tradition says a beacon signal was given for the slaughter to begin. This is now considered doubtful, since the essence of the deed was secrecy and surprise, and in any case the killing began simultaneously down the whole length of the glen, in some places out of sight of Signal Rock. But if anywhere in Scotland is haunted, it is Glen Coe.

Today, Glen Coe offers some of the finest rock climbs in Britain, and much of it is cared for by the National Trust for Scotland. Perhaps the best view of its savage splendour, and of the wild, bare peaks such as Bidean nam Bian and The Three Sisters of Glencoe, is from the rock platform called The Study, that stands above the road in the heart of the glen.

The A82 from Crianlarich runs the length of Glen Coe. It can also be reached by the A82 from Fort William.

Cb   Glen Garry

Not every visitor to the Highlands wants to climb the craggy peaks, so the well-laid-out trails in Glen Garry Forest are ideal for people who prefer a pleasant stroll to a scramble. The forest consists mainly of conifers that thrive even in the poor, peaty remnants of a soil largely destroyed by overgrazing and burning during past centuries. Specimen trees are labelled, and there is an observation point from which the conical peak of Ben Tee can be seen to the south through the trees. The nature trail features the great cascading falls, whose waters thunder majestically down a gorge. Well-protected viewing points allow a close look.

The entrance to the nature trail lies 2 miles west of Invergarry, along the A87.

THE THREE SISTERS The triple peaks on the south side of Glen Coe, one of Scotland's most impressive glens, were silent witnesses to the infamous massacre 300 years ago, when Scot slaughtered Scot in the valley below.

SUNSET TOUCH The raw beauty of the Great Glen is softened and mellowed as the setting sun brushes the peaks around Loch Oich with tints of gold. The loch is narrow here, squeezed to a mere quarter-mile width, and is joined by the river that winds through wooded Glen Garry.

Db   Glen Moriston

The Highlands are liberally sprinkled with caves traditionally held to have sheltered the Young Pretender after his flight from Culloden in 1746. But the one high in the far hills above Glen Moriston has a better pedigree than many. So if you have an appetite for walking, and a day to spare, you can follow the steps of the prince to the cave about a mile west of An Reithe's summit where, between August 24 and 28, 1746, he lay 'as comfortably lodged as if he had been in a royal palace'. Those less keen on mountain hiking will still find plenty to interest them on the lower stages of the trail.

It starts a short way past the Mackenzie Memorial cairn by a sign to Ceannacroc Lodge, where the River Doe meets the waters of the Moriston river, and leads north-west beside the Doe. The 'Private' sign notwithstanding, visitors are permitted free access. At first the road, too rough for motor vehicles, winds up through mixed woods containing some magnificent old pines. Cartridge cases in the undergrowth show that this is deerstalking country; from August to the end of February, find out before you set out whether it is safe to walk in the hills.

The road deteriorates into a track and continues across open and increasingly bleak countryside with a backdrop of distant mountains. After about 4 miles, the track peters out by a wooden bridge, and at the head of the valley, among rocks fallen from the ridge above, is the cave to which the prince came so long ago.

When you reach the head of the valley, you will have climbed to about 2,000 ft, and any urge to climb up to another cave that can be seen among

THE ALLT COIRE EÒGHAINN BELOW BEN NEVIS

the crags above should be resisted. The rocks are loose, slippery and dangerous, and help is a long way off.

The Mackenzie cairn and the road to Ceannacroc Lodge are roughly 14 miles along the 'Road to the Isles' – the A887 road leading through Glen Moriston from Invermoriston.

Bb   Glen Nevis

The glen cuts deep into the mountains along the steep western slopes of Ben Nevis, and in the variety of its scenery – a swift-flowing river, steep, tree-lined gullies and great rocky crags high above the valley – is the Highlands in

GLEN NEVIS The evening light turns the Water of Nevis iron-grey below the northern slopes of Stob Bàn (above). The river is fed by streams such as the Allt Coire Eòghainn (left), which flows down from Ben Nevis.

THE WATER OF NEVIS

microcosm. To complete the picture, the head of the glen is dominated by the graceful quartzite peaks of Sgurr a' Mhàim and Stob Bàn, both rising to more than 3,000 ft.

At the eastern end of the glen there is a spectacular waterslide, Allt Coire Eòghainn, a 1,250 ft gully of white water running down from below the summit of Ben Nevis. Just beyond the waterslide there is a car park from which a path runs through the splendid Nevis gorge to the Steall falls. This path divides once or twice at the beginning of the walk; keep to the upper branches for the best views.

High above the gorge, the track winds through pine, birch, oak and rowan. Below, the water crashes thunderously on boulders sculpted through the ages into wild forms. Suddenly, as you continue, the scene changes to a quiet meadow, at the end of which the white, feathery plumes of the Steall falls tumble from a valley high above.

For a flavour of adventure, climb at least some way up the tracks by the waterslide. These are perfectly safe, and a recognised route for experienced walkers to climb Ben Nevis. Even a few hundred feet above the road will give you that special feel of big mountains.

Glen Nevis is signposted from the north side of Fort William; the distance to the end of the glen is 6¼ miles.

Cb   Glen Roy

Most National Nature Reserves are devoted to wild plants and animals, but at Glen Roy it is the 'parallel roads' which have made this glen an area of 'exceptional geological interest'.

The 'parallel roads' are the three distinct horizontal stripes that can be seen clearly contouring the higher slopes on both sides of the glen. They show up as bright green against the darker shades of heather.

They are not highways, but the tidemarks left behind by ice-blocked lakes that once filled the glen. About 10,000 years ago, the last glaciers to cover the Highlands advanced up the Great Glen, and in doing so sealed off several side glens, including Glen Roy and the neighbouring glens of Gloy and Spean. With no means of drainage, the glens filled up and became huge lakes. The Glen Roy lake during its largest phase was 650 ft deep and 10 miles long.

The upper 'road' marks the shoreline of the lake when it was at its deepest. As the climate changed and the ice retreated, the lake dropped to successive new levels to where fresh outlets could balance the inflow of feed waters. The middle and lower 'roads' mark these newer and reduced shorelines.

The best place from which to see this remarkable phenomenon is a viewing point about 3 miles along the glen, passing the small crofting village of Bohuntinville on the way.

Roybridge, the entrance to the glen, is roughly 3 miles to the east of Spean Bridge along the A86.

Cb   Loch Arkaig

The 13 mile drive along the shores of Loch Arkaig ends among some of the wildest and most remote mountains in the Western Highlands. From the head of the loch, people wishing to get to Loch Morar or Loch Nevis have to do so on foot through the long, lonely passes of Glen Pean or Glen Dessarry. Perhaps because there is no through road, Loch Arkaig has remained one of the most beautiful stretches of water in Scotland; not only beautiful, but also huge and almost deserted.

Only the far-off hum of a small outboard engine, or the occasional sound of a car, discloses the presence of fishermen. This is water renowned for its fish – salmon, trout, pike and char. But of greater fame still is the Arkaig Treasure – gold landed here by the French in 1746 to bolster the already-defeated Jacobites. It is believed that some of the gold at least may still be buried somewhere along the lochside.

At the east end of the loch there are two small islands. One is the ancient burial-place of the Lochiels, the other is noted as having once been the nesting-place of ospreys. At this end of the loch – and indeed for most of its length – the surrounding hillsides are covered in mixed woodland reaching down to the water's edge. Across the loch are the gaunt remains of the original pine forest destroyed by a wartime blaze. But even this sad sight of desolation does not mar the overall scene. Numerous little sheltered bays provide delightful picnic places with very little chance of being disturbed. Further down the loch the scenery changes quite dramatically to that of bleaker, bare slopes and a grassy shore where blobs of white cotton-grass dance in the lightest of mountain breezes.

Loch Arkaig can be reached by following the B8005 north out of Gairlochy.

Bb   Lochan Lùnn Dà-Bhrà

This lonely little loch (whose name is pronounced 'Lundavra') lies hidden among the mountain fastnesses south of Fort William. It can be reached by car along an old military road whose lack of width almost seems planned to make the traveller slow down and admire the views.

There is an ancient stillness about the loch itself, with its two small islands, scattered clumps of pine and bare green hills sloping down to the water's edge. Only in spring is the scene transformed by a profusion of wild flowers.

The island off the north shore, which can be reached only by boat, has an oddly regular appearance and is strongly suspected to be a crannog, a man-made island stronghold that could have been constructed at any time between the Bronze and Middle Ages against enemies long forgotten. There

HIDDEN TREASURE Buried somewhere along the shores of lonely Loch Arkaig is a golden fortune, landed there – too late – to save the Young Pretender's cause.

are stories of an underground passage and soldiers' graves, but the place still awaits investigation. The southern island, however, is natural and quite charming; it can be visited by way of stepping-stones from the shore.

Lùnn Dà-Bhrà is utterly peaceful, its sounds a gentle orchestration of wind in the reeds, birdsong and the distant bleating of sheep. Permission to walk round the loch may be obtained from the farmhouse, Lundavra, which also issues fly-fishing permits, should you wish to try for some of the specially stocked brown and Loch Linnhe trout.

To reach the loch, take the Lundavra road signposted Upper Auchintore at the southern end of the A82 in Fort William; keep on until the road comes to an end – a distance of about 5¼ miles.

Db   Loch nan Lann

The scenery on the eastern side of Loch Ness differs considerably from the better-known views along the main Inverness to Fort William road along the western shore. After climbing steeply out of Fort Augustus, the old military road levels out and runs across a high plateau above the eastern side. The open heather-clad moor, from which a grouse may suddenly and noisily rise, is broken by a number of small lochans, each having its own particular charm.

One such is Loch nan Lann which lies off the beaten track at the foot of Beinn a' Bhacaidh. It can be found by following the signposted minor road to Knockie Lodge, which leaves the B862 about 6 miles north-east of Fort Augustus. Motorists should park along the edge of Loch Knockie, which appears on the right after a mile or so. The path to Loch nan Lann starts another quarter of a mile further on by the side of the lovely old white-painted shooting lodge – now a hotel.

The wooded path round the lochside provides an easy and pleasant walk, with only an occasional sudden splash or movement amongst the reeds to disturb the peaceful water.

More energetic walkers will enjoy crossing the stepping-stones at the end of the loch. From there the path can be followed down the deep gorge to the remote and isolated boat-house 600 ft below on the shore of Loch Ness.

Take the B862 from Fort Augustus towards Whitebridge. After 6 miles, a signposted minor road turns off west to Knockie Lodge and the loch.

Ab   Port Appin

Appin is the name generally given to the wild country that lies between Loch Creran and the meeting of lochs Leven and Linnhe. For centuries, this land was feuded over by the great clans, most bitterly by the Stewarts and the Campbells, the ramifications of whose quarrels would make three-dimensional chess seem simple by comparison. Their broadswords and targes have been long gathering dust on museum walls, but if you would catch the last faint echoes of battles long ago

NORTHERN VARIANTS

In June the northern eggar moth may be seen darting above the heather on northern moors – a darker relative of the southern oak eggar. The females scatter their eggs as they fly, but the caterpillars have no problem finding food plants such as heather and bramble. Cloudberry – a thornless relative of the bramble – is often abundant on damp heather moors in the north, although really an arctic plant. It flowers in June and July and its berries ripen to orange.

Northern eggar moth
(Lasiocampa callunae)
on cloudberry
(Rubus chamaemorus)

mingled with some magnificent scenery, then you could not do better than to make Port Appin your centre.

The little whitewashed village looks over to Mull, with the MacLean castle on Duart Point, and to Lismore with its ruined strongholds and its parish church that was once a cathedral, burned down during the Reformation. A little to the north is Portnacroish, facing the startlingly picturesque Castle Stalker (correctly *Stalcair*, 'Hunter's Castle'). Built on an offshore isle about 1300, it has reflected the Appin fortunes ever since. In 1450 it was James IV's hunting lodge, and 18 years later its castellan, Sir Dugald Stewart, fought a bloody mêlée for its possession in which Stewarts, MacLarens, Mac-

FEATHERED MONARCHS OF THE GLEN

As Scottish as whisky and haggis, the capercaillie was almost exterminated in Scotland during the 18th century due to the clearance of pine forests in which it lived. The species was reintroduced from Sweden in 1837 and now thrives again in the Central Highlands. Like its close 'look-alike' the black grouse, the male capercaillie has a flamboyant and aggressive courtship display during which the tail is fanned and the bird faces other males with a threatening posture. The rare osprey left Scotland for 50 years, but a few began breeding there again in 1959. One of the most spectacular hunters among birds of prey, it dives from a height of some 100 ft to snatch a fish in its talons, and can carry fish weighing up to 4½ lb back to its pine-top nest.

Capercaillie
(Tetrao urogallus)

Black grouse
(Lyrurus tetrix)

Osprey
(Pandion haliaetus)

Dougalls and MacFarlanes were involved. A stone in Portnacroish churchyard marks the spot.

Possession of the castle alternated between Stewarts and Campbells for centuries, the exchanges effected through battle, treachery, shifts in the political scene and once through a fit of drunken generosity when a Stewart swapped it with a Campbell for a rowing-boat. The Campbells held the castle for the Government in the '45 rising, and it did not become Stewart property again until 1908. It is now owned by Major Stewart Allward and is open to the public on certain days in summer by prior arrangement.

The hatred that existed between Campbells and Stewarts ensured that, whatever other issues were at stake, there was no possibility that they could serve on the same side in the Jacobite risings. Enmity was fanned in the aftermath of the '45 when 'Red Fox' Colin Campbell of Glenure was appointed Government agent for the sequestered lands of the Jacobite Stewarts of Appin. Someone – perhaps an evicted Stewart tenant – shot him from behind a tree on the road between Ballachulish and Kentallen. The name of the assassin remains a mystery to this day, but a rigged Campbell court convicted a Stewart smallholder named James of the Glens and hanged him at Ballachulish. Robert Louis Stevenson tells part of the story in *Kidnapped*, but perhaps the tale becomes even more haunting if you stand on the hillock behind the old ferry stage and look across the great expanse of Loch Linnhe to the mountains. This was the last sight that James saw before they hanged him.

Port Appin is reached by turning south-west from the A828 Oban–Fort William

WILD COUNTRY South-west of Port Appin, a rocky spur looks out to Loch Linnhe and the distant mountains of Kingairloch.

road at Tynribbie, a hamlet in the Strath of Appin.

Fb ### Rosemarkie

The green rolling hills of the Black Isle peninsula contrast strongly with the rugged Highland scenery a few miles inland. Here, the thick glacial deposits that came to rest on the Old Red Sandstone have produced a rich farming country that rises steeply out of the wide, clear waters of the Moray Firth.

This contrast between the wooded inland glens and the peninsula goes beyond mere scenic differences. This is an area of huge horizons, clear blue skies and one of the lowest rainfalls in the United Kingdom.

A few miles along the coast past Avoch and Fortrose is the pleasant village of Rosemarkie, where fishermen cast their drag-nets from the sandy beaches to catch the salmon.

A walk along the headland, populated mainly by rabbits that bob in and out of the undergrowth, is a delight, particularly in spring when gorse flares

yellow on the hills and the Nairn coast lies in blue-green serenity across the Moray Firth. A path where all this can be experienced leaves the narrow minor road along the headland about 4 miles out of Rosemarkie towards Cromarty. After skirting the side of a wood, it descends steeply through a bracken-covered hillside down to a remote fishing station on a deserted sandy shore. Here, your only likely companions will be sea-birds.

Rosemarkie lies on the A832, between Muir of Ord and Cromarty.

THE NORTH-WEST HIGHLANDS

A grand and savage landscape whose moods change
rapidly, according to the weather's whim

To a large extent it is the prodigious quantity of water that accounts for the North-west Highlands' special magic. Not just the waters of the great lochs or the famous and mighty falls, but those of the myriad springs and spouts that jet from every crevice in the rocks. Stop for a moment among the mountains and the first thing heard is water distant or water near – a far-off whisper or a wild roaring torrent leaping by the path. High, high above are the torrent's beginnings, stilled by distance into a white ribbon against the dark mountainside.

Water here creates mood, while the weather plays tricks with the light and the imagination: a wild snarling storm on one side of a mountain, and a bright golden quietness on the other. In moments the landscape can change from something old, bitter and savage to an innocent, sparkling world. And the contrasts are not all just imaginary. On the tattered, sea loch riven west coast for instance, compare the near luxuriance of Ardnamurchan with the desert of Inverpolly; or the little seal-haunted coves of Loch nan Uamh with dark Loch Torridon; or the gentle roundness of the Five Sisters of Kintail with the jagged sandstone fangs of the north, Stac Polly, Quinag and Suilven.

Though there are all kinds of exceptions – Caithness, the Black Isle, the country round the Dornoch Firth, for example – Scotland, north of

the Great Glen, is a wild and lonely place. It is best explored on foot, though a drive round the Highlands can be particularly rewarding. The National Trust for Scotland and the Forestry Commission have between them mapped out walks to suit all degrees of energy.

Much Highland history is still visible on the land's surface, with relics separated by thousands of years in time standing close by each other, built of the same stone and, at first glance, equally ageless. The relics are not plentiful, for this is a land where population has always been limited by lack of resources; but they are there, and between them they tell the Highland story. Ancient brochs, built to withstand an enemy long forgotten; Celtic crosses covering the dust of missionary saints; a castle on an islet that was the stronghold of a warlord. Not often visible, but very much a part of the landscape, are the water-horses and monsters, the mermaids and Little People, the mythical or part-mythical heroes whose existence tells of a society to which poetry was an integral part of life. Then there are the ruins and emptiness that tell of the Highlands' 400-year-long involvement with the House of Stuart, the remains of roads and barracks that were built to enforce the will of government upon the clans. Sad, roofless crofts in the glens and green patches on the hillsides mark the progress of the 19th-century Clearances, when thousands of people were driven from their homes, often with the acquiescence of their chiefs, to make way for sheep runs and deer forests. Finally, brooding romantically over the desolation, there are the castellated and turreted fantasies built when the extraordinary wave of sentiment for all things Scottish swept over the Victorians at just about the time the glens were being emptied, and their people setting forth for the New World.

NOON DREAM Clouds sleep over Glen Torridon and the mighty 4 mile long summit ridge of Liathach. By the head of Upper Loch Torridon – perhaps the loveliest of all north-western sea lochs – is Torridon village, famed among deer-stalkers and walkers alike.

Places to visit

Map ref. Aa Ardnamurchan

Like Cornwall and Caithness, Ardnamurchan has an air of separateness, often expressed by the inhabitants of all three in a note of faint surprise that anyone should ever bother to go anywhere else. All, of course, are peninsulas, Ardnamurchan being the westernmost in mainland Britain. From Point of Ardnamurchan beside the lighthouse, you can see Coll, Tiree, Rhum, Muck and Eigg, and on a clear day, far out, Barra and South Uist. Beyond there is nothing but America.

Ardnamurchan is threaded by the B8007 which runs off the A861 at Salen, and is fairly bumpy and swooping even by Western Highland singletrack standards. For a time it follows the shores of Loch Sunart, dressed at first in Forestry Commission larch and spruce, but these shortly give way to banks of azaleas, fuchsias and rhododendrons.

At this point the road switchbacks inland to skirt Ben Hiant – the Holy Mountain – an extinct volcano whose jagged ramparts are quite unlike the rounded tops of the other hills near by. Splendid views may be had from its upper slopes, but they should be shunned after August 15, when deer stalking begins.

The road returns to Loch Sunart again at Kilchoan, near which is the ruined Mingary Castle, a 13th-century stronghold that at various times was besieged or sacked by Campbells, MacDonalds and even the Spanish from the galleon that now lies with its treasure in Tobermory Bay. Hereabouts, and in other parts of the peninsula too, are a number of old black houses, either roofless or converted into animal pens. These are evidence of the Clearances which hit Ardnamurchan hard in the middle of the last century. One of those responsible was a tenant farmer named MacColl who lies in Kilchoan churchyard. He was cursed to eternal damnation by an old woman he had evicted, who also swore that grass would never grow on his grave; and, indeed, it does not.

Take the A830 from Fort William to Lochailort. Turn south on to the A861 and follow it to Salen, then take the B8007 to Glenborrodale and on into Ardnamurchan.

Bc Bealach na Bà

At the Loch Kishorn end of the Bealach na Bà – 'the Pass of the Cattle' – there is a large notice that reads: 'Applecross Scenic Route. This road rises to a height of 2,053 ft with gradients of 1 in 5 and hairpin bends. Not advised for learner drivers, very large vehicles or caravans after the first mile.' Which just about sums it up, though it is not nearly so formidable as it used to be. Only a few years ago, some of the gradients were 1 in 4 and barriers practically non-existent, making it possible to look out of the car down a drop of several hundred feet.

All the same, it is still one of the highest mountain roads in Britain, and

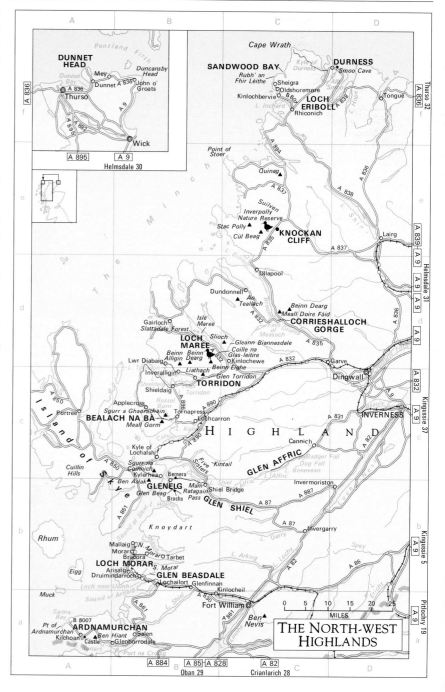

THE NORTH-WEST HIGHLANDS

perhaps the nearest thing to an Alpine pass that we have, especially in winter when it can become choked by snow. Until the building of the easier coast road from Shieldaig a few years ago, this was a serious matter for the inhabitants of Applecross, who had no other means of access except by sea.

The dramatic part of the drive is on the Loch Kishorn side, the slope down to Applecross being fairly gentle. But before beginning the climb, it is worth walking up the lower screes of Sgurr a Ghaorachain by the Russel Burn and looking back at Loch Kishorn. The road ascends high above, there is a sense of immense peace broken only by the splash of a little waterfall.

The sharpest hairpins are at the top of the pass where it runs between the peaks of Ghaorachain and Meall Gorm, when it becomes particularly incredible that this was the old cattle-drovers' route to the Lowland markets. Just beyond, there is a shattered rocky moonscape of a plateau with a viewing base from which, on the occasional clear day, you can see the Cuillins of Skye and the Outer Isles.

The Bealach na Bà lies on a minor road west from Tornapress on the A896 between Lochcarron and Shieldaig on Loch Torridon.

Cd Corrieshalloch Gorge

Corrieshalloch Gorge, with the Falls of Measach that pour through its entrance in a mighty 150 ft spout, is an extravaganza even by Highland standards – all the more so for being so completely unexpected. On either hand, the barren sentinel peaks of An Teallach and Beinn Dearg stand over the Ullapool road, where from a car park a steep, slippery path descends

through massed birch, rowan and hazel. At its end there is a little wooden platform which overhangs a world as lush as any Victorian conservatory. Rare ferns and mosses sprout from every crevice of the sheer rock walls; above them cling goat willow, guelder rose and bird cherry, and far below the River Droma tumbles.

The gorge itself is a box canyon – that is, it is as wide at the top as it is at

POINT OF THE GREAT OCEAN This is the meaning of Ardnamurchan, the westernmost peninsula of mainland Britain. It is a place of surprises – perfect bays such as Sanna and Port na Croisg and, inland, wild moors climbing high above great banks of rhododendrons.

PORT NA CROISG, ARDNAMURCHAN

SANNA BAY, ARDNAMURCHAN

the bottom, 200 ft below. A mile long and 100 ft wide, it was carved through solid metamorphic rock by floodwaters at the end of the last Ice Age.

Apart from the platform, a good view of the falls can also be obtained from the little suspension bridge that runs above them. This was built and presented by Sir John Fowler, co-designer of the Forth Bridge, towards the end of the last century. From it you can watch ravens and other birds make incredibly tight landings on the ledges and pinnacles among which they nest.

On the road to Dundonnell and Gairloch above the gorge there is another viewpoint that provides a splendid summary of the variety and contrasts of this part of the Highlands. Opposite, steep-crowding conifers clothe the lower slopes of Meall Doire Fàid, whose purple-brown 2,395 ft summit disappears into the mists above. Below, the gorge opens out into the gentle oak-dotted meadows of Strath More, threaded by the River Broom. At the river's end is Loch Broom and Ullapool, where trawlers from half Europe ride at anchor. Even the very road on which the viewpoint lies is part of the region's story; known throughout the Highlands as 'Destitution Road', it was built to give men work during the potato famine of 1851.

Corrieshalloch Gorge lies on the A835 Garve to Ullapool road, 12 miles south-east of Ullapool and ¼ mile north-west of the junction with the A832.

THE HOLY MOUNTAIN Ben Hiant looks down upon Loch Sunart and the Sound of Mull. Behind Camas nan Geall, the bay at its foot, there is an ancient cross dedicated to St Ciaran (d. 548) whom Columba called 'The light of this isle'.

Af Dunnet Head

Dunnet Head is the most northerly of the great capes that so dramatically terminate the Scottish mainland. It is easier of access than Cape Wrath, but feels much more remote than Duncansby Head with its John o' Groats. Dunnet Head is reached by a road crossing a wild sweep of moor that, when the heather is in bloom, is of a purple so intense that the colour seems to permeate the burns and the lochs, the peaty earth and even the sky.

When you reach the lookout point by the lighthouse – preferably at sunset – you are at the most northerly tip of mainland Britain. The Pentland Firth snores 340 ft below, or explodes at the foot of the cliff in bullets of spray that can easily reach your vantage place. Before you, anchored against the red-gold shoals of sunset, is the towering, sinister stack of the Old Man of Hoy backed by the humps of Orkney.

The scene changes hourly or, at times, in a matter of a few minutes. For everyone who remembers a Wagnerian storm, there are many others who recall the wide sands of Dunnet Bay, glittering under a calm sky. On such occasions it is easy to believe the story of the local fisher-lad who sleeps among all the treasures of all the ships that ever sank, in a cave somewhere in the bay. Apparently he was introduced to the treasures by a mermaid who dearly loved him, but when she found that he was dispensing them among earthly maidens, she wooed him to sleep with her singing. In the cave he remains, inactive but faithful, to this day.

Take the A836 from Thurso to John o' Groats; at Dunnet turn on to the B855 and follow the signposts to Dunnet Head.

HUNTERS AND HUNTED

Habitats are limited in the Highlands; consequently, bird species – at least those that live inland – tend to be limited, too. However, some species have adapted superbly. The golden eagle, which nests on crags up to 2,000 ft high, nails its victims to the ground with its talons after a 90 mph stoop. Among its prey is the red grouse which lives only in the British Isles, and whose diet consists mainly of heather shoots. The peregrine nests on cliffs and takes birds on the wing, while the redwing, our smallest thrush, resides in hillside birchwoods.

Redwing
(Turdus iliacus)

Red grouse
(Lagopus lagopus)

Golden eagle
(Aquila chrysaetos)

Peregrine falcon
(Falco peregrinus)

Df Durness and Loch Eriboll

A week or so after the end of the holiday season, motorists on the road that runs across the tip of Scotland to the Kyle of Durness begin to wave to one another. Doubtless each is relieved to discover that he is not the sole survivor of some cataclysm that has wiped every other human from the face of the earth. The moorlands hereabouts are very wild and very lonely, so that even the crofting hamlets at Durness seem bustling by comparison. There is a craft centre here and a roofless chapel; otherwise the principal attraction is the awesome Smoo Cave situated at the end of a deep cleft about 1½ miles east down the coast.

Actually there are three caves, but only one of them, the largest, is accessible without potholing equipment. A river, the Allt Smoo, emerges from its mouth behind which lies a tremendous cavern of cathedral-like proportions and appearance, some 200 ft deep and 120 ft high. For some reason, Bonnie Prince Charlie did not hide in the Smoo Cave but the Devil did. He was cornered there by the 17th-century Lord Reay, 'The Wizard of Reay', whose shadow Old Nick had stolen in Italy. Just as the wizard was about to settle accounts, the Devil blew a great hole in the roof and made his escape. By way of confirmation, the hole remains there to this day, though some prosaic people say it was really cut by the Allt Smoo which drops through the hole in an 80 ft waterfall to the cave floor. From there, it runs through the gully and out to the sea. This is an unspoiled and lovely place, calm even on a wild day, when the sea explodes in spray at the gully's entrance.

From the cave, the road runs off to Tongue, making a huge loop round Loch Eriboll, down one shore and up the other. This narrow-entranced sea loch cuts deep into the Sutherland mountains, creating a fine, easily defended anchorage, and was used as such by the Home Fleet during the Second World War. Now it is more or less deserted, a place of great sweeps of heather that swim in the heat of summer and pour mist on to the loch for most of the rest of the year. Here and there, however, and around nearby Loch Hope, tumbled traces of Pictish settlements show that the area was fairly populous in early times. Roofless crofts testify that it continued to be so for many centuries after, until the evictions of the 1800s, which in this district left thousands of people homeless.

But the present emptiness has one advantage in that the loch's solitude provides one of the very few mainland breeding grounds of the grey seal. The animals can be seen sometimes around the cliffs and caves of the south shore.

Durness and Loch Eriboll are about 40 miles due north-west of Lairg and can be approached on the A838, or A836 to Tongue and thence the A838.

Cc Glen Affric

If all the loveliest glens in the Highlands were distilled, then their yielded essence would be something very much like Glen Affric. It would be a traditional blend rather than a straight malt: two lochs, Affric and Benevean (correctly, Beinn a' Mheadhoin), a number of 'wild hanging woods and loud-roaring floods', and, for good measure, the fugitive memory of the Young Pretender, who found refuge in these parts after Culloden, in a cave above Badger Fall on the River Affric. The mountains are regular, graceful peaks wearing snowy mantles from early October. The glen was one of Landseer's favourite subjects. One of his paintings, dated 1887, shows a broken branch of Scots pine; the same branch can still be seen near the Affric bridge, below Dog Fall, and 'Monarchs of the Glen' still patrol the woods and high hills in abundance.

Glen Affric was part of the old road that cut through the Inverness-shire hills and ran across Scotland, and in fact there is still a fine long-distance path that goes all the way to Kintail. From the 16th to the early 20th centuries, the glen was Chisholm country, secured to some extent during the 1745 rising by a judicious hedging of bets. At

VICTORIAN IDEAL To Landseer, Dog Fall in Glen Affric was the very essence of romantic landscape; it figured frequently in his paintings.

LAST VIEW Here, at Loch nan Uamh, Prince Charles Edward took ship for France, never to see Scotland again.

Culloden, the chief of Clan Chisholm and a younger son fought for Charles, while two elder brothers faced them among the redcoat ranks opposite.

About 30 years ago, a hydroelectric dam was built across the eastern end of Loch Benevean, turning hillocks into islets crowned with pine. Those who remember the place in the days before the dam say that much of its beauty is gone for ever, in which case it must have been a paradise indeed, for there can be few more glorious valleys on the face of the planet.

The best way to see it is to take one of the Forestry Commission walks from Dog Fall – actually more of a tumbling rapid – or from the car park near the narrow spit of land that divides Benevean from Affric. The walks are from one to three hours' duration and offer splendid vistas of forest, dark lochs and rapids. Examples of almost every bird species in the Highlands nest here, and as well as red and roe deer there are foxes, badgers, wildcats and pine martens. Keep off the hills during the deer-stalking season, August to October;

otherwise, it is a gentle, friendly place.

Glen Affric is reached by branching off on the A831 at Cannich, from where a minor road leads south-west to the glen. Cannich is 23 miles west of Inverness.

Bb **Glen Beasdale**

As Glenfinnan was the pinnacle of the Jacobite rising of 1745, so Glen Beasdale was its beginning and its end, for it was on the shores of Loch nan Uamh, the little sea loch lying at the mouth of the glen, that the Young Pretender first

387

set foot on the Scottish mainland. And it was from there, too, that he departed, closing the final chapter of the story of the House of Stuart.

Beasdale Burn tumbles down from the mountains of South Morar in a series of waterfalls until it reaches the lower end of the glen, where it plunges deeply into woods as rich as any in southern England. Oaks descended from the ancient forest that once covered this part of the country grow here, mingled with rhododendrons, birches and larches. Mossy cushions coat the rocks, and pale green streamers of lichen hang from dead branches – all in astonishing contrast to the austere hills climbing above.

Near Arisaig House, where the trees arch over the road by the Borrodale Burn, there is a track signed 'Druimindarroch' angling down towards the shore. Take it, and abruptly the woods come to an end, opening out into the brightness of Loch nan Uamh, all lumpy green islets and isthmuses, with far to the west the bulks of Rhum and Eigg rising from the sea. There is a barn at the bottom of the track, and opposite, over a grassy beach crossable at low tide, a single wind-blown oak, beyond which lies 'Prince Charlie's Cave'. It is also possible to reach the cave by a longer track, but the beach route is more enjoyable. The chances are that a seal will stick his head out of the water and gaze at you, as fascinated by your presence as you are by his.

In September 1746, so tradition says, the Prince and a few companions hid in the 60 ft deep cave for ten days, awaiting a ship to France. He had been a wanderer and a fugitive ever since the Battle of Culloden six months earlier, and by now had grown a long red beard, was bare-footed, and was dressed in a

THE MYSTERY OF THE BROCHS

WHO built the brochs? The truth is, no one knows for certain. But quite possibly it was the race of big, red-haired men that the Roman general Agricola defeated at Mons Graupius, a hillside battlefield somewhere in north-east Scotland. Tacitus, the historian of the campaign, dubbed them Caledonians, but later they became known as Picts, a name that means simply 'the

DUN TELVE BROCH, NEAR GLENELG

painted ones'. Whether they were the aboriginal inhabitants of Scotland or migrants from some other part of Europe is unknown, and they have left few traces of their passing.

In fact, of all the major races that make up the British people, none has vanished more utterly than the Picts. From a few surviving place-names, among them the prefix 'Dun', it is known that they spoke a Celtic tongue, but it was not Gaelic, which was an import from Ireland. They had kings, but of their laws, system of government or religion, no direct evidence remains.

However, they were far from being the painted savages of legend. Their sculptures of birds, beasts, mounted warriors and strange abstract designs, found from Shetland to Fife, show that they had great artists among them. And if they did build the brochs, then they also possessed skilful engineers.

For a time, after the Romans left, Pictish kings with names such as Oengus and Kenneth ruled the entire country. But always they and their people lay trapped between the hammer of the Scots from Ireland and the anvil of the Norsemen. The Pictish nation was broken by the middle of the 9th century; the Scots spread north and east, crushing the last memories of the old customs and language. Only the brochs remain.

Bb Glenelg and Glen Shiel

The drive through Glen Shiel coming west from Invermoriston, with the mountains rising to 3,000 ft on either hand – so close you feel you could almost touch them – must be one of the most spectacular in Britain. And if you are inspired by it, you would not be the first, for it was here that Dr Johnson, riding with the faithful Boswell to Glenelg and Skye, conceived the idea of writing his *Journey to the Western Isles*.

The route they took is the same as that followed by the modern motorist, turning west at Shiel Bridge and climbing the old military road over the helter-skelter Mam Ratagain Pass. The view has been considerably obscured since Johnson's day by dark conifers, planted by the Forestry Commission, but in its usual courteous way it has made amends with a viewing base above the tree-line. Turn round, and the sight is at once breath-catching, almost too much to take in. Below in a pale green bowl lies little Loch Shiel, the head of Loch Duich and the toy shape of Shiel Bridge. Above them all, and the glen, tower the great billowing exuberant shapes of the grassy mountains known as the Five Sisters of Kintail. Wearing green in summer, old-gold in autumn and white in winter, with an occasional cloud veil to add a little mystery, they are among the loveliest of Highland hills.

The minor road west from Shiel Bridge runs on to Glenelg village and the Sound of Sleat, but just before reaching them, watch out for a jagged pile of grey masonry in a field on the right. This is the remains of Bernera Barracks, the reason for the military road over the Mam Ratagain Pass.

dirty shirt, a plaid and a ragged coat. However, he seemed in the best of spirits; fortitude in the face of adversity was always one of the Stuarts' most endearing traits.

Eventually, Charles and a number of his followers were picked up by the French ship *L'Heureux* from a cove some 2 miles east along the road. A cairn marks the spot, close by the place where he had landed with such high

hopes 14 months earlier. Yet, as one of the few inhabitants of Druimindarroch says with gentle sadness, as though the whole thing had happened yesterday: 'Perhaps it was a good thing he went away. He would never have agreed with democracy.'

Glen Beasdale runs north-east from the Sound of Arisaig towards Loch Morar. The A830 from Lochailort to Arisaig traverses part of it.

From 1722 to 1790, the barracks were occupied by Government troops engaged in the thankless task of pacifying the Highlands. Now the buildings stand roofless and neglected by the shore, grass and shrubs sprouting from the gaping windows.

Glenelg village is a cluster of cottages and fishing boats on the seaweed-draped shore south of the swift-flowing strait of Kyle Rhea. Opposite the village, on Skye, are the cottages of Kylerhea, scattered at the foot of a dark glen running between the peaks of Sgurr na Coinnich and Ben Aslak. Cattle used to be ferried from Skye here, and driven over Mam Ratagain to the Lowland markets. There is still a ferry for cars and people, but it shuts down in winter.

Inland and south from Glenelg, along a minor road into Glen Beag, there is a pair of those mysterious towers called brochs – Dun Telve and Dun Trodden – reputed to be the best-preserved of their kind on the mainland. Possibly built by Iron Age Picts as a defence against Norse sea-raiders, the outer wall of Dun Telve still rises in places to a sheer 33 ft of unmortared stone, pierced only by a 4 ft high door. Within, there is a second wall, rising up to join the outer one at the top, the lower space between them being filled with galleries and chambers. A pair of windows look down from the inner wall into a courtyard, some 33 ft across, that was perhaps a corral for cattle in times of trouble. Two ledges jut from a wall; but like so much else about the place, their purpose is a mystery.

Shiel Bridge is reached by the A87 from Invergarry or from Kyle of Lochalsh. Glenelg is on a minor road 9 miles west from Shiel Bridge.

Ce   ### Knockan Cliff

About 10 miles north of Ullapool the road is overhung by a mile-long dark cliff. This is the Knockan Cliff, a geological curiosity that a little over 100 years ago started an entirely new way of thinking about the origins of the world's mountain chains. Generally, in any rock formation, the oldest deposits are at the bottom, compressed and altered by the weight of the younger rocks above. But at Knockan Cliff in 1859, Professor Nicol, a geologist, observed that the topmost layer of Moine schists was considerably more compressed and altered in structure – and therefore probably older – than the limestone and quartzite on which it rests. This, it was deduced, was the result of a tremendous upheaval that took place in the earth's crust some 400 million years ago, thrusting up ancient rock from the depths to overlie the newer surface deposits. The discovery led to the investigation of similar phenomena elsewhere, and to a more profound understanding of the forces that shaped the great mountain ranges.

Knockan Cliff is now a nature trail,

'A TERRIBLE STEEP' So said Dr Johnson of Mam Ratagain Pass which looks over Glen Shiel to the Five Sisters of Kintail.

superbly marked out by the Nature Conservancy Council in 17 viewing points involving a 1½ mile walk and a climb to 1,050 ft. Each point illustrates some different aspect of the area – its geological formation, its views, its vegetation and flowers, its birds and beasts. There is even a 6,000-year-old pine root to suggest that the climate was much kinder here once, kind enough to permit the covering of the whole area by forest. This is not the case now, however, and the trail must not be taken lightly. Stout boots are essential, and it is strongly recommended, if the weather is wet and windy, that you should not proceed beyond Point 8.

The cliff looks out upon the Inverpolly Nature Reserve, an oddly gentle title for 27,000 acres of savage wilderness. Though it provides a variety of habitats from marine islands to birchwoods, lochs and rivers, much of it is a whisky-coloured wilderness of rock, peat bog and water. No one lives here, and you feel that probably no one ever has or ever will. The face of the land is covered by the old, leathery, unadorned hide of the planet, worn by aeons of ice and weather. It is not hostile, exactly; simply ancient and utterly indifferent.

Perhaps some of this impression comes from there being very few trees or large plants – at least in the area near the cliff – so that the land is forever still. Only the light and the cloud shapes change. Certainly not the old, old mountains – Cùl Beag, the sugar-loaf Suilven, or the worn, splintered Stac Polly. An uneasy place, but compelling and unforgettable.

Knockan Cliff and the Inverpolly Reserve lie 10 miles north from Ullapool on the A835.

Bd Loch Maree

Beinn Eighe is the earliest of the National Nature Reserves, set up in 1951 chiefly to conserve the fragment of the old Caledonian forest, Coille na Glas-leitire, 'the wood on the grey slopes', that runs along the southern shore of Loch Maree. It was not before time, since, as elsewhere in the Highlands, the hand of man has lain heavily on the forest this last 1,500 years and more. Vikings from Orkney built their ships of Highland timber and wantonly fired any stands about them that they did not use. In the 14th century, Alexander Stewart, the 'Wolf of Badenoch', is

LONELY HUNTER

Once common all over Britain, wildcats have been restricted to the Highlands since the 19th century, largely due to persecution by gamekeepers. Recent evidence, however, suggests they may now have extended their range as far south as Stirling. Numbers of true wildcats are difficult to assess, due to their shy, solitary habits and to their occasional cross-breeding with domestic cats which they somewhat resemble, though they are bigger and heavier and have bushier tails.

Wildcat
(Felis sylvestris grampia)

said to have burned the forests as an efficient means of persuading fugitives to emerge; so, too, did his grandfather, Robert Bruce, and many Highland chieftains in neighbourly squabbles. Sheep runs and lumbering both took massive toll, but now at Bienn Eighe and in other reserves, attempts are being made to regenerate not only the Scots pine forest, but the native stands of oak and birch as well.

The mountain trail at Bienn Eighe – steep and rough in places – explores the reserve and illuminates its history. Cairns mark points of particular interest and places where glimpses of wildcat, pine marten and ptarmigan may be seen if you are lucky. And as you climb there opens up the glorious 12 mile vista of Loch Maree with its raft-like islands and wild mountain scenery to the north. Dominating all is the peak of the aptly named Slioch, 'the spearhead', shadowing dark Gleann Biannasdale. Some way up the glen there are the remains of an ironworks that in the 17th century smelted iron from bog ore. The men who did the work were recruited from the south, and to this day part of the mouth of the glen, where it opens up on to the loch shore, is known as Cladh nan Sussanach, 'the grave of the English'.

Scots pine also clothes the loch's islands, and on one of the smallest of these, Isle Maree, the Irish St Maelrubha established a hermitage, later replaced by a chapel, the remains of which can still be seen. Possibly he did so to oust a local deity called Mourie, but if that was the case, his pious gesture had some odd repercussions. Maelrubha and Mourie became one in local legend, and as late as the 18th century people worshipped a tree and a well on the island, and sacrificed bulls there.

The waters of the well were held to have curative properties, especially in cases of insanity, being most potent on August 25, St Maelrubha's Day. There is a record of one such cure being attempted in 1852, with unknown results. But though the waters may no longer be effective, the little island itself is still regarded with affection and respect in the district.

The trails through Slattadale Forest at the western end of the loch provide an insight into modern forest management and the way it helps to preserve the wildlife of the area. One of the trails, Tollie Path, is fairly rough so make sure that your boots are adequate to its rigours.

The best approach to Loch Maree is by the A896 from Lochcarron, or by the A834 and A832 from Dingwall.

Bb Loch Morar

Above the hilly village of Morar there is an orange metal cross marking the spot where the first Irish missionary to these parts, said to be St Cumin, began his conversion of the local pagans. To the west, it looks out over the famous pure white quartzite sands of the beach to the dromedary humps of Rhum, and closer, to the war-galley prow of Eigg's headland; both islands lift out of the sea and disappear again in minutes, according to the whim of the weather.

Eastwards across a narrow neck of land there is the full 12 mile stretch of

MORAG'S LAIR A monster called Morag is said to live in Loch Morar. If she does she has plenty of room to manoeuvre, since towards its eastern end, the loch plunges to 1,017 ft, the deepest water in Britain or in its surrounding seas.

Loch Morar. If you take the narrow road to Bracora half a mile south of Morar, you come first to a thunderous weir on the short Morar river. This is the site of some once-mighty falls, but they have been largely tamed by a hydroelectric scheme. Beyond, the road opens out on to the loch's waters, which towards the eastern end fill the deepest abyss in Britain – 1,017 ft, a depth that does not occur again, even in the sea, until the edge of the Continental Shelf is reached near Rockall. It is thought that Morar's fearsome trench was scoured by a fast-moving glacier that spread and slowed towards the valley's broader western end. Certainly the loch is wider and shallower at this point.

For about 2 miles the road runs between little crofting meadows, oaks and rhododendrons, with crags above on which buzzards snatch at their breakfasts. However, a little beyond Bracora, mostly consisting of a post office and telephone kiosk, the road comes to an end. From here on, the way along the loch is on foot.

It is a fine, stony, adventurous path, constantly twisting and turning along the shore, constantly offering new vistas. For company there is the odd sheep and heron, fast-falling streams on the left and the quick-chopping splash of loch water on the right. There might also be a glimpse of Morag, Morar's monster, though she is less publicity-conscious than her relative in Loch Ness, and is said to appear only when the death of a MacDonald of Clanranald is imminent.

The mountains of North and South Morar lean over the shores of the loch and its scattering of islands, on which grow fragments of the ancient Caledonian Forest. On one of the islands

HIGHLAND PRACTICALITY

In Highland society, where hardship was never far away, it was essential to make the best possible use of whatever materials nature provided. The leaves and stems of cowberry, for example, were employed to make a yellow dye and the fruits made into a jelly. As long ago as the 15th century, the fruits of the pink-flowering bearberry, a favourite food of grouse, were pressed to make an astringent.

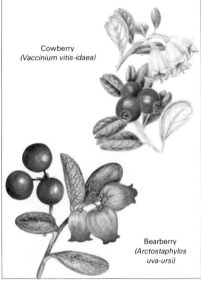

Cowberry
(Vaccinium vitis-idaea)

Bearberry
(Arctostaphylos
uva-ursi)

Simon Fraser, Lord Lovat, was captured in 1746 while hiding in a hollow tree; apparently he had omitted to conceal his legs. A double-dealing villain to whom the hedging of political bets was a way of life, he had chosen the wrong side for the first and last time in 1745. At his execution in London, he marvelled that so many folk had turned out to watch his old grey head roll.

After about 5 miles, the track turns left to Tarbet and the roadless splendours of Loch Nevis. Backed by the

mountains of Knoydart, the inner and outer lochs are grander and wilder than Morar, though they are accessible only to walkers and sailors. For those who prefer tougher hikes, there are also magnificent views of Lochs Nevis and Morar from some of the peaks east of the road to Mallaig.

Morar village lies on the A830, 30 miles north-west of Fort William and 3 miles south of Mallaig ferry harbour.

Cf   Sandwood Bay

The old Gaels claimed that Tir nan Og, 'the Land of Youth' – Paradise, in other words – lay somewhere far to the west, a place of quiet waters and gentle shores. Perhaps the model they had in mind was Sandwood Bay, the most north-westerly beach in mainland Britain, and one of the loveliest and most remote in all Scotland.

It is not easy of access. It is found by way of Loch Inchard and Kinlochbervie, a bright cluster of fishing boats backed by bungalows, fish sheds, a school and a hotel, all wrapped about by promontories and islands. From there, a rough road goes on to Oldshoremore with its cemetery overhanging a bay of white-gold sand and further still to Blairmore and Sheigra, at which point the road gives up in a peat bog. From a little before Sheigra, a path leads to the bay, over 4 miles of rock, peat and water, so go well-shod.

In fine weather Sandwood Bay is a paradise. An odd stillness lies upon the marram grass on the dunes and upon the freshwater loch behind. The sea is mirror-calm and, far off, the great bulk of Cape Wrath – the old Hvarf, or navigational turning point of the Vikings – stands bold against the horizon. But a wind can change it quickly into a

wild symphony of colour and sound. Pale green-white horses gallop in over the dark green Minch, smashing, clawing and exploding up the stacks of red Torridon rock as they race home to the beach. In either condition, there is seldom anyone there to observe it. A long way off, maybe, a stroller will be revealed by his vivid anorak, the universal Highland garb that has all but ousted the kilt.

In fair weather or foul there is a touch of the uncanny about Sandwood Bay. It has always had the reputation of being haunted, not by anything so mundane as ghosts but by shy and mysterious creatures from the sea. One such – a mermaid – startled a shepherd named Sandy Gunn in 1900; he told the story much later to MacDonald Robertson, the compiler of *Wade the River, Drift the Loch*. The mermaid had been stranded by the tide on a ledge at Rubh' an Fhir Léithe, about a mile down the coast from the bay, so Sandy was able to get a good look at her. She was bonnie, apparently, with reddish-yellow hair, green eyes, a yellowish complexion and, apart from a fishy tail and an arched back, looked just like a lovely human girl. Sandy and the mermaid stared at each other in equal amazement; then his dog let out a fearful howl and took off up the beach as though the Devil himself were after it. This broke the spell, and Sandy, suddenly terrifyingly aware of what he was looking at, also took to his heels.

However, it seems that the mermaid came to no harm, for she, or her descendants, have been seen many times since in and around the bay and in Loch Inchard. Sometimes she is in full view, but more often she is a swirl of golden hair just under the surface of the waves.

Kinlochbervie is on the B801, which is best approached by the A838 north-west out of Lairg, or by the A894 north from Ullapool, which joins the A838 4 miles south of the junction with the B801 at Rhiconich.

Torridon

Bc

For once throwing reserve to the winds, the National Trust for Scotland proclaims Glen Torridon and the wild mountains about it to be the loveliest mountain scenery in the country, Skye not even excepted. But at the same time, it should be remembered that this is not a place to take lightly. No one should attempt even a short expedition without proper equipment.

Those who are sensitive to landscape may feel that 'lovely' is hardly an adequate term for Torridon, which in its old, old age is awesome, majestic and faintly terrible. The phrase 'Before the hills in order stood' takes on a new dimension here, for you are looking at some of the oldest shapes on earth – the mighty ridge of Liathach, with its peaks, corries and crags, and the only slightly less impressive Beinn Alligin and Beinn Dearg. They are composed mainly of reddish Torridon sandstone, a substance laid down 750 million years ago and worn since by time, wind and rain into fantasy. By way of underlining the time scale involved, a number of the peaks are capped with white quartzite, in which are embedded the fossils of some of the first living creatures on the planet – half-inch worms.

The weather is by no means invariably sympathetic, and in any event the stiffer hill walks should be attempted only by experienced climbers. But the less ambitious walker can, for example, take the road from the scattering of white houses that is Torridon village, round the north shore of Upper Loch Torridon to Inveralligin. The mountains rise straight from the roadside, their gullies spilling cloud over the loch whose slaty calmness is streaked with the paler lines of currents.

From Inveralligin there runs a single-track switchback road that should satisfy the most ardent lover of mountain scenery. Justly named the Bealach na Gaoithe, 'the Pass of the Winds', it clambers around the lower slopes of Beinn Alligin, then soars and swoops to the little crofting hamlet of Lower Diabaig, among the loneliest habitations in Britain. About halfway up the pass there is a parking place. Before and around it there is the whole glorious panorama of rock and water – Loch Torridon, Loch Shieldaig and Loch Diabaig, the mountains of Shieldaig, Applecross and Torridon. Close by there is a little red letter-box. Who, you wonder, ever posts a letter here? And who collects it?

Torridon village is on a minor road off the A896, 6 miles east of Shieldaig. The A896 runs between Lochcarron and Kinlochewe.

ENCHANTED SANDS Sandwood Bay, north-westernmost of Scottish beaches, is claimed to be the haunt of a mermaid.

THE ISLANDS OF SCOTLAND

Wild, romantic, and steeped in history, each of the
remote islands has a personality of its own

Romance, like the sea, surrounds Orkney, Shetland and the Hebrides. They are worlds in miniature, islands off an island, the most remote and foreign parts of Britain. Such a roar and swirl of tidal water lies between Orkney and mainland Scotland that the currents are said to turn giant millstones beneath the waves, grinding the salt which flavours the sea. Another 50 miles further north from Orkney, the 100 or so rugged islands of Shetland straggle towards the Arctic, dividing the Atlantic from the North Sea and crouching below the salt-laden winds like wandering sea beasts turned to stone. Some 50 miles west of mainland Scotland are the Outer Hebrides, stretching 130 miles from north to south and rearing up like a worn grey rampart, breached but still tenacious, on the battered edge of the world.

There are great differences between the island groups, and even between individual islands lying close together. Shetland is mostly wild and treeless, with a coastline so broken and indented that no point is more than 3 miles from the sea. Bogs and peat moors are more common than farmland. The feeling that these are the Viking islands, the remote sea fortress of a fierce, seafaring people, is still strong despite the 20th-century promise of riches from North Sea oil. Orkney, by contrast, is gentle, softly undulating and domestic, more fertile than Shetland and pervaded with an extraordinary sense of prehistory. The

quantity of prehistoric remains throughout Orkney places the islands among Britain's richest archaeological treasure-houses.

The Hebrides are simply rock. The austere chain of the Outer Hebrides is composed almost entirely of gneiss, one of the hardest and most unyielding rocks in the world, and about 2,500 million years old in parts of the Uists and Benbecula. Here the landscapes range from the peat-land wilderness of Lewis, known as the Black Moor, through the mountains of North Harris to the long shell-sand beaches and the flower-strewn grassland called machair on the Atlantic coasts of South Harris and the Uists. In places the land lies half-drowned under an exploded jigsaw of inland lochs. Elsewhere, particularly in the east, the gneiss holds sway to such an extent that there is almost no soil at all. In the most barren but still inhabited areas, such as the east coast of South Harris, nothing of any value would ever grow, were it not for the tidy, cultivated beds which the crofters laboriously build up by piling peat and seaweed on the bare ground.

It is only a two-hour ferry journey between the Outer and Inner Hebrides, but in geological terms many hundreds of millions of years separate the two. The main bulk of the Inner Hebrides, from Skye to Mull, includes the youngest of the Scottish islands, and their landscapes are the most exuberant. Some 70 million years ago, the earth turned inside out where the islands now stand, exploding in a sequence of volcanic eruptions among the most savage and intense in Britain's geological history. There are parts of the Inner Hebrides as beautiful, serene and tranquil as anywhere in Britain. And yet they were born in an acrid rage of boiling rock, and given shape by slow erosion.

SKYE SHORELINE The heights of Meall na Suiramach overlook the rocky wilderness of Quiraing on the Trotternish peninsula in northern Skye. Beyond the waters of Staffin Bay and the Sound of Raasay lie the distant Highlands around Gairloch.

Places to visit

Kilchiaran, Islay

A ruined chapel, renovated but roofless, stands beside the track leading down to Kilchiaran Bay. A small stream lined with irises glides past it towards the sheltered sands. Highland cattle graze the green slopes at the side of the beach and sheep graze the darker hills beyond.

An oystercatcher flies past, shrilly piping; curlews call in the distance, sounding sweet but sad; jackdaws hop among the boulders and gulls rest on the waves. In the grass there are buttercups and clover, wild thyme, self-heal, eyebright and primroses. Piles of seaweed mark the tideline. It is a picture of perfect calm, changeless except for the turn of the seasons, untroubled except by the moods of the sea. Perhaps the calm can be attributed to Ciaran, a Celtic saint to whom the chapel is dedicated. For tradition maintains that even after his death in AD 548, Ciaran's calming effect was so great that St Columba once threw a handful of earth from his grave into the roaring Corryvreckan whirlpool at the northern tip of Jura, and the whirlpool instantly fell still.

A short distance north-east from the chapel, a narrow track turns left off the road, just before a curious, semi-circular steading, or farmstead. From the top of the track a walk leads round the hill, and down to the wide sands of Machir Bay. On the way it passes a high face of rock called Grannie's Rock, which has a profile like the face of an old woman, gazing out to sea. The tumbled remains of Dùn Chroisprig, an ancient Iron Age broch, can be reached by climbing up the slope 500 yds further on, and walking over the flat land to the inland cliffs.

Here, too, as on the sands of Kilchiaran and in the stony profile of the old lady, there is a sense of unchangeable calm, as if time had flown away.

Islay can be reached by car ferry from Kennacraig, northern Kintyre, to Port Askaig or Port Ellen. Kilchiaran is about 24 miles north-west of Port Ellen along the A846 and A847 and then a minor road west at Port Charlotte.

Loch Gruinart, Islay

In 1598 the argument about who owned the Rinns of Islay ended in a fierce clan battle between the MacDonalds and the MacLeans on the flats at the head of Loch Gruinart. Tradition maintains that all but 20 of the MacLeans were slaughtered. The survivors fled up the western shore towards the sea and safety, taking refuge for a time in Kilnave chapel. But the MacDonalds caught up with them there and burned the chapel; only one MacLean escaped, by climbing through the burning thatch.

The ruined chapel still stands, just a few yards from the shore, with a weathered but still beautiful 8th-century Celtic cross outside it. Nothing now disturbs the peace of the place – except the arrival of the barnacle geese each autumn. For Loch Gruinart's quiet waters and the surrounding pastures are one of the main British wintering grounds of barnacle geese; and when the birds fly in from their Arctic breeding grounds, the air rings with their dog-like yapping, and the empty spaces become crowded with life.

There are many delights in the area – the sand-dunes at the mouth of the loch, the quiet road along its east shore, and the curious castellated farmhouse that stands at the end of the western road, overlooking the tiny Ardnave Loch.

Perhaps the greatest delight is to sit on the hummock beyond the chapel, looking out over the flats when the tide is low. In the distance, waves roll between the dunes, balanced on the low horizon. Even the waves seem fixed in their setting, as if they have become frozen in time and would stay where they roll for ever.

Islay can be reached by car ferry from Kennacraig, northern Kintyre, to Port Ellen or Port Askaig. Loch Gruinart is about 14 miles west of Port Askaig along the A846, A847 and then the B8017 (narrow with passing places).

Calgary Bay, Mull

In the early 19th century many landowners in Mull, as elsewhere in the Highlands and islands, found sheep

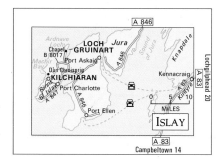

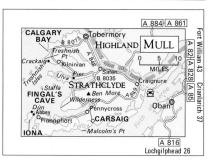

more profitable than people. Consequently, many families, mercilessly forced away from their crofts, took leave of their homeland at Calgary Bay. It is one of Mull's best-known beauty spots, but the brilliant white beach and soft green machair grass must have made bitter viewing from the rail of an emigrant ship setting sail for Canada.

Today the place presents a kinder aspect, a soothing balance of sea, sand and grass, protected by the wooded hillsides behind it. The trouble now is that so many people know of it, for unfortunately the number of visitors in summer has caused erosion of the machair grass.

Treshnish Point, at the southern end of the bay, can be reached either by walking round the coast or by driving down the long, rough track to Haunn; and though both ways have their share of difficulties, the journey is worth the trouble. The place is wild and lonely, but curiously gentle, like most of north Mull. There are fine views over the sea to the long islands of Tiree and Coll, and to the strange, volcanic humps of the Treshnish Isles. To the south, running 4 miles round the coast to Kilninian, is a raised beach caused by the uplift of land at the end of the last Ice Age, when it was relieved of the crushing weight of glaciers. There are two lines of cliffs, one higher and further inland than the other, forming a giant step down to the water. The lush, flower-strewn swath of grass between the cliffs is perfect for walking.

Inland, too, the district repays exploration. It is a deserted wilderness of spectacular beauty, with the tumbled remains of settlements such as Crackaig serving as nostalgic monuments to the crofters who sailed away.

Mull can be reached by car ferry from Oban to Craignure. Calgary Bay is about 10 miles west of Tobermory on the B8073. Tobermory is 20 miles north-west of Craignure along the A849 and A848 (narrow with passing places).

Carsaig, Mull

The first view of Carsaig is startling. The high moorland road from Pennycross enters the head of a valley and suddenly the view opens up ahead, as if the land had been cleft with an axe. Carsaig Bay lies far below, framed between steep, wooded hillsides. Then the road slides down into the woods, dropping sharply through a tunnel of trees until it re-emerges at the pier.

To the west lie the grey, volcanic sands of the bay, with a wild stretch of cliffs leading beyond them to Malcolm's Point. Two waterfalls tumble from the cliff-tops, separated by a sheer grassy slope called the Nuns' Pass. Flat beds of grey sandstone front the sea. The sandstone was quarried to make much of the ornamental stonework for the abbey on Iona, as well as for many chapels in Mull.

By following the track which begins just above the pier, it is possible to walk out to the bay, and then along the coast beneath the cliffs. There is an abun-

dance of wild flowers – such as herb Robert, lady's bedstraw, white stonecrop, thyme-leaved speedwell, skullcap and many others. Ravens nest on the cliffs and wheatears flit among the boulders or sit in the distance clicking out alarm calls. Just before the second waterfall, there is a cave tucked into the cliff-face at the top of a slope. It is called the Nuns' Cave, for the nuns of Iona are said to have taken refuge here after being driven from the island during the Reformation. Monks also used the cave as a workshop when they were quarrying stone from the nearby beds. It was probably the monks who carved the Celtic crosses in the west wall, and made the font that catches the drips over the entrance.

Mull can be reached by car ferry from Oban to Craignure. Carsaig is about 23 miles south-west of Craignure by road, off the A849 (narrow with passing places) along a minor road south-east at Pennycross.

Fingal's Cave, Staffa

The walls of the cave are a mass of elegant, black pillars; the perfectly jointed tops of broad, six-sided columns form a causeway into it, washed by the sea; the roof is finely arched and patterned. Waves fill the darkness with sound. 'Compared to this, what are the cathedrals and palaces built by men!' the naturalist Sir Joseph Banks wrote in 1772, and first drew the world's attention to these geological wonders.

Queen Victoria and Prince Albert visited Fingal's Cave, as did Sir Walter Scott, Keats, Wordsworth and Tennyson. Turner was inspired to make a painting of it, Mendelssohn to compose his *Hebrides Overture*. Between them they made Staffa one of the most

CANADIAN CONNECTION Sunset brings sparkle and shadow to Calgary Bay in north-west Mull, its sands ridged by the ebbing tide. Calgary is Gaelic for 'clear running water', and Calgary city in Canada takes its name from the bay.

famous small islands in the world, and Fingal's Cave became a place which every traveller to the Hebrides was bound to visit. The cave takes its name from the hero, Fionn macCumhaill, whom legend says constructed it.

The boat to Staffa sails from Ulva Ferry Pier, and turns out to sea through waters flanked by some of Mull's most magnificent scenery – to the north are the terraced hillsides and fragmented coastline of Ulva, to the south the aptly named Wilderness, impenetrable except on foot. It is a 45 minute journey from one style of beauty to another – from the sweeping romance of enormous landscapes dominated by Ben More, at 3,169 ft Mull's highest mountain, to the uniquely detailed marvels of Staffa.

Staffa lies alone in its waste of sea, half a mile long by a quarter of a mile wide. Grass-topped, it is uninhabited except by sheep and sea-birds. Pillars cram its southern face, leading into darkly yawning caves – for Fingal's Cave is only one of many. Seen from the sea the top of the island appears to be lifting from its base, stretching the rock between like rubber. Once ashore it is the geometrical precision of the rocks which is most impressive, and the way they fit together. Tens of millions of years ago they were a single mass of molten lava, exploding through a vent in the earth's crust. As it cooled to rock, the lava contracted, crystallised and acquired form – like a palace or

CARSAIG BAY Mull's empty shore below the green headlands was once busy with monks working as quarrymen. They came from Iona to hew grey sandstone from the sea's edge, then bore it back to their island to build the abbey.

cathedral building itself. Then the sea scooped out Fingal's Cave, 227 ft deep, and 66 ft high and 42 ft wide at its entrance. Standing in the dark of the cave – listening to it, looking at it, feeling it – such geological explanations seem unimportant. The cave leads into a world of the imagination.

Ulva Ferry lies 10 miles west of Salen, Mull, along the B8035 and B8073. Salen is about 12 miles north-west of Craignure on the A849, and there is a car ferry from Oban to Craignure.

Iona

It has become as much a state of mind as an island – Iona of St Columba's heart, Iona of his love, the cradle of Scottish Christianity and burial place of 60 kings. It is 3 miles long and never more than 1½ miles wide, a thin cut of land so steeped in religion that its hills and beaches are as hallowed as its abbey. The island is composed mainly of Lewisian gneiss, the most ancient and unchangeable of Hebridean rocks; it lies only a mile across the Sound of Iona from the younger, volcanic rocks of Mull, yet its landscapes pre-date those of Mull by millions of years.

Iona has two beauties: one, the beauty of the abbey, the ruined nunnery, St Oran's cemetery and all the other fabric of Christian endeavour; and the other, the spare beauty of the island itself, much of it hardly changed since St Columba arrived in AD 563.

The highest hill, Dùn, reaches only 332 ft above sea-level, but the island is so open that the views from Dùn sweep across an immense Hebridean panorama that stretches from the mountains of Mull to the Paps of Jura, and from Staffa and the Treshnish Isles to the distant heights of Rhum. On the coast,

especially in the north and west, machair grassland and dazzling beaches of shell-sand slope gently to the sea. All are within easy walking distance of the abbey.

Tradition maintains that when St Columba was old, he often used to visit the beach at the northern end of the island, sitting on the grassy mound behind it, alone with his thoughts. It is simple to follow in his footsteps, walking north from the abbey between the fields and hills, and along the quiet road to the sea; and simple also to sit as

FINGAL'S CAVE Close-set basalt columns line the southern shores of Staffa, curving to make a grand entrance for the largest cave on the island. Columns broken off short show how precise their hexagonal forms are.

FINGAL'S CAVE, STAFFA

THE BASALT PILLARS OF STAFFA

SAINT'S ISLE It is said that St Columba loved to sit alone above Iona's shore, meditating as he gazed out to sea.

history, like a faded picture sketched in stone. But the caretaker of the site knows the stones as if he had laid them out himself, and he tells the story of their grand beginnings with all the pride of the true Orcadian.

It is well worth climbing the slope beyond the ruins to the cliffs and lighthouse on the seaward side. There is an extraordinary springiness in the soft green turf, and in places it glows pink with a thick carpet of thrift. Puffins and many other sea-birds nest on the cliffs, which command views south past Marwick Head to the hills of Hoy, and east across the sea to Rousay and north-east to Westray. It is a lookout point fit for a great sea-earl, whose power depended on keeping secure his dominion over the sea.

Mainland, Orkney, can be reached by car ferry from Scrabster, near Thurso, to Stromness. There are also flights from Aberdeen and Wick to Kirkwall. Birsay lies about 1 mile north-west of the end of the A967, 13 miles north of Stromness.

he did, at the white edge of Iona, and be refreshed by the island's peace and tranquillity.

Iona can be reached by passenger ferry from Fionnphort, Mull. Fionnphort is about 35 miles west of Craignure by way of the A849 (narrow with passing places). Mull can be reached by car ferry from Oban to Craignure.

Birsay, Orkney

This tiny island was once Orkney's most holy place, a centre of Celtic Christianity established in the 7th or 8th centuries. In the 11th century it became the stronghold of Orkney's most powerful Viking earl, Thorfinn the Mighty, who built a church – Christ Church – on the grassy slopes above his palace.

In the 11th century Christ Church was consecrated as Orkney's first cathedral. Here the bones of Earl Magnus, the Norse ruler of Orkney, were laid to rest after his brutal murder by a rival earl in 1117. The grave became a centre of pilgrimage, a gathering place for all in need of miracles, until his remains were taken to Kirkwall in 1137 and placed in the cathedral of St Magnus.

The island can be reached only at low tide, across a causeway from the dunes on the mainland shore. When the tide rises, the sea runs in with surprising speed, quickly submerging the way across.

Slowly the insatiable sea is eroding the landward side of the island, where most of the ruins lie; the slipway where Earl Thorfinn would have hauled up his boats now ends abruptly well above the sea. The remains seem slight in comparison with their great

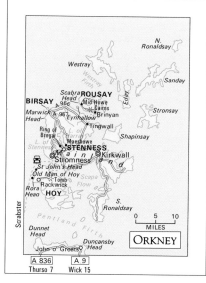

Hoy, Orkney

The name describes the place – Hoy, the high island, simply labelled by its first Norse settlers. It is like no other part of Orkney, but the huge, dark humps of its red-sandstone hills dominate many Orcadian views. For travellers from the south, the hills and magnificent cliffs on Hoy's western shore are the first image of Orkney – an imposing barrier behind which the other islands lie sheltered and concealed. As the ferry from Scrabster turns past Rora Head, Orkney's most celebrated geological freak comes clearly into view – the Old Man of Hoy, a 450 ft rock-stack standing rose-pink and solitary a short way out to sea.

There is no better way to appreciate the natural power of Hoy than to take the inter-island ferry from Stromness on Mainland and visit the island itself. Nowhere else in Orkney is so wild and silent as the glen road which crosses the island to reach Rackwick; no other prehistoric relic is so touched with strange magic as The Dwarfie Stane, an early Bronze Age tomb just south of the road. The tomb is hewn out of a single, isolated rock and is the only one of its kind in Britain. In a green valley at the end of the road, sloping gently down to a sandy bay, is the ancient Viking settlement of Rackwick, as poignant as it is picturesque, for it is almost deserted now except for a few crofts which have been turned into holiday homes.

From Rackwick a steep path leads up the hillside to Rora Head. Seen from the high moorland, a wilderness ruled over by great black-backed gulls and great skuas, the cliffs here seem much higher than they looked from the sea, and the Old Man of Hoy is an awesome

curiosity. St John's Head, 1,140 ft high, is one of the tallest vertical sea-cliffs in Britain, but only lovers of true wilderness will reach it. The land is wild and desolate, better suited to birds, sheep and mountain hares than to men. High above the hills a pair of golden eagles can sometimes be seen, soaring slowly on the wind; they are the only eagles in Orkney, and it is no surprise to discover that Hoy, the high island, is where they live.

Orkney can be reached by car ferry from Scrabster, near Thurso, to Stromness on Mainland. There are passenger flights from Aberdeen and Wick to Kirkwall on Mainland. Hoy can be reached by inter-island ferry from Stromness.

Rousay, Orkney

It is the stillness of Rousay which commands attention, as if time ends on its hillsides, among the cairns which held its ancient dead. There are so many burial chambers and other prehistoric remains on the island that it is sometimes called the Egypt of the North. It hardly seems to matter that the bones and burial goods were removed when the cairns were excavated, and taken to the National Museum of Antiquities in Edinburgh. The intense quiet among the cairns is like a spirit distilled from the wider quiet of the island.

The cairns express a people's fervent regard for the dead; they also demonstrate a powerful love of the land. It was the view from Taversoe Tuick which led to the cairns' rediscovery in 1898, when Lady Burroughs from nearby Trumland House decided to have a seat placed there, and part of the roof collapsed. Other nearby cairns, such as Blackhammer and Yarso, have equally impressive views; down the hillside

terraced by Ice Age glaciation, across the fertile coastal land where farmers since prehistoric times onwards have had their fields, and out across Eynhallow Sound to the island of Mainland.

Behind the western coast of Rousay another great concentration of remains includes the massive Mid Howe chambered tomb, 105 ft long by 42 ft wide, Mid Howe broch, two unexcavated brochs and a number of other burial mounds and more recent ruins. North from Mid Howe broch, a fine coastal walk leads along the cliffs and over Scabra Head into the wide, deserted Quandale district.

Amid the creaming waters between

Mainland and Rousay, across Eynhallow Sound, lies the uninhabited little island of Eynhallow, a holy island in the days when the Vikings ruled Orkney. The island, it is said, used to sail away sometimes, like the Vikings themselves, but from the shores of Rousay it looks still enough, fixed in the white rush of the tide.

Rousay, Orkney, can be reached from Mainland, Orkney, by passenger ferry from Tingwall, which lies about 13 miles north-west of Kirkwall or 15 miles north-east of Stromness by the A965 and the A966. From Brinyan, the Rousay ferry terminal, the chambered cairns lie between ½ mile and 2 miles west by the B9064.

RITUAL STONES Unearthly power seems to radiate from the Ring of Brogar by Loch of Stenness when a fiery sinking sun inches fingers of shadow across it. Sixty stones more than 7 ft tall made the Bronze Age ring; now 27 remain.

Stenness, Orkney

Around Orkney's two largest lochs, Stenness and Harray on the island of Mainland, there is a tantalising air of mystery – perhaps because in the wide plain which surrounds them, bordered by low hills, there is so little to hold the eye. It is strange, too, to find such great expanses of water enclosed within an island, and not even a distant view of the sea, as if a basic law of geography had suddenly been reversed – an island turned inside out.

The flatness of the land accentuates the flatness of the water; the lochs may be large – they are both about 4 miles long, and in places more than a mile wide – but they are also shallow. It seems a wonder that they are there at all, looking like twin mirages floating on the surface of the plain. The mute swans which grace their waters serve only to heighten the sense of illusion.

Travelling between the lochs – in the south-east only the narrowest strip of land separates them – adds to the air of mystery. Suddenly, eerily elegant standing stones appear in virtually every direction – the Stones of Stenness, the Ring of Brogar as well as many other isolated stones. They are the images of a forgotten people, a forgotten culture, and a forgotten religion. No one can explain the exact meaning or purpose of the stones, but their sombre aspect exactly matches the scenery.

There are many other prehistoric monuments scattered about this strange landscape, some suggesting invocations of the living, others clearly monuments to the dead. The most remarkable is Maeshowe chambered tomb, a green hump in a farmer's field just south-east of the Loch of Harray. Inside, the stonework reveals the building skills of prehistoric people. On the walls the runic graffiti, old Norse script left by the Vikings who first raided the tomb, bring past centuries crashing into the present with extraordinary clarity. One inscription reads, in translation: 'Ingigerd is the best woman of them all.' Another, carved with a Viking axe, says: 'Many a proud woman stooped to enter here.' For a moment the words of the fearsome Vikings speak a language all can understand.

Mainland, Orkney, can be reached by car ferry from Scrabster (near Thurso) to Stromness. There are also passenger flights from Aberdeen and Wick to Kirkwall. The lochs of Stenness and Harray are 4 miles north-east of Stromness by the A965, which follows the southern shore of Loch of Stenness and passes the main stone monuments.

Map ref. Ac Husinish, North Harris

For 17 miles the road to Husinish winds westwards from the head of West Loch Tarbert. It dips and rises and dips again, always narrow, sometimes blind, sometimes with long views ahead. The road passes a salmon leap where Lochan Beag tumbles towards the sea, and turns briefly through the grounds of Amhuinnsuidhe Castle, built by the Earl of Dunmore in 1868. Then suddenly, after passing inland behind a cluster of coastal lochs, the road rises over the crest of a hill and Husinish comes into sight. Below the hill, a flat bed of grassland backs a bay of silver sand, and the sombre colour of the hills gives way to brilliant green.

Husinish is a tiny crofting settlement at the neck of Husinish Point, and on its northern side it looks out across half a mile of tidal strait to the lovely island of Scarp. A century ago more than 200 people lived on the island; today it is completely deserted. In the 1930s it was the scene of a curious experiment in rocket-mail, a potential boon for islanders everywhere devised by a German inventor called Herr Zucker. But Herr Zucker's rocket, bound for the Harris shore, exploded on impact and shredded the mail, and the experiment was deemed a failure.

From the pier opposite Scarp, a beautiful walk leads north-east over the fringe of the hills to the long stretch of sand which lies beyond; by turning inland it is possible to walk over the dunes and through grassland to the lonely Loch na Cleavag. Even

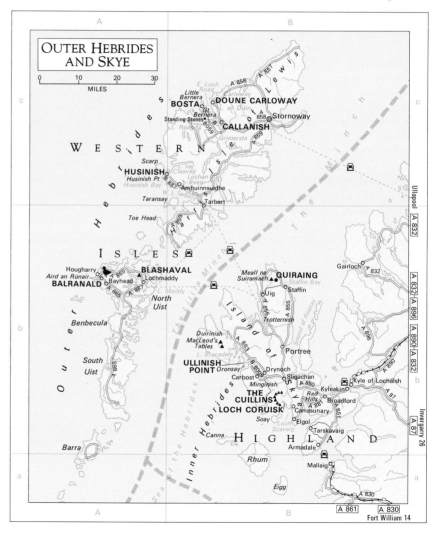

on a wet and windswept day, the loch is exhilarating in its wildness and isolation; and from the high land around it, or from the headland to the north, the view of the mountains north across the sea reveals Lewis in its most naked and desolate grandeur.

Harris can be reached by car ferry from Uig (Skye) to Tarbert. Husinish is about 17 miles north-west of Tarbert along the B887 (narrow with passing places).

Bc   Bosta, Lewis

So often in the islands of the Outer Hebrides there are burial places in the most beautiful locations, whether they are prehistoric cairns or more recent cemeteries; and Bosta on Great Bernera is no exception. Behind a pale, glimmering beach, there is a walled graveyard, serene and quiet and still in use. Below it the sea laps the empty sands, which are sheltered on either side by gentle headlands, and to the west a tiny stream lined with irises in summer tumbles down a softly curving, ice-hewn valley.

To reach Great Bernera, it is necessary to drive across the Atlantic, which is easier than it sounds, for here the ocean becomes a backwater of Loch Roag, and a bridge spans the gap from the shore of Lewis. The road that leads to the island is lonely and remote, running beside the Grimersta river – claimed by many fishermen to be one of the best salmon rivers in Scotland – before turning north among the rock-strewn hills to the coast.

Beyond the standing stones on the far side of the bridge it is lonelier still, as if the stones marked the edge of the known world. The road seems narrower than it was on Lewis, while the island is so fragmented by lochs and inlets from the sea that it is a puzzle how it holds together. But the island survives, and the little, bumpy road keeps going, and soon it comes safely past the last few crofts to the lovely beach at Bosta.

But Great Bernera is not the last of the islands, for Little Bernera lies beyond it, and beyond that lie smaller islands still. From the hills surrounding the beach, the panorama fades into the distance – a vista of hills and sands and a string of islands, untouched and untouchable in the blue-green sea.

Lewis can be reached by car ferry from Ullapool to Stornoway. There are also passenger flights to Stornoway from Inverness. Great Bernera lies about 22 miles west of Stornoway along the A858, B8011 and B8059 roads (narrow with passing places).

Bc   Callanish, Lewis

The standing stones of Callanish are visible from far away, silhouetted against the sky as the road approaches the village. So numerous and elegant are they that they look more like tall, cowled monks who came to admire the view, rather than large stones of unknown origin.

The stones stand just beyond the village of Callanish on a lonely promontory thrusting into East Loch Roag. They stand wide open to the sky, with hills, mountains, water and islands spread around them as if created by a painter's hand. In close up the stones are all shades of grey and pink, delicately streaked and patterned by the immense natural forces which first gave them form. Their power and beauty is unquestionable, like the power and beauty of the landscape which surrounds them. They are

HUSINISH BAY An empty beach of silver sand faces south and is sheltered from the Atlantic by the cliffs of Husinish Point to the west. In the east, a long rocky coastline leads the eye south past Taransay to Toe Head on the horizon.

known to have been quarried locally, and to have been raised some 4,000 years ago. But who raised them, and why, remains uncertain.

The stones are aligned like a Celtic cross, north to south and east to west, around a central circle. The remains of a cairn lie inside the circle. Perhaps this was a burial place or a centre for religious worship. Was the sun the supreme deity, or the moon, or a serpent or a dragon?

Another theory is that the stones were arranged as an astronomical observatory, one of whose purposes was to help maintain a calendar. The cairn at the centre may not have been a cairn at all, but the central observation point for an astronomer-priest.

One thing is certain. The landscape and weather have changed since prehistoric times – the sea-level was lower then, the land was more fertile, there was more sunshine, and there was less rain. Trees probably grew where now there is only peat-bog. So, whoever raised the Callanish stones, and the many other stone circles in the area, had time to spare from the basic struggle for survival. The stones suggest that Lewis in prehistory was a more comfortable land than it is today. In a whisper from long ago they speak of warmth and plenty.

Lewis can be reached by car ferry from Ullapool to Stornoway. There are also passenger flights from Inverness to Stornoway. Callanish lies about 16 miles west of Stornoway, west of the A858 (narrow with passing places).

CLUSTERED TOWERS The Cuillins rise in a jagged semicircle in the Skye distance, a towering mountain kingdom from a fairy-tale. Climbers find firm holds in the hard gabbro rock and stern challenges on the steep peaks.

Bc Doune Carloway, Lewis

In Lewis, people live at the edge of the land, for the interior of the island is an enormous waste of peat-bog, an uninhabitable wilderness half-drowned under hundreds of small, dark lochs. Even beyond the Black Moor, as it is called, there is little ease or comfort in the land – the soil is generally poor and everywhere grey rocks break through the grass as if they, not the grass, were growing. The wonder is not that people live here, but that so many people are able to live here.

The villages are known locally as townships, and Doune Carloway is as quiet, peaceful and pleasing to the eye as any of them. It is tucked away among the low hills south of Loch Carloway, a scattering of old and new buildings perched above the calm waters of Loch an Dùin. Between the hills there are views to other lochs, other hills and the sea. Muted colours back muted colours, fading as they recede into the distance. It is the sort of calm, unchanging place which no outsider would ever see, were it not for the broch which stands behind it.

Doune Carloway Broch is the most famous and best preserved of Lewis's Iron Age forts, built on an easily defended rock with commanding views of the surrounding countryside. Its circular, double walls still stand 30 ft high on the north-western side, with stairs and galleries inside them. It is a superbly evocative relic from some 2,000 years ago, a mysterious fortress in a hidden land, and today it brings outsiders in as once it must have kept them out.

Lewis can be reached by car ferry from Ullapool to Stornoway. There are also passenger flights from Inverness to Storno-

way. Doune Carloway Broch is about 24 miles west of Stornoway by way of the A858 (narrow with passing places).

Bb The Cuillins, Skye

The beauty of the mountains is matched by their danger and their stillness, a stillness that belies the raging of volcanoes and the grinding, destructive work of ice that formed them. They are bare, black and precipitous, but the jagged semicircle of peaks, 20 of them reaching more than 3,000 ft, is the crowning glory of the island. Sometimes they look like crushed velvet roughly folded against the sky; at other times they resemble the Ice Queen's palace; or they may look entirely unreal, like a painted backcloth.

Beside the sharp peaks and angular ridges, the gently rounded, scree-streaked summits of the adjacent Red Hills appear to be melting to the ground. The Cuillins are composed of black gabbro, the Red Hills of younger granites, and the contrast between them demonstrates clearly how different rocks, eroded by the same ice and weather, form different landscapes.

Only mountain climbers or the most determined walkers can see the Cuillins in close-up. Many climbers have made the 'Great Traverse', scaling all 20 major peaks in a single day. But it is distant viewpoints that have made the Cuillins so attractive. From Elgol or Tarskavaig to the south-east, from Sligachan or Carbost to the north, and

PILLARED STRONGHOLD The road through Quiraing's rocks is a mere thread for dwarfs in this landscape of giants – The Table, The Prison and The Needle – shaped by volcanic action and Ice Age glaciers.

from numberless other viewpoints on Skye, the Scottish mainland and other Hebridean islands, the mountains rise majestic against the sky. Their image becomes clear and recognisable, and then fades as the mountains draw clouds down over them like a veil. For Skye is known as the Isle of Mist, and the Cuillins are to blame for it.

Skye can be reached by car ferry from Mallaig to Armadale or from Kyle of Lochalsh to Kyleakin. There are also passenger flights from Inverness to Broadford. The Cuillins can be reached from Sligachan via the A863; turn on to the B8009 just east of Drynoch, and after 2 miles turn south on to a minor road.

Bb   Loch Coruisk, Skye

The rugged peaks of the Cuillins gather around Loch Coruisk as if no one should be allowed to see it; and very few people would, were it not for the little boat that plies across Loch Scavaig from Elgol. But the waters of Loch Scavaig are notoriously windswept, and often the boat cannot sail. The only other approaches require determination and much hard walking: round the shore from Camasunary, or down the glen and over the hills from Sligachan.

When the weather is fine, the 20 minute boat-trip across Loch Scavaig affords incomparable views of the Cuillins, and of the islands of Soay, Canna, Rhum and Eigg. Where the boat ties up at the mouth of the loch, the Scavaig river tumbles across a shallow sill into the sea. A short walk over the massive ice-worn rocks along the riverside leads round to the long, dark waters of Loch Coruisk, penetrating deep into the heart of the mountains.

The scene is a testament to the

SEA LOCH Viewed from the Cuillins of Skye, above the southern tip of Loch Coruisk, the wide blue expanse of Loch Scavaig – here only ruffled by the wind – stretches towards the island of Soay and the Sea of the Hebrides.

might of a retreating glacier, a water-filled trough 1½ miles long, ¼ mile wide and said to be more than 100 ft deep. Its intense silence is disturbed only by gulls and terns circling over the few small islands. The mountains form immense walls around its rock-strewn shores, gaunt and dark except where streams tumble down steep green slopes from higher corries. Loch Coruisk is the secret of the Cuillins, a raw memory of the Ice Age.

Skye can be reached by car ferry from Mallaig to Armadale or from Kyle of Lochalsh to Kyleakin. There are also passenger flights from Inverness to Broadford. Elgol lies about 15 miles south-west of Broadford by way of the A881.

Bb   Quiraing, Skye

The rocks at Quiraing are so dramatic and so spectacular in their setting that afterwards the memory of them seems like an illusion. Their names are simple, and yet they describe so much – Quiraing (the Gaelic for 'pillared stronghold'), The Needle, The Prison, The Table. It was a place which Victorian travellers never failed to visit, so well did it suit their taste for grandeur.

The easiest approach to the rocks is from the hill road between Uig and Staffin, following the footpath which starts above the steep, hairpin bend. The hillside falls away sharply below the path, and there are sweeping views

to the south and east. Above the path tower dark, inland cliffs, which extended much further east before the end of the last Ice Age. Quiraing and the landscape around it are the tumbled result of landslips – the slow, downward slide of layers of volcanic rock once held stable by the ice sheet.

At the end of the path, to the right, The Prison rises steeply, a brooding, castellated crag. To the left The Needle soars 120 ft into the sky, standing sentinel over the narrow gully which climbs towards The Table. This is the hardest part of the walk, a rough scramble past The Needle into the amphitheatre above, carpeted with grass and enclosed by shattered walls of rock. A final climb leads to The Table, where a platform of grass is said to be large enough to hold 4,000 head of cattle. Silent and private, The Table stands in its hall of rock. The views through the cleft windows sweep far out over coast and sea to the distant mountains of Scotland – views too wild and lovely to forget.

Skye can be reached by car ferry from Mallaig to Armadale or from Kyle of Lochalsh to Kyleakin. There are also passenger flights from Inverness to Broadford. Uig is 43 miles north-west of Broadford via the A850 and A856.

Bb   Ullinish Point, Skye

The best time to visit Ullinish Point is late on a summer evening, when the sun is setting over the twin, flat-topped hills known as MacLeod's Tables. When the tide is low it is possible to walk beyond the point, across the rocks and sand to the emerald-green islet of Oronsay. It will almost certainly be empty, except for a few sheep and birds, and silent except for the sounds of the sea. From here and from the point, only the last rays of sunlight crowd in, along with the views – Loch Bracadale and its scattering of islands, the wild peninsula of Duirinish, and the Cuillins and the Red Hills behind Minginish. As the sun sinks down behind MacLeod's Tables, the sky behind the Red Hills sometimes picks up the reflection of the last rays. For one moment the light seems to promise the impossible – sunset and sunrise with no night between.

MacLeod's Tables, like much of the Skye landscape, are relics from the savage volcanic eruptions which tore open this land some 70 million years ago; and the story told about them, if true, is an apt tribute to their splendour. In the 16th century Alasdair Crotach, the seventh chief of the Mac-Leods, was said to have been provoked, while visiting Edinburgh, with the taunt that Skye was a primitive place, with nowhere to banquet as fine as Holyrood Palace. He invited the scornful one back to Skye, and arranged for a magnificent feast to be laid out on the larger of the two hills, lit by scores of his clansmen bearing flaming torches. 'This is a roof grander than was ever made by human hands,' he is alleged to have remarked, standing under the starlit sky, 'And this table, you must confess, is more commodious than any that can be shown even in the royal court.' Looking across Loch Bracadale from Ullinish Point, it is easy to agree with him.

Skye can be reached by car ferry from Mallaig to Armadale and from Kyle of Lochalsh to Kyleakin. There are also passenger flights from Inverness to Broadford. Ullinish Point is about 32 miles north-west of Broadford by road, 1 mile west along a minor road off the A863.

Ab Balranald, North Uist

Behind Hougharry cemetery, the remote burial place of John Maccodrum, a famous 18th-century Uist bard, the land lies low, flat and wet – a rare example of undrained machair grassland. Looking down from the bard's grave, or south from the road to Hougharry, it is clear that the marsh

SWIFT AND STREAMLINED

Scotland's western isles are one of the last strongholds in Britain of the otter. It has disappeared from many parts because of river pollution and human encroachment on its habitat. About 4 ft long from nose to tail tip, otters are fast and skilful hunters on land or in water – lochs, rivers or the sea. They are also playful, and families keep in contact with a whistling call. By day, otters lay up in a tree hole, burrow or similar cavity. Their diet includes fish such as sea trout, which breed in fresh water in autumn and winter, then migrate to the sea.

Otter
(Lutra lutra)

Sea trout
(Salmo trutta)

and its shallow waters, rich with aquatic vegetation, are spectacular places for bird-watching. Coots and moorhens move slowly among the many species of wildfowl, including mallards, gadwalls, tufted ducks, teal and shovellers. Dabchicks, like dark flecks on the water, vanish suddenly from view as they dive for food. In the wet pasture there are lapwings, redshanks and other waders; and occasionally a bird of prey sweeps by, solitary and menacing, a hen-harrier perhaps, or a merlin, a short-eared owl or even a peregrine.

The delights of Balranald Nature Reserve are not confined to the birds of the marshland. The reserve also includes long stretches of beach, the rocky headland of Aird an Rùnair, and a large expanse of cultivated machair. In spring and autumn the beaches attract huge flocks of dunlins, ringed plovers and other migrant waders, while meadow pipits, curlews, golden plovers and greylag geese are among the many species which descend on the cornfields around harvest time. There are colonies of Arctic terns among the breeding species on the headland. The birds defend their territories by ferociously mobbing anyone who comes too near, so it is best to stay well away; also, predators are always waiting to snap up the eggs or young when the adults leave them to mob intruders.

Even in the still of a summer's night, birds still proclaim Balranald's charm. Sometimes from far away on the grassland, sometimes from a nearby hiding place, the rarely seen corncrake rasps out its song – a double croak that sounds like the incessant ringing of a telephone.

Balranald Nature Reserve is maintained by the Royal Society for the

Protection of Birds, and is open from April to August. Visitors should contact the Warden at Druim dhu Paiblesgarry, Bayhead.

North Uist can be reached by car ferry from Uig (Skye) to Lochmaddy. There are also passenger flights from Glasgow to Benbecula. Balranald is about 15 miles west of Lochmaddy via the A867 and A865 (both narrow with passing places).

Ab Blashaval, North Uist

An immense labyrinth of rock and water spreads in every direction at the foot of Blashaval, a hill which rises to 358 ft on the eastern side of North Uist in the Outer Hebrides. From its summit can be seen Loch Maddy, to the east, an inlet so strewn with little islands that it is estimated to have more than 70 miles of shore to every mile of its length. To the south and west the inland moor is so waterlogged that it is almost impossible to tell where one loch ends and the next begins – the lochs are every shape and size and far too numerous to count.

Blashaval is the first hill on the road north from Lochmaddy. Three standing stones on the north-west slope are, according to one tradition, the gravestones of three spies who were buried alive, but according to another they are the petrified bodies of three men from Skye who deserted their wives. White tufts of bog cotton rise above the heather, and the flowers on the hill include tormentil, milkwort and lousewort. Skylarks nest on the ground, or climb singing into the sky. Blashaval is small by comparison with the distant mountains of Harris to the north, and Skye to the east. But it is a simple, unbothered place, and a perfect vantage point from which to survey the half-drowned wilderness around it.

North Uist can be reached by car ferry from Uig (Skye) to Lochmaddy; Blashaval is about 2 miles north-west of Lochmaddy along the A865 (narrow with passing places). There are also flights from Glasgow to Benbecula airport, about 20 miles south-west of Lochmaddy by road.

Esha Ness, Shetland

From the unmanned lighthouse at Esha Ness, grassland rolls gently eastwards behind some of Shetland's most breathtaking cliff scenery. Here, at the meeting place of rock and ocean, the never-ending conflict between the two has created a superb spectacle of exhilarating power.

Just north of the lighthouse, the

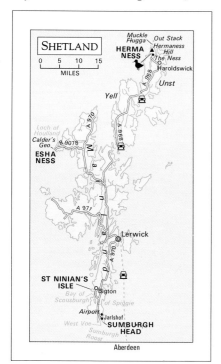

Atlantic has gouged the deep cleft of Calder's Geo from the dark, volcanic rock; further on, the rock becomes more shattered still, sculpted and eroded into thousands of dramatic shapes. It is a place to stop and wonder for a while, a wild frontier inhabited only by seals and sea-birds. Its profile on a fine summer's day conjures dreams of the mighty storms which shaped it, raging through the long darkness of winter.

Inland the scenery is more gentle, as if nature had exhausted itself on the battleground of the cliffs. The grassland runs by two small lochs, whose mysterious waters are quiet and still in comparison with the savage power of the ocean. Perhaps it was here that the water-horse lived, a malicious Shetland spirit which drowned anyone who tried to ride it. Or perhaps it was in the Loch of Houlland, which lies slightly further back from the shore. There is a ruined broch on the seaward bank, and a little sheep-grazed island which provides a breeding ground for a small colony of terns.

Between the loch and the sea lies the sinister Holes of Scraada, a sudden, sheer-sided gash in the land, fed by a stream from the loch and connected to the sea by a dark, subterranean tunnel. It is the sound more than the sight of the Holes of Scraada which stirs the imagination, as the Atlantic growls and grumbles up the tunnel, echoing liquid menace as the sea spills out into the open.

Mainland, Shetland, can be reached by car ferry from Aberdeen to Lerwick or by passenger flight from Aberdeen to Sumburgh. Esha Ness is about 35 miles north-west of Lerwick along the A970 and then the B9078 westwards (narrow with passing places).

BRITAIN'S NORTHERN EDGE Herma Ness rises from wild waters that extend unbroken by land until Siberia – in another continent beyond the North Pole's ice cap. Below the cliffs countless sea-birds squabble and fight for fish.

Herma Ness, Shetland

This is the ragged, northernmost tip of Britain – further north than Leningrad or Labrador, and on the same latitude as Cape Farewell in Greenland and the Kenai Peninsula in Alaska. In the summer sky, wild aerial battles take place between the great skuas, known locally as bonxies, and the gannets which throng the rock stacks and skerries. The gannets dive for fish, plunging into the sea from heights of 100 ft or more; the piratical skuas harry them to steal their catch. The other sea-birds which breed around the cliffs – the tens of thousands of puffins on the grassy slopes, the kittiwakes, guillemots, fulmars and shags – must protect their eggs and young from the bonxies,

which sometimes also strike down adult birds in flight.

Even visitors to the Hermaness National Nature Reserve are not spared the bonxies' ferocity. It takes about an hour to walk north from The Ness through the rough moorland to the top of Hermaness Hill, and down the steep grassy slopes to the cliffs; but under attack from the bonxies, which swoop down again and again in defence of their territory, it may take considerably longer. Many comments in the visitors' book in the shelter on the hill bear witness to the fact that it has never been easy to reach the top of Britain, whether because of the bonxies, or the wind, or a sudden mist, or just the climb through the heather and among the peat hags, or bogs. But the comments also confirm that the walk is well worth the trouble – partly for a close look at the bonxies, but also for the wild cliffs, and for the view. It reaches across the tide-race to the lighthouse on Muckle Flugga, and to Out Stack beyond it – the final fragment of Britain, a tiny island of rock defiantly angled against the storming of the sea.

Unst, Shetland, can be reached by passenger flight from Aberdeen via Sumburgh, Lerwick and Yell. There are also car ferries from Aberdeen to Lerwick, and inter-island boat and bus services from Lerwick. The Ness is about 3 miles northwest of Haroldswick, Unst, along the B9086 (narrow with passing places) and then along a minor road.

St Ninian's Isle, Shetland

Above the still, wide waters of the Loch of Spiggie and the beautiful sandy beach which sweeps round the southern shore of the Bay of Scousburgh, a narrow road runs north to the village of Bigton, through one of the most fertile areas of Shetland, rich, green crofting land sandwiched between moorland hills and the Atlantic. West of Bigton lies one of the scenic wonders of Shetland – St Ninian's Isle, uninhabited except by sheep, a few cattle, and a multitude of rabbits and birds. In fact it is not an island, for a narrow isthmus of sand links it to the mainland. Geographers call this double-edged beach a tombolo; locally it is known as an ayre. There are many other ayres in Shetland, a result of the rise in the sea-level since the last Ice Age and the drowning of the land. But of all the ayres, this one is the most beautiful, sweeping inwards in graceful curves of white sand set against the emerald-green

grass on either shore, and providing a path across the sea.

It is said that the Christian missionary St Ninian founded a chapel on the grassy slopes of the island in the 5th century AD, long before St Columba arrived in Iona. Apart from a stone wall across the centre of the island, the only signs of human presence are the foundations of a 12th-century chapel just above the isthmus, but excavation of the site in the 1950s revealed that the tradition about St Ninian might not be so far from the truth. The remains of a pre-Norse church were discovered, as well as a Bronze Age burial ground. But the greatest discovery was still to come; under a stone slab in the nave of the ruined chapel, a priceless treasure was found – a hoard of 8th-century Celtic silverware. It is not certain who buried the treasure, but one theory suggests that it was St Ninian's monks, threatened and perhaps wiped out by Viking raiders. Their treasure, like their treasure island, survived the centuries intact, and can now be seen in the National Museum of Antiquities in Edinburgh.

Mainland, Shetland, can be reached by car ferry from Aberdeen to Lerwick or by passenger flight from Aberdeen to Sumburgh. St Ninian's Isle lies about 14 miles south of Lerwick and 8 miles north of Sumburgh; it can be reached from Bigton, just off the B9122 (narrow with passing places).

Sumburgh Head, Shetland

The sheer cliffs and steeply banked hill of Sumburgh Head are the first view of Shetland, 25 miles north of the rocky, lonely island of Fair Isle and some 50 miles north-east of Orkney. By air the journey from Orkney takes barely half

SHARED ACCOMMODATION

Gannets are more numerous in the Scottish Islands than anywhere else in the world. They nest in raucous colonies on cliff ledges, each pair only just out of pecking range of the next, and jab with open beaks at any intruder. They drift and hang over the sea as they hunt for fish, then dive swiftly for the catch. The bullying great skuas, or bonxies – seen mostly in the Shetlands – often force other birds to disgorge their fish. Eiders feed mainly on blue mussels, and nest near the shore among rocks or heather. Their downy nest lining is collected for stuffing quilts and clothing.

Great skua
(Stercorarius skua)

Gannet
(Sula bassana)

Eider
(Somateria mollissima)

an hour: the plane dips and wheels over the headland, and there, tucked in behind it, is Sumburgh Airport. The runway extends from the shore of the North Sea to the shore of the Atlantic, on a narrow neck of flat land, one of Shetland's greatest rarities.

Since the oil bonanza began, the airport has become increasingly busy with traffic, and little of Shetland's sense of isolation remains here. But it takes only a few minutes to drive back to the headland, a short journey from modern civilisation to natural wilderness. In summer the wild cliffs below the lighthouse are thronged with nesting guillemots, razorbills, kittiwakes and other sea-birds; in spring and autumn, migrating birds in their thousands make a landfall on this hospitable headland.

Grey seals bask among the rocks, or cruise about in the water; while in the fierce tide-race of Sumburgh Roost, in the foreground of the view towards Fair Isle, there is always a chance of seeing dolphins, or even killer whales.

At the foot of Sumburgh Head, on the shore of West Voe, it is possible to step from the wilderness back through time, at the extraordinary archaeological site of Jarlshof. Here the bones of more than 4,000 years of Shetland history are laid bare in the sand, from the remains of Stone Age, Bronze Age, and Iron Age settlements, through Viking and medieval farmsteads, to the ruined 16th-century 'Laird's House', which Sir Walter Scott first christened Jarlshof. The stones jostle together in an eloquent collage of history.

Mainland, Shetland, can be reached by car ferry from Aberdeen to Lerwick or by passenger flight from Aberdeen to Sumburgh. Jarlshof and Sumburgh Head lie south of the airport along minor roads.

INDEX

Entries and page numbers in **bold** type identify main areas and features; page numbers alone in **bold** type indicate gazetteer entries. Page numbers in *italics* denote illustrations.

A

Index of plant and animal features

A

Adder 69
Alpine gentian 358
Alpine lady's mantle 213
Angular Solomon's seal 184
Annual rock-rose 310
Avocet 106

B

Bar-tailed godwit 124
Bearberry 392
Bee orchid 134
Bilberry 200
Bittersweet 325
Blackberry 154
Blackcap 45
Black grouse 378
Black poplar 131
Bloody cranesbill 25
Bluebell 51
Bogbean 351
Bog myrtle 351
Buck's-horn plantain 276
Burnet rose 241
Burnet saxifrage 134
Butcher's broom 270
Butterbur 343

C

Candytuft 172
Capercaillie 378
Carline thistle 152
Chalkhill blue butterfly 71
Cheddar pink 150
Cliff spurrey 276
Cloudberry 378
Common dog violet 36
Common sandpiper 209
Cormorant 308
Cornish heath 25
Cowberry 392
Crossbill 124
Cross-leaved heath 207
Crosswort 112
Crowberry 358
Curlew 183

D

Dark green fritillary butterfly 36
Dark red helleborine 184
Dartford warbler 63
Devil's-bit scabious 161
Dipper 217
Dorset heath 66
Dunlin 230
Dunnock 295

E

Eider 409

F

False brome grass 23
Field maple 112
Field poppy 112
Firecrest 82
Fulmar 194

G

Gannet 409
Garganey 124
Giant bellflower 237
Goldcrest 258
Golden eagle 386
Goldeneye 338
Golden plover 194
Goosander 248
Grass-of-Parnassus 213
Grass snake 69
Greater spearwort 260
Great skua 409
Great spotted woodpecker 318
Great wood-rush 51
Greylag goose 338
Grey seal 243
Grizzled skipper butterfly 56
Guillemot 277

H

Harebell 343
Heath spotted orchid 36
Hen harrier 353
Herring gull 277
Hoary plantain 134
Hobby 82

Honey buzzard 82
Hoopoe 89
Horseshoe vetch 71
Hottentot-fig 25

I

Italian lords and ladies 25

J

Jacob's ladder 237

K

Kestrel 58
Kingfisher 318
Kittiwake 308
Knapweed 166
Knot 124

L

Lapwing 113
Large skipper butterfly 23
Lesser black-backed gull 277
Linnet 82
Little tern 124
Lizard, Common 69
Lizard, Sand 69

M

Maidenhair fern 25
Manx shearwater 277
Marsh fritillary butterfly 161
Marsh frog 95
Marsh-marigold 343
May lily 200
Meadow thistle 260
Melancholy thistle 241
Merlin 183
Milk parsley 122
Monkeyflower 241
Montagu's harrier 18
Mossy saxifrage 302

N

Narrow-leaved lungwort 78
New Forest pony 82
Nightingale 89
Northern eggar moth 378
Nottingham catchfly 237

O

Oak, Pedunculate 93
Opposite-leaved golden
    saxifrage 51
Osprey 378
Otter 407
Oystercatcher 267

P

Pasque flower 140
Peacock butterfly 166
Peregrine falcon 386
Perennial centaury 276
Perforate St John's-wort 315
Ptarmigan 363
Puffin 277
Purple emperor butterfly 93

R

Raven 295
Razorbill 18
Red campion 207
Red grouse 386
Red kite 258
Red-legged partridge 113
Redpoll 194
Redwing 386
Reed warbler 113
Ringlet butterfly 154
Ring ouzel 217
Round-leaved sundew 78

S

Sand martin 124
Sandpiper, Common 209
Scottish dock 351
Scottish lupin 358
Sea bindweed 310
Sea buckthorn 112
Sea campion 107
Sea holly 310
Sea sandwort 107
Sea trout 407
Shag 277
Sheep's fescue 93
Silver-spotted skipper 93
Siskin 338
Skylark 133
Slow worm 69
Small tortoiseshell butterfly 152
Snake, Grass 69

Snake, Smooth 69
Snipe 290
Snow bunting 363
Soft-leaved rose 343
Sparrowhawk 45
Spotted flycatcher 82
Spring squill 241
Stinking iris 51
Stone bramble 207
Stonechat 32
Stone curlew 124
Swallowtail butterfly 122

T

Thrift 276
Tintern spurge 315
Tormentil 36
Treecreeper 147
Tree pipit 89
Turnstone 18
Twite 230

V

Violet, Common dog 36
Viper's bugloss 107

W

Water avens 260
Water horsetail 78
Welsh poppy 302
Western gorse 36
Whinchat 209
Wildcat 390
Wild strawberry 56
Willow warbler 209
Woodcock 217
Woodlark 18
Wood mellick 302
Wood warbler 32
Woolly thistle 140
Wryneck 89

Y

Yellow archangel 140
Yellow horned poppy 107
Yellow-necked mouse 291
Yellow pimpernel 325
Yellow wagtail 328
Yew 96

ACKNOWLEDGMENTS

The publishers express their thanks to the following people and organisations for their help in the preparation of this book:

British Tourist Authority; Countryside Commission; County Nature Conservation Trusts throughout Britain; English Tourist Board; Forestry Commission; J. M. Mullin, B.Sc.; the various National Park officers; The National Trust; The National Trust for Scotland; Nature Conservancy Council; J. R. Press, B.Sc.; Royal Society for Nature Conservation; Scottish Tourist Board; Welsh Tourist Board.

The illustrations in this book were provided by the following artists, photographers and agencies.

Except where stated, credits read from left to right down the page. Work commissioned by Reader's Digest is shown in *italics*:

1 *Jon Wyand*: **2–3** *Trevor Wood*: **4–5, 6–7, 9** *Michael Freeman*: **10** Neville Fox-Davies: **13–15** *Patrick Thurston*: **16** Neville Fox-Davies: **17** *Patrick Thurston*: **18** artists *Norman Arlott*: *Trevor Boyer*: *Trevor Boyer*: *Ken Wood*: **19–22** *Patrick Thurston*: **23** artist *Jill Tomblin*: **24** *Patrick Thurston*: **25** artists, top two *Colin Emberson*: centre *Wendy Brammal*: bottom two *Colin Emberson*: **26** *Jon Wyand*: **27** artist *Ivan Lapper*: **28–31** *Malcolm Aird*: **32** artist *Norman Arlott*: **33–35** *Malcolm Aird*: **36** artists, top left *Jill Tomblin*: top right *Ann Savage*: centre right *Stuart Lafford*: bottom right *Brenda Katte*: **37** *Malcolm Aird*: **38** *Paul Wakefield*: **41** West Air Photography: **42** The National Trust: **43** artist *Ivan Lapper*: **44–45** *Paul Wakefield*: **45** artists *Norman Arlott*: *Ken Wood*: **46** *John Robert Young*: **47** Mike Williams/Sefton Photo Library, Manchester: **48** artist *Ivan Lapper*: **49** artist *Richard Bonson*: Richard Jemmett: **50** *John Robert Young*: **51** artists, top two *Helen Senior*: centre right *Stuart Lafford*: bottom *Paul Wrigley*: **52** Jorge Lewinski: **55** *Malcolm Aird*: **56** artists, left *Ivan Lapper*: right *Jill Tomblin*: **57** *Malcolm Aird*: **58** artists, left *Ken Wood*: right *Richard Bonson*: **59** *Malcolm Aird*: **60** John Sims/Vision International: **63** *Nigel Cassidy*: artist *Norman Arlott*: **64** artist *Ivan Lapper*: **65** Jorge Lewinski: **66** artist *Colin Emberson*: **67** *Nigel Cassidy*: **68** artist *Richard Bonson*: **69** artists, left *Denis Ovenden*: right *Ivan Lapper*: **70** *Nigel Cassidy*: **71** artist *Jill Tomblin*: Robin Fletcher/Vision International: **73** John Bethell Photography: *Patrick Thurston*: *Michael Taylor*: *Patrick Thurston*: artist *Ivan Lapper*: **74** Robin Fletcher/Vision International: **77–78** *John Sims*: **78** artist *Wendy Brammal*: **79** Geoff Doré/Bruce Coleman Ltd: **80** *John Sims*: **81** artist *Brian Delf*: **82** Jane Burton/Bruce Coleman Ltd: artists, top three *Ken Wood*: bottom two *Norman Arlott*: **83** *John Sims*: **84** Jorge Lewinski: **84–85** Robin Fletcher/Vision International: **85** Jorge Lewinski: Robin Fletcher/Vision International: **86** *Patrick Thurston*: **89** artists, top right *Robert Morton*: top left *Norman Arlott*: *Denis Ovenden*: *Robert Morton*: **90** S. & O. Mathews: **91** Eric Crichton/Bruce Coleman Ltd: **92** *John Robert Young*: **93** artist *Jill Tomblin*: **95** artists, left *Linden Artists*: right *Ivan Lapper*: **96** artist *David Salariya*: **97** artist *Ivan Lapper*: **99** *Patrick Thurston*: John Bethell Photography: *Malcolm Aird*: **100** *Paul Wakefield*: **103–5** *Michael Freeman*: **106** artists, left *Robert Morton*: right *Jim Russell*: **107** artists, top left *Stuart Lafford*: top right *Helen Coucher*: bottom left *Josiane Campan*: bottom right *Wendy Brammal*: **108** Malcolm Aird: **111** *Martyn Adelman*: **112** artists *Shirley Felts*: *Ann Savage*: bottom left *Brenda Katte*: right *Helen Coucher*: **113** artists *Tim Hayward*: *Trevor Boyer*: *Norman Arlott*: **114** artist *Richard Bonson*: **115** *Martyn Adelman*: **116** *Paul Wakefield*: **119** *Michael Freeman*: I. Beames/Ardea, London: **120** *Michael Freeman*: **121** Eric Crichton/Bruce Coleman Ltd: **122** artist *Jill Tomblin*: **123** artist *Ivan Lapper*: **124** artists *Trevor Boyer*: *Trevor Boyer*: *Robert Morton*: *Robert Morton*: *John Francis*: bottom two *Robert Morton*: **125** *Nigel Cassidy*: **127** *Malcolm Aird*: artist *Ivan Lapper*: John Bethell Photography: **128** *Trevor Wood*: **131** artist *Brian Delf*: **132** *Trevor Wood*: **133** artist *Norman Arlott*: *Trevor Wood*: **134** artists, top *John Rignall*: left *Colin Emberson*: right *Sarah Fox-Davies*: **135** *Trevor Wood*: **136** *Paul Wakefield*: **139** *Trevor Wood*: **140** artists, left *Wendy Brammal*: right *Victoria Goman*: bottom *Brenda Katte*: **141** *Trevor Wood*: **142** Pictor International: **143–5** *Trevor Wood*: **146** Jorge Lewinski: **147** artist *Ken Wood*: **148** *John Sims*: **150** artist *Victoria Goman*: **151–2** *John Sims*: **152** artist *Jill Tomblin*: **153** *John Sims*: **154** *Patrick Thurston*: artist *Jill Tomblin*: **155** artist *Ivan Lapper*: **156** *Patrick Thurston*: **159** Steve Herr/Vision International: **160** artist *Ivan Lapper*: **161** artist *Jill Tomblin*: **162** Pictor International: **163** artist *Jim Russell*: **165–6** *Patrick Thurston*: **166** artist *Jill Tomblin*: **167** artist *Ivan Lapper*: **168** *Patrick Thurston*: **171** S. & O. Mathews: **172** artist *Wendy Brammal*: **173** artist *Jim Russell*: **174–5** *Nigel Cassidy*: **177** artist *Ivan Lapper*: inset, photo Howard Moore/Woodmansterne: Brian Seed/Aspect Picture Library: **178–83** *Michael Freeman*: **183** artists *Ken Wood*: *Robert Morton*: **184** Peter Wrigley/Vision International: artists *Line Mailhe*: others *Wendy Brammal*: **185–6** *Michael Freeman*: **187** artist *Ivan Lapper*: **188** artist *Richard Bonson*: **189–90** *Michael Freeman*: **193** artist *Ivan Lapper*: **194** artists *Trevor Boyer*: *Ken Wood*: *Trevor Boyer*: **195–8** *Michael Freeman*: **199** artist *Richard Bonson*: **200** *Michael Freeman*: **201** artists *Marie-Claire Nivoix*: *John Rignall*: **202–6** *Trevor Wood*: **207** artists, top two *Stuart Lafford*: *Marjory Saynor*: **208** *Trevor Wood*: **209** artists *Norman Arlott*: *Norman Arlott*: *John Francis*: **210** *Jon Wyand*: **213** artists *Stuart Lafford*: *Paul Wrigley*: **215–16** *John Wyand*: **217** artists *Tim Hayward*: others *Norman Arlott*: **218–25** *Jon Wyand*: **226** Derek Widdicombe: **229** artist *Ivan Lapper*: **230** artist *Trevor Boyer*: others *Ken Wood*: **230–6** *John Robert Young*: **237** artists *Helen Coucher*: others *John Rignall*: **238** *John Robert Young*: **241** artists *Helen Senior*: *Stuart Lafford*: *Helen Senior*: *Robert Hughes*: **242** *Patrick Thurston*: **243** artist *Graham Allen/Linden Artists*: **244–5** *John Robert Young*: **246** Geoff Doré/Bruce Coleman Ltd: **247** Jorge Lewinski: **248** artist *Robert Morton*: **249** artist *Ivan Lapper*: **251** artist *Ivan Lapper*: right Clive Coote: left Michael Ware: **252** Paul Wakefield: **255** Paul Wakefield: Colin Molyneux: **256** artist *Richard Bonson*: **257** *Colin Molyneux*: **258** artists *Ken Wood*: *Norman Arlott*: **259** Paul Wakefield: **260** artists *Wendy Brammal*: *Victoria Goman*: *Stuart Lafford*: **261–2** *Colin Molyneux*: **264** *Michael Freeman*: **267** artist *John Francis*: **268–9** *Michael Freeman*: **270** artist *Stuart Lafford*: **271** Colin Molyneux: Paul Wakefield/Bruce Coleman Ltd: **272–5** *Colin Molyneux*: **276** artists, top *Brenda Katte*: *John Rignall*: *Shirley Hooper*: *John Rignall*: **277** artists, centre far right *Tim Hayward*: others *Trevor Boyer*: **278** *Colin Molyneux*: **279** Gordon Langsbury/Bruce Coleman Ltd: **280–1** *Colin Molyneux*: **282** Bob Gibbons/Ardea, London: **283** *Colin Molyneux*: **284–8** Colin Molyneux: **289** Paul Wakefield: **290** artists, left *Tim Hayward*: right *Ivan Lapper*: **291** *John Robert Young*: artist *Graham Allen/Linden Artists*: **292** Paul Wakefield: **295** artists *Peter Barrett*: *Norman Arlott*: **296–9** Paul Wakefield: **300–1** Robert Eames: **302** artists *Marie-Claire Nivoix*: *Helen Coucher*: **302** artist *Paul Wrigley*: **303** Robert Eames: **304–8** *Robert Eames*: **308** artists *Tim Hayward*: *Trevor Boyer*: **309** Robert Eames: **310** *Robert Eames*: artists *John Rignall*: *Roger Hughes*: *Frankie Coventry*: **311** *Robert Eames*: *Colin Molyneux*: **312** *John Robert Young*: **315** artists, top right *Ivan Lapper*: *Paul Wrigley*: *John Rignall*: **317** *John Robert Young*: **318** artists *Robert Morton*: *Peter Barrett*: **319** *John Robert Young*: **320** Christina Gascoigne/Robert Harding Assoc: **323** *Patrick Thurston*: **324** *John Robert Young*: **325** artists *Barbara Walker*: *Line Mailhe*: **326** *Patrick Thurston*: **327** artist *Ivan Lapper*: **328** artist *Denis Ovenden*: **329** artist *Ivan Lapper*: **331** *Clive Coote*: artist *Ivan Lapper*: **332** *Jon Wyand*: **335** artist *Ivan Lapper*: **336** *Jon Wyand*: **337** Scottish Tourist Board: S. & O. Mathews: **338** artists *Robert Morton*: *Stephen Adams*: *Ken Wood*: **339–42** *Jon Wyand*: **343** artists *John Rignall*: *Sarah Fox-Davies*: *Stephanie Harrison*: *Maurice Esperance*: **344** *Michael Freeman*: **347** *Patrick Thurston*: **349** Derek Widdicombe: **350** artist *Ivan Lapper*: **351** artists *John Rignall*: *Guy Michel*: *Marjory Saynor*: **352** *Patrick Thurston*: **353** artist *Ken Wood*: **354–6** *Michael Freeman*: **358** artists, top *Victoria Goman*: *Wendy Brammal*: *Shirley Hooper*: **361** *Michael Freeman*: **362** artist *Richard Bonson*: **363** artists *Robert Morton*: *Tim Hayward*: **364–5** *Michael Freeman*: **366** artist *Ivan Lapper*: **367–76** *Michael Freeman*: **377** *Patrick Thurston*: **378** artists, far right *Jill Tomblin*: *Tim Hayward*: *Tim Hayward*: *Ken Wood*: **379** *Michael Freeman*: **380** Neville Fox-Davies: **383–5** *Michael Freeman*: **386** artists *Ken Wood*: *Tim Hayward*: *Ken Wood*: *Ken Wood*: **387–9** *Michael Freeman*: **390** artist *Graham Allen/Linden Artists*: **391** *Michael Freeman*: **392** artists *Marie-Claire Nivoix*: *Wendy Brammal*: **393** Neville Fox-Davies: **394–400** *Michael Freeman*: **401** Adam Woolfitt/Susan Griggs Agency: **403** Photo Library International, Leeds: **404–6** *Michael Freeman*: **407** artist *Graham Allen/Linden Artists*: **408** A. & E. Bomford/Ardea, London: **409** artists, top two *Trevor Boyer*: *Tim Hayward*: *Robert Morton*.

The publishers also acknowledge their indebtedness to the authors and publishers of the following works which were consulted for reference:

Along the Chiltern Ways G. R. Crosher (Cassell); *Archaeological Sites of Britain* P. Clayton (Weidenfeld and Nicolson); *Archaeology of the Industrial Revolution* B. Bracegirdle (Heinemann); *Around the Lizard* (Tor Mark Press); *The Atlas of British Breeding Birds in Britain and Ireland* J. T. R. Sharrock (T. and A. D. Poyser); *Atlas of the British Flora* F. H. Perring and S. M. Walters (Nelson and Sons Ltd); *Bedgebury Pinetum and Forest Plots* Forestry Commission (HMSO); *Berkshire* I. Yarrow (Robert Hale); *Blue Guide to England* (Ernest Benn Ltd); *Blue Guide to Scotland* (Ernest Benn Ltd); *Blue Guide to Wales* (Ernest Benn Ltd); *Border Guide* Forestry Commission (HMSO); *Bowland and Pendle Hill* W. R. Mitchell (Dalesman Books); *BP Handbook of Industrial Archaeology* N. Cossons (David and Charles); *Brecon Beacons National Park* Countryside Commission (HMSO); *Bristol and Gloucester District – British Regional Geology* (HMSO); *Britain in the Roman Empire* J. Liversedge (Routledge and Kegan Paul); *Britain's Green Mantle* A. G. Tansley (Allen and Unwin); *Britain's Structure and Scenery* Sir Dudley Stamp (Collins); *The British Amphibians and Reptiles* M. Smith (Collins); *British Battlefields* P. Warner (Osprey); *British Castles* (National Trust) P. Johnson (Weidenfeld and Nicolson); *British Poisonous Plants* A. A. Forsyth (HMSO); *The Broads* E. A. Ellis (Collins); *Butterfly Book for the Pocket* E. Samdars (OUP); *Cambrian Forests* Forestry Commission (HMSO); *Canals and Rivers of Britain* A. Darwin (Dent); *Castles of Britain* B. Gascoigne (Thames and Hudson); *Central England District – British Regional Geology* (HMSO); *The Changing Face of Britain* E. Hyams (Granada Publishing); *The Cinque Ports and Romney Marsh* M. Brentnall (John Gifford Ltd); *The Cleveland Way* A. Falconer (HMSO); *The Coast of North East England* J. Seymour (Collins); *Coming Down the Wye* R. Gibbings (Dent); *Cornish Shipwrecks* R. Larn and C. Carter (David and Charles); *Cornish Villages* D. R. Rowe (Robert Hale); *Cornwall Coast Path* E. C. Pyatt (HMSO); *Cornwall's Atlantic Coast* (Tor Mark Press); *Cornwall's Old Mines* H. V. Williams (Tor Mark Press); *Dartmoor* L. A. Harvey and D. St Leger-Gordon (Collins); *Dartmoor National Park* Countryside Commission (HMSO); *Derbyshire (Buildings of England)* N. Pevsner (Penguin); *Devon and Cornwall* D. Kay-Robinson (Bartholomew); *Domesday Geography of Eastern England* H. C. Darby (Cambridge University Press); *Dorset Coast Path* B. Jackman (HMSO); *The Drovers' Roads of Wales* F. Godwin and S. Toulson (Wildwood House); *East Anglia – British Regional Geology* (HMSO); *East Anglian Forests* Forestry Commission (HMSO); *East Yorkshire and Lincolnshire – British Regional Geology* (HMSO); *The Englishman's Flora* G. Grigson (Phoenix House); *Exmoor National Park* Countryside Commission (HMSO); *Explore the New Forest* Forestry Commission (HMSO); *Field Guide to Archaeology in Britain* E. S. Wood (Collins); *Flora of the British Isles* Clapham, Tutin and Warburg (Cambridge University Press); *Flowers of the Coast* I. Hepburn (Collins); *Galloway Forest Park* Forestry Commission (HMSO); *Geology and Scenery in England and Wales* A. E. Trueman (Pelican); *Glasgow* J. M. Reid (Batsford); *Grampian Highlands – British Regional Geology* (HMSO); *Grass and Grasslands* I. Moore (Collins); *Great Houses of Britain* N. Nicolson (Spring Books); *Guide to Prehistoric and Roman Monuments in England and Wales* J. Hawkes (Sphere Books); *Guide to Prehistoric England* N. Thomas (Book Club Associates); *Guide to the Prehistoric Remains in Britain* R. Wainwright (Book Club Associates); *Guide to Roman Remains in Britain* R. and A. Wilson (Constable); *Hampshire Basin – British Regional Geology* (HMSO); *The Handbook of British Mammals* ed. H. N. Southern (Blackwell Scientific Publications); *Hedgerow Plants* M. Hyde (Shire Publications); *History of Scotland* R. Mitchison (Methuen); *Illustrated Road Book of England and Wales* (Automobile Association); *Illustrated Road Book of Scotland* (Automobile Association); *The Islands of Western Scotland* W. H. Murray (Methuen); *The Lake Counties* W. G. Collingwood (Warne); *The Lake District* W. E. Pearsall and W. Pennington (Collins); *Lake District National Park* Countryside Commission (HMSO); *Lake District Walks for Motorists* J. Parker (Gerrard Publications); *Lincolnshire* W. Marsden (Batsford); *The Lion in the North* J. Prebble (Book Club Associates); *Literary Britain* F. Morley (Hutchinson); *London and Thames Valley – British Regional Geology* (HMSO); *The Lost Villages of England* M. Beresford (Lutterworth); *The Lowlands* I. Finlay (Batsford); *The Making of the English Landscape* W. G. Hoskins (Hodder and Stoughton); *Malvern Country* V. Waite (Phillimore); *Midland Valley of Scotland – British Regional Geology* (HMSO); *Moths of the British Isles* R. South (Warne); *Mountains and Moorlands* W. H. Pearsall (Collins); *The National Parks of England and Wales* R. Bush (Dent); *The National Trust Guide* ed. R. Fedden and R. Joekes (Cape); *The National Trust for Scotland Guide* ed. R. Prentice (Cape); *Nature Conservation in Britain* Sir Dudley Stamp (Collins); *Nature in Norfolk – A Heritage in Trust* (Jarrold and Sons); *Northern England – British Regional Geology* (HMSO); *Northern Highlands – British Regional Geology* (HMSO); *Northumberland National Park* Countryside Commission (HMSO); *North Wales – British Regional Geology* (HMSO); *The North West Highlands* W. H. Murray (Methuen); *North York Moors National Park* Countryside Commission (HMSO); *North Yorkshire Forests* Forestry Commission (HMSO); *Offa's Dyke Path* J. B. Jones (HMSO); *The Old Roads of England* Sir William Addison (Batsford); *One Man's England* W. G. Hoskins (BBC Publications); *Orkney and Shetlands – British Regional Geology* (HMSO); *Oxford Dictionary of Saints* D. H. Farmer (Clarendon Press); *The Peak District* K. C. Edwards (Collins); *Peak District National Park* Countryside Commission (HMSO); *Pembrokeshire Coast National Park* Countryside Commission (HMSO); *The Pembrokeshire Coast Path* J. H. Barrett (HMSO); *The Pennines – British Regional Geology* (HMSO); *The Pennine Way* T. Stephenson (HMSO); *A Plan for the Chilterns* (The Chilterns Standing Conference); *Pocket Guide to Wild Flowers* D. McClintock and R. S. Fitter (Collins); *Popular Handbook of British Birds* P. A. D. Hollom (H. F. and G. Wetherby); *Portrait of Exmoor* J. H. B. Peel (Robert Hale); *Prehistoric Britain* K. Brannigan (Spurbooks Ltd); *Queen Elizabeth Forest Park* Forestry Commission (HMSO); *Remains of a Revolution* A. Burton (Deutsch); *The Ridgeway* J. R. L. Anderson and F. Godwin (Wildwood House); *The Ridgeway Path* S. Jennett (HMSO); *Roman Roads in Britain* I. D. Margary (John Baker); *The Roof of Lancashire* H. C. Collins (Dent); *The Sea Coast* J. A. Steers (Collins); *The Shell County Guides* (Faber); *New Shell Guide to Scotland* D. L. Macnie and M. McLaren (Ebury Press); *Snowdonia Forest Park* Forestry Commission (HMSO); *The Snowdonia National Park* W. M. Condry (Collins); *Snowdonia National Park* Countryside Commission (HMSO); *South Downs Way* S. Jennett (HMSO); *South of Scotland – British Regional Geology* (HMSO); *South Wales – British Regional Geology* (HMSO); *South-West England – British Regional Geology* (HMSO); *Stone Circles of the British Isles* A. Burl (Yale University Press); *Tertiary Volcanic Districts – British Regional Geology* (HMSO); *Travellers' Guides to the British Isles* (Darton, Longman and Todd); *Trees, Woods and Man* H. L. Edlin (Collins); *Upland Britain* R. Millward and A. Robinson (David and Charles); *The Weald* S. W. Wooldridge and F. Goldring (Collins); *The Wealden District – British Regional Geology* (HMSO); *The Welsh Borderland* – British Regional Geology (HMSO); *Wild Flowers* J. Gilmour and M. Walters (Collins); *Wild Flowers of Chalk and Limestone* J. E. Lousley (Collins); *The Wolds Way* D. Rubinstein (Dalesman Books); *Woodland Birds* E. Simms (Collins); *Worth's Dartmoor* R. H. Worth (David and Charles); *Yorkshire (Buildings of England)* N. Pevsner (Penguin); *Yorkshire Dales National Park* Countryside Commission (HMSO).

Maps drawn by Thames Cartographic Services
Paper, printing and binding by Gilchrist Brothers Ltd, Leeds
Hazell, Watson & Viney Ltd, Aylesbury Ben Johnson & Co. Ltd, York
Litra Machine Plates Ltd, Edenbridge Leykam Murztaler, Graz
Vantage Photosetting Co. Ltd, Rownhams

01–020–1

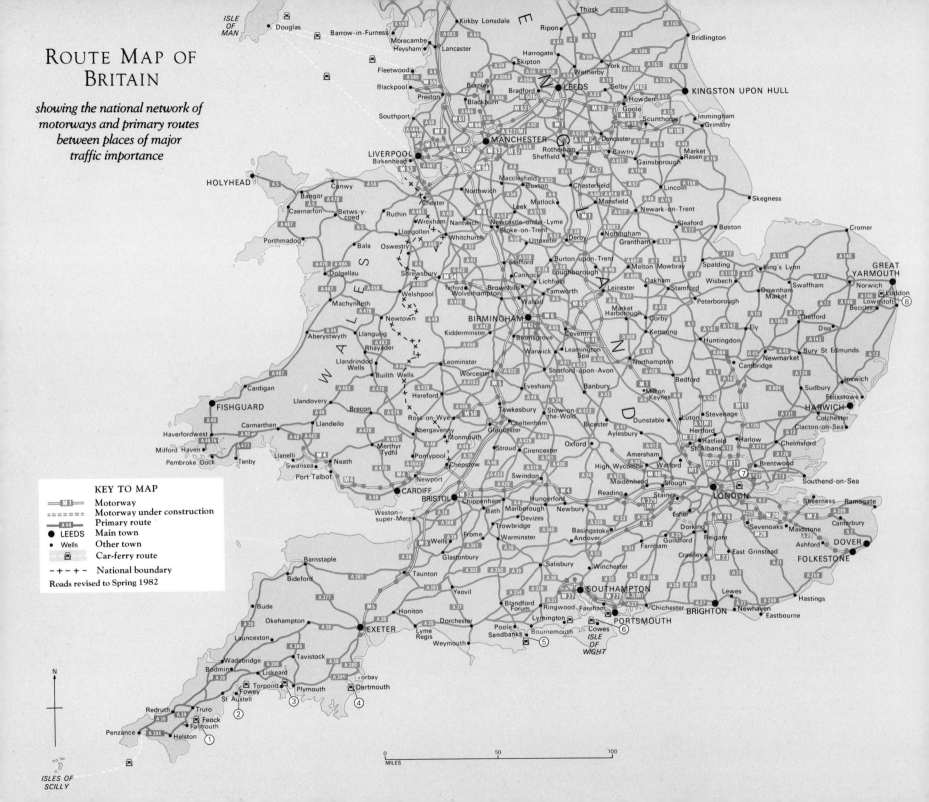